Mental Processes in the Human Brain

Mental Processes in the Human Brain

Edited by

JON DRIVER

PATRICK HAGGARD

AND

TIM SHALLICE

All at
UCL Institute of Cognitive Neuroscience
University College London
17 Queen Square, London

Originating from a Theme Issue first published in
Philosophical Transactions of the Royal Society B: Biological Sciences
http://publishing.royalsociety.org/philtransb

OXFORD

UNIVERSITY PRESS

Great Clarendon Street, Oxford OX2 6DP

Oxford University Press is a department of the University of Oxford.
It furthers the University's objective of excellence in research, scholarship,
and education by publishing worldwide in

Oxford New York

Auckland Cape Town Dar es Salaam Hong Kong Karachi
Kuala Lumpur Madrid Melbourne Mexico City Nairobi
New Delhi Shanghai Taipei Toronto

With offices in

Argentina Austria Brazil Chile Czech Republic France Greece
Guatemala Hungary Italy Japan Poland Portugal Singapore
South Korea Switzerland Thailand Turkey Ukraine Vietnam

Oxford is a registered trade mark of Oxford University Press
in the UK and in certain other countries

Published in the United States
by Oxford University Press Inc., New York

First published by Oxford University Press 2008

British Library Cataloguing in Publication Data

Data available

Library of Congress Cataloging-in-Publication Data

Data available

Typeset by Cepha Imaging Private Ltd., Bangalore, India
Printed in China
on acid-free paper through
Asia Pacific Offset

ISBN 978–0–19–923061–7

1 3 5 7 9 10 8 6 4 2

Contents

List of Contributors

Dr Donna Rose Addis Department of Psychology, Harvard University, Cambridge MA, USA

Professor Michael P Alexander Rotman Research Institute, Baycrest, Toronto, ON, CANADA and Beth Israel Deaconess Medical Center, Harvard Medical School, Boston, MA, USA

Dr. Jos Van Berkum Max Planck Institute for Psycholinguistics, Nijmegen, THE NETHERLANDS

Professor Paul Burgess UCL Institute of Cognitive Neuroscience, University College London, London, UK

Professor Jonathan D Cohen Department of Psychology and the Princeton Neuroscience Institute, Princeton University, Princeton NJ, USA

Professor Stanislas Dehaene Collège de France, Paris, and Inserm-CEA Cognitive Neuroimaging Unit, NeuroSpin Center, Gif sur Yvette, FRANCE

Professor Mark D'Esposito Helen Wills Neuroscience Institute, University of California Berkeley, Berkeley CA, USA

Professor Ray Dolan Wellcome Trust Centre for Neuroimaging, University College London, London, UK

Professor Jon Driver UCL Institute of Cognitive Neuroscience, University College London, London, UK

Dr Iroise Dumontheil UCL Institute of Cognitive Neuroscience and Psychology Department, University College London, UK

Dr Sam J Gilbert Institute of Cognitive Neuroscience and Psychology Department, University College London, UK

Professor Patrick Haggard UCL Institute of Cognitive Neuroscience, University College London, London, UK

Professor Peter Hagoort F C Donders Centre for Cognitive Neuroimaging, Radboud University Nijmegen, Nijmegen, THE NETHERLANDS

Dr Sid Kouider Ecole Normale Supérieure, Paris, FRANCE

Professor William Marslen-Wilson MRC Cognition and Brain Sciences Unit, Cambridge, UK

Dr Samuel M McClure Department of Psychology and Center for the Study of Brain, Mind and Behaviour, Princeton University, Princeton, NJ, USA

Dr Karalyn Patterson MRC Cognition and Brain Sciences Unit, Cambridge, UK

Professor Geraint Rees UCL Institute of Cognitive Neuroscience, University College London, London, UK

Professor Trevor Robbins Department of Experimental Psychology, University of Cambridge, Cambridge, UK

Professor Daniel Schacter Department of Psychology, Harvard University, Cambridge MA, USA

Professor Tim Shallice UCL Institute of Cognitive Neuroscience, University College London, London, UK

Professor Donald T Stuss Rotman Research Institute, Baycrest, Toronto ON, CANADA

Professor Lorraine K Tyler Centre for Speech, Language and the Brain, Department of Experimental Psychology, University of Cambridge, Cambridge, UK

Professor Patrik Vuilleumier Laboratory of Behavioural Neurology and Imaging of Cognition, Department of Neurosciences, University Medical Centre, Geneva, SWITZERLAND

Dr Angela J Yu Department of Psychology and Center for the Study of Brain, Mind and Behaviour, Princeton University, Princeton, NJ, USA

Introduction: Mental processes in the human brain

Jon Driver*, Patrick Haggard, and Tim Shallice

For centuries, the relation of the human mind to the brain has been debated. How can seemingly immaterial entities such as thoughts and memories arise from biological material? Advances in neuroscience have now led to wide acceptance in science and medicine that *all* aspects of our mental life—our perceptions, thoughts, memories, actions, plans, language, understanding of others and so on—in fact depend upon brain function.

In addition to being beneficiaries of the brain's complex functioning, people can also be victims of this. Many devastating and disabling conditions are a consequence of disrupted brain function, as in cases of dementia or following a stroke. Specific cognitive functions can be severely impaired, even while others remain intact in the same person. Disrupted brain function is also increasingly thought to underlie the major mental illnesses. Studies of human brain function (together with related animal studies) are thus critical for understanding major neurological and psychiatric disease. Hence, this field has become a key part of biomedical science.

In addition to the biomedical approach, studies of the human mind and brain have also benefited greatly from psychological approaches. These originally grew out of philosophy of mind, but then became determinedly experimental. More recently, a further key approach has involved computational modelling of cognitive functions in the brain. This approach has some historical roots in the development of intelligent machines during the computer revolution, but has since become a sophisticated mathematical branch of neuroscience. Nowadays, most cutting-edge research on human brain function fuses the three very different traditions or strands together (i.e. biomedical, psychological and computational), in a highly interdisciplinary field. Scientific study of the human mind and brain has apparently come of age in the past decade or so, with a series of remarkable methodological breakthroughs, and theoretical advances, in addition to an ever-growing number of empirical findings.

Space constraints here preclude a comprehensive review of how the current layout of the field has arisen for study of mental processes in the human brain. Nevertheless, several historical markers can be identified approximately. The computer revolution of the 1940s led in turn to a 'cognitive revolution' in psychology during the 1950s and 1960s, with the focus upon information processing (via analogies to computers and programs) leading to an interest in internal mental processes, rather than just in the overt behaviour that had been the dominant concern of the preceding 50 years.

While studies of lower-level sensory and motor processes have been fairly well integrated with underlying physiology for over a century, this was not always so for higher mental processes. A student in the mid-twentieth century might have been taught simply that 'association cortex' is involved in higher mental processes, in some non-specific (or 'mass action') way. This view often prevailed back then, even though Broca & Wernicke had reported on

*Author for correspondence (j.driver@ucl.ac.uk)

rather specific language deficits after particular brain damage in neurological patients considerably earlier (late nineteenth century). Several key developments were to bring the neuroscience of higher mental processes into focus again, with a particular emphasis on specificity in the underlying brain mechanisms.

One development was that advances from cognitive psychology, using its information-processing framework, led to new insights into the selective deficits of brain-damaged patients. The highly selective form of amnesia observed by Scoville & Milner (1957), after bilateral temporal lobe surgery in patient HM, provided one particularly striking example of specificity. Information-processing models from cognitive psychology were then used to provide further insights into highly selective cognitive deficits in a variety of domains, including not only long-term memory but also short-term memory, semantic memory, reading, planning and so on. This led to the new field of cognitive neuropsychology in the 1970s and 1980s (see McCarthy & Warrington 1988; Shallice 1988, for reviews).

In an overlapping period, an independent but equally critical development was that single-cell recording methods for studying neural activity in animals, which had originally been applied during anaesthesia (e.g. Hubel & Wiesel 1959), began to be used in awake behaving animals as they performed increasingly complex tasks. It became possible to relate response properties of neurons to more 'cognitive' issues, such as coding the particular place that an exploring animal was currently located in (e.g. O'Keefe & Dostrovsky 1971); perceptual discrimination (Newsome & Britten 1989); or even perceptual awareness (Logothetis & Schall 1989), as opposed to purely stimulus-driven responses; selective attention (Moran & Desimone 1985); working memory (Fuster *et al*. 1985) and so on.

As regards computational modelling, connectionist models of cognitive functions emerged in the 1980s. These sought to incorporate elementary aspects of cellular assemblies, using a so-called 'brain analogy', rather than the longstanding and rather literal computer analogy used hitherto by many information-processing approaches (e.g. McClelland & Rumelhart 1985). Connectionist models were also often strongly influenced by findings and topics from cognitive psychology and neuropsychology (e.g. Hinton & Shallice 1991). More recent computational theories now incorporate increasing cellular and neurotransmitter detail (e.g. Dayan & Abbot 2005; see also Cohen *et al*. 2007 and this volume). Indeed, it is arguably only since the 1990s that the biomedical, psychological and computational strands have become very closely interwoven. Prior to then, the methods of the time rarely allowed localization of function to be studied with high resolution in brain-damaged patients, while original connectionist models typically bore only a rather abstract similarity to actual neural populations.

A critical further development that has led to substantial advances, particularly for studies of the human brain, was the advent of new methods for non-invasive measurement of activity within the human brain. A series of technical breakthroughs led to increasingly widespread use of positron emission tomography (PET) in the 1980s and subsequently to functional magnetic resonance imaging (fMRI) from the 1990s. In addition to technological advances with such methods, a further key aspect was their application to human volunteers engaged in different cognitive tasks drawn from experimental psychology (Posner & Raichle 1994). Indeed, while there have since been many mathematical advances in the techniques used for analysing neuroimaging data (e.g. Valdes-Sosa *et al*. 2005), the combination of neural measures with psychological methods has remained critical. Even the most technically sophisticated neuroimaging approaches may be of little use for studying cognition, unless applied to carefully chosen paradigms designed to highlight one or another aspect of cognition, and to fractionate this into component processes. Methods from cognitive psychology and psychophysics (and, more recently, even from economics) have thus contributed much to recent advances in neuroimaging of human cognitive function, just as they have been critical for neuropsychology, in an increasingly inter-disciplinary field.

The advent of PET and fMRI triggered an explosion of interest in relating cognitive function to human brain activity. This also rekindled interest in some existing methods that can provide greater temporal resolution, such as electroencephalography (EEG), and related but technically more complex methods such as magnetoencephalography (MEG). At around the same time, separate developments in reductionist neuroscience studies at the molecular level, in relatively simple animals, were also being related to cognitive function (such as memory), with some spectacular successes (e.g. Kandel 2004). Molecular variations at the genetic level are now being related even to neural activity across the whole brain, in human neuroimaging (Hariri *et al.* 2006). Thus, there is an ever-increasing tendency for neuroscience studies at a variety of different levels to be related to each other, with all levels being linked to cognitive function. The study of mental processes in the human brain is now based on a convergence of scientific traditions, together with enabling methods and new technologies.

The interdisciplinarity of the current field is further illustrated by the growing importance of formal mathematical models for cognitive functions, which have evolved from the connectionist networks of the 1980s through to more detailed theoretical approaches that integrate data from cellular and neurotransmitter levels also (Dayan & Abbot 2005). Such formal models are increasingly being used to derive explicit predictions for neuroimaging studies, a development that we strongly welcome, as exemplified by several contributions in the present volume (e.g. Cohen *et al.* 2007; Dolan 2007; Kouider & Dehaene 2007; and this volume). Studies of specific cognitive deficits in patients with selective brain damage still continue to provide essential information (e.g. Burgess *et al.* 2007; D'Esposito 2007; Patterson 2007; Robbins 2007; Stuss & Alexander 2007; Vuilleumier & Driver 2007; and this volume), which can fruitfully be related to computational models of cognitive function and to neural networks. More recently, studies of brain-damaged patients can also include functional neuroimaging in the patients themselves, to assess the impact of their focal lesions upon function in remote but interconnected regions that survive the lesion (e.g. D'Esposito 2007; Vuilleumier & Driver 2007; and this volume). This provides a new approach for understanding network interactions between communicating brain areas.

A further methodological innovation involves the use of transcranial magnetic stimulation (TMS; Walsh & Pascual-Leone 2003), as a means for non-invasive stimulation of particular brain regions, which can have highly selective (and transient) effects on normal cognitive function. This method allows causal manipulation of activity in particular brain regions, offering perhaps the first such method for humans (albeit with rather less resolution than is allowed by more invasive interventions in animals, such as local cooling, pharmacological manipulation or even genetic intervention in a specific brain region). Moreover, it has now become possible for the first time to combine TMS online with fMRI in human studies (Vuilleumier & Driver 2007; and this volume), to study how manipulating activity in one specific brain region may influence others and to assess how this impacts causally on cognitive performance.

This brief survey shows that the past few decades have led to many remarkable advances in studies of brain function and of human cognition. But this Discussion meeting at the Royal Society, on Mental Processes in the Human Brain (held 16–17 October 2006), was not intended to provide a historical overview of how the field got here. Instead, we charged the speakers and contributors with surveying what is currently known, and what new challenges and opportunities arise for the foreseeable future. We were inspired by several prior Royal Society Discussion meetings on related topics (including Broadbent & Weiskrantz 1982; Roberts *et al.* 1996;

Parker *et al.* 2002, among others). But, we deliberately set out to organize this particular meeting along somewhat different lines. The Broadbent & Weiskrantz (1982) meeting had focused on cognitive neuropsychology in patient studies, whereas here we deliberately interleave studies of normality with pathology. Roberts *et al.* (1996) focused primarily on the frontal lobe in particular, whereas we had no such restriction. Parker *et al.* (2002) focused primarily (but not exclusively) on physiological studies of cognitive function in animals, with some emphasis on sensory function. We focused instead on so-called higher-level cognitive functions (e.g. memory, language, awareness, attention, executive function) in humans.

All these topics provide unequivocally 'cognitive' domains that feature prominently in human mental life, and that in some cases (e.g. for language) may have no direct animal homologue. Since no prior Royal Society discussion meeting had focused extensively on the advances, new possibilities and possible shortcomings of functional neuroimaging, we address these in some detail here. This seemed appropriate, as the advent of neuroimaging has provided arguably the biggest sea change in studies of human cognitive and brain function in recent years (albeit not always without its critics; see Coltheart 2006). We were not able to cover all of the recent developments in the field. For instance, there is relatively little here on the growth of so-called social neuroscience, nor on developmental aspects. Such aspects are covered elsewhere (e.g. Frith & Frith 2003; Emery *et al.* 2007).

Hagoort & van Berkum (2007), Marslen-Wilson & Tyler (2007) and Patterson (2007) provide insights here into how the new methods and theories have influenced studies of human language function, including mental representation in the brain of semantics, syntax, morphemes and even of pragmatic contextual constraints during communication. D'Esposito (2007), Dolan (2007) and Schacter & Addis (2007) survey recent developments for different aspects of memory and learning. Burgess *et al.* (2007), Cohen *et al.* (2007), Robbins (2007) and Stuss & Alexander (2007) present advances in the study of so-called 'executive functions' (or top-down cognitive control), relating not only to frontal cortex, but also to the many systems that specific frontal regions interconnect with, and to pharmacological modulation of such loops (Robbins 2007; see also Dolan 2007). Kouider & Dehaene (2007), Rees (2007) and Vuilleumier & Driver (2007) report on recent studies of perceptual awareness and attention in the human brain. They highlight both theoretical (Kouider & Dehaene 2007) and methodological advances (Rees 2007; Vuilleumier & Driver 2007), in addition to several key findings.

Although the presentations from all these contributors were organized into four separate sessions at the meeting (on language, memory, awareness, attention/executive function), there is often much striking overlap between the subtopics. For instance, frontal cortex features not only in the executive functions topic, but also in the language contribution by Hagoort & van Berkum (2007); in Dolan's (2007) account of how learning and affect impact upon conditioned responses and decision making; and in the three contributions on awareness and attention (Kouider & Dehaene 2007; Rees 2007; Vuilleumier & Driver 2007). Equally, D'Esposito's (2007) contribution is arguably concerned as much with executive function as it is with short-term or working memory and so on. All of the contributions emphasize the need to go beyond just the particular contribution of each distinct brain area, to understand further how the various regions may interact causally in network terms, a topic that receives particular attention from Vuilleumier & Driver (2007).

There was much lively discussion at the meeting, which was the best attended ever in the history of Royal Society discussion meetings to date (with the audience spilling out into four overflow rooms!). We think that this exceptional attendance is a testament to the excitement and rapid rate of progress in this field, and to the intrinsic interest of our mental lives and their neural basis. All of the extended discussions that took place at the meeting have fed back into this volume.

There has been no better time to study the neural basis of human cognitive function. We hope that the present volume captures this, by illustrating the recent advances, excitement and future potential in this field.

We thank all participants at the discussion meeting; the speakers and contributors; Uta Frith FRS for chairing the language session; Jay McClelland for provocative comments; Rosalyn Lawrence from the UCL Institute of Cognitive Neuroscience, and Laura Howlett and many Royal Society staff for administrative help; James Joseph at the Phil. Trans. B editorial office; and our many colleagues at the UCL Institute of Cognitive Neuroscience and neighbouring centres in Queen Square, all of whom share our passion for studying mental processes in the human brain. We also thank participants at the separate Festscrift for Tim Shallice held at UCL on 18 October 2006, subsequent to the Royal Society Discussion meeting. A video recording of the discussion meeting is available at: http://www.royalsoc.ac.uk/page.asp?id=1110

References

For all references to *Phil.Trans.R.Soc.B* **362**, pp. 757–942, see also this volume.

Broadbent, D. E., Weiskrantz, L. (eds). 1982 The neuropsychology of cognitive function. Proceedings of a Royal Society Discussion Meeting Held on 18 and 19 November 1981. *Phil. Trans. R. Soc. B* **298**(1089).

Burgess, P. W., Gilbert, S. J. & Dumontheil, I. 2007 Function and localization within rostral prefrontal cortex (area 10). *Phil. Trans. R. Soc. B* **362,** 887–899. (doi:10.1098/rstb. 2007.2095)

Cohen, J. D., McClure, S. M. & Yu, A. J. 2007 Should I stay or should I go? How the human brain manages the tradeoff between exploitation and exploration. *Phil. Trans. R. Soc. B* **362,** 933–942. (doi:10.1098/rstb.2007.2098)

Coltheart, M. 2006 What has functional neuroimaging told us about the mind (so far)? *Cortex* **42,** 323–331.

Dayan, P. & Abbot, L. F. 2005 *Theoretical neuroscience*. Cambridge, MA: MIT Press.

D'Esposito, M. 2007 From cognitive to neural models of working memory. *Phil. Trans. R. Soc. B* **362,** 761–772. (doi:10.1098/rstb.2007.2086)

Dolan, R. J. 2007 The human amygdala and orbital prefrontal cortex in behavioural regulation. *Phil. Trans. R. Soc. B* **362,** 787–799. (doi:10.1098/rstb.2007.2088)

Emery, N., Clayton, N. & Frith, C. 2007 Introduction. Social intelligence: from brain to culture. *Phil. Trans. R. Soc. B.* **362,** 485–488. (doi:10.1098/rstb.2006.2022)

Frith, U. & Frith, C. D. 2003 Development and neurophysiology of mentalizing. *Phil. Trans. R. Soc. B* **358,** 459–473. (doi:10.1098/rstb.2002.1218)

Fuster, J. M., Bauer, R. H. & Jervey, J. P. 1985 Functional interactions between inferotemporal and prefrontal cortex in a cognitive task. *Brain Res.* **330,** 299–307. (doi:10.1016/0006-8993(85)90689-4)

Hagoort, P. & van Berkum, J. 2007 Beyond the sentence given. *Phil. Trans. R. Soc. B* **362,** 801–811. (doi:10.1098/rstb.2007.2089)

Hariri, A. R., Drabant, E. M. & Weinberger, D. R. 2006 Imaging genetics. *Biol. Psychiatry* **59**, 888–897. (doi:10.1016/j.biopsych.2005.11.005)

Hinton, G. & Shallice, T. 1991 Lesioning an attractor network: investigations of acquired dyslexia. *Psychol. Rev.* **98**, 74–95. (doi:10.1037/0033-295X.98.1.74)

Hubel, D. H. & Wiesel, T. N. 1959 Receptive fields of single neurones in the cat's striate cortex. *J. Physiol.* **148.** 574–591.

Kandel, E. R. 2004 The molecular biology of memory storage: a dialog between genes and synapses. *Biomed. Life Sci.* **24**, 475–522.

Kouider, S. & Dehaene, S. 2007 Levels of processing during non-conscious perception: a critical review of visual masking. *Phil. Trans. R. Soc. B* **362**, 857–875. (doi:10.1098/rstb.2007.2093)

Logothetis, N. K. & Schall, J. D. 1989 Neuronal correlates of subjective visual perception. *Science* **245**, 761–763. (doi:10.1126/science.2772635)

Marslen-Wilson, W. D. & Tyler, L. K. 2007 Morphology, language and the brain: the decompositional substrate for language comprehension. *Phil. Trans. R. Soc. B* **362**, 823–836. (doi:10.1098/rstb.2007.2091)

McCarthy, R. A. & Warrington, E. K. 1988 *Cognitive neuropsychology*. London, UK: Academic Press.

McClelland, J. L. & Rumelhart, D. E. 1985 Distributed memory and the representation of general and specific information. *J. Exp. Psychol. Gen.* **114**, 159–188. (doi:10.1037/0096-3445.114.2.159)

Moran, J. & Desimone, R. 1985 Selective attention gates visual processing in the extrastriate cortex. *Science* **229**, 782–784. (doi:10.1126/science.4023713)

Newsome, W. T. & Britten, K. H. 1989 Neural correlates of a perceptual decision. *Nature* **341**, 52–54. (doi:10.1038/341052a0)

O'Keefe, J. & Dostrovsky, J. 1971 The hippocampus as a spatial map: preliminary evidence from unit activity in the freely moving rat. *Brain Res.* **34**, 171–175. (doi:10.1016/0006-8993(71)90358-1)

Parker, A., Derrington, A. & Blakemore, C. 2002 The physiology of cognitive processes. *Phil. Trans. R. Soc. B* **357**, 959–961. (doi:10.1098/rstb.2002.1115)

Patterson, K. 2007 The reign of typicality in semantic memory. *Phil. Trans. R. Soc. B* **362**, 813–821. (doi:10.1098/rstb.2007.2090)

Posner, M. I. & Raichle, M. E. 1994 *Images of mind*. San Francisco, CA: Freeman and company.

Rees, G. 2007 Neural correlates of the contents of visual awareness in humans. *Phil. Trans. R. Soc. B* **362**, 877–886. (doi:10.1098/rstb.2007.2094)

Robbins, T. W. 2007 Shifting and stopping: fronto-striatal substrates, neurochemical modulation and clinical implications. *Phil. Trans. R. Soc. B* **362**, 917–932. (doi:10.1098/rstb.2007.2097)

Roberts, A. C., Robbins, T. W. R. & Weiskrantz, L. 1996 Executive and cognitive functions of the prefrontal cortex. *Phil. Trans. R. Soc. B* **351**, 1389–1395. (doi:10.1098/rstb.1996.0122)

Schacter, D. L. & Addis, D. R. 2007 The cognitive neuroscience of constructive memory: remembering the past and imagining the future. *Phil. Trans. R. Soc. B* **362**, 773–786. (doi:10.1098/rstb.2007.2087)

Scoville, W. B. & Milner, B. 1957 Loss of recent memory after bilateral hippocampal lesions. *J. Neurol. Neurosurg. Psychiatry* **20**, 11–21.

Shallice, T. 1988 *From neuropsychology to mental structure*. Cambridge, UK: Cambridge University Press.

Stuss, D. T. & Alexander, M. P. 2007 Is there a dysexecutive syndrome? *Phil. Trans. R. Soc. B* **362**, 901–915. (doi:10.1098/rstb.2007.2096)

Valdes-Sosa, P. A., Koptter, R. & Friston, K. J. 2005 Introduction: multimodal neuroimaging of brain connectivity. *Phil. Trans. R. Soc. B* **360**, 865–867. (doi:10.1098/rstb.2005.1655)

Vuilleumier, P. & Driver, J. 2007 Modulation of visual processing by attention and emotion: windows on causal interactions between human brain regions. *Phil. Trans. R. Soc. B* **362**, 837–855. (doi:10.1098/rstb.2007.2092)

Walsh, V. & Pascual-Leone, A. 2003 *Transcranial magnetic stimulation*. Cambridge, MA: MIT Press.

2

From cognitive to neural models of working memory

Mark D'Esposito *

Working memory refers to the temporary retention of information that was just experienced or just retrieved from long-term memory but no longer exists in the external environment. These internal representations are short-lived, but can be stored for longer periods of time through active maintenance or rehearsal strategies, and can be subjected to various operations that manipulate the information in such a way that makes it useful for goal-directed behaviour. Empirical studies of working memory using neuroscientific techniques, such as neuronal recordings in monkeys or functional neuroimaging in humans, have advanced our knowledge of the underlying neural mechanisms of working memory. This rich dataset can be reconciled with behavioural findings derived from investigating the cognitive mechanisms underlying working memory. In this paper, I review the progress that has been made towards this effort by illustrating how investigations of the neural mechanisms underlying working memory can be influenced by cognitive models and, in turn, how cognitive models can be shaped and modified by neuroscientific data. One conclusion that arises from this research is that working memory can be viewed as neither a unitary nor a dedicated system. A network of brain regions, including the prefrontal cortex (PFC), is critical for the active maintenance of internal representations that are necessary for goal-directed behaviour. Thus, working memory is not localized to a single brain region but probably is an emergent property of the functional interactions between the PFC and the rest of the brain.

Keywords: working memory; short-term memory; executive function; cognitive control; prefrontal cortex; functional magnetic resonance imaging

2.1 Introduction

What is the neural basis of working memory? To answer this question, one must begin with a proper definition of the term 'working memory'. To me, working memory refers to the temporary retention of information that was just experienced but no longer exists in the external environment, or was just retrieved from long-term memory. These internal representations are short-lived, but can be stored for longer periods of time through active maintenance or rehearsal strategies, and can be subjected to various operations that manipulate the information in ways that make it useful for goal-directed behaviour. Thus, working memory is critically important in cognition and seems necessary for many cognitive abilities, such as reasoning, language comprehension, planning and spatial processing. However, it is clear from the numerous empirical studies of working memory that are published each year that it is an evolving construct, one that has come a long way over the past 30 years, since Baddeley & Hitch (1974) introduced their highly influential cognitive model of working memory.

Within a cognitive framework, Baddeley conceptualized working memory as a cognitive system comprising multiple components that support executive control (see also Burgess *et al.* 2007; Robbins 2007; Stuss & Alexander 2007; this volume) as well as active maintenance of

*despo@berkeley.edu

temporarily maintained information (Baddeley 1986). Thus, a 'central executive system' was proposed as a system that could actively regulate the distribution of limited attentional resources   and coordinate information within limited capacity verbal and spatial memory storage buffers. The central executive system, based on the analogous supervisory attentional system introduced by Norman & Shallice (1986), was proposed to take control over cognitive processing when novel tasks are engaged and/or when existing behavioural routines have to be overridden. Empirical studies of working memory using neuroscientific techniques, such as neuronal recordings in monkeys (e.g. Funahashi *et al*. 1989) and functional neuroimaging in humans (e.g. Curtis *et al*. 2004),have provided a rich dataset that can be reconciled with behavioural findings derived by testing cognitive models of working memory such as the one proposed by Baddeley. In this paper, I review the progress that has been made towards this effort by illustrating how investigations of the neural mechanisms underlying working memory can be influenced by cognitive models and, in turn, how cognitive models can be shaped and modified by neuroscientific data.

2.2 Traditional cognitive models of working memory

A critical component of Baddeley's working memory model is the existence of verbal and spatial storage buffers. The cognitive concept of a buffer translated into neural terms would propose that temporary retention of task-relevant information requires transfer of that information to a part of the brain that is dedicated to the storage of information. Presumably, such buffers are analogous to a computer's RAM, which serves as a cache for information transferred from the hard drive that is processed by a CPU. Consistent with this interpretation of a working memory 'buffer', many descriptions of cognitive models of working memory refer to the information being 'in' or 'out' of working memory. For example, in a recent review of working memory, Repovs & Baddeley (2006) state that 'the function of the articulatory rehearsal process is to retrieve and rearticulate the contents held *in* this phonological store and in this way to refresh the memory trace. Further, while speech input *enters* the phonological store automatically, information from other modalities enters the phonological store only through recoding into phonological form, a process performed by articulatory rehearsal'. Later, the authors refer to 'focal shifts of attention to memorized locations that provide a rehearsal-like function of maintaining information active *in* spatial working memory'. Thus, one question that neuroscientific data can address regarding how the brain implements working memory processes is whether such buffers or storage sites exist in distinct parts of the brain to support the active maintenance of task-relevant information.

Another cognitive model of working memory, put forth by Cowan (1988, 1999), proposes that the 'contents of working memory' are not maintained within dedicated storage buffers, but rather are simply the subset of information that is within the focus of attention at a given time. He describes an embedded-processes model where working memory comes from hierarchically arranged faculties comprising long-term memory, the subset of working long-term memory that is currently activated and the subset of activated memory that is the focus of attention. These ideas are similar to that put forth by Anderson (1983) who referred to working memory as those representations currently at a high level of activation. Thus, task-relevant representations are not in working memory, but they do have levels of activation that can be higher or lower. After use, for example, representations may be temporarily more active or 'primed'. In this formulation, working memory does not have a size, or maximum number of items, as a structural feature. Instead, performance on working memory tasks is determined by the level of activation of relevant representations, and the discriminability of activation levels between relevant and irrelevant representations (Kimberg *et al.* 1997).

Again, in neural terms, Cowan or Anderson's cognitive model of working memory would predict that information that is represented throughout the brain is not transferred to an independent buffer or storage site, but rather that temporary retention of task-relevant information is mediated by the activation of the neural structures that represent the information being maintained or stored (for a further discussion of these and related ideas see Ruchkin *et al.* (2003) and the commentary that followed). In other words, the temporary retention of a face, for example, would require activation of cortical areas that are involved in the perceptual processing of faces.

It is not possible in this paper to consider all cognitive models of working memory (for an excellent starting point, the reader is referred to Miyake & Shah 1999). However, based on the models put forth by Baddeley and Cowan as prototypes, one can begin to consider how the cognitive mechanisms proposed by such models are implemented in the brain. Thus, with these cognitive models in mind, I review evidence that begins to provide some insight into the neural mechanisms regarding how relevant information is temporarily stored in the service of goal-directed behaviour.

From a neuroscience perspective, it is counterintuitive that all temporarily stored information during goal-directed behaviour requires specialized dedicated buffers. Clearly, there could not be a sufficient number of independent buffers to accommodate the infinite types of information that need to be actively maintained to accommodate all potential or intended actions. In a system with only two buffers, such as verbal and visuospatial, how would the retention of odours or tactile sensations, which cannot always be recoded into verbal or visuospatial representations, be accomplished? More recently, an additional episodic buffer has been proposed to be a store capable of multidimensional coding that allows the binding of information to create an integrated episode (Baddeley 2000). However, even with the addition of this buffer, Baddeley's working memory model cannot accommodate storage of all possible types of information processed by the human brain (it is important to note, however, that this was not probably the original intent of this model). Alternatively, in Cowan's proposal, which does not rely on the concept of specialized dedicated storage buffers, active maintenance or storage of task-relevant representations could be implemented with a neural system where memory storage occurs in the very same brain circuitry that supports the perceptual representation of information. Such a neural system presumably would be more flexible and efficient than one that transfers information back and forth between dedicated storage buffers. Can studies of brain function, either in animal or man, test these competing hypotheses?

2.3 Neural models of working memory

For over 30 years, the results of experiments in behaving monkeys using recordings from single neurons within the lateral prefrontal cortex (PFC, figure 2.1*a*) have consistently found persistent, sustained levels of neuronal firing during the retention interval in tasks that require a monkey to retain information over a brief period of time (e.g. Fuster & Alexander 1971; Kubota & Niki 1971; Funahashi *et al.* 1989). This sustained activity is thought to provide a bridge between the stimulus cue (e.g. the location of a flash of light) and its contingent

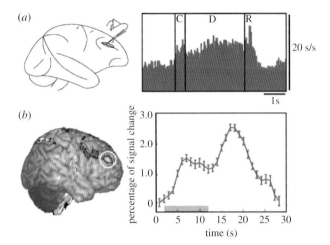

Fig. 2.1 Neural activity in the monkey and the human lateral PFC during the retention interval of a spatial oculomotor delayed response (ODR) task. (*a*) Macaque: average of single-unit recordings from 46 neurons with delay-period activity from the monkey lateral PFC (brain area (BA) area 46; adapted from Funahashi *et al*. 1989). C, cue; D, delay; R, response. (*b*) Human: significant delay-period activity (left) and average (±s.e.) fMRI signal (right) from right lateral PFC (BA area 46; circled) in a human performing an ODR task (unpublished data from my laboratory). The grey bar represents the length of the delay interval. Note that how in both cases the level of PFC activity persists throughout the delay, seconds after the stimulus cue has disappeared.

response (e.g. a later delayed saccade to the remembered location). These results have been supported by the functional neuroimaging studies in humans, and there is now a critical mass of studies that find lateral PFC activity in humans during delay tasks (for review, see Curtis & D'Esposito 2003). For example, in a functional magnetic resonance imaging (fMRI) study using an oculomotor delay task identical to that used in monkey studies, we observed not only the frontal cortex activity during the retention interval (figure 2.1*b*), but also the magnitude of the activity correlated positively with the accuracy of the memory-guided saccade that followed later. This relationship suggests that the fidelity of the actively maintained location is reflected in the delay-period activity (Curtis *et al*. 2004). Thus, the existence of persistent neural activity during blank memory intervals of delay tasks is a powerful empirical finding, which lends strong support for the hypothesis that such activity represents a neural mechanism for the active maintenance or storage of task-relevant representations. The necessity of the PFC for the active maintenance of task-relevant representations has been demonstrated by studies that have found impaired performance on delay tasks in monkeys with selective lesions of the lateral PFC (Bauer & Fuster 1976; Funahashi *et al*. 1993).

However, monkey physiology studies recording from other brain areas and human fMRI studies of working memory have also found that the PFC is not the only region that is active during the temporary retention of task-relevant information. For example, we also observed in the previously mentioned fMRI study (Curtis *et al*. 2004) that different brain regions were involved during the performance of the oculomotor delayed response task. Specifically, different brain regions were active depending on whether the task required the temporary maintenance of retrospective (e.g. past sensory events) or prospective (e.g. representations of anticipated action and preparatory set) codes. During the performance of this task, participants in the study were biased towards or against the use of a prospective motor code. In one condition (match trials), the participants were able to plan a saccade to the target as soon as the cue appeared and then they could simply postpone the initiation of the saccade until after the delay. During these trials, delay-period activity should reflect this strategy, i.e. the maintenance of a prospective motor code. In a comparison condition (non-match trials), a saccade was made after the retention interval to an unpredictable location that did not match the location of the sample. The participants still had to remember the location of the sample so that they could discern between the matching and non-matching targets. Since a saccade was never made to the sample location and the non-matching location was unpredictable, we expected that, during these trials, the participants were biased away from maintaining a motor code during the delay. Instead, the nature of these trials encouraged the maintenance of a retrospective sensory code. We found that delay-period activity was greater for the match when compared with non-match trials within oculomotor regions; whereas delay-period activity for non-match trials was greater

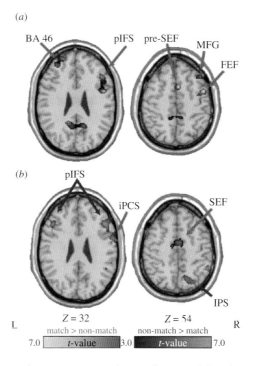

Fig. 2.2 Statistical parametric *t*-maps contrasting oculomotor delayed matching-to-sample versus non-matching-to-sample delay period-specific activity (Curtis *et al.* 2004). Activity during the (*a*) early and (*b*) late delay periods is shown. Warm colours depict regions with greater delay-period activity on matching than non-matching trials. Cool colours depict regions with greater delay-period activity on non-matching than matching trials. BA, brain area; FEF, frontal eye fields; SEF, supplementary eye fields; MFG, middle frontal gyrus; pIFS, posterior inferior frontal sulcus; iPCS, inferior precentral sulcus; IPS, intraparietal sulcus.

in frontal and parietal regions (figure 2.2). Thus, this study demonstrated not only that many different brain regions exhibit persistent neural activity during active maintenance of task-relevant information, but also that a unique network of brain regions are recruited depending on the type of information being actively maintained. Our fMRI data also support the notion that even within the domain of spatial information, separable neural mechanisms are engaged for the active maintenance of 'motor' plans versus 'spatial' codes. Moreover, given that our task only required the oculomotor system, it is probable that distinct neural circuitry will be recruited when the motor act involves other modalities, such as speech or limb output (e.g. Hickok *et al.* 2003). Thus, this is the first piece of evidence presented in this review that the concept of specialized buffers (for, say, verbal versus spatial information) may not map adequately onto neural architecture. Rather, the findings appear more consistent with a system in which active maintenance involves the recruitment of the same circuitry that represents the information itself, with different circuits for different types of spatial information (e.g. visual versus oculomotor).

Similar findings exist when the 'visual' component of working memory is investigated with neuroscientific methods. For example, in another fMRI study (Ranganath *et al.* 2004), we asked the participants to learn a series of faces, houses and face–house associations and they were scanned while performing a delayed match-to-sample (DMS) and delayed paired-associate (DPA) task with these stimuli. Results showed that delay-period activity within category-selective inferior temporal subregions reflected the type of information that was being actively maintained—the fusiform gyrus showed enhanced activity when participants maintained previously shown faces on DMS trials, and when subjects recalled faces in response to a house cue on DPA trials. Likewise, the parahippocampal gyrus showed enhanced activity when participants maintained previously shown houses on DMS trials and when they recalled houses in response to a face cue on DPA trials (figure 2.3). These fMRI findings are consistent with several monkey neurophysiological studies which have also shown that temporal lobe neurons exhibit persistent stimulus-selective activity in tasks requiring the active maintenance of visual object information across short delays (Miyashita & Chang 1988; Miller *et al.* 1993; Nakamura & Kubota 1995). Again, like spatial and motor codes, active maintenance of visual stimuli is mediated by the activation of cortical regions that also support processing of that information, perceptual in this case.

2.4 Is phonological working memory special?

Neuroscientific studies of verbal working memory, which has been most extensively studied by behavioural methods (Vallar & Shallice 1990), provide a similar view regarding the neural mechanisms underlying working memory. Consistently, performance on tasks that tap the 'phonological loop', as conceptualized by Baddeley, engage a set of brain regions that are thought to be involved in phonological processing. For example, using functional neuroimaging techniques during verbal working memory tasks, the left inferior parietal lobe, posterior inferior frontal gyrus (Broca's area), premotor cortex and the cerebellum are typically activated (e.g. Paulesu *et al.* 1993; Awh *et al.* 1996).

However, is this network of brain regions also responsible for the active maintenance of non-phonological language representations (e.g. lexical-semantic)? For visual word recognition, a functionally specialized processing stream is thought to exist within inferior temporal cortex, representing visual words at increasingly higher levels of abstraction along a posterior-to-anterior axis (Cohen & Dehaene 2004). Intracranial electrophysiological recordings (Nobre

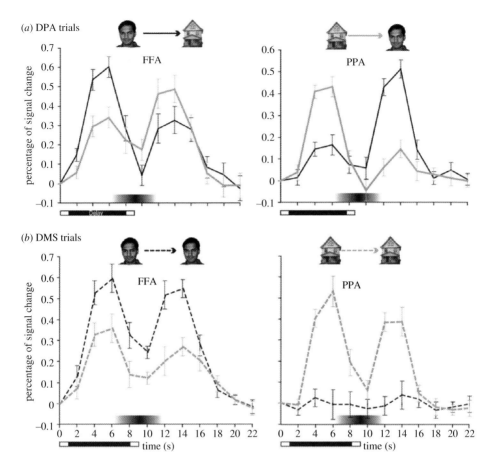

Fig. 2.3 Human inferior temporal cortex activity during visual working memory maintenance and associative memory retrieval (Ranganath *et al.* 2004). (*a*) DPA trials: on DPA trials, activity during the cue phase in the FFA (left) and PPA (right) was enhanced when each region's preferred stimulus was presented (black line, face stimuli; grey line, house stimuli). However, during the delay period, activity in these regions reflected the type of information that was active in memory, rather than the previously presented cue stimulus, i.e. delay activity in the FFA was greater when a face was recalled in response to a house cue and delay activity in the PPA was greater when a house was recalled in response to a face cue. (*b*) DMS trials: on DMS trials, cue and delay-period activity in the FFA and PPA was enhanced when subjects maintained each region's preferred stimulus type (black dashed line, face stimuli; grey dashed line, house stimuli).

et al. 1994), for example, show that posterior inferior temporal cortex differentiates letter strings from non-linguistic complex visual objects. Brain activity in more anterior inferior temporal cortical regions, in contrast, distinguishes words from non-words and is affected by the semantic context of words, indicating that anterior inferior temporal cortex holds more elaborate linguistic representations (see also Marslen-Wilson & Tyler 2007; Patterson 2007). To demonstrate that there is distinct neural circuitry supporting the active maintenance of non-phonological language representations, we explored the role of language regions within the left inferotemporal cortex (ITC) that are involved in visual word recognition and word-related semantics. Using fMRI, we first localized a visual 'word form' area within inferior temporal cortex area and then demonstrated that this area was involved in the active maintenance of visually presented words during a delay task (Fiebach *et al.* 2006). Specifically, we found that this area was recruited more for the active maintenance of words than pseudowords (i.e. orthographically legal and pronounceable non-words). Maintenance of pseudo-words should not elicit strong sustained activation in such brain regions, as no stored representations preexist for these items. These results suggest that verbal working memory may be conceptualized as involving sustained activation of all relevant pre-existing cortical language (phonological, lexical or semantic) representations.

If working memory maintenance processes reflect the prolonged activation of the same brain regions that support online processing, evidence for cortical activity in the absence of stimuli should be evident not only in association cortex (as discussed thus far) but also within primary cortical regions. This indeed is the case as such effects have been observed in primary olfactory (Zelano *et al.* 2005), visual (Klein *et al.* 2000; Silver *et al.* 2006) and auditory cortex (Calvert *et al.* 1997; Kraemer *et al.* 2005). Thus, the neuroscientific data presented in this paper are consistent with most or all neural populations being able to retain information that can be accessed and kept active over several seconds, via persistent neural activity in the service of goal-directed behaviour.

2.5 Neural mechanisms of active maintenance of task-relevant representations

The observed persistent neural activity during delay tasks may reflect active rehearsal mechanisms. Active rehearsal is hypothesized to consist of the repetitive selection of relevant representations or recurrent direction of attention to those items. Subvocal articulations probably mediate the rehearsal of verbalizable memoranda (Baddeley 1986) since articulatory suppression (e.g. uttering 'the...the...the' during a retention interval), which interferes with rehearsal, degrades memory performance (Murray 1968). In addition, the ventrolateral frontal cortex (i.e. Broca's area) is often activated in working memory tasks where subvocal rehearsal is the main strategy for maintenance (Bench *et al.* 1993; Awh *et al.* 1996). Similar mechanisms may be involved in the active maintenance of visual information such as objects, which may be represented by their visual features (e.g. size, colour, texture, shape) as well as verbal information associated by an individual with a visual stimulus (Postle *et al.* 2005). The mechanisms underlying rehearsal of non-verbalizable material like spatial locations have been more difficult to resolve, but are likely to involve related motor and/or attentional processes (Awh *et al.* 1999; Awh & Jonides 2001). Positional information might be represented in oculomotor coordinates, where the memorized location might be maintained in terms of a saccade vector that acquires the target. Therefore, rehearsal of locations could simply be the reactivations of oculomotor programmes without actually making overt eye movements and can account for consistent activation of the frontal eye fields during spatial working memory tasks (Courtney *et al.* 1998). Thus, the rehearsal may be one mechanism by which transiently activated representations can be reactivated and refreshed.

Active maintenance (or rehearsal) of task-relevant representations clearly requires interactions between brain regions (Goldman-Rakic 1988; Fuster 1995, 2003). Such interactions could support working memory maintenance processes via synaptic reverberations in recurrent circuits (Durstewitz *et al.* 2000*b*; Wang 2001) or synchronous oscillations between neuronal populations (Singer & Gray 1995; Engel *et al*. 2001). Owing to the limitations in available methodology, only a few studies to date have been able to assess if and how neurons and brain regions interact to facilitate active maintenance processes (Fuster *et al*. 1985; Chafee & Goldman-Rakic 1998; Tomita *et al*. 1999; Funahashi & Inoue 2000; Constantinidis *et al*. 2001; Tallon-Baudry *et al*. 2001), although this is a critical issue for the future (see also Vuilleumier & Driver 2007). In other words, neither single neuron recordings nor standard univariate analysis of fMRI data, in which each neuron or voxel or brain region is analysed independently of all others, reveal more than the nature of isolated activity within these regions. Thus, only indirect evidence exists to support the assertion that working memory maintenance processes are implemented by the interaction of nodes within a neural network. Human functional neuroimaging, however, is ideally and uniquely suited to explore network interactions, since this method simultaneously records correlates of neural activity throughout the entire functioning brain with high spatial resolution. Thus, multivariate analyses have been developed to analyse neuroimaging data (Friston *et al*. 1993; McIntosh 1998), which thus far have been used to investigate functional connectivity in many cognitive domains, such as learning (Buchel *et al*. 1999; Toni *et al*. 2002), attention (Friston & Buchel 2000; Rowe *et al*. 2002) and long-term memory (Maguire *et al*. 2000).

Recently, we developed a new multivariate method designed specifically to characterize functional connectivity in an event-related fMRI dataset and measure interregional correlations during the individual stages of a delay task (Rissman *et al*. 2004). Using this method, we specifically sought to characterize the network of brain regions associated with the maintenance of the representation of a visual stimulus over a short-delay interval. To accomplish this, we re-analysed two previously published event-related fMRI datasets (Ranganath & D'Esposito 2001; Druzgal & D'Esposito 2003) that employed similar delayed recognition paradigms on different groups of subjects and used a functionally defined region of visual association cortex as the exploratory seed. Since both tasks required the maintenance of face stimuli, the fusiform face area (FFA), a visual region that is selective for viewing faces (Kanwisher *et al*. 1997), was used as the seed. By pooling the correlation data from these two datasets into a single group-level analysis, we identified the network of brain regions that was most consistently correlated with the FFA seed during the delay period and hence associated with the active maintenance of the represented stimulus (figure 2.4). The presence of significant delay-period correlations between the FFA and regions of the prefrontal and parietal cortex regions supports models of working memory which suggest that higher-order association cortices interact with posterior sensory regions to facilitate the active maintenance of a sensory percept. The correlation between the FFA and these high-order regions appears to be initially established during the encoding of the cue stimulus, and these correlations are largely sustained during the delay period, despite a dramatic decrease in the level of univariate activity. Similarly, we have also found that language-related visual association areas involved in the maintenance of words (as described earlier), in the absence of visual input, also exhibit increased functional connectivity with the PFC (Fiebach *et al*. 2006). In summary, all of these empirical findings extend neural mechanisms of maintenance processes from the finding of persistent isolated neural activity within functionally specialized brain regions to encompass the concept of persistent functional connectivity between brain regions.

As discussed earlier, physiological and behavioural data suggest that each brain region, although forming part of a functional network, may contribute different elements to active maintenance by the nature of the representations that are coded within each region. However, different brain regions within a functional network probably differ only in their degree of

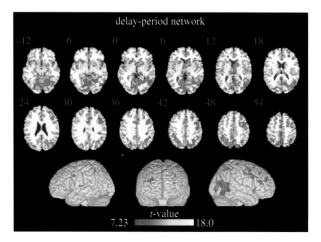

Fig. 2.4 Delay-period correlation map with right FFA seed (N=17; Gazzaley *et al.* 2004). Activations are thresholded at p<0.05 (corrected) and shown overlaid on both axial slices and a three-dimensionally rendered MNI template brain. The colour scale indicates the magnitude of the *t*-values.

participation in a manner that is dependent on the context of the operation being actively performed (Fuster 1995, 2003; McIntosh 2000). This is immediately evident by noting, for example, that the same regions which are involved in temporarily maintaining a representation are often also engaged during the encoding and retrieval of that information (e.g. Funahashi *et al.* 1989). Further understanding of such neural interactions will require investigating the influence of hypothesis-driven task design manipulations on the functional connectivity between brain regions. For example, we have investigated functional connectivity during a delay task with distracting stimuli aimed at increasing active maintenance demands (Yoon *et al.* 2006). During the performance of a delayed face recognition task, selective interference was evident behaviourally when face stimuli were presented as distractors during the delay period, relative to a condition in which scene stimuli were presented as distractors. Event-related fMRI data showed that maintenance-related functional connectivity between the lateral PFC and FFAs was perturbed during these face distraction trials. These data provide additional support for the notion that a plausible mechanism for the active maintenance is the coupling of abstracted, higher-order information in the PFC and stimuli-specific sensory information in the visual association cortex through reverberant activity between these areas. Finally, it is important to note that correlational data such as these need to be complemented with techniques to establish the functional necessity of network nodes, through methods such as lesions studies in animals and man (e.g. Fuster *et al.* 1985; Mottaghy *et al.* 2002; D'Esposito *et al.* 2006; see also Vuilleumier & Driver 2007).

2.6 Is there a central executive in the brain?

Further understanding of the neural mechanisms underlying the active maintenance of task-relevant information may hinge on our ability to resolve the nature of stored representations in addition to the types of operations performed on such representations (Wood & Grafman 2003). 'Representations' are symbolic codes for information activated either transiently or permanently within neuronal networks. 'Operations' are processes or computations performed on representations. As we have reviewed thus far, models of working memory (e.g. Fuster 1985; Goldman-Rakic 1987; Petrides 1994; Kieras *et al.* 1999; D'Esposito & Postle 2000; Miller & Cohen 2001) vary substantially in the relative importance given to representations and operations. Baddeley's original advance was to move us from the concept of short-term memory that accounted only for the storage of representations, to the concept of working memory as a multi-component system that allows for both storage and processing of temporarily active representations. Likewise, Logie (1995) considered working memory as a 'mental workspace' that cannot only hold but is also able to manipulate activated representations. In a recent peer review of an empirical paper we submitted to a journal, the following comment was offered: 'one concern is conceptual in that the authors describe their tasks as involving working memory when it is basically a letter memory task that primarily emphasizes storage with little or no processing. If working memory is defined as simultaneous storage and processing, then these tasks would probably be considered to assess short-term memory rather than working memory'. Thus, it is probably fair to say that the concept of working memory as a non-unitary system that allows for both storage and processing has gained popular acceptance in our field. However, in my opinion, less progress has been made regarding the neural mechanisms underlying the 'processing' component of working memory as compared with the 'storage' component (although see Petrides 2005).

Based on the data we have reviewed thus far, we propose that any population of neurons within primary or unimodal association cortex can exhibit persistent neuronal activity, which serves to actively maintain the representations coded by those neuronal populations. Areas of multimodal cortex, such as PFC and parietal cortex, which are in a position to integrate representations through connectivity to unimodal association cortex, are also critically involved in the active maintenance of task-relevant information (see also Burgess *et al.* 2007; Stuss & Alexander 2007). Miller & Cohen (2001) have proposed that in addition to the recent sensory information, integrated representations of task contingencies and even abstract rules (e.g. if this object then this later response) are also maintained in the PFC. This is similar to what Fuster (1997) has long emphasized, namely that the PFC is critically responsible for temporal integration and the mediation of events that are separated in time but contingent on one another. In this way, the PFC may exert 'control' in that the information it represents can bias posterior unimodal association cortex in order to keep neural representations of behaviourally relevant sensory information activated when they are no longer present in the external environment (Fuster 2000; Ranganath *et al.* 2004; Miller & D'Esposito 2005; Postle 2005). In a real world example, when a person is looking at a crowd of people, the visual scene presented to the retina may include a myriad of angles, shapes, people and objects. However, if that person is a police officer looking for an armed robber escaping through the crowd, some mechanism of suppressing irrelevant visual information while enhancing task-relevant information is necessary for an efficient and effective search. Thus, neural activity throughout the brain that is generated by input from the outside world may be differentially enhanced or suppressed, presumably from top-down signals emanating from integrative brain regions such as PFC, based on the context of the situation. Thus, in this formulation, the processing component of working memory is that the control of actively maintained representations within primary and unimodal association cortex stems from the representational power of multimodal association cortex, such as the PFC, parietal cortex and/or hippocampus. If the PFC, for example, stores the rules and goals, then the activation of such PFC representations will be necessary when behaviour must be guided by internal states or intentions. As Miller & Cohen (2001) elegantly state, putative top-down signals originating in PFC may permit 'the active maintenance of patterns of activity that represent goals and the means to achieve them. They provide bias signals throughout much of the rest of the brain, affecting visual processes and other sensory modalities, as well as systems responsible for response execution, memory retrieval, emotional evaluation, etc. The aggregate effect of these bias signals is to guide the flow of neural activity along pathways that establish the proper mappings between inputs, internal states and outputs needed to perform a given task'. Computational models of this type of system have created a PFC module (e.g. O'Reilly *et al*. 2002) that consists of 'rule' units whose activation leads to the production of a response other than the one most strongly associated with a given input. Thus, 'this module is not responsible for carrying out input–output mappings needed for performance. Rather, this module influences the activity of other units whose responsibility is making the needed mappings' (e.g. Cohen *et al*. 1990). Thus, there is no need to propose the existence of a homunculus (e.g. central executive) in the brain that can perform a wide range of cognitive operations which are necessary for the task at hand (for a further discussion of this issue, see Shallice 1988; see also Hazy *et al*. 2006).

We have used a delay task to directly study the neural mechanisms underlying top-down modulation by investigating the processes involved when participants were required to enhance relevant and suppress irrelevant information (Gazzaley *et al*. 2005*b*). During each trial, participants observed sequences of two faces and two natural scenes presented in a randomized order. The tasks differed in the instructions informing the participants how to process the stimuli: (i) remember faces and ignore scenes, (ii) remember scenes and ignore faces, or (iii) passively view faces and scenes without attempting to remember them. In each task, the period in which the cue stimuli were presented was balanced for bottom-up visual information, thus allowing us to probe the influence of goal-directed behaviour on neural activity (top-down modulation). In the two memory tasks, the encoding of the task-relevant stimuli requires selective attention and thus permits the dissociation of physiological measures of enhancement and suppression relative to the passive baseline. Also in the memory tasks, after a short-delay period, the participants were tested on their ability to recognize a probe stimulus as being one of the task-relevant cues, yielding a behavioural measure of memory performance. These experiments were performed using both event-related fMRI and electroencephalography (event-related potentials (ERP)) to record correlates of neural activity while the participants performed the task. This allowed us to capitalize on the high spatial resolution of fMRI and the high temporal resolution of ERP.

We investigated activity measures of enhancement and suppression obtained from the visual association cortex of young healthy participants. For fMRI, we used an independent functional localizer to identify both the stimulus-selective face and scene regions in the FFA and the parahippocampal/lingual gyrus, respectively. For ERP, we used a face-selective ERP component, the N170, which is localized to posterior occipital electrodes and is thought to reflect visual association cortex activity with some face specificity (Bentin *et al*. 1996). Our fMRI and ERP data revealed top-down modulation of both activity magnitude and processing speed that occurred above or below the perceptual baseline depending on task instruction (figure 2.5).

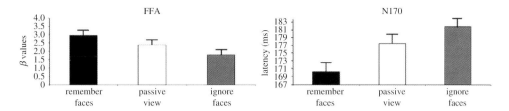

Fig. 2.5 (*a*) fMRI and (*b*) ERP data during the performance of a face/scene delay task in healthy human individuals (Gazzaley *et al*. 2005*a*). The left-hand graph shows fMRI signal from the right FFA during the three behavioural conditions. fMRI signal is greatest during the 'remember faces' condition and least during the 'ignore faces' condition. The right-hand graphs show the average N170 peak latency values during the three behavioural conditions. N170 latency is earliest during the 'remember faces' condition and latest during the 'ignore faces'condition.

In other words, during the encoding period of the delay task, FFA activity was enhanced, and the N170 occurred earlier, when faces had to be remembered as compared with a condition where they were passively viewed. Likewise, FFA activity was suppressed, and the N170 occurred later, when faces had to be ignored (with scenes now being retained instead across the delay interval) compared with a condition where they were passively viewed.

Thus, there appears to be at least two types of top-down signal, one that serves to enhance task-relevant information and another that serves to suppress task-relevant information. It is well documented that the nervous system uses interleaved inhibitory and excitatory mechanisms throughout the neuroaxis (e.g. spinal reflexes, cerebellar outputs and basal ganglia movement control networks). Thus, it may not be surprising that enhancement and suppression mechanisms may exist to control cognition (Knight *et al*. 1999; Shimamura 2000). By generating contrast via both enhancements and suppressions of activity magnitude and processing speed, top-down signals bias the likelihood of successful representation of relevant information in a competitive system.

Though it has been proposed that the PFC provides a major source of the types of top-down signals that we have described, this hypothesis largely originates from suggestive findings rather than direct empirical evidence. However, a few studies lend direct causal support to this hypothesis (see also Vuilleumier & Driver 2007). For example, Fuster *et al*. (1985) investigated the effect of cooling inactivation of specific parts of the PFC upon spiking activity in ITC neurons, during a DMS colour task. During the delay interval in this task—when persistent stimulus-specific activity in ITC neurons is observed—inactivation caused attenuated spiking profiles and a loss of stimulus specificity of ITC neurons. These two alterations of ITC signalling strongly implicate the PFC as a source of top-down signals necessary for maintaining robust sensory representations in the absence of bottom-up sensory activity. Tomita *et al*. (1999) isolated top-down signals during the retrieval of paired associates in a visual memory task. Spiking activity was recorded from stimulus-specific ITC neurons as cue stimuli were presented to the ipsilateral hemifield. This experiment's unique feature was the ability to separate bottom-up sensory signals from a top-down mnemonic reactivation, using a posterior split-brain procedure that limited hemispheric crosstalk to the anterior corpus callosum connecting each PFC. When a probe stimulus was presented ipsilaterally to the recording site, thus restricting bottom-up visual input to the contralateral hemisphere, stimulus-specific neurons became activated at the recording site approximately 170 ms later. Since these neurons received no bottom-up visual signals of the probe stimulus, with the only route between the two hemispheres being via the PFC, this experiment showed that PFC neurons were sufficient to trigger the reactivation of object-selective representations in ITC regions in a top-down manner. The combined lesion/electrophysiological approach in humans has rarely been implemented (though see Vuilleumier & Driver 2007). However, Chao & Knight (1998) studied patients with lateral PFC lesions during DMS tasks. It was found that when distracting stimuli are presented during the delay period, the amplitude of the recorded ERP from posterior electrodes was markedly increased in patients compared with controls. These results were interpreted to show disinhibition of sensory processing and support a role of the PFC in suppressing the representation of stimuli that are irrelevant for current behaviour.

Clearly, there are other areas of multimodal cortex such as posterior parietal cortex, and the hippocampus, that can also be the source of top-down signals. For example, the hippocampus has been proposed to be specialized for 'rapid learning of arbitrary information which can be recalled in the service of controlled processing' (O'Reilly *et al*. 1999). Moreover, input from brainstem neuromodulatory systems probably plays a critical role in modulating goal-directed behaviour (see also Robbins 2007). For example, the dopaminergic system probably plays a critical role in cognitive control processes (for a review, see Cools & Robbins 2004). Specifically, it is proposed that phasic bursts of dopaminergic neurons may be critical for updating currently activated task-relevant representations whereas tonic dopaminergic activity serves to stabilize such representations (e.g. Durstewitz *et al*. 2000*a*; Cohen *et al*. 2002). Empirical studies in animals and man have provided support for a role of dopamine in working memory (e.g. Sawaguchi 2001; Gibbs & D'Esposito 2005).

2.7 Conclusions

The overall goal of cognitive neuroscience as a discipline is to determine the biological basis of the mind. As an interdisciplinary discipline that has evolved from both neuroscience and psychology, cognitive neuroscientists consume data derived from each of these disciplines in their attempt to advance cognitive theory as well as determine how the brain implements cognitive function. Advances made in understanding the cognitive and neural basis of working memory provide examples of this synergy. In my opinion, future studies must continue to consider both cognitive and neural data in the way that has been briefly illustrated in this review. Research thus far suggests that working memory can be viewed as neither a unitary nor a dedicated system. A network of brain regions, including the PFC, is critical for the active maintenance of internal representations that are necessary for goal-directed behaviour. Thus, working memory is not localized to a single brain region but probably is an emergent property of the functional interactions between the PFC and the rest of the brain.

I would like to express my sincere appreciation to all of my former and current students and postdocs for their invaluable contributions to the formulation of the ideas presented in this paper.

References

Anderson, J. R. 1983 *The architecture of cognition*. Cambridge, MA: Harvard University Press.
Awh, E. & Jonides, J. 2001 Overlapping mechanisms of attention and spatial working memory. *Trends Cogn. Sci* **5**, 119–126. (doi:10.1016/S1364-6613(00)01593-X)

Awh, E., Jonides, J., Smith, E. E., Schumacher, E. H., Koeppe, R. A. & Katz, S. 1996 Dissociation of storage and rehearsal in verbal working memory: evidence from PET. *Psychol. Sci.* **7**, 25–31. (doi:10.1111/j.1467-9280.1996.tb00662.x)

Awh, E., Jonides, J., Smith, E. E., Buxton, R. B., Frank, L. R., Love, T., Wong, E. C. & Gmeindl, L. 1999 Rehearsal in spatial working memory: evidence from neuroimaging. *Psychol. Sci.* **10**, 433–437. (doi:10.1111/1467-9280.00182)

Baddeley, A. 1986 *Working memory*. New York, NY: Oxford University Press.

Baddeley, A. 2000 The episodic buffer: a new component of working memory? *Trends Cogn. Sci.* **4**, 417–423. (doi:10.1016/S1364-6613(00)01538-2)

Baddeley, A. & Hitch, G. J. 1974 Working memory. In *Recent advances in learning and motivation*, vol. 8 (ed. G. Bower), pp. 47–89. New York, NY: Academic Press.

Bauer, R. H. & Fuster, J. M. 1976 Delayed-matching and delayed-response deficit from cooling dorsolateral prefrontal cortex in monkeys. *Q. J. Exp. Psychol.* B **90**, 293–302.

Bench, C. J., Frith, C. D., Grasby, P. M., Friston, K. J., Paulesu, E., Frackowiak, R. S. J. & Dolan, R. J. 1993 Investigations of the functional anatomy of attention using the Stroop test. *Neuropsychologia* **31**, 907–922. (doi:10.1016/0028-3932(93)90147-R)

Bentin, S., Allison, T., Puce, A., Perez, E. & McCarthy, G. 1996 Electrophysiological studies of face perception in humans. *J. Cogn. Neurosci.* **8**, 551–565.

Buchel, C., Coull, J. T. & Friston, K. J. 1999 The predictive value of changes in effective connectivity for human learning. *Science* **283**, 1538–1541. (doi:10.1126/science. 283.5407.1538)

Burgess, P. W., Gilbert, S. J. & Dumontheil, I. 2007 Function and localization within rostral prefrontal cortex (area 10). *Phil. Trans. R. Soc. B* **362**, 887–899. (doi:10.1098/rstb. 2007.2095)

Calvert, G. A., Bullmore, E. T., Brammer, M. J., Campbell, R., Williams, S. C., McGuire, P. K., Woodruff, P. W., Iversen, S. D. & David, A. S. 1997 Activation of auditory cortex during silent lipreading. *Science* **276**, 593–596. (doi:10.1126/science.276.5312.593)

Chafee, M. V. & Goldman-Rakic, P. S. 1998 Matching patterns of activity in primate prefrontal area 8a and parietal area 7ip neurons during a spatial working memory task. *J. Neurophysiol.* **79**, 2919–2940.

Chao, L. & Knight, R. 1998 Contribution of human prefrontal cortex to delay performance. *J. Cogn. Neurosci.* **10**, 167–177. (doi:10.1162/089892998562636)

Cohen, L. & Dehaene, S. 2004 Specialization within the ventral stream: the case for the visual word form area. *Neuroimage* **22**, 466–476. (doi:10.1016/j.neuroimage. 2003.12.049)

Cohen, J. D., Braver, T. S. & Brown, J. W. 2002 Computational perspectives on dopamine function in prefrontal cortex. *Curr. Opin. Neurobiol.* **12**, 223–229. (doi:10.1016/S0959-4388(02)00314-8)

Constantinidis, C., Franowicz, M. N. & Goldman-Rakic, P. S. 2001 Coding specificity in cortical micro-circuits: a multiple-electrode analysis of primate prefrontal cortex. *J. Neurosci.* **21**, 3646–3655.

Cools, R. & Robbins, T. W. 2004 Chemistry of the adaptive mind. *Phil. Trans. R. Soc. A* **362**, 2871–2888. (doi:10. 1098/rsta.2004.1468)

Courtney, S. M., Petit, L., Maisog, J. M., Ungerleider, L. G. & Haxby, J. V. 1998 An area specialized for spatial working memory in human frontal cortex. *Science* **279**, 1347–1351. (doi:10.1126/science. 279.5355.1347)

Cowan, N. 1988 Evolving conceptions of memory storage, selective attention, and their mutual constraints within the human information processing system. *Psychol. Bull.* **104**, 163–171. (doi:10.1037/0033-2909.104.2.163)

Cowan, N. 1999 An embedded-process model of working memory. In *Models of working memory: mechanisms of active maintenance and executive control* (eds A. Miyake & P. Shah), pp. 62–101. Cambridge, UK: Cambridge University Press.

Cohen, J. D., Dunbar, K. & McClelland, J. L. 1990 On the control of automatic processes: a parallel distributed processing account of the Stroop effect. *Psychol. Rev.* **97**, 332–361.

Curtis, C. E. & D'Esposito, M. 2003 Persistent activity in the prefrontal cortex during working memory. *Trends. Cogn. Sci.* **7**, 415–423. (doi:10.1016/S1364-6613(03)00197-9)

Curtis, C. E., Rao, V. Y. & D'Esposito, M. 2004 Maintenance of spatial and motor codes during oculomotor delayed response tasks. *J. Neurosci.* **24**, 3944–3952. (doi:10.1523/ JNEUROSCI.5640-03.2004)

D'Esposito, M., Postle, B. R. & Rypma, B. 2000 Prefrontal cortical contributions to working memory: evidence from event-related fMRI studies. *Exp. Brain Res.* **133**, 3–11. (doi:10.1007/s002210000395)

D'Esposito, M., Cooney, J. W., Gazzaley, A., Gibbs, S. E. & Postle, B. R. 2006 Is the prefrontal cortex necessary for delay task performance? Evidence from lesion and FMRI data. *J. Int. Neuropsychol. Soc.* **12**, 248–260.

Druzgal, T. J. & D'Esposito, M. 2003 Dissecting contributions of prefrontal cortex and fusiform face area to face working memory. *J. Cogn. Neurosci.* **15**, 771–784. (doi:10.1162/089892903322370708)

Durstewitz, D., Seamans, J. K. & Sejnowski, T. J. 2000*a* Dopamine-mediated stabilization of delay-period activity in a network model of prefrontal cortex. *J. Neurophysiol.* **83**, 1733–1750.

Durstewitz, D., Seamans, J. K. & Sejnowski, T. J. 2000*b* Neurocomputational models of working memory. *Nat. Neurosci.* **3**, 1184–1191. (doi:10.1038/81460)

Engel,A.K., Fries,P. & Singer,W.2001 Dynamic predictions: oscillations and synchrony in top-down processing. *Nat. Rev. Neurosci.* **2**, 704–816. (doi:10.1038/35094565)

Fiebach, C. J., Rissman, J. & D'Esposito, M. 2006 Modulation of inferotemporal cortex activation during verbal working memory maintenance. *Neuron* **51**, 251–261. (doi:10.1016/j.neuron.2006.06.007)

Friston, K. J. & Buchel, C. 2000 Attentional modulation of effective connectivity from V2 to V5/MT in humans. *Proc. Natl Acad. Sci. USA* **97**, 7591–9596. (doi:10.1073/pnas. 97.13.7591)

Friston, K. J., Frith, C. D., Liddle, P. F. & Frackowiak, R. S. 1993 Functional connectivity: the principal-component analysis of large (PET) data sets. *J. Cereb. Blood Flow Metab.* **13**, 5–14.

Funahashi, S. & Inoue, M. 2000 Neuronal interactions related to working memory processes in the primate prefrontal cortex revealed by cross-correlation analysis. *Cereb. Cortex* **10**, 535–551. (doi:10.1093/cercor/10.6.535)

Funahashi, S., Bruce, C. J. & Goldman-Rakic, P. S. 1989 Mnemonic coding of visual space in the monkey's dorsolateral prefrontal cortex. *J. Neurophysiol.* **61**, 331–349.

Funahashi, S., Bruce, C. J. & Goldman-Rakic, P. S. 1993 Dorsolateral prefrontal lesions and oculomotor delayed-response performance: evidence for mnemonic "scotomas". *J. Neurosci.* **13**, 1479–1497.

Fuster, J. M. (ed.) 1985 *The prefrontal cortex and temporal integration cerebral cortex: vol. 4, association and auditory cortices*. New York, NY: Plenum Press.

Fuster, J. M. 1995 *Memory in the cerebral cortex*. Cambridge, UK: The MIT Press.

Fuster, J. 1997 *The prefrontal cortex: anatomy, physiology, and neuropsychology of the frontal lobes*. New York, NY: Raven Press.

Fuster, J. M. 2000 Cortical dynamics of memory. *Int. J. Psychophysiol.* **35**, 155–164. (doi:10.1016/S0167-8760(99)00050-1)

Fuster, J. M. 2003 *Cortex and mind*. New York, NY: Oxford University Press.

Fuster, J. M. & Alexander, G. E. 1971 Neuron activity related to short-term memory. *Science* **173**, 652–654. (doi:10.1126/science.173.3997.652)

Fuster, J. M., Bauer, R. H. & Jervey, J. P. 1985 Functional interactions between inferotemporal and prefrontal cortex in a cognitive task. *Brain Res.* **330**, 299–307. (doi:10.1016/ 0006-8993(85)90689-4)

Gazzaley, A., Rissman, J. & Desposito, M. 2004 Functional connectivity during working memory maintenance. *Cogn. Affect. Behav. Neurosci.* **4**, 580–599.

Gazzaley, A., Cooney, J. W., McEvoy, K., Knight, R. T. & D'Esposito, M. 2005*a* Top-down enhancement and suppression of the magnitude and speed of neural activity. *J. Cogn. Neurosci.* **17**, 507–517. (doi:10.1162/0898929053279522)

Gazzaley, A., Cooney, J. W., McEvoy, K., Knight, R. T. & D'Esposito, M. 2005*b* Top-down enhancement and suppression of the magnitude and speed of neural activity. *J. Cogn. Neurosci.* **17**, 1–11. (doi:10.1162/0898929053279522)

Gibbs, S. E. & D'Esposito, M. 2005 A functional MRI study of the effects of bromocriptine, a dopamine receptor agonist, on component processes of working memory. *Psychopharmacology (Berlin)* **180**, 644–653. (doi:10.1007/ s00213-005-0077-5)

Goldman-Rakic, P. S. 1987 Circuitry of the prefrontal cortex and the regulation of behavior by representational memory. In *Handbook of physiology. Sec 1. The nervous system*, vol. 5, section I (eds F. Plum & V. Mountcastle), pp. 373–417. Bethesda, MD: American Physiological Society.

Goldman-Rakic, P. 1988 Topography of cognition: parallel distributed networks in primate association cortex. *Annu. Rev. Neurosci.* **11**, 137–156. (doi:10.1146/annurev.ne.11.030188.001033)

Hazy, T. E., Frank, M. J. & O'Reilly, R. C. 2006 Banishing the homunculus: making working memory work. *Neuroscience* **139**, 105–118. (doi:10.1016/j.neuroscience.2005.04.067)

Hickok, G., Buchsbaum, B., Humphries, C. & Muftuler, T. 2003 Auditory-motor interaction revealed by fMRI: speech, music, and working memory in area Spt. *J. Cogn. Neurosci.* **15**, 673–682.

Kanwisher, N., McDermott, J. & Chun, M. M. 1997 The fusiform face area: a module in human extrastriate cortex specialized for face perception. *J. Neurosci.* **17**, 4302–4311.

Kieras, D. E., Meyer, D. E., Mueller, S. & Seymour, T. 1999 Insights into working memory from the perspective of the EPIC architecture for modeling skilled perceptual-motor and cognitive human performance. In *Models of working memory: mechanisms of active maintenance and executive control* (eds A. Miyake & P. Shah), pp. 183–223. Cambridge, UK: Cambridge University Press.

Kimberg, D. Y., D'Esposito, M. & Farah, M. J. 1997 Cognitive functions in the prefrontal cortex-working memory and executive control. *Curr. Dir. Psychol. Sci.* **6**, 185–192. (doi:10.1111/1467-8721. ep10772959)

Klein, I., Paradis, A. L., Poline, J. B., Kosslyn, S. M. & Le Bihan, D. 2000 Transient activity in the human calcarine cortex during visual-mental imagery: an event-related fMRI study. *J. Cogn. Neurosci.* **12**(Suppl. 2), 15–23. (doi:10.1162/089892900564037)

Knight, R. T., Staines, W. R., Swick, D. & Chao, L. L. 1999 Prefrontal cortex regulates inhibition and excitation in distributed neural networks. *Acta. Psychol. (Amst)* **101**, 159–178. (doi:10.1016/ S0001-6918(99)00004-9)

Kraemer, D. J., Macrae, C. N., Green, A. E. & Kelley, W. M. 2005 Musical imagery: sound of silence activates auditory cortex. *Nature* **434**, 158. (doi:10.1038/434158a)

Kubota, K. & Niki, H. 1971 Prefrontal cortical unit activity and delayed alternation performance in monkeys. *J. Neurophysiol.* **34**, 337–347.

Logie, R. H. 1995 *Visuo-spatial working memory.* Hove, UK: Erlbaum.

Maguire, E. A., Mummery, C. J. & Buchel, C. 2000 Patterns of hippocampal–cortical interaction dissociate temporal lobe memory subsystems. *Hippocampus* **10**, 475–482. (doi:10.1002/1098-1063(2000)10:4<475::AID-HIPO14>3.0.CO;2-X)

Marslen-Wilson, W. D. & Tyler, L. K. 2007 Morphology, language and the brain: the decompositional substrate for language comprehension. *Phil. Trans. R. Soc. B* **362**, 823–836. (doi:10.1098/ rstb.2007.2091)

McIntosh, A. R. 1998 Understanding neural interactions in learning and memory using functional neuroimaging. *Ann. NY Acad. Sci.* **855**, 556–571. (doi:10.1111/j.1749-6632.1998.tb10625.x)

McIntosh, A. R. 2000 Towards a network theory of cognition. *Neural Netw.* **13**, 861–870. (doi:10.1016/S0893-6080(00) 00059-9)

Miller, B. T. & D'Esposito, M. 2005 Searching for "the top" in top-down control. *Neuron* **48**, 535–538. (doi:10.1016/ j.neuron.2005.11.002)

Miller, E. K. & Cohen, J. D. 2001 An integrative theory of prefrontal cortex function. *Annu. Rev. Neurosci.* **4**, 167–202. (doi:10.1146/annurev.neuro.24.1.167)

Miller, E. K., Li, L. & Desimone, R. 1993 Activity of neurons in anterior inferior temporal cortex during a short-term memory task. *J. Neurosci.* **13**, 1460–1478.

Miyake, A. & Shah, P. (eds) 1999 *Models of working memory: mechanisms of active maintenance and executive control.* Cambridge, UK: Cambridge University Press.

Miyashita, Y. & Chang, H. S. 1988 Neuronal correlate of pictorial short-term memory in the primate temporal cortex. *Nature* **331**, 68–70. (doi:10.1038/331068a0)

Mottaghy, F. M., Gangitano, M., Sparing, R., Krause, B. J. & Pascual-Leone, A. 2002 Segregation of areas related to visual working memory in the prefrontal cortex revealed by rTMS. *Cereb. Cortex* **12**, 369–375. (doi:10.1093/cercor/12.4.369)

Murray, D. J. 1968 Articulation and acoustic confusability in short-term memory. *J. Exp. Psychol.* **78**, 679–684. (doi:10.1037/h0026641)

Nakamura, K. & Kubota, K. 1995 Mnemonic firing of neurons in the monkey temporal pole during a visual recognition memory task. *J. Neurophysiol.* **74**, 162–178.

Nobre, A. C., Allison, T. & McCarthy, G. 1994 Word recognition in the human inferior temporal lobe. *Nature* **372**, 260–263. (doi:10.1038/372260a0)

Norman, D. A. & Shallice, T. 1986 Attention to action: willed and automatic control of behavior. In *Consciousness and self-regulation*, vol. 4 (eds R. J. Davidson, G. E. Schwartz & D. Shapiro), pp. 1–18. New York, NY: Plenum Press.

O'Reilly, R.C., Braver, T. S. & Cohen, J. D. 1999 A biologically based computational model of working memory. In *Models of working memory: mechanisms of active maintenance and executive control* (eds A. Miyakw & P. Shah), pp. 62–101. Cambridge, UK: Cambridge University Press.

O'Reilly, R. C., Noelle, D. C., Braver, T. S. & Cohen, J. D. 2002 Prefrontal cortex and dynamic categorization tasks: representational organization and neuromodulatory control. *Cereb. Cortex* **12**, 246–257. (doi:10.1093/cercor/12.3.246)

Patterson, K. 2007 The reign of typicality in semantic memory. *Phil. Trans. R. Soc. B* **362**, 813–821. (doi:10.1098/rstb.2007.2090)

Paulesu, E., Frith, C. D. & Frackowiak, R. S. 1993 The neural correlates of the verbal component of working memory. *Nature* **362**, 342–345. (doi:10.1038/362342a0)

Petrides, M. 1994 Frontal lobes and working memory: evidence from investigations of the effects of cortical excisions in nonhuman primates. In *Handbook of neuropsychology*, vol. 9 (eds F. Boller & J. Grafman), pp. 59–84. Amsterdam, The Netherlands: Elsevier Science B.V.

Petrides, M. 2005 Lateral prefrontal cortex: architectonic and functional organization. *Phil. Trans. R. Soc. B* **360**, 781–795. (doi:10.1098/rstb.2005.1631)

Postle, B. R. 2005 Delay-period activity in the prefrontal cortex: one function is sensory gating. *J. Cogn. Neurosci.* **17**, 1679–1690. (doi:10.1162/089892905774589208)

Postle, B. R., Desposito, M. & Corkin, S. 2005 Effects of verbal and nonverbal interference on spatial and object visual working memory. *Mem. Cogn.* **33**, 203–212.

Ranganath, C. & D'Esposito, M. 2001 Medial temporal lobe activity associated with active maintenance of novel information. *Neuron* **31**, 865–873. (doi:10.1016/S0896-6273(01)00411-1)

Ranganath, C., Cohen, M. X., Dam, C. & D'Esposito, M. 2004 Inferior temporal, prefrontal, and hippocampal contributions to visual working memory maintenance and associative memory retrieval. *J. Neurosci.* **24**, 3917–3925. (doi:10.1523/JNEUROSCI.5053-03.2004)

Repovs, G.& Baddeley, A. 2006 The multi-component model of working memory: explorations in experimental cognitive psychology. *Neuroscience* **139**, 5–21. (doi:10.1016/j.neuroscience.2005.12.061)

Rissman, J., Gazzaley, A. & D'Esposito, M. 2004 Measuring functional connectivity during distinct stages of a cognitive task. *Neuroimage* **23**, 752–763. (doi:10.1016/j.neuroimage.2004.06.035)

Robbins, T. W. 2007 Shifting and stopping: fronto-striatal substrates, neurochemical modulation and clinical implications. *Phil. Trans. R. Soc. B* **362**, 917–932. (doi:10.1098/rstb.2007.2097)

Rowe, J., Friston, K., Frackowiak, R. & Passingham, R. 2002 Attention to action: specific modulation of corticocortical interactions in humans. *Neuroimage* **17**, 988–998. (doi:10.1016/S1053-8119(02)91156-0)

Ruchkin, D. S., Grafman, J., Cameron, K. & Berndt, R. S. 2003 Working memory retention systems: a state of activated long-term memory. *Behav. Brain Sci.* **26**, 709–728, discussion 728–777.

Sawaguchi, T. 2001 The effects of dopamine and its antagonists on directional delay-period activity of prefrontal neurons in monkeys during an oculomotor delayed-response task. *Neurosci. Res.* **41**, 115–128. (doi:10.1016/S0168-0102(01)00270-X)

Shallice, T. 1988 *From neuropsychology to mental structure*. Cambridge, UK: Cambridge University Press.

Shimamura, A. P. 2000 The role of the prefrontal cortex in dynamic filtering. *Psychobiology* **28**, 207–218.

Silver, M. A., Ress, D. & Heeger, D. J. 2006 Neural correlates of sustained spatial attention in human early visual cortex. *J. Neurophysiol.* **97**, 229–237. (doi:10.1152/jn.00677.2006)

Singer, W. & Gray, C. M. 1995 Visual feature integration and the temporal correlation hypothesis. *Annu. Rev. Neurosci.* **18**, 555–586. (doi:10.1146/annurev.ne.18.030195.003011)

Stuss, D. T. & Alexander, M. P. 2007 Is there a dysexecutive syndrome? *Phil. Trans. R. Soc. B* **362**, 901–915. (doi:10.1098/rstb.2007.2096)

Tallon-Baudry, C., Bertrand, O. & Fischer, C. 2001 Oscillatory synchrony between human extrastriate areas during visual short-term memory maintenance. *J. Neurosci.* **21**, RC177.

Tomita, H., Ohbayashi, M., Nakahara, K., Hasegawa, I. & Miyashita, Y. 1999 Top-down signal from prefrontal cortex in executive control of memory retrieval. *Nature* **401**, 699–703. (doi:10.1038/44372)

Toni, I., Rowe, J., Stephan, K. E. & Passingham, R. E. 2002 Changes of cortico-striatal effective connectivity during visuomotor learning. *Cereb. Cortex* **12**, 1040–1047. (doi:10.1093/cercor/12.10.1040)

Vallar, G. & Shallice, T. 1990 *Neuropsychological impairments of short-term memory*. Cambridge, UK: Cambridge University Press.

Vuilleumier, P. & Driver, J. 2007 Modulation of visual processing by attention and emotion: windows on causal interactions between human brain regions. *Phil. Trans. R. Soc. B* **362**, 837–855. (doi:10.1098/rstb.2007.2092)

Wang, X. J. 2001 Synaptic reverberation underlying mnemonic persistent activity. *Trends Neurosci.* **24**, 455–463. (doi:10.1016/S0166-2236(00)01868-3)

Wood, J. N. & Grafman, J. 2003 Human prefrontal cortex: processing and representational perspectives. *Nat. Rev. Neurosci.* **4**, 139–147. (doi:10.1038/nrn1033)

Yoon, J. H., Curtis, C. E. & D'Esposito, M. 2006 Differential effects of distraction during working memory on delay-period activity in the prefrontal cortex and the visual association cortex. *Neuroimage* **29**, 1117–1126. (doi:10.1016/j.neuroimage.2005.08.024)

Zelano, C., Bensafi, M., Porter, J., Mainland, J., Johnson, B., Bremner, E., Telles, C., Khan, R. & Sobel, N. 2005 Attentional modulation in human primary olfactory cortex. *Nat. Neurosci.* **8**, 114–120. (doi:10.1038/nn1368)

3

The cognitive neuroscience of constructive memory: remembering the past and imagining the future

Daniel L. Schacter* and Donna Rose Addis

Episodic memory is widely conceived as a fundamentally constructive, rather than reproductive, process that is prone to various kinds of errors and illusions. With a view towards examining the functions served by a constructive episodic memory system, we consider recent neuropsychological and neuroimaging studies indicating that some types of memory distortions reflect the operation of adaptive processes. An important function of a constructive episodic memory is to allow individuals to simulate or imagine future episodes, happenings and scenarios. Since the future is not an exact repetition of the past, simulation of future episodes requires a system that can draw on the past in a manner that flexibly extracts and recombines elements of previous experiences. Consistent with this *constructive episodic simulation* hypothesis, we consider cognitive, neuropsychological and neuroimaging evidence showing that there is considerable overlap in the psychological and neural processes involved in remembering the past and imagining the future.

Keywords: constructive memory; false recognition; mental simulation; neuroimaging; amnesia; Alzheimer's disease;

3.1 Introduction

The analysis of human memory comprises a variety of approaches, conceptual frameworks, theoretical ideas and empirical findings. Despite the wealth of contrasting and sometimes conflicting ideas, there are some basic observations on which memory researchers can agree. One of the least controversial—but most important—observations is that memory is not perfect. Instead, memory is prone to various kinds of errors, illusions and distortions. For instance, it has been proposed that memory's imperfections can be classified into seven basic categories or 'sins' (Schacter 1999, 2001). Each of the memory sins has important practical implications, ranging from annoying everyday instances of absent-minded forgetting to misattributions and suggestibility that can distort eyewitness identifications. But for memory researchers, such imperfections are most important because they provide critical evidence for the fundamental idea that memory is not a literal reproduction of the past, but rather is a constructive process in which bits and pieces of information from various sources are pulled together; memory errors are thought to reflect the operation of specific components of this constructive process. This characterization of memory dates at least to the pioneering ideas of Bartlett (1932) and has been a major influence in contemporary cognitive psychology for nearly 40 years.

The situation is rather different when we turn to cognitive neuroscience approaches, which attempt to elucidate the neural underpinnings of memory. Here, sustained interest in constructive aspects of memory has developed only more recently. Such interest has been driven mainly

* Author for correspondence (dls@wjh.harvard.edu).

by observations concerning the memory distortion known as confabulation, in which patients with damage to various regions within prefrontal cortex and related regions produce vivid but highly inaccurate 'recollections' of events that never happened (e.g. Johnson 1991; Moscovitch 1995; Burgess & Shallice 1996; Dalla Barba *et al.* 1999; Schnider 2003; Moulin *et al.* 2005). During the past decade, investigations of memory distortions in other patient populations, as well as neuroimaging studies of accurate versus inaccurate remembering in healthy individuals, have contributed to an increase in research on the cognitive neuroscience of constructive memory (for reviews, see Schacter *et al.* 1998a; Schacter & Slotnick 2004).

In the present paper, we focus on episodic memory, the system that enables people to recollect past experiences (Tulving 1983, 2002). We consider some recent work concerning the neural basis of memory construction with a view to addressing a question concerning its function: why does memory involve a constructive process of piecing together bits and pieces of information, rather than something more akin to a replay of the past? Several researchers have grappled with this issue and proposed various reasons why human memory, in contrast to video recorders or computers, does not store and retrieve exact replicas of experience (e.g. Bjork & Bjork 1988; Anderson & Schooler 1991; Schacter 1999, 2001). We focus on one hypothesis concerning the origins of a constructive episodic memory: that an important function of this type of memory is to allow individuals to simulate or imagine future episodes, happenings and scenarios. As we discuss later, a number of investigators have recently articulated a broad view of memory that not only considers the ability of individuals to re-experience past events, but also focuses on the capacity to imagine, simulate or pre-experience episodes in the future (Tulving 1983, 2002, 2005; Suddendorf & Corballis 1997; Atance & O'Neill 2001, 2005; Klein & Loftus 2002; Suddendorf & Busby 2003, 2005; D'Argembeau & Van der Linden 2004; Dudai & Carruthers 2005; Hancock 2005; Buckner & Carroll 2007; Schacter & Addis 2007). This latter ability has been referred to by such terms as prospection (Gilbert 2006; Buckner & Carroll 2007) and episodic future thinking (Atance & O'Neill 2001, 2005). Since the future is not an exact repetition of the past, simulation of future episodes may require a system that can draw on the past in a manner that flexibly extracts and recombines elements of previous experiences—a constructive rather than a reproductive system. If this idea has merit, then there should be considerable overlap in the psychological and neural processes involved in remembering the past and imagining the future. We consider some recent cognitive, neuropsychological and neuroimaging evidence that is consistent with this hypothesis.

3.2 Constructive memory: from cognitive psychology to cognitive neuroscience

Any discussion of constructive memory must acknowledge the pioneering ideas of Bartlett (1932), who rejected the notion that memory involves a passive replay of a past experience via the awakening of a literal copy of experience. Although Bartlett did not advocate the extreme position sometimes ascribed to him that memory is always inaccurate (Ost & Costall 2002), he clearly rejected the importance of reproductive memory: 'the first notion to get rid of is that memory is primarily or literally reduplicative, or reproductive. In a world of constantly changing environment, literal recall is extraordinarily unimportant…if we consider evidence rather than supposition, memory appears to be far more decisively an affair of construction rather than one of mere reproduction' (Bartlett 1932, pp. 204–205). Bartlett emphasized the dependence of remembering on schemas, which he defined as 'an active organization of past reactions, or of past experiences' (p. 201). Though usually adaptive for the organism, the fact that remembering relies heavily on construction via a schema also has a downside: 'condensation, elaboration and invention are common features or ordinary remembering, and these all very often involve the mingling of materials belonging originally to different 'schemata' (p. 205).

Bartlett's (1932) ideas have influenced countless modern attempts to conceive of memory as a constructive rather than a reproductive process. For example, Schacter *et al.* (1998*a*) described a 'constructive memory framework' that links ideas about memory construction from cognitive psychology with various brain systems. Schacter *et al.* noted evidence supporting the idea that representations of new experiences should be conceptualized as patterns of features in which different features represent different facets of encoded experience, including outputs of perceptual systems that analyse specific physical attributes of incoming information and interpretation of these attributes by conceptual or semantic systems analogous to Bartlett's schemas. In this view, constituent features of a memory are distributed widely across different parts of the brain, such that no single location contains a literal trace or engram that corresponds to a specific experience (cf. Squire *et al.* 2004; Thompson 2005). Retrieval of a past experience involves a process of pattern completion (Marr 1971; McClelland *et al.* 1995; Norman & O'Reilly 2003), in which the rememberer pieces together some subset of distributed features that comprise a particular past experience, including perceptual and conceptual/interpretive elements.

Since a constructive memory system is prone to error, it must solve many problems to produce sufficiently accurate representations of past experience. For example, the disparate features that constitute an episode must be linked or bound together at encoding; failure to adequately bind together appropriate features can result in the common phenomenon of source memory failure, where people retrieve fragments of an episode but do not recollect, or misrecollect, how or when the fragments were acquired, resulting in various kinds of memory illusions and distortions (e.g. Johnson *et al.* 1993; Schacter 1999). Furthermore, bound episodes must be kept separate from one another in memory: if episodes overlap extensively with one another, individuals may recall the general similarities or gist (Brainerd & Reyna 2005) common to many episodes, but fail to remember distinctive item-specific information that distinguishes one episode from another, resulting in the kinds of gist-based distortions that Bartlett (1932) and many others have reported. Similarly, retrieval cues can potentially match stored experiences other than the sought-after episode, thus resulting in inaccurate memories that blend elements of different experiences (McClelland 1995), so retrieval often involves a preliminary stage in which the rememberer forms a more refined description of the characteristics of the episode to be retrieved (Burgess & Shallice 1996; Norman & Schacter 1996). Breakdowns in this process of formulating a retrieval description as a result of damage to the frontal cortex and other regions can sometimes produce striking memory errors, including confabulations regarding events that never happened (e.g. Burgess & Shallice 1996; Dab *et al.* 1999; Ciaramelli *et al.* 2006; Gilboa *et al.* 2006).

During the past decade, research in cognitive neuroscience has made use of neuroimaging and neuropsychological approaches to address questions concerning memory errors and distortions that bear on constructive aspects of memory (for a review, see Schacter & Slotnick 2004). We do not attempt an exhaustive review here, but instead focus on two lines of research that are most relevant to our broader claims regarding a possible functional basis for constructive aspects of memory. First, we will consider research concerning false recognition in patients with memory disorders that provides evidence indicating that false recognition–rather than reflecting the operation of a malfunctioning or flawed memory system–is sometimes a marker of a healthy memory system, such that damage to the system can reduce, rather than increase, the incidence of this memory error. Second, we consider neuroimaging studies that provide insight into the extent to which accurate and inaccurate memories depend on the same underlying brain regions. A growing body of evidence indicates that there is indeed extensive overlap in the brain regions that support true and false memories, at least when false memories are based on what we refer to as general similarity or gist information.

3.3 False recognition in amnesia and dementia

As noted earlier, patients with damage to regions of prefrontal cortex and related brain areas sometimes exhibit the memory distortion known as confabulation. Such patients also sometimes show pathological levels of false recognition, claiming incorrectly that novel information is familiar (e.g. Delbecq-Derouesné *et al*. 1990; Schacter *et al*. 1996a; Ward *et al*. 1999). The fact that brain damage can increase the incidence of memory distortion leads naturally to the view that recollective errors reflect the operation of a diseased or malfunctioning system. By contrast, however, two related lines of research that have emerged during the past decade indicate that some types of memory distortion reflect the adaptive operation of a healthy memory system. These studies of amnesic and demented patients have examined the incidence of robust false recognition effects, in which healthy people exhibit high levels of false alarms after studying a series of semantically or perceptually related words or pictures. For example, in the Deese–Roediger–McDermott (DRM) paradigm (Deese 1959; Roediger & McDermott 1995), participants study lists of words (e.g. *tired*, *bed*, *awake*, *rest*, *dream*, *night*, *blanket*, *doze*, *slumber*, *snore*, *pillow*, *peace*, *yawn* and *drowsy*) that are related to a non-presented lure word (e.g. *sleep*). On a subsequent old–new recognition test containing studied words (e.g. *tired* and *dream*), new words that are unrelated to the study list items (e.g. *butter*) and new words that are related to the study list items (e.g. *sleep*), participants frequently claim that they previously studied the related lure words. In many instances, false recognition of the related lure words is indistinguishable from the true recognition rate of studied words (for review of numerous DRM studies, see Gallo 2006).

A number of studies have consistently revealed that amnesic patients with damage to the hippocampus and related structures in the medial temporal lobe (MTL) show significantly reduced false recognition of non-studied lure words that are either semantically or perceptually related to previously studied words (figure 3.1; Schacter *et al*. 1996c, 1997, 1998b; Melo *et al*. 1999; Ciaramelli *et al*. 2006). This false recognition 'deficit' roughly parallels patients' true recognition deficit and occurs even though amnesics typically show similar or even increased levels of false recognition to unrelated lure words. Amnesics also show reduced false recognition of non-studied visual shapes that are perceptually similar to previously presented shapes (Koutstaal *et al*. 1999). Parallel studies have been reported in patients with Alzheimer's disease (AD), who typically have neuropathology that includes, but is not limited to, MTL regions. Like amnesics, AD patients show reduced false recognition of lure items that are either semantically or perceptually related to previously studied items (Balota *et al*. 1999; Budson *et al*. 2000, 2001, 2003).

One interpretation of this pattern of results is that healthy controls form and retain a well-organized representation of the semantic or perceptual gist of a list of related study items. Related lures that match semantic or perceptual features of this representation are likely to be

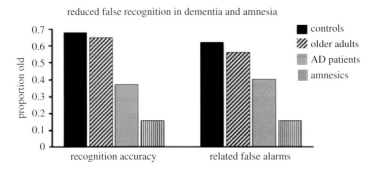

Fig. 3.1 Performance of patients with amnesia and Alzheimer's disease on the Deese–Roediger–McDermott (DRM) paradigm (Roediger & McDermott 1995). Participants study lists of words (e.g. *tired*, *bed*, *awake*, *rest*, *dream*, *night*, etc.) that are related to a non-presented lure word (e.g. *sleep*). A subsequent old–new recognition test contains studied words (e.g. *tired*, *dream*), new words that are unrelated to the study list items (e.g. *butter*) and new words that are related to the study list items (e.g. *sleep*). Both patient groups show significantly reduced recognition accuracy (i.e. hits—false alarms to new unrelated words) and also make fewer related false alarms (i.e. false alarms to new related words—false alarms to new unrelated words) relative to age-matched controls. Note that the 'controls' were the age-matched control group for the amnesic patients (data for controls and amnesics are obtained from Schacter *et al.* 1996*c*) and the 'older adults' were the age-matched control group for Alzheimer's patients (data for older adults and Alzheimer's patients are obtained from Budson *et al.* 2000). AD, Alzheimer's disease.

falsely recognized, while unrelated words that do not match it are likely to be correctly rejected. As a result of MTL damage, amnesic and AD patients may form and retain only a weak or degraded gist representation and thus make fewer false alarms to semantic associates or perceptually similar items than do controls. Support for this interpretation comes from a study that used a modified version of the DRM semantic associates procedure (Verfaellie *et al.* 2002). Participants were instructed to call 'old' any item that is semantically related to the theme or gist of a previously studied list, even if the item itself had not appeared on the list. Evidence from the healthy controls suggests that such a task provides a more direct probe of gist information than a standard old/new recognition task (Brainerd & Reyna 1998; Schacter *et al.* 2001). Verfaellie *et al.* (2002) reported that even in this meaning test, amnesic patients provided fewer 'old' responses to semantically related lure words than do controls, thereby supporting the idea of a degraded gist representation. Budson *et al.* (2006) reported similar results in patients with AD, using a paradigm in which participants studied categorized pictures and were given a version of a 'meaning test' in which they were instructed to respond 'yes', when either a studied or non-studied picture came from a studied category.

In the foregoing studies, involving meaning tests, participants were asked to remember explicitly aspects of previously presented materials; it is well known that both amnesic and AD patients exhibit deficits on explicit memory tasks. Thus, it is conceivable that patients do form and retain a normal gist representation, but do not express this information on explicit tests. Since amnesic patients can show intact priming effects on various implicit or indirect memory tasks (for review, see Schacter *et al.* 2004), Verfaellie *et al.* (2005) examined whether use of an implicit task might reveal intact retention of gist information in amnesics. They did so by having patients and controls study lists of semantic associates (e.g. *resort*, *sun*, *beach*, *parties*, etc.) that were all associated to a non-presented related lure word (e.g. *vacation*). On the subsequent stem completion test, participants were provided three-letter word beginnings that had multiple possible completions; some could be completed with previously studied words (e.g. bea___) and some with related lures (e.g. vac___). Previous research using a similar paradigm with healthy subjects revealed the existence of a 'false priming' effect: compared with a baseline condition, participants were more likely to complete stems of related lures with the lure item following study of a list of semantic associates (not surprisingly, priming was also observed for previously studied words, e.g. McDermott 1997; McKone & Murphy 2000). Verfaellie *et al.* reported that amnesic patients showed intact priming for previously studied words, replicating earlier results, but showed no priming for related lures. By contrast, controls showed significant priming for both studied words and related lure words.

These results further strengthen the idea that impaired false recognition of similar words and objects in amnesic and AD patients reflects an impoverished or diminished gist representation, while suggesting that the deficit extends beyond the strict confines of episodic memory. They also support the idea that this type of memory error in control populations reflects the normal operation of healthy adaptive memory processes. This latter conclusion is also supported by the results of functional neuroimaging studies.

3.4 Neuroimaging studies of true and false recognition

In a number of studies using positron emission tomography (PET) and functional magnetic resonance imaging (fMRI), subjects studied lists of DRM semantic associates and were later scanned while making judgements about old words, related lures and unrelated lures. Consistent with the results from amnesic and AD patients, these studies have revealed significant and comparable levels of activation in the MTL, including the hippocampus, during both true and false recognition of related lures (e.g. Schacter *et al.* 1996*b*; Cabeza *et al.* 2001; for more detailed review, see Schacter & Slotnick 2004).

More recent neuroimaging studies of gist-based false recognition using paradigms other than the DRM procedure have replicated and extended these results. Slotnick & Schacter (2004) used a prototype recognition paradigm in which the critical materials were abstract, unfamiliar shapes; all shapes in the study list were visually similar to a non-presented prototype (figure 3.2). Participants made significantly more 'old' responses to studied shapes than to new related shapes and also made significantly more 'old' responses to new related shapes (i.e. prototypes) than to new unrelated shapes. This latter result confirms the presence of a false recognition effect that was presumably driven by memory for the 'perceptual gist' of the studied exemplars that resembled the prototype. Slotnick & Schacter documented that a number of regions previously implicated in true recognition, including MTL, fusiform cortex, lateral parietal cortex and multiple regions in dorsolateral and inferior prefrontal cortex, showed significant and comparable levels of activity during false recognition of new related shapes and true recognition of studied shapes (figure 3.2).

Garoff-Eaton *et al.* (2006) also used abstract shapes as target items in a slightly different experimental paradigm that focused on the relationship between processes underlying related and unrelated false recognition. In both types of false recognition, subjects respond 'old' to new items. However, in related false recognition, semantic or perceptual overlap between the new item and a previously studied item drives the false recognition response, whereas the basis for 'old' response to unrelated items is unclear. Standard signal detection models of memory typically do not distinguish between related and unrelated false alarms: both are seen

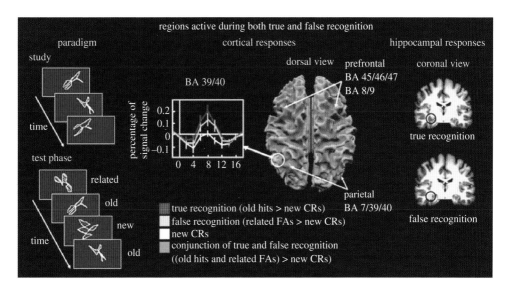

Fig. 3.2 Neural regions engaged during both true and false recognition (adapted from Slotnick & Schacter 2004). A prototype recognition paradigm was employed; all stimuli presented during study were abstract, unfamiliar shapes. During recognition testing, participants made recognition judgements about old studied shapes, new prototypical shapes visually related to studied shapes and new shapes unrelated to studied shapes. A number of regions previously implicated in true recognition, including hippocampus, lateral parietal cortex, and dorsolateral and inferior prefrontal cortex, showed significant and comparable levels of activity during false recognition of new related shapes (i.e. prototypes) and true recognition of studied shapes compared with correct rejections of new unrelated shapes. The percentage of signal changed extracted from the left lateral parietal cortex is also shown. BA, Brodmann area; CR, correct rejection; FA, false alarm.

to result from a single underlying process that supports familiarity or memory strength sufficient to surpass a subject's criterion for saying 'old' (e.g. Miller & Wolford 1999; Slotnick & Dodson 2005; but see, Wixted & Stretch 2000). However, data from studies of false recognition in amnesic patients reviewed earlier point towards different mechanisms underlying related and unrelated false recognition, because amnesics typically show reduced related false recognition compared with controls, together with either increased or unchanged unrelated false recognition.

In the experiment by Garoff-Eaton *et al.* (2006), subjects studied abstract shapes drawn from the same set as those developed by Slotnick & Schacter (2004). On a subsequent recognition test, they were presented either with the same shape from the study list, a related shape that was visually similar to one of the studied shapes or a new unrelated shape. Participants were instructed to respond 'same' when a test shape was identical to a previously studied shape, 'similar' when a new shape was visually similar to a previously studied one and 'new' to unrelated novel shapes. Behavioural data revealed significantly more 'same' responses (0.59) to same shapes than to either new related or new unrelated shapes, and significantly more 'same' responses to related (0.31) than to unrelated (0.20) shapes. A conjunction analysis of the fMRI data that assessed common neural activity during true recognition (i.e. 'same'/same) and related false recognition (i.e. 'same'/related new) compared with unrelated false recognition (i.e. 'same'/new) indicated significant activity in a network of regions previously associated with episodic remembering, including hippocampus/ MTL, several regions within prefrontal cortex, medial and inferior parietal lobes and ventral temporal/ occipital regions. In striking contrast, a conjunction analysis that assessed common activity during related and unrelated false recognition, in comparison with true recognition, showed no significant activity in any region. When contrasting unrelated false recognition with true recognition and related false recognition, significant activity was observed in regions of left superior and middle temporal gyri (BA 22/38), regions previously associated with language processing. Unrelated false recognition may have occurred when subjects mistakenly applied a verbal label generated during the study list to a novel shape, whereas related false recognition was driven largely by perceptual similarity between studied shapes and related new shapes.

Overall, these data strengthen the argument that related or gist-based false recognition depends on many of the same neural processes as true recognition and shares relatively little in common with unrelated false recognition. Of course, we do not wish to imply that gist-based false recognition is neurally indistinguishable from true recognition. A number of PET and fMRI studies have provided evidence that brain activity can distinguish between true recognition and related false recognition (for review, see Schacter & Slotnick 2004). Some of these studies have supported what Schacter & Slotnick (2004) termed the sensory reactivation hypothesis, which holds that true memories contain more sensory and perceptual details than do related false memories (e.g. Mather *et al.* 1997; Norman & Schacter 1997). Slotnick & Schacter (2004; see also Kahn *et al.* 2004) provided some of the strongest evidence for this hypothesis: they showed increased activation in early visual areas, when subjects made recognition decisions about previously studied shapes compared with related new shapes. Interestingly, this early visual area activity for old shapes occurred equally strongly when subjects responded 'old' and when they responded 'new' to the studied shapes, suggesting that this putative sensory reactivation effect reflected some type of non-conscious or implicit memory (Slotnick & Schacter 2004; for further evidence, see Slotnick & Schacter 2006).

In summary, both neuropsychological and neuroimaging studies of gist-based false recognition support the idea that this type of memory error reflects, to a very large extent, the healthy operation of constructive processes that support the ability to remember what has actually happened in the past.

3.5 Remembering the past and imagining the future: what kind of overlap?

The foregoing research provides not only insights into the constructive nature of episodic memory, but also some clues regarding the functional basis of constructive memory processes. Although memory errors such as false recognition may at first seem highly dysfunctional, especially given the havoc that memory distortions can wreak in real-world contexts (Loftus 1993; Schacter 2001), we have seen that they sometimes reflect the ability of a normally functioning memory system to store and retrieve general similarity or gist information, and that false recognition errors often recruit some of the same processes that support accurate memory decisions. Indeed, several researchers have argued that the memory errors involving forgetting or distortion serve an adaptive role (cf. Bjork & Bjork 1988; Anderson & Schooler 1991; Schacter 1999, 2001). For example, Anderson & Schooler (1991) contend that memory is adapted to retain information that is most likely to be needed in the environment in which it operates. Since we do not frequently need to remember all the exact details of our experiences, an adapted system need not slavishly preserve all such details as a default option; instead, it should record and preserve such details over time only when circumstances indicate that they are likely to be needed, as human memory tends to do. Similarly, memory for gist, which is sometimes responsible for false recognition, is also crucial for such adaptive capacities as categorization and comprehension and may facilitate transfer and generalization across tasks (McClelland 1995).

We attempt to build on this type of argument by suggesting that the constructive nature of episodic memory is highly adaptive for performing a major function of this system: to draw on past experiences in a way that allows us to imagine and simulate episodes that might occur in our personal futures. Thinking about the future plays a critical role in mental life (Gilbert 2006), and students of brain function have long recognized the important role of frontal cortex in allowing individuals to anticipate or plan for the future (e.g. Ingvar 1985; Stuss & Benson 1986; Fuster 1989; Shallice & Burgess 1996; Mesulam 2002). Tulving (1983, 2002, 2005) has argued that episodic memory affords the ability to engage in 'mental time travel', which involves projecting oneself into both the past and the future. From this perspective, representations of both past and future events may be richly detailed, vivid and contextually specific. Furthermore, a number of investigators have recognized that information about past experiences is useful only to the extent that it allows us to anticipate what may happen in the future (e.g. Atance & O'Neill 2001, 2005; Suddendorf & Busby 2003, 2005; Hancock 2005; Buckner & Carroll 2007). Indeed, Anderson & Schooler's (1991) analysis of adaptive forgetting supports the idea that information about the past is retained when it is likely to be useful in the future.

However, future events are rarely, if ever, exact replicas of past events. Thus, a memory system that simply stored rote records of what happened in the past would not be well suited to simulating future events, which will probably share some similarities with past events while differing in other respects. We think that a system built along the lines of the constructive principles that we and others have attributed to episodic memory is better suited to the job of simulating future happenings. Such a system can draw on elements of the past and retain the general sense or gist of what has happened. Critically, it can flexibly extract, recombine and reassemble these elements in a way that allows us to simulate, imagine or 'pre-experience' (Atance & O'Neill 2001) events that have never occurred previously in the exact form in which we imagine them. We will refer to this idea as the *constructive episodic simulation* hypothesis: the constructive nature of episodic memory is attributable, at least in part, to the role of the episodic system in allowing us to mentally simulate our personal futures (for similar perspectives, see Suddendorf & Corballis 1997; Suddendorf & Busby 2003; Dudai & Carruthers 2005).

The constructive episodic simulation hypothesis does not imply that the only function of episodic memory is to allow us to simulate future events, nor do we believe that its role in simulation of the future constitutes the sole reason why episodic memory is primarily constructive rather than reproductive. Episodic memory also functions to help us make sense of the past and the present. Furthermore, considerations such as economy of storage are no doubt relevant to understanding why the system does not simply preserve rote records of all experience: compressing information into a gist-like representation may protect the memory system from overload (Schacter 2001). We nonetheless endorse Suddendorf & Busby's (2003, p. 393) suggestion that 'episodic reconstruction is just an adaptive feature of the future planning system'. Moreover, exploring the possible link between constructive aspects of memory and simulation of the future may help to provide fresh perspectives on such fundamental questions as why imagination is sometimes confused with memory and, more generally, why memories can be badly mistaken.

If the constructive episodic simulation hypothesis has merit, then remembering the past and imagining the future should show a number of similar characteristics and depend on some of the same neural substrates. We next consider cognitive, neuropsychological, psychopathological and neuroimaging data that bear on this hypothesis.

3.6 Cognitive studies of past and future events

In contrast to the extensive cognitive literature on episodic memory of past experiences, there is little evidence concerning simulation of future episodes and a virtual absence of direct comparisons between remembering the past and imagining the future. While there has been a great deal of research concerning prospective memory—remembering to do things in the future (e.g. Brandimonte *et al*. 1996)—this line of research has been concerned with such topics as the formulation and retention of intentions (e.g. Goschke & Kuhl 1993) or differences between event-based versus time-based prospective memory (e.g. Einstein & McDaniel 1990) and has not focused specifically on episodic simulation and imagining of future events. Research on the topic of affective forecasting—which examines how people predict, and often mispredict, future happiness (Gilbert 2006)—has revealed important interactions between memory of past events and predictions of future happiness. For example, Morewedge *et al*. (2005) found that people sometimes base predictions of future happiness on atypical past experiences that are highly memorable but not highly predictive of what is likely to occur in the future.

More directly related to the constructive episodic simulation hypothesis, D'Argembeau & Van der Linden (2004) directly compared 're-experiencing' past episodes and 'pre-experiencing' episodes in the future. They investigated how the valence of events and their temporal distance from the present affect phenomenological qualities of past and future autobiographical events. Subjects were asked to either remember a specific event from their past or imagine a specific event that could plausibly happen to them in the future. For each of several past and future events that participants provided, they rated a number of phenomenological qualities using a variant of the memory characteristics questionnaire (Johnson *et al*. 1988), including perceptual details, valence and intensity of emotions involved, and clarity of spatial information. Participants also indicated the nature of their visual perspective on the event: observer (i.e. they 'saw' themselves in their representation of the event) or field (i.e. they saw the scene from their own perspective). Subjects were also asked to date past events and estimate the temporal proximity of future events.

D'Argembeau and van der Linden found that remembered past events were associated with richer and more vivid sensory and contextual details than were imagined future events, consistent with previous observations concerning phenomenological qualities of remembered versus imagined events (e.g. Johnson *et al*. 1988). Importantly, however, they also reported several notable commonalities between remembering the past and imagining the future. When compared with negative events, positive events were associated with subjective ratings of greater re-experiencing for past events and greater pre-experiencing for future events. Temporally close events in either the past or future included more sensory and contextual details, and were associated with greater feelings of re-experiencing and pre-experiencing, than temporally distant events (cf. Trope & Liberman 2003). Furthermore, participants were more likely to adopt a field than observer perspective for temporally close than temporally distant events in both the past and the future. More recently, D'Argembeau & Van der Linden (2006) extended these results by showing that individual differences in imagery ability and emotion regulation strategies are similarly related to past and future events. Overall, these results are consistent with the constructive episodic simulation hypothesis inasmuch as they highlight strong similarities between remembering the past and imagining the future.

3.7 Past and future events in neuropsychological and psychopathological patients

It is well known that patients with damage to the hippocampus and related structures in the MTL have impairments of episodic memory (e.g. Squire *et al.* 2004). Much less is known about the capacity of amnesic patients to imagine future experiences. However, consistent with the constructive episodic simulation hypothesis, the existing evidence indicates that at least some amnesics have great difficulty imagining their personal futures. Some early observations along these lines were reported concerning patient K. C., who suffered from total loss of episodic memory as a result of closed head injury that produced damage to a number of brain regions, including the medial temporal and frontal lobes (Tulving *et al.* 1988; Rosenbaum *et al.* 2005). K. C. was unable to provide a description of his personal future for any time period asked about: 'this afternoon'; 'tomorrow'; or 'next summer'. Instead, K. C. provided the same response when asked to think about any part of his personal future or past, describing his mental state as 'blank' (Tulving 1985; Tulving *et al.* 1988).

A later investigation in another patient, D. B., who became amnesic as a result of cardiac arrest and consequent anoxia revealed that he, like K. C., exhibited deficits in both retrieving past events and imagining future events (Klein & Loftus 2002). Klein and Loftus developed a 10-item questionnaire in which they probed past and future events that were matched for temporal distance from the present (e.g. What did you do yesterday? What are you going to do tomorrow?). One problem with assessing responses to questions about the personal future is that it is not entirely clear what constitutes a correct answer. Klein and Loftus evaluated D. B.'s responses in light of information provided by his family. Thus, when D. B. was asked 'When will be the next time you see a doctor?', his response ('Sometime in the next week')was judged correct because his daughter confirmed that he did have a doctors' appointment the next week. However, when D. B. was asked 'Who are you going to see this evening?', and indicated that he was going to visit his mother, this response was judged to be confabulatory because his mother had died nearly two decades earlier.

D. B. was highly impaired on both the past and future versions of this task. In fact, he provided only 2 of 10 responses on the future task that were judged correct by family members, providing five confabulatory responses and three 'don't know' responses to the other items. Control subjects provided correct responses to all questions regarding their personal pasts and futures. D. B.'s deficit in thinking about the future seemed specific to his *personal* future: he had little difficulty imagining possible future developments in the public domain (e.g. political events and issues), performing similar to control subjects. Note, however, that many of the items concerning the public domain did not inquire about specific events, so the evidence for a personal/public distinction is somewhat equivocal. Moreover, little information was provided concerning the precise location of D. B.'s lesion.

A more recent study by Hassabis *et al*. (2007) examined the ability of five patients with documented bilateral hippocampal amnesia to imagine new experiences. Patients and matched control subjects were cued to construct everyday imaginary experiences such as 'Imagine you are lying on a white sandy beach in a beautiful tropical bay'. Subjects were specifically instructed not to provide a memory of a past event, but to construct something new. Participants described their imaginary scenarios in the presence of a cue card to remind them of the task, and experimenters occasionally probed subjects for further details and elaboration. Protocols were scored based on the content, spatial coherence and subjective qualities of the partici-pants' imagined scenarios. Overall, the constructions of the hippocampal patients were greatly reduced in richness and content when compared with those of controls. The impairment was especially pronounced for the measure of spatial coherence, indicating that the constructions of the hippocampal patients tended to consist of isolated fragments of information rather than connected scenes. Four of the five patients showed an impaired ability to imagine new experi-ences; the one patient who performed normally exhibited some residual hippocampal sparing that might have supported intact performance.

In a related line of research, Dalla Barba *et al*. (1997, 1999) have found that patients who confabulate about their personal pasts also confabulate about their personal futures. Taken together, the pattern of deficits in these patients suggests that imagining personal future events may involve processes above and beyond the general processes involved in constructing non-personal events and generating images, and shares common processes with episodic remembering.

Studies of another population exhibiting episodic memory impairments—suicidally depressed individuals—also reveal commonalities between remembering the past and imagin-ing the future (Williams *et al*. 1996). When given word cues and instruction to recall an epi-sode from the past or imagine a future episode, depressed patients showed reduced specificity in their retrieval of both past and future autobiographical events. Importantly, the reduction in specificity of past and future events was significantly correlated. Moreover, Williams and col-leagues demonstrated that in healthy individuals, manipulations that reduced the specificity of past events (e.g. instructions or cues which induce a general retrieval style) also reduced the specificity of subsequently generated future events.

3.8 Neuroimaging of past and future events

Cognitive and patient studies provide evidence, suggesting that retrieving past events and sim-ulating future events rely on common processes. Three recent neuroimaging studies have dem-onstrated that past and future events engage common neural regions (Okuda *et al*. 2003; Addis *et al*. 2007; Szpunar *et al*. 2007), providing further support for the constructive episodic simu-lation hypothesis.

In the first of these studies, Okuda *et al*. (2003) instructed participants to talk freely about their past or future during a PET scan, with the only constraint being the time period to report on: either the near (i.e. the last or next few days) or the distant (i.e. the last or next few years) past or future. Regardless of time period, both the past and future conditions elicited shared activity in bilateral frontopolar cortex, probably reflecting the self-referential nature of both types of event representations (Craik *et al*. 1999; Gusnard *et al*. 2001). Further, there was evi-dence of common MTL activity, and Okuda *et al*. interpreted this outcome as reflecting the retrieval of past events during both tasks; as explicitly required by the past event task, and as arguably necessary for the simulation of future episodic events. The effect of temporal distance on neural activity in these two regions was also examined, and remarkably, in eight out of the nine foci the same neural response to temporal distance (i.e. either an increase or a decrease with increasing distance) was evident for both past and future events. The only region exhibiting an interaction between temporal direction (i.e. past versus future) and distance (i.e. near versus distant) was an inferior region in left parahippocampal gyrus (BA 36). Despite these marked similarities, Okuda *et al.* (2003) also demonstrated that right frontopolar activity exhibited strong positive correlations with the amount of intentional information produced during the future task, consistent with studies implicating this region in prospective memory (Bechara *et al.* 1994; Okuda *et al.* 1998; Burgess *et al.* 2001*b*).

Although participants in this study talked about their personal past or future, it is unclear whether these events were episodic in nature, i.e. unique events specific in time and place (Tulving 1983), rather than reflecting general or semantic information about one's past or future. Moreover, even if specific episodic events were localizable within a participant's narrative, the use of a block design, as necessitated by PET, prevented analysis of neural activity associated with specific events. Given that others have shown that specificity of past events can alter neural activity during retrieval (Addis *et al.* 2004), the specificity of events in Okuda *et al.*'s study, or lack thereof, may have influenced the pattern of results.

More recent fMRI studies have attempted to overcome this limitation using event-related designs to yield information regarding the neural bases of specific past and future events. For instance, Szpunar *et al.* (2007) instructed participants to remember specific past events, imagine specific future events or imagine specific events involving a familiar individual (Bill Clinton) in response to event cues (e.g. past birthday, retirement party). Again, there was striking overlap in activity associated with past and future events in the bilateral frontopolar and MTL regions reported by Okuda *et al.* (2003), as well as posterior cingulate cortex. Importantly, these regions were not activated to the same magnitude when imagining events involving Bill Clinton, demonstrating a neural signature that is unique to the construction of events in one's *personal* past or future and is not shared by the construction of event representations *per se*. This result dovetails with the suggestive findings considered earlier from amnesic patients who cannot remember or imagine events in their personal past or future despite some ability to remember and imagine non-personal information. Together, these data suggest that there is a core network of neural structures that commonly supports the generation of event representations from one's personal past or future, in line with the constructive episodic simulation hypothesis.

A direct comparison of activity associated with past and future events identified several regions that were significantly more active for future relative to past events, including bilateral premotor cortex and left precuneus. The authors argue that this pattern of findings may reflect a more active type of imagery processing required by future events. One must not only construct and maintain the image, but also manipulate the image to create a novel scenario.

In a study from our laboratory, Addis *et al.* (2007) divided the past and future tasks into two phases: (i) an initial construction phase during which participants generated a past or future event in response to an event cue (e.g. 'dress') and made a button press when they had an event in mind and (ii) an elaboration phase during which participants generated as much detail as possible about the event (for related evidence from an electrophysiological study of remembered and imagined events that also distinguished between construction and elaboration phases, see Conway *et al.* 2003). We argued that specific cognitive processes contributing to the completion of such past and future tasks could be differentially engaged during the different phases of the task. Thus, if a particular neural difference between past and future events is only evident during one phase, collapsing across both phases in a block design or sampling neural activity during another phase in an event-related design could potentially obscure such differences. The same logic also applies to the search for common neural activity, if the common network is engaged during only one, but not another, phase of the task. Furthermore, we confirmed that past and future events were of equivalent phenomenology with both objective and subjective measures, thus enabling the interpretation of past–future differences as reflecting differences in temporal orientation and engagement of task-specific processes. We compared activity during the past and future tasks with control tasks that required semantic and imagery processing, respectively.

Consistent with the constructive episodic simulation hypothesis, there was indeed striking overlap between the past and future tasks. This overlap was most apparent during the elaboration phase, when participants are focused on generating details about the remembered or imagined event (figures 3.3 and 3.4). For instance, both event types were associated with activity in left anterior temporal cortex, a region thought to mediate conceptual and semantic information about the self and one's life (e.g. familiar people, common activities, Graham *et al.* 2003; Addis *et al.* 2004). Event representations also contained episodic and contextual imagery, perhaps related to activation of precuneus (e.g. Fletcher *et al.* 1995) and parahippocampal/retrosplenial cortices (e.g. Bar & Aminoff 2003), respectively. There was common activity in the left frontopolar cortex, reflecting the self-referential nature of past and future events (e.g. Craik *et al.* 1999), and in the left hippocampus, possibly reflecting the retrieval and/or integration of additional event details into the representation. Interestingly, this common past–future network is remarkably similar to the network consistently implicated in the retrieval of episodic memories of past autobiographical events (Maguire 2001), again consistent with the constructive episodic simulation hypothesis.

The construction phase was associated with some common past–future activity in posterior visual regions and left hippocampus, which may reflect the initial interaction between visually

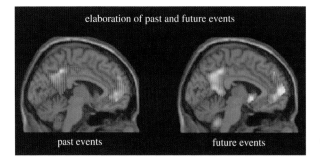

Fig. 3.3 Sagittal slice (*x* = −4) illustrating the striking commonalities in the medial left prefrontal and parietal regions engaged when (*a*) remembering the past and (*b*) imagining the future (adapted from Addis *et al.* 2007). These marked similarities of activation were also evident in areas of the medial temporal lobe (bilateral parahippocampal gyrus) and lateral cortex (left temporal pole and left bilateral inferior parietal cortex). This extensive pattern of common activity was not present during the construction of past and future events (figure 3.4); it only emerged during the elaboration of these events (shown here, relative to elaboration phase of a semantic and an imagery control task).

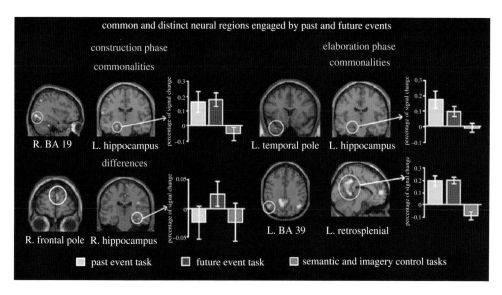

Fig. 3.4 Common and distinct regions engaged by the construction and elaboration of past and future events (Addis et al. 2007). A conjunction analysis of activity during the construction of past and future events revealed a few regions exhibiting common activity, such as left hippocampus and right occipital gyrus (BA 19). Contrast analyses identified a number of regions exhibiting differentially more activity for future events, including the right frontal pole and hippocampus. The elaboration phase was marked by striking overlap between past and future events, including left hippocampus, left temporal pole, bilateral parietal lobule (BA 39) and retrosplenial cortex. Plots of per cent signal change during the past event, future event and control (semantic and imagery) tasks are also shown. BA, Brodmann area.

presented cues and hippocampally mediated pointers to memory traces (Moscovitch 1992). Even so, this phase was characterized by considerable neural differentiation of past and future events. In particular, higher levels of activity during the future task were evident in the right frontopolar cortex, consistent with the association of this region with prospective memory (Burgess *et al.* 2001*b*; see also Burgess *et al.* 2007 and this volume), and in the left inferior frontal gyrus, a region mediating generative processing (Poldrack *et al.* 1999). Furthermore, the right hippocampus was differentially engaged by the future event task, which may reflect the novelty of future events and/or additional relational processing required when one must recombine disparate details into a coherent event. This latter finding fits nicely with the observations noted earlier from Hassabis *et al.* (2007), indicating that hippocampal amnesics have difficulty imagining new experiences: the hippocampus may play a key role in recombining details of previous experiences into a coherent new imagined construction.

Notably, in all regions exhibiting significant past–future differences, future events were associated with more activity than past events, as also observed by Szpunar *et al.* (2007). We propose that this apparent regularity across neural regions and across studies reflects the more intensive constructive processes required by imagining future events relative to retrieving past events. Both past and future event tasks require the retrieval of information from memory, engaging common memory networks. However, only the future task requires that event details gleaned from various past events are flexibly recombined into a novel future event and, further, that this event is plausible given one's intentions for the future. Thus, additional regions supporting these processes are recruited by the future event task.

Many questions remain to be addressed regarding the nature of brain activity related to past and future events. For example, some of the regions that we found to be strongly activated when people imagine future events, including hippocampus and parahippocampal cortex, have been linked with imagery for spatial scenes (e.g. Burgess *et al.* 2001*a*; Byrne *et al.* 2007). According to the constructive episodic simulation hypothesis, the adaptive nature of such activity is specifically related to its role in simulating the future. But to what extent do the activations associated with simulating future events specifically reflect the requirement to imagine a *future* event, as opposed to general imaginings that are not linked to a particular time frame? A critical task for research in this area is to attempt to distinguish between the specifically temporal component of episodic simulations and more general imaginative activity.

3.9 Concluding comments

Much research has focused on elucidating the constructive nature of episodic memory, and a growing number of recent investigations have recognized the close relationship between remembering the past and imagining the future. However, the possible relationship between constructive memory and past–future issues remains almost entirely unexplored. A major purpose of the present paper is to emphasize that this relationship constitutes a promising area for research (see also, Suddendorf & Corballis 1997; Dudai & Carruthers 2005; Hassabis *et al.* 2007). For example, according to the constructive episodic simulation hypothesis, it should be possible to document a direct link between processes underlying memory distortion and those underlying mental simulations of the future. It is already well known that imagining experiences can result in various kinds of memory distortions (e.g. Johnson *et al.* 1988, 1993; Garry *et al.* 1996; Goff & Roediger 1998; Loftus 2003); we think it will be quite informative to focus specifically on the link between imagining future events and memory distortion. Indeed, the scope of this research is probably even broader than that covered here. In a thoughtful review that elucidates the relationship between, and neural basis of, remembering the past and thinking about the future, Buckner & Carroll (2007) point out that neural regions that show common activation for past and future tasks closely resemble those that are activated during 'theory of mind' tasks, where individuals simulate the mental states of other people (e.g. Saxe & Kanwisher 2003).Buckner & Carroll note that such findings suggest that the commonly activated regions may be 'specialized for, and engaged by, mental acts that require the projection of oneself in another time, place, or perspective', resembling what Tulving (1985) referred to as autonoetic consciousness. Such observations highlight the importance of thinking broadly about the functions of episodic memory in constructing our personal and social worlds.

Preparation of this paper was supported by grants from the NIA (AG08441) and NIMH (MH060941). We thank Moshe Bar, Randy Buckner, Dan Gilbert, Itamar Kahn, Jason Mitchell and Gagan Wig for comments on the paper, and Alana Wong for invaluable aid in preparation of the manuscript.

References

Addis, D. R., McIntosh, A. R., Moscovitch, M., Crawley, A. P. & McAndrews, M. P. 2004 Characterizing spatial and temporal features of autobiographical memory retrieval networks: a partial least squares approach. *Neuroimage* **23**, 1460–1471. (doi:10.1016/j.neuroimage.2004.08.007)

Addis, D. R., Wong, A. T. & Schacter, D. L. 2007 Remembering the past and imagining the future: common and distinct neural substrates during event construction and elaboration. *Neuropsychologia* **45**, 1363–1377. (doi:10.1016/j.neuropsychologia.2006.10.016)

Anderson, J. R. & Schooler, L. J. 1991 Reflections of the environment in memory. *Psychol. Sci.* **2**, 396–408. (doi:10.1111/j.1467-9280.1991.tb00174.x)

Atance, C. M. & O'Neill, D. K. 2001 Episodic future thinking. *Trends Cogn. Sci.* **5**, 533–539. (doi:10.1016/S1364-6613(00)01804-0)

Atance, C. M. & O'Neill, D. K. 2005 The emergence of episodic future thinking in humans. *Learn. Motiv.* **36**, 126–144. (doi:10.1016/j.lmot.2005.02.003)

Balota, D. A., Cortese, M. J., Duchek, J. M., Adams, D., Roediger, H. L., McDermott, K. B. & Yerys, B. E. 1999 Veridical and false memories in healthy older adults and in dementia of the Alzheimer's type. *Cogn. Neuropsychol.* **16**, 361–384. (doi:10.1080/026432999380834)

Bar, M. & Aminoff, E. 2003 Cortical analysis of visual context. *Neuron* **38**, 347–358. (doi:10.1016/S0896-6273(03)00167-3)

Bartlett, F. C. 1932 *Remembering*. Cambridge, UK: Cambridge University Press.

Bechara, A., Damasio, A. R., Damasio, H. & Anderson, S. W. 1994 Insensitivity to future consequences following damage to human prefrontal cortex. *Cognition* **50**, 7–15. (doi:10.1016/0010-0277(94)90018-3)

Bjork, R. A. & Bjork, E. L. 1988 On the adaptive aspects of retrieval failure in autobiographical memory. In *Practical aspects of memory: current research and issues* (eds M. M. Gruneberg, P. E. Morris & R. N. Sykes). Chichester, UK: Wiley.

Brainerd, C. J. & Reyna, V. F. 1998 When things that were never experienced are easier to "remember" than things that were. *Psychol. Sci.* **9**, 484–489. (doi:10.1111/1467-9280.00089)

Brainerd, C. J. & Reyna, V. F. 2005 *The science of false memory.* New York, NY: Oxford University Press.

Brandimonte, M., Einstein, G. O. & McDaniel, M. A. 1996 *Prospective memory: theory and applications. Mahwah*, NJ: Erlbaum.

Buckner, R. L. & Carroll, D. C. 2007 Self-projection and the brain. *Trends Cogn. Sci.* **11**, 49–57. (doi:10.1096/j.tics. 2006.11.004)

Budson, A. E., Daffner, K. R., Desikan, R. & Schacter, D. L. 2000 When false recognition is unopposed by true recognition: gist-based memory distortion in Alzheimer's disease. *Neuropsychology* **14**, 277–287. (doi:10.1037/0894-4105.14.2.277)

Budson, A. E., Desikan, R., Daffner, K. R. & Schacter, D. L. 2001 Perceptual false recognition in Alzheimer's disease. *Neuropsychology* **15**, 230–243. (doi:10.1037/0894-4105. 15.2.230)

Budson, A. E., Sullivan, A. L., Daffner, K. R. & Schacter, D. L. 2003 Semantic versus phonological false recognition in aging and Alzheimer's disease. *Brain Cogn.* **51**, 251–261. (doi:10.1016/S0278-2626(03)00030-7)

Budson, A. E., Todman, R. W. & Schacter, D. L. 2006 Gist memory in Alzheimer's disease: evidence from categorized pictures. *Neuropsychology* **20**, 113–122. (doi:10.1037/0894-4105.20.1.113)

Burgess, P. W. & Shallice, T. 1996 Confabulation and the control of recollection. *Memory* **4**, 359–411. (doi:10.1080/096582196388906)

Burgess, N., Becker, S., King, J. A. & O'Keefe, J. 2001a Memory for events and their spatial context: models and experiments. *Phil. Trans. R. Soc. B* **356**, 1493–1503. (doi:10.1098/rstb. 2001.0948)

Burgess, P. W., Quayle, A. & Frith, C. D. 2001b Brain regions involved in prospective memory as determined by positron emission tomography. *Neuropsychologia* **39**, 545–555. (doi:10.1016/S0028-3932(00)00149-4)

Burgess, P. W., Sam, J. G. & Dumontheil, I. 2007 Function and localization within rostral prefrontal cortex (area 10). *Phil. Trans. R. Soc. B* **362**, 887–899. (doi:10.1098/rstb.2007.2095)

Byrne, P., Becker, S. & Burgess, N. 2007. Remembering the past and imagining the future: a neural model of spatial memory and imagery. *Psychol. Rev.* **114**, 340–371.

Cabeza, R., Rao, S. M., Wagner, A. D., Mayer, A. R. & Schacter, D. L. 2001 Can medial temporal lobe regions distinguish true from false? An event-related fMRI study of veridical and illusory recognition memory. *Proc. Natl Acad. Sci. USA* **98**, 4805–4810. (doi:10.1073/pnas.081082698)

Ciaramelli, E., Ghetti, S., Frattarelli, M. & Ladavas, E. 2006 When true memory availability promotes false memory: evidence from confabulating patients. *Neuropsychologia* **44**, 1866–1877. (doi:10.1016/j.neuropsychologia.2006. 02.008)

Conway, M. A., Pleydall-Pearce, C. W., Whitecross, S. E. & Sharpe, H. 2003 Neurophysiological correlates of memory for experienced and imagined events. *Neuropsychologia* **41**, 334–340. (doi:10.1016/S0028-3932(02)00165-3)

Craik, F. I., Moroz, T. M., Moscovitch, M., Stuss, D. T., Winocur, G., Tulving, E. & Kapur, S. 1999 In search of the self: a positron emission tomography study. *Psychol. Sci.* **10**, 26–34. (doi:10.1111/1467-9280.00102)

Dab, S., Claes, T., Morais, J. & Shallice, T. 1999 Confabulation with a selective descriptor process impairment. *Cogn. Neuropsychol.* **16**, 215–242. (doi:10.1080/026432999380771)

Dalla Barba, G., Cappelletti, Y. J., Signorini, M. & Denes, G. 1997 Confabulation: remembering "another" past, planning "another" future. *Neurocase* **3**, 425–436. (doi:10.1093/neucas/3.6.425)

Dalla Barba, G., Nedjam, Z. & Dubois, B. 1999 Confabulation, executive functions, and source memory in Alzheimer's disease. *Cogn. Neuropsychol.* **16**, 385–398. (doi:10.1080/026432999380843)

D'Argembeau, A. & Van der Linden, M. 2004 Phenomenal characteristics associated with projecting oneself back into the past and forward into the future: influence of valence and temporal distance. *Conscious. Cogn.* **13**, 844–858. (doi:10.1016/j.concog.2004.07.007)

D'Argembeau, A. & Van der Linden, M. 2006 Individual differences in the phenomenology of mental time travel. *Conscious. Cogn.* **15**, 342–350. (doi:10.1016/j.concog. 2005.09.001)

Deese, J. 1959 On the prediction of occurrence of particular verbal intrusions in immediate recall. *J. Exp. Psychol.* **58**, 17–22. (doi:10.1037/h0046671)

Delbecq-Derouesné, J., Beauvois, M. F. & Shallice, T. 1990 Preserved recall versus impaired recognition. *Brain* **113**, 1045–1074.

Dudai, Y. & Carruthers, M. 2005 The Janus face of mnemosyne. *Nature* **434**, 823–824. (doi:10.1038/434823a)

Einstein, G. O. & McDaniel, M. A. 1990 Normal aging and prospective memory. *J. Exp. Psychol. Learn. Mem. Cogn.* **16**, 717–726. (doi:10.1037/0278-7393.16.4.717)

Fletcher, P., Frith, C., Baker, S. C., Shallice, T., Frackowiak, R. S. & Dolan, R. 1995 The mind's eye—precuneus activation in memory-related imagery. Neuroimage 2, 195–200. (doi:10.1006/nimg. 1995.1025)

Fuster, J. M. 1989 The prefrontal cortex: anatomy, physiology, and the frontal lobe. New York, NY: Raven Press.

Gallo, D. A. 2006 Associative illusions of memory. New York, NY: Taylor & Francis.

Garoff-Eaton, R. J., Slotnick, S. D. & Schacter, D. L. 2006 Not all false memories are created equal: the neural basis of false recognition. *Cereb. Cortex* **16**, 1645–1652. (doi:10. 1093/cercor/bhj101)

Garry, M., Manning, C. G., Loftus, E. F. & Sherman, S. J. 1996 Imagination inflation: Imagining a childhood event inflates confidence that it occurred. *Psychon. Bull. Rev.* **3**, 208–214.

Gilbert, D. T. 2006 Stumbling on happiness. New York, NY: Alfred A. Knopf.

Gilboa, A., Alain, C., Stuss, D. T., Melo, B., Miller, S. & Moscovitch, M. 2006 Mechanisms of spontaneous confabulations: a strategic retrieval account. *Brain* **129**, 1399–1414. (doi:10.1093/brain/awl093)

Goff, L. M. & Roediger, H. L. 1998 Imagination inflation for action events: repeated imaginings lead to illusory recollections. *Mem. Cogn.* **26**, 20–33.

Goschke, T. & Kuhl, J. 1993 The representation of intentions: persisting activation in memory. J. Exp. *Psychol. Learn. Mem. Cogn.* **19**, 1211–1226. (doi:10.1037/0278-7393.19.5.1211)

Graham, K. S., Lee, A. C., Brett, M. & Patterson, K. 2003 The neural basis of autobiographical and semantic memory: new evidence from three PET studies. *Cogn. Affect. Behav. Neurosci.* **3**, 234–254.

Gusnard, D. A., Akbudak, E., Shulman, G. L. & Raichle, M. E. 2001 Medial prefrontal cortex and self-referential mental activity: relation to a default mode of brain function. *Proc. Natl Acad. Sci. USA* **98**, 4259–4264. (doi:10.1073/pnas.071043098)

Hancock, P. A. 2005 Time and the privileged observer. *KronoScope* **5**, 176–191. (doi:10.1163/15685240 577485 8744)

Hassabis, D., Kumaran, D., Vann, S. D. & Maguire, E. A. 2007 Patients with hippocampal amnesia cannot imagine new experiences. *Proc. Natl Acad. Sci. USA* **104**, 1726–1735. (doi:10.1073/pnas.0610561104)

Ingvar, D. H. 1985 'Memory of the future': an essay on the temporal organization of conscious awareness. Hum. *Neurobiol.* **4**, 127–136.

Johnson, M. K. 1991 Reality monitoring: evidence from confabulation in organic brain disease patients. In *Awareness of deficit after brain injury: clinical and theoretical issues* (eds G. P. Prigatano & D. L. Schacter), pp. 176–197. New York, NY: Oxford University Press.

Johnson, M. K., Foley, M. A., Suengas, A. G. & Raye, C. L. 1988 Phenomenal characteristics of memories for perceived and imagined autobiographical events. *J. Exp. Psychol. Gen.* **117**, 371–376. (doi:10.1037/0096-3445.117.4.371)

Johnson, M. K., Hashtroudi, S. & Lindsey, D. S. 1993 Source monitoring. *Psychol. Bull.* **114**, 3–28. (doi:10.1037/0033-2909.114.1.3)

Kahn, I., Davachi, L. & Wagner, A. D. 2004 Functional-neuroanatomic correlates of recollection: implications for models of recognition memory. *J. Neurosci.* **24**, 4172–4180. (doi:10.1523/JNEUROSCI.0624-04.2004)

Klein, S. B. & Loftus, J. 2002 Memory and temporal experience: the effects of episodic memory loss on an amnesic patient's ability to remember the past and imagine the future. *Soc. Cogn.* **20**, 353–379. (doi:10.1521/soco.20.5.353.21125)

Koutstaal, W., Schacter, D. L., Verfaellie, M., Brenner, C. & Jackson, E. M. 1999 Perceptually-based false recognition of novel objects in amnesia: effects of category size and similarity to prototype. *Cogn. Neuropsychol.* **16**, 317–342. (doi:10.1080/026432999380816)

Loftus, E. F. 1993 The reality of repressed memories. *Am. Psychol.* **48**, 518–537. (doi:10.1037/0003-066X.48.5. 518)

Loftus, E. F. 2003 Make-believe memories. *Am. Psychol.* **58**, 867–873. (doi:10.1037/0003-066X.58.11.867)

Maguire, E. A. 2001 Neuroimaging studies of autobiographical event memory. *Phil. Trans. R. Soc. B* **356**, 1441–1451. (doi:10.1098/rstb.2001.0944)

Mather, M., Henkel, L. A. & Johnson, M. K. 1997 Evaluating characteristics of false memories: remember/know judgments and memory characteristics questionnaire compared. *Mem. Cogn.* **25**, 826–837.

Marr, D. 1971 Simple memory: a theory for archicortex. *Phil. Trans. R. Soc. B* **262**, 23–81. (doi:10.1098/rstb.1971.0078)

McClelland, J. L. 1995 Constructive memory and memory distortions: a parallel-distributed processing approach. In *Memory distortion: how minds, brains and societies reconstruct the past* (ed. D. L. Schacter), pp. 69–90. Cambridge, MA: Harvard University Press.

McClelland, J. L., McNaughton, B. L. & O'Reilly, R. C. 1995 Why there are complementary learning systems in the hippocampus and neocortex: insights from the successes and failures of connectionist models of learning and memory. *Psychol. Rev.* **102**, 419–457. (doi:10.1037/0033-295X.102.3.419)

McDermott, K. B. 1997 Priming on perceptual implicit memory test can be achieved through presentation of associates. *Psychon. Bull. Rev.* **4**, 582–586.

McKone, E. & Murphy, B. 2000 Implicit false memory: effects of modality and multiple study presentations on long lived semantic priming. *J. Mem. Lang.* **43**, 89–109. (doi:10.1006/jmla.1999.2702)

Melo, B., Winocur, G. & Moscovitch, M. 1999 False recall and false recognition: an examination of the effects of selective and combined lesions to the medial temporal lobe/diencephalon and frontal lobe structures. *Cogn. Neuropsychol.* **16**, 343–359. (doi:10.1080/026432 999380825)

Mesulam, M. M. 2002 The human frontal lobes: transcending the default mode through contingent encoding. In *Principles of frontal Lobe function* (eds D. T. Stuss & R. T. Knight), pp. 8–30. New York, NY: Oxford University Press.

Miller, M. B. & Wolford, G. L. 1999 The role of criterion shift in false memory. *Psychol. Rev.* **106**, 398–405. (doi:10.1037/0033-295X.106.2.398)

Morewedge, C. K., Gilbert, D. T. & Wilson, T. D. 2005 The least likely of times: how remembering the past biases forecasts of the future. *Psychol. Sci.* **16**, 626–630. (doi:10.1111/j.1467-9280.2005.01585.x)

Moscovitch, M. 1992 Memory and working-with-memory: a component process model based on modules and central systems. *J. Cogn. Neurosci.* **4,** 257–267.

Moscovitch, M. 1995 Confabulation. In *Memory distortion: how minds, brains, and societies reconstruct the past* (ed. D. L. Schacter), pp. 226–254. Cambridge, MA: Harvard University Press.

Moulin, C. J. A., Conway, M. A., Thompson, R. G., James, N. & Jones, R. W. 2005 Disordered memory awareness: recollective confabulation in two cases of persistent deja vecu. *Neuropsychologia* **43,** 1362–1378. (doi:10.1016/ j.neuropsychologia.2004.12.008)

Norman, K. A. & O'Reilly, R. C. 2003 Modeling hippocampal and neocortical contributions to recognition memory: a complementary learning systems approach. *Psychol. Rev.* **110,** 611–646. (doi:10.1037/ 0033-295X.110.4.611)

Norman, K. A. & Schacter, D. L. 1996 Implicit memory, explicit memory, and false recollection: a cognitive neuroscience perspective. In *Implicit memory and metacognition* (ed. L. M. Reder), pp. 229–257. Hillsdale, NJ: Erlbaum.

Norman, K. A. & Schacter, D. L. 1997 False recognition in young and older adults: exploring the characteristics of illusory memories. *Mem. Cogn.* **25,** 838–848.

Okuda, J., Fujii, T., Yamadori, A., Kawashima, R., Tsukiura, T., Fukatsu, R., Suzuki, K., Itoh, M. & Fukuda, H. 1998 Participation of the prefrontal cortices in prospective memory: evidence from a PET study in humans. *Neurosci. Lett.* **253,** 127–130. (doi:10.1016/ S0304-3940(98)00628-4)

Okuda, J. et al. 2003 Thinking of the future and the past: the roles of the frontal pole and the medial temporal lobes. *Neuroimage* **19,** 1369–1380. (doi:10.1016/S1053-8119 (03)00179-4)

Ost, J. & Costall, A. 2002 Misremembering Bartlett: a study in serial reproduction. *Br. J. Psychol.* **93,** 243–255. (doi:10. 1348/000712602162562)

Poldrack, R., Wagner, A. D., Prull, M. W., Desmond, J. E., Glover, G. H. & Gabrieli, J. D. 1999 Functional specialization for semantic and phonological processing in the left inferior prefrontal cortex. *Neuroimage* **10,** 15–35. (doi:10.1006/nimg.1999.0441)

Roediger, H. L. & McDermott, K. B. 1995 Creating false memories: remembering words not presented in lists. J. Exp. Psychol. Learn. *Mem. Cogn.* **21,** 803–814. (doi:10.1037/0278-7393.21.4.803)

Rosenbaum, R. S., Kohler, S., Schacter, D. L., Moscovitch, M., Westmacott, R., Black, S. E., Gao, F. & Tulving, E. 2005 The case of K. C.: contributions of a memory-impaired person to memory theory. *Neuropsychologia* **43,** 989–1021. (doi:10.1016/j.neuropsychologia.2004.10.007)

Saxe, R. & Kanwisher, N. 2003 People thinking about thinking people. The role of the temporo-parietal junction in "theory of mind". *Neuroimage* **19,** 1835–1842. (doi:10.1016/S1053-8119 (03)00230-1)

Schacter, D. L. 1999 The seven sins of memory: insights from psychology and cognitive neuroscience. *Am. Psychol.* **54,** 182–203. (doi:10.1037/0003-066X.54.3.182)

Schacter, D. L. 2001 *The seven sins of memory: how the mind forgets and remembers.* Boston, MA; New York, NY: Houghton Mifflin.

Schacter, D. L. & Addis, D. R. 2007. The ghosts of past and future. *Nature* **445,** 27. (doi:10.1038/ 445027a)

Schacter, D. L. & Slotnick, S. D. 2004 The cognitive neuroscience of memory distortion. *Neuron* **44,** 149–160. (doi:10.1016/j.neuron.2004.08.017)

Schacter, D. L., Curran, T., Galluccio, L., Milberg, W. & Bates, J. 1996a False recognition and the right frontal lobe: a case study. *Neuropsychologia* **34,** 793–808. (doi:10.1016/0028-3932(95)00165-4)

Schacter, D. L., Reiman, E., Curran, T., Sheng Yun, L., Bandy, D., McDermott, K. B. & Roediger, H. L. 1996b Neuroanatomical correlates of veridical and illusory recognition memory: evidence from positron emission tomography. *Neuron* **17,** 1–20. (doi:10.1016/S0896-6273(00)80158-0)

Schacter, D. L., Verfaellie, M. & Pradere, D. 1996c The neuropsychology of memory illusions: false recall and recognition in amnesic patients. *J. Mem. Lang.* **35,** 319–334. (doi:10.1006/ jmla.1996.0018)

Schacter, D. L., Verfaellie, M. & Anes, M. D. 1997 Illusory memories in amnesic patients: conceptual and perceptual false recognition. *Neuropsychology* **11,** 331–342. (doi:10. 1037/0894-4105.11.3.331)

Schacter, D. L., Norman, K. A. & Koutstaal, W. 1998a The cognitive neuroscience of constructive memory. *Annu. Rev. Psychol.* **49,** 289–318. (doi:10.1146/annurev.psych. 49.1.289)

Schacter, D. L., Verfaellie, M., Anes, M. & Racine, C. 1998b When true recognition suppresses false recognition: evidence from amnesic patients. *J. Cogn. Neurosci.* **10**, 668–679. (doi:10.1162/089892998563086)

Schacter, D. L., Cendan, D. L., Dodson, C. S. & Clifford, E. R. 2001 Retrieval conditions and false recognition: testing the distinctiveness heuristic. *Psychon. Bull. Rev.* **8**, 827–833.

Schacter, D. L., Dobbins, I. G. & Schnyer, D. M. 2004 Specificity of priming: a cognitive neuroscience perspective. *Nat. Rev. Neurosci.* **5**, 853–862. (doi:10.1038/nrn1534)

Schnider, A. 2003 Spontaneous confabulation and the adaptation of thought to ongoing reality. *Nat. Rev. Neurosci.* **4**, 662–671. (doi:10.1038/nrn1179)

Shallice, T. & Burgess, P. 1996 The domain of supervisory processes and the temporal organization of behaviour. *Phil. Trans. R. Soc. B* **351**, 1405–1411. (doi:10.1098/rstb. 1996.0124)

Slotnick, S. D. & Dodson, C. S. 2005 Support for a continuous (single-process) model of recognition memory and source memory. *Mem. Cogn.* **33**, 151–170.

Slotnick, S. D. & Schacter, D. L. 2004 A sensory signature that distinguishes true from false memories. *Nat. Neurosci.* **7**, 664–672. (doi:10.1038/nn1252)

Slotnick, S. D. & Schacter, D. L. 2006 The nature of memory related activity in early visual areas. *Neuropsychologia* **44**, 2874–2886. (doi:10.1016/j.neuropsychologia.2006.06.021)

Squire, L. R., Stark, C. E. & Clark, R. E. 2004 The medial temporal lobe. *Annu. Rev. Neurosci.* **27**, 279–306. (doi:10. 1146/annurev.neuro.27.070203.144130)

Stuss, D. T. & Benson, D. F. 1986 *The frontal lobes*. New York, NY: Raven Press.

Suddendorf, T. & Busby, J. 2003 Mental time travel in animals? *Trends Cogn. Sci.* **7**, 391–396. (doi:10.1016/S1364-6613(03)00187-6)

Suddendorf, T. & Busby, J. 2005 Making decisions with the future in mind: developmental and comparative identification of mental time travel. *Learn. Motiv.* **36**, 110–125. (doi:10.1016/j.lmot.2005.02.010)

Suddendorf, T. & Corballis, M. C. 1997 Mental time travel and the evolution of the human mind. *Genet. Soc. Gen. Psychol. Monogr.* **123**, 133–167.

Szpunar, K. K., Watson, J. M. & McDermott, K. B. 2007 Neural substrates of envisioning the future. Proc. *Natl Acad. Sci. USA* **104**, 642–647. (doi:10.1073/pnas.0610082104)

Thompson, R. F. 2005 In search of memory traces. *Annu. Rev. Psychol.* **56**, 1–23. (doi:10.1146/annurev. psych.56.091103.070239)

Trope, Y. & Liberman, N. 2003 Temporal construal. *Psychol. Rev.* **110**, 401–421.

Tulving, E. 1983 *Elements of episodic memory*. Oxford, UK: Clarendon Press.

Tulving, E. 1985 Memory and consciousness. *Can. Psychol.* **26**, 1–12.

Tulving, E. 2002 Episodic memory: from mind to brain. *Annu. Rev. Psychol.* **53**, 1–25. (doi:10.1146/annurev. psych.53.100901.135114)

Tulving, E. 2005 Episodic memory and autonoesis: uniquely human? In *The missing link in cognition: origins of self-reflective consciousness* (eds H. S. Terrace & J. Metcalfe), pp. 3–56. New York, NY: Oxford University Press.

Tulving, E., Schacter, D. L., McLachlan, D. R. & Moscovitch, M. 1988 Priming of semantic autobiographical knowledge: a case study of retrograde amnesia. *Brain Cogn.* **8**, 3–20. (doi:10.1016/0278-2626(88)90035-8)

Verfaellie, M., Schacter, D. L. & Cook, S. P. 2002 The effect of retrieval instructions on false recognition: exploring the nature of the gist memory impairment in amnesia. *Neuropsychologia* **40**, 2360–2368. (doi:10.1016/S0028-3932(02)00074-X)

Verfaellie, M., Page, K., Orlando, F. & Schacter, D. L. 2005 Impaired implicit memory for gist information in amnesia. *Neuropsychology* **19**, 760–769. (doi:10.1037/0894-4105.19.6.760)

Ward, J., Parkin, A. J., Powell, G., Squires, E. J., Townshend, J. & Bradley, V. 1999 False recognition of unfamiliar people: "Seeing film stars everywhere". *Cogn. Neuropsychol.* **16**, 293–315. (doi:10.1080/026432999380807)

Williams, J. M., Ellis, N. C., Tyers, C., Healy, H., Rose, G. & MacLeod, A. K. 1996 The specificity of autobiographical memory and imageability of the future. *Mem. Cogn.* **24**, 116–125.

Wixted, J. T. & Stretch, V. 2000 The case against a criterion-shift account of false memory. *Psychol. Rev.* **107**, 368–376. (doi:10.1037/0033-295X.107.2.368)

4

The human amygdala and orbital prefrontal cortex in behavioural regulation

R. J. Dolan*

Survival in complex environments depends on an ability to optimize future behaviour based on past experience. Learning from experience enables an organism to generate predictive expectancies regarding probable future states of the world, enabling deployment of flexible behavioural strategies. However, behavioural flexibility cannot rely on predictive expectancies alone and options for action need to be deployed in a manner that is responsive to a changing environment. Important moderators on learning-based predictions include those provided by context and inputs regarding an organism's current state, including its physiological state. In this paper, I consider human experimental approaches using functional magnetic resonance imaging that have addressed the role of the amygdala and prefrontal cortex (PFC), in particular the orbital PFC, in acquiring predictive information regarding the probable value of future events, updating this information, and shaping behaviour and decision processes on the basis of these value representations.

Keywords: emotion; decision making; reward; fMRI; amygdala: orbital prefrontal cortex

4.1 Amygdala encoding of value

A general consensus that the human amygdala plays an important role in emotional processing begs a broader question as to the features of the sensory world to which it is responsive. There is a widely held view that emotion is reducible to dimensions of arousal and valence (Russell 1980; Lang 1995). Within this framework, an enhanced amygdala response to emotional stimuli has been proposed to reflect a specialization for processing emotional intensity (a surrogate for arousal), as opposed to processing valence. Consequently, amygdala activation by stimulus intensity, but not stimulus valence (Anderson & Sobel 2003; Small et al. 2003), is interpreted as supporting a view that external sensory events activate this structure by virtue of their arousal-inducing capabilities (McGaugh *et al.* 1996; Anderson & Sobel 2003; Hamann 2003).

If arousal is a critical variable in mediating the emotional value of sensory stimuli, then a prediction is that blockade of an arousal response should impair key functional characteristics of emotional stimuli, such as their ability to enhance episodic memory encoding. One means to experimentally influence an arousal response is by a pharmacological manipulation. Substantial evidence indicates that enhanced memory for emotional events engages a β-adrenergic central arousal system (Cahill & McGaugh 1998). β-Adrenergic blockade with the $\beta_1\beta_2$-receptor antagonist propranolol selectively impairs long-term human episodic memory for emotionally arousing material without affecting the memory for neutral material (Cahill *et al.* 1994). This modulation of emotional memory by propranolol is centrally mediated because

*r.dolan@fil.ion.ucl.ac.uk

peripheral β-adrenergic blockade has no effect on emotional memory function (van Stegeren *et al.* 1998). The fact that human amygdala lesions also impair emotional, but not non-emotional, memory (Cahill et al. 1995; Phelps *et al.* 1998) points to this structure as a critical locus for emotional effects on memory.

To test the impact of blockading arousal in response to emotional stimuli on episodic memory encoding, as well as to determine the locus of this effect, we presented human subjects with 38 lists of 14 nouns under either placebo or propranolol (Strange *et al.* 2003). Each list comprised 12 emotionally neutral nouns of the same semantic category, a perceptual oddball in a novel font, and an aversive emotional oddball of the same semantic category and perceptually equivalent to neutral nouns. As predicted from previous studies, we observed enhanced subsequent free recall for emotional nouns, relative to both control and perceptual oddball nouns. Furthermore, propranolol eliminated this enhancement such that memory for emotional nouns equated that for neutral nouns. Propranolol had no influence on memory for perceptual oddball items indicating that its effect was not related to an influence on oddball processing. Consequently, this finding supports the idea that arousal provides a key element in enhanced mnemonic processing, in this case encoding of emotional stimuli.

To determine the locus of this effect, we conducted an event-related functional magnetic resonance imaging (fMRI) experiment using identical stimulus sets. Twenty-four subjects received 40 mg of either propranolol or placebo in a double-blind experimental design (Strange & Dolan 2004). There were two distinct scanning sessions corresponding to encoding and retrieval, respectively. Drug/placebo was administered in the morning with the encoding scanning session coinciding with propranolol's peak plasma concentration. The retrieval session that took place 10 h later was not contaminated by the presence of drug. In the placebo group, successful encoding of emotional oddballs, as assessed by successful retrieval 10 h later, engaged left amygdala relative to forgotten items. Under propranolol, amygdala activation no longer predicted subsequent memory for emotional nouns. Even more convincingly, the amygdala exhibited a significant three way interaction for remembered versus forgotten emotional nouns, versus the same comparison for either control nouns or perceptual oddballs, under conditions of placebo compared with propranolol. Thus, adrenergic-dependent amygdala responses do not simply reflect oddball encoding, but unambiguously show that successful encoding-evoked amygdala activation is β-adrenergic dependent. These findings fit with animal data demonstrating that inhibitory avoidance training increases noradrenaline/noradrenergic (NA) levels in the amygdala, where actual NA levels in individual animals correlate highly with later retention performance (McGaugh & Roozendaal 2002).

The fact that blockade of central arousal by propranolol impairs both emotional encoding and amygdala activation might seem to support an idea that an amygdala response indexes arousal. However, this conclusion is limited by the fact that most investigations, including the aforementioned, are predicated on the idea that valence effects in respect of amygdala activation are linear. Few investigations have taken account of an alternative possibility, namely a nonlinearity of response such that effects of arousal are expressed only at the extremes of valence. One difficulty in addressing this question relates to the absence of a range of standard stimuli that have high arousal/intensity but are of neutral or low valence. Conveniently, it turns out that odour stimuli provide a means of unravelling these competing views as they can be independently classified in terms of hedonics (valence; Schiffman 1974) or intensity (an index of arousal; Bensafi *et al.* 2002). Valence as used in the present context is assumed to operate along a linear continuum of pleasantness, with stimuli of low (i.e. more negative) valence representing a less pleasant sensory experience than those of higher (i.e. more positive) valence.

Given that chemosensory strength or intensity takes on greater importance when a stimulus is pleasant or unpleasant, then a nonlinearity in response would predict that amygdala activation to intensity should be expressed maximally at valence extremes.

We tested two competing models of amygdala function. On a valence-independent hypothesis, amygdala response to intensity is similar at all levels of valence. We contrasted this with a valence-dependent model in which the amygdala is sensitive to intensity only at the outer bounds of valence. Using event-related functional magnetic resonance imaging, we then measured amygdala responses to high- and low-concentration variants of pleasant, neutral and unpleasant odours. Our key finding was that amygdala exhibits an intensity–valence interaction in olfactory processing (figure 4.1). Put simply, the effect of intensity on amygdala activity is not the same across all levels of valence and amygdala responds differentially to high (versus low)-intensity odour for pleasant and unpleasant smells, but not for neutral smells (Winston *et al.* 2005). This finding indicates that the amygdala codes neither intensity nor valence per se, but an interaction between intensity and valence, a combination we suggest reflects the overall emotional value of a stimulus. This suggestion is in line with more general theories of amygdala function which suggest that this structure contributes to encoding of salient events that are likely to invoke action (Whalen *et al.* 2004).

4.2 Flexible learning of stimulus–reward associations

Associative learning provides a phylogenetically highly conserved means to predict future events of value, such as the likelihood of food or danger, on the basis of predictive sensory cues. A key contribution of the amygdala to emotional processing relates to its role in acquiring associative or predictive information. In Pavlovian conditioning, a previously neutral item

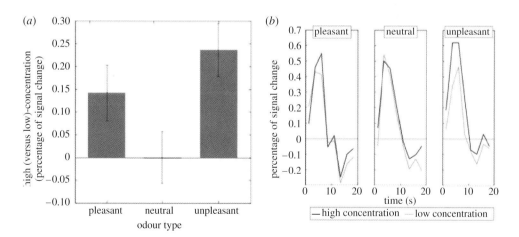

Fig. 4.1 Interaction between odour valence and intensity in the amygdala. (*a*) Plots represent the group-averaged peak fMRI signal in amygdala for high (versus low)-concentration odours at each valence level. An effect of intensity is evident for the pleasant and unpleasant, but not neutral, odours. This is reflected in a significant concentration–type interaction. (*b*) Time courses of amygdala activation for each level of odour concentration and odour type. Data highlight the effects of intensity on amygdala activity that are expressed only at the extremes of odour valence.

(the conditioned stimulus or CS+) acquires predictive significance by pairing with a biologically salient reinforcer (the unconditioned stimulus or UCS). An example of this type of associative learning is a study where we scanned 13 healthy, hungry subjects using fMRI, while they learnt an association between arbitrary visual cues and two pleasant food-based olfactory rewards (vanilla and peanut butter), both before and after selective satiation (Gottfried *et al.* 2003). Arbitrary visual images comprised the two conditioned stimuli (target and non-target CS+) that were paired with their corresponding UCS on 50% of all trials, resulting in paired (CS+p) and unpaired (CS+u) event types, enabling us to distinguish learning-related responses from sensory effects of the UCS (Cahill *et al.* 1994). A third visual image type was never paired with odour (the non-conditioned stimulus or CS–). One odour was destined for reinforcer devaluation (target UCS), while the other odour underwent no motivational manipulation (non-target UCS) (Gottfried *et al.* 2003).

Olfactory associative learning engaged amygdala, rostromedial orbitofrontal cortex (OFC), ventral midbrain, primary olfactory (piriform) cortex, insula and hypothalamus, highlighting the involvement of these regions in acquiring picture–odour contingencies. While these contingencies enable the generation of expectancies in response to sensory cues, it is clear that these predictions have limitations in optimizing future behaviour. The value of the states associated with predictive cues can change in the absence of pairing with these cues, for example when the physiological state of the organism changes. Consequently, it is important for an organism to have a capability of maintaining accessible and flexible representations of the current value of sensory–predictive cues.

Reinforcer devaluation offers an experimental methodology for dissociating among stored representations of value accessed by a CS+. For example, in animals, food value can be decreased by pairing a meal with a toxin. In humans, a more acceptable way of achieving the same end is through sensory-specific satiety, where the reward value of a food eaten to satiety is reduced (devalued) more than to foods not eaten. Animal studies of appetitive (reward-based) learning show that damage to amygdala and OFC interferes with the behavioural expression of reinforcer devaluation (Hatfield *et al.* 1996; Malkova *et al.* 1997; Gallagher *et al.* 1999; Baxter *et al.* 2000). We reasoned that if amygdala and OFC maintain representations of predictive reward value, then CS+-evoked neural responses within these regions should be sensitive to their current reward value and, by implication, to experimental manipulations that devalue a predicted reward. On the other hand, insensitivity to devaluation would indicate that the role of these areas relates more to associative learning that is independent of, or precedes linkage to, central representations of their reward value.

When we compared responses elicited by CS+ stimuli associated with a post-training devalued and non-devalued reward outcome, we found significant response decrements in left amygdala, and both rostral and caudal areas of OFC in relation to the predictive cue that signalled a devalued outcome (Gottfried *et al.* 2003).

Thus, activity in the amygdala and OFC showed a satiety-related decline for target CS+u activity but remained unchanged for the non-target CS+u activity, paralleling the behavioural effects of satiation. Conversely, satiety-sensitive neural responses in ventral striatum, insular cortex and anterior cingulate exhibited a different pattern of activity, reflecting decreases to the target CS+u, which contrasted with increases to the non-target CS+u (figure 4.2). Thus, amygdala and OFC activities evoked by the target CS+u decreased from pre- to post-satiety in a manner that paralleled the current reward value of the target UCS. This response pattern within amygdala and OFC suggests that these regions are involved in representing reward value of predictive stimuli in a flexible manner, observations that accord with animal

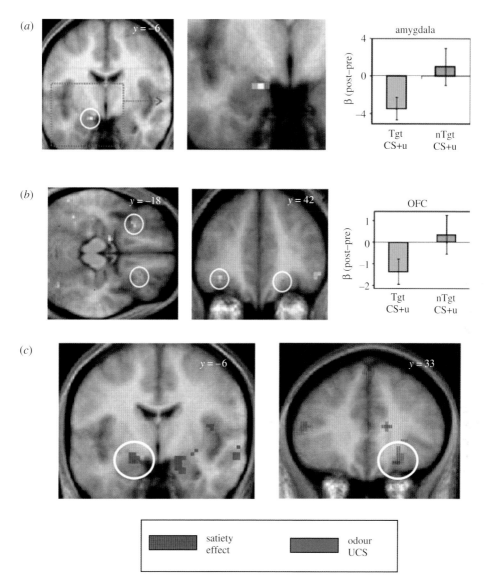

Fig. 4.2 (*a*) Dorsal amygdala region showing altered response to a predictive stimulus that was devalued (CS + Tgt) compared with a control non-devalued stimulus (CS + nTgt). (*b*) Region of orbital prefrontal cortex showing altered response to a predictive stimulus that was devalued (CS + Tgt) compared with a control non-devalued stimulus (CS + nTgt). (*c*) Areas of overlap in amygdala and OFC for responses to UCS (blue) and devaluation (satiety) effects (red). Tgt, target; nTgt, non-target.

data demonstrating that amygdala and OFC lesions impair the effects of reinforcer devaluation (Hatfield *et al.* 1996; Malkova *et al.* 1997; Gallagher *et al.* 1999; Baxter *et al.* 2000).

A question raised by these findings is whether satiety-related devaluation effects reflect the ability of a CS+ to access UCS representations of reward value. Evidence in support of this is our finding that devaluation effects are expressed in the same regions that encode representations of the odour UCS (figure 4.2). Similarly, brain regions that encode predictive reward value participated in the initial acquisition of stimulus–reward contingencies (Gottfried *et al.* 2003) as evidenced by common foci of CS+-evoked responses at initial learning, and during reinforcer devaluation, in amygdala and OFC. The inference from these data is that brain regions maintaining representations of predictive reward are a subset of those that actually participate in associative learning.

Computational models of reward learning postulate motivational 'gates' that facilitate information flow between internal representations of CS+ and UCS stimuli (Dayan & Balleine 2002; Ikeda *et al.* 2002). These are the targets of motivational signals and determine the likelihood that stimulus–reward associations activate appetitive systems. The observation that neural responses evoked by a CS+ in amygdala and OFC are directly modulated by hunger states indicates that these regions underpin Pavlovian incentive behaviour in a manner that accords with specifications of a motivation gate. These findings also inform an understanding of the impact of pathologies within mediotemporal and basal orbitofrontal lobes. Damage to these regions causes a wide variety of maladaptive behaviours. Defective encoding of (or impaired access to) updated reward value in amygdala and OFC could explain the inability of such patients to modify their responses when expected outcomes change (Rolls *et al.* 1981). Thus, these findings can potentially explain the feeding abnormalities observed in both the Kluver–Bucy syndrome (Bechara *et al.* 1994) and frontotemporal dementias (Terzian & Ore 1955). Patients with these conditions may show increased appetite, indiscriminate eating, food cramming, change in food preference, hyperorality and even attempts to eat non-food items. Our data suggest that, in these pathologies, food cues no longer evoke updated representations of their reward value. A disabled anatomical network involving OFC and amygdala would result in food cues being unable to recruit motivationally appropriate representations of food-based reward value.

4.3 Emotional learning evokes a temporal difference teaching signal

There are a number of theoretical accounts of emotional learning; among them the most notable have been based on the Rescorla–Wagner rule (Rescorla 1972). These models, and their real-time extensions, provide some of the best descriptions of computational processes underlying associative learning (Sutton & Barto 1981). The characteristic teaching signal within these models is the prediction error, which is used to direct acquisition and refine expectations relating to cues. In simple terms, a prediction error records change in an expected affective outcome and is expressed whenever predictions are generated, updated or violated. The usefulness of a computational approach in fostering an understanding of biological processes ultimately rests on an empirical test of the degree to which these processes are approximated in real biological systems (Sutton & Barto 1981).

To determine whether emotional learning is implemented using a temporal difference learning algorithm, we used fMRI to investigate the brain activity in healthy subjects as they learned to predict the occurrence of phasic relief or exacerbations of background tonic pain, using a first-order Pavlovian conditioning procedure with a probabilistic (50%) reinforcement schedule (Seymour *et al.* 2005). Tonic pain was induced using the capsaicin thermal hyperalgesia model, while visual cues (abstract coloured images) acted as Pavlovian-conditioned stimuli such that subjects learned that certain images tended to predict either imminent relief or exacerbation of pain. We implemented a computational learning model, the temporal difference (TD) model, which generates a prediction error signal, enabling us to identify brain responses that correlated with this signal. The temporal difference model learns the predictive values (expectations) of neutral cues by assessing their previous associations with appetitive or aversive outcomes.

We treated relief of pain as a reward and exacerbation of pain as a negative reward. Usage of the temporal difference algorithm to represent positive and negative deviations of pain intensity from a tonic background level approximates a class of reinforcement learning model termed average-reward models (Price 1999; O'Doherty *et al.* 2001; Tanaka *et al.* 2004). In these models, predictions are judged relative to the average level of pain, rather than some absolute measures; a comparative approach consistent with both neurobiological and economic accounts of homeostasis that rely crucially on change in affective state (Small *et al.* 2001; Craig 2003). The individual sequence of stimuli given to each subject provides a means to calculate both the value of expectations (in relation to the cues) and the prediction error as expressed at all points throughout the experiment. The use of a partial reinforcement strategy, in which the cues are only 50% predictive of their outcomes, ensures constant learning and updating of expectations, generating both positive and negative prediction errors throughout the course of the experiment.

Using a TD model, as described earlier, to index a representation of an appetitive (reward/relief) prediction error in the brain, we found that activity in left amygdala and left midbrain, a region encompassing the substantia nigra, correlated with this prediction error signal. Time-course analysis of the average pattern of response associated with the different trial types in this area showed a strong correspondence with the average pattern of activity predicted by the model. These data allow two general inferences. Firstly, the functions of the amygdala are not only confined to learning about aversive events, but also reflect learning about rewarding events. Secondly, predictive learning in the amygdala involves a neuronal signature that accords with the outputs of a TD computational model involving a prediction error teaching signal. This suggests that emotional learning in the amygdala involves implementation of a TD-like learning algorithm.

4.4 Learning to avoid danger

Predictive learning may be temporally specific and a cue that predicts danger at one time may not predict danger at a subsequent future time. It would clearly be maladaptive if an organism continued to be governed by these earlier predictions. How cues that no longer signal threat are disregarded can be studied using extinction paradigms. During extinction, successive presentations of a non-reinforced CS+ (following conditioning) diminish conditioned responses (CRs). Animal research indicates that extinction is not simply unlearning an original contingency, but evokes new learning that opposes, or inhibits, expression of conditioning (Rescorla 2001; Myers & Davis 2002). This account proposes that extinction leads to the formation of two distinct memory representations: a 'CS : UCS' excitatory memory and a 'CS : no UCS' inhibitory memory. Which competing memory is activated by a given CS+ is influenced by a range of contingencies including sensory, environmental and temporal contexts (Bouton 1993; Garcia 2002; Hobin *et al.* 2003).

In rodent models of extinction, both ventral prefrontal cortex (PFC) (White & Davey 1989; Repa *et al.* 2001; Milad & Quirk 2002) and amygdala (Herry & Garcia 2002; Hobin *et al.* 2003;

Quirk & Gehlert 2003) are implicated in extinction-related processes. The most interesting mechanistic account of extinction is a proposal that excitatory projections from medial PFC to interneurons in lateral amygdaloid nucleus (Mai *et al.* 1997; Rosenkranz *et al.* 2003) or neighbouring intercalated cell masses (Pearce & Hall 1980; Quirk *et al.* 2003) gate excitatory impulses into the central nucleus of the amygdala in a manner that attenuates the expression of CRs.

To assess how extinction learning is expressed in the human brain, we measured region-specific brain activity in human subjects who had undergone olfactory aversive conditioning (Gottfried & Dolan 2004). This involved pairing two CS faces repetitively with two different UCS odours, while two other faces were never paired with odour and acted as non-conditioned control stimuli (CS-1 and CS-2). This manipulation was followed in the same session by extinction, permitting direct comparison between neural responses evoked during conditioning and extinction learning. In a further manipulation, we used a revaluation procedure to alter, post-conditioning and pre-extinction, the value of one target odour reinforcer using UCS inflation, resulting in target and non-target CS+ stimuli (Falls *et al.* 1992; Critchley *et al.* 2002). In effect, we presented subjects a more intense and aversive exemplar of this UCS, a manipulation that enabled us to tag this CS : UCS memory and index its persistence during the extinction procedure.

We again showed that neural substrates associated with learning involved the amygdala (Gottfried & Dolan 2004) with additional activations seen in ventral midbrain, insula, caudate and ventral striatum, comprising structures previously implicated in associative learning (Morgan *et al.* 1993; Gottfried *et al.* 2002; O'Doherty *et al.* 2002). The crucial finding in this study was our observation that significant activations in rostral and caudal OFC, ventromedial PFC (VMPFC) and lateral amygdala were evident during extinction. Strikingly, these findings implicate similar regions highlighted in animal studies of extinction learning, with the caveat that there are difficulties in identifying homologies between human and rodent models (White & Davey 1989; Repa *et al.* 2001; Herry & Garcia 2002; Milad & Quirk 2002; Hobin *et al.* 2003; Quirk & Gehlert 2003).

One obvious question that arises from these data is whether neural substrates of extinction learning overlap those involved in acquisition? Areas mutually activated across both conditioning and extinction contexts included medial amygdala, rostromedial OFC, insula, and dorsal and ventral striatum. In comparison, a direct contrast of extinction–conditioning allowed us to test for functional dissociations between these sessions. This analysis indicated that neural responses in lateral amygdala, rostromedial OFC and hypothalamus were preferentially enhanced during extinction learning, over and above any conditioning-evoked activity for both CS+ types. These peak activations occurred in the absence of significant interactions between phase (conditioning versus extinction) and CS+ type (target versus non-target).

The above findings do not enable a distinction between CS+-evoked activation of UCS memory traces and those related more generally to extinction learning. The fact that we used UCS inflation to create an updated trace of UCS value meant it could be selectively indexed during extinction. The logic here is that CRs subsequently elicited by the corresponding CS+ should become accentuated, as the predictive cue accesses an updated and inflated representation of UCS value. The contrast of target CS+u versus non-target CS+u at extinction (each minus their respective CS –) demonstrated a significant activity in left lateral OFC, with an adjacent area of enhanced activity evident when we examined the interaction between phase (extinction versus conditioning) and CS+ type (target versus non-target). Furthermore, a significant positive correlation was evident between lateral OFC activity and ratings of target CS+ aversiveness, implying that relative magnitude of predictive (aversive) value is encoded, and updated, within this structure. Note that as UCS inflation enhanced target CS+ aversiveness, the non-target CS+ concurrently became less aversive, relative to the target CS+. In this respect, post-inflation value of the non-target UCS became relatively more rewarding. Consequently, when we compared non-target and target CS+ activities at extinction (minus CS− baselines) to index areas sensitive to predictive reward value (i.e., relatively 'less aversive' value), we found significant VMPFC activity driven by the non-target CS+u response at extinction. Regression analysis demonstrated that neural responses in ventromedial PFC were significantly and negatively correlated with differential CS+ aversiveness.

These findings indicate that discrete regions of OFC, including lateral/medial and rostral sectors, as well as lateral amygdala are preferentially activated during extinction learning. However, these findings cannot be attributed to general mechanisms of CS+ processing, as extinction-related activity was selectively enhanced in these areas over and above that evoked during conditioning. Thus, CS+-evoked recruitment of an OFC–amygdala network provides the basis for memory processes that regulate expression of conditioning. Our findings suggest that ventral PFC supports dual mnemonic representations of UCS value, which are accessible to a predictive cue. The presence of a dual representational system that responds as a function of the degree of preference (or non-preference) could provide a basis for fine-tuned regulation over conditioned behaviour and other learned responses. Indeed, an organism that needs to optimize its choices from among a set of different predictive cues would be well served by a system that integrates information about their relative values in such a parallel and differentiated manner. The general idea that orbital PFC synthesizes sensory, affective and motivational cues in the service of goal-directed behaviour also accords well with animal (Tremblay & Schultz 1999; Arana *et al.* 2003; Pickens *et al.* 2003; Schoenbaum *et al.* 2003) and human (Morgan *et al.* 1993; Gottfried *et al.* 2003) studies of associative learning and incentive states.

Medial–lateral dissociations in ventral PFC activity have been described in the context of a diverse set of rewards and punishments. Pleasant and unpleasant smells (Hatfield *et al.* 1996; O'Doherty *et al.* 2003) and tastes (Malkova *et al.* 1997), as well as more abstract valence representations (Gallagher *et al.* 1999; Gottfried *et al.* 2002), all exhibit functional segregation along this axis. On neuroanatomical grounds, these regions can be regarded as distinct functional units with unique sets of cortical and subcortical connections (Baxter *et al.* 2000). Notably, projections between OFC and amygdala are reciprocal (Baxter *et al.* 2000; Morris & Dolan 2004) and it is thus plausible that differences in input patterns from amygdala might contribute to the expression of positive and negative values in medial and lateral prefrontal subdivisions, respectively.

4.5 Contextual control in the expression of emotional memory

The idea that extinction represents a form of new learning, while leaving intact associations originally established during conditioning, receives strong support from animal studies. As we have seen, the VMPFC is strongly implicated in the storage and recall of extinction memories (Morgan & LeDoux 1995; Milad & Quirk 2002; Phelps *et al.* 2004; Milad *et al.* 2005) and this region may exert control in conditioned memory expression via suppression of the amygdala (Quirk *et al.* 2003; Rosenkranz *et al.* 2003).

Conditioning has usually been discussed within a framework of associative models, but an alternative perspective invokes the concept of decision making (Wasserman & Miller 1997; Gallistel & Gibbon 2000). Consequently, extinction is proposed to reflect a decision mechanism designed to detect change in the rate of reinforcement attributed to a CS where recent experience is inconsistent with earlier experience. Background context is a critical regulatory variable in this decision process (Bouton 2004) such that, with extinction training, the subsequent recall of an extinction memory with CS presentation (i.e. the CR) shows a relative specificity to contexts that resemble those present during extinction training ('extinction context').

We used context-dependency in recall of extinction memory to study its neurobiological underpinnings in human subjects using a within-subject AB–AB design consisting of Pavlovian fear conditioning in context A and extinction in context B on day 1 with testing of CS-evoked responses in both a conditioning (A) and extinction (B) context on day 2 (delayed recall of extinction) (Kalisch et al. 2006). The two CSs (CS +, which was occasionally paired with the UCS, and a CS−, which was never paired with a UCS) consisted of one male and one female face, while contexts were distinguished by background screen colour and auditory input. Conditioned fear responses were extinguished by presenting the CSs in the same fashion as

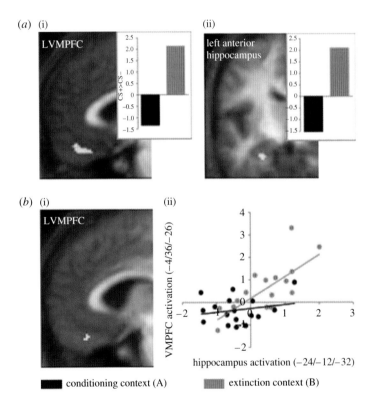

Fig. 4.3 (a) Recall of extinction memory: figure (i) displays a region of orbital prefrontal cortex (left ventromedial prefrontal cortex: LVMPFC) showing enhanced activity during contextual recall of extinction memory (in other words signalling that a sensory stimulus that had earlier predicted an aversive event no longer predicts its occurrence). Figure (ii) shows a region of left hippocampus where there is also enhanced activity during extinction memory recall. (b) Context-specific correlation: (i and ii) region of OFC where there is a significant correlation in activity with hippocampal regions (as highlighted in (a)) that is expressed solely in an extinction context.

during conditioning but now omitting shock. We reasoned that areas supporting context-dependent recall of extinction memory would show a contextual modulation of CS+-evoked activation. We examined this by testing for a categorical CS−context interaction (CS+ >CS−)$_B$>(CS+ >CS−)$_A$ on day 2 (delayed recall of extinction).

We found a significant interaction in OFC and left anterior hippocampus driven by a relatively greater activation to the CS+ than to the CS− in the extinction (figure 4.3). Thus, CS+-evoked activation of OFC and (left anterior) hippocampus was specifically expressed in an extinction context. The hippocampus is known to process contextual information supporting recall of memory (Delamater 2004) and our data suggest that it uses this information to confer (extinction) context dependency on CS+-evoked VMPFC activity. Thus, contextually regulated recall of extinction memory in humans seems to be mediated by a network of brain areas including the OFC and the anterior hippocampus. Our data indicate that these regions form a neurobiological substrate for the context-dependence of extinction recall (Bouton 2004). The finding of extinction context-specific relative activations in our study, as opposed to the extinction-related deactivations observed previously by LaBar & Phelps (2005), supports the general idea that extinction (and its recall) is not simply a process of forgetting the CS−UCS association, but consists of active processes that encode and retrieve a new CS–no UCS memory trace (Myers & Davis 2002; Bouton 2004; Delamater 2004).

4.6 Instrumental behaviour and value representations

Optimal behaviour relies on using past experience to guide future decisions. In behavioural economics, expected utility (a function of probability, magnitude and delay to reward) provides a guiding perspective on decision making (Camerer 2003). Despite limitations, the utility theory of Neumann–Morgenstern (Loomes 1988) continues to dominate models of decision making and converges with reinforcement learning on the idea that decision making involves integration of reward, reward magnitude and reward timing to provide a representation of action desirability (Glimcher & Rustichini 2004). On this basis, a key variable in optimal decision, particularly under conditions of uncertainty, reflects the use of information regarding the likely value of distinct courses of actions. As we have already seen, there is good evidence from studies of associate learning that OFC is involved in representing value and in updating value representations in a flexible manner.

A key question that arises is whether such representations guide more instrumental-type actions where reward values of options for action are unknown or can only be approximated. Classically, these situations pose a conflict between exploiting what is estimated to be the current best option versus sampling an uncertain, but potentially more rewarding, alternative (see also Cohen *et al.* 2007 and this volume). This scenario is widely known as the explore–exploit dilemma. We studied this class of decision making while subjects performed an *n*-armed bandit task with four slots that paid money as reward (Daw *et al.* 2006). Simultaneous data on brain responses were acquired using fMRI. Pay-offs for each slot varied from trial to trial around a mean value corrupted by Gaussian noise. Thus, information regarding the value of an individual slot can only be obtained by active sampling. As the values of each of the actions cannot be determined from single outcomes, subjects need to optimize their choices by exploratory sampling of each of the slots in relation to a current estimate of what is the optimal or greedy slot.

We characterized subjects' exploratory behaviour by examining a range of reinforcement learning models of exploration, where the best approximation was what is known as a softmax rule.

A softmax solution implies that actions are chosen as a ranked function of their estimated value. This rule ensures that the action with the highest value is still selected in an exploitative manner, with other actions chosen with a frequency that reflects a ranked estimate of their value. Using the softmax model, we could calculate value predictions, prediction errors and choice probabilities for each subject on each trial. These regressors were then used to identify brain regions where activity was significantly correlated with the model's internal signals.

Implementing this computational approach to our fMRI data analysis demonstrated that activity in medial OFC correlated with the magnitude of the obtained pay-off, a finding consistent with our previous evidence that this region codes the relative value of different reward stimuli, including abstract rewards (O'Doherty *et al.* 2001; O'Doherty 2004). Furthermore, activity in medial and lateral OFC, extending into VMPFC, correlated with the probability assigned by the model to the action actually chosen trial-to-trial. This probability provides a relative measure of the expected reward value of the chosen action, and the associated profile of activity is consistent with a role for orbital and adjacent medial PFC in encoding predictions of future reward as indicated in our studies of devaluation (Gottfried *et al.* 2003; Tanaka *et al.* 2004). Thus, these data accord with a general framework wherein action choice is optimized by accessing the likely future reward value of chosen actions.

A crucial aspect of our model is that it affords a characterization of neural activity as exploratory as opposed to exploitative. Consequently, we classified subjects' behaviour according to whether the actual choice was one predicted by the model to be determined by the dominant slot machine with the highest expected value (exploitative) or a dominated machine with

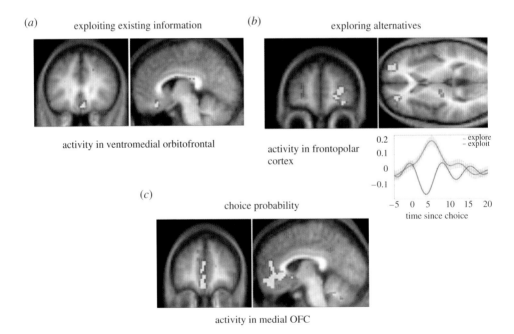

(*a*)   exploiting existing information   (*b*)   exploring alternatives

activity in ventromedial orbitofrontal   activity in frontopolar cortex

(*c*)   choice probability

activity in medial OFC

Fig. 4.4 (*a*) Regions of ventromedial prefrontal cortex where activity increases as a function of actual reward received. (*b*) Regions of left and right frontopolar cortex where activity increases during trials that are exploratory. (*c*) Regions of medial and lateral OFC and adjacent medial prefrontal cortex where activity correlates with the probability assigned by the computational model to subject's choice of slot.

a lower expected value (exploratory). Comparing the pattern of brain activity associated with these exploratory and exploitative trials showed right anterior frontopolar cortex (BA 10) as more active during decisions classified as exploratory (figure 4.4). This anterior frontopolar cortex activity indicates that this region provides a control mechanism facilitating switching between exploratory and exploitative strategies. Indeed, this fits with what is known about the role of this most rostral prefrontal region in high-level control (Ramnani & Owen 2004), mediating between different goals, subgoals (Braver & Bongiolatti 2002) or cognitive processes (Ramnani & Owen 2004; see also Burgess *et al.* 2007 and this volume)

The conclusions from these data are that choices under uncertainty are strongly correlated with activity in the OFC, emphasizing the key role played by this structure in behavioural control. Within the context of an instrumental task, activity in the OFC encodes the value, and indeed relative value, of individual actions. More rostral PFC (BA 10), activated during exploratory choices, would seem to represent a control region that can override decisions based solely on value to allow a less deterministic sampling of the environment and possibly reveal a richer seam of rewards.

4.7 Emotional biases on decision making

Decision-making theory emphasises the role of analytic processes based upon utility maximisation, which incorporates the concept of reward, in guiding choice behaviour. There is now good evidence that more intuitive, or emotional responses, play a key role in human decision-making (Damasio *et al.* 1994; Loewenstein *et al.* 2001; Greene & Haidt 2002). In particular, decisions under conditions when available information is incomplete or overly complex can invoke simplifying heuristics, or efficient rules of thumb, rather than extensive algorithmic processing (Gilovich *et al.* 2002). Deviations from predictions of utility theory can, in some instances, be explained by emotion, as proposed by disappointment (Bell 1985; Loomes & Sugden 1986) and regret theory (Bell 1982; Loomes & Sugden 1983). Disappointment is an emotion that occurs when an outcome is worse than an outcome one would have obtained under a different state of reward. Regret is the emotion that occurs when an outcome is worse than what one would have experienced, had one made a different choice. It has been shown that an ability to anticipate emotions, such as disappointment or regret, has consequences for future options for action and profoundly influences our decisions (Mellers *et al.* 1999). In other words, when faced with mutually exclusive options, the choice we make is influenced not only by what we hope to gain (expected value or utility) but also by how we anticipate we will feel after the choice (Payne *et al.* 1992).

Counterfactual thinking is a comparison between obtained and unattained outcomes that determines the quality and intensity of the ensuing emotional response. Neuropsychological studies have shown that this effect is abolished by lesions to OFC (Camille *et al.* 2004). A cumulative regret history can also exert a biasing influence on the decision process, such that subjects are biased to choose options likely to minimize future regret, an effect mediated by the OFC and amygdala (Coricelli *et al.* 2005). Theoretically, these findings can be seen as approximating a forward model of choice that incorporates predictions regarding future emotional states as inputs into decision processes.

While there is now good evidence that emotion can bias decision making, there are other striking instances of the effects of emotion on rationality. A key assumption in rational decision making is logical consistency across decisions, regardless of how choices are presented.

This assumption of description invariance (Tversky & Kahneman 1986) is now challenged by a wealth of empirical data (McNeil *et al*. 1982; Kahneman & Tversky 2000), most notably in the 'framing effect', a key component within Prospect Theory (Kahneman & Tversky 1979; Tversky & Kahneman 1981). One theoretical consideration is that the framing effect results from a systematic bias in choice behaviour arising from an affect heuristic underwritten by an emotional system (Slovic *et al*. 2002; Gabaix, 2003).

We investigated the neurobiological basis of the framing effect using fMRI and a novel financial decision-making task. Participants were shown a message indicating the amount of money that they would initially receive in that trial (e.g. 'You receive £50'). Subjects then had to choose between a 'sure' or a 'gamble' option presented in the context of two different 'frames'. The sure option was formulated as either the amount of money retained from the initial starting amount (e.g. keep £20 of a total of £50—'Gain' frame), or as the amount of money lost from the initial amount (e.g. lose £30 of a total of £50—'Loss' frame). The gamble option was identical in both frames and represented as a pie chart depicting the probability of winning or losing (De Martino *et al*. 2006).

Subjects' behaviour in this task showed a marked framing effect evident in being risk-averse in the Gain frame, tending to choose the sure option over the gamble option (gambling on 42.9% trials; significantly different from 50%, $p<0.05$), and risk-seeking in the Loss frame, preferring the gamble option (gambling on 61.6% trials; significantly different from 50%). This effect was consistently observed across different probabilities and initial endowment amounts. During simultaneous acquisition of fMRI data on regional brain activity, we observed bilateral amygdala activity when subjects' choices were influenced by the frame. In other words, amygdala activation was significantly greater when subjects chose the sure option in the Gain frame (G_sure–G_gamble), and the gamble option in the Loss frame (L_gamble–L_sure). When subjects made choices that ran counter to this general behavioural tendency, there was enhanced activity in anterior cingulate cortex (ACC), suggesting an opponency between two neural systems. Activation of ACC in these situations is consistent with the detection of conflict between more 'analytic' response tendencies and an obligatory effect associated with a more 'emotional' amygdala-based system (Botvinick *et al*. 2001; Balleine & Killcross 2006).

A striking feature of our behavioural data was a marked inter subject variability in susceptibility to the frame. This variability allowed us to index subject specific differences in neural activity associated with a decision by frame interaction. Using a measure of overall susceptibility of each subject to the frame manipulation, we constructed a 'rationality index' and found a significant correlation between decreased susceptibility to the framing effect and enhanced activity in orbital and medial PFC (OMPFC) and VMPFC. In other words, subjects who acted more rationally exhibited greater activation in OMPFC and VMPFC associated with the frame effect.

We have already seen that the amygdala plays a key role in value-related prediction and learning, both for negative (aversive) and positive (appetitive) outcomes (LeDoux 1996; Baxter & Murray 2002; Seymour *et al*. 2005). Furthermore, in simple instrumental decision making tasks in animals, the amygdala appears to mediate biases in decision that come from value-related predictions (Paton *et al*. 2006). In humans, the amygdala is also implicated in the detection of emotionally relevant information present in contextual and social emotional cues. Increased activation in amygdala associated with subjects' tendency to be risk-averse in the Gain frame and risk-seeking in the Loss frame supports the hypothesis that the framing effect is driven by an affect heuristic underwritten by an emotional system.

The observation that the frame has such a pervasive impact on complex decision making supports the emerging central role for the amygdala in decision making (Kim *et al*. 2004; Hsu *et al*. 2005). These data extend the role of the amygdala to include processing contextual positive or negative emotional information communicated by a frame. Note that activation of amygdala was driven by the combination of a subject's decision in a given frame, rather than by the valence of the frame *per se*. It would seem that frame-related valence information is incorporated into the relative assessment of options to exert control over the apparent risk sensitivity of individual decisions.

An intriguing question is why is the frame so potent in driving emotional responses that engender deviations from rationality? Information about motivationally important outcomes may come from a variety of sources, not only from those based on analytic processes. In animals, the provision of cues that signal salient outcomes, for example, Pavlovian contingencies, can have a strong impact on ongoing instrumental actions. Intriguingly, interactions of the impact of Pavlovian cues on instrumental performance involve brain structures such as the amygdala. Similar processes may be involved in the 'framing effect' where an option for action is accompanied by non-contingent affective cues. Such affective cues ('frames') invoke risk, typically either positive (you could win £x) or negative (you might lose £y), and may cause individuals to adjust how they value distinct options. From the perspective of economics, the resulting choice biases seem irrational, but in real-life decision-making situations, sensitivity to these cues may provide a valuable source of additional information.

Susceptibility to the frame showed a robust correlation with neural activity in OMPFC across subjects consistent with the idea that this region and the amygdala each contributes distinct functional roles in decision making. As already argued, the OFC, by incorporating inputs from the amygdala, represents the motivational value of stimuli (or choices), which allows it to integrate and evaluate the incentive value of predicted outcomes in order to guide future behaviour (Rolls *et al*. 1994; Schoenbaum *et al*. 2006). Lesions of the OFC cause impairments in decision making, often characterized as an inability to adapt behavioural strategies according to current contingencies (as in extinction) and consequences of decisions expressed in forms of impulsivity (Winstanley *et al*. 2004; Bechara *et al*. 1994). One interpretation of enhanced activation with increasing resistance to the frame is that more 'rational' individuals have a better and more refined representation of their own emotional biases. Such a representation would allow subjects to modify their behaviour appropriate to circumstances, as for example when such biases might lead to suboptimal decisions. In this model, OFC evaluates and integrates emotional and cognitive information that underpins more 'rational' behaviour, operationalized here as description-invariant.

4.8 Conclusions

The amygdala and orbital PFC have a pivotal role in emotional processing and guidance of human behaviour. The rich sensory connectivity of the amygdala provides a basis for its role in encoding predictive value for both punishments and rewards. Acquisition of value representations by the amygdala would appear to involve implementation of a TD-like reinforcement learning algorithm. On the other hand, the OFC appears to provide the basis for a more flexible representation of value that is sensitive to multiple environmental factors, including context and internal physiological state (e.g. state satiety). Flexible representation of value in OFC also provides a basis for optimization of behaviour on the basis of reward value accruing from individual choice behaviour. There are suggestions that OFC may integrate value over both short and long time frames (Cohen *et al*. 2007). An intriguing, though as yet unanswered, question is whether there are distinct regions within OFC that encode different aspects of value such as reward and punishment. Our findings indicate that a more rostral PFC region appears to exert control of action, enabling switching between actions that are exploitative and those that allow exploratory sampling of other options for action (see also Cohen *et al*. 2007). However, high-level behaviour is also susceptible to more low-level influences from the amygdala, perhaps mediated via low-level Pavlovian processing, and these influences can bias choice behaviour in a manner that is rationally suboptimal as seen in regret and in the framing effect.

The author's research was supported by the Wellcome Trust.

REFERENCES

Anderson, A. K. & Sobel, N. 2003 Dissociating intensity from valence as sensory inputs to emotion. Neuron 39, 581–583. (doi:10.1016/S0896-6273(03)00504-X)

Arana, F. S., Parkinson, J. A., Hinton, E., Holland, A. J., Owen, A. M. & Roberts, A. C. 2003 Dissociable contributions of the human amygdala and orbitofrontal cortex to incentive motivation and goal selection. *J. Neurosci*. **23**, 9632–9638.

Balleine, B. W. & Killcross, S. 2006 Parallel incentive processing: an integrated view of amygdala function. *Trends Neurosci*. **29**, 272–279. (doi:10.1016/j.tins.2006.03.002)

Baxter, M. G. & Murray, E. A. 2002 The amygdala and reward. *Nat. Rev. Neurosci*. **3**, 563–573. (doi:10.1038/nrn875)

Baxter, M. G., Parker, A., Lindner, C. C., Izquierdo, A. D. & Murray, E. A. 2000 Control of response selection by reinforcer value requires interaction of amygdala and orbital prefrontal cortex. *J. Neurosci*. **20**, 4311–4319.

Bechara, A., Damasio, A. R., Damasio, H. & Anderson, S. W. 1994 Insensitivity to future consequences following damage to human prefrontal cortex. *Cognition* **50**, 7–15. (doi:10.1016/0010-0277 (94)90018-3)

Bell, D. 1982 Regret and decision making under uncertainty. *Oper. Res*. **30**, 961–981.

Bell, D. E. 1985 Disappointment in decision making under uncertainty. *Oper. Res*. **33**, 1–27.

Bensafi, M., Rouby, C., Farget, V., Bertrand, B., Vigouroux, M. & Holley, A. 2002 Autonomic nervous system responses to odours: the role of pleasantness and arousal. *Chem. Senses* 27, 703–709. (doi:10.1093/chemse/27.8.703)

Botvinick, M. M., Braver, T. S., Barch, D. M., Carter, C. S. & Cohen, J. D. 2001 Conflict monitoring and cognitive control. *Psychol. Rev*. **108**, 624–652. (doi:10.1037/0033-295X.108.3.624)

Bouton, M. E. 1993 Context, time, and memory retrieval in the interference paradigms of Pavlovian learning. *Psychol. Bull*. 114, 80–99. (doi:10.1037/0033-2909.114.1.80)

Bouton, M. E. 2004 Context and behavioral processes in extinction. *Learn. Mem*. **11**, 485–494. (doi:10.1101/ lm.78804)

Braver, T. S. & Bongiolatti, S. R. 2002 The role of frontopolar cortex in subgoal processing during working memory. *Neuroimage* 15, 523–536. (doi:10.1006/nimg.2001.1019)

Burgess, P. W., Gilbert, S. J. & Dumontheil, I. 2007 Function and localization within rostral prefrontal cortex (area 10). *Phil. Trans. R. Soc. B* **362**, 887–899. (doi:10.1098/rstb. 2007.2095)

Cahill, L. & McGaugh, J. L. 1998 Mechanisms of emotional arousal and lasting declarative memory. *Trends Neurosci*. **21**, 294–299. (doi:10.1016/S0166-2236(97)01214-9)

Cahill, L., Prins, B., Weber, M. & McGaugh, J. L. 1994 Beta-adrenergic activation and memory for emotional events. *Nature* 371, 702–704. (doi:10.1038/371702a0)

Cahill, L., Babinsky, R., Markowitsch, H. J. & McGaugh, J. L. 1995 The amygdala and emotional memory. *Nature* 377, 295–296. (doi:10.1038/377295a0)

Cahill, L., Haier, R. J., Fallon, J., Alkire, M. T., Tang, C., Keator, D., Wu, J. & McGaugh, J. L. 1996 Amygdala activity at encoding correlated with long-term, free recall of emotional information. *Proc. Natl Acad. Sci. USA* **93**, 8016–8021. (doi:10.1073/pnas.93.15.8016)

Camerer, C. F. 2003 *Behavioral gain theory*. New Jersey, NJ: Princeton University Press.

Camille, N., Coricelli, G., Sallet, J., Pradat-Diehl, P., Duhamel, J. R. & Sirigu, A. 2004 The involvement of the orbitofrontal cortex in the experience of regret. *Science* **304**, 1167–1170. (doi:10.1126/science.1094550)

Cohen, J., McLure, S. M. & Yu, A. 2007 Should I stay or should I go? How the human brain manages the tradeoff between exploration and exploitation. *Phil. Trans. R. Soc. B* **362**, 933–942. (doi:10.1098/rstb.2007.2098)

Coricelli, G., Critchley, H. D., Joffily, M., O'Doherty, J. P., Sirigu, A. & Dolan, R. J. 2005 Regret and its avoidance: a neuroimaging study of choice behavior. *Nat. Neurosci.* **8**, 1255–1262. (doi:10.1038/nn1514)

Craig, A. D. 2003 A new view of pain as a homeostatic emotion. *Trends Neurosci.* **26**, 303–307. (doi:10.1016/S0166-2236(03)00123-1)

Critchley, H. D., Mathias, C. J. & Dolan, R. J. 2002 Fear conditioning in humans: the influence of awareness and autonomic arousal on functional neuroanatomy. *Neuron* **33**, 653–663. (doi:10.1016/S0896-6273(02)00588-3)

Damasio, H., Grabowski, T., Frank, R., Galaburda, A. M. & Damasio, A. R. 1994 The return of Phineas Gage: clues about the brain from the skull of a famous patient. *Science* **264**, 1102–1105. (doi:10.1126/science.8178168) [Erratum in *Science* 1994 **265**, 1159.]

Daw, N. D., O'Doherty, J. P., Dayan, P., Seymour, B. & Dolan, R. J. 2006 Cortical substrates for exploratory decisions in humans. *Nature* **441**, 876–879. (doi:10.1038/nature04766)

Dayan, P. & Balleine, B. W. 2002 Reward, motivation, and reinforcement learning. *Neuron* **36**, 285–298. (doi:10. 1016/S0896-6273(02)00963-7)

De Martino, B., Kumaran, D., Seymour, B. & Dolan, R. J. 2006 Frames, biases, and rational decision-making in the human brain. *Science* **313**, 684–687. (doi:10.1126/science. 1128356)

Delamater, A. R. 2004 Experimental extinction in Pavlovian conditioning: behavioural and neuroscience perspectives. *Q. J. Exp. Psychol.* B 57, 97–132. (doi:10.1080/02724 990344000097)

Falls, W. A., Miserendino, M. J. & Davis, M. 1992 Extinction of fear-potentiated startle: blockade by infusion of an NMDA antagonist into the amygdala. *J. Neurosci.* **12,** 854–863.

Gallagher, M., McMahan, R. W. & Schoenbaum, G. 1999 Orbitofrontal cortex and representation of incentive value in associative learning. *J. Neurosci.* **19**, 6610–6614.

Gallistel, C. R. & Gibbon, J. 2000 Time, rate, and conditioning. *Psychol. Rev.* **107**, 289–344. (doi:10.1037/0033-295X.107.2.289)

Garcia, R. 2002 Postextinction of conditioned fear: between two CS-related memories. *Learn. Mem.* **9**, 361–363. (doi:10.1101/lm.56402)

Gilovich, T., Griffin, D. W. & Kahneman, D. 2002 *Heuristics and biases: the psychology of intuitive judgment*. New York, NY: Cambridge University Press.

Glimcher, P. W. & Rustichini, A. 2004 Neuroeconomics: the consilience of brain and decision. *Science* **306**, 447–452. (doi:10.1126/science.1102566)

Gottfried, J. A. & Dolan, R. J. 2004 Human orbitofrontal cortex mediates extinction learning while accessing conditioned representations of value. *Nat. Neurosci.* 7, 1144–1152. (doi:10.1038/nn1314)

Gottfried, J. A., O'Doherty, J. & Dolan, R. J. 2002 Appetitive and aversive olfactory learning in humans studied using event-related functional magnetic resonance imaging. *J. Neurosci.* **22**, 10 829–10 837.

Gottfried, J. A., O'Doherty, J. & Dolan, R. J. 2003 Encoding predictive reward value in human amygdala and orbitofrontal cortex. *Science* **301**, 1104–1107. (doi:10.1126/ science.1087919)

Greene, J. & Haidt, J. 2002 How (and where) does moral judgment work? *Trends Cogn. Sci.* **6**, 517–523. (doi:10.1016/S1364-6613(02)02011-9)

Hamann, S. 2003 Nosing in on the emotional brain. *Nat. Neurosci.* **6**, 106–108. (doi:10.1038/nn0203-106)

Hatfield, T., Han, J. S., Conley, M., Gallagher, M. & Holland, P. 1996 Neurotoxic lesions of basolateral, but not central, amygdala interfere with Pavlovian second-order conditioning and reinforcer devaluation effects. *J. Neurosci.* **16**, 5256–5265.

Herry, C. & Garcia, R. 2002 Prefrontal cortex long-term potentiation, but not long-term depression, is associated with the maintenance of extinction of learned fear in mice. *J. Neurosci.* **22**, 577–583.

Hobin, J. A., Goosens, K. A. & Maren, S. 2003 Context-dependent neuronal activity in the lateral amygdala represents fear memories after extinction. *J. Neurosci.* **23**, 8410–8416.

Hsu, M., Bhatt, M., Adolphs, R., Tranel, D. & Camerer, C. F. 2005 Neural systems responding to degrees of uncertainty in human decision-making. *Science* **310**, 1680–1683. (doi:10.1126/science.1115327)

Ikeda, M., Brown, J., Holland, A. J., Fukuhara, R. & Hodges, J. R. 2002 Changes in appetite, food preference, and eating habits in frontotemporal dementia and Alzheimer's disease. *J. Neurol. Neurosurg. Psychiatry* **73**, 371–376. (doi:10.1136/jnnp.73.4.371)

Kahneman, D. & Tversky, A. 1979 Prospect theory: an analysis of decision under risk. *Econometrica* **47**, 263–291. (doi:10.2307/1914185)

Kahneman, D. & Tversky, A. 2000 *Choices, values, and frames.* New York, NY: Cambridge University Press.

Kalisch, R., Korenfeld, E., Stephan, K. E., Weiskopf, N., Seymour, B. & Dolan, R. J. 2006 Context-dependent human extinction memory is mediated by a ventromedial prefrontal and hippocampal network. *J. Neurosci.* **26**, 9503–9511. (doi:10.1523/JNEUROSCI.2021-06.2006)

Kim, H., Somerville, L. H., Johnstone, T., Polis, S., Alexander, A. L., Shin, L. M. & Whalen, P. J. 2004 Contextual modulation of amygdala responsivity to surprised faces. *J. Cogn. Neurosci.* **16**, 1730–1745. (doi:10.1162/0898929042947865)

LaBar, K. S. & Phelps, E. A. 2005 Reinstatement of conditioned fear in humans is context dependent and impaired in amnesia. *Behav. Neurosci.* **119**, 677–686. (doi:10.1037/0735-7044.119.3.677)

Lang, P. J. 1995 The emotion probe. Studies of motivation and attention. Am. *J. Psychol.* **50**, 372–385. (doi:10.1037/0003-066X.50.5.372)

LeDoux, J. E. 1996 The emotional brain. New York, NY: Simon and Schuster.

Loewenstein, G. F., Weber, E. U., Hsee, C. K. & Welch, N. 2001 Risk as feelings. *Psychol. Bull.* **127**, 267–286. (doi:10.1037/0033-2909.127.2.267)

Loomes, G. 1988 Further evidence of the impact of regret and disappointment in choice under uncertainty. *Econometrica* **55**, 47–62.

Loomes, G. & Sugden, R. 1983 A rationale for preference reversal. *Am. Econ. Rev.* **73**, 428–432.

Loomes, G. & Sugden, R. 1986 Disappointment and dynamic consistency in choice under uncertainty. *Rev. Econ. Stud.* **53**, 272–282.

Mai, J. K., Assheuer, J. & Paxinos, G. 1997 *Atlas of the human brain.* San Dieto, CA: Academie Press.

Malkova, L., Gaffan, D. & Murray, E. A. 1997 Excitotoxic lesions of the amygdala fail to produce impairment in visual learning for auditory secondary reinforcement but interfere with reinforcer devaluation effects in rhesus monkeys. *J. Neurosci.* **17**, 6011–6020.

McGaugh, J. L. & Roozendaal, B. 2002 Role of adrenal stress hormones in forming lasting memories in the brain. *Curr. Opin. Neurobiol.* **12**, 205–210. (doi:10.1016/S0959-4388 (02)00306-9)

McGaugh, J. L., Cahill, L. & Roozendaal, B. 1996 Involvement of the amygdala in memory storage: interaction with other brain systems. *Proc. Natl Acad. Sci. USA* **93**, 13 508–13 514. (doi:10.1073/pnas.93.24.13508)

McNeil, B. J., Pauker, S. G., Sox, H. C. & Tversky, A. 1982 On the elicitation of preferences for alternative therapies. *N. Engl. J. Med.* **306**, 1259–1262.

Mellers, B., Ritov, I. & Schwartz, A. 1999 Emotion-based Choice. *J. Exp. Psychol. General* **128**, 332–345. (doi:10.1037/0096-3445.128.3.332)

Milad, M. R. & Quirk, G. J. 2002 Neurons in medial prefrontal cortex signal memory for fear extinction. *Nature* **420**, 70–74. (doi:10.1038/nature01138)

Milad, M. R., Quinn, B. T., Pitman, R. K., Orr, S. P., Fischl, B. & Rauch, S. L. 2005 Thickness of ventromedial prefrontal cortex in humans is correlated with extinction memory. *Proc. Natl Acad. Sci. USA* **102**, 10 706–10 711. (doi:10.1073/pnas.0502441102)

Morgan, M. A. & LeDoux, J. E. 1995 Differential contribution of dorsal and ventral medial prefrontal cortex to the acquisition and extinction of conditioned fear in rats. *Behav. Neurosci.* **109**, 681–688. (doi:10.1037/0735-7044.109.4.681)

Morgan, M. A., Romanski, L. M. & LeDoux, J. E. 1993 Extinction of emotional learning: contribution of medial prefrontal cortex. *Neurosci. Lett.* **163**, 109–113. (doi:10. 1016/0304-3940(93)90241-C)

Morris, J. S. & Dolan, R. J. 2004 Dissociable amygdala and orbitofrontal responses during reversal fear conditioning. *Neuroimage* **22**, 372–380. (doi:10.1016/j.neuroimage. 2004.01.012)

Myers, K. M. & Davis, M. 2002 Behavioral and neural analysis of extinction. *Neuron* **36**, 567–584. (doi:10.1016/ S0896-6273(02)01064-4)

O'Doherty, J. P. 2004 Reward representations and reward-related learning in the human brain: insights from neuroimaging. *Curr. Opin. Neurobiol.* **14**, 769–776. (doi:10.1016/j.conb.2004.10.016)

O'Doherty, J., Kringelbach, M. L., Hornak, J., Andrews, C. & Rolls, E. T. 2001 Abstract reward and punishment representations in the human orbitofrontal cortex. *Nat. Neurosci.* **4**, 95–102. (doi:10.1038/82959)

O'Doherty, J. P., Deichmann, R., Critchley, H. D. & Dolan, R. J. 2002 Neural responses during anticipation of a primary taste reward. *Neuron* **33**, 815–826. (doi:10.1016/S0896-6273 (02)00603-7)

O'Doherty, J., Critchley, H., Deichmann, R. & Dolan, R. J. 2003 Dissociating valence of outcome from behavioral control in human orbital and ventral prefrontal cortices. *J. Neurosci.* **23**, 7931–7939.

Paton, J. J., Belova, M. A., Morrison, S. E. & Salzman, C. D. 2006 The primate amygdala represents the positive and negative value of visual stimuli during learning. *Nature* **439**, 865–870. (doi:10.1038/ nature04490)

Payne, J. W., Bettman, J. R. & Johnson, E. J. 1992 Behavioral decision research: a constructive processing pespective. *Annu. Rev. Psychol.* **43**, 87–131. (doi:10.1146/annurev.ps.43.020192.000511)

Pearce, J. M. & Hall, G. 1980 A model for Pavlovian learning: variations in the effectiveness of conditioned but not of unconditioned stimuli. *Psychol. Rev.* **87**, 532–552. (doi:10.1037/0033-295X. 87.6.532)

Phelps, E. A., LaBar, K. S., Anderson, A. K., O'Connor, K. J., Fulbright, R. K. & Spencer, D. D. 1998 Specifying the contributions of the human amygdala to emotional memory: a case study. *Neurocase* **4**, 527–540. (doi:10.1093/neucas/4.6.527)

Phelps, E. A., Delgado, M. R., Nearing, K. I. & LeDoux, J. E. 2004 Extinction learning in humans: role of the amygdala and vmPFC. *Neuron* **43**, 897–905. (doi:10.1016/j.neuron. 2004.08.042)

Pickens, C. L., Saddoris, M. P., Setlow, B., Gallagher, M., Holland, P. C. & Schoenbaum, G. 2003 Different roles for orbitofrontal cortex and basolateral amygdala in a reinforcer devaluation task. *J. Neurosci.* **23**, 11 078–11 084.

Price, D. D. 1999 *Psychological mechanisms of pain and analgesia*. Seattle, WA: IASP.

Quirk, G. J. & Gehlert, D. R. 2003 Inhibition of the amygdala: key to pathological states? *Ann. NY Acad. Sci.* **985**, 263–272.

Quirk, G. J., Likhtik, E., Pelletier, J. G. & Pare, D. 2003 Stimulation of medial prefrontal cortex decreases the responsiveness of central amygdala output neurons. *J. Neurosci.* **23**, 8800–8807.

Ramnani, N. & Owen, A. M. 2004 Anterior prefrontal cortex: insights into function from anatomy and neuroimaging. *Nat. Rev. Neurosci.* **5**, 184–194. (doi:10.1038/nrn1343)

Repa, J. C., Muller, J., Apergis, J., Desrochers, T. M., Zhou, Y. & LeDoux, J. E. 2001 Two different lateral amygdala cell populations contribute to the initiation and storage of memory. *Nat. Neurosci.* **4**, 724–731. (doi:10.1038/89512)

Rescorla, R. A. 1972 "Configural" conditioning in discretetrial bar pressing. *Q. J. Exp. Psychol. B* **79**, 307–317.

Rescorla, R. A. 2001 Experimental extinction. In *Handbook of contemporary learning theories* (eds R.R.Mowrer & S. Klein), pp. 119–154. Mahwah, NJ: Lawrence Erlbaum.

Rolls, B. J., Rolls, E. T., Rowe, E. A. & Sweeney, K. 1981 Sensory specific satiety in man. *Physiol. Behav.* **27,** 137–142. (doi:10.1016/0031-9384(81)90310-3)

Rolls, E. T., Hornak, J., Wade, D. & McGrath, J. 1994 Emotion-related learning in patients with social and emotional changes associated with frontal lobe damage. *J. Neurol. Neurosurg. Psychiatry* **57**, 1518–1524.

Rosenkranz, J. A., Moore, H. & Grace, A. A. 2003 The prefrontal cortex regulates lateral amygdala neuronal plasticity and responses to previously conditioned stimuli. *J. Neurosci.* **23**, 11 054–11 064.

Russell, J. 1980 A circumplex model of affect. *J. Pers. Soc. Psychol.* **39**, 1161–1178. (doi:10.1037/ h0077714)

Schiffman, S. S. 1974 Physicochemical correlates of olfactory quality. *Science* **185**, 112–117. (doi:10.1126/science.185. 4146.112)

Schoenbaum, G., Setlow, B., Saddoris, M. P. & Gallagher, M. 2003 Encoding predicted outcome and acquired value in orbitofrontal cortex during cue sampling depends upon input from basolateral amygdala. *Neuron* **39**, 855–867. (doi:10.1016/S0896-6273(03)00474-4)

Schoenbaum, G., Roesch, M. R. & Stalnaker, T. A. 2006 Orbitofrontal cortex, decision-making and drug addiction. *Trends Neurosci.* **29**, 116–124. (doi:10.1016/j.tins.2005.12. 006)

Seymour, B., O'Doherty, J. P., Koltzenburg, M., Wiech, K., Frackowiak, R., Friston, K. & Dolan, R. 2005 Opponent appetitive-aversive neural processes underlie predictive learning of pain relief. *Nat. Neurosci.* **8**, 1234–1240. (doi:10.1038/nn1527)

Slovic, P., Finucane, M., Perers, E. & MacGregor, D. 2002 The affect heuristic. In *Heuristics and biases: the psychology of intuitive judgment* (eds T. Gilovich, D. W. Griffin & D. Kahneman), pp. 397–421. New York, NY: Cambridge University Press.

Small, D. M., Zatorre, R. J., Dagher, A., Evans, A. C. & Jones-Gotman, M. 2001 Changes in brain activity related to eating chocolate: from pleasure to aversion. *Brain* **124,** 1720–1733. (doi:10.1093/brain/124.9.1720)

Small, D. M., Gregory, M. D., Mak, Y. E., Gitelman, D., Mesulam, M. M. & Parrish, T. 2003 Dissociation of neural representation of intensity and affective valuation in human gustation. *Neuron* **39**, 701–711. (doi:10.1016/ S0896-6273(03)00467-7)

Strange, B. A. & Dolan, R.J. 2004 Beta-adrenergic modulation of emotional memory-evoked human amygdala and hippocampal responses. *Proc. Natl Acad. Sci. USA* **101,** 11 454–11 458. (doi:10.1073/pnas.0404282101)

Strange, B. A., Hurlemann, R. & Dolan, R. J. 2003 An emotion induced retrograde amnesia in humans is amygdala- and β-adrenergic-dependent. *Proc. Natl Acad. Sci. USA* **100,** 13 626–13 631. (doi:10.1073/pnas.1635116100)

Sutton, R. S. & Barto, A. G. 1981 Toward a modern theory of adaptive networks: expectation and prediction. *Psychol. Rev.* **88**, 135–170. (doi:10.1037/0033-295X.88.2.135)

Tanaka, S. C., Doya, K., Okada, G., Ueda, K., Okamoto, Y. & Yamawaki, S. 2004 Prediction of immediate and future rewards differentially recruits cortico-basal ganglia loops. *Nat. Neurosci.* 7, 887–893. (doi:10.1038/nn1279)

Terzian, H. & Ore, G. D. 1955 Syndrome of Kluver and Bucy; reproduced in man by bilateral removal of the temporal lobes. *Neurology* **5**, 373–380.

Tremblay, L. & Schultz, W. 1999 Relative reward preference in primate orbitofrontal cortex. *Nature* **398**, 704–708. (doi:10.1038/19525)

Tversky, A. & Kahneman, D. 1981 The framing of decisions and the psychology of choice. *Science* **211**, 453–458. (doi:10.1126/science.7455683)

Tversky, A. & Kahneman, D. 1986 Rational choice and the framing of decisions. *Business* **59**, 251–278. (doi:10.1086/296365)

van Stegeren, A. H., Everaerd, W., Cahill, L., McGaugh, J. L. & Gooren, L. J. 1998 Memory for emotional events: differential effects of centrally versus peripherally acting beta-blocking agents. *Psychopharmacology (Berlin)* **138**, 305–310. (doi:10.1007/s002130050675)

Wasserman, E. A. & Miller, R. R. 1997 What's elementary about associative learning? *Annu. Rev. Psychol.* **48,** 573–607. (doi:10.1146/annurev.psych.48.1.573)

Whalen, P. J. *et al.* 2004 Human amygdala responsivity to masked fearful eye whites. *Science* **306**, 2061. (doi:10.1126/science.1103617)

White, K. & Davey, G. C. 1989 Sensory preconditioning and UCS inflation in human 'fear' conditioning. *Behav. Res. Ther.* **27**, 161–166. (doi:10.1016/0005-7967(89)90074-0)

Winstanley, C. A., Theobald, D. E., Cardinal, R. N. & Robbins, T. W. 2004 Contrasting roles of basolateral amygdala and orbitofrontal cortex in impulsive choice. *J. Neurosci.* **24**, 4718–4722. (doi:10.1523/JNEUROSCI. 5606-03.2004)

Winston, J. S., Gottfried, J. A., Kilner, J. M. & Dolan, R. J. 2005 Integrated neural representations of odor intensity and affective valence in human amygdala. *J. Neurosci.* **25,** 8903–8907. (doi:10.1523/JNEUROSCI.1569-05.2005)

5

Beyond the sentence given

Peter Hagoort* and Jos Van Berkum

A central and influential idea among researchers of language is that our language faculty is organized according to Fregean compositionality, which states that the meaning of an utterance is a function of the meaning of its parts and of the syntactic rules by which these parts are combined. Since the domain of syntactic rules is the sentence, the implication of this idea is that language interpretation takes place in a two-step fashion. First, the meaning of a sentence is computed. In a second step, the sentence meaning is integrated with information from prior discourse, world knowledge, information about the speaker and semantic information from extra-linguistic domains such as co-speech gestures or the visual world. Here, we present results from recordings of event-related brain potentials that are inconsistent with this classical two-step model of language interpretation. Our data support a one-step model in which knowledge about the context and the world, concomitant information from other modalities, and the speaker are brought to bear immediately, by the same fast-acting brain system that combines the meanings of individual words into a message-level representation. Underlying the one-step model is the immediacy assumption, according to which all available information will immediately be used to co-determine the interpretation of the speaker's message. Functional magnetic resonance imaging data that we collected indicate that Broca's area plays an important role in semantic unification. Language comprehension involves the rapid incorporation of information in a 'single unification space', coming from a broader range of cognitive domains than presupposed in the standard two-step model of interpretation.

Keywords: language; event-related brain potentials; functional magnetic resonance imaging; discourse; semantic unification; Broca's area

5.1 Introduction

As a result of the Chomskyan revolution in linguistics (Chomsky 1957), theories about human language comprehension often assume that the sentence is not only the core unit of syntactic analysis, but also the core unit of language interpretation. The assumption follows from the fact that the sentence is the domain of syntactic analysis coupled with two dominant ideas in mainstream generative grammar: (i) the truly relevant combinatorics of language are coded in the syntax and (ii) the semantic interpretation of an expression is derived from its syntactic structure. The latter idea is what Culicover & Jackendoff (2006) have recently referred to as Fregean compositionality, the claim that the overall meaning of an utterance is a function of the meaning of its parts and of the syntactic rules by which they are combined.

The implication of this idea is that language interpretation takes place in a two-step fashion. First, the context-free meaning of a sentence is computed by combining fixed word meanings

* Author for correspondence (peter.hagoort@fcdonders.ru.nl).

in ways specified by the syntax. In a second step, the sentence meaning is integrated with information from prior discourse, world knowledge, information about the speaker and semantic information from extra-linguistic domains such as co-speech gestures or the visual world. The latter step is needed because interpretation is clearly shaped by factors beyond the sentence given. That is, listeners interpret language not only by combining stored word meanings in accordance with the grammar, but also by taking into consideration their knowledge about the speaker (Clark 1996), their knowledge of the world (Jackendoff 2003) and the available information from the other input modalities (Tanenhaus *et al.* 1995).

There is widespread agreement that such additional 'contextual' factors help to fix the final interpretation of a sentence. However, there is disagreement over whether such factors can also immediately co-determine the initial interpretation of sentence-level expressions. The standard two-step model of interpretation prohibits such immediate contextualization of meaning (e.g. Grice 1975; Fodor 1983; Sperber & Wilson 1995; Cutler & Clifton 1999; Lattner & Friederici 2003). For instance, in their blueprint of the listener, Cutler & Clifton (1999) assume that, based on syntactic analysis and thematic processing, utterance interpretation takes place first, in a next processing step integration into a discourse model follows. Along similar lines, Lattner & Friederici (2003) recently argued that mismatches between spoken message and speaker are detected relatively late, in slow pragmatic computations that are different from the rapid semantic computations in which word meanings are combined. Adherents of a one-step model of language interpretation, in contrast, take the immediacy assumption as their starting point (cf. Just & Carpenter 1980), i.e. the idea that every source of information that constrains the interpretation of an utterance (syntax, prosody, word-level semantics, prior discourse, world knowledge, knowledge about the speaker, gestures, etc.) can in principle do so immediately (e.g. Crain & Steedman 1985; Garrod & Sanford 1994; MacDonald *et al.* 1994; Tanenhaus & Trueswell 1995; Clark 1996; Altmann 1997; Van Berkum *et al.* 1999; Jackendoff 2002; Zwaan 2004).

In our contribution, we review the results of a number of studies that aimed to determine the processing principles of language understanding beyond the sentence level and that are directly relevant to the issue of one- versus two-step language interpretation. We looked at the influence of discourse, world knowledge and co-speech gestures on the integration of lexical information into a coherent mental model of what is being talked about ('situation model'; Zwaan & Radvansky 1998). In most of these studies, we made use of event-related brain potentials (ERPs), an average measure of electroencephalogram (EEG) activity associated with particular critical events. Because ERPs provide a direct and qualitative informative record of neuronal activity, with almost 0 ms delay, they allow one to keep track of the various processes in language comprehension with high temporal resolution. For several of the studies discussed below, we also briefly report functional magnetic resonance imaging (fMRI) data collected with the same experimental design to identify crucial cortical contributions to language interpretation.

5.2 The domain of semantic unification: sentence versus discourse

To investigate the different claims of the one-step and the two-step models empirically, we first conducted an ERP study aiming to unravel how and when the language comprehension system relates an incoming spoken word to semantic representations of the unfolding local sentence and the wider discourse (Van Berkum *et al.* 2003). For this and most of the other studies discussed here, we exploited the characteristics of the so-called N400 component in the ERP waveform. Kutas & Hillyard (1980) were the first to observe this negative-going potential with an onset at approximately 250 ms and a peak at approximately 400 ms (hence the N400), whose amplitude was increased when the semantics of the eliciting word (i.e. *socks*) mismatched with the semantics of the sentence context, as in *He spread his warm bread with socks*.

Since its original discovery in 1980, much has been learned about the processing nature of the N400 (for extensive overviews, see Kutas & Van Petten 1994; Osterhout & Holcomb 1995; Kutas *et al.* 2006; Osterhout *et al.* in press). In particular, as Hagoort & Brown (1994) and many others have observed, the N400 effect does not depend on a semantic violation. For example, subtle differences in semantic expectancy, as between *mouth* and *pocket* in the sentence context 'Jenny put the sweet in her *mouth/pocket* after the lesson', can also modulate the N400 amplitude (Hagoort & Brown 1994). Specifically, as the degree of semantic fit between a word and its context increases, the amplitude of the N400 goes down. Owing to such subtle modulations, the word-elicited N400 is generally viewed as reflecting the processes that integrate the meaning of a word into the overall meaning representation constructed for the preceding language input (Osterhout & Holcomb 1992; Brown & Hagoort 1993).

In our discourse experiment (Van Berkum *et al.* 2003; see Van Berkum *et al.* (1999) for a written-language variant), listeners heard short stories of which the last sentence sometimes contained a critical word that was semantically anomalous with respect to the wider discourse (e.g. *Jane told the brother that he was exceptionally slow* in a discourse context where he had in fact been very quick). Relative to a discourse-coherent counterpart (e.g. *quick*), these discourse-anomalous words (*slow* in the example sentence) elicited a large N400 effect (i.e. a negative shift in the ERP that began at approximately 150–200 ms after spoken word onset and peaked around 400 ms; figure 5.1*a*).

Next to the discourse-related anomalies, standard sentence-semantic anomaly effects were elicited under comparable experimental conditions (figure 5.1*b*). The ERP effects elicited by both types of anomalies were highly similar. Relative to their coherent counterparts, discourse- and sentence-anomalous words elicited an N400 effect with an identical time course and scalp topography (figure 5.1). The similarity of these effects, particularly in polarity and scalp distribution, is compatible with the claim that they reflect the activity of a largely overlapping or identical set of underlying neural generators, indicating similar functional processes. In related studies, we have furthermore found that like sentence-dependent N400 effects, discourse-dependent N400 effects can also be elicited by coherent words that are simply somewhat less expected (Van Berkum *et al.* 2005; Otten & Van Berkum 2007).

In line with other work (e.g. St George *et al.* 1994), our discourse ERP studies provide no indication whatsoever that the language comprehension system is slower in relating a new word to the semantics of the wider discourse than in relating it to local sentence context. Our findings thus do not support the idea that new words are related to the discourse model after they have been evaluated in terms of their contribution to local sentence semantics. Furthermore, the speed with which discourse context affects processing of the current sentence appears to be at odds with estimates of how long it would take to retrieve information about prior discourse from long-term memory. In the material of Van Berkum and colleagues, the relative coherence of a critical word usually hinged on rather subtle information that was implicit in the discourse and required considerable inferencing about the discourse topic and the situation it described. Kintsch (Ericsson & Kintsch 1995; Kintsch 1998) has suggested that

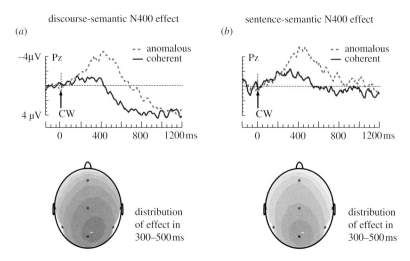

Fig. 5.1 N400 effects triggered by (*a*) discourse-related and (*b*) sentence-related anomalies. Waveforms are presented for a representative electrode site (Pz). The latencies of the N400 effect in discourse and sentence contexts (both onset and peak latencies) are the same (after Van Berkum *et al*. 2003).

during online text comprehension, such subtle discourse information is not immediately available and must be retrieved from memory when needed. This is estimated to take some 300–400 ms at least. However, the results of our experiments suggest that the relevant discourse information can sometimes be brought to bear on local processing within a mere 150 ms after spoken word onset.

As discussed elsewhere (Van Berkum *et al*. 1999, 2003), the observed identity of discourse- and sentence-level N400 effects can be accounted for in terms of a processing model that abandons the distinction between sentence- and discourse-level semantic unification. One viable way to do this (in our view) is by invoking the notion of 'common ground' (Stalnaker 1978, Clark 1996). Linguistic analyses have demonstrated that the meaning of utterances cannot be determined without taking into account the knowledge that speaker and listener share and mutually believe they share. This common ground includes a model of the discourse itself (i.e. a situation model as well as a record of the exchange, 'a discourse record' or 'textbase'; Clark 1996), which is continually updated as the discourse unfolds. If listeners and readers always immediately evaluate new words relative to the discourse model and the associated information in common ground (i.e. immediately compute 'contextual meaning'), the identity of the ERP effects generated by sentence- and discourse anomalies has a natural explanation. With a single sentence, the relevant common ground only includes whatever discourse and world knowledge has just been activated by the sentence fragment presented so far. With a sentence presented in discourse context, the relevant common ground will be somewhat richer, now also including information elicited by the specific earlier discourse. But the unification process that integrates incoming words with the relevant common ground should not really care about where the interpretive constraints came from. We suspect that the N400 effects observed by Van Berkum *et al*. (2003) reflect the activity of this single conceptual unification process.

Of course, this is not to deny the relevance of sentential structure for semantic interpretation. In particular, how the incoming words are related to the discourse model is co-constrained by sentence-level syntactic devices (such as word order, case marking, local phrase structure or agreement) and the associated mapping onto thematic roles. However, this is fully compatible with the claim that there is no separate stage during which word meaning is exclusively evaluated with respect to 'local sentence meaning', independent of the discourse context in which that sentence occurs.

The idea that language interpretation involves the immediate mapping of incoming word meanings onto the widest interpretive domain available has also received supported from eye tracking data with readers (e.g. Hess *et al.* 1995) and listeners (e.g. Altmann & Kamide 1999; Hanna *et al.* 2003; see Trueswell & Tanenhaus (2005) for review). However, unlike eye movements, brain potentials provide clear cues to the identity of the processes involved, and therefore allow for stronger inferences about whether or not two sources of information are recruited by the same neuronal system (Van Berkum 2004). It is due to this feature that ERP data can make a unique contribution to debates about the (non) equivalence of specific processes.

Particularly strong ERP evidence for the immediate integration of lexical-semantic information into a discourse model has recently been provided by Nieuwland & Van Berkum (2006). They had subjects listening to short stories in which the inanimate protagonist was attributed with different animacy characteristics. Here is an example of the materials, with the critical words in italics:

> A woman saw a dancing peanut who had a big smile on his face. The peanut was singing about a girl he had just met. And judging from the song, the peanut was totally crazy about her. The woman thought it was really cute to see the peanut singing and dancing like that. The peanut was *salted/in love*, and by the sound of it, this was definitely mutual. He was seeing a little almond.

As can be seen in figure 5.2, the canonical inanimate predicate (salted) for this inanimate object (peanut) elicited a larger N400 than the locally anomalous, but contextually appropriate predicate (i.e. a peanut that is in love).

These results show that discourse context can completely overrule constraints provided by animacy, a feature claimed to be part of the evolutionary hardwired aspects of conceptual knowledge (Caramazza & Shelton 1998), and often mentioned as a prime example of the semantic primitives involved in the computation of context-free sentence meaning (cf. Fregean compositionality). As such, these ERP results provide strong evidence against the standard two-step model of language interpretation.

5.3 Knowledge of the speaker

In interpreting a speaker's utterance, we not only take the preceding utterances into consideration, but also our knowledge of the speaker. For instance, we know that a toddler is unlikely to say 'I studied quantum physics during my holidays', and that it is really odd for a man to say 'I think I am pregnant because I feel sick every morning'. As examples such as these reveal, at some point during language comprehension, people combine the information that is represented in the contents of a sentence with the information they have about the speaker. The question again concerns exactly when the pragmatic information about the speaker is having its impact on the unfolding interpretation of the utterance.

In an ERP experiment (Van Berkum *et al.* in press), people listened to sentences, some of which contained a speaker inconsistency, a specific word at which the message content became at odds with inferences about the speaker's sex, age and social status, as inferred from the

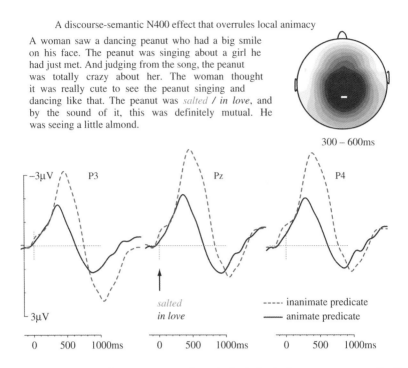

Fig. 5.2 N400 effects triggered by a correct predicate (*salted*) that is, however, contextually disfavoured in comparison to an incorrect predicate (*in love*). Waveforms are presented for representative electrode sites, time locked to the onset of the critical inanimate/animate predicate in the fifth sentence (after Nieuwland & Van Berkum 2006).

speaker's voice. One example was: 'I have a large *tattoo* on my back' spoken in an upper-class accent. For comparison, other sentences contained a standard semantic anomaly, a specific word whose meaning did not fit the semantic context established by the preceding words, as in 'The Earth revolves around the *trouble* in a year'.

If voice-based inferences about the speaker are recruited by the same early unification process that combines word meanings, then speaker inconsistencies and semantic anomalies should elicit the same N400 effect (though not necessarily of the same size). But if, as predicted by the two-step model of semantic interpretation, contextual information about the speaker is handled in a distinct second phase of interpretation (cf. Lattner & Friederici 2003), then speaker inconsistencies should elicit a delayed and possibly quite different ERP effect. As can be seen in figure 5.3, speaker inconsistencies elicited a small but clear N400 effect with a classical posterior maximum. Moreover, its onset latency is the same as for the standard N400 effect. Importantly, reliable effects of speaker inconsistency were already found in the 200–300 ms latency range after word onset. The same latency effects were obtained in this experiment for the straightforward semantic anomalies.

According to our ERP results, the brain integrates message content and speaker information within some 200–300 ms after the acoustic onset of a relevant word. Also, speaker inconsistencies elicited the same type of brain response as semantic anomalies, an N400 effect. That is, voice inferred information about the speaker is taken into account by the same early language interpretation mechanisms that construct 'sentence-internal' meaning based on just the words.

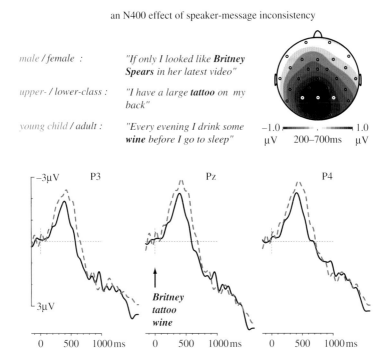

Fig. 5.3 N400 effects triggered by a critical word (in bold) that rendered the spoken sentence inconsistent with voice-based inferences about the speaker. Three representative electrode sites are shown (speaker-inconsistent waveforms are in red) as well as the topographic distribution of the N400 effect (Van Berkum *et al.* in press).

These findings therefore demonstrate again that linguistic meaning depends on the pragmatics of the communicative situation right from the start. However, by revealing an immediate impact of what listeners infer about the speaker, the present results add a distinctly social dimension to the mechanisms of online language interpretation. What we see is that language users immediately model the speaker to help determine what is being said. This ERP finding converges with linguistic analyses of conversation (Clark 1996) as well as with evidence from eye movements for the rapid use of speaker-related information during comprehension (e.g. Hanna *et al.* 2003; Trueswell & Tanenhaus 2005).

In addition, in an fMRI version of this experiment, we found that the increased unification load of combining incompatible speaker information and message content resulted in increased activation of the left inferior frontal gyrus (LIFG), the area that has been found to be of importance for unification operations in many other neuro imaging studies (cf. Hagoort 2005).

5.4 World knowledge versus semantic knowledge

At least since Frege (1892, see Seuren 1998), theories of meaning make a distinction between the semantics of an expression and its truth-value in relation to our mental representation of the state of affairs in the world (Jackendoff 2002). For instance, the sentence 'The present

Queen of England is divorced' has a coherent semantic interpretation, but contains a proposition that is false in the light of our knowledge in memory that Her Majesty is married to Prince Phillip. The situation is different for the sentence 'The favorite palace of the present Queen of England is divorced'. Under default interpretation conditions, this sentence has no coherent semantic interpretation, since the predicate *is divorced* requires an animate argument. This sentence mismatches with our representation of the world in memory, because the descriptive features of the purported state of affairs are inherently in conflict. The difference between these two sentences points to the distinction that can be made between facts of the world and the words of our language, including their meaning (lexical semantics). In the standard two-step model of interpretation, only the latter type of knowledge feeds into the construction of initial sentence meaning; the integration of pragmatic or world knowledge information would be delayed and handled by a different system (e.g. Sperber & Wilson 1986).

Hagoort *et al*. (2004) performed a combined EEG/ MRI study that speaks to this issue. While participants' brain activity was recorded, they read three versions of sentences such as: 'The Dutch trains are *yellow/white/ sour* and very crowded.' (the critical words are in italics). It is a well-known fact among Dutch people that Dutch trains are yellow and, therefore, the first version of this sentence is correctly understood as true. However, the linguistic meaning of the alternative colour term *white* applies equally well to trains as the predicate *yellow*. It is world knowledge about trains in Holland that makes the second version of this sentence false. This is different for the third version, where (under standard interpretation conditions) the core semantic features of the predicate *sour* do not fit the semantic features of its argument *trains*. One could thus argue that the third sentence is false or incoherent for semantic-internal reasons: it is our knowledge about the words of our language and their linguistic meaning that poses a problem. If semantic interpretation precedes verification against world knowledge, the effects of the semantic violations should be earlier and might invoke other brain areas than the effects of the world knowledge violations.

Figure 5.4 presents an overview of the results. As expected, the classic N400 effect was obtained for the semantic violations. For the world knowledge violations, a clear N400 effect was observed as well. Crucially, this effect was identical in onset and peak latency, and very similar in amplitude and topographic distribution to the semantic N400 effect. This finding is strong empirical evidence that lexical-semantic knowledge and general world knowledge are both integrated in the same time-frame during sentence interpretation, starting at approximately 300 ms after word onset. Furthermore, the fMRI data (figure 5.4*b*), time locked to the onset of the critical words, revealed a common activation increase in LIFG for both semantic and world knowledge violations, when compared with correct sentences, observed in Brodmann's areas 45 and 47.

Both word meaning and world knowledge are thus recruited and integrated very rapidly, that is within some 400 ms, during online sentence comprehension. The LIFG, including Broca's area, seems to be critical both in the computation of meaning and in the verification of linguistic expressions. Although Frege (1892) made an important distinction between the sense of a proposition and relating it to the states of affairs in the world, the processing consequences of a lexical-semantic and world-knowledge problem appear to be immediate and parallel.[1] The results of our world-knowledge experiments, therefore, provide further evidence against a non-overlapping two-step unification process in which first the meaning of a sentence is determined, and only then its meaning is verified in relation to our knowledge of the world. Semantic interpretation is not separate from its integration with non-linguistic elements of meaning.

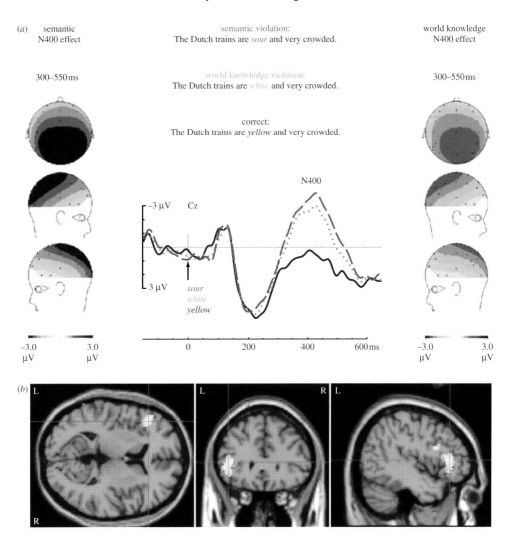

Fig. 5.4 (*a*) Grand average ERPs for a representative electrode site (Cz) for correct condition (black line), world knowledge violation (green dotted line) and semantic violation (red dashed line). ERPs are time locked to the presentation of the critical words (in italic). Spline-interpolated isovoltage maps display the topographic distributions of the mean differences from 300 to 550 ms between semantic violation and control (left); and between world knowledge violation and control (right). Topographic distributions of the N400 effect are not significantly different between semantic and world knowledge violation ($p = 0.9$). (*b*) The common activation for semantic and world knowledge violations compared with the correct condition based on the results of a minimum-T-field conjunction analysis. Both violations resulted in a single common activation ($p = 0.043$, corrected) in the LIFG (in, or in the vicinity of, Brodmann's area 45 ([x, y, z] = [–44, 30, 8]; $Z = 4.87$) and brain area (BA 47) ([x, y, z] = [–48, 28, – 12]; $Z = 4.15$). The cross hair indicates the voxel of maximal activation and has the following coordinates [x, y, z] = [–44, 30, 8] (left BA 45).

5.5 The integration of co-speech gestures

In ordinary face-to-face conversation, language users not only hear speech but also see the speaker's hand, mouth and body movements. This concurrent visual information often bears on the message conveyed. For example, when talking about drinking a glass of whisky, speakers sometimes perform a concomitant drink gesture (i.e. C shaped hand moved towards the mouth) as they utter the verb 'drink' in their spoken utterance. The listener's brain therefore continuously integrates spoken language information with several streams of visual information, including information from the lips, the eyes and, crucially, semantic information from the hand gestures, that accompany speech (McNeill 1992). Yet, until recently, nothing was known about whether and how listeners integrate the semantic information from co-speech gestures online into the discourse model, and about how this compares to the discourse-model integration of spoken words.

In two recent ERP and fMRI studies (Özyürek *et al*. 2007; Willems *et al*. in press), we have begun to address the issue by focusing on iconic gestures that convey information about the shape, size, motion and action characteristics of the events described in the spoken utterance. To determine the nature of the integration of verbal and gestural semantic information, we manipulated the semantic fit of speech (i.e. a critical verb) and/or gesture in relation to the preceding part of the sentence, as well as the semantic relations between the temporally overlapping gesture and speech (table 5.1).

Movie clips of the iconic gestures were temporally aligned to the critical verbs in the sentences. This manipulation resulted in four conditions (table 5.1): in the language 'mismatch' condition, the critical verb was harder to fit semantically to the preceding context while the co-occurring gesture matched the sentence context perfectly. In the gesture mismatch condition, the gesture was harder to integrate to previous context, while the critical verb matched the spoken sentence context. In the condition in which both verb and gesture were less expected, both the gesture and the word were difficult to integrate to the previous sentence context. Note that in the conditions in which either the verb or the gesture were less expected, the critical verb and the overlapping gesture locally mismatched (i.e. speech, roll; gesture, walk, and vice-versa), while in the language and gesture less expected condition they locally matched (i.e. both walk). This extra manipulation allowed us to investigate and compare the effects of local and global integration of speech and gesture in sentence context.

Table 5.1 An example of the stimulus materials. (In brackets is a verbal description of the iconic gesture. Gestures were time locked to the onset of the critical verb (underlined). ERPs were time locked to the beginning of the critical word and the gesture in each sentence. The condition coding (G + L +; G + L−, etc.) refers to the semantic fit of either the verb (language: L) or the gesture (gesture: G) to the preceding sentence context, with a minus sign indicating a semantically less expected continuation (mismatch). Less expected continuations of the preceding context are indicated in bold. Conditions B and C also contain local mismatches where the concurrent speech and gesture are different. All stimuli were in Dutch.)

(A)	Language and gesture match (correct condition): L + G +	He slips on the roof and <u>rolls</u> down (roll down)
(B)	Language mismatch: G + L +	He slips on the roof and <u>walks</u> to the other side (roll down)
(C)	Gesture mismatch: G−L+	He slips on the roof and rolls down (<u>walk</u> across)
(D)	Double mismatch: G−L −	He slips on the roof and <u>walks</u> to the other side (walk across)

If the immediacy assumption also applies to the unification of linguistic and extra-linguistic visual information, we expect a similar latency and amplitude of the N400 effect for all types of semantic 'mismatches' (i.e. language, gesture and double), revealing that the brain integrates information from both speech and gesture at the same time. Furthermore, according to the immediacy assumption, we do not expect differences across conditions with local mismatches (language and gesture mismatches) and the condition with the local match (double mismatch), since integration takes place immediately in relation to a discourse model and not in multiple steps from lower to higher levels of semantic organization. According to this view, the gesture and the concurrent speech segment (i.e. the verb) are integrated in parallel into the preceding context and not after they first formed a common semantic object.

Figure 5.5 shows the ERP results. In terms of their latency and amplitude characteristics, the effects are similar to the well-known N400 effect that is observed if word meaning violates the semantic context (Kutas & Hillyard 1980). However, the waveforms show a clearly biphasic morphology and the effects have a more anterior distribution than is reported for the classical N400 effect. The first negative peak in the biphasic negativity is reminiscent of the N300 that has been reported before for visual materials, and which has been found to be more negative for unrelated than for related pictures (Barrett & Rugg 1990; Holcomb & McPherson 1994; McPherson & Holcomb 1999). The N300 effect might be related to the presence of the visual-gestural information.

For the N400, an anterior distribution has been observed before for visual information such as pictures (e.g. Federmeier & Kutas 2001; West & Holcomb 2002). In the current study, the visual characteristics of the gestures might have elicited a frontal distribution. The finding that all conditions with a semantically unexpected continuation have similar topographic distributions suggests that semantic integration of information from both modalities (i.e. speech and gesture) might be instantiated by overlapping neuronal sources. Interestingly, it suggests that with respect to contextual integration there is no reason to distinguish between visual semantics and verbal semantics.

Next to our ERP study, we also performed an fMRI study (Willems *et al*. 2007), using the same stimuli in a design with the same conditions. The fMRI data (figure 5.6) revealed that all conditions with a semantically unexpected continuation activated the LIFG, and specifically

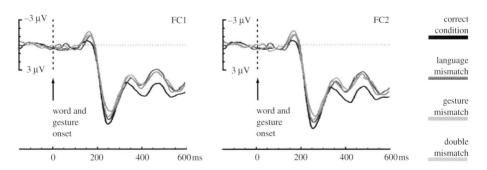

Fig. 5.5 Grand-average waveforms for ERPs elicited in the three semantic mismatch conditions and the correct condition at two representative electrode sites (FC1 and FC2). Negativity is plotted upwards. Waveforms are time locked to the onset of spoken verb and gesture (0 ms).

Broca's area. This area has been claimed to be crucial for the integration of semantic information into the previous context (Hagoort 2003; 2005; Hagoort *et al.* 2004).

Together with the ERP results, the fMRI data suggest that the semantic integration of both
speech and gesture semantics to sentence context involves very similar processes, and that the
underlying semantic representations might be amodal in nature, in spite of the differences in
input modality.

In conclusion, when understanding an utterance, the brain does not restrict itself to
language information alone, but also integrates semantic information conveyed through other
modalities, such as co-speech gestures. Furthermore, the neuronal sources and the time course
of the integration processes seem to be similar across gesture and language semantics.
Both constrain the interpretation domain simultaneously during online processing. This opens
the interesting possibility that language comprehension involves the incorporation of
information in a 'single unification space' (Hagoort 2003, 2005; Hagoort *et al.* 2004), coming
from a broader range of cognitive domains than is presupposed in the standard two-step
model of interpretation.

5.6 Making sense of language: immediate use of all relevant constraints

In traditional linguistic theories about meaning, a distinction is often made between the
context-free rule-based combination of fixed word meanings ('sentence meaning') and the
contributions made by the communicative context, such as what has been said before, who is
speaking, co-speech gestures or other concomitant visual information, and the listener's
background knowledge about the topic of conversation. In psycholinguistics, this analysis of
meaning has evolved into the standard two-step model of language interpretation, according
to which listeners (and readers) first compute a local, context-independent meaning for the

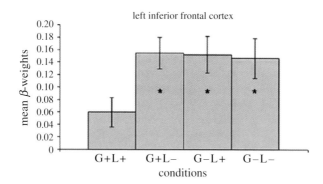

Figure 6. Gesture and speech in a sentence context. Mean activation levels (β weights) for the four experimental conditions in left inferior frontal cortex (BA 45/47). The activation levels are averaged over participants. An asterisk indicates a significant difference of the activation level of that condition compared with
the correct condition (G + L +), at an α level of $p<0.05$. Error bars are standard error of the mean. G + L +,
correct condition; G + L–, language mismatch; G–L +, gesture mismatch; G–L–, double mismatch.

sentence, and only then work out what it really means given the wider communicative context and the particular speaker.

We have discussed a wide range of ERP and fMRI findings that collectively do not sit well with this two-step model. Instead, the findings consistently point to a one-step model of language interpretation. Not only core linguistic information about the phonology, syntax and semantics of single words and sentences, but also discourse information, world knowledge and non-linguistic context information immediately conspire in determining the interpretation of compound expressions. Language input seems to be mapped onto a discourse model that takes all communicative acts, including eye gaze, iconic gestures, smiles and pointing, into consideration (Clark 1996). This is in line with the immediacy assumption, which states that these information types are brought to bear on language interpretation as soon as they become available, without giving priority, on principled grounds, to the syntax-constrained combination of lexical-semantic information (Fregean compositionality).

Our neuroimaging findings converge with and extend behavioural observations (e.g. Trueswell & Tanenhaus 2005), and they provide support for architectures of language comprehension that allow for the rapid parallel use of multiple constraints (e.g. MacDonald *et al.* 1994; Tanenhaus & Trueswell 1995; Jackendoff 2002). Our results also converge with recent linguistic observations that the notion of context-free sentence meaning is in fact highly problematic, and that linguistic meaning is always coloured by the pragmatics of the communicative situation (Clark 1996; Perry 1997; Kempson 2001) and the wider knowledge of the world (Jackendoff 2002). The meaning of so-called 'indexicals' like 'I' and 'you', e.g. inevitably depends on who is the speaker and who is the listener (e.g. Perry 1997), and the meaning of the verb phrase 'finished X' differs, based on our world knowledge, for 'Mary finished the book' and 'the goat finished the book' (Jackendoff 2002).

Formal semantic models have been proposed that are in line with our findings. For instance, the event calculus of Van Lambalgen & Hamm (2004) assumes that the ability to construct a discourse model is derived from our ability to compute plans for achieving a given goal (Baggio *et al.* in press). This model specifies the event structure of narratives. It accounts for the fact that many core aspects of language, such as tense and aspect, really play their role beyond the sentence given at the discourse level. Moreover, one can show that even tense and aspect cannot by themselves completely determine the event structure and must recruit world knowledge (for examples, see Baggio *et al.* in press).

All this does not imply that syntax disappears in the face of discourse. Clearly, whether a language has SVO (subject verb object) or SOV (subject object verb) as its basic structure is a matter of syntax and not of semantics. Likewise, the fact that German has case morphology and English does not cannot reduce to the semantics of discourse. All we are saying here is that language processing is operating under unification principles in which linguistic information (phonology, syntax, semantics) as well as pragmatic information coming from knowledge about the context, the speaker and states of affairs in the world are handled in parallel, with a direct mapping onto an event structure (or discourse model) that goes beyond the sentence given.

Our neuroimaging studies suggest that the left inferior frontal cortex, including Broca's area, is an important node in the semantic unification network. Moreover, this area is not language specific but acts as a single unification space (as postulated in the *MUC* framework; Hagoort 2003, 2005; Hagoort *et al.* 2004), integrating the semantic consequences of a broader range of cognitive domains than is usually thought. Of course, the fact that various constraints on interpretation all recruit LIFG does not mean that conceptual processing during language comprehension only recruits LIFG. In fact, some recent work suggests that the resolution of referential ambiguity recruits a very different network of brain areas (Nieuwland *et al*. 2007). Crucially, however, the data reviewed here do not support the idea that some types of constraints (lexical-semantic) are handled by an early sentence-internal sense-making process whereas others (pragmatic constraints) can only be brought to bear during later computations. Knowledge about the context, concomitant information from other modalities and the speaker are immediately brought to bear on utterance interpretation, by the same fast-acting brain system that combines the meanings of individual words into a larger whole.

5.7 Endnote

[1] Note that problems with establishing reference in discourse (i.e., finding out to what or whom a linguistic expression refers) recruit different neuronal ensembles than the two problems with meaning discussed here. Whereas lexical-semantic and world knowledge violations both generate the N400 effect and both activate LIFG, referential ambiguity elicits a sustained frontal negativity in ERPs (Nref effect; see Van Berkum *et al*. 2007) and recruits a non-overlapping set of brain areas. Thus, although as suggested by the recurring N400 effects and LIFG activations, constraints from various types of domains all rapidly affect interpretation, other neural systems can also be involved in making sense of language.

References

Altmann, G. T. M. 1997 *The ascent of Babel: an exploration of language, mind, and understanding*. Oxford, UK: Oxford University Press.

Altmann, G. T. M. & Kamide, Y. 1999 Incremental interpretation at verbs: restricting the domain of subsequent reference. *Cognition* **73**, 247–264. (doi:10.1016/ S0010-0277(99)00059-1)

Baggio, G., Van Lambalgen, M. & Hagoort, P. In press. Language, linguistics and cognition. In *Handbook of philosophy of linguistics* (eds M. Stokhof & J. Groenendijk).

Barrett, S. E. & Rugg, M. D. 1990 Event-related potentials and the semantic matching of pictures. *Brain Cogn.* **14**, 201–212. (doi:10.1016/0278-2626(90)90029-N)

Brown, C. & Hagoort, P. 1993 The processing nature of the N400: evidence from masked priming. *J. Cogn. Neurosci.* **5**, 34–44.

Caramazza, A. & Shelton, J. R. 1998 Domain-specific knowledge systems in the brain the animate–inanimate distinction. *J. Cogn. Neurosci.* **10**, 1–34. (doi:10.1162/ 089892998563752)

Chomsky, N. 1957 *Syntactic structures*. The Hague, The Netherlands: Mouton & Co.

Clark, H. H. 1996 *Using language*. Cambridge, UK: Cambridge University Press.

Crain, S. & Steedman, M. 1985 On not being led up the garden path: the use of context by the psychological parser. In *Natural language parsing* (eds D. R. Dowty, L. Karttunen & A. M. N. Zwicky), pp. 320–358. Cambridge, UK: Cambridge University Press.

Culicover, P. W. & Jackendoff, R. 2006 The simpler syntax hypothesis. *Trends Cogn.* Sci. **10**, 413–418. (doi:10.1016/ j.tics.2006.07.007)

Cutler, A. & Clifton, C. E. 1999 Comprehending spoken language: a blueprint of the listener. In *The neurocognition of language* (eds C. M. Brown & P. Hagoort), pp. 123–166. Oxford, UK: Oxford University Press.

Ericsson, K. A. & Kintsch, W. 1995 Long-term working memory. *Psychol. Rev.* **102**, 211–245. (doi:10.1037/0033-295X.102.2.211)

Federmeier, K. D. & Kutas, M. 2001 Meaning and modality: influences of context, semantic memory organization, and perceptual predictability on picture processing. *J. Exp. Psychol. Learn. Mem. Cogn.* **27**, 202–224. (doi:10.1037/ 0278-7393.27.1.202)

Fodor, J. D. 1983 *The modularity of mind*. Cambridge, MA: MIT Press.

Frege, G. 1892 Uber Sinn und Bedeutung. *Zeitschrift für Philosophie und philosophische Kritik* **100**, 25–50.

Garrod, S. & Sanford, A. J. 1994 Resolving sentences in a discourse context: how discourse representation affects language understanding. In *Handbook of psycholinguistics* (ed. M. Gernsbacher), pp. 675–698. New York, NY: Academic Press.

Grice, H. P. 1975 Logic and conversation. In *Syntax and semantics: speech acts* (eds P. Cole & J. L. Morgan), pp. 41–58. New York, NY: Academic Press.

Hagoort, P. 2003 How the brain solves the binding problem for language: a neurocomputational model of syntactic processing. *Neuroimage* **20**, S18–S29. (doi:10.1016/ j.neuroimage.2003.09.013)

Hagoort, P. 2005 On Broca, brain, and binding: a new framework. *Trends Cogn. Sci.* **9**, 416–423.

Hagoort, P. & Brown, C. 1994 Brain responses to lexical ambiguity resolution and parsing. In *Perspectives on sentence processing* (eds C. Clifton, L. Frazier & K. Rayner), pp. 45–81. Hillsdale, NJ: Lawrence Erlbaum Associates.

Hagoort, P., Hald, L., Bastiaansen, M. & Petersson, K. M. 2004 Integration of word meaning and world knowledge in language comprehension. *Science* **304**, 438–441. (doi:10.1126/science.1095455)

Hanna, J. E., Tanenhaus, M. K. & Trueswell, J. C. 2003 The effects of common ground and perspective on domains of referential interpretation. *J. Mem. Lang.* **49**, 43–61. (doi:10.1016/S0749-596X (03)00022-6)

Hess, D. J., Foss, D. J. & Carroll, P. 1995 Effects of global and local context on lexical processing during language comprehension. *J. Exp. Psychol. Learn. Mem. Cogn.* **124**, 62–82.

Holcomb, P. J. & McPherson, W. B. 1994 Event-related brain potentials reflect semantic priming in an object decision task. *Brain Cogn.* **24**, 259–276. (doi:10.1006/brcg.1994. 1014)

Jackendoff, R. 2002 *Foundations of language: brain, meaning, grammar, evolution.* Oxford, UK: Oxford University Press.

Jackendoff, R. 2003 Précis of foundations of language: brain, meaning, grammar, evolution. *Behav. Brain Sci.* **26**, 651–707.

Just, M. A. & Carpenter, P. A. 1980 A theory of reading: from eye fixations to comprehension. *Psychol. Rev.* **87**, 329–354. (doi:10.1037/0033-295X.87.4.329)

Kempson, R. 2001 Pragmatics: language and communication. In *The handbook of linguistics* (eds M. Aronoff & J. Rees-Miller), pp. 394–427. Cambridge, MA: MIT Press.

Kintsch, W. 1998 *Comprehension: a paradigm for cognition.* Cambridge, UK: Cambridge University Press.

Kutas, M. & Hillyard, S. A. 1980 Reading senseless sentences: brain potentials reflect semantic anomaly. *Science* **207**, 203–205. (doi:10.1126/science.7350657)

Kutas, M. & Van Petten, C. K. 1994 Psycholinguistics electrified: event-related brain potential investigations. In *Handbook of psycholinguistics* (ed. M. A. Gernsbacher), pp. 83–143. San Diego, CA: Academic Press.

Kutas, M., Van Petten, C. & Kluender, R. 2006 Psycholinguistics electrified II: 1994–2005. In *Handbook of psycholinguistics* (eds M. Traxler & M. A. Gernsbacher), 2nd edn. New York, NY: Elsevier.

Lattner, S. & Friederici, A. D. 2003 Talker's voice and gender stereotype in human auditory sentence processing—evidence from event-related brain potentials. *Neurosci. Lett.* **339**, 191–194. (doi:10.1016/ S0304-3940(03)00027-2)

MacDonald, M. C., Pearlmutter, N. J. & Seidenberg, M. S. 1994 Lexical nature of syntactic ambiguity resolution. *Psychol. Rev.* **101**, 676–703. (doi:10.1037/0033-295X. 101.4.676)

McNeill, D. 1992 *Hand and mind: what gestures reveal about thought.* Chicago, IL. University of Chicago Press.

McPherson, W. B. & Holcomb, P. J. 1999 An electrophysiological investigation of semantic priming with pictures of real objects. *Psychophysiology* **36**, 53–65. (doi:10.1017/ S0048577299971196)

Nieuwland, M. S. & Van Berkum, J. J. A. 2006 When peanuts fall in love: N400 evidence for the power of discourse. *J. Cogn. Neurosci.* **18**, 1098–1111. (doi:10.1162/jocn. 2006.18.7.1098)

Nieuwland, M. S., Petersson, K. M. & Van Berkum, J. J. A. 2007. On sense and reference: examining the functional neuroanatomy of referential processing. *NeuroImage* **37**, 993–1004.

Osterhout, L. & Holcomb, P. J. 1992 Event-related brain potentials elicited by syntactic anomaly. *J. Mem. Lang.* **31**, 785–806. (doi:10.1016/0749-596X(92)90039-Z)

Osterhout, L. & Holcomb, P. J. 1995 Event-related potentials and language comprehension. In *Electrophysiology of mind* (eds M. D. Rugg & M. G. H. Coles), pp. 171–215. Oxford, UK: Oxford University Press.

Osterhout, L., Kim, A. & Kuperberg, G. 2007. The neurobiology of sentence comprehension. In *The Cambridge handbook of psycholinguistics* (eds M. Spivey, M. Joanaisse & K. McRae). Cambridge, UK: Cambridge University Press.

Otten, M. & Van Berkum, J. J. A. 2007. What makes a discourse constraining? Comparing the effects of discourse message and scenario fit on the discourse-dependent N400 effect. *Brain Res* **1153**, 166–177.

Özyürek, A., Willems, R. M., Kita, S. & Hagoort, P. In press. On-line integration of semantic information from speech and gesture: insights from event-related brain potentials. *J. Cogn. Neurosci* **19**, 605–616.

Perry, J. 1997 Indexicals and demonstratives. In *Companion to the philosophy of language* (eds C. Wright & R. Hale), pp. 586–612. Oxford, UK: Blackwell.

Seuren, P. A. M. 1998 *Western linguistics: an historical introduction.* Oxford, UK: Blackwell.

Sperber, D. & Wilson, D. 1986 *Relevance.* Cambridge, MA: Harvard University Press.

Sperber, D. & Wilson, D. 1995 *Relevance: communication and cognition.* Oxford, UK: Blackwell.

Stalnaker, R. C. 1978 Assertion. In *Syntax and semantics 9: pragmatics* (ed. P. Cole), pp. 315–332. New York, NY: Academic Press.

St George, M., Mannes, S. & Hoffman, J. E. 1994 Global semantic expectancy and language comprehension. *J. Cogn. Neurosci.* 6, 70–83.

Tanenhaus, M. K. & Trueswell, C. 1995 Sentence comprehension. In *Speech, language, and communication* (eds J. L. Miller & P. D. Eimas), pp. 217–262. San Diego, CA: Academic Press.

Tanenhaus, M. K., Spivey-Knowlton, M. J., Eberhard, K. M. & Sedivy, J. C. 1995 Integration of visual and linguistic information in spoken language comprehension. *Science* 268, 1632–1634. (doi:10.1126/science.7777863)

Trueswell, J. & Tanenhaus, M. (eds) 2005 *Approaches to studying world-situated language use: bridging the language-as-product and language-action traditions.* Cambridge, MA: MIT Press.

Van Berkum, J. J., Hagoort, P. & Brown, C. M. 1999 Semantic integration in sentences and discourse: evidence from the N400. *J. Cogn. Neurosci.* **11**, 657–671. (doi:10. 1162/089892999563724)

Van Berkum, J. J., Zwitserlood, P., Hagoort, P. & Brown, C. M. 2003 When and how do listeners relate a sentence to the wider discourse? Evidence from the N400 effect. *Cogn. Brain Res.* **17**, 701–718. (doi:10.1016/S0926-6410(03)00196-4)

Van Berkum, J. J. A. 2004 Sentence comprehension in a wider discourse: can we use ERPs to keep track of things? In *The on-line study of sentence comprehension: eyetracking, ERPs and beyond* (eds M. Carreiras & C. Clifton), pp. 229–270. New York, NY: Psychology Press.

Van Berkum, J. J. A., Brown, C. M., Zwitserlood, P., Kooijman, V. & Hagoort, P. 2005 Anticipating upcoming words in discourse: evidence from ERPs and reading times. *J. Exp. Psychol. Learn.* **31**, 443–467. (doi:10.1037/ 0278-7393.31.3.443)

Van Berkum, J. J. A., Koornneef, A. W., Otten, M. & Nieuwland, M. S. In press. Establishing reference in language comprehension: an electrophysiological perspective. *Brain Res* **1146**, 158–171.

Van Berkum, J. J. A., Van den Brink, D., Tesink, C., Kos, M. & Hagoort, P. in press. The neural integration of speaker and message. *J. Cog. Neurosci.*

Van Lambalgen, M. & Hamm, F. 2004 *The proper treatment of events.* Oxford, UK: Blackwell.

West, W. C. & Holcomb, P. J. 2002 Event-related potentials during discourse-level semantic integration of complex pictures. *Brain Res. Cogn. Brain. Res.* **13**, 363–375. (doi:10.1016/S0926-6410(01)00129-X)

Willems, R. M., Özyürek, A. & Hagoort, P. 2007. When language meets action: the neural integration of gesture and speech. *Cereb. Cortex.* **17**, 2322–2333.

Zwaan, R. A. 2004 The immersed experiencer: toward an embodied theory of language comprehension. In *The psychology of learning and motivation*, vol. 44 (ed. B. H. Ross), pp. 35–62. New York, NY: Academic Press.

Zwaan, R. A. & Radvansky, G. A. 1998 Situation models in language comprehension and memory. *Psychol. Bull.* **123**, 162–185. (doi:10.1037/0033-2909.123.2.162)

6

The reign of typicality in semantic memory

*Karalyn Patterson**

This paper begins with a brief description of a theoretical framework for semantic memory, in which processing is inherently sensitive to the varying typicality of its representations. The approach is then elaborated with particular regard to evidence from semantic dementia, a disorder resulting in relatively selective deterioration of conceptual knowledge, in which cognitive performance reveals ubiquitous effects of typicality. This applies to frankly semantic tasks (like object naming), where typicality can be gauged by the extent to which an object or concept is characterized by shared features in its category. It also applies in tasks apparently requiring only access to a 'surface' representation (such as lexical decision) or translation from one surface representation to another (like reading words aloud), where typicality is defined in terms of the structure of the surface domain(s). The effects of surface-domain typicality also appear early in the time course of word and object processing by normal participants, as revealed in event-related potential studies. These results suggest that perceptual and conceptual processing form an interactive continuum rather than distinct stages, and that typicality effects reign throughout this continuum.

Keywords: perceptual versus conceptual processing; receptive versus expressive tasks; modality-specific versus modality-general representations; semantic disorders; connectionist networks; event-related potentials

Things say in one language and mean in another. No getting across that gap without the ultimate transitive, to translate.

(Powers 1992, p. 487)

6.1 Introduction and theoretical framework

Why has a paper about semantic memory come to roost in the Language section of this special issue? Although the paper could have nested in the Memory section, it also seems at home in Language, because semantic memory—although encompassing much more than language—is intimately tied to language function in humans. This link was acknowledged in Greek mythology. As one might infer from her name, Mnemosyne (daughter of Zeus and mother of the nine muses) signified memory, but she was also credited with 'giving names to everything, so that we can describe them, and converse about them without seeing them'. And Plato's *Critias* apparently urged gratitude to the memory goddess, Mnemosyne, as the source of practically all of the most important aspects of language.

Over approximately the past decade, our transatlantic research group has been developing an account of semantic memory that is framed in connectionist principles and at least parts of which are instantiated in connectionist simulations (e.g. Lambon Ralph *et al.* 2001; Plaut 2002; McClelland & Rogers 2003; Rogers & McClelland 2004; Rogers *et al.* 2004*a*). This account was developed in part as an alternative to the proposal (e.g. by Collins & Quillian 1969) that

*karalyn.patterson@mrc-cbu.cam.ac.uk

semantic memory might be represented in terms of discrete, hierarchically organized categories of concepts and propositions about them. In this hierarchy, subordinate levels would automatically inherit the propositions applying to their superordinates, such that—having represented the fact that birds can fly—(i) one would not need to learn explicitly that owls can fly and (ii) one would need to store the fact that the ostrich, though a bird, cannot fly. As presaged by Warrington (1975) and outlined in detail by McClelland & Rogers (2003) and Rogers & McClelland (2004), the hierarchical approach encounters a variety of difficulties in accounting for the results of a body of research on conceptual knowledge, both normal and impaired. Many of these difficulties seem to be resolved in connectionist models where concepts correspond to distributed representations occupying positions in a multidimensional semantic space.

Hinton (1981) and Hinton *et al*. (1986) were the first to lay out the basic logic of capturing semantic similarity in terms of overlap among microfeatures that characterize similar concepts. This principle was then expanded by Rumelhart & Todd (1993) in their important work on the learning of semantic representations. As Rumelhart & Todd (1993) described it:

> Because learning in a distributed-representation network occurs as modification of connections among microfeatures rather than among concepts directly, generalization and transfer of learning between concepts is inescapable. When similar concepts should be responded to similarly ….the system must learn which common microfeatures similar concepts share. When important distinctions must be made between concepts that are very similar …, it must learn distinctive microfeatures that differentiate otherwise similar concepts.
>
> (Rumelhart & Todd 1993, p. 7).

A natural consequence of this kind of system bent on discovering the important generalizations is that the most typical concepts in any category, which share the greatest number of microfeatures with other members of the category, will be robustly represented, efficiently recognized or retrieved and relatively resistant to disruption by brain disease/injury.

6.2 Typicality from the perspective of neuropsychology

Semantic dementia (SD), a neurodegenerative disorder associated with atrophy of the anterior temporal lobes, is characterized by striking, and relatively selective, deterioration of semantic memory (Hodges *et al*. 1992). There are many fascinating things about the neuropsychology, neuroanatomy and neuropathology of SD, but one of the most intriguing aspects of its cognitive profile is the ubiquitous and potent impact of typicality. Two comprehensive and thoughtful early experimental studies of a few SD patients (Warrington 1975; Schwartz *et al*. 1979), conducted before the condition was given its SD label by Snowden *et al*. (1989), already provided strong hints that typicality might be an important factor. More recent research establishes just how important typicality is—not only in its impact on SD patients' degree of success/failure in virtually any cognitive domain, but also in its capacity to make sense of what can otherwise seem like inconsistent and messy data.

For an example of what typicality means here, and also an example of the way in which this variable can create order out of apparent confusion, take the case of lexical decision in SD. Lexical decision, a task created in the late 1960s/early 1970s by experimental psychologists interested in both language and memory, requires the participant to decide whether a verbal stimulus (sometimes spoken, more often written) constitutes a real word in his or her own language. CAKE is a word in English; DAKE could have been a word but is not; and the fact that people can accurately and rapidly judge the lexical status of such letter strings is considered theoretically informative. There has also been considerable controversy as to how such decisions are made. As usual in our discipline, researchers address the question of mechanism or process, at least in part, by attempting to determine which experimental manipulations affect performance. Because lexical decision is such a popular experimental task, a fair bit is now known about the variables that influence it. Some of these are straightforward and predictable: for example, people are significantly faster to make correct 'yes' judgements to high- rather than to low-frequency words, and also significantly faster to make correct judgements to words if the non-words in the experiment are not very word-like.

6.3 How do people, and patients, recognize words/objects?

What happened when neuropsychologists applied the task of lexical decision to patients with a deficit of semantic memory? It appears that, with two praiseworthy exceptions (Bub *et al.* 1985; Diesfeldt 1992), these researchers tended to neglect what was already known about factors that affect normal performance and are perhaps even more likely to affect SD performance. At the time that we (Rogers *et al.* 2004*b*) were preparing to write up our first experiment on lexical decision in SD, we could find about eight publications that offered data on this topic. Now, it is true that (i) SD, like all disorders, varies in its severity (in this case, because it is a progressive disease, much of this variation is attributable to stage of decline), (ii) many of these reports were single case studies, and individual patients with the same condition—even with approximately the same degree of severity—do not always behave in the same way (though SD is a more homogeneous disorder than most), and (iii) no two of these eight studies used the same lexical decision test. Nevertheless, the outcome could be described as messy and puzzling, because this literature review told us that SD patients' success at lexical decision could vary from essentially normal, to impaired-but-above-chance, to chance level.

Our experiment (Rogers *et al.* 2004*a,b*), in keeping with the two notable exceptions mentioned above, demonstrated that success at lexical decision in the selfsame SD patient could vary from essentially normal to impaired-but-above-chance to chance level (or below), depending on the characteristics of the words and non-words. We tested 22 SD patients on a two-alternative forced-choice lexical decision task, with four of these patients participating at two different stages of decline, resulting in 26 observations for each of four conditions. For a group of normal control participants, matched to the patients in age and years of education, proportions correct for the four conditions ranged from 0.99 to 0.96. By contrast—to give just two examples of individual patient data (from table 6.3, p. 338 of Rogers *et al.* 2004*b*)—JTh's proportions correct for the four conditions were 1.0, 1.0, 0.89 and 0.44 (the latter being chance), and the same values for patient AT were 0.94, 0.67, 0.61 and 0.22 (the latter being significantly below chance-level performance of 0.5).

What was it that varied across the conditions to yield this huge range of scores for the patients? Unsurprisingly, word frequency had a significant impact, but even more dramatically, it was the typicality of the words and non-words that determined success or failure. Typicality in this case means orthographic 'goodness' or word-likeness, as scaled by bigram and trigram frequencies. CHEESE is a nice orthographically typical word in English; SEIZE is atypical; and each of these words can be reclad in the other one's spelling pattern to yield a non-word that is either more or less orthographically typical than the real word (CHEIZE and SEESE). Asked to decide whether CHEESE or CHEIZE is the real word, almost all SD patients at any stage of severity select the correct alternative. Asked to decide between pairs like SEIZE versus SEESE, on the other hand, many patients prefer the typical non-word to the atypical real word. This preference is exacerbated when word frequency is low or stage of disease is fairly advanced or especially both, such that (as indicated above for AT) performance can go significantly below chance.

This pattern, in which success is a joint function of patient severity, item familiarity and the degree to which the item in question is typical of the relevant domain, has been documented for a single group of 14 SD patients on six different tasks (Patterson *et al.* 2006). Four of the six tasks used words as stimuli: reading aloud; spelling to dictation; producing the past-tense forms of verbs from their stem (present-tense) forms; and lexical decision. The other two tasks, object decision and delayed copy drawing, used line drawings of familiar objects as stimuli. Put another way: four of the six tasks were expressive or production tasks (reading aloud, spelling, past-tense generation and delayed copy), while the other two (lexical decision and object decision) were receptive. Since that study, the same pattern has been demonstrated for SD patients on two additional tasks, one non-verbal and one verbal, both receptive. The non-verbal task is selection of the correct colour for objects that have a conventionally associated colour (Adlam *et al.* 2006): in certain semantic domains, there is a typical but not universal colour (e.g. brown for animals, green for vegetables), so that one can—just as in the lexical and object decision studies described above—construct pairs in which the correctly coloured object is either more or less typical of its domain than the incorrect alternative. The verbal task is selection of the correct gender for nouns in Spanish (Sage *et al.* 2006). Some noun endings in Spanish, like -o and -a, have an almost completely predictable associated gender (masculine for -o, feminine for -a); but others are 'quasi-regular' and thus only somewhat predictable (e.g. for nouns ending in -e, 83% are masculine and 17% are feminine).

Table 6.1 lists these eight tasks and briefly describes the nature of the typicality manipulation in each. It should be noted that the importance of graded typicality of spelling–sound correspondences in reading aloud was first highlighted in normal performance by Glushko (1979) and in acquired surface dyslexia by Shallice *et al.* (1983). Figure 6.1 demonstrates the impact of three factors—patient severity, stimulus familiarity and typicality—on SD performance in two of the language tasks, one productive (reading aloud) and the other receptive (lexical decision). Similar to the previous report described above (Rogers *et al.* 2004*b*), the SD

Table 6.1 Eight different tasks, spanning a range of verbal versus non-verbal content and expressive versus receptive format, in which success by SD patients is significantly determined by typicality as well as frequency.

task	typicality manipulation	typical examples	atypical examples
reading aloud	spelling–sound correspondences	*sea hint*	*sew pint*
spelling to dictation	sound– spelling correspondences	*couch swerve*	*cough suave*
past-tense generation	past tense formed by + ed or change to stem?	*save (saved) laugh (laughed)*	*steal (stole) lose (lost)*
forced-choice lexical decision	real word or non-word more orthographically typical?	*cheese/cheize drew/driew*	*seize/seese view/vew*
forced-choice noun gender (Spanish)	phonological/orthographic ending of noun	*el conde el lacre*	*la nave la sierpe*
forced-choice object decision	real or non-real object more typical of object domain?	*jackal without/with a hump*	*camel with/without a hump*
delayed copy drawing	object typical of its domain?	*jackal*	*camel*
forced-choice colour decision	animal brown or not; vegetable green or not	*brown/pink bear green/purple asparagus*	*pink/brown flamingo purple/green aubergine*

patients' lexical decision performance from Patterson *et al.* (2006) spanned the range from nearly normal when all three of these factors were 'positive' (milder patients; higher-frequency words; words more orthographically typical than their non-word counterparts) to below chance when all three of these factors were 'negative' (more severe patients; less familiar words; words less orthographically typical than their non-word mates).

The atypical items in all of these tasks are not only vulnerable to error: as predicted, the manner in which the patients err turns the atypical stimulus into a more typical response. The two-alternative forced-choice tests (lexical decision, object decision, colour decision and Spanish noun-gender decision) cannot exactly demonstrate this point since, if the patients do make errors, they can only choose the incorrect alternatives that the test offers them; but, of course, when the incorrect alternatives offered are less typical than the correct ones, the patients make few errors. And in all of the productive tasks, the errors of commission follow the predicted pattern. Figure 6.2 presents the mean proportions of three types of responses,

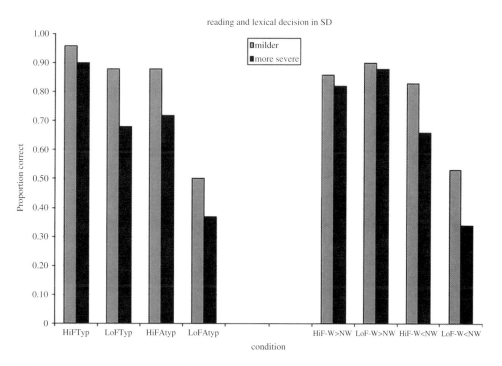

Fig. 6.1 Results demonstrating how SD patients' success in two verbal tasks, one productive and one receptive, varies as a function of word frequency, stimulus typicality and patient severity. For both tasks, severity refers to the fact that the 14 patients have been divided into two equal subgroups on the basis of scores on a word + picture comprehension test. For the task of reading aloud (on the left), all stimuli were words, and the condition labels refer to a combination of the words' frequency (HiF, high frequency; LoF, low frequency) and their spelling–sound typicality (Typ means that the word's pronunciation is typical for its spelling and Atyp that the pronunciation is atypical for or unpredictable from the word's spelling). For the task of lexical decision (on the right), each trial consisted of a word + non-word pair. HiF and LoF in the condition labels refer to the frequency of the real word. The remaining part of each label refers to the relative orthographic typicality of the word/non-word pairs in that condition: W > NW means that the word had more typical orthographic structure than the non-word, W < NW means the reverse.

across the 14 SD patients in Patterson *et al.* (2006), in each of the four conditions of the three productive verbal tasks. Correct responses are self-explanatory. LARC errors (standing for legitimate alternative rendering of components; Patterson *et al.* 1995) are called 'legitimate' alternatives because the response would be correct if the stimulus word were typical rather than atypical. Examples of LARC errors for the three tasks are as follows: in reading aloud, *sew* → 'sue'; in spelling to dictation, 'cough' → *coff*; in past-tense generation, 'lose' → 'losed' ('loozed'). 'Other errors' is a summary label for any incorrect responses that are not LARC errors. The figure demonstrates that in all tasks other errors remain fairly constant across the four conditions of the task, but as the condition shifts along from easiest (high frequency typical) to hardest (low frequency atypical), correct responses gradually decline and are replaced by LARC errors.

The tasks in which we specifically manipulate the typicality of stimuli and of response alternatives are of special value in revealing the impact of this variable on SD patients' success/failure rates; but, the simple tasks used commonly by neuropsychologists, such as object/ picture naming or concept definitions, provide corroborating evidence. Table 6.2 illustrates picture naming by an SD patient in response to 25 different animals from the Snodgrass and Vanderwart picture set. Among several different points of interest that one could extract from this simple dataset are the facts: (i) that the patient's only correct responses occurred to the four most typical (also the most familiar) animals, (ii) that three of these typical animal names were assigned incorrectly to a large number of other animals—basically, the mammals—that have reasonably typical animal features, (iii) that, although all of the pictures as shown to the

Table 2. Picture-naming responses by patient DG.

stimulus picture	naming response
dog	dog
cat	cat
horse	horse
cow	cow
pig	dog
squirrel	dog
sheep	dog
deer	dog
goat	dog
fox	dog
leopard	dog
tiger	dog
skunk	dog
racoon	dog
mouse	cat
rabbit	cat
monkey	cat
lion	horse
zebra	horse
rhino	horse
bear	horse
snake	long thing
seahorse	little thing
fish	don't know
frog	don't know

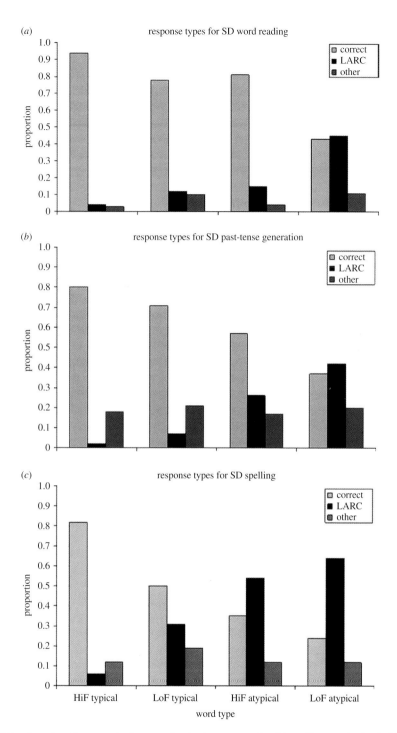

Fig. 6.2 SD patients' performance in three productive language tasks: (a) reading words aloud; (b) generating the past tense of verbs from their stem (present-tense) forms; (c) spelling words to dictation. For each of the four conditions formed by crossing word frequency with domain typicality, the figure shows, across the group of 14 patients, the proportions of responses that were correct, LARC errors or some other type of error. LARC stands for legitimate alternative rendering of components, and indicates that, although the patient's response to the stimulus is incorrect, it would be correct if the stimulus were a similar one from the same domain. Such errors mainly occur to atypical items, where the response represents a more typical rendering of the stimulus (e.g. reading the word hood as if it rhymed with 'food'); but LARC errors can and occasionally do occur to typical items (e.g. reading the word food to rhyme with 'hood').

patient were approximately the same size, her 'choice' of a more typical incorrect label seemed somewhat appropriate to the size of the stimulus animal in real life, and, most importantly, (iv) that pictures of the atypical animals (listed at the end) were not assigned her favoured typical names. Finally, here is a single example from the concept definitions task that seems to say it all: when SD patient AM was asked 'Can you tell me what a seahorse is?', he replied 'I didn't know they had horses in the sea'.

6.4 The interaction between perceptual and conceptual processing

One of the messages to be derived from these findings on SD is germane to a debate about the relationship between perceptual and semantic processing. One position in this debate holds that the human brain contains structural representations or descriptions of familiar words and objects against which a stimulus can be matched to produce 'recognition'. Such structural representations are not only construed as meaning-free, but they are also thought to be a sufficient basis for recognition decisions (as in lexical or object decision) without reference to meaning (Coltheart 2004). Such a view seems to be seriously challenged by our SD data. Other findings demonstrate that SD patients succeed well at tasks requiring perceptual processing, such as matching different views of the same object (Hovius *et al.* 2003) or matching upper- and lower-case versions of the same letter (Cumming *et al.* 2006). This is as one might expect, at least on the basis that the relatively focal anterior temporal lobe atrophy in SD does not extend to the posterior regions of the brain generally thought to be crucial for perceptual processing of written words (left occipitotemporal cortex; Dehaene *et al.* 2002) or of seen objects (right posterior temporal cortex; Gerlach *et al.* 1999; Kellenbach *et al.* 2005). More to the point, however, our claim is that the distinction between perceptual and conceptual processing is nothing like as sharp as traditional psychology textbooks might lead one to believe. As Gloor (1997, p.270) charmingly put it: '… Teuber's (1968) definition of agnosia as a normal percept stripped of its meaning, attractive as it is by its concise lapidarity, owes more to our traditional linear way of logical reasoning than to an appreciation of the underlying neurobiological mechanisms involved'.

To rephrase Gloor's (and our) position in Teuber's terms: agnosia is a percept stripped of its meaning, which is very unlikely to be a normal percept. One of our goals in studying SD has been to try to specify the nature of meaning-diminished percepts by determining what kinds of behaviours they can and cannot support. We do not claim to have a complete understanding or taxonomy with regard to this issue, but the data suggest that such meaning-diminished percepts are sufficient to cope with tasks only at the very perceptual end of this putative perceptual-to-conceptual continuum. Relevant examples here include abilities like the ones mentioned above, e.g. simultaneous matching of different views of a real object—which, after all, people can do with nonsense objects as well as real ones—or matching upper- and lower-case letters. Even these abilities turn out to be somewhat vulnerable to semantic impairment if one introduces some perceptual 'stress' or memory requirement into the tasks, such as a short filled delay between the presentations of the two different object views to be matched (Ikeda *et al.* 2006), or brief-and-masked presentation of the first of two sequentially presented different case letters to be matched (Cumming *et al.* 2006).

Perhaps the most dramatic example of how an apparently perceptual task is 'invaded' by conceptual knowledge—meaning that performance of the task is supported by a meaningful percept in normal participants and disrupted by a meaning-diminished percept in

SD patients—is delayed copy drawing. One of the abilities often taken to demonstrate relative preservation of both visuoperceptual processing and episodic memory in SD is the combination of copy and recall of the complex meaningless Rey figure. Initially, the person is asked to copy this figure with it in full view. SD patients almost invariably do this as well as age-matched controls; indeed, when we see patients in the clinic in Cambridge, impairment on copy of the Rey figure is virtually grounds on its own for rejecting a clinical diagnosis of SD. The second component of the task is that, approximately half to three-quarters of an hour later, participants are asked, without prior alerting, to reproduce the figure from memory. Normal people are not so brilliant at this kind of literal visual recall: there is a strict scoring scheme designed to capture the completeness and accuracy of the features reproduced, and control subjects' scores for delayed recall are often around 50% of the full marks achieved for direct copy. The point germane to the current discussion is that, at least in mild-to-moderate SD, not only direct copy but also delayed recall of the Rey complex figure tends to be normal: although the patients' scores are sometimes at the lower end of the normal range, they are certainly not several standard deviations below it as is consistently observed even in very early Alzheimer's disease. If SD patients achieve reasonably normal success in both copying and recalling meaningless figures, one might predict that they would do the same with line drawings of real, familiar objects. This prediction is, however, wrong or at least half wrong: the patients' ability to copy is fine but their recall is not.

We do this experimental task in a somewhat different manner to the procedure for administering the Rey figure. In one test session, we ask the patient to copy line drawings of objects, such as a rhinoceros or a watering can, with the stimulus picture present. On a different day, we show them each picture and let them study it for perhaps 5 s so that they have a good idea of what it looks like; they are not asked to name it, nor does the experimenter name it for them. The drawing is then removed from view and the patient counts aloud from 1 to 15, which takes patients (and controls) only approximately 10 s. The patient is then asked to draw what he or she was looking at before counting (again, no name mentioned). Figure 6.3, an example from Bozeat *et al.* (2003), illustrates both an SD patient's copy of the rhinoceros and his recall of it a mere 10 s later. The direct reproduction would perhaps not win any awards, but it qualifies as a thoroughly recognizable facsimile. The delayed copy, on the other hand, has lost virtually all of its unique features and looks like a much more generic animal shape, perhaps a pig or a long-snouted dog.

How can one explain the discrepancy, both between SD patients' direct and delayed copy of meaningful objects and between their delayed recall of meaningless and meaningful figures? Our proposal is that the two tasks that they perform with essentially normal accuracy are at the very perceptual end of the perceptual ↔ conceptual continuum. Direct copy of a meaningful figure, like simultaneous matching of two different views of an object, can be done without reference to conceptual knowledge, as witnessed by the fact that both normal people and patients can do these tasks on nonsense figures. Delayed recall of meaningless figures can be done (though not all that skilfully by either patients or controls) without reference to conceptual knowledge because it has to be: there are no obvious concepts to refer to in performing this task. But delayed recall of a meaningful drawing—which would presumably be as difficult as recall of a meaningless figure if it were being performed solely on the basis of literal stimulus memory—can invoke, indeed probably cannot avoid invoking, conceptual knowledge. Normal participants, in delayed copy drawing of a rhinoceros, do not need to rely on literal visual memory in order to draw its horns: once they have recognized the stimulus picture as a rhino, semantic memory insists that it must have horns. Our hypothesis is that exactly the

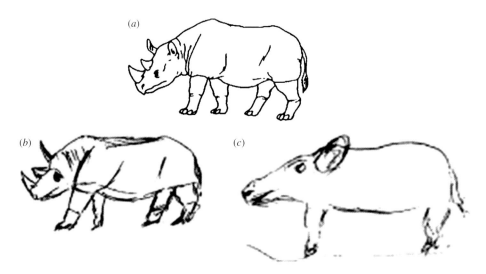

Fig. 6.3 Drawings by an SD patient (DS) of (*a*) the stimulus picture of a rhinoceros: (*b*) the drawing is DS's copy of the picture with it present and (*c*) the drawing is his copy of the picture approximately 10 s after it had been removed from view.

same reliance on semantic knowledge occurs, cannot fail to occur, in SD patients; but, because their conceptual knowledge is significantly degraded, they have only recognized the rhino as some kind of generic animal, and that is what their delayed reproduction represents. This is agnosia as redefined by Gloor (1997) and by us: a percept that is stripped of its meaning and is accordingly abnormal.

The hornless, armourless rhinoceros in figure 6.3 may seem like a particularly striking example, and, of course, not all of the SD patients' delayed copy drawings are quite so unfaithful to their stimuli; however, there are many other examples like the rhino, including humpless camels and four-legged ducks (Lambon Ralph & Howard 2000; Bozeat *et al.* 2003). What, apart from patient severity, modulates success when SD patients do this task? Our old friend typicality. Rogers *et al.* (2004*a*,*b*) established that the patients are likely both to omit distinctive properties of objects that should have such unusual features, and to intrude common properties when they attempt to recall objects that happen not to possess such shared features. Rhinoceros horns and camel humps are, of course, atypical, distinctive features, and while no birds have four legs, the most typical animals (of the cat–dog– horse ilk) all do. If SD patients' conceptual recognition of a duck amounts basically to 'animal', then it is not all that surprising that, once the duck has disappeared, they assign it four legs. Such errors in the patients' drawings could be considered a non-verbal parallel of the LARC errors described above by which the patients render words more typical in reading aloud, spelling or past-tense inflection.

6.5 Where does typicality have its impact? Evidence from brain imaging

Patients with SD have a relatively selective disorder of conceptual knowledge, and we have in the past argued that—even in tasks seeming to require minimal access to semantic information, such as reading single words aloud or delayed copy drawing—all deficits observed in SD stem from the central semantic degradation (Rogers *et al.* 2004*a*,*b*; Patterson *et al.* 2006; Woollams *et al.* 2007). The sections above were designed to illustrate the pervasive impact of typicality on performance in SD, in both more and less obviously semantic tasks (e.g. object naming and reading aloud, respectively). If we attribute all of the patients' deficits to the central semantic disorder, then it would seem logical to assume that the typicality effect derives from the structure of semantic memory, as indeed we have in the past also argued (McClelland *et al.* 1995; Rogers *et al.* 2004*a*,*b*). On the other hand, if there is no sharp distinction between perceptual and conceptual processing of the meaningful things (objects and words) that people encounter every minute of their waking lives, is it correct to attribute the typicality effect entirely to the conceptual end of processing?

Functional imaging in normal individuals might be helpful in answering this question, since it would allow the researcher to ask where/when typicality manipulations affect patterns of brain activity. There is as yet no evidence from a technique with high spatial resolution, like functional magnetic resonance imaging (fMRI), on where in the brain typicality effects might be observed. There is, however, some evidence from two event-related potential (ERP) studies (Hauk *et al.* 2006, 2007); these were motivated by our lexical decision and object decision experiments on typicality effects in SD patients and, like them, independently manipulated the typicality and the lexicality or authenticity of the stimuli. Apart from the neurological normality of the participants and the recording of ERPs, these studies differed from the SD experiments primarily in using a yes/no rather than a forced-choice procedure. Presentation of each word and non-word (or real and non-real object) as a separate event rather than in pairs was necessary to measure the time course of ERP signals, and estimate their brain sources, separately for the different experimental conditions.

In the lexical decision study (Hauk *et al.* 2006), there was a very early significant effect of typicality, at approximately 100 ms post-stimulus onset, where both words and non-words with atypical orthographic patterns (e.g. *yacht*, *cacht*) elicited stronger activation than words and non-words with typical spelling patterns (e.g. *yart*, *cart*). Acknowledging that there are always limits on the precision with which one can determine the sources of ERP effects, our procedure for source estimation (the 'minimum norm solution'; see Hauk 2004 for details) highlighted relatively focal activation in the left mid-posterior temporal lobe in association with the early typicality effect. In other words, although *yacht* is a familiar word and *yart* is not, at this stage of the word recognition process and in this region of the brain, *yart* appears to be processed more efficiently. This left mid-posterior temporal area may correspond to the region that, in fMRI experiments, responds significantly more to the written forms of both words and pseudowords than to letter strings (like a series of consonants) that are not possible words (Dehaene *et al.* 2002; McCandliss *et al.* 2003). Of major interest here are the facts that this ERP typicality effect: (i) occurred so soon following stimulus presentation and (ii) was 'blind' to lexicality. A significant main effect of lexicality, in the form of a stronger ERP response to pseudowords than real words, was observed later at 200 + ms. These facts suggest that substantial sensitivity to stimulus typicality is characteristic of early perceptual processing as well as later semantic processing. The one remaining ERP finding of particular salience in Hauk *et al.* (2006) is that, about midway between the typicality effect at approximately 100 ms and the lexicality effect at approximately 200 ms post-stimulus, there was a significant interaction of these two variables, with stronger activation for atypical than typical words, and the source estimation for this effect was in the left anterior temporal cortex, in or near the location of major atrophy in SD. This finding is compatible with, although it does not in any sense confirm, the hypothesis that the convergence centre of the semantic system works harder on atypical than typical familiar things before deciding that they are real/meaningful.

Our ERP study on object decision (Hauk *et al.* 2007) yielded a strikingly similar time course of ERP effects, although the difference between real and non-real objects (the equivalent of the lexicality effect in lexical decision, which we have termed an authenticity effect for object decision) occurred much later, at approximately 480 ms. This difference can probably be explained in terms of the far greater visual complexity of line drawings of objects relative to printed words. Similar to the lexical decision study, we obtained an early effect, at 116 ms post-stimulus, of typicality: atypical line drawings, whether authentic or not, produced greater activation than typical drawings, and source estimation localized this effect to bilateral occipitotemporal cortex. Once again, in other words, the evidence suggests that typicality has a pervasive influence that is early and perceptual as well as later and semantic.

6.6 Concluding comments

Some other things, that there was insufficient time/ space to discuss here, are already known about the impact of typicality on both normal and abnormal cognition. But §5 of this little treatise, concerning the impact of typicality on more perceptual versus more conceptual processing, is a good example of how much remains to be understood about the nature of typicality and the manner in which it affects representations of different kinds of information, at different locations in the brain. What is gradually becoming clear, however, is: (i) how pervasive the influence of typicality seems to be and (ii) how well-suited connectionist models—like Rogers *et al.* (2004*a,b*)—are to capturing and explaining such effects.

Acknowledgements

If I had included, as co-authors, everyone who contributed significantly to the work discussed here, the author list would be a whole paragraph. I would particularly like to acknowledge important contributions, of many varieties, from Jay McClelland, Tim Rogers, Matt Lambon Ralph, Anna Woollams, David Plaut, John Hodges, Olaf Hauk and Sharon Davies.

References

Adlam, A.-L. R., Patterson, K., Rogers, T. T., Nestor, P., Salmond, C. H., Acosta-Cabronero, J. & Hodges, J. R. 2006 Semantic dementia and fluent primary progressive aphasia: two sides of the same coin? *Brain* **129**, 3066–3080. (doi:10.1093/brain/awl285)

Bozeat, S., Lambon Ralph, M. A., Graham, K. S., Patterson, K., Wilkin, H., Rowland, J., Rogers, T. T. & Hodges, J. R. 2003 A duck with four legs: Investigating the structure of conceptual knowledge using picture drawing in semantic dementia. *Cogn. Neuropsychol.* **20**, 27–47. (doi:10.1080/02643290244000176)

Bub, D., Cancelliere, A. & Kertesz, A. 1985 Whole-word and analytic translation of spelling to sound in a nonsemantic reader. In *Surface dyslexia* (eds K. Patterson, J. C. Marshall & M. Coltheart), pp. 15–34. Hillsdale, NJ: Erlbaum.

Collins, A. M. & Quillian, M. R. 1969 Retrieval time from semantic memory. *J. Verb. Learn. Verb. Behav.* **8**, 240–247. (doi:10.1016/S0022-5371(69)80069-1)

Coltheart, M. 2004 Are there lexicons? *Q. J. Exp. Psychol. A: Hum. Exp. Psychol.* **57**, 1153–1171.

Cumming, T., Patterson, K., Verfaellie, M. & Graham, K. S. 2006 One bird with two stones: letter-by-letter reading in pure alexia and semantic dementia. *Cogn. Neuropsychol.* **23**, 1130–1161. (doi:10.1080/02643290600674143)

Dehaene, S., Le Clec'H, G., Poline, J. B., Le Bihan, D. & Cohen, L. 2002 The visual word form area: a prelexical representation of visual words in the fusiform gyrus. *Neuroreport* **13**, 321–325. (doi:10.1097/00001756-200203040-00015)

Diesfeldt, H. F. A. 1992 Impaired and preserved semantic memory functioning in dementia. In *Memory functioning in dementia* (ed. L. Backman). Amsterdam, The Netherlands: Elsevier.

Gerlach, C., Law, I., Gade, A. & Paulson, O. B. 1999 Perceptual differentiation and category effects in normal object recognition: a PET study. *Brain* **122**, 2159–2170. (doi:10.1093/brain/122.11.2159)

Gloor, P. 1997 *The temporal lobe and limbic system.* New York, NY; Oxford, UK: OUP.

Glushko, R. J. 1979 The organization and activation of lexical knowledge in reading aloud. *J. Exp. Psychol. Hum. Percept. Perform.* **5**, 674–691. (doi:10.1037/0096-1523.5.4.674)

Hauk, O. 2004 Keep it simple: a case for using classical minimum norm estimation in the analysis of EEG and MEG data. *Neuroimage* **21**, 1612–1621. (doi:10.1016/ j.neuroimage.2003.12.018)

Hauk, O., Patterson, K., Woollams, A., Pulvermuller, F., Watling, L. & Rogers, T. T. 2006 [Q]: When would you prefer a SOSSAGE to a SAUSAGE? [A]: At about 100 ms. ERP correlates of orthographic typicality and lexicality in written word recognition. *J. Cogn. Neurosci.* **18**, 818–832. (doi:10.1162/jocn.2006.18.5.818)

Hauk, O., Patterson, K., Woollams, A., Pye, E., Pulvermuller, F. & Rogers, T. T. 2007. How the camel lost its hump: the impact of typicality on ERP signals in object decision. *J. Cogn. Neurosci.* **19**, 1338–1353.

Hinton, G. E. 1981 Implementing semantic networks in parallel hardware. In *Parallel models of associative memory* (eds G. E. Hinton & J. A. Anderson), pp. 161–188. Hillsdale, NJ: Erlbaum.

Hinton, G. E, McClelland, J. L. & Rumelhart, D. E. 1986 Distributed representations. In *Parallel models of associative memory*, vol. 1 (eds D. E. Rumelhart, J. L. McClelland & the PDP Research Group). Cambridge MA: MIT Press.

Hodges, J. R., Patterson, K., Oxbury, S. & Funnell, E. 1992 Semantic dementia: progressive fluent aphasia with temporal lobe atrophy. *Brain* **115**, 1783–1806. (doi:10. 1093/brain/115.6.1783)

Hovius, M., Kellenbach, M. L., Graham, K. S., Hodges, J. R. & Patterson, K. 2003 What does the object decision task measure? Reflections on the basis of evidence from semantic dementia. *Neuropsychology* **17**, 100–107. (doi:10. 1037/0894-4105.17.1.100)

Ikeda, M., Patterson, K., Graham, K. S., Lambon Ralph, M. A. & Hodges, J. R. 2006 "A horse of a different colour": do patients with semantic dementia recognise different versions of the same object as the same? *Neuropsychologia* **44**, 566–575. (doi:10.1016/j.neuropsychologia.2005.07.006)

Kellenbach, M. L., Hovius, M. & Patterson, K. 2005 A PET study of visual and semantic knowledge about objects. *Cortex* **41**, 107–118.

Lambon Ralph, M. A. & Howard, D. 2000 Gogi aphasia or semantic dementia? Simulating and assessing poor verbal comprehension in a case of progressive fluent aphasia. *Cogn. Neuropsychol.* **17**, 437–465. (doi:10.1080/0264 32900410784)

Lambon Ralph, M. A., McClelland, J. L., Patterson, K., Galton, C. J. & Hodges, J. R. 2001 No right to speak? The relationship between object naming and semantic impairment: neuropsychological evidence and a computational model. *J. Cogn. Neurosci.* **13**, 341–356. (doi:10. 1162/08989290151137395)

McCandliss, B. D., Cohen, L. & Dehaene, S. 2003 The visual word form area: expertise for reading in the fusiform gyrus. *Trends Cogn. Sci.* **7**, 293–299. (doi:10.1016/S1364-6613(03)00134-7)

McClelland, J. L. & Rogers, T. T. 2003 The parallel distributed processing approach to semantic cognition. *Nat. Rev. Neurosci.* **4**, 310–322. (doi:10.1038/nrn1076)

McClelland, J. L., McNaughton, B. L. & O'Reilly, R. C. 1995 Why there are complementary learning systems in the hippocampus and neocortex: insights from the successes and failures of connectionist models of learning and memory. *Psychol. Rev.* **102**, 419–457. (doi:10.1037/0033-295X.102.3.419)

Patterson, K., Suzuki, T., Wydell, T. & Sasanuma, S. 1995 Progressive aphasia and surface alexia in Japanese. *Neurocase* **1**, 155–165. (doi:10.1093/neucas/1.2.155)

Patterson, K., Lambon Ralph, M. A., Jefferies, E., Woollams, A., Jones, R., Hodges, J. R. & Rogers, T. T. 2006 'Pre-semantic' cognition in semantic dementia: six deficits in search of an explanation. *J. Cogn. Neurosci.* **18**, 169–183. (doi:10.1162/jocn.2006.18.2.169)

Plaut, D. C. 2002 Graded modality-specific specialization in semantics: a computational account of optic aphasia. *Cog. Neuropsychol.* **19**, 603–639. (doi:10.1080/02643290 244000112)

Powers, R. 1992 *The Gold Bug Variations*. London, UK: Harper Perennial.

Rogers, T. T. & McClelland, J. L. 2004 *Semantic cognition*: *a parallel distributed processing approach*. Cambridge, MA: MIT Press.

Rogers, T. T., Lambon Ralph, M. A., Garrard, P., Bozeat, S., McClelland, J. L., Hodges, J. R. & Patterson, K. 2004*a* The structure and deterioration of semantic memory: a neuropsychological and computational investigation. *Psychol. Rev.* **111**, 205–235. (doi:10.1037/0033-295X. 111.1.205)

Rogers, T. T., Lambon Ralph, M. A., Hodges, J. R. & Patterson, K. 2004*b* Natural selection: the impact of semantic impairment on lexical and object decision. *Cogn. Neuropsychol.* **21**, 331–352. (doi:10.1080/0264329034 2000366)

Rumelhart, D. E. & Todd, P. M. 1993 Learning and connectionist representations. In *Attention and performance XIV: synergies in experimental psychology, artificial intelligence, and cognitive neuroscience* (eds D. E. Meyer & S. Kornblum), pp. 3–30. Cambridge, MA: MIT Press.

Sage, K., Heredia, C. G., Berthier, M. & Lambon Ralph, M. A. 2006 The impact of semantic impairment on lexical gender in Spanish. Paper presented to the British Neuropsychological Society, October.

Schwartz, M. F., Marin, O. S. & Saffran, E. M. 1979 Dissociations of language function in dementia: a case study. *Brain Lang.* **7**, 277–306. (doi:10.1016/0093-934X(79)90024-5)

Shallice, T., Warrington, E. K. & McCarthy, R. 1983 Reading without semantics. *Q. J. Exp. Psychol.* **35A**, 111–138.

Snowden, J. S., Goulding, P. J. & Neary, D. 1989 Semantic dementia: a form of circumscribed temporal atrophy. *Behav. Neurol.* **2**, 167–182.

Warrington, E. K. 1975 Selective impairment of semantic memory. *Q. J. Exp. Psychol.* **27**, 635–657.

Woollams, A. M., Lambon Ralph, M. A., Plaut, D. C. & Patterson, K. 2007. SD-Squared: on the association between semantic dementia and surface dyslexia. *Psychol. Rev.* **114**, 316–339.

7

Morphology, language and the brain: the decompositional substrate for language comprehension

William D. Marslen-Wilson* and Lorraine K. Tyler

This paper outlines a neurocognitive approach to human language, focusing on inflectional morphology and grammatical function in English. Taking as a starting point the selective deficits for regular inflectional morphology of a group of non-fluent patients with left hemisphere damage, we argue for a core decompositional network linking left inferior frontal cortex with superior and middle temporal cortex, connected via the arcuate fasciculus. This network handles the processing of regularly inflected words (such as *joined* or *treats*), which are argued not to be stored as whole forms and which require morpho-phonological parsing in order to segment complex forms into stems and inflectional affixes. This parsing process operates early and automatically upon all potential inflected forms and is triggered by their surface phonological properties. The predictions of this model were confirmed in a further neuroimaging study, using event-related functional magnetic resonance imaging (fMRI), on unimpaired young adults. The salience of grammatical morphemes for the language system is highlighted by new research showing that similarly early and blind segmentation also operates for derivationally complex forms (such as *darkness* or *rider*). These findings are interpreted as evidence for a hidden decompositional substrate to human language processing and related to a functional architecture derived from non-human primate models.

Keywords: language; morphology; regular inflection; neural decomposition

7.1 Introduction

The fundamental challenge for cognitive neuroscience is to construct explanatory accounts of the major human cognitive systems in a neurobiological framework. Most such systems—vision, attention, emotion and memory—have straightforward non-human precursors, so that studies of these processes in other species can provide a relatively straightforward input to our understanding and analysis of their human equivalents. A recent example of this is the way that the emerging story about the ventral visual object processing stream in non-human primates (e.g. Ungerleider & Mishkin 1982) has proved to be informative and predictive in constructing a neurobiologically rooted account of human visual object perception (e.g. Simmons & Barsalou 2003; Tyler *et al*. 2004).

Human language, in contrast, stands in a more ambiguous and less direct relationship to its neurobiological precursors. Non-human primates have well-developed systems for processing complex auditory objects, including conspecific vocal calls. Furthermore, as will be seen later,

*Author for correspondence (w.marslen-wilson@mrc-cbu.cam.ac.uk).

recent research into the properties of these networks is proving to be influential and informative in thinking about the neurofunctional architecture of the homologous human systems. Nonetheless, no matter how well we understand, for example, macaque systems for processing conspecific vocal communication, these are not remotely comparable to human language in their range of expressive capacities. Human language has functional properties that go far beyond those exhibited by the macaque or closer primate relatives. The focus of this chapter will be on one hypothesis about the nature of this difference—that it lies in the grammatical aspects of human language function—which we will investigate in the context of regular inflectional morphology, a major source of grammatical information during language comprehension and production.

In developing this hypothesis, nonetheless, an important constraint will be the view of the basic architecture of primate auditory processing systems that has emerged from recent research in this domain (Kaas & Hackett 1999; Romanski *et al.* 1999; Rauschecker & Tian 2000; Petkov *et al.* 2006), and is shown in figure 7.1. This represents the application to auditory object processing of the dorsal/ventral processing stream model long established for primate visual processes. Neuroanatomical and neurophysiological evidence clearly shows that at least two major processing streams leave macaque auditory cortex (itself a close homologue of the human equivalent), with the dorsal stream leaving posteriorly and looping round to connect to areas in inferior frontal cortex. The ventral stream travels forward, down the superior temporal gyrus, and also connects to inferior frontal areas.[1] This division into processing streams, which has been taken up in detail in the human domain (e.g. Hickok & Poeppel 2000;

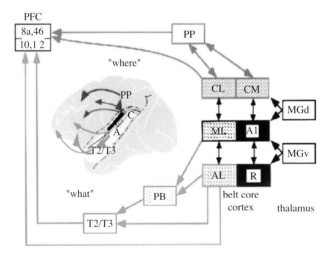

Fig. 7.1 Ventral and dorsal auditory object processing streams in the macaque brain. The dorsal stream (red) connects caudolateral (CL) and caudomedial (CM) regions in auditory cortex to prefrontal cortex (PFC) either directly or via posterior parietal cortex (PP). The ventral stream (green) connects mediolateral (ML) and anterolateral (AL) regions in auditory cortex to PFC, via parabelt cortex (PB) and areas T2/T3 in the anterior superior temporal gyrus (reprinted with permission from Rauschecker & Tian 2000, copyright 2000 National Academy of Sciences).

Scott & Johnsrude 2003), has major implications for the characterization of human language function.

Cognitive approaches to the functional structure of the system for mapping from sound to meaning (and vice versa) have typically assumed that a single unitary process (or succession of processes) carries out these mappings. However, the neurobiological evidence suggests that the underlying neural system is not organized along these lines, and that multiple parallel processing streams are involved, extending hierarchically outwards from the auditory cortex. In this respect, speech and language analysis might be brought into closer alignment with long held assumptions about the organization of primate perceptual processing systems, where separable sub-processes analyse different aspects of the sensorimotor environment.

A recent report (Gil-da-costa *et al.* 2006) brings the apparent parallels between macaque and human functional architecture even closer (see also Ghazanfar & Miller 2006). This was a positron emission tomography (PET) activation study on awake monkeys, where the subjects heard a mixture of species-specific vocal calls and acoustically matched non-biological sounds. The vocal calls were found to preferentially activate areas in the macaque brain (ventral premotor cortex and temporo-parietal cortex) that are argued to be homologues of two key language areas (Broca's and Wernicke's, respectively) in the classical view of the human system (figure 7.2). This was despite the absence of hemispheric lateralization in these data, contrary to earlier studies (e.g. Poremba *et al.* 2004). Gil-da-costa *et al.* (2006) argue that this joint involvement of temporal and frontal cortex reflects the need to embed the interpretation of conspecific calls in the context of their social and environmental significance. Since macaques and human branched off from each other about 25 million years ago, these parallels imply a distant common ancestor whose brain already possessed key organizational features that would eventually develop, in the human case, into the substrate for complex language function. These ancient architectural and functional commonalities bring into even sharper

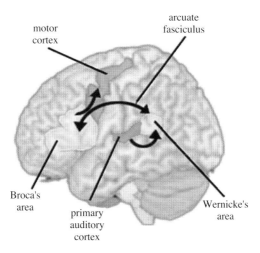

Fig. 7.2 Classical Broca–Wernicke neurological diagram of the human language system. Note the absence of a ventral processing stream.

focus the question of how human language nonetheless differs so markedly in its apparent properties from those of our evolutionary relatives.

The functional answer, unsurprisingly, must lie in the grammatical domain—the powerful and flexible set of devices, for organizing the flow of linguistic information and its interpretation that every human language possesses and for which there is no convincing evidence in any non-human communication system (Hauser *et al.* 2002). Language is more than a string of social signals or a list of symbols that stand for things and events in the world—this much, arguably, it may have in common with its primate ancestry. These semantic and referential aspects of linguistic communication, conveyed primarily by content words and morphemes, are embedded in a profusion of linguistic devices that indicate the grammatical relationships between these words, the temporal properties of the events being described, aspects of the speaker's attitude towards the addressee and many other similar functions.

The focus of this chapter is on the neural systems that underpin one particular aspect of these grammatical functions (cf. Ullman 2007). Combining research on brain-damaged patients with neuroimaging studies of normal adults, we will argue for a specific left hemisphere (LH) fronto-temporal sub-system, tuned to the properties of grammatical morphemes. This may constitute a separate decompositional processing stream, as part of the complementary streams of processing activity underlying human language function. We begin with a sketch of the linguistic environment in which these linguistic devices occur, since understanding their functional role is critical to asking the right questions about how the neurocognitive system supports them.

7.2 Grammatical morphemes in English: linguistic background

Human linguistic communication requires two kinds of information to be conveyed between speakers and listeners: semantic information, about meanings and their instantiation in the world; and a wide range of syntactic information, specifying grammatical relationships, tense, aspect and so forth. These different kinds of linguistic information are associated with specific lexical entities, called *morphemes*, which are defined as the minimal meaning-bearing linguistic elements. These are assembled together, in different ways in different languages, to convey the necessary mix of semantic and syntactic cues to the intended meaning as the speech input is heard over time (or as a written text is read).

In a language like English, a high proportion of semantic and syntactic morphemes can occur as phonologically separate entities—as individual words like *the* or *dog*—so that the distinction between word and morpheme is neutralized. Nonetheless, this is by no means the case for the language as a whole, with the frequent occurrence of complex words made up of the combination of different morphemes, especially those involving *bound* morphemes. These latter are grammatical affixes, like {-ness} or {-s}, which cannot occur as words on their own, but only in combination with content word stems, as in forms like *darkness* ({dark} + {-ness}) or *smiles* ({smile} + {-s}). In common with many other languages, English has two modes of affixal word combination—*inflectional* and *derivational morphology*, where a stem is combined with a derivational or an inflectional morpheme (as in the *darkness* and *smiles* examples). Here, we will focus primarily on inflectional morphology, which is exclusively syntactic in its function, as opposed to derivational morphology (to which we return at the end of the paper), whose primary role is lexical in nature, creating new words in the language.

Inflectional morphology is the combination of a stem with one or more inflectional affixes—in English, examples are regular noun plurals (*cats*—{cat} + {-s}) and the regular past tense (*walked*—{walk} + {-ed}). Although the precise definition of an inflectional morphological process is controversial, there are some core properties of inflectional morphology that are generally accepted and of critical significance to a proper neurocognitive approach. First, inflectional morphology does not, by definition, create new words requiring new lexical entries. Rather, the prototypical inflectional functions—marking number, tense, aspect, gender, case and so forth—produce new forms of the same word and not new different words. Inflectional variants like *cat* and *cats* or *walk* and *walked* are not listed as separate headwords in standard dictionaries. If inflectional morphemes do modify the semantics of a word—as in the noun plural—they do not change the basic meaning of the stem to which they attach, nor do they change its grammatical category.

The second key characteristic of inflections is that they are responsive, in a regular and predictable way, to the properties of the grammatical environment in which they occur (e.g. Anderson 1992; Bickel & Nichols 2006). This is clear, for example, where inflectional morphemes express agreement—as in the third person singular {-s} for English verbs (*he walks*), or, in many other languages, when morphological case is used to express the grammatical role of a noun as subject, object, indirect object and so forth. Similarly, the presence of the regular past tense in English verbs (*they walked*) is dictated by the role of the verb in the context of the utterance and its wider temporal and aspectual properties. The information carried by the inflection is not just about the stem itself, but about the processes of phrasal and sentential interpretation to which that stem relates.

We will argue in this paper that these two functional properties—of meaning preservation and context sensitivity—are directly reflected in the properties of the neurocognitive language system. Regularly inflected forms, such as *joined*, *treats* or *agreed*, are not stored or processed as whole forms, since their morphemic components are relevant to different aspects of the interpretation process and their lexical content—the semantic and syntactic properties of the stem—is fully recoverable from the representation of the stem on its own. This means that access to lexical content is via the stem (*join*, *treat* and *agree*), which in turn requires morpho-phonological parsing of the complex form in order to separate the stem from its affix. This decompositional access process, consistent with the psycholinguistic functions of regularly inflected forms in English, seems to apply early and automatically to all potentially decomposable inputs and may be specifically dependent on the dorsal processing network linking posterior temporal lobe regions to LH inferior temporal cortex.

This emphasis on the morphological decomposition of regular inflected forms clearly allies the account presented here with the 'Words and Rules' (e.g. Clahsen 1999; Pinker 1999) and the procedural/declarative (e.g. Ullman 2004) approaches, in distinction to non-decompositional, usually connectionist approaches, which deny the existence of separable stem and inflectional morphemes and argue instead that inflected forms are processed and represented as overlapping whole forms sharing certain semantic and phonological similarities (e.g. Rumelhart & McClelland 1986; McClelland & Patterson 2002). Unlike Pinker and colleagues, however, we do not assume that the presence or absence of grammatical morphemes implicates differences in the nature of mental computation, while our treatment of inflectional morphology cuts across Ullman's declarative/procedural dichotomy.[2]

Our initial evidence for a decompositional scenario, as laid out in the next section, comes from neuropsychological research on patients with LH damage which affects primary grammatical functions. These patient data make explicit what are the core, neurally irreplaceable functions of the LH grammatical processing system and demonstrate the separability of the systems processing stem morphemes from those involved in the access and analysis of regular inflectional morphemes.

7.3 Neuropsychological evidence for stem-based access and obligatory decomposition

A linked set of experiments demonstrate, first, that the neurocognitive processes mediating access for isolated stems (and any other lexical entity that is accessed as a non-decomposed whole form) are separable from those mediating access for complex forms made up of a stem and an inflectional affix—as in cases like *joined* or *agreed*, analysable, respectively, as {*join*} + {*-ed*} and {*agree*} + {*-ed*}. The first of these experiments (Marslen-Wilson & Tyler 1997; Tyler *et al.* 2002*a*) used auditory–auditory immediate repetition priming to demonstrate a selective impairment for the decompositional aspects of inflectional morphology. Left hemi-sphere non-fluent patients, typically with damage that included inferior frontal regions, showed normal priming for irregular past-tense pairs like *found/find*, but significantly reduced priming for regular pairs like *joined/join*.[3] The significance of the English irregulars here is that they are fully matched to the regulars in terms of their general syntactic and semantic properties, but do not require (or allow) segmentation into a stem + affix format. An irregular past tense like *found*, given its idiosyncratic and unpredictable surface form, must be learned, stored and accessed as a whole form— in the same way as morphologically simple forms like *sound* or *round*.[4] The fact that priming is intact for these irregular forms indicates that the impairment for the regulars is specific to their decompositional properties.

This inference is strengthened by the results of a subsequent experiment with similar patients using a semantic priming task (again auditory–auditory), where prime and target are semantically rather than morphologically related (Longworth *et al.* 2005). Here, we contrasted regular past tense pairs (*blamed/accuse*), verb stem pairs (*hope/wish*) and irregular past tense pairs like *shook/tremble*. This is a task where successful priming requires rapid access to the meaning of the prime, followed by equally rapid access to the form and meaning of the target, such that the semantic relatedness between the two can be accessed and used to facilitate responses to the target. The fact that these LH patients show unimpaired priming for the stem pairs and the irregular past pairs (figure 7.3) is a confirmation that they retain apparently nor-mal and effective systems for mapping stems and whole forms onto lexical representations of form and content. At the same time, the absence of semantic priming for the regularly inflected pairs, in the same patients, confirms their problems with forms requiring decompositional processing.[5]

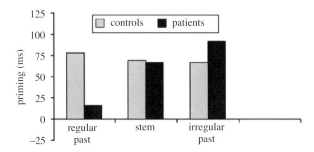

Fig. 7.3 Priming effects (the difference in milliseconds between responses to targets following related versus unrelated prime words) for non-fluent patients and controls in an auditory–auditory semantic prim-ing task for three types of prime word—regularly inflected past tenses (regular past); uninflected stems (stem); and irregularly inflected past tenses (irregular past). For details, see Longworth *et al.* (2005).

What these results also mean is that the regular inflected 'whole form' cannot be stored as the perceptual target for lexical access. If the access route for *joined* were via a representation of *joined* as a whole form, then there would be no reason for access to fail here when it was succeeding for other whole-form representations like *found* or stem representations like *hope*. This, in turn, means that inflected regular forms must be subjected to some form of morpho-phonological parsing, which breaks down the surface full form into its stem + affix components. Without such decomposition, the full inflected form is an ill-formed input to the lexical access process, not matching fully with any stored representation.

Further work with the same type of LH non-fluent patients sheds additional light on these decompositional processes, showing them to be applied early and obligatorily to the speech input and highlighting the priority that the system seems to assign to the detection of inflectional morphemes and their separation from their stems. The evidence for this comes from an auditory same–different task, where patients were presented with two successive words (or non-words), spoken in a male and a female voice, and asked to judge whether the second word/non-word in each pair was the same as the first (Tyler *et al.* 2002*b*).

Successful performance in this apparently simple task requires the participant to construct a stable internal representation of the first stimulus heard, so that this can be held in memory for comparison with the second member of the pair. The pattern of successes and failures for the non-fluent patients indicates the importance of morpho-phonological parsing in constructing these representations. The patients had problems not only with regularly inflected real words—in pairs like *played/play*—but also with any other stimulus pairs—even non-words like *snade/snay*— that ended in the characteristic phonetic pattern associated with regular inflectional morphology in English and which were therefore potentially decomposable. This pattern—the presence of a coronal consonant (d, t, s, z) that agrees in voice with the preceding phoneme—holds without exception for the two dominant regular inflectional paradigms in English, the past tense {-d} and the {-s} inflection. We have labelled this the English *inflectional rhyme pattern* (IRP).

In the experiment, we compared performance on real regular pairs (*played/play*)[6] with two other sets that shared this IRP. These were pseudo-regular pairs like *trade/tray*, where *trade* is homophonous with the potential but non-existent past tense of the noun *tray*, and non-word regular pairs like *snade/snay*, where neither is a word in English, but where *snade* could be the past tense of the (non-existent) stem *snay*. These three sets contrast with two sets of word/non-word pairs which are matched to the inflectional sets in terms of consonant–vowel (CV) structure, with the final phoneme being dropped in the second member of the pair, but where this final phoneme is not a possible inflectional affix in English—as in pairs like *claim/clay* or *blane/blay*. Although *claim* contains the imbedded word *clay*, much as *trade* contains *tray*, it cannot be interpreted as a morphologically complex form and does not invite morpho-phonological parsing and decomposition. For the non-word *blane*, there is similarly no indication that it is the inflected form of a potential real stem.

The results show a striking divergence between the inflectional sets and the additional phoneme sets. Although patients perform worst on the real regulars, they also perform remarkably poorly on the pseudo-regular and non-word regular sets, while being close to normal on the two additional phoneme sets. These effects show up significantly in their response times, but can be seen most dramatically in the pattern of errors (defined as a failure to detect a difference; figure 7.4). In the context of near-zero error rates for the age-matched controls (means of 1.7% for non-words and 0.6% for real words), the patients fail to detect a *played/play* difference over 30% of the time, with error rates well above 20% for the pseudo-regular and the

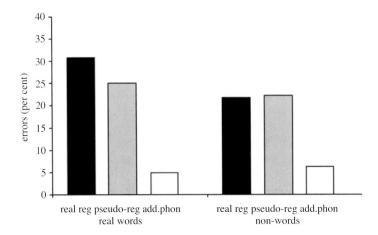

Fig. 7.4 Per cent error rates (for different pairs only) for non-fluent patients in a same–different judgement task, comparing real regular, pseudo-regular and additional phoneme pairs in real word and non-word conditions (data replotted from Tyler *et al.* 2002*a*).

non-word conditions. In contrast, they make less than 5% errors on the matched additional phoneme conditions.[7]

This pattern of deficits gives us a kind of 'negative image' of the properties of the underlying intact system for processing regular inflectional forms in English. First of all, it confirms that this is a decompositional process, and that regular inflected forms are not treated or stored as whole forms. Otherwise, there would be no reason for a non-word like *snade* to create significant problems when *blane* does not. It is only in a decompositional context, where whole forms are not stored, that a string like *snade* needs to be analysed to determine whether it is a form like *played*—also not stored—which is an inflected form of a stem that does exist and which is stored.

Second, and relatedly, this potential internal structure seems to be signalled by the presence of a specific acoustic–phonetic pattern in the input, that triggers morpho-phonological parsing processes independent of the actual lexical status of the string being decomposed. It is this that selects out *snade* for analysis, in contrast to items like *blane*—or indeed items like *trade* in contrast to *claim*. This tuning of the parsing process to the distributional properties of English inflectional morphemes, and the fact that such parsing evidently operates blindly and obligatorily, vividly brings out the priority that the system must place on the identification of inflectional morphemes in the speech stream.

This neuropsychological behavioural data illuminates for us, therefore, the functional outlines of a hidden decompositional processing system that operates beneath the surface of the language interpretation process. However, owing to the heterogeneous nature of the lesions involved and the size of the left perisylvian lesions in some of these patients, this patient group is only weakly informative about how these functions relate to specific brain systems. To move beyond this, in order to establish an adequate neurocognitive model of these phenomena, we need to: (i) map these processes onto an anatomically more specific neural substrate and (ii) carry out the appropriate tests, using behavioural and neuroimaging techniques, to evaluate these claims in the context of the undamaged brain. These goals are the focus of the following sections of this paper.

7.4 Towards a normal neurocognitive model

As we have shown above, behavioural priming tasks allow us to segment the damaged system in functional terms, with different kinds of priming relationships being differentially sensitive to different aspects of cognitive and psycholinguistic function. In tests with the non-fluent patients, for example, we see a selective impairment for stimuli containing a regular inflectional morpheme. In other experiments, we see selective impairments for semantic priming, in patients with semantic disorders (Marslen-Wilson & Tyler 1997; Tyler & Moss 1998).

This behavioural selectivity can be used, together with whole brain structural magnetic resonance imaging (MRI) of patients' lesions, in a novel analysis procedure that allows us to pinpoint the brain areas that are most critical for the performance of the behavioural functions indexed by these tasks. This procedure correlates variations in behavioural performance on specific tasks with whole-brain voxel-by-voxel variations in MRI signal intensity (Tyler *et al.* 2005a). These variations in signal strength reflect variations in tissue density within each voxel, and these, relative to a population norm, reflect the integrity of the tissue involved. Lower signal intensity reflects damage to the brain, either directly (e.g. in the area affected by an infarct or following surgery) or indirectly, through effects of damage elsewhere on grey and white matter density in connected areas.

This is a much more sensitive technique than conventional lesion overlap methods and is proving remarkably successful in delineating highly specific brain–behaviour relationships (e.g. Tyler *et al.* 2005c; Bright *et al.* 2006). Here, we focus on the outcome of a study correlating structural MRIs for a sample of 22 brain-damaged patients with their performance on the same auditory–auditory repetition priming task described earlier, where a stem target is primed by a regularly inflected stem (*joined/join*), together with other priming conditions for irregular past tenses (*found/find*), semantically related pairs (*swan/goose*) and a phonological control condition (*clamp/clam*), matched to the regularly inflected pairs in amount of phonetic overlap between prime and target (Tyler *et al.* 2002a, 2005a). The patients tested, with predominantly LH lesions, were not pre-selected on the basis of their linguistic performance but simply according to the requirement that (i) they were able to have a structural MRI and (ii) they could perform the priming task, where lexical decision responses to the targets were required.

The results for regular inflected primes (figure 7.5a) selectively pick out key areas of the perisylvian language system in the left inferior frontal gyrus (LIFG). At the highest statistical threshold ($p < 0.001$ voxel, $p < 0.05$ cluster levels), variations in priming performance for regular pairs correlate with variations in tissue density in Broca's area, with the maxima in BA 47, extending superiorly into BA 45. This is a part of the brain long thought to be implicated in grammatical aspects of linguistic performance (Grodzinsky 2000). The scatterplot in figure 7.5b gives the distribution of priming scores for the patient group at the peak voxel for this analysis, showing a strong positive correlation with signal intensity ($r = 0.75$, $p < 0.01$). As signal intensity diminishes with increasing damage, the size of the priming effect falls off. For comparison, the scores for the phonological control condition (*clamp/clam*) are also included. These do not correlate significantly with damage in these areas ($r = 0.29$, n.s.) and are significantly weaker than the effects for the regulars. Instead, performance on the phonological pairs correlates with a more medial LH area, the insula, known on independent grounds to be involved in aspects of phonological processing (Noesselt *et al.* 2003), and where a significant effect for the regulars is not seen.

What figure 7.5a also shows is that when the correlation with regular priming scores is plotted at a slightly lower statistical threshold ($p < 0.01$ voxel level), we see a more extensive

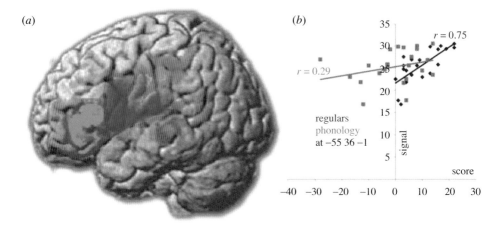

Fig. 7.5 Structural correlates of regular inflection. (*a*) Three-dimensional reconstruction of a T1-weighted MRI image showing brain areas where variations in signal density (for grey and white matter) correlate with priming for regularly inflected words at three significance levels: $p < 0.001$ (green); $p < 0.01$ (blue); and $p < 0.05$ (red) voxel thresholds. The clusters shown survived correction at $p < 0.05$ cluster level adjusted for the entire brain. The statistical peak $(-55, 36, -1)$ is in the LIFG (BA 47), and the cluster extends superiorly into BA 45. At lower thresholds, the cluster extends from Broca's to Wernicke's areas and includes the arcuate fasciculus. (*b*) The scatter plot showing the relationship between variations in signal intensity at the most significant voxel, and individual behavioural scores in the regular past tense condition and the non-morphological phonological overlap condition (reprinted with permission from Tyler *et al.* 2005*a*, copyright 2005 National Academy of Sciences).

region of the LH being implicated. This region included the left superior temporal gyrus, extending posteriorly from primary auditory cortex into the anterior extent of Wernicke's area (BA 41, 42) and anteriorly along the left superior temporal gyrus. When the threshold is reduced further ($p < 0.05$ voxel level), the cluster now includes all of Wernicke's area, looping around to include the arcuate fasciculus and including BAs 47, 44 and 45.

These patterns of correlation correspond closely both to the classical Broca–Wernicke–Lichtheim model of language function (figure 7.2), where the white matter tract of the arcuate fasciculus connects superior temporal and inferior frontal regions, and to the dorsal route identified in more recent neurobiological accounts (figure 7.1). This is not only consistent with previous reports implicating damage to the dorsal route in impairments of regular inflectional morphology, but also allows us to make the stronger inference, given the selectivity of the priming task, that this impairment is specific to the decompositional aspects of regular inflection—especially since priming patterns for the irregulars correlate with quite different posterior temporo-parietal brain regions (Tyler *et al.* 2005*a*).

In terms of an initial statement of a neurocognitive model of the processing of spoken regularly inflected words in English, these results point to a core decompositional network involving LIFG and posterior left temporal regions, centred around the dorsal processing stream and less critically dependent on other processing streams—either the proposed ventral processing stream (Scott *et al.* 2000; Davis & Johnsrude 2003) or a potential third stream of processing (e.g. Rodd *et al.* 2005), possibly linked to an inferior temporal 'basal language area' (Price 2000). This dorsal decompositional network would be engaged in two types of interdependent processing activity triggered by a regularly inflected stem combined with an inflectional affix. These are processes of stem and affix access and of morpho-phonological segmentation of the original complex form.[8]

These functions are distributed over a partially left lateralized fronto-temporal language system, with some differentiation of function between frontal and temporal areas. Access to lexico-semantic content is likely to be mediated by temporal lobe structures, centred around the posterior superior and middle temporal gyri and linking sensory inputs to stem-based representations of morphemic form and meaning (cf. Binder *et al.* 2000; Wise *et al.* 2001). If these brain regions are intact, we see preserved phonological and semantic processing of both monomorphemic forms (like *jump* or *dog*) and irregular forms (like *gave* or *taught*) that have to be accessed as whole forms. Note that considerable neuropsychological and neuroimaging evidence suggests that access for these morphologically simple forms is supported bilaterally, in RH and LH temporal lobes.

The successful access, in contrast, of regularly inflected forms requires a further left-lateralized process of morpho-phonological parsing, which segments potential complex forms into stems and grammatical affixes. This segmentation, on one hand, allows the isolated stem to access successfully the appropriate stem representation, and, on the other hand, allows the inflectional affix to access the representations and processes relevant to its successful interpretation. The processes supporting this parsing process seem to require intact left inferior frontal cortex and intact processing links between these areas and left superior and middle temporal cortex. A striking feature, finally, of these segmentation processes is that they are apparently triggered by any input, word or non-word, that shares the diagnostic properties (the IRP) of an inflectional affix in English (Tyler *et al.* 2002*b*).

The specific features of this decompositional grammatical processing model, both neural and functional, have been inferred from the results of research into the damaged system. In a series of experiments with intact young adults, we have started to examine the predictions of this model for performance in the normal brain, primarily using neuro-imaging techniques.

7.5 Modulation of fronto-temporal interactions by morpho-phonological cues

The key claims of the neurocognitive model concern the interplay of stem access and affixal decomposition, modulated by the IRP, across left temporal and inferior frontal cortex. We probed these, in the normal brain, by running a version of the same–different experiment (Tyler *et al.* 2002*b*) in an event-related functional MRI (fMRI) paradigm (Tyler *et al.* 2005*b*). The stimulus set for this study (Table 7.1), although restricted in scope by the constraints of

Table 7.1 Stimulus conditions for the speeded same–different judgement task.

	conditions		real word	non-word
1	regular past	(+IRP)	played/play	crade/crey
2	pseudo- regular	(+IRP)	trade/tray	drade/drey
3	irregular past	(−IRP)	taught/teach	hort/heach
4	pseudo- irregular	(−IRP)	port/peach	gort/geach
5	additional phoneme	(−IRP)	claim/clay	blain/blay

the neuroimaging environment, allowed us to evaluate a range of neurocognitive effects. To do so, we used both standard subtractive analyses, and a functional connectivity analysis of the dependencies between different processing regions (Stama-takis *et al.* 2005).

The same–different task, as noted earlier, requires the listener to construct a stable representation of the first member of each pair, so that this can be held in memory for comparison with the incoming information about the second target word. Further, as the earlier experiment with the patients demonstrated, this process is dependent on an intact LH fronto-temporal system for those pairs where the first member of the pair ends with the English IRP. This implies that the stimulus types that caused the most severe problems to the patients should be those that generate the strongest fronto-temporal activation in normals. The first contrast in the current study, therefore, is between the (+IRP) sets—the real regulars and pseudo-regulars, with their matched non-word counter-parts—and the (−IRP) sets, consisting of real irregulars, pseudo-irregulars and additional phoneme pairs, also with non-word counterparts (Table 7.1). For the (+IRP) sets, the model predicts stronger LIFG activation, since the presence of the IRP should trigger decompositional activity for which LIFG involvement is required. It may also generate increased temporal lobe activity, especially for real regulars, where the presence of the IRP is claimed to lead to a reanalysis of forms like *played* into *play* + *-ed*, allowing *play* to access its stem representation.

The second broad contrast is in lexicality, with a comparison between real word and non-word pairs across all five conditions. Since none of the non-word pairs (like *snade/snay*) correspond to stored lexical representation, this should lead to reduced temporal lobe activity relative to the real words. The latter should engage lexical access mechanisms much more strongly, especially when they have an embedded competitor (as in *trade/tray* or *claim/clay*). Lexicality, however, should not interact with IRP, which should trigger LIFG activity irrespective of the status of the stem.

The third contrast, finally, allows us to compare whole word and decompositional access for pairs matched for semantic and syntactic complexity— namely the regular/irregular contrast, including pseudo-regular/irregular and non-word conditions. Both the real regulars and the real irregulars are inflectionally marked for the past tense, and seem to be fully equivalent in terms of their syntactic implications. To the extent that LIFG activation associated with regular past tense inflection is driven by the syntactic interpretation of these markers, the regular and irregular forms would generate equivalent levels of activation. If, however, as the patient data suggest, LIFG activity is primarily driven by the processing demands associated with morpho-phonological decomposition, then LIFG activation should be stronger for the regulars.

These three contrasts interact in an illuminating manner to support and extend the model. Across the board, we see stronger activations in temporal cortex bilaterally for (+ IRP) conditions, coupled with significant LIFG effects. These effects are modulated by lexicality and decompositionality. We consider first the regular/irregular comparison, which compares decomposable and non-decomposable forms while holding syntactic properties constant. Overall, there is stronger superior/middle temporal gyrus (STG/MTG) activation bilaterally for all regulars (real, pseudo- and non-word) when compared with all irregulars, coupled with significantly greater LIFG activation (and no effects in the reverse direction). In addition, as shown in figure 7.6, the real regular/irregular contrast shows a further focus of activation in the left anterior cingulate (with some RH involvement). This activation, reflected in an interaction between past tense type (regular/irregular) and word type (real past/pseudo-past), seems specific to the real regulars (*played/play*)—namely, those stimuli which are genuinely segmentable into a stem and an inflectional affix, as opposed to pseudo-affixed pairs like *trade/tray*.

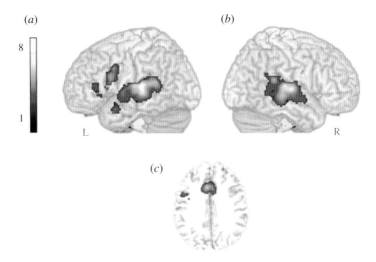

Fig. 7.6 fMRI data: significant activations for the contrast of real regulars minus real irregulars. Significant clusters were found in the right superior temporal gyrus (RSTG), left superior temporal gyrus (LSTG), left anterior cingulate cortex (LACC), and left inferior frontal gyrus (LIFG) (data redrawn from Tyler *et al.* 2005*b*).

The appearance of this anterior cingulate activation is significant, since it potentially relates to control processes that regulate the proposed processing relationship between left frontal and temporal regions. Several lines of evidence suggest that the integration of information between superior temporal and left frontal areas may be modulated by anterior midline structures including the anterior cingulate. Work with non-human primates shows that the anterior cingulate projects to or receives connections from most regions of frontal cortex (Barbas & Pandya 1989) and superior temporal cortex (Pandya *et al.* 1981). Recent neuroimaging data not only implicate the anterior cingulate in the modulation of fronto-temporal integration (Fletcher *et al.* 1999), but also show it to be active in situations requiring the monitoring of interactions between different information processing pathways (Braver *et al.* 2001).

In this view, the increased activation of the anterior cingulate by real regular inflected forms (figure 7.6) may reflect the greater demands made on this monitoring function when complex forms such as *jumped* need to be parsed into a stem + affix, with the bare stem then able to act as a well-formed input to temporal lobe lexical access processes. The properties of this potential anterior cingulate contribution were examined in more detail in a subsequent functional connectivity analysis (Stamatakis *et al.* 2005) carried out on the same data, using the PPI (psycho-physiological interaction) approach developed by Friston *et al.* (1997). This allowed us to address more directly the functional relationship between regions in the fronto-temporal language system.

The resulting connectivity analysis shows that the LH regions in the LIFG and anterior cingulate identified by the subtractive analyses (figure 7.6*a,c*) covary with activity in the left posterior MTG more for regularly inflected forms compared with irregularly inflected forms (*played* versus *taught*). This fronto-temporal interaction was reduced when the words were phonologically similar to the regular and irregular past tense but were not themselves morphologically complex (e.g. for contrasts like *trade* versus *port*). This suggests that the modulatory effects we found for the regulars reflect the stronger dependency between components of the fronto-temporal language system required for processes of morpho-phonological decomposition and analysis, rather than being attributable to the phonetic differences between the regular and irregular pairs.[9] The greater activation for real as opposed to pseudo-regulars means that a form like *played* triggers more activity than *trade*, both in terms of its consequences for the lexical access process, with the assignment of the stem morpheme (*play*) and the grammatical morpheme (*-ed*) to different processing destinations, and in terms of morpho-syntactic analysis processes. These latter processes will presumably be engaged more strongly when the evidence suggests that a grammatical morpheme is indeed present.

These results, showing connectivity between inferior frontal and middle temporal regions, are consistent with anatomical connectivity dorsally via the arcuate fasciculus between frontal and temporal regions, but also between orbito-frontal and anterior temporal regions via ventral connections (Petrides & Pandya 1988; Morris *et al.* 1999). They are also consistent with recent *in vivo* analyses of anatomical connections in the human brain, using diffusion tensor imaging to visualize white matter tracts connecting different brain areas (Catani *et al.* 2005; Parker *et al.* 2005). One indication that the connectivity implied by our analyses was via dorsal rather than ventral connections is that the LIFG seed for these analyses was the more superior of the two activation foci seen in the subtractive analyses, being located in BA 44 pars opercularis (figure 7.6*a*). Studies on humans and macaques suggest that neurons in the dorsal stream project to regions of superior LIFG which overlap with area BA 44 and its macaque homologue (Kaas & Hackett 1999; Scott & Johnsrude 2003).

Returning to the original subtractive analyses of the same–different task, the second main contrast was between the regulars and the additional phoneme conditions. The results here, under conditions where the two sets could be closely matched in their phonetic properties, are also consistent with the view that LH fronto-temporal interactions in speech processing are modulated by morpho-phonological cues to potential inflectional affixes. As shown in figure 7.7, we again see increased temporal activation bilaterally together with increased LIFG activation for the real regulars and non-word regulars, compared to the additional phoneme sets (*claim*/*clay*, *blane*/*blay*). This difference seems to depend on the presence of the IRP contrast between the regular and additional phoneme conditions. When the irregulars are compared with the additional phoneme condition, where neither set carries the IRP, there is no sign of the left fronto-temporal pattern seen for comparisons involving the regulars.

Finally, and reinforcing the view that the IRP triggers decompositional activity blindly and obligatorily, irrespective of the lexical status of the stem to which it is attached, we see signifi-

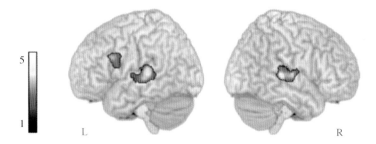

Fig. 7.7 fMRI data: significant activations for the contrast of regulars (real, non-word) minus additional phoneme (real, non-word). Clusters were found in the RSTG, LSTG and LIFG (data redrawn from Tyler *et al.* 2005*b*).

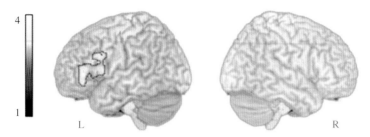

Fig. 7.8 fMRI data: significant activations for the contrast of regular non-words minus additional pho-neme non-words. Clusters were found in the LIFG (data redrawn from Tyler *et al*. 2005*b*).

cant LIFG activity, but no differential temporal lobe activity (figure 7.8) in a specific compari-son between regular non-words (*snade/snay*) and additional phoneme non-words (*blain/blay*). Here, there are no real stems, either embedded or inflected, so that there is no basis for sub-stantial differences in stem-based access processes in either type of material. Nonetheless, the IRP is still present for the regular non-words, and this is still effective as a cue to potential decomposition, engaging similar LIFG regions to the real regulars.

In summary, this experiment is consistent with our basic hypotheses for an underlying grammatically driven neurocognitive system, instantiated in a left lateralized fronto-temporal network linking temporal and inferior frontal areas, which prioritizes the identification and interpretation of inflectional morphemes. Functional connectivity analyses point to the dynamic modulatory relationships across this network, consistent with the view that the func-tional properties of such a network emerge from cooperation between anatomically distant areas.

Additional evidence for dynamic fronto-temporal interactions, operating on millisecond time-scales, comes from studies using electroencephalography (EEG) and magnetoencepha-lography (MEG) techniques, which allow us to track brain events with high temporal resolution. Research across a variety of languages shows additional left fronto-temporal activity associated with the presence of grammatical morphemes. This holds for contrasts between isolated function and content words (e.g. Pulvermüller & Mohr 1996), and for several EEG studies examining the effects of morphological violations involving regular and irregular inflected forms, typically as they occur in sentence contexts (e.g. Münte *et al*. 1999; Rodriguez-Fornells *et al*. 2001; Lück *et al*. 2006), using both written and spoken materials.

Recent MEG experiments using the mismatch negativity (MMN) paradigm demonstrate with spatial as well as temporal precision the dynamic properties of the fronto-temporal links underpinning inflectional processes. Pulvermüller *et al*. (2006), using modern source localization techniques, are able to discriminate a left superior/middle temporal burst of activation, triggered by successful word recognition, from a second burst of activity in left inferior temporal regions that follows within approximately 20 ms. This is for inflected verbal forms in Finnish, where a stem like {tuo-} is accompanied by the inflectional suffix {-t}, giving the surface form *tuot*, 'you bring'. Other MEG research using the MMN paradigm indicates that this left frontal activation reflects the status of the final phoneme as an inflectional affix (e.g. Shtyrov & Pulvermüller 2002; Shtyrov *et al*. 2005). This is consistent with the fMRI research described previously (Tyler *et al*. 2005*b*), where a marked increase in left inferior frontal activation is stimulated by the presence of an inflectional affix.

Running through all the research discussed so far is the theme that identifying inflectional morphemes is a major priority for the language processing system. Evidence is now emerging that this is a truly general property of language interpretation, and that the other major class of grammatical affixes—derivational morphemes—are also prioritized by the system for early blind identification. In secton 6 of the paper, we examine this novel and complementary evidence for the salience of grammatical information in the early stages of language comprehension.

7.6 Early segmentation of derivational morphemes

Derivational affixes—forms in English like {-ness}, {-er} and {-ize}—function primarily to create new lexical items, combining with existing free or bound content morphemes to create words like *darkness*, *builder* and *radicalize*. These derived forms are generally treated in the language as new words, with different meanings from their stems and very often with different syntactic categories—*builder*, for example, is a noun, formed from the verb stem *build*. Compelling evidence is now emerging that all potential derivationally complex words undergo an initial obligatory process of segmentation into their morphemic components, irrespective of whether the words actually are morphologically complex—paralleling the kind of obligatory early decomposition we have seen for inflectionally complex forms. Although this obligatory early decomposition was initially proposed over 30 years ago (Taft & Forster 1975), the recent wider acceptance of this view reflects new experiments, across a range of languages, using the visual masked priming technique (for a recent review, see Marslen-Wilson 2007)—and contrasting, therefore, with the primarily auditory focus of the research on inflectional morphology described previously.

Masked priming is an experimental situation where a visual prime word (preceded by a pattern mask and followed by a visual target) is presented so briefly that the reader is not aware that the prime is present and simply makes a lexical decision to the target (Forster & Davis 1984). Several experiments using this task provide converging evidence cross-linguistically for the dominance of morphological factors in the early analysis of derivational complex forms (e.g. Frost *et al.* 1997; Forster & Azuma 2000; Boudelaa & Marslen-Wilson 2004). This dominant role for morphology is underlined by a further series of experiments which show that this early segmentation is conducted independently of the stored lexical properties of the forms in question. Several studies in English (Rastle *et al.* 2000, 2005; Marslen-Wilson *et al.* in press) show strong masked priming not only between transparent pairs like *bravely/brave*, which are genuinely morphologically related, but also between pairs like *hardly/hard*, which are not transparently morphologically related in modern English, and even for pseudo-derived pairs like *corner/corn*, where *corner* clearly has no morphological interpretation as {corn+-er}. The process underlying these effects is nonetheless morphologically sensitive, since pairs like *harpoon/harp*, where '-oon' is not a derivational affix in English, do not show priming.

Similar patterns are reported for French by Longtin and colleagues, who not only replicate the results of Rastle *et al.* (2000), but also go on to show that non-word primes (such as *rapidifier*) can prime their real word pseudo-stem (*rapide*, 'rapid') just as well as transparent real-word primes (*rapidement*, 'rapidly'), but only if the pseudo-stem co-occurs with an existing French suffix (Longtin *et al.* 2003; Longtin & Meunier 2005). Thus *rapiduit*, where -*uit* is not a possible suffix in French, does not prime *rapide*. These results not only support a lexically blind early segmentation account of masked morphological priming (non-words, by definition, cannot have a stored lexical representation), but also confirm that this early segmentation is sensitive to morphological factors. Only if the potential stem is paired with an actual suffix in the language do we see priming.

In summary, these masked priming results point to an early phase of the visual lexical access process, where all morphologically decomposable surface forms are segmented into potential stems and affixes by a process which is blind to higher-order lexical structure (cf. Shallice & Saffran 1986; McKinnnon *et al.* 2003). Given the ample evidence for masked priming between inflectionally related pairs (e.g. Forster *et al.* 1987; Drews & Zwitserlood 1995; Pastizzo & Feldman 2002), this undoubtedly extends to inflectionally complex forms as well. In terms of the neural substrate for these early segmentation processes, a strong candidate is the left fusiform gyrus—a LH brain region known as the visual word form area (cf. Cohen *et al.* 2002; McCandliss *et al.* 2003), which plays an important role in the early interpretation of orthographic inputs.

Consistent with this, a recent paper by Devlin *et al.* (2004) reports masked priming effects in exactly this area, using an event-related fMRI approach, for a mixture of semantically opaque and pseudo-derived stimuli (such as *department*/*depart*, *hardly*/*hard* and *slipper*/*slip*). The behavioural priming effect for these materials was identical in size to the effect for morphologically transparent pairs like *teacher*/*teach*, consistent with the masked priming literature. The neural priming effect, however, was stronger in the visual word form area for the opaque and pseudostem pairs than for the transparent pairs, consistent with the view that activation at this level primarily reflects pre-lexical segmentation processes.[10]

Neuroimaging data from a different study (Bozic *et al.* 2007) indicate that the effects of these early analyses propagate more widely than the Devlin *et al.* (2004) data would suggest. Using delayed repetition priming in an event-related fMRI paradigm, Bozic *et al.* compared effects for transparent and opaque morphologically decomposable pairs (*bravely*/*brave*, *archer*/*arch*) with appropriate form and meaning controls (*harpoon*/*harp*, *accuse*/*blame*). Second presentations of morphologically related words produced significantly reduced activation in left inferior frontal regions, whether the pairs were semantically transparent or opaque. No effects were observed for the form and meaning control conditions. The appearance of these frontal morphologically driven effects at long repetition delays, for opaque as well as for transparent pairs, suggests that potential morphemic segmentations are widely evaluated in the neural language system.

7.7 Implications and speculations

The research discussed here provides a preliminary glimpse of the processing networks underlying human language comprehension, framed in the broader context of how linguistic inputs convey meaning through the sequential packaging of syntactic and semantic morphemes, and constrained by a general neurobiological processing architecture. The empirical picture that has emerged for inflectional and derivational morphology, though still quite fragmentary, underlines the importance of morpheme-level analysis across the language comprehension process. It seems to be one of the highest priorities of the system, as soon as orthographic or phonological information starts to accumulate, to identify possible stems and possible grammatical morphemes.

In the case of inflectional morphology, where the neurocognitive picture is better established, the basic process of lexical access for stems interacts with morpho-phonological parsing processes which identify the presence of potential grammatical morphemes. Regular inflected forms do not seem to participate in language comprehension as whole forms, but rather as bearers of inflectional morphemes relevant to basic phrasal and sentential interpretation, and of stem morphemes conveying further semantic and syntactic information.[11]

The neuropsychological nature of the evidence for this underlyingly decompositional system points strongly to the separability of these processes, tied to core LH language networks, from more broadly based and robust systems for whole form lexical access and interpretation. Patients who are unable to access lexical semantic information from regular inflected stems can still do so with essentially normal efficiency from equivalent non-inflected stems, even in cases where there is substantial damage to much of the LH perisylvian language system. Although the evidence here is not fully developed, this robustness must in large part reflect the bilateral lexical representation of content words and bilateral mechanisms for accessing these representations (e.g. Mohr *et al.* 1994). Our same–different study on normal young adults, for example, showed strong lexically related RH as well as LH temporal activation in contrasts between different types of real word stimuli (figures 7.6 and 7.7).

Consistent with this, when we analyse the fMRI activation patterns and resulting functional connectivity for a severe LH patient performing the same–different task (Tyler & Marslen-Wilson 2007), we see an enhanced RH fronto-temporal pattern of connectivity, with increased activity in the anterior temporal lobes in both hemispheres. Earlier voxel-based lesion–behaviour correlation studies (Tyler *et al.* 2005*c*) show that the temporal poles, bilaterally, play a key causal role in word recognition performance. At the same time, however, although such patients' reorganized lexical processing system performs well in speeded priming tasks (Longworth *et al.* 2005), and they have good spoken language comprehension, they still exhibit a significant syntactic deficit, as well as persistent problems with regularly inflected words. These grammatical functions depend on an intact LH perisylvian system, and the homologous RH structures seem unable to compensate, in this respect, for damage on the left.

This brings us back to the issues, raised at the beginning of this paper, of how to characterize the neurobiological framework for human language and whether this has special properties not found in non-human primate systems for auditory object processing and conspecific vocal communication. The fronto-temporal organization detected by Gil-da-costa *et al.* (2006) clearly holds for the human language system, although it is doubtful how informative this apparent homology is without a better understanding of both the functional properties of these connections in the human and the macaque, and the basis for the strong lateralization of core language functions in the human brain. Indeed, since the left lateralized fronto-temporal system in humans seems to handle grammatical and possibly combinatorial functions that are arguably only seen in human language, it may be that no direct precursors for these functions will be seen in the macaque. Instead, as Dehaene and others (e.g. Dehaene 2005; Dehaene *et al.* 2005) have argued for the left fusiform gyrus—that it provides a suitable processing substrate for the representation and analysis of abstract visual forms such as letters and words—it may be that the primate fronto-temporal system provides a suitable processing substrate, in ways as yet unknown, for exaptation in the process of human linguistic evolution.[12]

Finally, it is worth considering how far the notion of different processing streams is helpful in illuminating the organization of the human language system. While the evidence is not definitive, there are several hints in the data that the decompositional morphemic processes focusing on grammatical affixes are particularly dependent on dorsal pathways, linking left temporal and inferior frontal regions via the arcuate fasciculus (cf. Catani *et al.* 2005). Damage to these pathways has also been shown to affect syntactic function (Tyler & Marslen-Wilson 2007). The ventral route, in contrast, seen as resembling the classical 'what' pathway in primate vision, seems to be more engaged in processes of semantic interpretation (e.g. Scott *et al.* 2000; Davis & Johnsrude 2003), being sensitive to the intelligibility of the speech stream.

This is a highly interconnected system of pathways, in both time and space, but if the role of grammatical constraints is to orchestrate and direct the interpretation of semantic and pragmatic information carried by content words and morphemes, in the general pragmatic context of speaking, then one could suggest some division of labour along these lines, between dorsal and ventral processing streams, and heavily dependent on frontal control processes. This would be consistent with the evidence for the separability of morpho-syntactic function on one hand, and semantic and pragmatic interpretation on the other, which is clearly seen in the online performance of patients with damage to the core LH system, and would point to a neurobiologically constrained basis for future research into this most complex of neurocognitive systems.

Acknowledgements

This research was supported by MRC programme grants awarded to L.K.T, and by the MRC grant-in-aid to the MRC Cognition and Brain Sciences Unit. We thank, in particular, Emmanuel Stamatakis and Billi Randall for their many contributions to the work reviewed here. We also thank Tim Shallice, Natasha Sigala and two anonymous reviewers for their comments on the manuscript.

Endnotes

1 This is a simplification of a neuroanatomically much more complicated story (e.g. Petrides & Pandya 1994).
2 Ullman (2004) distinguishes a memorized 'mental lexicon' and a computational 'mental grammar', mapping onto a more basic distinction between declarative and procedural neurocognitive systems. On our view, however, the 'lexicon' is intrinsically both 'memorized' and 'computed', built around a set of fronto-temporal circuits that permanently link brain areas that Ullman primarily assigns to either procedural or declarative functions.
3 In all of these neuropsychological studies, unless indicated otherwise, we are working with small sets of patients (typically four or five) treated both individually and as small groups.
4 We refer here to the phonological access representation for these irregular forms. The whole form, once accessed, may well link to an abstract underlying morpheme corresponding to the stem.
5 Extensive testing for possible phonetic differences between regular inflected forms and stem or irregular forms showed no effects of these variables on priming, tying the effects instead to the morpho-phonological properties of the regulars.
6 Patients heard both same (*played/played*) and different (*played/play*) pairs in equal proportions. Since they only made 'different' responses (to minimize task demands), we focus here just on the different stimuli. The experiment also contained sets of irregular and pseudo-irregular pairs. Responses to these are not directly relevant to the current discussion (patients performed very well) and are not presented here. For further details, see Tyler *et al.* (2002*b*).
7 Note that an account of these results in terms of deficits in phonetic (as opposed to morpho-phonological) processing (cf. Joanisse & Seidenberg 1999; Bird *et al.* 2003) is unlikely for two reasons. First, the regular and the additional phoneme sets were matched in terms of phonological complexity. Second, patients performed poorly on the regular sets even when they did not have deficits in phonetic processing as standardly assessed (Tyler *et al.* 2002b).
8 The dorsal network may also be engaged in the morpho-syntactic interpretation of the grammatical implications of the inflectional affix.
9 Note that, as discussed in Tyler *et al.* (2005*b*), these data on their own do not allow us to exclude an account of the ACC involvement in terms of differences in task requirements between regular and

other conditions—although RT and error data suggest that there is no major difference in difficulty between, for example, regular and pseudo-regular forms.

10 Devlin *et al.* (2004) themselves interpret these results quite differently, since they regard their pseudo-derived/semantically opaque condition (*department/depart, hardly/hard*) as a purely orthographic control for their morphologically related condition (*teacher/teach*). This does not seem tenable to us, given the ample evidence (cited above) for the morphologically driven processing elicited by opaque and pseudo-derived pairs of exactly this type.

11 For derivational morphology, where we also see very early identification of morphemic structure, for both transparent and opaque derived forms, it is unlikely that this leads to a disassembly of the complex form into its morphemic components for the purposes of subsequent analysis (for further discussion, see Marslen-Wilson 2007).

12 'Exaptation' is the reutilization, during phylogenesis, of biological mechanisms for a new function different from the one for which they evolved (Gould & Vrba 1982).

References

Anderson, S. R. 1992 *A-morphous morphology*. Cambridge, UK: Cambridge University Press.

Barbas, H. & Pandya, D. N. 1989 Architecture and intrinsic connections of the prefrontal cortex in the rhesus monkey. *J. Comp. Neurol.* **286**, 353–375. (doi:10.1002/cne.902860306)

Bickel, B. & Nichols, J. 2006 Inflectional morphology. In *Language typology and syntactic description* (ed. T. Shopen). Cambridge, UK: Cambridge University Press.

Binder, J. R., Frost, T. A., Hammeke, P. S. F., Bellgowan, P. S. F., Springer, J. A., Kaufman, J. N. & Possing, E. T. 2000 Human temporal lobe activation by speech and nonspeech sounds. *Cereb. Cortex* **10**, 512–528. (doi:10.1093/cercor/10.5.512)

Bird, H., Lambon Ralph, M. A., Seidenberg, M. S., McClelland, J. L. & Patterson, K. 2003 Deficits in phonology and past tense morphology: what's the connection? *J. Mem. Lang.* **48**, 502–526. (doi:10.1016/S0749-596X(02)00538-7)

Boudelaa, S. & Marslen-Wilson, W. D. 2004 Abstract morphemes and lexical representation: the CV-skeleton in Arabic. *Cognition* **92**, 271–303. (doi:10.1016/j.cognition.2003.08.003)

Bozic, M., Marslen-Wilson, W. D., Stamatakis, E., Davis, M. H. & Tyler, L. K. 2007. Differentiating morphology, form, and meaning: neural correlates of morphological complexity. *J. Cogn. Neurosci.* **19**, 1464–1475.

Braver, T. S., Barch, D. M., Gray, J. R., Molfese, D. L. & Snyder, A. 2001 Anterior cingulate cortex and response conflict: effects of frequency, inhibition and errors. *Cereb. Cortex* **11**, 825–836. (doi:10.1093/cercor/11.9.825)

Bright, P., Moss, H. E., Longe, O., Stamatakis, E. A. & Tyler, L. K. 2006 Conceptual structure modulates anteromedial temporal involvement in processing verbally presented object properties. *Cereb. Cortex*. June 13 [Epub ahead of print]. (doi:10.1093/cercor/bhl016)

Catani, M., Jones, D. K. & Ffytche, D. H. 2005 Perisylvian language networks of the human brain. *Ann. Neurol.* **57**, 8–16. (doi:10.1002/ana.20319)

Clahsen, H. 1999 Lexical entries and rules of language: a multidisciplinary study of German inflection. *Behav. Brain Sci.* **22**, 991–1060. (doi:10.1017/S0140525X99002228)

Cohen, L., Lehericy, S., Chochon, F., Lemer, C., Rivard, S. & Dehaene, S. 2002 Language-specific tuning of visual cortex? Functional properties of the visual word form area. *Brain* **125**, 1054–1069. (doi:10.1093/brain/awf094)

Davis, M. H. & Johnsrude, I. S. 2003 Hierarchical processing in spoken language comprehension. *J. Neurosci.* **23**, 3423–3431.

Dehaene, S. 2005 Evolution of human cortical circuits for reading and arithmetic: the 'neuronal recycling' hypothesis. In *From monkey brain to human brain* (eds S. Dehaene, J.-R. Duhamel,M.D.Hauser & G.Rizzolatti), pp. 133–158. Cambridge, MA: MIT Press.

Dehaene, S., Cohen, L., Sigman, M. & Vinckier, F. 2005 The neural code for written words: a proposal. *Trends Cogn. Sci.* **9**, 335–341. (doi:10.1016/j.tics.2005.05.004)

Devlin, J. T., Jamison, H. L., Matthews, P. M. & Gonnerman, L. 2004 Morphology and the internal struc-ture of words. *Proc. Natl Acad. Sci. USA* **101**, 14 984–14 988. (doi:10.1073/pnas.0403766101)

Drews, E. & Zwitserlood, P. 1995 Effects of morphological and orthographic similarity in visual word recognition. *J. Exp. Psychol. Hum. Percept. Perform.* **21**, 1098–1116. (doi:10.1037/0096-1523. 21.5.1098)

Fletcher, P., McKenna, P. J., Friston, K. J., Frith, C. D. & Dolan, R. J. 1999 Abnormal cingulate modulation of fronto-temporal connectivity in schizophrenia. *Neuroimage* **9**, 337–342. (doi:10.1006/nimg. 1998.0411)

Forster, K. I. & Azuma, T. 2000 Masked priming for prefixed words with bound stems: does submit prime permit? *Lang. Cogn. Process.* **14**, 539–561.

Forster, K. I. & Davis, C. 1984 Repetition priming and frequency attenuation in lexical access. *J. Exp. Psychol. Learn. Mem. Cogn.* **10**, 680–698. (doi:10.1037/0278-7393.10.4.680)

Forster, K. L., Davis, C., Schoknecht, C. & Carter, R. 1987 Masked priming with graphemically related forms: repetition or partial activation? *Q. J. Exp. Psychol. A* **39**, 211–251.

Friston, K. J., Buechel, C., Fink, G. R., Morris, J., Rolls, E. & Dolan, R. J. 1997 Psychophysiological and modulatory interactions in neuroimaging. *Neuroimage* **6**, 218–229. (doi:10.1006/nimg.1997.0291)

Frost, R., Forster, K. I. & Deutsch, A. 1997 What can we learn from the morphology of Hebrew? A masked-priming investigation of morphological representation. *J. Exp. Psychol. Learn. Mem. Cogn.* **23**, 829–856. (doi:10.1037/0278-7393.23.4.829)

Ghazanfar, A. A. & Miller, C. T. 2006 Language evolution: loquacious monkey brains. *Curr. Biol.* **16**, R879–R881. (doi:10.1016/j.cub.2006.09.026)

Gil-da-costa, R., Martin, A., Lopez, M. A., Munoz, M., Fritz, J. B. & Braun, A. R. 2006 Species-specific calls activate homologs of Broca's and Wernicke's areas in the macaque. *Nat. Neurosci.* **9**, 1064–1070. (doi:10.1038/nn1741)

Gould, S. J. & Vrba, E. S. 1982 Exaptation: a missing term in the science of form. *Paleobiology* **8**, 4–15.

Grodzinsky, Y. 2000 The neurology of syntax: language use without Broca's area. *Behav. Brain Sci.* **23**, 1–21. (doi:10.1017/S0140525X00002399)

Hauser, M. D., Chomsky, N. & Fitch, W. T. 2002 The faculty of language: what is it, who has it, and how did it evolve. *Science* **298**, 1569–1579. (doi:10.1126/science.298.5598.1569)

Hickok, G. & Poeppel, D. 2000 Towards a functional neuroanatomy of speech perception. *Trends Cogn. Sci.* **4**, 131–138. (doi:10.1016/S1364-6613(00)01463-7)

Joanisse, M. F. & Seidenberg, M. S. 1999 Impairments in verb morphology after brain injury. *Proc. Natl Acad. Sci. USA* **96**, 7592–7597. (doi:10.1073/pnas.96.13.7592)

Kaas, J. H. & Hackett, T. A. 1999 'What' and 'where' processing in auditory cortex. *Nat. Neurosci.* **2**, 1045–1047. (doi:10.1038/15967)

Longtin, C.-M. & Meunier, F. 2005 Morphological decomposition in early visual word processing. *J. Mem. Lang.* **53**, 26–41. (doi:10.1016/j.jml.2005.02.008)

Longtin, C.-M., Segui, J. & Hallé, P. A. 2003 Morphological priming without morphological relation-ship. *Lang. Cogn. Process.* **18**, 313–334. (doi:10.1080/01690960244000036)

Longworth, C. E., Marslen-Wilson, W. D., Randall, B. & Tyler, L. K. 2005 Getting to the meaning of the regular past tense: evidence from neuropsychology. *J. Cogn. Neurosci.* **17**, 1087–1097. (doi:10.1162/0898929054475109)

Lück, M., Hahne, A. & Clahsen, H. 2006 Brain potentials to morphologically complex words during listening. *Brain Res.* **1077**, 144–152. (doi:10.1016/j.brainres.2006.01.030)

Marslen-Wilson, W. D. 2007. Morphological processes in language comprehension. In *Handbook of psycholinguistics* (ed. G. Gaskell). Oxford, UK: Oxford University Press.

Marslen-Wilson, W. D. & Tyler, L. K. 1997 Dissociating types of mental computation. *Nature* **387**, 592–594. (doi:10.1038/42456)

Marslen-Wilson, W. D., Bozic, M. & Randall, B. In press. Early decomposition in visual word recogni-tion: dissociating morphology, form, and meaning. *Lang. Cogn. Process.*

McCandliss, B. D., Cohen, L. & Dehaene, S. 2003 The visual word form area: expertise for reading in the fusiform gyrus. *Trends Cogn. Sci.* **7**, 2003. (doi:10.1016/S1364-6613(03)00134-7)

McClelland, J. & Patterson, K. 2002 Rules or connections in past-tense inflections: what does the evidence rule out? *Trends Cogn. Sci.* **6**, 465–472. (doi:10.1016/S1364-6613(02)01993-9)

McKinnnon, R., Allen, M. & Osterhout, L. 2003 Morphological decomposition involving non-productive morphemes: ERP evidence. *Neuroreport* **14**, 883–886. (doi:10.1097/00001756-20030 5060-00022)

Mohr, B., Pulvermüller, F. & Zaidel, E. 1994 Lexical decision after left, right and bilateral presentation of content words, function words, and non-words: evidence for interhemispheric interaction. *Neuropsychologia* **32**, 105–124. (doi:10.1016/0028-3932(94)90073-6)

Morris, R., Pandya, D. N. & Petrides, M. 1999 Fiber system linking the mid-dorsolateral frontal cortex with the retrosplenial/presubicular region in the rhesus monkey. *J. Comp. Neurol.* **407**, 183–192. (doi:10.1002/(SICI)1096-9861 (19990503)407:2<183::AID-CNE3>3.0.CO;2-N)

Münte, T. F., Say, T., Schiltz, K., Clahsen, H. & Kutas, M. 1999 Decomposition of morphologically complex words in English: evidence from event-related brain potentials. *Cogn. Brain Res.* **7**, 241–253.

Noesselt, T., Shah, N. & Jancke, L. 2003 Top-down and bottom-up modulation of language related areas—an fMRI study. *BMC Neurosci.* **4**, 13. (doi:10.1186/1471-2202-4-13)

Pandya, D. N., Hoesen, G. W. & Mesulam, M.-M. 1981 Efferent connections of the cingulate gyrus in the rhesus monkey. *Exp. Brain Res.* **42**, 319–330. (doi:10.1007/ BF00237497)

Parker, G. J. M., Luzzi, S., Alexander, D. C., Wheeler-Kingshott, C. A. M., Ciccarelli, O. & Lambon Ralph, M. A. 2005 Lateralization of ventral and dorsal auditory-language pathways in the human brain. *Neuroimage* **24**, 656–666. (doi:10.1016/j.neuroimage.2004.08.047)

Pastizzo, M. J. & Feldman, L. B. 2002 Discrepancies between orthographic and unrelated baselines in masked priming undermine a decompositional account of morphological facilitation. *J. Exp. Psychol. Learn. Mem. Cogn.* **28**, 244–249. (doi:10.1037/0278-7393.28.1.244)

Petkov, C. L., Kayser, C., Augath, M. & Logothetis, N. K. 2006 Functional imaging reveals numerous fields in the monkey auditory cortex. *PLoS Biol.* **4**, e215. (doi:10.1371/journal.pbio.0040215)

Petrides, M. & Pandya, D. N. 1988 Association fiber pathways to the frontal cortex from the superior temporal region in the rhesus monkey. *J. Comp. Neurol.* **273**, 52–66. (doi:10.1002/cne.902730106)

Petrides, M. & Pandya, D. N. 1994 Comparative architectonic analysis of human and macaque frontal cortex. In *Handbook of neuropsychology*, vol. 9 (eds F. Boller & J. Grafman), pp. 17–58. Amsterdam, The Netherlands: Elsevier Science.

Pinker, S. 1999 *Words and rules: the ingredients of language*. New York, NY: Harper Collins.

Poremba, A., Malloy, M., Saunders, R. C., Carson, R. E., Hescovitch, P. & Mishkin, M. 2004 Species-specific calls evoke asymmetric activity in the monkey's temporal poles. *Nature* **427**, 448–551. (doi:10.1038/nature02268)

Price, C. J. 2000 The anatomy of language: contributions from functional neuroimaging. *J. Anat.* **197**, 335–359. (doi:10.1046/j.1469-7580.2000.19730335.x)

Pulvermüller, F. & Mohr, B. 1996 The concept of transcortical cell assemblies: a key to the understanding of cortical localisation and interhemispheric interaction. *Neurosci. Biobehav. Rev.* **20**, 557–566. (doi:10.1016/0149-7634(95)00068-2)

Pulvermüller, F., Shtyrov, Y., Ilmoniemi, R. & Marslen-Wilson, W. D. 2006 Tracking speech comprehension in space and time. *Neuroimage* **31**, 1297–1305. (doi:10.1016/j.neuroimage.2006.01.030)

Rastle, K., Davis, M. H., Marslen-Wilson, W. D. & Tyler, L. K. 2000 Morphological and semantic effects in visual word recognition: a time-course study. *Lang. Cogn. Process.* **15**, 507–537. (doi:10.1080/01690960050119689)

Rastle, K., Davis, M. H. & New, B. 2005 The broth in my brother's brothel: morphoorthographic segmentation in visual word recognition. *Psychon. Bull. Rev.* **11**, 1090–1098.

Rauschecker, J. P. & Tian, B. 2000 Mechanisms and streams for processing of 'what' and 'where' in auditory cortex. *Proc. Natl Acad. Sci. USA* **97**, 11 800–11 806. (doi:10.1073/pnas.97.22.11800)

Rodd, J., Davis, M. & Johnsrude, I. 2005 The neural mechanisms of speech comprehension: fMRI studies of semantic ambiguity. *Cereb. Cortex* **15**, 1261–1269. (doi:10.1093/cercor/bhi009)

Rodriguez-Fornells, A., Clahsen, H., Lleo, C., Zaake, W. & Münte, T. F. 2001 Event related brain responses to morphological violations in Catalan. *Cogn. Brain Res.* **11**, 47–58. (doi:10.1016/ S0926-6410(00)00063-X)

Romanski, L. M., Tian, B., Fritz, J., Mishkin, M., Goldman-Rakic, P. & Rauschecker, J. P. 1999 Dual streams of auditory afferents target multiple domains in the primate prefrontal cortex. *Nature* **2**, 1131–1136.

Rumelhart, D. E. & McClelland, J. L. 1986 On learning the past tenses of English verbs. In *Parallel distributed processing: explorations in the microstructure of cognition*, vol. 2 (eds D. E. Rumelhart, J. L. McClelland & P. R. Group). Cambridge, MA: MIT Press.

Scott, S. K. & Johnsrude, I. S. 2003 The neuroanatomical and functional organization of speech perception. *Trends Neurosci.* **26**, 100–107. (doi:10.1016/S0166-2236(02)00037-1)

Scott, S. K., Blank, C. C., Rosen, S. & Wise, R. J. S. 2000 Identification of a pathway for intelligible speech in the left temporal lobe. *Brain* **123**, 2400–2406. (doi:10.1093/brain/123.12.2400)

Shallice, T. & Saffran, E. 1986 Lexical processing in the absence of explicit word identification: evidence from a letter-by-letter reader. *Cogn. Neuropsychol.* **3**, 429–458.

Shtyrov, Y. & Pulvermuller, F. 2002 Memory traces for inflectional affixes as shown by the mismatch negativity. *Eur. J. Neurosci.* **15**, 1085–1091. (doi:10.1046/j.1460-9568.2002.01941.x)

Shtyrov, Y., Pihko, E. & Pulvermuller, F. 2005 Determinants of dominance: is language laterality determined by physical or linguistic features of speech? *Neuroimage* **27**, 37–47. (doi:10.1016/j.neuroimage.2005.02.003)

Simmons, W. K. & Barsalou, L. W. 2003 The similarity-in-topography principle: reconciling theories of conceptual deficits. *Cogn. Neuropsychol.* **20**, 451–486. (doi:10.1080/02643290342000032)

Stamatakis, E. A., Marslen-Wilson, W. D., Tyler, L. K. & Fletcher, P. C. 2005 Cingulate control of fronto-temporal integration reflects linguistic demands: a three way interaction in functional connectivity. *Neuroimage* **15**, 115–121. (doi:10.1016/j.neuroimage.2005.06.012)

Taft, M. & Forster, K. I. 1975 Lexical storage and retrieval of prefixed words. *J. Verbal Learn. Verbal Behav.* **15**, 638–647. (doi:10.1016/S0022-5371(75)80051-X)

Tyler, L. K. & Marslen-Wilson, W. D. 2007. Fronto-temporal brain systems supporting spoken language comprehension. *Phil. Trans. R. Soc. B.* (doi: 10.1098/rstb.2007.2158)

Tyler, L. K. & Moss, H. E. 1998 Going, going, gone …? Implicit and explicit tests of conceptual knowledge in a longitudinal study of semantic dementia. *Neuropsychologia* **36**, 1313–1323. (doi:10.1016/S0028-3932(98)00029-3)

Tyler, L. K., Randall, B. & Marslen-Wilson, W. D. 2002a Phonology and neuropsychology of the English past tense. *Neuropsychologia* **40**, 1154–1166. (doi:10.1016/S0028-3932(01)00232-9)

Tyler, L. K., de Mornay Davies, P., Anokhina, R., Longworth, C., Randall, B. & Marslen Wilson, W. D. 2002b Dissociations in processing past tense morphology: neuropathology and behavioural studies. *J. Cogn. Neurosci.* **14**, 79–95. (doi:10.1162/089892902317205348)

Tyler, L. K., Stamatakis, E. A., Bright, P., Acres, K., Abdallah, S., Rodd, J. M. & Moss, H. E. 2004 Processing objects at different levels of specificity. *J. Cogn. Neurosci.* **16**, 351–362. (doi:10.1162/089892904322926692)

Tyler, L. K., Marslen-Wilson, W. D. & Stamatakis, E. A. 2005a Differentiating lexical form, meaning and structure in the neural language system. *Proc. Natl Acad. Sci. USA* **102**, 8375–8380. (doi:10.1073/pnas.0408213102)

Tyler, L. K., Stamatakis, E. A., Post, B., Randall, B. & Marslen-Wilson, W. D. 2005b Temporal and frontal systems in speech comprehension: an fMRI study of past tense processing. *Neuropsychologia* **43**, 1963–1974. (doi:10.1016/j.neuropsychologia.2005.03.008)

Tyler, L. K., Marslen-Wilson, W. D. & Stamatakis, E. A. 2005c Dissociating neuro cognitive component processes: voxel-based correlational methodology. *Neuropsychologia* **43**, 771–778. (doi:10.1016/j.neuropsychologia.2004.07.020)

Ullman, M. T. 2004 Contributions of memory circuits to language: the declarative/procedural model. *Cognition* **92**, 231–270. (doi:10.1016/j.cognition.2003.10.008)

Ullman, M. T. 2007. The biocognition of the mental lexicon. In *Handbook of psycholinguistics* (ed. G. Gaskell). Oxford, UK: Oxford University Press.

Ungerleider, L. G. & Mishkin, M. 1982 Two cortical visual systems. In *Analysis of visual behavior* (eds D. J. Ingle, M. A. Goodale & R. J. W. Mansfield). Cambridge, MA: The MIT Press.

Wise, R., Scott, S., Blank, C., Mummery, C., Murphy, K. & Warburton, E. 2001 Separate neural systems within "Wernicke's area". *Brain* **124**, 83–95. (doi:10.1093/brain/124.1.83)

8

Modulation of visual processing by attention and emotion: windows on causal interactions between human brain regions

Patrik Vuilleumier* and Jon Driver

Visual processing is not determined solely by retinal inputs. Attentional modulation can arise when the internal attentional state (current task) of the observer alters visual processing of the same stimuli. This can influence visual cortex, boosting neural responses to an attended stimulus. Emotional modulation can also arise, when affective properties (emotional significance) of stimuli, rather than their strictly visual properties, influence processing. This too can boost responses in visual cortex, as for fear-associated stimuli. Both attentional and emotional modulation of visual processing may reflect distant influences upon visual cortex, exerted by brain structures outside the visual system *per se*. Hence, these modulations may provide windows onto causal interactions between distant but interconnected brain regions. We review recent evidence, noting both similarities and differences between attentional and emotional modulation. Both can affect visual cortex, but can reflect influences from different regions, such as fronto-parietal circuits versus the amygdala. Recent work on this has developed new approaches for studying causal influences between human brain regions that may be useful in other cognitive domains. The new methods include application of functional magnetic resonance imaging (fMRI) and electroencephalography (EEG) measures in brain-damaged patients to study distant functional impacts of their focal lesions, and use of transcranial magnetic stimulation concurrently with fMRI or EEG in the normal brain. Cognitive neuroscience is now moving beyond considering the putative functions of particular brain regions, as if each operated in isolation, to consider, instead, how distinct brain regions (such as visual cortex, parietal or frontal regions, or amygdala) may mutually influence each other in a causal manner.

Keywords: attention; emotion; vision; transcranial magnetic stimulation; functional magnetic resonance imaging; electroencephalography

8.1. Introduction

Prior to the recent advent of functional neuroimaging, the traditional approach for attributing particular cognitive functions to particular structures in the human brain (often referred to as 'functional localization'), was to relate specific types of brain damage (originally studied post-mortem but now also with high-resolution structural MRI, e.g. Rorden & Karnath 2004) to patterns of selective cognitive deficit (Damasio & Damasio 1989; Farah 1990; Grüsser & Landis 1991; Shallice 1988). Putative functions were thereby tentatively assigned to particular brain regions, as for Broca's and Wernicke's celebrated ascription of speech production or speech reception to distinct regions of left frontal or temporal cortex. Analogously, early neu-

* Author for correspondence(patrik.vuilleumier@medecine.unige.ch).

roimaging studies with positron emission tomography (PET) and then functional magnetic resonance imaging (fMRI) also sought to assign particular functions to particular brain areas (Petersen *et al.* 1988; Kanwisher *et al.* 1997; Epstein *et al.* 1999). Some commentators critiqued such work for merely confirming or refining what was already known from neuropsychology, now via neuroimaging. But when such confirmation or refinement did arise (which was not always the case!), this provided a useful step in validating the new methods. Moreover, we think that neuroimaging has now moved well beyond mere confirmation or refinement of neuropsychology, with the development of advanced neuroimaging tools. These include use of multiple converging tests to probe operations and representations for specific brain areas (e.g. To n g *et al.* 2000); use of well-defined cognitive methods for studying internal representations, as for those derived from the psychological repetition priming literature (Grill-Spector & Malach 2001; Naccache & Dehaene 2001; Vuilleumier *et al.* 2002*b*); the advent of higher resolution fMRI (Grill-Spector *et al.* 2006); and development of sophisticated multivariate statistical analyses for assessing patterns of activity within particular brain areas (Norman *et al.* 2006; see also Rees 2007 and this volume).

Another traditional perspective in neuropsychology and behavioural neurology, beyond strict 'functional localization', also finds an echo in recent functional neuroimaging work. Clinicians have often argued on the basis of lesion evidence from brain-damaged patients that complex cognitive functions, such as memory, attention or language, are not each reliant on any single brain area but instead reflect a 'distributed network' of contributing areas (e.g. Mesulam 1990) and cognitive components (e.g. Shallice 1988). Cognitive neuropsychology led to numerous multi-component models of particular domains in cognition (e.g. Bruce & Young 1986; Hinton & Shallice 1991). Functional neuroimaging has contributed further to the identification and refinement of cognitive networks. For instance, recent fMRI studies have identified brain networks associated with different aspects of attention, including not only superior and inferior circuits in fronto-parietal cortex (Corbetta & Shulman 2002), but also circuits in medial regions of the frontal and parietal lobes (Raichle *et al.* 2001). As another example, recent fMRI work (along with neuropsychological patient studies) has emphasized not only that some regions of ventral visual cortex may be particularly involved in processing faces (e.g. the so-called fusiform face area (FFA); Kanwisher *et al.* 1997), but also that an extensive ensemble of further areas contribute to face processing also (e.g. superior temporal sulcus, amygdala, retrosplenial cortex and the putative occipital face area; Haxby *et al.* 2000; Vuilleumier & Pourtois 2007). Results from human neuroimaging have thus enriched traditional neuropsychological approaches from both 'functional localization' and 'distributed network' perspectives.

In this article we emphasize that, in combination with other methods, human functional neuroimaging is now embarking on a new critical next step. Rather than merely characterizing the possible functions of particular brain areas, or identifying a distributed network associated with a particular domain of cognition, many current studies now seek to identify how remote but interconnected regions within a particular network may influence each other causally. This combines (and thus goes beyond) both the functional localization perspective *and* the distributed network perspective, by seeking to determine the functional contributions of a given area to activity taking place in other interconnected regions of the network. Such issues are sometimes referred to as concerning 'functional integration' (e.g. Friston 1998, 2002) rather than functional localization *per se*.

Some pioneering work has already used various forms of 'effective connectivity' analyses of imaging data (from PET or fMRI, but also electroencephalography, EEG or magnetoencephalogram, MEG) to illustrate the importance of dynamic interactions between brain areas (Friston *et al.* 2003; Penny *et al.* 2004; Valdes-Sosa *et al.* 2005), and their possible modulation by state- or context-dependent influences (Coull *et al.* 1999; Buchel & Friston 2000). These approaches typically involve sophisticated mathematical models of neuroimaging data that inevitably must rely on various assumptions when searching for putatively causal influences between brain areas. The time has now come to address causal interactions between human brain regions more directly also, by combining neuroimaging measures (e.g. fMRI, EEG, MEG) with 'interventional' manipulations, such as transcranial magnetic stimulation (TMS), pharmacology, or focal lesions in neurological patients. In addition, other causal interventions are possible in animal studies (e.g. transient inactivation of a given brain area by cooling, or highly local drug application, selective deafferentation by tractotomy, genetic manipulation, viral transfection, etc.).

Here, we will illustrate new approaches in human studies that are non-invasive, yet still introduce a causal dimension. One approach applies neuroimaging in patients with focal brain lesions to uncover the functional effect of damage to one particular area upon neural activity in other surviving areas. Pharmacological fMRI is also a growing area of research for assessing causal effects of interventions in human studies (e.g. Bentley *et al.* 2003; Wise & Tracey 2006). Finally, it is now possible to target specific human brain regions online with TMS, actually during fMRI or PET scanning (or EEG), while assessing the causal impact on activity in remote but interconnected regions (e.g. Bestmann *et al.* 2005, 2006; Paus 2005; Ruff *et al.* 2006).

8.2 Attentional and emotional modulation of visual processing: paradigm cases of causal interplay between different brain regions?

There are many aspects of human cognition (perhaps all) for which causal influences between remote brain areas may apply. Here, we illustrate the issue of causal interplay between different brain regions for two specific situations: attentional and emotional modulation of visual processing. In both domains, remote influences between brain regions are implicated in influencing perceptual processing and awareness. In both cases, our understanding of such network interactions has improved through the combination of functional neuroimaging with more interventional techniques. We argue that both attentional and emotional effects on visual perception concern influences upon visual cortex from brain regions beyond visual cortex. In this sense, the effects are analogous. But the critical brain regions and pathways producing causal influences upon visual cortex may be different for the two cases, in accord with the different psychological factors involved. Thus, we will present evidence that the amygdala (among other regions) contributes to emotional modulation of visual processing; while the frontal eye fields (FEF), among other regions, including some parietal areas, contribute to attentional modulation. While there are many previous suggestions of such possible influences from the amygdala or FEF in the literature, here we will concentrate on how true influences of one region upon others might be directly demonstrated for the human brain.

What we mean by 'modulation of visual processing' can be illustrated not only by human neuroimaging, as below, but also by direct single-cell recording studies in awake behaving monkeys. Figure 8.1*a* shows an example for attentional modulation of visual responses (neural firing rates) in inferior temporal visual cortex (adapted from Chelazzi *et al.* 1998). Similarly, figure 8.1*b* shows an example of emotional modulation of visual processing, also from neurons in temporal visual cortex (adapted from Sugase *et al.* 1999). In the attentional case (Figure 8.1*a*), firing of neurons with particular visual preferences is enhanced and prolonged for a given display when the preferred stimulus within it is attended as task-relevant (corresponding to the current item to be searched for by the animal), relative to when that preferred stimulus is task-irrelevant (and a non-preferred stimulus is attended, instead, for the same visual display). In the emotional case (Figure 8.1*b*), the response to a stimulus that matches the neuron's visual preference (here a preference for face images) is enhanced and prolonged when the seen face conveys an emotional rather than neutral expression. Note that in both cases (Figure 8.1*a,b*), the initial rise in firing rate seems comparable regardless of attentional

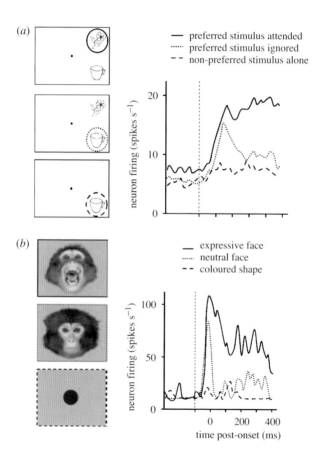

Fig. 8.1 Single-cell recordings in the monkey illustrate two different types of modulation of visual responses. (*a*) Illustration of attentional effects for neurons in inferior temporal visual cortex (adapted from Chelazzi *et al.* 1998). When the 'preferred' stimulus is presented, responses are enhanced and prolonged if attention is directed to the stimulus as task-relevant (red), but weaker and more transient if attention is directed to another stimulus instead, with the preferred stimulus now being task-irrelevant (green). In this case, later components of the response can then be similar to when the preferred stimulus is absent (blue). (*b*) Illustration of emotional effects on face-selective neurons in superior temporal sulcus (adapted from Sugase *et al.* 1999). The pattern and time-course of emotional effects appear rather analogous to those of attention, with enhanced and prolonged responses when the seen face has an emotional expression (red), but weaker with a more transient peak when the seen face is neutral (green).

or emotional status, with the impact of the latter factors acting to boost and sustain neuronal activity from approximately 100 ms into the neural response.

Both of these effects have tentatively been attributed to 'top-down' or 'feedback' influences from other areas (specifically, from fronto-parietal regions in the case of attentional modulation, and from limbic regions such as the amygdala for emotional effects). However, no direct evidence for this could be derived from studies (such as Chelazzi *et al.* 1998; or Sugase *et al.* 1999) that recorded only from the affected visual region. Moreover, it is not inconceivable that both examples could, in principle, be considered as reflecting the same general 'attentional' phenomenon. For instance, one might argue that an emotional face becomes more attended than a neutral face, possibly even due to recruitment of fronto-parietal attention circuits. Hence, decisive experiments are required to determine the causal origins of such visual modulations.

Below we turn to human neuroimaging and neuropsychological studies of attentional or emotional effects on visual processing. These effects in humans have several analogies to the monkey single-cell phenomena illustrated in figure 8.1. While providing some overview of the literature, we focus particularly on studies that may show direct causal influences of remote brain areas upon visual cortex, and that introduce new methods for doing so.

8.3 Selective attention and modulation of sensory processing

Findings from both human and animal neuroscience provide abundant evidence that top-down modulations of sensory processing play a key role in selective attention and perceptual awareness (Driver *et al.* 2003; Kanwisher & Wojciulik 2000, for reviews). Across a wide range of paradigms it has been shown that, while holding stimulus displays constant, directing attention towards or away from a particular stimulus (by making it task-relevant or irrelevant) will affect sensory neural processing for that stimulus. This is observed when recording individual neurons and/or local field potentials in awake behaving monkeys (e.g. Gottlieb 2002), and for fMRI, EEG or MEG measures in humans (e.g. Kastner & Ungerleider 2000). Moreover, these attentional modulations of sensory processing can have strong corresponding effects on perceptual judgements and awareness (e.g. Cameron *et al.* 2002). Typically, sensory responses or activations are enhanced for a given stimulus when attended, relative to the same stimulus when ignored. Such effects have now been found with human fMRI for all areas of retinotopic visual cortex (Hopfinger *et al.* 2000; Kastner & Ungerleider 2000), including V1 (Ghandi *et al.* 1999), and even for human lateral geniculate nucleus (O'Connor *et al.* 2002). Attentional modulations have also been found for feature-selective responses in visual areas (e.g. when attending to colour versus motion, Corbetta *et al.* 1990; Chawla *et al.* 1999) and for particular directions of motion (Saenz *et al.* 2002), together with differential responses to particular stimulus categories, such as visual words versus objects (Rees *et al.* 1999) or faces versus houses in the FFA and parahippocampal place area (PPA), respectively (Wojciulik *et al.* 1998; O'Craven *et al.* 1999). Figure 8.2 illustrates that the FFA shows a stronger response to displays including face stimuli when those faces are attended (for a perceptual comparison task) rather than ignored (with the comparison task now performed on concurrent house stimuli instead), even though retinal stimulation remains the same in both conditions.

Likewise, in EEG studies, sensory components such as P1 and N1 potentials are typically found to exhibit a greater amplitude for attended relative to unattended stimuli (e.g. Heinze *et al.* 1994; Martinez *et al.* 2001). Taken together, all these data indicate that selective attention

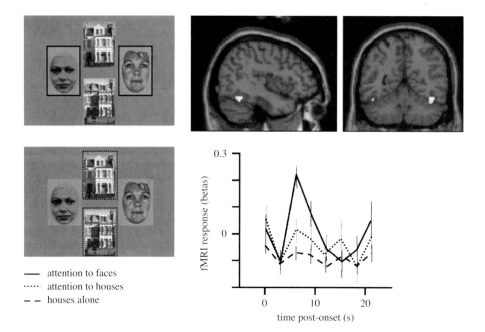

— attention to faces
····· attention to houses
– – houses alone

Fig. 8.2 Example of fMRI results showing modulation of fusiform cortex responses to faces by spatial attention in the human brain (adapted from Vuilleumier *et al.* 2001*a*). Subjects saw displays that always contained a pair of faces (aligned either vertically or horizontally), together with a pair of houses, but concentrated on one pair only to perform a picture-matching task. The lateral face-selective fusiform area (FFA) was more strongly activated when faces appeared at the task-relevant location (red), while responses were strongly reduced when faces were task-irrelevant (green), although the visual displays were physically comparable in both conditions (and equated by counterbalancing). In comparison, FFA was not responsive to pictures of houses (blue), obtained in a separate localizer fMRI scan. Units for fMRI activation (betas) correspond to parameters estimates for event-related changes in BOLD signal.

acts on sensory processing by enhancing neural responses to task-relevant stimuli, with corresponding enhancements of perceptual awareness, whereas unattended information evokes a reduced response or in some extreme cases no differential response (e.g. Rees *et al.* 1999).

8.4 Possible sources of attentional modulation

As described above, there are now many clear demonstrations that top-down effects of attention (i.e. of task-relevance) on visual processing can apply at many 'sites' within the visual system, ranging from early retinotopic areas through to higher level ventral and dorsal regions. This has led to the new question of which neural system(s) may impose such modulations upon visual pathways, providing the causal 'sources' for attentional modulation. A common suggestion is that a broad network of frontal–parietal regions contributes to this, collectively instantiating attentional control in 'attentional network(s)' (Mesulam 1999; Driver & Frackowiak 2001; Kastner & Ungerleider 2001; Corbetta & Shulman 2002) that modulate sensory processing in relation to current task demands, by providing top-down signals or biases that influence visual cortex.

Several different types of evidence implicate frontal– parietal areas in such attentional control of sensory processing. Here, we consider how directly causal such evidence may be, noting that in many cases the current evidence is often more correlational than strictly causal or interventionist. Numerous recent neuroimaging studies have highlighted the role of a putative large-scale 'attention network' (or networks), involving several areas in parietal and frontal cortex (figure 8.3), often with some right-hemisphere predominance, typically activated when comparing conditions that require attention shifting to those that do not (e.g. Corbetta *et al.* 2000; Hopfinger *et al.* 2000), or conditions requiring active judgements of sensory inputs versus those posing less attentional demand with the same stimulation (e.g. Pinsk *et al.* 2004; Schwartz *et al.* 2005). Strikingly, a common network is often found across rather different tasks, whenever visual processing requires more selective attention (figure 8.3*a*, *b*).

Usually many different areas are activated by such comparisons, but some subsets might be associated with distinct roles. Recent neuroimaging work on attentional control has sought to make increasingly subtle comparisons, leading to various suggestions of distinct subsystems within attentional control. For instance, there may be more 'anterior' and 'posterior' attention systems (Posner & Dehaene 1994), possibly with more 'executive' functions being associated with the former (see also Burgess *et al.* 2007; Stuss & Alexander 2007). More 'dorsal' and 'ventral' attention networks have also been suggested (Corbetta& Shulman 2002), possibly with the former involved in directing attention according to the current task set, and the latter involved in interrupting this or serving as a 'circuit-breaker' when required. Other putative distinctions between spatial and non-spatial attention (Husain & Rorden 2003), between selective attention versus alerting/arousal (Robertson 1999), or between supramodal versus modal-

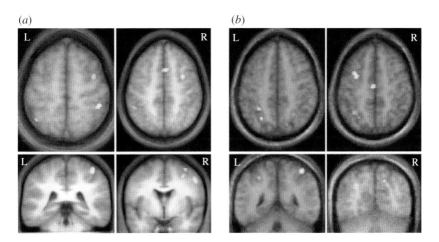

Fig. 8.3 Examples showing activation of attentional-control networks within frontal and parietal cortex in two different visual tasks. (*a*) Blood oxygen level-dependent (BOLD) fMRI activity is increased in bilateral intraparietal sulcus (IPS), middle frontal gyrus (possibly corresponding to the frontal eye field, FEF) and anterior cingulate cortex (ACC), when subjects have to focus their attention at fixation for a difficult visual task (rapid sequential visual presentation of targets among a stream of distractors, with high attention load), relative to an easy task at fixation with the same stimuli (low attentional load). Adapted from Schwartz *et al.* (2005). (*b*) A similar and overlapping network is activated during a visual search task, with increased activation when subjects have to detect a novel target (with different colour and different location) relative to a repeated target (with same colour but different location). Adapted from Kristjansson *et al.* (2006).

ity-specific attention (Macaluso & Driver 2001) have been made for various frontal and parietal circuits.

However, a limitation of such neuroimaging findings arises here. When considered as a single method, in isolation from other approaches, neuroimaging is essentially a correlative approach. This can make it hard to assess whether certain activations are essential for performing a particular cognitive function, or merely associated with it, perhaps epiphenomenally. Moreover, merely demonstrating activation of a putative attention network across frontal and parietal cortex, in a situation where attentional modulation of visual cortex also arises (e.g. Kastner & Ungerleider 2000), cannot in itself establish that the observed modulation of visual cortex was causally imposed by particular regions within the fronto-parietal network. Some work using effective connectivity analyses of fMRI data has provided initial evidence in support of dynamic interactions between areas (Buchel & Friston 2000; Friston *et al*. 2003). But such approaches rely on several assumptions or simplifications in their mathematical models and as yet may fall short of demonstrating strict causality. Below we consider how such causal issues might be addressed more directly.

8.5 Implication of frontal and parietal cortex in attentional control

Some longstanding evidence that frontal and parietal regions might be involved in attentional effects upon visual perception and visual awareness arises from brain-damaged patients. Many neurological and neuropsychological reports (Heilman *et al*. 1970; Heilman & Valenstein 1979; Mesulam 1981, 1999; Damasio *et al*. 1987) concern patients with lesions in (often large) frontal and/or parietal regions (possibly also involving superior temporal cortex, Karnath *et al*. 2001). These patients can manifest symptoms and deficits that appear to reflect deficits in attention and awareness for incoming stimuli. For instance, in the intriguing 'spatial neglect' syndrome (Driver & Vuilleumier 2001; Karnath *et al*. 2003; Vallar *et al*. 2003; Driver *et al*. 2004), patients with extensive unilateral lesions in perisylvian regions (usually on the right side) can appear oblivious to information towards the contralesional side of space, even when they have no primary sensory or motor deficit for that side (e.g. still have intact visual fields). Areas commonly damaged in neglect patients (Figure 8.4) often overlap with those activated in fMRI studies of attentional control in healthy subjects, although some disputes continue about how and why the typical lesion and activation sites may relate. Lesions in some parts of this network may lead to functional disruptions in surviving areas elsewhere in the network (Corbetta & Shulman 2002; Corbetta *et al*. 2005).

Contralesional deficits in patients with spatial neglect are often exacerbated by the presence of concurrent competing stimuli on the ipsilesional side, as observed for the phenomenon of perceptual 'extinction' during double simultaneous stimulation. Patients may correctly perceive a stimulus presented alone in their left visual field, but fail to detect the same stimulus when paired with another simultaneous event in the right visual field (Bender & Teuber 1946; Heilman *et al*. 1970). Such deficits have long been considered to involve pathological biases and/or limited capacities in attention, leading to a contralesional stimulus escaping awareness only when it must compete for attentional resources with an ipsilesional event (Heilman & Valenstein 1979; Mesulam 1981; Driver & Vuilleumier 2001; Geeraerts *et al*. 2005). Space constraints preclude a comprehensive review of neglect or extinction here (Driver & Vuilleumier 2001), but we can briefly emphasize that in manifesting pathological losses in perceptual awareness, such patients illustrate that regions well beyond visual cortex (i.e. parietal, frontal

(a)   (b)

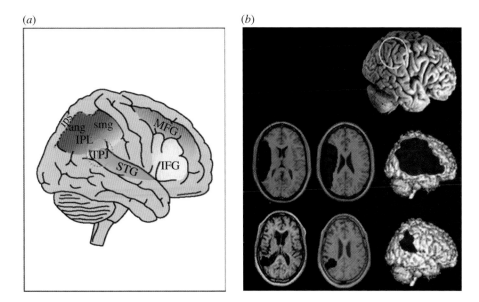

Fig. 8.4 Common lesion sites in patients with unilateral spatial neglect. (a) Damage may involve different regions in both parietal and frontal lobes, most often the inferior parietal lobule (IPL) and temporo-parietal junction (TPJ), but also the middle frontal gyrus (MFG) and inferior frontal gyrus (IFG) and possibly the superior temporal gyrus (STG). These regions overlap with many of those areas associated with attentional control by fMRI studies in normals (cf. Figure 8.3). (b) Lesions may have very different extents in different neglect patients, as shown here for two example cases (adapted from Driver & Vuilleumier 2001), often involving more than just one brain area within the attentional network.

and possibly superior temporal areas, all remote from posterior and ventral visual areas) can make some critical contributions to visual attention and awareness, leading to pathological losses when damaged.

Such lesions beyond the conventional visual system may have functional effects upon vision precisely because they disrupt top-down or recursive causal influences from those regions upon visual cortex (Driver & Vuilleumier 2001; Driver *et al.* (2001); Kastner & Ungerleider 2001; Corbetta *et al.* 2005). But alternative possibilities have not always been ruled out. For instance, the mere observation that parietal and/or frontal lesions can lead to pathological losses in visual awareness might, on its own, be consistent with disruption to purely feedforward processes, which normally operate when occipital areas project to higher regions, but inevitably fail at subsequent processing stages when higher regions are lesioned. However, neural processing is increasingly regarded as highly recursive, rather than involving only one-way traffic (Bullier *et al.* 2001; Pascual-Leone & Walsh 2001). Such issues can be addressed by assessing directly whether focal lesions (or transient disruption) of 'higher-level' regions (e.g. in parietal or frontal cortex) lead causally to functional changes in the visual responses of 'lower' intact occipital regions, and whether this may relate to the pathological losses in visual awareness in patients.

There have been relatively few such studies to date for neglect and extinction patients. It is only fairly recently that non-invasive measures of neural activity, such as EEG, SPECT or fMRI, have been applied to study visual responses in patients with such deficits after lesions centred on right inferior parietal cortex (though for some pioneering attempts with EEG, see Lhermitte *et al.* 1985; Spinelli *et al.* 1994; Viggiano *et al.* 1995). Several fMRI studies have now demonstrated, via event-related responses to pictures of faces and/or houses, that some residual visual activations can still be found for extinguished stimuli in the contralesional (left) visual field of these patients. Such activations were found not only in right striate and extrastriate cortex (Figure 8.5), but also in some category-selective regions, such as the FFA (Rees *et al.* 2000, 2002; Vuilleumier *et al.* 2001*b*, 2002*a*). These activations typically became significantly greater and extended into higher-order areas, when the same stimuli were consciously seen by the patients rather than extinguished, as determined by their perceptual report (Vuilleumier *et al.* 2001*b*; Rees *et al.* 2002). The greater activations in visual cortex were also associated with concomitant activations of (and functional coupling with) parietal and frontal regions in the intact left hemisphere (Vuilleumier *et al.* 2001*b*). Similarly, event-related potential (ERP) recordings in such patients have also revealed some residual but reduced evoked potentials from visual cortex for visual stimuli extinguished due to parietal lesions (Marzi *et al.* 2000; Driver *et al.* 2001; Vuilleumier *et al.* 2001*b*), as opposed to when consciously seen by the same patients. Thus, while these studies have revealed unconscious responses to neglected or extinguished stimuli in parietal patients, they have also demonstrated

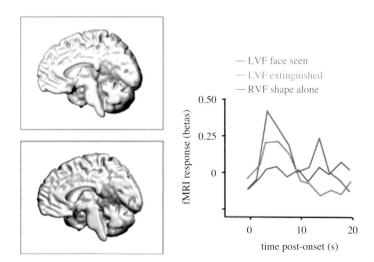

Fig. 8.5 Effects of right parietal damage on visual cortex activation in a patient with left spatial neglect and visual extinction. Face stimuli were presented in the contralesional left hemifield with another distractor shape in the ipsilesional right hemifield, such that the faces were either perceived on some trials or extinguished from awareness on other trials (adapted from Vuilleumier *et al.* 2001*a*). When perceived, contralesional faces evoked significant BOLD fMRI responses in intact right occipital and temporal visual areas (red, here for a region of inferior temporal cortex posterior to FFA). Residual activation was still observed when contrale-sional faces were extinguished (green), relative to when there was no stimulus in the contralesional field (blue), but such activation was reduced relative to perceived faces (red). These data indicate that parietal damage may have significant functional consequences on the activation of intact visual areas in relation to conscious perception. Units for fMRI activation (betas) correspond to parameters estimates for event-related changes in BOLD signal.

that some visual activations may be reduced by lesions outside visual areas and that such neural changes may relate to impaired conscious perception.

More recent work from our group (Vuilleumier *et al*. 2004*a*) used fMRI retinotopic-mapping procedures (Sereno *et al*. 1995) in right-parietal patients with left neglect and extinction to characterize the responsivity of intact visual cortex and any effects of attentional demand on these areas in more detail. We mapped cortical areas V1 through to V4 for each hemisphere and recorded their fMRI responses to peripheral flickering checkerboards in either visual field. In the main experiment (which was analogous to a study of normal visual attention by Schwartz *et al*. 2005), the patients had to fixate a stream of successive central stimuli to perform one of the two tasks with varying attentional demand (low or high load; see Lavie *et al*. 2004; Schwartz *et al*. 2005), while ignoring peripheral checkerboard stimuli. In normal observers, increasing attentional load at fixation reduces visual activations for the (task-irrelevant) peripheral visual checkerboard, but does so symmetrically (i.e. similar effect of attentional load on both peripheral visual fields). Our fMRI results in right-parietal patients showed a striking pattern. Whereas, visual responses of V1–V4 appeared normal under low attentional load in these patients, even for the left visual field, increasing attentional load at fixation produced a significant asymmetry in visual activation to peripheral stimuli across all successive stages of the visual system. This was found from V1 onwards, but with the largest effect in higher visual areas (Vuilleumier *et al*. 2004*b*; Schwartz *et al*. 2005), such that right V4 no longer responded to a left checkerboard when foveal attentional load was high. These results suggest that early retinotopic cortex for the disrupted side may respond normally under low attentional demands at fixation, but pathologically when attention is engaged by other stimuli. This may lead to corresponding effects on visual awareness (Walker *et al*. 1991). Indeed, we have now confirmed behaviourally (in collaboration with Jason Mattingley & Chris Rorden) that increased attentional load at fixation can disrupt visual reports for items in the peripheral left visual field more than the right visual field in neglect patients (Lavie & Robertson 2001). More importantly for present purposes, these new retinotopic fMRI data in right-parietal patients indicate that disruptions of visual perception due to lesions in attention-related brain areas may not merely reflect disrupted feedforward access to the (lesioned) higher-level representations. Instead they can involve changes in visual processing within early occipital areas: changes that are functionally caused by the parietal damage and that depend on attentional state.

Frontal lesions in humans can also produce some functional changes in processing within visual cortex, although relatively few studies have directly addressed this. Some reports (Barcelo *et al*. 2000; Gehring & Knight 2002) indicate that while lesions to dorsolateral prefrontal cortex (DLPFC) do not usually produce persistent signs of the neglect syndrome, they can produce failures to detect visual targets (e.g. 'oddballs') in the contralesional hemifield during monitoring tasks. One study applied visual ERP measures to frontal-lesioned patients (Barcelo *et al*. 2000). Patients were shown rapid visual streams of bilateral stimuli, concurrently in both visual fields. Those with DLPFC damage showed a reduction in relatively early visual ERPs (starting with the P1 component thought to arise from extrastriate cortex), specifically for visual targets in the field contralesional to their DLPFC injury. Such abnormalities extended from approximately 120 ms after stimulus onset for a more sustained period lasting approximately 500 ms, and correlated with behavioural deficits in target detection. These findings indicate that prefrontal cortex may also impose some regulatory influences upon neural activity in extrastriate visual cortex, and that such influences may be necessary for normal visual target detection (Yago *et al*. 2004).

Taken together, these fMRI and EEG studies of patients with parietal or frontal lesions, focusing on the impact upon processing in visual cortex, illustrate that combining the lesion approach with neural measures of activity (for intact regions) may reveal truly causal influences of parietal or frontal regions upon visual cortex, in relation to attentional or task-related manipulations. Any differences between frontal and parietal influences still remain largely unknown, so further studies should implement comparable tasks in different lesion groups. Related studies are now being conducted in non-human primates (e.g. Orban *et al.* 2006).

8.6 Fronto-parietal influences on attentional control in the normal brain: combining brain-stimulation with measures of remote neural activity

Interventional approaches to studying causal influences between remote but interconnected brain regions may not need to rely on lesions only. Another approach is to use 'neuro-disruption' techniques (Chambers & Mattingley 2005) to manipulate activity in one brain region, while recording from other interconnected regions. An elegant example comes from recent work by Moore and colleagues (Moore *et al.* 1998; Moore & Armstrong 2003; Moore & Fallah 2004), who applied microstimulations to the macaque FEF. Single-cell recording work indicates that the FEF are involved not only in saccadic behaviour, but also in selective visual processing, particularly in relation to target–non-target distinctions in search tasks (Bichot *et al.* 2001; Schall 2004). Moreover, in humans, the FEF are often activated (Figure 8.3) as part of the putative attention network (Kastner & Ungerleider 2000; Corbetta & Shulman 2002), and are also implicated in the lesions of some neglect patients (Mesulam 1999).

Moore and colleagues (Moore *et al.* 1998; Moore & Armstrong 2003; Moore & Fallah 2004) took advantage of the spatial precision with which saccades can be triggered by FEF microstimulation in monkeys. In this way, they could map out the 'motor field' for each of their particular stimulation sites within FEF. Critically, they then stimulated at the mapped site, but now below the threshold level needed to trigger a saccade, while studying the impact of this on visual performance by the monkey during a target-detection task (Moore *et al.* 1998), or on responses to visual stimuli in V4 neurons with receptive fields that either did or did not correspond spatially with the motor field of the FEF microstimulation (Moore & Armstrong 2003). The striking finding was that subthreshold FEF microstimulation could enhance both visual performance by the monkey and also visual responses in V4, provided there was a spatial correspondence between the visual target (and V4 receptive field) with the motor field of the stimulated FEF site. This provides a direct causal demonstration that (stimulated) activity in FEF can produce spatially corresponding modulations of visual processing in extrastriate cortex, with a corresponding impact on visual performance also.

Microstimulation with implanted electrodes will rarely be available in human subjects (though see Blanke *et al.* 2000; Zumsteg *et al.* 2006). However, TMS provides a non-invasive method for causally manipulating neural activity at a targeted site, whose effects are increasingly well studied and understood (Pascual-Leone *et al.* 2000; Pascual-Leone & Walsh 2001; Paus 2005). Moreover, it is now possible to combine application of TMS to human cortical sites while concurrently recording brain activity with PET, fMRI or EEG, although this can be technically challenging, especially for concurrent fMRI (Bestmann *et al.* 2005, 2006; Ruff *et al.* 2006). Ruff *et al.* (2006) recently applied TMS to human FEF while recording fMRI activity from visual cortex and retinotopically mapping areas V1 through V4.

Increased intensity of FEF–TMS led to enhanced activation of peripheral visual field representations, and relative suppression of central visual field representations, for all retinotopic areas of visual cortex, including V1 (Figure 8.6). TMS applied to a control site (vertex) had no such effects. Thus, circuits originating in the human FEF can causally modulate activity in visual cortex, as previously suggested (see above) on the basis of much less direct, less causal evidence. Ruff and colleagues also found that psychophysical visual judgements were modulated by FEF–TMS, in a manner that accorded with their fMRI findings for early visual cortex. Under high intensity FEF–TMS, peripheral visual stimuli were judged as higher in contrast relative to foveal visual stimuli, analogously to the enhanced fMRI responses for peripheral visual field in the visual cortex caused by FEF–TMS.

In another recent study applying TMS to human FEF, Taylor *et al.* (2007) recorded ERPs during a task requiring direction of visual attention to the expected side of an upcoming visual target. TMS over FEF (but not over a control site, posterior to motor cortex) modulated ERPs recorded from occipital electrodes over visual cortex, both prior to and during the visual stimulus presentation. Fuggetta *et al.* (2006) also recently combined TMS with ERP recordings during a visual-attention task (in their case, visual search). They found that the early phase of the N2pc component, often associated with focusing of visual attention (Luck 1995), was eliminated over the right-hemisphere by TMS to right posterior parietal cortex.

Taken together, the recent studies that combine TMS to frontal or parietal sites, together with neural measures of activity in or over occipital cortex, illustrate the potential fruitfulness of a new causal approach that manipulates particular candidate attentional-control regions with neuro-disruption techniques, while studying the impact on remote but interconnected

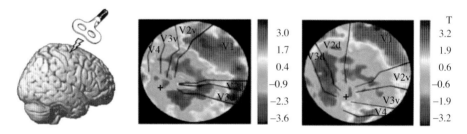

Fig. 8.6 Illustration of concurrent TMS–fMRI study by Ruff *et al.* (2006), with example results from retinotopic visual cortex. TMS was applied over human right frontal-eye fields (see cartoon at left, depicting TMS stimulator held over this brain region). TMS stimulation was applied inside the MR scanner, interleaved with MR slice-acquisition, with procedures to prevent MR artefacts. Example fMRI results are shown for two participants, in 'flat-map' depictions of retinotopically mapped visual cortical areas. Borders between adjacent areas (e.g. V1 with ventral V2 ('V2v'), or with dorsal V2 ('V2d') and so on) are drawn in black, with areas labelled. Foveal confluence is marked with a cross, with increased retinal eccentricity running out from here within each marked visual area. The 'hot' colours correspond to increased fMRI activity with higher TMS intensity to FEF; 'cold' colours represent decreased activity instead. The consistent pattern in all subjects was that, for all retinotopic areas (V1–V4), representations of the peripheral visual field showed enhanced fMRI activity with increased FEF-TMS intensity, while the central visual field (nearer the foveal cross) showed reduced activity. This confirms that human FEF can causally modulate activity in retinotopic visual cortex. Ruff *et al.* (2006) also derived and confirmed the psychophysical prediction, based on these fMRI data, that TMS should enhance peripheral relative to central vision, for perceived contrast.

regions of visual cortex, and any corresponding impacts upon visual performance and awareness.

In summary thus far, many studies show that visual processing and neural activity measured in or over occipital cortex can be modulated by selective attention. Fronto-parietal circuits have been implicated in this modulation, albeit with relatively few causal demonstrations hitherto. But more causal demonstrations of influences from frontal and/or parietal regions upon visual cortex are now forthcoming. These arise from new methodological combinations, including application of neural measures of visual processing to lesioned patients, or in healthy individuals undergoing non-invasive stimulation of particular cortical areas via TMS.

8.7 Emotional modulation of visual processing

As mentioned earlier, attentional factors related to task-relevance are not the only modulatory influences upon visual processing. The emotional value of a stimulus may also produce some analogous effects (Figure 8.7), typified by relatively enhanced and/or sustained neural responses for emotional relative to neutral stimuli in functional neuroimaging studies (Vuilleumier 2005; Pourtois & Vuilleumier 2006). But the potential sources for imposing these modulations upon visual processing may involve distinct brain structures than attentional control by task-relevance, outside of parietal and frontal cortex. For instance, some converging evidence from both animal and human research suggests that emotion-related modulation of visual processing involves the amygdala, an almond-shaped nucleus in the anterior medial temporal lobe, known to be critically implicated in fear processing and fear-related

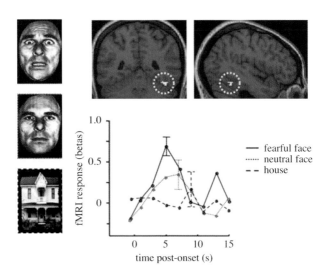

Fig. 8.7 Example of emotional modulation of activation in FFA. Results from fMRI in normal subjects show that FFA exhibits selective responses to pictures of faces (green), not to houses (blue), but also exhibits a further increase to emotionally salient facial expression, particularly when fearful or threat-related (red). Data from P.Vuilleumier & G.Pourtois (2005, unpublished); see also Vuilleumier *et al.* 2001*a*). Units for fMRI activation (betas) correspond to parameters estimates for event-related changes in BOLD signal.

learning (LeDoux 2000; Phelps&LeDoux2005),and perhapsother social-affective appraisal processes (Sander *et al*. 2003; Rosen & Donley 2006).

A longstanding behavioural literature has considered processing of emotion-related stimuli, in both normal and clinical populations (Wells & Matthews 1994; Mogg & Bradley 1998). In the past decade, such work has been supplemented by a growing body of neuroimaging data concerning possible emotional influences upon perceptual processing (e.g. Lang *et al*. 1990; Lane *et al*. 1999; Sabatinelli *et al*. 2005; for review see Vuilleumier *et al*. 2003). Some of these findings have proved so replicable that they have led to standard procedures in neuroimaging assessments of clinical groups and genetic subpopulations (e.g. Bertolino *et al*. 2005; Hariri *et al*. 2005; Meyer-Lindenberg *et al*. 2005). In particular, fMRI studies of face processing have repeatedly shown that emotional facial expressions can produce significant increases in activation for the amygdala, and also for face-responsive regions within visual cortex (e.g. FFA in lateral fusiform gyrus). Such increases are typically greater for negative facial expressions associated with possible threat, such as fear (Vuilleumier *et al*. 2001*a*; Surguladze *et al*. 2003), although some similar effects have also been reported for other emotional expressions, including positive emotions such as happiness (Winston *et al*. 2003). Analogously, increased visual activation for complex emotional visual scenes (e.g. mutilations, assaults, etc), relative to neutral scenes, has been found in lateral occipital cortical areas involved in object processing (Lane *et al*. 1999; Sabatinelli *et al*. 2005). Such increases in visual activation triggered by emotional information are usually quite specific, affecting those visual regions selectively activated by the current stimulus category, rather than a non-specific arousal effect that influences all brain areas. Thus, in a study where pictures of emotional or neutral faces were presented concurrently with pictures of houses, displays with emotional faces produced an increased activation in face-selective areas (the FFA) but not in PPA house-selective areas (Vuilleumier *et al*. 2001*a*).

Analogously, a recent study found (Peelen *et al*. submitted) that movies showing emotional body movements (relative to neutral body movements) produced selective increases in the extrastriate body area, as well as in the fusiform body area (FBA, that partly overlaps with the FFA but shows body-selective rather than face-selective responses; Peelen & Downing 2005). Within fusiform cortex, increased activation to emotional versus neutral bodies was significantly correlated on a voxel-wise basis with the degree of body-selectivity for that voxel, but was not correlated with face-selectivity (both forms of selectivity being defined relative to a third category of objects). This suggests that emotional signals from seen body movements specifically modulate neural populations involved in processing seen bodies selectively, rather than having a more diffuse arousal-like effect on the visual system. Furthermore, in audition, the emotional prosody of voices has been found to boost activation (relative to neutral prosody) within a restricted region of superior temporal cortex known to be selective for human voices (Grandjean *et al*. 2005).

Taken together, all these findings show that emotion can produce activations strikingly analogous to those due to selective attention, now enhancing the representation of emotionally relevant (rather than strictly task-relevant) stimuli in specific regions of sensory cortex. One interpretation might be that emotional stimuli are simply more 'attended'. But we argue below that the findings for emotional stimuli may typically reflect modulation imposed by different circuits than those typically involved in modulations due to selective attention or task-relevance (cf. the frontal and parietal results above).

The data from human neuroimaging showing emotional modulation of visual processing converge with monkey single-cell results, demonstrating for instance that emotional facial expressions (figure 8.1*b*) can modulate the response of face-selective neurons in temporal cortex (Sugase *et al*. 1999). Those single-cell recordings revealed that the initial phase of firing in such neurons was driven by global distinctions such as face–non-face category, while a subsequent phase (starting approx. 50–100 ms later) showed enhanced firing for faces with particular expressions (or with preexisting familiarity, for some other neurons). Formal information-analyses of neural activity confirmed that the same neurons can carry different information about the same stimulus at distinct latencies, with early activity coding for object category and later activity for emotional value (Oram & Richmond 1999; Sugase *et al*. 1999). Such emotional boosting of face-selective neurons by expressions and/or affective relevance is reminiscent of the boosting produced by selective attention. But while this has been similarly ascribed to top-down or re-entrant feedback influences from remote brain areas (Sugase *et al*. 1999; Vuilleumier *et al*. 2004*a*), different areas have been hypothesized to play a crucial role for emotional influences, such as limbic regions involved in affect and memory (e.g. the amygdala), instead of parietal or frontal cortex.

Recent EEG recordings in humans also indicate potential analogies between emotion and attention effects on sensory responses. Several studies found a higher amplitude of visual evoked potentials for emotional versus neutral faces (Eimer & Holmes 2002; Pizzagalli *et al*. 2002; Eger *et al*. 2003; Ashley *et al*. 2004), including an enhancement of the P1 component at approximately 120 ms that is thought to be generated in extrastriate cortex (Batty & Taylor 2003; Pourtois *et al*. 2005), together with later more sustained effects (Krolak-Salmon *et al*. 2001). Such enhancements of P1 amplitude are often considered as the hallmark for gain modulation of visual processing by selective attention (Hillyard *et al*. 1998; Martinez *et al*. 1999). It remains unclear whether this early P1 enhancement for emotional faces may be intrinsically related to processing of emotional facial features in particular (Batty & Taylor 2003), or to other mod-ulatory processes (Moratti *et al*. 2004; Pourtois *et al*. 2004). But in either case, the P1 effect demonstrates that some emotional-related modulation may arise in visual cortex, either prior to or concomitant with the processing stages traditionally associated with face perception or object recognition (i.e. approx. 170 ms, when the well-known N170 component specifically related to face-processing arises; Bentin & Deouell 2000; Pizzagalli *et al*. 2002; Holmes *et al*. 2003).

8.8 Specific subcortical sources for emotional influences on visual processing

Which circuits lead to emotion-related modulation of visual processing, as in the examples above? How distinct (or common) are these circuits in relation to those imposing task-related modulations of selective attention? One possible candidate for emotion-related modulations was first highlighted by anatomical tracing studies (Amaral & Price 1984; Amaral *et al*. 2003), showing dense feedback connections between the amygdala and cortical sensory areas. This led to proposals that such pathways might regulate perceptual analysis of emotional stimuli, particularly when these are threat-related. As indirect support for this idea, electrical stimulation of amygdala nuclei in the rat can produce desynchronization of EEG activity in remote cortical areas, including visual cortex (Kapp *et al*. 1994; Dringenberg *et al*. 2001). Furthermore, in rats, lesions of the amygdala after auditory fear-conditioning can suppress a late amplification exhibited by auditory cortex neurons for fear-conditioned tones relative to neutral tones, while leaving the initial auditory response unchanged (Armony *et al*. 1998).

But perhaps the strongest evidence for a truly causal role of the amygdala in modulation of sensory processing by emotional factors has come from human neuroimaging of patients. A recent fMRI study of patients whose focal lesions could include the amygdala revealed distant functional consequences of these lesions for face processing in visual cortex (Vuilleumier *et al.* 2004*a*). In this study, we selected a group of patients with epileptic disease characterized by medial temporal-lobe sclerosis, for whom structural imaging showed that their sclerotic damage involved either the amygdala and hippocampus or just the hippocampus sparing the amygdala. Visual cortex was completely intact in all cases. Both groups of patients performed a task with fearful and neutral faces, in which faces were either task-relevant (attended) or task-irrelevant (unattended), analogous to the attention manipulation shown earlier in Figure 8.2*a*. Patients with hippocampal damage but intact amygdala showed (figure 8.8) a normal enhancement in fusiform face-selective areas for fearful versus neutral faces, as found in a healthy control group (figure 8.6) and in two other previous studies (Vuilleumier *et al.* 2001*a*; Bentley *et al.* 2003). By contrast, patients having the same temporal lobe disease (and medical treatment) but with additional structural damage affecting the amygdala showed no differential responses to fearful versus neutral faces in fusiform cortex (figure 8.8).

Moreover, there was a significant inverse correlation between the severity of structural amygdala damage and enhancement of fusiform activity by fearful faces, observed selectively within each hemisphere (i.e. greater right amygdala damage led to a decreased boost of right fusiform activity for fearful expressions and analogously for the impact of left amygdala damage on left fusiform activity), without any such correlation between hemispheres (e.g. right amygdala damage did not predict left fusiform activity for fearful faces). This strongly suggests that increases in fusiform activity for fearful faces depend on ipsilateral intra-hemispheric influences from the amygdala upon fusiform cortex. This is consistent with anatomical evidence for such ipsilateral connections (Amaral *et al.* 2003). A further important feature of our patient fMRI study (Vuilleumier *et al.* 2004*a*) was that, in both patient groups,

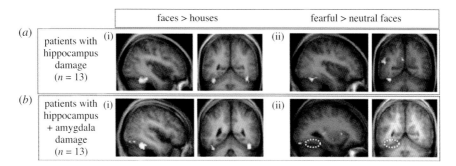

Fig. 8.8 Effect of amygdala lesion on fMRI BOLD responses to emotional faces in visual cortex (adapted from Vuilleumier *et al.* 2004*a*). Patients with medial temporal-lobe sclerosis, whose lesions involved either (*a*) the hippocampus alone or (*b*) the hippocampus plus amygdala, performed a picture-matching task similar to that illustrated in Figure 8.2. Seen faces could be fearful or neutral and task-relevant or not. Patients with hippocampal damage alone (*a*) showed normal activation of fusiform cortex for fearful versus neutral faces (*a*(ii)), as for healthy subjects also (not shown). Patients with additional damage to the amygdala (*b*) showed no effect of fearful expression in visual cortex. By contrast, in both patient groups, fusiform cortex was normally activated by attention to task-relevant faces (*a*(i), *b*(i)). These results indicate distant functional consequences for visual cortex responses to fearful faces, caused by amygdala damage.

bilateral fusiform face-responsive areas were normally activated by faces relative to houses, and normally modulated by selective attention when the faces were task-relevant (versus task-irrelevant) for the required behavioural discrimination task (cf. Figure 8.2). The latter two effects confirm that visual cortex itself and attentional influences from other regions upon it (presumably arising from fronto-parietal circuits representing task-set control, see above) were still operating normally.

Taken together, these data (Vuilleumier *et al.* 2004*a*) provide direct evidence that the amygdala can influence processing in remote visual cortical areas, normally boosting the representation of fear-related faces in fusiform cortex, in a way that is disrupted after amygdala damage. The results also confirm that the emotional influence of fearful expressions in boosting fusiform activation to faces can be separated from (i.e., disrupted by amygdala damage independently from) the attentional effect of task-relevance upon fusiform activations.

More recent work using EEG in similar patients has extended these fMRI data by showing that amygdala damage (but not hippocampal damage) can also reduce or eliminate the enhancement usually found in the P1 component for fearful faces relative to neutral faces (Rotshtein *et al.* 2006). This finding accords with the fMRI results above, but add temporal specificity that further confirms a role for the amygdala in modulation of a relatively early extrastriate response to fear. Other EEG studies in patients have shown that amygdala damage may also disrupt later cortical modulations by emotional expressions arising approximately 300 ms after stimulus onset (Krolak-Salmon *et al.* 2001, 2004), while orbitofrontal damage may impair both early and late ERP effects (Ashley *et al.* 2003).

Future research using intracranial recordings in epileptic patients (with electrodes implanted on clinical grounds, for presurgical assessment) may prove useful for further investigating the exact nature and timing of such distant interactions between areas, in relation to emotional situations (Kawasaki *et al.* 2001; Krolak-Salmon *et al.* 2004). Such recordings with implants are usually limited by clinical constraints. Nevertheless, even single-cell recordings can now take place in some patients (Kreiman *et al.* 2002; Oya *et al.* 2002), and will shed further light on emotional and attentional modulation of visual processing. In addition, transient electrical stimulation or post-seizure suppression of activity in amygdala or other limbic regions may provide a further tool to identify inter-regional interactions, in patients investigated for epilepsy prior to surgery (Bartolomei *et al.* 2005; Lanteaume *et al.* 2006). Non-invasive approaches with TMS may be more limited in this context, due to insufficient access to deep limbic brain structures in the medial temporal lobe and ventral prefrontal regions. Nevertheless, TMS studies of more lateral cortical regions involved in controlling attention in the presence of emotional stimuli (e.g. Dolcos & McCarthy 2006; Dolcos *et al.* 2006) may provide further opportunities to study consequences of such causal interventions upon neural activations within limbic pathways.

8.9 Possible relations between attentional and emotional modulation of visual processing

Several behavioural observations have been taken to suggest that emotional stimuli may tend to 'capture' attention (Öhman 1986; Mogg *et al.* 1997; Fox *et al.* 2000; Vuilleumier & Schwartz 2001*a,b*; Anderson 2005). Might the emotional modulations of visual processing described here (e.g. increased activation of fusiform cortex for faces with fearful expressions, and so on) perhaps simply reflect enhanced 'attention' *per se* (e.g. Öhman 1986; Ohman *et al.* 2001; see also Pourtois *et al.* 2005)? An alternative perspective, that we favour, may be that emotional modulations (e.g. from amygdala) can boost the processing of particular stimuli to give them added 'competitive strength' in neural representation (Desimone & Duncan 1995; Kastner & Ungerleider 2001) against other incoming stimuli. This could arise for different reasons (and with different causal neurobiological sources) than attentional signals related to task-relevance *per se*.

As noted above, fMRI results in temporal-lobe patients (Vuilleumier *et al.* 2004*a*) have shown that amygdala lesions can abolish enhancement of the fusiform response for fearful versus neutral faces, yet without disrupting the normal boost (Wojciulik *et al.* 1998) for task-relevant versus task-irrelevant faces in the same fusiform region for the same patients. Moreover, in normal subjects, we found (Vuilleumier *et al.* 2001*a*) that orthogonal manipulations of emotion (fearful versus neutral) or task-relevance (faces versus houses judged) were additive in their impacts on the fusiform response to faces. The amygdala response to fearful expressions did not depend on attention in that particular paradigm. However, some other studies have suggested that, under sufficiently attention-demanding conditions, the amygdala response to fearful faces might be reduced when those faces are unattended (Pessoa *et al.* 2002): for instance, under conditions of attentional load that are strong enough to eliminate the fusiform response to the faces. But such a pattern might be reconciled with attentional modulations due to task-relevance having different causal modulatory sources than emotional modulations of visual processing (even though both types of modulation can affect the same structure). Such a pattern might simply imply that attentional modulation can sometimes be strong enough (e.g. under high perceptual load, Lavie 2005; Schwartz *et al.* 2005) to override any apparent emotional influences.

The literature shows that, in several situations, emotional modulations can still arise from task-irrelevant stimuli (e.g. Critchley *et al.* 2000; Pasley *et al.* 2004; Williams *et al.* 2004; Keil *et al.* 2005). A recent fMRI study (Jiang & He 2006) showed that when face images are rendered invisible by interocular suppression, activity in FFA is reduced to both neutral and fearful faces (although it is still measurable) while activity in the amygdala may be reduced for neutral but not fearful faces. Several EEG studies have manipulated attentional (task-relevance) and emotional (e.g. fearful versus neutral facial expression) factors orthogonally, analogous to our fMRI design described above (Vuilleumier *et al.* 2001*a*, 2004*a*). Holmes *et al.* (2003) found that task-relevance modulated face processing at a relatively late stage (from approx. 170–180 ms onwards), following the face-specific N170 component (Bentin & Deouell 2000); this was later than the earliest component modulated by fearful expression (P1 component, arising at approx. 120 ms). This appears consistent with some emotional modulation arising in extrastriate visual cortex (the likely source of the P1) prior to task-related attentional selection (Luck 1995), and prior to full completion of cortical face processing. Another EEG study (Keil *et al.* 2005) used a different paradigm, with emotional scenes presented in either hemifield (right or left) while participants directed attention to detect a target on one or other side selectively. The results again demonstrated additive effects of emotion and attention on visual evoked potentials. Other studies have reported emotional increases in visual ERPs to affective scenes (Sato *et al.* 2001; Schupp *et al.* 2003).

Further evidence that may be compatible with separate causal sources for emotional or attentional modulation comes from neuropsychological and neuroimaging studies in patients with right parietal damage and consequent left neglect/extinction. As we described earlier, mechanisms of spatial attention are thought to be pathologically biased in such patients, resulting in perceptual extinction and unawareness of contrale-sional stimuli when these must compete with ipsilesional inputs (Driver & Vuilleumier 2001; Driver *et al.* 2004). The fMRI data in such patients show that residual activation evoked by unseen (extinguished) faces in fusiform cortex can still be modulated by the emotional expression of the unseen faces, with a similar boosting of fusiform response to that observed for fearful versus neutral faces when consciously seen (Vuilleumier *et al.* 2002*a*). Thus, when a face was presented in the contralesional (left) hemifield of a right-parietal patient, together with a distractor (house) in the ipsilesional right hemifield, fusiform activation was not only found to be greater during conscious detection of the contralesional face (as opposed to trials where it was extinguished from awareness, see earlier sections), but was also greater for fearful than neutral faces regardless of whether the face was seen or extinguished. Fearful expressions also activated the amygdala and orbitofrontal cortex (OFC), again regardless of awareness. Such a pattern echoes the additive effects of emotion and attention that we have observed in healthy subjects (Vuilleumier *et al.* 2001*a*); and it accords with the notion that emotional modulation of the fusiform may reflect modulatory signals from amygdala, that can still operate despite deficient spatial attention following damage to parietal systems. Moreover, in keeping with this preserved emotional modulation, parietal patients can show significantly less severe extinction overall for emotional stimuli relative to neutral stimuli (Vuilleumier & Schwartz 2001*a,b*; Fox 2002), presumably because emotional modulation of visual processing can still enhance the perceptual weight of such stimuli in any competition for awareness, thus partly compensating for reduced attention to contralesional inputs caused by the parietal lesion. Furthermore, unconscious perception of facial emotions has also been found to produce 'implicit' or indirect behavioural priming effects in parietal patients with visual extinction, even when they fail consciously to detect the contralesional face (Williams & Mattingley 2004).

In summary, just as attentional modulation of visual processing (due to task-relevance) can have major consequences for perceptual awareness (Mack & Rock 1998; Beck *et al.* 2001; Driver 2001; Chun & Marois 2002), by providing top-down biases that affect sensory representations of currently task-relevant information, emotional modulations may also analogously affect perception and awareness, by imposing a distinct source of bias upon sensory representations, but now based on signals of affective relevance. Just as frontal and/or parietal damage can disrupt attentional control to dramatically alter perceptual awareness in patients, so too amygdala dysfunction may not only cause difficulties in emotional or affective learning tasks, but may also have some distinct impacts on perceptual processing and awareness (e.g. eliminating detection advantages for emotional stimuli, Anderson & Phelps 2001, see below).

8.10 Emotional influences on perceptual tasks

Many behavioural studies have shown that, in healthy normal subjects, emotional stimuli can often be detected better and quicker than neutral stimuli. For instance, visual search can be speeded for emotional faces (Fox *et al.* 2000; Eastwood *et al.* 2001), while the attentional blink is reduced for emotional words (Anderson & Phelps 2001; Anderson 2005). Spatial cueing effects, in paradigms classically used to study selective attention, can also be enhanced when cues involve emotional or threat-related stimuli rather than neutral stimuli (Pourtois *et al.* 2004; Phelps *et al.* in press). But importantly, such effects of emotion on perceptual performance and on associated competitive advantages can be eliminated in patients with amygdala lesions (e.g. Anderson & Phelps 2001), providing further causal evidence that lesions in emotion-related regions of the brain may not only impair emotion processing, but can also have some specific effects on vision, especially in competitive situations with several visual events.

In contrast to amygdala patients, increased rather than decreased perceptual effects of emotional stimuli are often seen in patients with anxiety disorders (Mathews *et al.* 1990; Mogg *et al.* 1991; Fox *et al.* 2001; Yiend & Mathews 2001). Moreover, such individuals may show enhanced amygdala activation to threat-related stimuli (Bishop *et al.* 2004*a,b*; Etkin *et al.* 2004), and increased emotional enhancement in visual cortex (Sabatinelli *et al.* 2005). Such observations may accord with classic cognitive accounts of anxiety disorders that have emphasized the role of 'attentional biases' in these patients (Mathews *et al.* 1990; Mogg *et al.* 1991). But here, we emphasize again that the neurobiological sources for emotional modulation of sensory processing may differ from those for attentional modulation in the sense of task-relevance (see above).

Further approaches to such issues in the future will concern pharmacological interventions intended to target potential sources of emotional modulation, separately from potential sources for task-related attentional influences. Initial pharmacological fMRI studies, manipulating cholinergic neuromodulatory transmission, were found to affect attention-related activations but not emotion-related effects in visual cortex (Bentley *et al.* 2003). Other drugs acting on adrenergic or benzodiazepine systems, as well as neuropeptides (Kirsch *et al.* 2005) and neurohormones (van Stegeren *et al.* 2007), might produce important regulatory effects on emotion-related responses instead (Robbins 2007 and this volume).

Finally, we should note that although we focused for simplicity on just the amygdala in our review of emotional modulation, it is unlikely to be the sole source for emotional modulation of sensory processing (just as the FEF is unlikely to be the sole source for task-related attention, but was likewise emphasized for simplicity above). OFC and the striatum (Robbins 2007; Dolan 2007) are also potential candidates likely to play important roles in emotional or motivational modulation of sensory processing (Ashley *et al.* 2003). Moreover, there is now some initial evidence that, under some circumstances, reward-related information can modulate parietal neurons thought to play a role in the control of selective attention, or in the direction of saccades (Platt & Glimcher 1999; Maunsell 2004; Sugrue *et al.* 2004). This could provide a potential functional link for rewards to interface with attentional systems. There is also some new emerging evidence that rewards might directly affect sensory processing in early cortical regions, including even primary visual cortex (Shuler & Bear 2006). For both parietal and sensory cortex, it seems likely that the effective reward signals would probably be conveyed to neurons in parietal or sensory areas by remote brain areas implicated in emotional and motivational processes, such as OFC, striatum and/or amygdala (Cavada & Goldman-Rakic 1989). The sources of such reward-related signals might be identified in future by combining lesion studies with imaging or neurophysiological measures in remote and intact sensory cortices, as we illustrated here for attention and emotion. Moreover, in animals, inactivation or stimulation methods targeting specific nuclei (e.g. in the amygdala, or in distinct regions of OFC) might be performed while recording functional consequences for remote sensory areas.

8.11 Concluding remarks

We have considered attentional and emotional modulation of visual processing as two complementary examples. In both cases, processing in some regions (e.g. visual cortex) may be causally influenced by remote but interconnected areas (e.g. fronto-parietal circuits for attentional influences; or limbic circuits involving the amygdala for emotional influences). Both kinds of modulation can have analogous consequences at the neural and behavioural levels, including enhanced visual responses and competitive strength for more attended or more emotional stimuli. But while it is often said that emotional stimuli may 'capture attention', we suggest that emotional and attentional modulations of vision may often reflect independent effects, imposed by separate circuits, albeit influencing some common regions such as visual cortex. Thus, these findings indicate that sources of top-down biases can provide multiple influences on perceptual systems, rather than there being just a single unified source of modulation (Vuilleumier 2005).

Here, we have illustrated these points by new approaches, including the combination of functional neuroimaging with either lesion studies in brain-damaged patients or online neuro-disruption methods such as TMS, to address causal impacts on remote but interconnected regions. As fMRI can now be applied to studies in monkeys or rodents also, combining such interventional manipulations with neuroimaging may provide an important link between human cognitive neuroscience and animal research in future. These new approaches illustrate the increasing shift in cognitive neuroscience from considering the role of single brain areas in isolation, to a focus on how different regions may influence each other causally. For the particular case of visual processing, such studies reveal that even basic perceptual processing can be substantially influenced by higher-level factors, such as task-relevance or affective status. Although the visual system was once considered to comprise cognitively impenetrable 'modules' that would proceed automatically, regardless of higher-level influences, a much more interactive and recursive interplay between different brain systems seems to apply.

Acknowledgements

Our research is supported by grants from the Swiss National Science Foundation and NCCR in Affective Sciences to P.V.; and by MRC, Wellcome Trust and Royal Society awards to J.D. in the UK. We thank our collaborators; the patients who have participated in our research; plus a Tim Shallice and Geraint Rees for helpful comments.

References

Amaral, D. G. & Price, J. L. 1984 Amygdalo-cortical projections in the monkey (*Macaca fascicularis*). *J. Comp. Neurol.* **230**, 465–496. (doi:10.1002/cne.902300402)

Amaral, D. G., Behniea, H. & Kelly, J. L. 2003 Topographic organization of projections from the amygdala to the visual cortex in the macaque monkey. *Neuroscience* **118**, 1099–1120. (doi:10.1016/S0306-4522(02)01001-1)

Anderson, A. K. 2005 Affective influences on the attentional dynamics supporting awareness. *J. Exp. Psychol. Gen.* **134**, 258–281. (doi:10.1037/0096-3445.134.2.258)

Anderson, A. K. & Phelps, E. A. 2001 Lesions of the human amygdala impair enhanced perception of emotionally salient events. *Nature* **411**, 305–309. (doi:10.1038/ 35077083)

Armony, J. L., Quirk, G. J. & LeDoux, J. E. 1998 Differential effects of amygdala lesions on early and late plastic components of auditory cortex spike trains during fear conditioning. *J. Neurosci.* **18**, 2646–2652.

Ashley, V., Vuilleumier, P. & Swick, D. 2003 Effects of orbitofrontal lesions on the recognition of emotional facial expressions. *Abstract presented at Cognitive Neuroscience Society Meeting*. New York, NY: MIT Press.

Ashley, V., Vuilleumier, P. & Swick, D. 2004 Time course and specificity of event-related potentials to emotional expressions. *Neuroreport* **15**, 211–216. (doi:10.1097/ 00001756-200401190-00041)

Barcelo, F., Suwazono, S. & Knight, R. T. 2000 Prefrontal modulation of visual processing in humans. Nat. *Neurosci.* 3, 399–403. (doi:10.1038/73975)

Bartolomei, F., Trebuchon, A., Gavaret, M., Regis, J., Wendling, F. & Chauvel, P. 2005 Acute alteration of emotional behaviour in epileptic seizures is related to transient desynchrony in emotion-regulation networks. *Clin. Neurophysiol.* **116**, 2473–2479. (doi:10.1016/j.clinph. 2005.05.013)

Batty, M. & Taylor, M. J. 2003 Early processing of the six basic facial emotional expressions. *Brain Res. Cogn. Brain Res.* **17**, 613–620. (doi:10.1016/S0926-6410(03)00174-5)

Beck, D. M., Rees, G., Frith, C. D. & Lavie, N. 2001 Neural correlates of change detection and change blindness. *Nat. Neurosci.* **4**, 645–650. (doi:10.1038/88477)

Bender, M. B. & Teuber, H. L. 1946 Phenomena of fluctuation, extinction, and completion in visual perception. *Arch. Neurol. Psychiatry* **55**, 627–658.

Bentin, S. & Deouell, L. Y. 2000 Structural encoding and identification in face processing: ERP evidence for separate mechanisms. *Cognitive Neuropsychol.* **17**, 35–54. (doi:10.1080/026432900380472)

Bentley, P., Vuilleumier, P., Thiel, C. M., Driver, J. & Dolan, R. J. 2003 Cholinergic enhancement modulates neural correlates of selective attention and emotional processing. *Neuroimage* **20**, 58–70. (doi:10.1016/S1053-8119(03) 00302-1)

Bertolino, A. *et al.* 2005 Variation of human amygdala response during threatening stimuli as a function of 5 HTTLPR genotype and personality style. *Biol. Psychiatry* **57**, 1517–1525. (doi:10.1016/j.biopsych.2005.02.031)

Bestmann, S., Baudewig, J., Siebner, H. R., Rothwell, J. C. & Frahm, J. 2005 BOLD MRI responses to repetitive TMS over human dorsal premotor cortex. *Neuroimage* **28**, 22–29. (doi:10.1016/j.neuroimage.2005.05.027)

Bestmann, S., Oliviero, A., Voss, M., Dechent, P., Lopez-Dolado, E., Driver, J. & Baudewig, J. 2006 Cortical correlates of TMS-induced phantom hand movements revealed with concurrent TMS–fMRI. *Neuropsychologia* **44**, 2959–2971. (doi:10.1016/j.neuropsychologia.2006.06.023)

Bichot, N. P., Thompson, K. G., Chenchal, R. S. & Schall, J. D. 2001 Reliability of macaque frontal eye field neurons signaling saccade targets during visual search. *J. Neurosci.* **21**, 713–725.

Bishop, S., Duncan, J., Brett, M. & Lawrence, A. D. 2004*a* Prefrontal cortical function and anxiety: controlling attention to threat-related stimuli. *Nat. Neurosci.* **7**, 184–188. (doi:10.1038/nn1173)

Bishop, S. J., Duncan, J. & Lawrence, A. D. 2004*b* State anxiety modulation of the amygdala response to unattended threat-related stimuli. *J. Neurosci.* **24**, 10 364–10 368. (doi:10.1523/JNEUROSCI.2550-04.2004)

Blanke, O., Spinelli, L., Thut, G., Michel, C. M., Perrig, S., Landis, T. & Seeck, M. 2000 Location of the human frontal eye field as defined by electrical cortical stimulation: anatomical, functional and electrophysiological characteristics. *Neuroreport* **11**, 1907–1913. (doi:10.1097/ 00001756-200006260-00021)

Bruce, V. & Young, A. W. 1986 Understanding face recognition. *Br. J. Psychol.* **77**, 305–327.

Buchel, C. & Friston, K. 2000 Assessing interactions among neuronal systems using functional neuroimaging. *Neural Netw.* **13**, 871–882.

Bullier, J., Hupe, J. M., James, A. C. & Girard, P. 2001 The role of feedback connections in shaping the responses of visual cortical neurons. *Prog. Brain Res.* **134**, 193–204.

Burgess, P. W., Gilbert, S. J. & Dumontheil, I. 2007 Function and localization within rostral prefrontal cortex (area 10). *Phil. Trans. R. Soc. B* **362**, 887–899. (doi:10.1098/rstb. 2007.2095)

Cameron, E. L., Tai, J. C. & Carrasco, M. 2002 Covert attention affects the psychometric function of contrast sensitivity. *Vision Res.* **42**, 949 967. (doi:10.1016/S0042-6989(02)00039-1)

Cavada, C. & Goldman-Rakic, P. S. 1989 Posterior parietal cortex in rhesus monkey: II. Evidence for segregated corticocortical networks linking sensory and limbic areas with the frontal lobe. *J. Comp. Neurol.* **287**, 422–445. (doi:10.1002/cne.902870403)

Chambers, C. D. & Mattingley, J. B. 2005 Neurodisruption of selective attention: insights and implications. *Trends Cogn. Sci.* **9**, 542–550. (doi:10.1016/j.tics.2005.09.010)

Chawla, D., Rees, G. & Friston, K. J. 1999 The physiological basis of attentional modulation in extrastriate visual areas. *Nat. Neurosci.* **2**, 671–676. (doi:10.1038/10230)

Chelazzi, L., Duncan, J., Miller, E. K. & Desimone, R. 1998 Responses of neurons in inferior temporal cortex during memory-guided visual search. *J. Neurophysiol.* **80**, 2918–2940.

Chun, M. M. & Marois, R. 2002 The dark side of visual attention. *Curr. Opin. Neurobiol.* **12**, 184–189. (doi:10. 1016/S0959-4388(02)00309-4)

Corbetta, M. & Shulman, G. L. 2002 Control of goal-directed and stimulus-driven attention in the brain. *Nat. Rev. Neurosci.* **3**, 201–215. (doi:10.1038/nrn755)

Corbetta, M., Meizin, F. M., Dobmeyer, S., Shulman, G. L. & Petersen, S. E. 1990 Selective attention modulates neural processing of shape, color and velocity in humans. *Science* **248**, 1556–1559. (doi:10.1126/science.2360050)

Corbetta, M., Kincade, J. M., Ollinger, J. M., McAvoy, M. P. & Shulman, G. L. 2000 Voluntary orienting is dissociated from target detection in human posterior parietal cortex. *Nat. Neurosci.* **3**, 292–297. (doi:10.1038/73009)

Corbetta, M., Kincade, M. J., Lewis, C., Snyder, A. Z. & Sapir, A. 2005 Neural basis and recovery of spatial attention deficits in spatial neglect. *Nat. Neurosci.* **8**, 1603–1610. (doi:10.1038/nn1574)

Coull, J. T., Buchel, C., Friston, K. J. & Frith, C. D. 1999 Noradrenergically mediated plasticity in a human attentional neuronal network. *Neuroimage* **10**, 705–715. (doi:10.1006/nimg.1999.0513)

Critchley, H. *et al.* 2000 Explicit and implicit neural mechanisms for processing of social information from facial expressions: a functional magnetic resonance imaging study. *Hum. Brain Mapp.* **9**, 93–105. (doi:10.1002/(SICI)1097-0193(200002)9:2<93::AID-HBM4>3.0.CO;2-Z)

Damasio, H. & Damasio, A. R. 1989 *Lesion analysis in neuropsychology*. New York, NY: Oxford.

Damasio, A. R., Damasio, H. & Chui, H. C. 1987 Neglect following damage to frontal lobe or basal ganglia. *Neuropsychologia* **18**, 123–132. (doi:10.1016/0028-3932(80)90058-5)

Desimone, R. & Duncan, J. 1995 Neural mechanisms of selective visual attention. *Annu. Rev. Neurosci.* **18**, 193–222. (doi:10.1146/annurev.ne.18.030195.001205)

Dolan, R. J. 2007 The human amygdala and orbital prefrontal cortex in behavioural regulation. *Phil. Trans. R. Soc. B* **362**, 787–799. (doi:10.1098/rstb.2007.2088)

Dolcos, F. & McCarthy, G. 2006 Brain systems mediating cognitive interference by emotional distraction. *J. Neurosci.* **26**, 2072–2079. (doi:10.1523/JNEUROSCI. 5042-05.2006)

Dolcos, F., Kragel, P., Wang, L. & McCarthy, G. 2006 Role of the inferior frontal cortex in coping with distracting emotions. *Neuroreport* **17**, 1591–1594. (doi:10.1097/01.wnr.0000236860.24081.be)

Dringenberg, H. C., Saber, A. J. & Cahill, L. 2001 Enhanced frontal cortex activation in rats by convergent amygdaloid and noxious sensory signals. *Neuroreport* **12**, 2395–2398. (doi:10.1097/00001756-200108080-00022)

Driver, J. 2001 A selective review of selective attention research from the past century. *Br. J. Psychol.* **92 Part 1**, 53–78. (doi:10.1348/000712601162103)

Driver, J. & Frackowiak, R. S. 2001 Neurobiological measures of human selective attention. *Neuropsychologia* **39**, 1257–1262. (doi:10.1016/S0028-3932(01)00115-4)

Driver, J. & Vuilleumier, P. 2001 Perceptual awareness and its loss in unilateral neglect and extinction. *Cognition* **79**, 39–88. (doi:10.1016/S0010-0277(00)00124-4)

Driver, J., Vuilleumier, P., Eimer, M. & Rees, G. 2001 Functional magnetic resonance imaging and evoked potential correlates of conscious and unconscious vision in parietal extinction patients. *Neuroimage* **14**, S68–S75. (doi:10.1006/nimg.2001.0842)

Driver, J., Eimer, M., Macaluso, E. & Velzen, V. 2003 Neurobiology of human spatial attention; modulation, generation and integration. In *Functional imaging of visual cognition*: *attention and performance*, vol. XX (eds N. Kanwisher & J. Duncan). Oxford, UK: Oxford University Press.

Driver, J., Vuilleumier, P. & Husain, M. 2004 Spatial neglect and extinction. In *The new cognitive neurosciences* (ed. M. Gazzaniga), pp. 589–606. Cambridge, MA: MIT Press.

Eastwood, J. D., Smilek, D. & Merikle, P. M. 2001 Differential attentional guidance by unattended faces expressing positive and negative emotion. *Percept. Psychophys.* **63**, 1004–1013.

Eger, E., Jedynak, A., Iwaki, T. & Skrandies, W. 2003 Rapid extraction of emotional expression: evidence from evoked potential fields during brief presentation of face stimuli. *Neuropsychologia* **41**, 808–817. (doi:10.1016/S0028-3932 (02)00287-7)

Eimer, M. & Holmes, A. 2002 An ERP study on the time course of emotional face processing. *Neuroreport* **13**, 427–431. (doi:10.1097/00001756-200203250-00013)

Epstein, R., Harris, A., Stanley, D. & Kanwisher, N. 1999 The parahippocampal place area: recognition, navigation, or encoding? *Neuron* **23**, 115–125. (doi:10.1016/S0896-6273(00)80758-8)

Etkin, A., Klemenhagen, K. C., Dudman, J. T., Rogan, M. T., Hen, R., Kandel, E. R. & Hirsch, J. 2004 Individual differences in trait anxiety predict the response of the basolateral amygdala to unconsciously processed fearful faces. *Neuron* **44**, 1043–1055. (doi:10.1016/j.neuron. 2004.12.006)

Farah, M. J. 1990 *Visual agnosia: disorders of object recognition and what they tell us about normal vision*. Cambridge, MA: MIT Press.

Fox, E. 2002 Processing of emotional facial expressions: the role of anxiety and awareness. *Cogn. Affect. Behav. Neurosci.* **2**, 52–63.

Fox, E., Lester, V., Russo, R., Bowles, R. J., Pichler, A. & Dutton, K. 2000 Facial expressions of emotion: are angry faces detected more efficiently? *Cognition Emotion* **14**, 61–92. (doi:10.1080/026999300378996)

Fox, E., Russo, R., Bowles, R. J. & Dutton, K. 2001 Do threatening stimuli draw or hold visual attention in subclinical anxiety? *J. Exp. Psychol. Gen.* **130**, 681–700. (doi:10.1037/0096-3445.130.4.681)

Friston, K. J. 1998 Imaging neuroscience: principles or maps? *Proc. Natl Acad. Sci. USA* **95**, 796–802. (doi:10. 1073/pnas.95.3.796)

Friston, K. 2002 Beyond phrenology: what can neuroimaging tell us about distributed circuitry? *Annu. Rev. Neurosci.* **25**, 221–250. (doi:10.1146/annurev.neuro.25. 112701.142846)

Friston, K. J., Harrison, L. & Penny, W. 2003 Dynamic causal modelling. *Neuroimage* **19**, 1273–1302. (doi:10.1016/ S1053-8119(03)00202-7)

Fuggetta, G., Pavone, E. F., Walsh, V., Kiss, M. & Eimer, M. 2006 Cortico-cortical interactions in spatial attention: a combined ERP/TMS study. *J. Neurophysiol.* **95**, 3277–3280. (doi:10.1152/jn.01273.2005)

Geeraerts, S., Lafosse, C., Vandenbussche, E. & Verfaillie, K. 2005 A psychophysical study of visual extinction: ipsilesional distractor interference with contralesional orientation thresholds in visual hemineglect patients. *Neuropsychologia* **43**, 530–541. (doi:10.1016/j.neuropsycho logia.2004. 07.012)

Gehring, W. J. & Knight, R. T. 2002 Lateral prefrontal damage affects processing selection but not attention switching. *Brain Res. Cogn. Brain Res.* **13**, 267–279. (doi:10.1016/S0926-6410(01)00132-X)

Ghandi, S., Heeger, D. & Boyton, G. 1999 Spatial attention affects brain activity in human primary visual cortex. *Proc. Natl Acad. Sci. USA* **96**, 3314–3319. (doi:10.1073/pnas. 96.6.3314)

Gottlieb, J. 2002 Parietal mechanisms of target representation. *Curr. Opin. Neurobiol.* **12**, 134–140. (doi:10.1016/ S0959-4388(02)00312-4)

Grandjean, D., Sander, D., Pourtois, G., Schwartz, S., Seghier, M. L., Scherer, K. R. & Vuilleumier, P. 2005 The voices of wrath: brain responses to angry prosody in meaningless speech. *Nat. Neurosci.* **8**, 145–146. (doi:10. 1038/nn1392)

Grill-Spector, K. & Malach, R. 2001 fMR-adaptation: a tool for studying the functional properties of human cortical neurons. *Acta Psychol. (Amst)* **107**, 293–321. (doi:10. 1016/ S0001-6918(01)00019-1)

Grill-Spector, K., Sayres, R. & Ress, D. 2006 High-resolution imaging reveals highly selective nonface clusters in the fusiform face area. *Nat. Neurosci.* **9**, 1177–1185. (doi:10. 1038/nn1745)

Grüsser, O. J. & Landis, T. 1991 Visual agnosias and other disturbances of visual perception and cognition. In *Vision and visual dysfunction*, vol. **12** (ed. J. Grouly-Dillon). London, UK: MacMillan.

Hariri, A. R., Drabant, E. M., Munoz, K. E., Kolachana, B. S., Mattay, V. S., Egan, M. F. & Weinberger, D. R. 2005 A susceptibility gene for affective disorders and the response of the human amygdala. *Arch. Gen. Psychiatry* **62**, 146–152. (doi:10.1001/archpsyc.62.2.146)

Haxby, J. V., Hoffman, E. A. & Gobbini, M. I. 2000 The distributed human neural system for face perception. *Trends Cogn. Neurosci.* **4**, 223–232. (doi:10.1016/S1364-6613(00)01482-0)

Heilman, K. M. & Valenstein, E. 1979 Mechanisms underlying hemispatial neglect. *Ann. Neurol.* **5**, 166–170. (doi:10.1002/ana.410050210)

Heilman, K. M., Pandya, D. M. & Geschwind, N. 1970 Trimodal inattention following parietal lobe ablations. *Trans. Am. Neurol. Assoc.* **95**, 259–268.

Heinze, H. J. *et al.* 1994 Combined spatial and temporal imaging of brain activity during visual selective attention in humans. *Nature* **372**, 543–546. (doi:10.1038/372543a0)

Hillyard, S. A., Teder-Sälerärvi, W. A. & Münte, T. F. 1998 Temporal dynamics of early perceptual processing. *Curr. Opin. Neurobiol.* **8**, 202–210. (doi:10.1016/S0959-4388 (98)80141-4)

Hinton, G. E. & Shallice, T. 1991 Lesioning an attractor network: investigations of acquired dyslexia. *Psychol. Rev.* **98**, 74–95. (doi:10.1037/0033-295X.98.1.74)

Holmes, A., Vuilleumier, P. & Eimer, M. 2003 The processing of emotional facial expression is gated by spatial attention: evidence from event-related brain potentials. *Brain Res. Cogn. Brain Res.* **16**, 174–184. (doi:10.1016/S0926-6410(02)00268-9)

Hopfinger, J. B., Buonocore, M. H. & Mangun, G. R. 2000 The neural mechanisms of top-down attentional control. *Nat. Neurosci.* **3**, 284–291. (doi:10.1038/72999)

Husain, M. & Rorden, C. 2003 Non-spatially lateralized mechanisms in hemispatial neglect. *Nat. Rev. Neurosci.* **4**, 26–36. (doi:10.1038/nrn1005)

Jiang, Y. & He, S. 2006 Cortical responses to invisible faces: dissociating subsystems for facial-information processing. *Curr. Biol.* **16**, 2023–2029. (doi:10.1016/j.cub.2006.08.084)

Kanwisher, N. & Wojciulik, E. 2000 Visual attention: insights from brain imaging. *Nat. Rev. Neurosci.* **1**, 91–100. (doi:10.1038/35039043)

Kanwisher, N., McDermott, J. & Chun, M. M. 1997 The fusiform face area: a module in human extrastriate cortex specialized for face perception. *J. Neurosci.* **17**, 4302–4311.

Kapp, B. S., Supple, W. F. & Whalen, P. J. 1994 Effects of electrical stimulation of the amygdaloid central nucleus on neocortical arousal in the rabbit. *Behav. Neurosci.* **108**, 81–93. (doi:10.1037/0735-7044.108.1.81)

Karnath, H. O., Ferber, S. & Himmelbach, M. 2001 Spatial awareness is a function of the temporal not the posterior parietal lobe. *Nature* **411**, 950–953. (doi:10.1038/ 35082075)

Karnath, H. O., Milner, A. D. & Vallar, G. 2003 *The cognitive and neural bases of spatial neglect.* Oxford, UK: Oxford University Press.

Kastner, S. & Ungerleider, L. G. 2000 Mechanisms of visual attention in the human cortex. *Annu. Rev. Neurosci.* **23**, 315–341. (doi:10.1146/annurev.neuro.23.1.315)

Kastner, S. & Ungerleider, L. G. 2001 The neural basis of biased competition in human visual cortex. *Neuropsychologia* **39**, 1263–1276. (doi:10.1016/S0028-3932(01)00116-6)

Kawasaki, H., Kaufman, O., Damasio, H., Damasio, A. R., Granner, M., Bakken, H., Hori, T., Howard, M. A. & Adolphs, R. 2001 Single-neuron responses to emotional visual stimuli recorded in human ventral prefrontal cortex. *Nat. Neurosci.* **4**, 15–16. (doi:10.1038/82850)

Keil, A., Moratti, S., Sabatinelli, D., Bradley, M. M. & Lang, P. J. 2005 Additive effects of emotional content and spatial selective attention on electrocortical facilitation. *Cereb. Cortex* **15**, 1187–1197. (doi:10.1093/cercor/bhi001)

Kirsch, P. *et al.* 2005 Oxytocin modulates neural circuitry for social cognition and fear in humans. *J. Neurosci.* **25**, 11 489–11 493. (doi:10.1523/JNEUROSCI.3984-05.2005)

Kreiman, G., Fried, I. & Koch, C. 2002 Single-neuron correlates of subjective vision in the human medial temporal lobe. *Proc. Natl Acad. Sci. USA* **99**, 8378–8383. (doi:10.1073/pnas.072194099)

Kristjansson, A., Vuilleumier, P., Schwartz, S., Macaluso, E. & Driver, J. 2006 Neural basis for priming of pop-out during visual search revealed with fMRI. *Cereb. Cortex* Sep 7 [Epub ahead of print]. (doi:10.1093/cercor/bhl072)

Krolak-Salmon, P., Fischer, C., Vighetto, A. & Mauguiere, F. 2001 Processing of facial emotional expression: spatiotemporal data as assessed by scalp event-related potentials. *Eur. J. Neurosci.* **13**, 987–994. (doi:10.1046/j.0953-816x. 2001.01454.x)

Krolak-Salmon, P., Henaff, M. A., Vighetto, A., Bertrand, O. & Mauguiere, F. 2004 Early amygdala reaction to fear spreading in occipital, temporal, and frontal cortex: a depth electrode ERP study in human. *Neuron* **42**, 665–676. (doi:10.1016/S0896-6273(04)00264-8)

Lane, R. D., Chua, P. M.-L. & Dolan, R. J. 1999 Common effects of emotional valence, arousal, and attention on neural activation during visual processing of pictures. *Neuropsychologia* **37**, 989–997. (doi:10.1016/S0028-3932(99)00017-2)

Lang, S. F., Nelson, C. A. & Collins, P. F. 1990 Event-related potentials to emotional and neutral stimuli. *J. Clin. Exp. Neuropsychol.* **12**, 946–958.

Lanteaume, L., Khalfa, S., Regis, J., Marquis, P., Chauvel, P. & Bartolomei, F. 2006 Emotion induction after direct intracerebral stimulations of human amygdala. *Cereb. Cortex*, July 31 [Epub ahead of print].

Lavie, N. 2005 Distracted and confused? selective attention under load. *Trends Cogn. Sci.* **9**, 75–82. (doi:10.1016/j.tics. 2004.12.004)

Lavie, N. & Robertson, I. H. 2001 The role of perceptual load in neglect: rejection of ipsilesional distractors is facilitated with higher central load. *J. Cogn. Neurosci.* **13**, 867–876. (doi:10.1162/089892901753165791)

Lavie, N., Hirst, A., de Fockert, J. W. & Viding, E. 2004 Load theory of selective attention and cognitive control. *J. Exp. Psychol. Gen.* **133**, 339–354. (doi:10.1037/0096-3445. 133.3.339)

LeDoux, J. E. 2000 Emotion circuits in the brain. *Annu. Rev. Neurosci.* **23**, 155–184. (doi:10.1146/annurev. neuro. 23.1.155)

Lhermitte, F., Turell, E., LeBrigand, D. & Chain, F. 1985 Unilateral visual neglect and wave P300. *Arch. Neurol.* **42**, 567–573.

Luck, S. J. 1995 Multiple mechanisms of visual-spatial attention: recent evidence from human electrophysiology. *Behav. Brain Res.* **71**, 113–123. (doi:10.1016/0166-4328 (95)00041-0)

Macaluso, E. & Driver, J. 2001 Spatial attention and crossmodal interactions between vision and touch. *Neuropsychologia* **39**, 1304–1316. (doi:10.1016/S0028-3932(01)00119-1)

Mack, A. & Rock, I. 1998 *Inattentional blindness*. Cambridge, MA: MIT Press.

Martinez, A. *et al.* 1999 Involvement of striate and extrastriate visual cortical areas in spatial attention. *Nat. Neurosci.* **2**, 364–369. (doi:10.1038/7274)

Martinez, A., DiRusso, F., Anllo-Vento, L., Sereno, M. I., Buxton, R. B. & Hillyard, S. A. 2001 Putting spatial attention on the map: timing and localization of stimulus selection processes in striate and extrastriate visual areas. *Vision Res.* **41**, 1437–1457. (doi:10.1016/S0042-6989(00) 00267-4)

Marzi, C., Girelli, M., Miniussi, C., Smania, N. & Maravita, A. 2000 Electrophysiological correlates of conscious vision: evidence from unilateral extinction. *J. Cogn. Neurosci.* **12**, 869–877. (doi:10.1162/089892900562471)

Mathews, A., May, J., Mogg, K. & Eysenck, M. 1990 Attentional bias in anxiety: selective search or defective filtering? *J. Abnorm. Psychol.* **99**, 166–173. (doi:10.1037/ 0021-843X.99.2.166)

Maunsell, J. H. 2004 Neuronal representations of cognitive state: reward or attention? *Trends Cogn. Sci.* **8**, 261–265. (doi:10.1016/j.tics.2004.04.003)

Mesulam, M. M. 1981 A cortical network for directed attention and unilateral neglect. *Ann. Neurol.* **4**, 309–325. (doi:10.1002/ana.410100402)

Mesulam, M. M. 1990 Large-scale neurocognitive networks and distributed processing for attention, language, and memory. *Ann. Neurol.* **28**, 597–613. (doi:10.1002/ana. 410280502)

Mesulam, M. M. 1999 Spatial attention and neglect: parietal, frontal and cingulate contributions to the mental representation and attentional targeting of salient extrapersonal events. *Phil. Trans. R. Soc. B* **354**, 1325–1346. (doi:10. 1098/rstb.1999.0482)

Meyer-Lindenberg, A., Hariri, A. R., Munoz, K. E., Mervis, C. B., Mattay, V. S., Morris, C. A. & Berman, K. F. 2005 Neural correlates of genetically abnormal social cognition in Williams syndrome. *Nat. Neurosci.* **8**, 991–993. (doi:10. 1038/nn1494)

Mogg, K. & Bradley, B. P. 1998 A cognitive-motivational analysis of anxiety. *Behav. Res. Ther.* **36**, 809–848. (doi:10. 1016/S0005-7967(98)00063-1)

Mogg, K., Mathews, A., Eysenck, M. & May, J. 1991 Biased cognitive operations in anxiety: artefact, processing priorities or attentional search? *Behav. Res. Ther.* **29**, 459–467. (doi:10.1016/0005-7967 (91)90130-U)

Mogg, K., Bradley, B. P., de Bono, J. & Painter, M. 1997 Time course of attentional bias for threat information in non-clinical anxiety. *Behav. Res. Ther.* **35**, 297–303. (doi:10.1016/ S0005-7967 (96)00109-X)

Moore, T. & Armstrong, K. M. 2003 Selective gating of visual signals by microstimulation of frontal cortex. *Nature* **421**, 370–373. (doi:10.1038/nature01341)

Moore, T. & Fallah, M. 2004 Microstimulation of the frontal eye field and its effects on covert spatial attention. *J. Neurophysiol.* **91**, 152–162. (doi:10.1152/jn.00741.2002)

Moore, T., Tolias, A. S. & Schiller, P. H. 1998 Visual representations during saccadic eye movements. *Proc. Natl Acad. Sci. USA* **95**, 8981–8984. (doi:10.1073/pnas.95.15.8981)

Moratti, S., Keil, A. & Stolarova, M. 2004 Motivated attention in emotional picture processing is reflected by activity modulation in cortical attention networks. *Neuroimage* **21**, 954–964. (doi:10.1016/j.neuroimage.2003.10.030)

Naccache, L. & Dehaene, S. 2001 The priming method: imaging unconscious repetition priming reveals an abstract representation of number in the parietal lobes. *Cereb. Cortex* **11**, 966–974. (doi:10.1093/cercor/11.10.966)

Norman, K. A., Polyn, S. M., Detre, G. J. & Haxby, J. V. 2006 Beyond mind-reading: multi-voxel pattern analysis of fMRI data. *Trends Cogn. Sci.* **10**, 424–430. (doi:10.1016/j.tics.2006.07.005)

O'Connor, D. H., Fukui, M. M., Pinsk, M. A. & Kastner, S. 2002 Attention modulates responses in the human lateral geniculate nucleus. *Nat. Neurosci.* **5**, 1203–1209. (doi:10.1038/nn957)

O'Craven, K., Downing, P. & Kanwisher, N. 1999 fMRI evidence for objects as the units of attentional selection. *Nature* **401**, 584–587. (doi:10.1038/44134)

Öhman, A. 1986 Face the beast and fear the face: animal and social fears as prototypes for evolutionary analyses of emotion. *Psychophysiology* **23**, 123–145. (doi:10.1111/j.1469-8986.1986.tb00608.x)

Ohman, A., Flykt, A. & Esteves, F. 2001 Emotion drives attention: detecting the snake in the grass. *J. Exp. Psychol. Gen.* **130**, 466–478. (doi:10.1037/0096-3445.130.3.466)

Oram, M. W. & Richmond, B. J. 1999 I see a face – a happy face. *Nat. Neurosci.* **2**, 856–858. (doi:10.1038/13149)

Orban, G. A., Claeys, K., Nelissen, K., Smans, R., Sunaert, S., Todd, J. T., Wardak, C., Durand, J. B. & Vanduffel, W. 2006 Mapping the parietal cortex of human and non-human primates. *Neuropsychologia* **44**, 2647–2667. (doi:10.1016/j.neuropsychologia.2005.11.001)

Oya, H., Kawasaki, H., Howard, M. A. & Adolphs, R. 2002 Electrophysiological responses in the human amygdala discriminate emotion categories of complex visual stimuli. *J. Neurosci.* **22**, 9502–9512.

Pascual-Leone, A. & Walsh, V. 2001 Fast backprojections from the motion to the primary visual area necessary for visual awareness. *Science* **292**, 510–512.

Pascual-Leone, A., Walsh, V. & Rothwell, J. 2000 Transcranial magnetic stimulation in cognitive neuroscience—virtual lesion, chronometry, and functional connectivity. *Curr. Opin. Neurobiol.* **10**, 232–237. (doi:10.1016/S0959-4388(00)00081-7)

Pasley, B. N., Mayes, L. C. & Schultz, R. T. 2004 Subcortical discrimination of unperceived objects during binocular rivalry. *Neuron* **42**, 163–172. (doi:10.1016/S0896-6273 (04)00155-2)

Paus, T. 2005 Inferring causality in brain images: a perturbation approach. *Phil. Trans. R. Soc. B* **360**, 1109–1114. (doi:10.1098/rstb.2005.1652)

Peelen, M. V. & Downing, P. E. 2005 Selectivity for the human body in the fusiform gyrus. *J. Neurophysiol.* **93**, 603–608. (doi:10.1152/jn.00513.2004)

Peelen, M., Atkinson, A., Andersson, F. & Vuilleumier, P. Submitted. Emotional modulation of body-selective visual areas.

Penny, W. D., Stephan, K. E., Mechelli, A. & Friston, K. J. 2004 Modelling functional integration: a comparison of structural equation and dynamic causal models. *Neuroimage* **23**(Suppl. 1), S264–S274. (doi:10.1016/j.neuro-image.2004.07.041)

Pessoa, L., McKenna, M., Gutierrez, E. & Ungerleider, L. G. 2002 Neural processing of emotional faces requires attention. *Proc. Natl Acad. Sci. USA* **99**, 11 458–11 463. (doi:10.1073/pnas.172403899)

Petersen, S. E., Fox, P. T., Posner, M. I., Mintun, M. & Raichle, M. E. 1988 Positron emission tomographic studies of the cortical anatomy of single-word processing. *Nature* **331**, 585–589. (doi:10.1038/331585a0)

Phelps, E. A. & LeDoux, J. E. 2005 Contributions of the amygdala to emotion processing: from animal models to human behavior. *Neuron* **48**, 175–187. (doi:10.1016/ j.neuron.2005.09.025)

Phelps, E. A., Ling, S. & Carrasco, M. 2006 Emotion facilitates perception and potentiates the perceptual benefits of attention. *Psychol. Sci.* **17**, 292–299. (doi:10. 1111/j.1467-9280.2006.01701.x)

Pinsk, M. A., Doniger, G. M. & Kastner, S. 2004 Push–pull mechanism of selective attention in human extrastriate cortex. *J. Neurophysiol.* **92**, 622–629. (doi:10.1152/jn. 00974.2003)

Pizzagalli, D. A., Lehmann, D., Hendrick, A. M., Regard, M., Pascual-Marqui, R. D. & Davidson, R. J. 2002 Affective judgments of faces modulate early activity (approximately 160 ms) within the fusiform gyri. *Neuroimage* **16**, 663–677. (doi:10.1006/nimg.2002.1126)

Platt, M. L. & Glimcher, P. W. 1999 Neural correlates of decision variables in parietal cortex. *Nature* **400**, 233–238. (doi:10.1038/22268)

Posner, M. I. & Dehaene, S. 1994 Attentional networks. *Trends Neurosci.* **17**, 75–79. (doi:10.1016/0166-2236(94) 90078-7)

Pourtois, G. & Vuilleumier, P. 2006 Dynamics of emotional effects on spatial attention in the human visual cortex. *Prog. Brain Res.* **156**, 67–91.

Pourtois, G., Grandjean, D., Sander, D. & Vuilleumier, P. 2004 Electrophysiological correlates of rapid spatial orienting towards fearful faces. *Cereb. Cortex* **14**, 619–633. (doi:10.1093/cercor/bhh023)

Pourtois, G., Thut, G., Grave de Peralta, R., Michel, C. & Vuilleumier, P. 2005 Two electrophysiological stages of spatial orienting towards fearful faces: early temporoparietal activation preceding gain control in extrastriate visual cortex. *Neuroimage* **26**, 149–163. (doi:10.1016/ j.neuroimage. 2005.01.015)

Raichle, M. E., MacLeod, A. M., Snyder, A. Z., Powers, W. J., Gusnard, D. A. & Shulman, G. L. 2001 A default mode of brain function. *Proc. Natl Acad. Sci. USA* **98**, 676–682. (doi:10.1073/ pnas. 98.2.676)

Rees, G., Russell, C., Frith, C. & Driver, J. 1999 Inattentional blindness versus inattentional amnesia for fixated but ignored words. *Science* **286**, 2504–2507. (doi:10.1126/science.286.5449.2504)

Rees, G., Wojciulik, E., Clarke, K., Husain, M., Frith, C. D. & Driver, J. 2000 Unconscious activation of visual cortex in the damaged right hemisphere of a parietal patient with extinction. *Brain* **123**, 1624–1633. (doi:10.1093/brain/123.8.1624)

Rees, G., Wojciulik, E., Clarke, K., Husain, M., Frith, C. & Driver, J. 2002 Neural correlates of conscious and unconscious vision in parietal extinction. *Neurocase* **8**, 387–393. (doi:10.1093/neucas/8.5.387)

Rees, G. 2007 Neural correlates of the contents of visual awareness in humans. *Phil. Trans. R. Soc. B* **362**, 877–886. (doi:10.1098/rstb.2007.2094)

Robbins, T. W. 2007 Shifting and stopping: fronto-striatal substrates, neurochemical modulation and clinical implications. *Phil. Trans. R. Soc. B* **362**, 917–932. (doi:10.1098/ rstb.2007.2097)

Robertson, I. H. 1999 Cognitive rehabilitation: attention and neglect. *Trends Cogn. Sci.* **3**, 385–393. (doi:10.1016/ S1364-6613(99)01378-9)

Rorden, C. & Karnath, H. O. 2004 Using human brain lesions to infer function:a relic from a past era in the fMRI age? *Nat. Rev. Neurosci.* **5**, 813–819. (doi:10.1038/nrn1521)

Rosen, J. B. & Donley, M. P. 2006 Animal studies of amygdala function in fear and uncertainty: relevance to human research. *Biol. Psychol.* **73**, 49–60. (doi:10.1016/ j.biopsycho.2006.01.007)

Rotshtein, P., Richardson, M., Winston, J., Kiebel, S., Quayle, A., Eimer, M., Driver, J. & Dolan, R. 2006 Early brain responses to fearful faces are modulated by amygdala lesion. *Abstract Organisation for Human Brain Mapping*. Florence.

Ruff, C. C. *et al.* 2006 Concurrent TMS–fMRI and psychophysics reveal frontal influences on human retinotopic visual cortex. *Curr. Biol.* **16**, 1479–1488. (doi:10. 1016/j.cub.2006.06.057)

Sabatinelli, D., Bradley, M. M., Fitzsimmons, J. R. & Lang, P. J. 2005 Parallel amygdala and inferotemporal activation reflect emotional intensity and fear relevance. *Neuroimage* **24**, 1265–1270. (doi:10.1016/j.neuroimage. 2004.12.015)

Sander, D., Grafman, J. & Zalla, T. 2003 The human amygdala: an evolved system for relevance detection. *Rev. Neurosci.* **14**, 303–316.

Saenz, M., Buracas, G. T. & Boynton, G. M. 2002 Global effects of feature-based attention in human visual cortex. *Nat. Neurosci.* **5**, 631–632. (doi:10.1038/nn876)

Sato, W., Kochiyama, T., Yoshikawa, S. & Matsumura, M. 2001 Emotional expression boosts early visual processing of the face: ERP recording and its decomposition by independent component analysis. *Neuroreport* **12**, 709–714. (doi:10.1097/00001756-200103260-00019)

Schall, J. D. 2004 On the role of frontal eye field in guiding attention and saccades. *Vision Res.* **44**, 1453–1467. (doi:10.1016/j.visres.2003.10.025)

Schupp, H. T., Junghofer, M., Weike, A. I. & Hamm, A. O. 2003 Attention and emotion: an ERP analysis offacilitated emotional stimulus processing. *Neuroreport* **14**, 1107–1110. (doi:10.1097/00001756-200306110-00002)

Schwartz, S., Vuilleumier, P., Hutton, C., Maravita, A., Dolan, R. J. & Driver, J. 2005 Attentional load and sensory competition in human vision: modulation of fMRI responses by load at fixation during task-irrelevant stimulation in the peripheral visual field. *Cereb. Cortex* **15**, 770–786. (doi:10.1093/cercor/bhh178)

Sereno, M. I., Dale, A. M., Reppas, J. B., Kwong, K. K., Belliveau, J. W., Brady, T. J., Rosen, B. R. & Tootell, R. B. 1995 Borders of multiple visual areas in humans revealed by functional magnetic resonance imaging. *Science* **268**, 889–893. (doi:10.1126/science.7754376)

Shallice, T. 1988 *From neuropsychology to mental structure*. Cambridge, MA: Cambridge University Press.

Shuler, M. G. & Bear, M. F. 2006 Reward timing in the primary visual cortex. *Science* **311**, 1606–1609. (doi:10. 1126/science.1123513)

Spinelli, D., Burr, D. C. & Morrone, M. C. 1994 Spatial neglect is associated with increased latencies of visual evoked potentials. *Vis. Neurosci.* **11**, 909–918.

Stuss, D. T. & Alexander, M. P. 2007 Is there a dysexecutive syndrome? *Phil. Trans. R. Soc. B* **362**, 901–915. (doi:10. 1098/rstb.2007.2096)

Sugase, Y., Yamane, S., Ueno, S. & Kawano, K. 1999 Global and fine information coded by single neurons in the temporal visual cortex. *Nature* **400**, 869–873. (doi:10. 1038/23703)

Sugrue, L. P., Corrado, G. S. & Newsome, W. T. 2004 Matching behavior and the representation of value in the parietal cortex. *Science* **304**, 1782–1787. (doi:10.1126/ science.1094765)

Surguladze, S. A., Brammer, M. J., Young, A. W., Andrew, C., Travis, M. J., Williams, S. C. & Phillips, M. L. 2003 A preferential increase in the extrastriate response to signals of danger. *Neuroimage* **19**, 1317–1328. (doi:10. 1016/S1053-8119(03)00085-5)

Taylor, P. C., Nobre, A. C. & Rushworth, M. F. 2007 FEF TMS affects visual cortical activity. *Cereb. Cortex* **17**, 391–399. (doi:10.1093/cercor/bhj156)

Tong, F., Nakayama, K., Moscovitch, M., Weinrib, O. & Kanwisher, N. 2000 Response properties of the human fusiform face area. *Cognitive Neuropsych.* **17**, 257–279. (doi:10.1080/026432900380607)

Valdes-Sosa, P. A., Kotter, R. & Friston, K. J. 2005 Introduction: multimodal neuroimaging of brain connectivity. *Phil. Trans. R. Soc. B* **360**, 865–867. (doi:10.1098/ rstb.2005.1655)

Vallar, G., Bottini, G. & Paulesu, E. 2003 Neglect syndromes: the role of the parietal cortex. In The parietal lobes, vol. 93 (eds A. M. Siegel, R. A. Andersen, H. J. Freund & D. D. Spencer), pp. 219–315. London, UK: Lippincott, Williams & Wilkins.

van Stegeren, A. H., Wolf, O. T., Everaerd, W., Scheltens, P., Barkhof, F. & Rombouts, S. A. 2007 Endogenous cortisol level interacts with noradrenergic activation in the human amygdala. *Neurobiol. Learn. Mem.* **87**, 57–66. (doi:10. 1016/j.nlm.2006.05.008)

Viggiano, M. P., Spinelli, D. & Mecacci, L. 1995 Pattern reversal visual evoked potentials in patients with hemi-neglect syndrome. *Brain Cogn.* **27**, 17–35. (doi:10.1006/ brcg.1995.1002)

Vuilleumier, P. 2005 How brains beware: neural mechanisms of emotional attention. *Trends Cogn. Sci.* **9**, 585–594. (doi:10.1016/j.tics.2005.10.011)

Vuilleumier,P. & Pourtois, G. 2007 Distributed and interactive brain mechanisms during emotion face perception:evidence from functional neuroimaging. *Neuropsychologia* **45**, 174–194. (doi:10.1016/ j.neuropsychologia.2006.06.003)

Vuilleumier, P. & Schwartz, S. 2001a Beware and be aware: capture of attention by fear-relevant stimuli in patients with unilateral neglect. *Neuroreport* **12**, 1119–1122. (doi:10.1097/ 00001756-200105080-00014)

Vuilleumier, P. & Schwartz, S. 2001b Emotional facial expressions capture attention. *Neurology* **56**, 153–158.

Vuilleumier, P., Armony, J. L., Driver, J. & Dolan, R. J. 2001a Effects of attention and emotion on face processing in the human brain: an event-related fMRI study. *Neuron* **30**, 829–841. (doi:10.1016/ S0896-6273(01)00328-2)

Vuilleumier, P., Sagiv, N., Hazeltine, E., Poldrack, R., Swick, D., Rafal, R. & Gabrieli, J. 2001*b* Neural fate of seen and unseen faces in unilateral spatial neglect: a combined event-related fMRI and ERP study of visual extinction. *Proc. Natl Acad. Sci. USA* **98**, 3495–3500. (doi:10.1073/ pnas. 051436898)

Vuilleumier, P., Armony, J., Clarke, K., Husain, M., Driver, J. & Dolan, R. 2002*a* Neural response to emotional faces with and without awareness: event-related fMRI in a parietal patient with visual extinction and spatial neglect. *Neuropsychologia* **40**, 2156–2166. (doi:10.1016/ S0028-3932(02)00045-3)

Vuilleumier, P., Henson, R., Driver, J. & Dolan, R. J. 2002*b* Multiple levels of visual object constancy revealed by event-related fMRI of repetition priming. *Nat. Neurosci.* **5**, 491–499. (doi:10. 1038/nn839)

Vuilleumier, P., Armony, J. & Dolan, R. 2003 Reciprocal links between emotion and attention. In *Human brain functions* (eds K. J. Friston, C. D. Frith, R. J. Dolan, C. Price, J. Ashburner, W. Penny, S. Zeki & R. S. J. Frackowiak), pp. 419–444. San Diego, IL: Academic Press.

Vuilleumier, P., Richardson, M., Armony, J., Driver, J. & Dolan, R. J. 2004*a* Distant influences of amygdala lesion on visual cortical activation during emotional face processing. *Nat. Neurosci.* **7**, 1271–1278. (doi:10.1038/ nn1341)

Vuilleumier, P., Schwartz, S., Maravita, A., Rees, G., Hutton, C., Husain, M., Dolan, R. J. & Driver, J. 2004*b* Functional changes in activation of retinotopic visual cortex in patients with right parietal damage and left visuospatial neglect. In *Human brain mapping*. Budapest: Neuroimage.

Walker, R., Findlay, J. M., Young, A. W. & Welch, J. 1991 Disentangling neglect and hemianopia. *Neuropsychologia* **29**, 1019–1027. (doi:10.1016/0028-3932(91)90065-G)

Wells, A. & Matthews, G. 1994 *Attention and emotion: a clinical perspective*. Hove, UK: Lawrence Erlbaum.

Williams, M. A. & Mattingley, J. B. 2004 Unconscious perception of non-threatening facial emotion in parietal extinction. *Exp. Brain Res.* **154**, 403–406. (doi:10.1007/ s00221-003-1740-x)

Williams, M. A., Morris, A. P., McGlone, F., Abbott, D. F. & Mattingley, J. B. 2004 Amygdala responses to fearful and happy facial expressions under conditions of binocular suppression. *J. Neurosci.* **24**, 2898–2904. (doi:10.1523/ JNEUROSCI.4977-03.2004)

Winston, J. S., O'Doherty, J. & Dolan, R. J. 2003 Common and distinct neural responses during direct and incidental processing of multiple facial emotions. *Neuroimage* **20**, 84–97. (doi:10.1016/S1053-8119(03)00303-3)

Wise, R. G. & Tracey, I. 2006 The role of fMRI in drug discovery. *J. Magn. Reson. Imaging* **23**, 862–876. (doi:10. 1002/jmri.20584)

Wojciulik, E., Kanwisher, N. & Driver, J. 1998 Covert visual attention modulates face-specific activity in the human fusiform gyrus: fMRI study. *J. Neurophysiol.* **79**, 1574–1578.

Yago, E., Duarte, A., Wong, T., Barcelo, F. & Knight, R. T. 2004 Temporal kinetics of prefrontal modulation of the extrastriate cortex during visual attention. *Cogn. Affect. Behav. Neurosci.* **4**, 609–617.

Yiend, J. & Mathews, A. 2001 Anxiety and attention to threatening pictures. *Q. J. Exp. Psychol. A* **54**, 665–681. (doi:10.1080/02724980042000462)

Zumsteg, D., Lozano, A. M. & Wennberg, R. A. 2006 Depth electrode recorded cerebral responses with deep brain stimulation of the anterior thalamus for epilepsy. *Clin. Neurophysiol.* **117**, 1602–1609. (doi:10.1016/j.clinph.2006. 04.008)

9

Levels of processing during non-conscious perception: a critical review of visual masking

Sid Kouider* and Stanislas Dehaene

Understanding the extent and limits of non-conscious processing is an important step on the road to a thorough understanding of the cognitive and cerebral correlates of conscious perception. In this article, we present a critical review of research on subliminal perception during masking and other related experimental conditions. Although initially controversial, the possibility that a broad variety of processes can be activated by a non-reportable stimulus is now well established. Behavioural findings of subliminal priming indicate that a masked word or digit can have an influence on perceptual, lexical and semantic levels, while neuroimaging directly visualizes the brain activation that it evokes in several cortical areas. This activation is often attenuated under subliminal presentation conditions compared to consciously reportable conditions, but there are sufficiently many exceptions, in paradigms such as the attentional blink, to indicate that high activation, *per se*, is not a sufficient condition for conscious access to occur. We conclude by arguing that for a stimulus to reach consciousness, two factors are jointly needed: (i) the input stimulus must have enough strength (which can be prevented by masking) and (ii) it must receive top-down attention (which can be prevented by drawing attention to another stimulus or task). This view leads to a distinction between two types of non-conscious processes, which we call subliminal and preconscious. According to us, maintaining this distinction is essential in order to make sense of the growing neuroimaging data on the neural correlates of consciousness.

Keywords: consciousness; subliminal perception; priming; brain imaging; review

9.1 Introduction

To what extent can non-conscious perception affect our behaviours? This issue, one of the most controversial in psychology (e.g. Sidis 1898; Eriksen 1960; Dixon 1971; Holender 1986; Merikle & Daneman 1998), has been predominantly addressed through the use of subliminal stimulation methods, in which a stimulus is presented below the 'limen' or threshold for conscious perception. Subliminal perception is inferred when a stimulus is demonstrated to be invisible while still influencing thoughts, feelings, actions, learning or memory.

Construction of a convincing empirical demonstration of subliminal processing has constituted a challenging task. Indeed, this topic has faced some of the most complex problems of experimental psychology, not only technically (e.g. How to present stimuli that are invisible but still processed?), but also methodologically (e.g. How to measure non-conscious influences from a stimulus? How to demonstrate an absence of conscious perception?), theoretically (e.g. Should we trust introspective subjective measures or rather rely on objective measures?) and epistemologically (e.g. Why do so many subliminal perception experiments

*Author and address for correspondence: Ecole Normale Supérieure, 46 rue d'Ulm, 75005 Paris, France (sid.kouider@ens.fr).

fail to be replicated?). Such difficulties, among others, are the reasons why the topic of perception without awareness has taken so long to achieve respectability.

Nowadays, while the existence of subliminal perception is no longer denied, the controversy has shifted to the depth of processing of invisible stimuli. While it is largely accepted that lower levels of processing (e.g. motor reflexes, sensory analysis) do not necessitate perceptual awareness, the existence of non-conscious computations at higher levels (e.g. semantic or inferential processing) remains debated. The claim of subliminal semantic activation has been cyclically acclaimed or rejected (Eriksen 1960; Dixon 1971; Holender 1986; Greenwald 1992).

In parallel, conflicting theoretical positions have been adopted regarding the differences between conscious and non-conscious processing. Some authors continue to argue in favour of the classical notion that mental representations and consciousness go hand in hand, thus leaving little room for the possibility of non-conscious levels of representation (Dulany 1997; Perruchet & Vinter 2002; Holender & Duscherer 2004). According to this 'mentalistic' perspective, non-conscious processes exist, but are non-representational and thus, by definition, cannot involve semantic representations. Conversely, several authors have argued that all information processing can proceed without conscious experience, at least in principle, and that consciousness may therefore be of an altogether different, perhaps non-computational nature (Chalmers 1996). This perspective meshes well with the hypothesis that non-conscious processes can attain the highest levels of representation, a position advocated for instance by Marcel (1983, p. 238): 'non-conscious perceptual processes automatically redescribe sensory data into every representational form and to the highest levels of description available to the organism'.

In between these two extreme positions, an intermediate and widely held view proposes that a stimulus first involves a non-conscious analysis associated with the lower levels of processing, and then a second conscious stage associated with higher levels of representations. According to this view, non-conscious processes exist but are limited in depth. To follow Greenwald's (1992) terminology, non-conscious processes should be considered as 'dumb' rather than 'smart' in comparison to conscious processes. The two-stage position suggests a rigid limit between non-conscious and conscious levels of processing, the former involving an automatic activation of information while the latter are associated with strategic processes under volitional control (Posner & Snyder 1975; Schneider & Shiffrin 1977). According to this position, it is strictly an empirical problem to determine whether semantic-level processes fall below or above the hypothetical limit of subliminal processing depth.

Nowadays, two-stage accounts have evolved into a more dynamical view, which considers the notion of 'conscious access' as a central concept. In the global neuronal workspace framework (Dehaene & Naccache 2001; Dehaene & Changeux 2004), which extends Baars' (1988) cognitive theory of consciousness, the human brain is viewed as a collection of specialized processors that mostly operate non-consciously, but whose content can be consciously accessed whenever they are linked to a global, metastable assembly involving distant prefrontal and parietal neurons with long-range axons. According to this view, there is no fixed limit between conscious and non-conscious processing but, rather, subjects at any given moment can attend to one of the several (though not necessarily all) levels of representation and bring the corresponding information into consciousness.

With these conflicting theories in mind, the present article provides an overview of past and current researches on non-conscious perception. We initially focus on subliminal masking paradigms, then extend our review to discuss other forms of non-conscious perception such as those induced by inattention. In section 9, we outline a theoretical framework that may account for the differences between these two types of non-conscious perception.

9.2 A historical perspective on subliminal perception

It is primarily via the demonstration of semantic activation from invisible stimuli that research-ers have tried to define the limits of non-conscious perception. This approach consists of test-ing the hypothesis that the meaning of a stimulus is extracted while the subject cannot consciously identify it or even detect its presence. Stimuli are usually made subliminal by the joint use of brief presentations and masking techniques. A direct measure such as identifica-tion, discrimination or detection is used to show null sensitivity on the masked stimulus. An indirect measure is used to show that, nevertheless, this stimulus influences behaviour. The most common indirect measure is masked priming, in which a highly visible target stimulus is processed more efficiently when preceded by a related and heavily masked prime than by an unrelated prime. Figure 9.1 provides examples of established subliminal priming methods in the domain of visual words, faces and speech perception.

As we review below, characterization of the processes involved in subliminal masked priming has remained controversial. The development of this field of research can be divided into five periods.

9.3 Period 1: On demonstrating perception without awareness

The study of non-conscious perception appeared simultaneously with the emergence of psychology and its separation from philosophy during the nineteenth century. Several scientists evoked the possibility that mental life extended beyond conscious processing. Johann Herbart (1776–1841) introduced the word 'subliminal' to describe ideas that compete below the limen for consciousness. According to Hermann Von Helmholtz (1821–1894), visual perception mostly resulted from the operation of non-conscious inferential processes. On the other hand, under the influence of Wilhelm Wundt during the second part of the nineteenth century, introspective reports were considered as a scientifically valid measure for studying mental states. Contrary to Herbart and Von Helmholtz's perspective, this position considered that all mental states are potentially accessible to conscious report. In spite of its limits, this played a helpful role in developing methods for measuring aspects of conscious experience.

The introspective approach was used in a landmark paper by Pierce & Jastrow (1884). In their study, subjects (Peirce and Jastrow themselves) received a first pressure on a finger and then a second slightly stronger or slightly weaker one. They judged which one seemed the more intense by rating their estimation on a 0–3 scale, where '0 denoted absence of any prefer-ence for one answer over its opposite, so that it seemed nonsensical to answer at all' (Pierce & Jastrow 1880, p. 78). They also performed a forced-choice discrimination task between the two possibilities. Peirce and Jastrow found that under subjective estimations of null awareness they could still discriminate the two alternatives well above the 50% criterion for chance per-formance, suggesting the existence of non-conscious influences on behaviour. Along the same lines, Sidis (1898) presented cards containing alphanumeric characters at a distance, such that subjects reported they barely saw a dim, blurred spot. Yet, subjects were better than chance not only at discriminating whether the stimulus was a digit or a letter in a forced-choice task, but also in guessing its identity. Stroh *et al.* (1908) extended these findings to the auditory modal-ity, by showing that subjects were better than chance at guessing whispered letter names under conditions where they reported not hearing any sound.

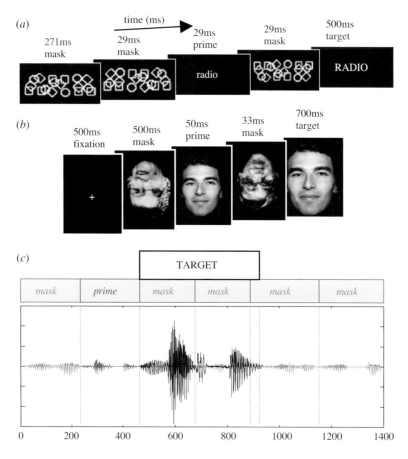

Fig. 9.1 Schematic description of three masked priming methods for which objective direct measures have demonstrated prime invisibility or inaudibility. (*a*) Visual word repetition priming across case (Dehaene *et al.* 2001). (*b*) Repetition priming for faces (Kouider *et al.* submitted). Masks are made of overlaid and reversed faces and the prime size is reduced by 80% when compared with the target. (*c*) Repetition priming for spoken words (Kouider & Dupoux 2005). Masks made from backward speech and the prime are attenuated (−15 dB) and time compressed to 35% of their original duration.

These pioneering studies were followed by a few other similar demonstrations during the first half of the twentieth century (see Adams 1957, for a review). Claims of subliminal influences on behaviour became especially popular during the mid-1950s, when a few advertising companies initiated the fallacious belief that it can have long-term effects on consumer's choice (see Pratkanis 1992, for a review).

The end of this first period can be attributed to Eriksen's (1960) criticism of the scientific literature on subliminal perception. Basically, he argued against the use of introspection as a valid measure of awareness. Subjective measures might reflect response bias rather than the genuine subjective experience of the observer owing to the so-called 'underconfidence phenomenon' (Bjorkman *et al.* 1993). Subjects may partially or even fully see the stimulus, yet claim that they have not seen it because they need a higher level of certainty. This confidence criterion depends on the expectations that the experimenter is imposing on the subject. Furthermore, experimenters might have a tendency to underestimate awareness as a function of the hypothesis at hand (S. Kouider 2002, unpublished doctoral thesis). Eriksen further argued that the objective threshold for consciousness should be defined as a situation where forced-choice discrimination is at chance. According to this new operational definition of awareness, the discrimination tasks previously used as indirect measures thought to prove non-conscious influences now became the direct measure thought to index awareness of the stimulus. Of course, such a new definition of awareness left researchers with the difficult problem of inventing new indirect measures of subliminal processing.

9.4 Period 2: On demonstrating subliminal semantic influences

The second phase of research started with the use of semantic influences as an indirect measure of perception, primarily with the seminal work of Marcel (1974, 1980, 1983). Marcel used the method of visual masking to render stimuli invisible and provided two types of experimental evidence for non-conscious semantic processing. First, he argued that under presentation conditions, where subjects could not detect the presence or absence of a masked word, this stimulus nevertheless produced semantic biases. Subsequently to a masked word (e.g. 'salt'), subjects were presented with two alternatives, one which was semantically related (e.g. 'pepper') and the other unrelated (e.g. 'lotus'). Subjects preferred to choose the former alternative, suggesting the presence of semantic influences from invisible words. Similarly, Allport (1977) found that when subjects failed to correctly recognize a masked word, many of their errors were semantically related to the masked word. Second, Marcel (1980, 1983) provided evidence that semantic priming—the facilitation of the processing of a target word by another semantically related 'prime' word—remained present under heavy masking conditions that render the primes subliminal.

At that time, mainly owing to Eriksen's (1960) critical review, the scientific community was extremely sceptical regarding the existence of subliminal perception, not to mention the existence of subliminal activation at the semantic level. Yet, by the early 1980s, several other authors started to report similar results. Semantic priming from masked stimuli was replicated not only with words (Fowler *et al.* 1981; Balota 1983) but also with pictures (McCauley *et al.* 1980; Carr *et al.* 1982). However, as we will see below, all these studies without exception suffered from serious methodological flaws.

9.5 Period 3: The hunt for artefacts

Holender (1986) published a detailed and intensively argued criticism of masked priming studies. The article stressed the need to carefully control the methods used to argue for the existence of subliminal semantic processing. He mainly argued that the issue of awareness was not properly addressed and was largely underestimated in past studies. After Holender's article, scepticism regarding the existence of subliminal semantic activation became the rule. It was also motivated by several other studies that pointed to serious methodological flaws in demonstrations of subliminal semantic influences. We summarize these different problems below.

(a) The need for methodological controls

First, the semantic biases in the choice of alternatives observed by Marcel (1983) could have been due to the absence of counterbalancing for the experimental and control word lists.

Subjects tend to report that the prime is pepper rather than lotus not only if the prime is salt but also when there is no prime at all (Fowler *et al*. 1981)! Along the same lines, although it is true that subjects can sometimes erroneously report a semantic associate of a masked word (Allport 1977), this need not happen more often than what would be expected from chance (Ellis & Marshall 1978; Williams & Parkin 1980; however, see Gaillard *et al*. 2006*a* for a clear case of semantic influence on verbal reports).

Second, Merikle (1982) used signal detection theory to show that the small sample of items frequently used to evaluate the threshold for conscious perception (not more than 20 trials) is not statistically reliable. Under statistically valid conditions, Marcel's experiments could no longer be replicated (Cheesman & Merikle 1984).

Third, prime visibility was largely underestimated. Indeed, the first studies of Marcel and others used tachistoscopic presentations for which the display parameters were fixed in a preliminary phase, before the proper indirect measure (e.g. priming) started. A method of descending threshold was used, consisting of decreasing the delay between the prime and a brief backward mask until subjects performed at a chance level on the direct measure. These parameters were then considered as subliminal during the subsequent indirect measure. However, subjects were differentially adapted to darkness during the two phases. During the threshold definition, only brief (e.g. 50 ms) primes and backward masks were presented, while subjects also received a long (e.g. 800 ms) and visible target during the indirect measure. This had the consequence of increasing dark adaptation, and thus increasing prime identification from 0 to 70% as shown by Purcell *et al*. (1983). Moreover, they found that when luminance is controlled carefully, semantic priming fully correlated with prime visibility. Similarly, Nolan & Caramazza (1982) asked subjects to perform the direct and indirect measures on the same trials and also found that semantic effects correlated with performance on the prime detection task. These studies suggest that stimulus visibility should not be established before but, rather, during or after the indirect measure and, furthermore, that the same display conditions should be used.

Fourth, Bernstein *et al*. (1989) found that the semantic context can modulate prime visibility. This finding is based on the fact that unmasked semantic priming reflects not only classical or proactive priming, i.e. semantic activation from the prime representation to the target representation, but also backward or retroactive priming, i.e. semantic activation from the target to the prime (see Neely 1991, for a review). Evidence for retroactive priming comes from studies showing that priming occurs for semantically related pairs for which an association exists from the target to the prime, but not from the prime to the target (Koriat 1981; Chwilla *et al*. 1998). Since semantically related target stimuli can increase, retrospectively, the identification of masked primes (Bernstein *et al*. 1989), the absence of any target stimuli during threshold definition procedures in the experiments of Marcel and others probably underestimated prime visibility. In fact, many other studies have found that semantic priming, prime reportability and retroactive priming are interdependent (Briand *et al*. 1988; Dark 1988; Dark & Benson 1991; Van Voorhis & Dark 1995). Semantic relatedness increases, retrospectively, the reportability of the prime, which in turns leads to semantic priming. Accordingly, in these studies, masked semantic priming occurred only when subjects were able to identify the masked primes: in the absence of retroactive priming, prime reportability decreased and masked semantic priming vanished. It is of note, however, that Durante & Hirshman (1994) found the reverse correlation: proactive semantic priming decreased when retroactive priming increased. It remains unclear why the results of this study are discordant with others.

(b) On the status of qualitative dissociations

According to some authors (e.g. Dixon 1971, 1981), another way of demonstrating subliminal influences is to show that subliminal and conscious perception afford qualitatively different processes. Marcel (1980) used this process-dissociation logic and reported that context effects on semantic priming for homographs depend on prime awareness. He presented subject with word triplets corresponding to the context/prime/target presentation sequence and for which the first and last words were either congruent (hand/palm/wrist) or incongruent (tree/palm/wrist). If the prime was clearly visible, he found facilitation for congruent trials and interference for incongruent trials. By contrast, Marcel reported that no context bias occurs when the prime is not visible, leading to facilitation for both congruent and incongruent trials. These results were considered as evidence for a dissociation between non-conscious and conscious processes.

A similar dissociation logic was used by Merikle *et al.* with the goal of avoiding exceeding reliance on objective measures of consciousness. While all the above studies used objective measures of awareness, in accord with Eriksen's (1960) criticism, Cheesman & Merikle (1986) privileged subjective measures, as in the earliest research on subliminal perception. Their main argument against the use of objective measures was that they can lead to above-chance performance due to non-conscious influences, thus making the definition of an objective threshold an extremely conservative measure of conscious access. To address this problem, Cheesman & Merikle (1986), using a process-dissociation logic, argued that the definition of a subjective limit between conscious and subliminal perception would be validated if they gave rise to qualitatively different forms of processing. They used a priming version of the Stroop task in which, compared with a neutral condition, subjects are slower to respond to a target colour patch if it is preceded by a prime word denoting a different colour (e.g. the word 'blue' preceding a red patch) and faster if the prime and target denote the same colour. In accord with past studies (Taylor 1977), they found that if the proportion of congruent trials increased (for instance, from 25 to 75%), then facilitation and interference increased. Indeed, in this case, the prime is the same as the target in most cases, and subjects can use this information to anticipate the identity of the target during the appearance of the prime. However, when prime duration was decreased from 250 ms to a shorter duration at which subjects denied perceiving the primes, priming was still found and, importantly, it ceased to be affected by predictive strategies. According to Cheesman & Merikle, this dissociation demonstrates that subjects are genuinely unaware of the primes with brief prime durations. In later work, Merikle and colleagues (Merikle *et al.* 1995; Merikle & Joordens 1997) showed that under some conditions, predictive strategies could even reverse the Stroop effect, leading to faster reaction times for incongruent primes. Here too, this was the case only for rather long prime duration (e.g. 150 ms), but not for shorter durations (e.g. 50 ms).

However, as outlined by Holender (1986), the problem with this logic is that qualitative dissociations need not reflect a dissociation between conscious and subliminal processing. One must ensure that they do not occur merely owing to other confounded differences, for instance because the SOA is much shorter in the subliminal case, as was the case in the studies of both Marcel (1980) and Cheesman & Merikle (1986). As argued by S. Kouider (2002, unpublished doctoral thesis), it is well known from the unmasked priming literature that even clearly visible primes produce qualitative differences as a function of the prime-target delay. For instance, Swinney (1979) has shown that context effects on semantic priming of homographs depend on the time course of prime processing, not prime visibility *per se*. Thus, rather than being due to visibility, these qualitative dissociations could be due to differences in the time or resources needed to strategically process the prime. In the case of Merikle and colleagues' studies, in which subjects are explicitly asked to try to identify the primes before responding to the target, primes that are difficult to identify would require attentional resources that otherwise could be used for predictive strategies. As recently shown by Kouider & Dupoux (2004), predictive strategies can no longer be used with short prime duration owing to the difficulty in identifying the primes, not because the primes are rendered subliminal. In fact, when the primes are not just difficult to perceive but genuinely invisible, then Stroop priming disappears as well (Tzelgov *et al.* 1997; Kouider & Dupoux 2004).

The process-dissociation method was later extended through the use of inclusion–exclusion tasks (Debner & Jacoby 1994; Merikle *et al.* 1995; Merikle & Joordens 1997). In a typical exclusion task, subjects have to complete a target fragment (e.g. 'YE____') with any word that comes to mind, except the prime (e.g. 'yellow'). Debner & Jacoby (1994) have shown that exclusion is no longer possible when primes are masked and presented for a brief duration (50 ms). Instead, subjects frequently complete the fragment with the prime word itself. This failure to exclude masked primes while being influenced by them suggests a process-dissociation between conscious and subliminal perception (Debner & Jacoby 1994; Merikle *et al.* 2001). Yet, one should be cautious before making this conclusion because the results may be imputed to partial conscious perception. Indeed, it is possible that subjects were only aware of some letters of the prime such as 'llow' and then completed the fragment 'YE___' onto 'yellow' while faithfully complying with the instruction to avoid reporting a seen word. In fact, recent investigations have shown that when an orthographic baseline (e.g. 'billow') is used, then there is a similar probability to complete 'YE___' onto 'yellow' (Hutchison *et al.* 2004). Although the authors used this result to argue that non-conscious influences occur at the orthographic level with this task, it may as well mean that it results from partial conscious perception of the primes. Further studies will be needed to demonstrate that perceptual influences on the exclusion task are of a genuinely subliminal nature.

9.6 Period 4: Methodological improvements and recovery from scepticism

In the late 1980s, subliminal perception was no longer an isolated domain in the study of non-conscious processing, given the emergence of great interest in implicit memory and implicit learning at that time (e.g. Kihlstrom 1987; Schacter 1987). While these topics also suffered from similar difficulties, especially regarding the assessment of awareness (Shanks & St. John 1994), they largely contributed to reinstate the study of non-conscious processing from a cognitive rather than a psychoanalytic perspective (Greenwald 1992). Furthermore, despite Holender's massive criticism, or perhaps under its admonition, new and stronger paradigms of subliminal priming emerged.

(a) Insights from psycholinguistics

In the hands of Forster and Humphreys, masked priming became a powerful method to study visual word recognition (Evett & Humphreys 1981; Forster & Davis 1984). These authors did not focus on semantic activation, but rather on lexical processing. They used masked priming with the assumption that a minimal perceptual awareness of the word stimulus allows study of its automatic, strategy-free processing (e.g. Posner & Snyder 1975). They primarily relied on orthographic and repetition priming, not semantic priming, to address several issues that are more directly relevant to psycholinguistics than to subliminal perception (e.g. Is masked repetition priming affected by word frequency? Is priming lexical or sub-lexical? Can it occur at a phonological level? Do orthographic neighbours inhibit or facilitate word recognition? And so forth). We first describe the paradigm introduced by Humphreys and colleagues, as well as its implications, and then turn to the one introduced by Forster and colleagues.

(i) Humphreys' masked priming method

The masked priming method of Humphreys and colleagues (Evett & Humphreys 1981; Humphreys *et al.* 1982, 1988) comprised the presentation of four events: a forward mask (i.e. random letter fragments), the prime in lower case, the target in upper case and then a backward mask. All these events were presented for a very short duration (e.g. 25–50 ms) such that the prime could not be identified, while the target could be correctly identified on about half of the trials. The measure here was whether perceptual identification of the target improved when preceded by a related prime. Yet, since the presentation parameters were estimated for each subject during a preceding threshold definition session, this methodology did not fully escape Holender's criticism (see above).

The research mostly investigated whether masked written words can contact the phonological level of representations. Although the first answer provided by Evett & Humphreys (1981) was negative, later studies found that, under some conditions, phonological effects can be found in addition to orthographic priming (e.g. Humphreys *et al.* 1982). Perfetti and colleagues (Perfetti *et al.* 1988; Perfetti & Bell 1991; Berent & Perfetti 1995) later developed a backward priming variant, in which the prime follows, rather than precedes, the target and in which robust phonological priming effect can be found.

Nonetheless, this methodology has been less popular than the one introduced by Forster and colleagues (described below) for two main reasons. First, given that not only the prime but also the target is presented very briefly in this paradigm, subjects sometimes report the prime instead of the target and tend to mix their letters during identification, suggesting conscious access to at least partial information regarding the primes (Brysbaert & Praet 1992; Perry & Ziegler 2002). As shown by Perry & Ziegler (2002), phonological effects in this paradigm can result from partial awareness rather than subliminal processing. Second, as shown by Davis & Forster (1994), priming in this paradigm might be entirely due to differences in terms of target legibility, which results from a physical fusion between the prime and target stimuli and is higher for orthographically related words. Importantly, when the target duration is relatively long, as in the Forster and Davis method, low-level physical integration disappears (Davis & Forster 1994).

(ii) Forster and Davis' masked priming method

The masked priming method by Forster and colleagues (Forster & Davis 1984, 1991) is simpler because it has no backward mask, the target being itself considered a very strong mask. The display typically consists of a 500 ms forward mask (e.g. ######), a lower-case prime for a brief duration (60 ms or below) and an upper-case target for another 700 ms. Priming with this method has been found not only at the orthographic level (Forster *et al.* 1987), but also at the level of morphology (easier processing of cars-CAR compared with card-CAR; Forster *et al.* 1987; Rastle *et al.* 2000), phonology (easier processing of klip-CLIP compared with plip-CLIP; Ferrand & Grainger 1992, 1993; Lukatela *et al*. 1998), cross-modal repetitions (visual-to-auditory priming; Kouider & Dupoux 2001) and, importantly, for semantically related words (Sereno 1991; Perea & Gotor 1997; Rastle *et al*. 2000) and translations (Gollan *et al*. 1997; Grainger & Frenck-Mestre 1998).

Nevertheless, the problem with all these studies is that most of them do not provide an index of prime awareness, making it difficult to assess whether the primes were visible or not. Kouider & Dupoux (2001) assessed prime awareness in this method across several prime durations and showed that a prime can be considered as genuinely invisible only if its duration is below 50 ms. Although orthographic and morphological priming are found at such durations, priming usually vanishes below 50 ms for semantic (Perea & Gotor 1997; Rastle *et al*. 2000) and phonological relations (Ferrand & Grainger 1992, 1993). In a recent auditory version of this masked priming procedure (figure 9.1*c*), Kouider & Dupoux (2005) found word repetition priming in the absence of prime audibility, while semantic priming was found only for audible primes. The results seem stronger for translation priming (Gollan *et al*. 1997; Grainger & Frenck-Mestre 1998; especially when the prime is in the first language and the target in the second language; Jiang 1999), possibly because translation equivalents are more strongly associated at the semantic level. Yet, a clear demonstration that primes were genuinely subliminal has not been provided.

Whether phonological priming occurs in masked priming remains a debated issue in psycholinguistics (Rastle & Bryasbert 2006), and it is unfortunate that the possibility that prime awareness might account for some of the conflicting results is not taken seriously. Of course, it might also be that phonological priming requires a longer prime duration because it requires longer processing regardless of conscious perception (Ferrand & Grainger 1992).

In a recent functional magnetic resonance imaging (fMRI) study, we studied the behavioural and neural distinction between priming from visible and priming from invisible stimuli (Kouider *et al*. in press). Moreover, we compared orthographic and phonological priming in a semantic decision task while the prime duration was kept constant (i.e. 43 ms). We found orthographic priming for both visible and invisible primes. By contrast, we found phonological priming only for visible primes. At the neural level, only for visible primes we observed phonological repetition enhancement in the left inferior frontal cortex and anterior insula, two regions usually associated with phonological and articulatory processing. This study thus adds to the evidence that visibility may be needed for the emergence of phonological priming. Yet, it does not mean that subliminal phonological effects cannot occur under conditions that emphasize phonological processing of the prime. Rather, we prefer to argue that these effects are very fragile and that they increase drastically during conscious perception. It is possible that subliminal phonological priming is more reliable when the task explicitly requires phonological recoding from orthographic inputs, such as in the naming task (Shen & Forster 1999), under special masking conditions that allow for longer prime durations while keeping the prime invisible (Grainger *et al*. 2003), or when using an orthography with a high degree of transparency, such as the Kana Japanese syllabary (Nakamura *et al*. 2006).

In summary, from the psycholinguistic literature on masked priming, one can infer that some forms of orthographic and lexical processing clearly occur under subliminal conditions. By contrast, phonological and semantic masked priming effects appear rather fragile and sometimes difficult to replicate, especially when using short prime durations to prevent conscious perception.

(b) Semantic congruity evoked by subliminal primes

By the mid-1990s, a renewal of interest for subliminal semantic activation became apparent in the scientific community. Two articles claiming that genuinely invisible primes could influence processing at the semantic level appeared in *Science* and *Nature* (Greenwald *et al*. 1996; Dehaene *et al*. 1998).

Greenwald *et al*. (1996; see also Draine & Greenwald 1998) proposed two methodological improvements in order to obtain robust subliminal priming. The first one was to use a response-window procedure that forced subjects to respond extremely quickly to the target stimulus. This response-window procedure was thought to improve the sensitivity of the indirect measure because priming is short-lived under subliminal conditions. The second improvement was statistical. Instead of demonstrating chance performance on objective measures of awareness for all subjects, they proposed to use a regression method that uses the visibility measure as a predictor of the priming effect. The intercept of the regression was then used to evaluate the amount of priming for null performance on prime visibility (Greenwald *et al*. 1995). The main advantage of this method is that subliminal priming can be evaluated even when some of the subjects show better-than-chance performance in the visibility test. In a typical experiment performed by Greenwald and colleagues, subjects classified target words as pleasant (e.g. 'happy') or unpleasant (e.g. 'vomit') and these words were preceded by a congruent prime (i.e. a word from the same category, such as 'love' preceding the target happy) or an incongruent prime (vomit preceding happy). Subjects were faster for congruent trials when compared with incongruent trials, even under conditions where they could not perform the affective evaluation on the prime.

As discovered later by Klinger *et al*. (2000), the priming effect found by Greenwald and colleagues depends on whether the prime and target are congruent or incongruent, not on whether they are semantically (or affectively) related or unrelated. It means that subliminal priming results from a competition between the prime and target categories and thus reflects categorical congruity rather than semantic priming in the classical sense of spreading activation theories (Collins & Loftus 1975; McNamara 1992, 1994).

A similar demonstration of a subliminal congruity effect was made by Dehaene *et al*. (1998) who further proposed that subliminal processing depends on strategic rather than automatic processing. According to them, subliminal semantic processing can be found under conditions where the task performed on the target stimuli is strategically applied to the prime. In order to provide evidence for this possibility, they asked subjects to classify numbers, presented in spelled-out or Arabic form, as smaller or larger than the reference number 5. These numbers were preceded by subliminal number primes that were also smaller or larger than 5. Subjects were faster when both the prime and the target belonged to the same category than when they belonged to opposite categories. Moreover, this study was the first one to use brain imaging (fMRI and event-related potentials (ERPs)) to show that subliminal stimuli can elicit not only a behavioural influence, but also a detectable neural activity in the motor cortex due to response competition (we return to this aspect below).

In summary, all these studies suggested, by the end of the 1990s, that priming from genuinely subliminal stimuli is a real phenomenon that can be studied without suffering from all the methodological criticisms made earlier on the underestimation of prime visibility. However, as we will see in section 7, which covers contemporary research, although the existence of subliminal perception is largely acknowledged today, some researchers still debate the semantic interpretation of these experiments.

9.7 Period 5: Outline and status of contemporary research

(a) Semantic versus alternative interpretations of congruity effects

Although the evidence for subliminal semantic priming by Greenwald *et al.* (1996) and Dehaene *et al.* (1998) renewed the interest in non-conscious perception, it also did not take long before non-semantic interpretations were proposed (Abrams & Greenwald 2000; Damian 2001). Basically, it was argued that congruity effects reflect conflicting stimulus–response associations rather than competition between semantic categories. This assumption is based on the direct motor specification hypothesis according to which an adequate response is unconsciously associated with a stimulus without having to be mediated by the semantic level (Neumann & Klotz 1994). Research on sensorimotor processing has shown that subliminal primes (e.g. ») can elicit competition with an opposite target (e.g. «; Neumann & Klotz 1994; Eimer & Schlaghecken 1998). In this case, motor congruity effects from a subliminal prime result from a learned stimulus–response mapping because the prime stimulus was previously presented as a target. In both the studies of Greenwald *et al.* (1996) and Dehaene *et al.* (1998), owing to the use of a restricted set of items, the masked primes were also used as target stimuli. For instance, Dehaene *et al.* (1998) used only the numbers 1, 4, 6 and 9 that appeared repeatedly both as primes and targets during the experiment. Thus, it could be argued that the observed subliminal congruity effects did not imply semantic mediation.

Damian (2001) claimed that subliminal priming occurred only for practised primes. Novel primes (i.e. primes that had not received a prior response) did not give rise to any effect. At the same time and independently, Abrams & Greenwald (2000) also showed that their own past work (e.g. Greenwald *et al.* 1996) should be totally reinterpreted as implying no semantic mediation. They showed that subliminal priming not only did not generalize to novel words, but in fact resulted from a learned association between fragments of the word primes and the response. For instance, in an affective evaluation task where the target words 'smut' and 'bile' were repeatedly classified as unpleasant, subliminal presentation of the prime word 'smile' (made of smut and bile) initiated an unpleasant response. These results suggested that in Greenwald's original paradigm, subliminal words were analysed only in terms of their ortho-graphic constituents, not as a whole and thus probably not up to the semantic level. Nevertheless, Abrams *et al.* (2002) also disconfirmed the motor specification hypothesis. They found that subliminal priming for words results from the learned mapping between stimulus fragments and a semantic category rather than to a motor response. Abrams *et al.* (2002) showed that the valence (i.e. pleasant versus non-pleasant) activated by the primes followed a reversal of key assignment. For instance, if subjects had to categorize a pleasant word such as smile with the left hand, and were then told to use the right hand for pleasant words, the subliminal prime smile would now facilitate right-hand responses. This result suggests that subliminal priming for words goes beyond the level of motor processing *per se*. Yet, priming for words was still restricted to practised items and, thus, provides little support for semantic interpretations.

Dehaene *et al.*'s (1998) claim of subliminal semantic priming for numbers turned out to resist better under scrutiny. Naccache & Dehaene (2001*a*) found that subliminal priming extended to novel number stimuli. As in their previous work, they found priming for practised primes (the numbers 1, 4, 6 and 9), but they also found priming for unpractised primes (2, 3, 7 and 8), although the former led to a stronger effect. These results suggested that subliminal priming for numbers was mediated, at least in part, by semantic representations. Several studies using numbers have since found that subliminal priming can extend to novel stimuli, suggesting that it can be mediated by semantic codes (Greenwald *et al.* 2003; Reynvoet *et al.* 2005).

However, Kunde *et al.* (2003) proposed an intermediate interpretation to account for the restriction to number stimuli. According to Kunde *et al.* (2003), subjects prepare action triggers in order to quickly associate each possible experimental stimulus with its appropriate response in minimal time. The setting of action triggers happens during the instructions or practice phase and depends on the stimulus set size, as it is efficient only for narrow categories (e.g. Arabic numbers from 1 to 9). According to this account, even novel primes (e.g. 2 and 3) may prime the appropriate response not because the meaning of these primes has been extracted, but rather because the adequate response to these stimuli was consciously prepared in advance (see Forster 2004, for a similar account). Kunde *et al.* (2003) provided evidence for this account by showing in several experiments that priming in numerical judgment paradigms (Dehaene *et al.* 1998) does not extend to novel primes that fall outside the expected numerical target range, or when primes occur in an unexpected format (Arabic instead of verbal or vice versa). Thus, priming was found only for the set of stimuli that subjects expected to see as targets, suggesting that the subliminal primes did not receive a semantic analysis.

As of today, the issue of whether subliminal priming reflects action-triggers or genuine semantic activation from subliminal primes remains intensely debated (Van Opstal *et al.* 2005*a*,*b*; Kunde *et al.* 2005). Van Opstal and colleagues argue that considerable evidence cannot be accounted for by the action-trigger model and suggests that, at least with certain types of masking procedures, genuine subliminal semantic priming occurs (e.g. Reynvoet *et al.* 2002, 2005; Reynvoet & Brysbaert 2004). Kunde and colleagues argue that such effects result from inefficient masking of the primes, leading to the conditions of conscious rather than subliminal perception.

It is important, however, to note that at least one study on congruity effects induced by subliminal primes does not appear to suffer from these criticisms and provides strong evidence for subliminal semantic processing. In this study, Dell'Acqua & Grainger (1999) asked subjects to categorize pictures of objects as referring to living things or artefacts and found a prime-target congruity effect even under conditions where the primes never appeared as targets during the experiment (ruling out stimulus–response interpretations) and were part of a large set of 252 objects (ruling out action-triggers interpretations). Although it is rather isolated, this study represents a clear-cut demonstration of congruity effects at the semantic level. One possibility is that pictures have a more direct access to meaning representations and thus lead to stronger semantic effects under subliminal conditions.

(b) Brain imaging and levels of representation for invisible stimuli

Another approach to the study of subliminal perception is to use brain activity rather than behavioural influences as an indirect measure of subliminal influences. This logic consists in finding whether cerebral regions or electrophysiological components associated with a given level of representations (i.e. motor, orthographic, semantic, etc.) are activated by subliminal stimuli. We first describe studies using ERPs, then turn to research using fMRI and intracranial recordings (see figure 9.2 for illustrations).

(i) Evidence from event-related potentials

Several studies have used ERPs in conjunction with priming paradigms induced by congruity effects. ERP correlates of priming are revealed through the use of the 'lateralized readiness potential' (LRP), an index of left-and right-hand movement preparation, which is computed by comparing the differential activity between the right and left hemispheres (Coles *et al.* 1988).

Congruent trials induce a greater LRP because both the prime and the target favour the same response side. By contrast, incongruent trials induce a decrease in the LRP, and the difference between the two types of LRP can be used as an electrophysiological index of priming. Dehaene *et al.* (1998) and Eimer & Schlaghecken (1998), using numbers and arrows, respectively, have shown that the LRP index can be modulated by priming from invisible stimuli. Moreover, the temporal resolution of the ERPs allowed to see that the subliminal prime first induced a LRP, then modulated the LRP induced by the target depending on whether it was congruent or incongruent (see also Leuthold & Kopp 1998; Jaskowski *et al.* 2002).

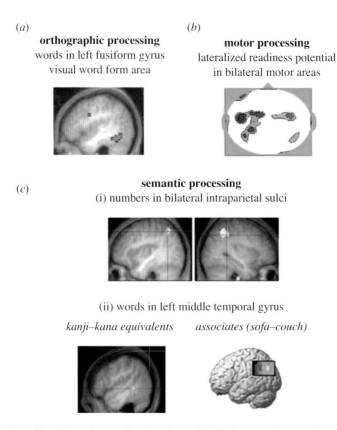

Fig. 9.2 Examples of brain imaging studies showing subliminal processing at orthographic, motor and semantic levels of processing for words and numbers. (*a*) The left occipitotemporal region is sensitive to repetition priming from masked words, independently of the case in which words are presented, and with a sensitivity to orthographic similarity (Dehaene *et al.* 2001; Devlin *et al.* 2004). (*b*) Subliminal digits can prime a motor response during a number comparison task, as revealed by the LRP measured with ERPs (Dehaene *et al.* 1998). (*c*, i) The bilateral intraparietal sulcus is sensitive to subliminal repetition priming of numbers, independently of whether they are presented as words or as digits (Naccache & Dehaene 2001*b*); other experiments indicate a dependency on numerical distance, suggesting that this region may encode the semantic dimension of numerical magnitude. (*c*, ii) The left middle temporal gyrus (with blown-up inset shown) is sensitive to priming by synonym words (Devlin *et al.* 2004) as well as priming by repetition of words presented in the Kanji and Kana Japanese writing systems (Nakamura *et al.* 2005), suggesting that this region encodes words at a semantic level.

Surprisingly, Eimer & Schlaghecken (1998) also discovered that this congruity effect can be totally reversed, resulting in a 'negative compatibility effect'. At the behavioural levels, it leads to longer reaction times for congruent trials and faster reaction times for incongruent trials. At the level of ERPs, they found that at around 300 ms the LRP activated by the prime was massively reversed. According to them, such a paradoxical effect would be the result of a supplementary inhibition mechanism applied on invisible primes. As of today, whether this negative compatibility effect, observed solely with arrow primes, really reflects central inhibition of the primes or, rather, a confound due to the resemblance of masks with prime stimuli remains a controversial issue (Lleras & Enns 2004; Verleger *et al.* 2004; Schlaghecken & Eimer 2006). In any case, all these studies consensually show that invisible stimuli can elicit motor responses.

Regarding word processing, Brown & Hagoort (1993) were the first to compare semantic priming for visible and invisible primes using ERPs. Semantic priming produced an attenuation of the N400, an ERP component thought to reflect either lexical or semantic integration of information (Kutas & Hillyard 1980; Holcomb 1993). However, this N400 attenuation was obtained only for visible primes. Brown & Hagoort (1993) concluded that the N400 reflects conscious post-lexical processing rather than automatic processing. Schnyer *et al.* (1997) found an N400 modulation for masked repetition rather than semantic priming. Although, some of the subjects reported conscious perception of the primes in this study, this finding was replicated in later studies controlling more carefully for the absence of visibility (Misra & Holcomb 2003; Holcomb *et al.* 2005). Moreover, Holcomb *et al.* (2005) recently compared masked repetition and semantic priming as a function of prime visibility. They found that, by contrast to repetition priming, the N400 modulation induced by semantic priming totally correlates with prime awareness.

By contrast, several other studies have reported that the N400 is modulated by semantic priming even for invisible primes (Deacon *et al.* 2000; Kiefer & Spitzer 2000; Kiefer 2002; Kiefer & Brendel 2006). Some of these studies might have underestimated conscious perception because they used a preliminary threshold definition procedure (Deacon *et al.* 2000) or because too few trials were used for the objective measure (Deacon *et al.* 2000; Kiefer 2002). Yet even when prime awareness was controlled carefully, subliminal semantic priming was reflected in both the reaction times and the N400 component, as shown recently by Kiefer & Brendel (2006).

In summary, the literature on the ERP correlates of subliminal priming strongly suggests that subliminal stimuli can reach motor and lexical levels of processing. Some studies show that it can reach the semantic level, whereas others find that the semantic level is involved only during conscious perception. The reason for this discrepancy remains an open question for future research.

(ii) Evidence from fMRI and intracranial recordings

Dehaene *et al.* (1998) used subliminal priming in the numerical judgment task presented above in conjunction with fMRI. They used an equivalent of the LRP component labelled the 'lateralized BOLD response'. This index, which reflects the differential BOLD activity between the left and right motor cortices, allowed them to show that subliminal congruity effects occur in motor cortex.

Again with fMRI, Dehaene *et al.* (2001) showed that subliminal repetition priming induces repetition suppression (a decrease in neural activity; Naccache & Dehaene 2001*b*; Henson 2003) in the occipital extrastriate cortex and in a region of the posterior fusiform gyrus corresponding to the visual word form area (VWFA). Occipital regions responded only to physical repetition (e.g. for 'radio–radio', but not for 'radio–RADIO'), whereas the VWFA, which is thought to encode abstract orthographic knowledge (Cohen *et al.* 2000), was insensitive to case change (e.g. repetition suppression was equivalent for radio–radio and radio–RADIO). This brain imaging study provided evidence that invisible stimuli are processed at least to the level of abstract orthographic representations. Dehaene *et al.* (2004) used anagram words to distinguish whether this repetition priming effect in the VWFA reflects processing at the single-letter level or at the level of larger orthographic units. In their study, for instance, the French target word 'REFLET' was preceded by the prime word 'trefle', such that almost all of the middle letters (r, e, f, l, e) could be repeated. Moreover, a shift in letter position allowed to present these middle letters at the same spatial position (e.g. 'trefle_'–'_REFLET'). Dehaene *et al.* (2004) found that the posterior part of the VWFA responded specifically to the repetition of letters at the same location, whereas the anterior part of the VWFA was more invariant and responsive to larger letter-sequence units. Kouider *et al.* (in press) used orthographically related primes and targets (garape-GARAGE) and found also priming in the posterior part of the VWFA. Along the same lines, Gaillard *et al.* (2006*b*) used intracranial recording to show that several areas in the ventral stream, including the VWFA, are activated by invisible word stimuli.

All these fMRI (or intracranial) studies provided evidence that invisible stimuli can reach orthographic, lexical and motor levels of representation. Three studies further indicate that subliminal priming can also tap semantic regions. For numbers, Naccache & Dehaene (2001*b*) observed a notation-independent repetition suppression effect in bilateral intraparietal cortices, at a site thought to encode numerical magnitudes. For other types of words, Devlin *et al.* (2004) used priming of semantic associates and we used, in Nakamura *et al.* (2005), cross-script priming of Japanese Kanji and Kana equivalents. Both studies led to repetition suppression in the left middle temporal gyrus, a region thought to be involved in semantic processing or words and objects (e.g. Tyler *et al.* 2003). Thus, these studies provide convergent evidence that subliminal perception can reach the semantic level of processing.

fMRI was also used to demonstrate emotional processing of masked stimuli (Morris *et al.* 1998; Whalen *et al.* 1998). In these experiments, subjects saw brief (e.g. 33 ms) fearful or fear-associated faces followed by a clearly visible neutral face that also served as a backward mask. Both studies found that the processing of these emotional faces was associated with an increased activity in the amygdala relative to neutral stimuli (see also Vuilleumier & Driver 2007), while subjects reported no subjective experience of these faces after the experiment. Since then, these studies have been replicated with faces as well as other types of stimuli (e.g. fearful animals; see Ohman 2002 for a review).

However, most studies in this field do not provide stringent demonstrations that the masked faces were genuinely subliminal. The assumption that the stimuli were not visible depended rather on the argument that their duration was short enough (e.g. 33 ms; Pessoa 2005). As shown recently by Pessoa *et al.* (2005), about 60% of subjects are able to report whether the masked stimulus is fearful or not under presentation conditions that were previously argued to reflect perception without awareness. More recently, Pessoa *et al.* (2006) showed that, when stimulus visibility is controlled carefully, the amygdala does not always seem to be activated under conditions of subliminal face processing. Should we thus conclude that emotional processing in the amygdala cannot be activated from subliminal stimuli? Before making such a strong assumption, one would need to check that in the study by Pessoa *et al.* (2006), masking was not too strong to prevent any form of processing, even at the lowest levels of visual processing.

Recently, Kouider *et al.* (submitted) developed a new method that allows for efficient masking of faces conjoined with subliminal repetition priming effects (figure 9.1*b*). They found repetition suppression in several occipitotemporal areas, including the fusiform face area. It would be interesting to use the same procedure to test whether invisible fearful faces can activate the amygdala. Robust evidence for genuinely subliminal emotional processing has been found in a recent study using word stimuli and intracranial recordings of the amygdala. Naccache *et al.* (2005) found that masked words that are threatening (e.g. 'danger') increase the activity in the amygdala compared with neutral words (e.g. 'cousin'). Crucially, in this case, subjects were totally at chance in categorizing these masked words as threatening or neutral. Unexpectedly, in this study, the latency of activation of the amygdala was relatively late (around 800 ms after stimulus presentation). According to Naccache *et al.* (2005), before reaching the amygdala, words have to pass through several levels of processing, including visual, lexical and, crucially, semantic levels of processing. In summary, this study provides evidence that areas coding for an emotional semantic dimension can indeed be activated by subliminal words.

(c) Subliminal perception is modulated by attention

Until recently, attention was considered the main 'gatekeeping' mechanism of consciousness (Posner 1994). Subliminal priming was assumed to involve automatic processes and thus to be unaffected by conscious controlled processes (Posner & Snyder 1975). Recently, however, several studies have shown that even subliminal processing may be modulated by spatial and temporal attention.

For temporal attention, Naccache *et al.* (2002) used an extension of the numerical decision paradigm (Dehaene *et al.* 1998) and found that subliminal congruity effects vanished if the prime did not appear at temporally predictable moments, and therefore did not fall into the temporal window of attention. Kiefer & Brendel (2006) used the same experimental logic (predictable versus unpredictable targets) with masked priming of semantic associates and found that the N400 modulation induced by semantic priming is reduced for unattended primes.

For spatial attention, Dupoux *et al.* (2003) used masked auditory priming under dichotic conditions. Subjects were asked to pay attention to words in the attended ear (e.g. the right ear) in order to perform a lexical decision task and to ignore the unattended ear (e.g. the left ear), which contained prime stimuli. Except under conditions where the prime stimuli could pop out from the auditory signal and attract subjects' attention, auditory repetition priming disappeared under dichotic conditions, suggesting that masked priming requires spatial attention. Lachter *et al.* (2004) reached a similar conclusion for the visual domain. In a series of word repetition priming experiments, they used presentation condition where the prime and target could appear either at the same location or one below the other. Here also, repetition priming was found only at attended locations. Along the same lines, Sumner *et al.* (2006) used a precueing procedure to manipulate attention to a subliminal prime and found that it substantially increased priming effects.

In summary, all these studies suggest that attention increases the processing of invisible stimuli at both perceptual and semantic levels. This conclusion contrasts largely with the classical view of automatic processing, by which all levels of non-conscious representations are mandatorily and passively involved during perception (Posner & Snyder 1975; Schneider & Shiffrin 1977). Nonetheless, it remains an open question for further research whether attention modulates subliminal priming even at the lowest levels of sensory processing.

9.8 Comparison with non-conscious perception during inattention

While this review focuses on subliminal masking paradigms, where the evidence for semantic processing is limited to specific experimental conditions, it is also interesting to consider other paradigms where non-conscious perception is induced by inattention. Indeed, there is a large consensus that in such cases, semantic processing can occur in the absence of conscious perception. In these paradigms, stimuli fail to be seen because the subject's attention is occupied on a different task and/or with another stimulus. It is important to note that it constitutes a drastically different situation compared with subliminal masking paradigms, because in this case it involves supraliminal stimuli that can be reported when they are attended. To make stimuli invisible in masking paradigms, where the subject's attention is focused on the stimuli, the experimenter must drastically reduce the amount of sensory input, for instance, by using short stimulus durations. Under conditions of inattention, however, the stimulus can be presented for a long duration, with only late masking (attentional blink) or no masking at all (inattentional blindness), and yet remain unreportable. As a result, much stronger non-conscious effects are observed.

In the attentional blink paradigm, focused attention to a first item (T1) hinders the subsequent identification of a second item (T2) presented a few hundred milliseconds later (Raymond *et al.* 1992). Yet, failure to consciously perceive T2 does not prevent its semantic processing. Shapiro *et al.* (1997) used a semantic priming version of the attentional blink by having a third word T3 that was either semantically related or unrelated to T2. They found that semantic priming increased the identification of T3 not only when T2 was reported, but also when it was missed, although priming was smaller for missed items (see also Martens *et al.* 2002).

In an ERP study by Luck *et al.* (1996), T1 and T2 were preceded by a context word that was either semantically related or unrelated to T2. The N400 was modulated by the semantic relation between T1 and T2, not only when T2 was reported, but also when it was missed. Surprisingly, the N400 induced by reported and missed targets was identical in amplitude, suggesting that, even under non-conscious conditions, semantic processing can remain entirely unaffected. Rolke *et al.* (2001) replicated this N400 semantic modulation for missed stimuli, although, in this study, it was smaller than for reported stimuli. Sergent *et al.* (2005) recorded the entire sequence of ERP components evoked by unseen T2s, and found unaffected P1 and N1 components as well as a preserved but reduced N400. In summary, studies using semantic priming in conjunction with the attentional blink have provided strong evidence for the existence of semantic activation during non-conscious perception. Mack & Rock (1998) report similar, though scarcer, evidence from the inattentional blindness paradigm, where a single, totally unexpected task-unrelated target is presented foveally without any masking. Under such conditions, a word can remain undetected, yet subsequently cause priming, for instance, in a stem completion task.

Neuropsychological deficits such as unilateral neglect also offer the possibility to study perception under conditions of inattention (Driver & Vuilleumier 2001). Neglect patients may fail to report stimuli on the side of space contralateral to their damaged hemisphere, when this stimulus competes with another ipsilateral stimulus (extinction). Since the stimulus can be reported if attention is cued towards it, neglect is considered as a loss of awareness resulting from a lack of attention, not a lack of sensory processing (Posner *et al.* 1984; Driver & Vuilleumier 2001). In a pioneering study on non-conscious processing during extinction, Volpe *et al.* (1979) showed that although neglect patients could not report the identity of a stimulus (i.e. a word or an object) in the contralateral field, they were still able to guess whether it had the same or a different name as the stimulus in the ipsilateral field. Above-chance guessing in the absence of subjective report of the contralateral stimuli was taken as evidence for non-conscious perception. Berti *et al.* (1992) extended this finding to higher levels of processing. They showed that patients could guess that the objects presented on the two sides had the same name even when different views were displayed. In addition, they argued that guessing could involve choosing between exemplars from the same or a different semantic category. These results were taken as evidence that the stimulus in the neglected field primed the category of the stimulus in the intact field. Nevertheless, two major points of caution should be raised. First, stimuli from the same semantic category tended to be much more similar physically than exemplars from different categories. Second, the approach suffers from the same criticisms raised against the early studies of subliminal perception (Eriksen 1960). Above-chance performance on discrimination could reflect partial or even full conscious perception in the presence of the under-confidence phenomenon during the subjective measure of conscious perception. Along these lines, Farah *et al.* (1991) matched the difficulty of the direct and indirect measure by having subjects performing a two-alternative forced-choice task on the neglected stimuli, rather than identification. Under conditions where discrimination performance on the neglected stimuli was at chance, patients were no longer able to match it to the stimulus in the intact field.

A more promising approach has been to use priming as the indirect measure of non-conscious influences. Audet *et al.* (1991) used a priming task in which neglect patients had to identify one of the two target stimuli presented at central fixation (the letter 'T' or 'K') preceded by peripheral stimuli that were either identical (T preceded by T), incongruent (T preceded by K) or neutral (T preceded by O). As shown by Taylor (1977), normal subjects in this task show facilitation on repeated trials and interference on incongruent trials relative to the neutral condition. In the study by Audet *et al.* (1991), the prime could be presented on the left (i.e. in the neglected field) or above the target (i.e. reportable at central fixation). As with normal subjects, they found both facilitation and interference, but only as long as the prime appeared in the intact field. When the prime was presented in the neglected side, the general pattern of results was facilitation in the absence of interference. Nevertheless, interference was found in one of the four experiments reported, when the subject was told to explicitly use the prime to predict the target. Following the same logic, Cohen *et al.* (1995) asked patients to judge the colour of a central target (e.g. green), surrounded by a repeated (e.g. green), incongruent (e.g. red) or neutral (e.g. blue) prime presented either in the ipsi- or in the contralateral side. In this study, Cohen and colleagues not only found interference from the neglected field, but also that it was just as large as interference from the intact field.

Unfortunately, a problem with these two studies is that awareness was not fully controlled. Audet and colleagues relied only on subjective reports, which can be criticized for the above-mentioned reasons. Cohen and colleagues used a colour decision on the peripheral rather than on the central stimulus and found that patients had much more difficulty in identifying the contralateral than the ipsilateral stimulus, which allowed them to demonstrate that patients indeed suffered from extinction. However, patients remained much better than chance for contralateral stimuli, and thus it remains possible that the effects were due to conscious perception.

Fuentes & Humphreys (1996) relied on the negative priming phenomenon and controlled more rigorously for potential influences from conscious perception. Subjects received on each trial a first display with a central letter to identify (e.g. 'T') and a distractor (e.g. 'M') to ignore on the right side of fixation (e.g. '+T M') or on the left side (e.g. 'MT+'). Then they received a second display in which, compared to the distractor on the first display, the central letter was identical (e.g. '+M L') or different (e.g. '+B L'). Contrary to the classical facilitatory priming effect, repetition leads here to lower accuracy and longer reaction times (i.e. negative priming) because the distractor in the first display receives active suppression (Tipper 1985). Fuentes & Humphreys (1996) replicated this negative priming with distractors in the intact field of a neglect patient. However, priming from the contralateral field was positive rather than negative. Moreover, Fuentes & Humphreys showed that this repetition effect occurred across a case change, suggesting the involvement of abstract letter representations. In addition, they used an objective measure to assess the awareness of distractors. Subjects were asked to either report the central stimulus that was presented alone, or the number of displayed letters when a distractor was added. Importantly, the task was provided only after the display, such that subjects were primarily paying attention to the central stimulus, as in the priming experiment. Patients easily reported the presence of two letters when the distractor was on the right side (e.g. '+TM'), but failed when the distractor was on the left side. Fuentes & Humphreys (1996) concluded that perception occurs without awareness in neglect patients and involves levels of representation above simple visual sensory processing. By contrast, according to them, inhibitory processes require conscious perception.

Recently, Rusconi et al. (2006) extended the results of Fuentes & Humphreys by providing evidence for the extraction of arithmetic information from neglected number stimuli. Their subjects were instructed to perform a parity judgment task with a target number that was preceded by two prime numbers. When the product of the two primes was equal to the target (e.g. 2###7 followed by 14), then normal subjects were slower to perform the parity judgment task. Rusconi and colleagues replicated this result in a neglect patient. However, when the primes appeared in the neglected field, then interference turned into facilitation. Rusconi and colleagues used an identification task to show that none of the stimuli in the neglect field could be identified. These results suggest that associations between numbers can be activated without conscious perception and that, as in the study by Fuentes & Humphreys (1996), inhibitory processes require, by contrast, conscious processing.

Other studies concentrated on the semantic level of processing. Berti & Rizzolatti (1992) asked patients to categorize drawings as referring to animals or vegetables. Patients were presented with two drawings, one on the neglected side followed by another on the intact field, that either referred to the same category or was incongruent. Berti & Rizzolati found a congruence effect even when restricting the analysis to patients reporting having seen only one stimulus on each trial, not two. At first glance, this result suggests a non-conscious semantic influence. Yet, given that the stimulus set was very narrow (i.e. 14 in total) and that the prime stimuli could appear as target stimuli, this experiment does not unequivocally provide evidence for non-conscious semantic processing, but could reflect motor congruity effects (Damian 2001; see above). Moreover, here subjective reports can also be largely criticized due to the potential confound with confidence criteria.

Two other studies used priming with semantic associates and controlled more carefully for the absence of conscious perception. Ladavas et al. (1993) used word stimuli, whereas McGlinchey-Berroth et al. (1993) relied on picture primes and word targets. In both cases, semantic priming was obtained from primes in the neglected field. Moreover, McGlinchey-Berroth and colleagues compared the amount of priming from the neglected and intact field and found no difference, suggesting that semantic processing can remain entirely unaffected during non-conscious perception by inattention. Importantly, both studies showed that under similar presentation conditions, patients were at chance in several objective measures of conscious perception of the primes, such as lexical decision, semantic categorization, detection (Ladavas *et al.* 1993) and two-alternative forced-choice (McGlinchey-Berroth *et al.* 1993). It is of note, however, that the presentation conditions were not identical in the direct and indirect measures, because the target was omitted during the measure of conscious prime perception. Thus, it might be argued that conscious perceptibility was higher during the priming experiment owing to retroactive semantic priming (Briand *et al.* 1988; Dark 1988; Bernstein *et al.* 1989; see above for details). Nevertheless, those experiments, together with those on the attentional blink, constitute some of the best evidence to date for semantic-level processing without conscious perception.

9.9 Theoretical conclusions

We have reviewed evidence for the depth of non-conscious processing in two categories of experimental conditions: masked priming paradigms and inattention paradigms. The depth of processing seems to differ in those two conditions. In masked priming, while orthographic and lexical levels are easily contacted, evidence for phonological and semantic processing, although real, is much more restricted. Subliminal semantic priming effects can be very small, indeed much smaller than under conscious conditions. However, in inattention paradigms, while effect sizes vary according to experimental conditions, strong semantic effects can be observed. Under the most favourable conditions of the attentional blink, where spatial attention is focused onto the stimulus location, but central executive attention is occupied by a secondary task, there may be little or no difference between semantic-level processing under conditions of conscious versus blinked (Luck *et al.* 1996) or extinguished (McGlinchey-Berroth *et al.* 1993) stimulus processing.

In this concluding section, we would like to argue that those results fit with the tripartite distinction of subliminal, preconscious and conscious processing that one of us has recently proposed (Dehaene *et al.* 2006). According to the global neuronal workspace theory, sensory information is consciously accessed whenever a bidirectional, self-sustained activation loop is established between the relevant posterior sensory processors and an assembly of workspace neurons with long-distance axons, distributed through the brain, but particularly dense in associative cortical areas, most notably prefrontal cortex (Dehaene *et al.* 1998, 2001, 2003). Thus, for a stimulus to reach consciousness, two factors are jointly needed: first, the input stimulus must have enough strength to cross a dynamic threshold for global reverberation (which can be prevented by stimulus degradation or competition with other stimuli, i.e. masking); and second, it must receive top-down amplification by distant neurons (which can be prevented by drawing these neurons into another stimulus or task). Accordingly, conscious access may fail for two quite distinct reasons, leading to a distinction between two types of non-conscious processes, which we call subliminal and preconscious, respectively (figure 9.3).

According to the theory, subliminal processing is a condition of information inaccessibility where the bottom-up, stimulus-induced activation itself is insufficient to trigger large-scale reverberation. Thus, subliminal information is information that cannot be brought into consciousness, in spite of all efforts of focused attention. This does not mean, of course, that subliminal processing is independent of the subject's attention and strategies. As we have seen, whichever task and attentional sets are prepared consciously can orient and amplify the processing of a subliminal stimulus, even if its bottom-up strength remains insufficient for global conscious access.

On the other hand, preconscious processing occurs when processing is limited by top-down access rather than bottom-up strength. According to the theory, preconscious processes potentially carry enough activation for conscious access, but are temporarily buffered in a non-conscious store owing to a lack of top-down attentional amplification (for instance, owing to transient occupancy of the central workspace system). As shown by the attentional blink and inattentional blindness paradigms, even strong visual stimuli can remain temporarily precon-scious. They are potentially visible (contrary to subliminal stimuli, they could quickly gain access to conscious report if they were attended), but they are not consciously seen at the moment. However, they are clearly maintained in a sensory buffer for a few hundreds of milli-seconds, since they may ultimately achieve conscious access once the central workspace is freed (as exemplified by the psychological refractory period paradigm, in which one task is put

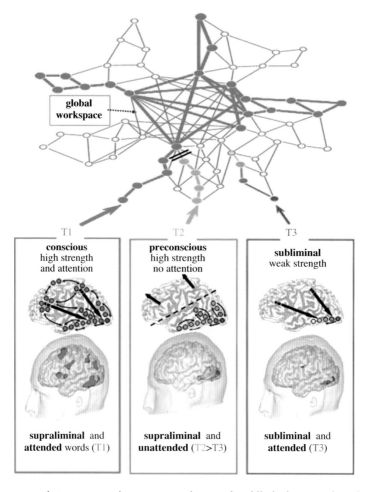

Fig. 9.3 Taxonomy between conscious, preconscious and subliminal processing, based on the theoretical proposal by Dehaene *et al.* (2006). This distinction stipulates the existence of three types of brain states associated with conscious report, non-conscious perception due to inattention (preconscious state; Kouider *et al.* in press) and non-conscious perception due to masking (subliminal perception; Dehaene *et al.* 2001, 2006).

on hold while another task is being processed). This sensory buffer can be erased by other competing stimuli, however, in which case a preconscious stimulus may never gain access to conscious processing (as achieved by late masking in the attentional blink paradigm).

We have argued that maintaining this distinction is essential in order to make sense of the growing neuro-imaging data on the neural correlates of consciousness (Dehaene *et al.* 2006; Kouider *et al.* in press). Here, we add that consideration of the neural bases of subliminal and preconscious states may then help in understanding why they differ in the depth of non-conscious processing. During subliminal processing, brain imaging and neurophysiological data indicate that masking prevents the efficient propagation of bottom-up stimulus activation in successive perceptual areas, leaving only a short pulse of activity whose amplitude decreases at each synaptic step (Kovacs *et al.* 1995; Thompson & Schall 1999; Dehaene *et al.* 2001; Lamme 2003). Thus, although behavioural priming effects can be detected at a distance from sensory systems, they are expected to decrease with synaptic distance and become very small and frequently undetectable in distant phonological and semantic areas. On the other hand, during preconscious processing (defined as suprathreshold stimulation under conditions of inattention), neuroimaging data shows a much increased and durable activation in posterior occipitotemporal cortices, probably corresponding to the activation of local reverberatory loops forming a sensory buffer, yet without extension into a global brain-scale parietofrontal ignition (Tse *et al.* 2005; Kouider *et al.* in press). It is therefore not surprising that such a durable and extended activity state should be capable of causing greater priming at multiple processing levels. Indeed at the cerebral level, repetition suppression and repetition enhancement effects can be seen in a much wider cortical network that includes areas known to be involved in phonology and semantics (Kouider *et al.* in press), owing to precon-scious processing.

As increasingly reliable paradigms are being designed to create such preconscious states and to collect the subject's own assessment of their degree of consciousness (Sergent *et al.* 2005), we suspect that researchers will discover increasingly reliable evidence for non-conscious activation of broad perceptual, lexical, phonological and semantic networks. Accordingly, research should progressively shift to another crucial issue, that of understanding which cognitive processes, if any, are the exclusive privilege of conscious processing. The global neuronal workspace model makes the clear prediction that they should bear the characteristics of a 'central executive' parietofrontal system: long-lasting maintenance of information; flexible recombination and exchange of intermediate results across processors; and intentional effortful control should be deployed only during conscious processing (Dehaene & Naccache 2001). While highly suggestive evidence already exists (e.g. Kunde 2003), the testing of this prediction remains a key issue for further research.

References

Abrams, R. L. & Greenwald, A. G. 2000 Parts outweigh the whole (word) in unconscious analysis of meaning. *Psychol. Sci.* **11**, 118–124. (doi:10.1111/1467-9280.00226)

Abrams, R. L., Klinger, M. R. & Greenwald, A. G. 2002 Subliminal words activate semantic categories (not automated motor responses). *Psychon. Bull. Rev.* **9**, 100–106.

Adams, J. K. 1957 Laboratory studies of behavior without awareness. *Psychol. Bull.* **54**, 383–405. (doi:10.1037/ h0043350)

Allport, A. 1977 On knowing the meaning of words we are unable to report: the effects of visual masking. In *Attention and performance*, vol. 6 (ed. D. S. Dornic), pp. 505–534. London, UK: Academic Press.

Audet, T., Bub, D. & Lecours, A. R. 1991 Visual neglect and left-sided context effects. *Brain Cogn.* **16**, 11–28. (doi:10. 1016/0278-2626(91)90082-J)

Baars, B. J. 1988 *A cognitive theory of consciousness.* New York, NY: Cambridge University Press.

Balota, D. A. 1983 Automatic semantic activation and episodic memory encoding. *J. Verb. Learn. Verb. Behav.* **22**, 88–104. (doi:10.1016/S0022-5371(83)80008-5)

Berent, I. & Perfetti, C. A. 1995 A rose is a REEZ: the two-cycles model of phonology assembly in reading English. *Psychol. Rev.* **102**, 146–184. (doi:10.1037/0033-295X. 102.1.146)

Bernstein, I. H., Bissonnette, V., Vyas, A. & Barclay, P. 1989 Semantic priming: subliminal perception or context? *Percept. Psychophys.* **45**, 153–161.

Berti, A. & Rizzolatti, G. 1992 Visual processing without awareness: evidence from unilateral neglect. *J. Cogn. Neurosci.* **4**, 345–351.

Berti, A., Allport, A., Driver, J., Dienes, Z., Oxbury, J. & Oxbury, S. 1992 Level of processing for stimuli in an "extinguished" visual field. *Neuropsychologia* **30**, 403–415. (doi:10.1016/0028-3932(92)90088-4)

Bjorkman, M., Juslin, P. & Winman, A. 1993 Realism of confidence in sensory discrimination: the underconfidence phenomenon. *Percept. Psychophys.* **54**, 75–81.

Briand, K., den Heyer, K. & Dannenbring, G. L. 1988 Retroactive semantic priming in a leixcal decision task. *Q. J. Exp. Psychol. A* **40**, 341–359.

Brown, C. & Hagoort, P. 1993 The processing nature of the N400: evidence from masked priming. *J. Cogn. Neurosci.* **5**, 34–44.

Brysbaert, M. & Praet, C. 1992 Reading isolated words: no evidence for automatic incorporation of the phonetic code. *Psychol. Res.* **54**, 91–102. (doi:10.1007/BF00937137)

Carr, T. H., McCauley, C., Sperber, R. D. & Parmalee, C. M. 1982 Words, pictures, and priming: on semantic activation, conscious identification, and the automaticity of information processing. *J. Exp. Psychol. Hum. Percept. Perform.* **8**, 757–777. (doi:10.1037/0096-1523.8.6.757)

Chalmers, D. 1996 *The conscious mind: in search of a fundamental theory.* Oxford, UK: Oxford University Press.

Cheesman, J. & Merikle, P. M. 1984 Priming with and without awareness. *Percept. Psychophys.* **36**, 387–395.

Cheesman, J. & Merikle, P. M. 1986 Distinguishing conscious from unconscious perceptual processes. *Can. J. Psychol.* **40**, 343–367.

Chwilla, D. J., Hagoort, P. & Brown, C. M. 1998 The mechanism underlying backward priming in a lexical decision task: spreading activation versus semantic matching. *Q. J. Exp. Psychol. A* **51**, 531–560. (doi:10.1080/ 027249898391521)

Cohen, A., Ivry, R., Rafal, R. & Kohn, C. 1995 Response code activation by stimuli in the neglected visual field. *Neuropsychology* **9**, 165–173. (doi:10.1037/0894-4105.9. 2.165)

Cohen, L., Dehaene, S., Naccache, L., Lehericy, S., Dehaene-Lambertz, G., Henaff, M.-A. & Michel, F. 2000 The visual word form area: spatial and temporal characterization of an initial stage of reading in normal subjects and posterior split-brain patients. *Brain* **123**, 291–307. (doi:10.1093/ brain/123.2.291)

Coles, M. G. H., Gratton, G. & Donchin, E. 1988 Detecting early communication: using measures of movement-related potentials to illuminate human information processing. *In Event-related potential investigations of cognition* (eds B. Renault, M. Kutas, M. G. H. Coles & A. W. K. Gaillard), pp. 69–89. Amsterdam, The Netherlands: North-Holland. (Published as Volume 26, Nos. 1–3 of Biological Psychology.)

Collins, A. M. & Loftus, E. F. 1975 A spreading-activation theory of semantic processing. *Psychol. Rev.* **82**, 407–428. (doi:10.1037/0033-295X.82.6.407)

Damian, M. 2001 Congruity effects evoked by subliminally presented primes: automaticity rather than semantic processing. *J. Exp. Psychol. Hum. Percept. Perform.* **27**, 154–165. (doi:10.1037/0096-1523.27.1.154)

Dark, V. J. 1988 Semantic priming, prime reportability, and retroactive priming are interdependent. *Mem. Cogn.* **16**, 299–308.

Dark, V. J. & Benson, K. 1991 Semantic priming and identification of near threshold primes in a lexical decision task. *Q. J. Exp. Psychol. A* **43**, 53–78.

Davis, C. & Forster, K. I. 1994 Masked orthographic priming: the effect of prime-target legibility. *Q. J. Exp. Psychol. A* **47**, 673–697.

Deacon, D., Hewitt, S., Yang, C.-M. & Nagata, M. 2000 Event-related potential indices of semantic priming using masked and unmasked words: evidence that the N400 does not reflect a postlexical process. *Cogn. Brain Res.* **9**, 137–146. (doi:10.1016/S0926-6410(99)00050-6)

Debner, J. A. & Jacoby, L. L. 1994 Unconscious perception: attention, awareness, and control. *J. Exp. Psychol. Learn. Mem. Cogn.* **20**, 304–317. (doi:10.1037/0278-7393.20. 2.304)

Dehaene, S. & Changeux, J.-P. 2004 Neural mechanisms for access to consciousness. In *The cognitive neurosciences* (ed. M. Gazzaniga), 3rd edn. Cambridge, MA: MIT Press.

Dehaene, S. & Naccache, L. 2001 Towards a cognitive neuroscience of consciousness: basic evidence and a workspace framework. *Cognition* **79**, 1–37. (doi:10.1016/ S0010-0277(00)00123-2)

Dehaene, S., Naccache, L., Le Clec'H, G., Koechlin, E., Mueller, M., Dehaene-Lambertz, G., van de Moortele, P. F. & Le Bihan, D. 1998 Imaging unconscious semantic priming. *Nature* **395**, 597–600. (doi:10.1038/26967)

Dehaene, S., Naccache, L., Cohen, L., Le Bihan, D., Mangin, J.-F., Poline, J.-B. & Rivière, D. 2001 Cerebral mechanisms of word masking and unconscious repetition priming. *Nat. Neurosci.* **4**, 752–758. (doi:10. 1038/89551)

Dehaene, S., Sergent, C. & Changeux, J.-P. 2003 A neuronal network model linking subjective reports and objective physiological data during conscious perception. *Proc. Natl Acad. Sci. USA* **1001**, 8520–8525. (doi:10.1073/pnas. 1332574100)

Dehaene, S., Jobert, A., Naccache, L., Ciuciu, P., Poline, J. B., Le Bihan, D. & Cohen, L. 2004 Letter binding and invariant recognition of masked words. *Psychol. Sci.* **15**, 307–313. (doi:10.1111/j.0956-7976.2004.00674.x)

Dehaene, S., Changeux, J.-P., Naccache, L., Sackur, J. & Sergent, C. 2006 Conscious, preconscious, and subliminal processing: a testable taxonomy. *Trends Cogn. Sci.* **10**, 204–211. (doi:10.1016/ j.tics.2006.03.007)

Dell'Acqua, R. & Grainger, J. 1999 Unconscious semantic priming to pictures. *Cognition* **73**, B1–B15. (doi:10.1016/ S0010-0277(99)00049-9)

Devlin, J. T., Jamison, H. L., Matthews, P. M. & Gonnerman, L. M. 2004 Morphology and the internal structure of words. *Proc. Natl Acad. Sci. USA* **101**, 14 984–14 988. (doi:10.1073/pnas.0403766101)

Dixon, N. F. 1971 *Subliminal perception: the nature of a controversy.* London, UK: McGraw-Hill.

Dixon, N. F. 1981 *Preconscious processing.* New York, NY: Wiley.

Draine, S. C. & Greenwald, A. G. 1998 Replicable unconscious semantic priming. *J. Exp. Psychol. Gen.* **127**, 286–303. (doi:10.1037/0096-3445.127.3.286)

Driver, J. & Vuilleumier, P. 2001 Perceptual awareness and its loss in unilateral neglect and extinction. *Cognition* **79**, 39–88. (doi:10.1016/S0010-0277(00)00124-4)

Dulany, D. E. 1997 Consciousness in the explicit (deliberative) and implicit (evocative). In *Scientific approaches to consciousness* (eds J. Cohen & J. Schooler), pp. 179–211. Mahwah, NJ: Lawrence Erlbaum Associates.

Dupoux, E., Kouider, S. & Mehler, J. 2003 Lexical access without attention? Exploration using dichotic priming. *J. Exp. Psychol. Hum. Percept. Perform.* **29**, 172–183. (doi:10.1037/ 0096-1523.29.1.172)

Durante, R. & Hirshman, E. 1994 Retrospective priming and masked semantic priming: the interfering effects of prime activation. *J. Mem. Lang.* **33**, 112–127. (doi:10.1006/jmla. 1994.1006)

Eimer, M. & Schlaghecken, F. 1998 Effects of masked stimuli on motor activation: behavioral and electrophysiological evidence. *J. Exp. Psychol. Hum. Percept. Perform.* **24**, 1737–1747. (doi:10.1037/0096-1523.24.6.1737)

Ellis, A. W. & Marshall, J. C. 1978 Semantic errors or statistical flukes? A note on Allport's "Onknowing the meanings of words we are unable to report". *Q. J. Exp. Psychol.* **30**, 569–575.

Eriksen, C. W. 1960 Discrimination and learning without awareness: a methodological survey and evaluation. *Psychol. Rev.* **67**, 279–300. (doi:10.1037/h0041622)

Evett, L. J. & Humphreys, G. W. 1981 The use of abstract graphemic information in lexical access. *Q. J. Exp. Psychol.* **33**, 325–350.

Farah, M. J., Monheit, M. A., Brunn, J. L. & Wallace, M. A. 1991 Unconscious perception of "extinguished" visual stimuli: reassessing the evidence. *Neuropsychologia* **29**, 949–958. (doi:10.1016/0028-3932(91)90059-H)

Ferrand, L. & Grainger, J. 1992 Phonology and orthography in visual word recognition: evidence from masked non-word priming. *Q. J. Exp. Psychol. A* **45**, 353–372.

Ferrand, L. & Grainger, J. 1993 The time course of orthographic and phonological code activation in the early phases of visual word recognition. *Bull. Psychonom. Soc.* **31**, 119–122.

Forster, K. I. 2004 Category size revisited: frequency and masked priming effects in semantic categorization. *Brain Lang.* **90**, 276–286. (doi:10.1016/S0093-934X(03) 00440-1)

Forster, K. I. & Davis, C. 1984 Repetition priming and frequency attenuation in lexical access. *J. Exp. Psychol. Learn. Mem. Cogn.* **10**, 680–698. (doi:10.1037/0278-7393.10.4.680)

Forster, K. I. & Davis, C. 1991 The density constraint on form-priming in the naming task: interference from a masked prime. *J. Mem. Lang.* **30**, 1–25. (doi:10.1016/0749-596X (91)90008-8)

Forster, K. I., Davis, C., Schoknecht, C. & Carter, R. 1987 Masked priming with graphemically related forms: repetition or partial activation? *Q. J. Exp. Psychol.* **39**, 211–251.

Fowler, C. A., Wolford, G., Slade, R. & Tassinary, L. 1981 Lexical access with and without awareness. *J. Exp. Psychol. Gen.* **110**, 341–362. (doi:10.1037/0096-3445.110.3.341)

Fuentes, L. J. & Humphreys, G. W. 1996 On the processing of "extinguished" stimuli in unilateral visual neglect: an approach using negative priming. *Cogn. Neuropsychol.* **13**, 111–136. (doi:10.1080/026432996382088)

Gaillard, R., Del Cul, A., Naccache, L., Vinckier, F., Cohen, L. & Dehaene, S. 2006a Nonconscious semantic processing of emotional words modulates conscious access. *Proc. Natl Acad. Sci. USA* **103**, 7524–7529. (doi:10.1073/pnas. 0600584103)

Gaillard, R. *et al.* 2006b Direct intracranial, fMRI and lesion evidence for the causal role of left inferotemporal cortex in reading. *Neuron* **50**, 191–204. (doi:10.1016/j.neuron. 2006.03.031)

Gollan, T. H., Forster, K. I. & Frost, R. 1997 Translation priming with different scripts: masked priming with cognates and non-cognates in Hebrew-English bilinguals. *J. Exp. Psychol. Learn. Mem. Cogn.* **23**, 1122–1139. (doi:10.1037/0278-7393.23.5.1122)

Grainger, J. & Frenck-Mestre, C. 1998 Masked translation priming in bilinguals. *Lang. Cogn. Process.* **13**, 601–623. (doi:10.1080/016909698386393)

Grainger, J., Diependaele, K., Spinelli, E., Ferrand, L. & Farioli, F. 2003 Masked repetition and phonological priming within and across modalities. *J. Exp. Psychol. Learn. Mem. Cogn.* **29**, 1256–1269. (doi:10.1037/0278-7393.29.6.1256)

Greenwald, A. G. 1992 New Look 3: reclaiming unconscious cognition. *Am. Psychol.* **47**, 766–779. (doi:10.1037/0003-066X.47.6.766)

Greenwald, A. G., Klinger, M. R. & Schuh, E. S. 1995 Activation by marginally perceptible ("subliminal") stimuli: dissociation of unconscious from conscious cognition. *J. Exp. Psychol. Gen.* **124**, 22–42. (doi:10. 1037/0096-3445.124.1.22)

Greenwald, A. G., Draine, S. C. & Abrams, R. L. 1996 Three cognitive markers of unconscious semantic activation. *Science* **273**, 1699–1702. (doi:10.1126/science.273.5282. 1699)

Greenwald, A. G., Abrams, R. L., Naccache, L. & Dehaene, S. 2003 Long-term semantic memory versus contextual memory in unconscious number processing. *J. Exp. Psychol. Learn. Mem. Cogn.* **29**, 235–247. (doi:10.1037/ 0278-7393.29.2.235)

Henson, R. N. A. 2003 Neuroimaging studies of priming. *Prog. Neurobiol.* **70**, 53–81. (doi:10.1016/S0301-0082(03) 00086-8)

Holcomb, P. J. 1993 Semantic priming and stimulus degradation: implications for the role of the N400 in language processing. *Psychophysiology* **30**, 47–61.

Holcomb, P. H., Reder, L., Misra, M. & Grainger, J. 2005 The effects of prime visibility on ERP measures of masked priming. *Cogn. Brain Res.* **24**, 155–172. (doi:10.1016/ j.cogbrainres.2005.01.003)

Holender, D. 1986 Semantic activation without conscious identification in dichotic listening, parafoveal vision, and visual masking: a survey and appraisal. *Behav. Brain Sci.* **9**, 1–23.

Holender, D. & Duscherer, K. 2004 Unconscious perception: the need for a paradigm shift. *Percept. Psychophys.* **66**, 872–881.

Humphreys, G. W., Evett, L. J. & Taylor, D. E. 1982 Automatic phonological priming in visual word recognition. *Mem. Cogn.* **10**, 576–590.

Humphreys, G. W., Besner, D. & Quinlan, P. T. 1988 Event perception and the word repetition effect. *J. Exp. Psychol. Gen.* **117**, 51–67. (doi:10.1037/0096-3445.117.1.51)

Hutchison, K. A., Neely, J. H., Neill, W. T. & Walker, P. 2004 Lexical and sub-lexical contributions to unconscious identity priming. *Conscious. Cogn.* **13**, 512–538. (doi:10. 1016/j.concog.2004.05.001)

Jaskowski, P., van der Lubbe, R. H., Schlotterbeck, E. & Verleger, R. 2002 Traces left on visual selective attention by stimuli that are not consciously identified. *Psychol. Sci.* **13**, 48–54. (doi:10.1111/1467-9280.00408)

Jiang, N. 1999 Testing explanations for asymmetry in cross-language priming. *Bilingual. Lang. Cogn.* **2**, 59–75. (doi:10.1017/S1366728999000152)

Kiefer, M. 2002 The N400 is modulated by unconsciously perceived masked words: further evidence for a spreading activation account of N400 priming effects. *Cogn. Brain Res.* **13**, 27–39. (doi:10.1016/S0926-6410(01)00085-4)

Kiefer, M. & Spitzer, M. 2000 Time course of conscious and unconscious semantic brain activation. *Neuroreport* **11**, 2401–2407. (doi:10.1097/00001756-200008030-00013)

Kiefer, M. & Brendel, D. 2006 Attentional modulation of unconscious 'automatic' processes: evidence from event-related potentials in a masked priming paradigm. *J. Cogn. Neurosci.* **18**, 184–198. (doi:10.1162/jocn.2006.18.2.184)

Kihlstrom, J. F. 1987 The cognitive unconscious. *Science* **237**, 1445–1452. (doi:10.1126/science.3629249)

Klinger, M. R., Burton, P. C. & Pitts, G. S. 2000 Mechanisms of unconscious priming I: response competition not spreading activation. *J. Exp. Psychol. Learn. Mem. Cogn.* **26**, 441–455. (doi:10.1037/0278-7393.26.2. 441)

Koriat, A. 1981 Semantic facilitation in lexical decision as a function of prime-target association. *Mem. Cogn.* **9**, 587–598.

Kouider, S. & Dupoux, E. 2001 A functional disconnection between spoken and visual word recognition: evidence from unconscious priming. *Cognition* **82**, B35–B49. (doi:10.1016/S0010-0277(01)00152-4)

Kouider, S. & Dupoux, E. 2004 Partial awareness creates the "Illusion" of subliminal semantic priming. *Psychol. Sci.* **15**, 75–81. (doi:10.1111/j.0963-7214.2004.01502001.x)

Kouider, S. & Dupoux, E. 2005 Subliminal speech priming. *Psychol. Sci.* **16**, 617–625. (doi:10.1111/j.1467-9280. 2005.01584.x)

Kouider, S., Dehaene, S., Jobert, A. & Le Bihan, D. In press. Cerebral bases of subliminal and supraliminal priming during reading. *Cereb. Cortex.*

Kouider, S., Eger, E., Dolan, R. & Henson, R. Submitted. Non-conscious face processing in the ventral stream.

Kovacs, G., Vogels, R. & Orban, G. A. 1995 Cortical correlate of pattern backward masking. *Proc. Natl Acad. Sci. USA* **92**, 5587–5591. (doi:10.1073/pnas.92.12.5587)

Kunde, W. 2003 Sequential modulations of stimulus-response correspondence effects depend on awareness of response conflict. *Psychon. Bull. Rev.* **10**, 198–205.

Kunde, W., Kiesel, A. & Hoffmann, J. 2003 Conscious control over the content of unconscious cognition. *Cognition* **88**, 223–242. (doi:10.1016/S0010-0277(03) 00023-4)

Kunde, W., Kiesel, A. & Hoffmann, J. 2005 On the masking and disclosure of unconscious elaborate processing. A reply to van Opstal, Reynvoet & Verguts. *Cognition* **97**, 99–105. (doi:10.1016/j.cognition.2005.03.005)

Kutas, M. & Hillyard, S. A. 1980 Event-related brain potentials to semantically inappropriate and surprisingly large words. *Biol. Psychol.* **11**, 99–116. (doi:10.1016/0301-0511(80)90046-0)

Lachter, J., Forster, K. I. & Ruthruff, E. 2004 Forty years after Broadbent: still no identification without attention. *Psychol. Rev.* **111**, 880–913. (doi:10.1037/0033-295X. 111.4.880)

Ladavas, E., Paladini, R. & Cubelli, R. 1993 Implicit associative priming in a patient with left visual neglect. *Neuropsychologia* **31**, 1307–1320. (doi:10.1016/0028-3932 (93)90100-E)

Lamme, V. A. 2003 Why visual attention and awareness are different. *Trends Cogn. Sci.* **7**, 12–18. (doi:10.1016/S1364-6613(02)00013-X)

Leuthold, H. & Kopp, B. 1998 Mechanisms of priming by masked stimuli: inferences from event-related brain potentials. *Psychol. Sci.* **9**, 263–269. (doi:10.1111/1467-9280.00053)

Lleras, A. & Enns, J. T. 2004 Negative compatibility or object updating? A cautionary tale of mask-dependent priming. *J. Exp. Psychol. Gen.* **133**, 475–493. (doi:10.1037/0096-3445.133.4.475)

Luck, S. J., Vogel, E. K. & Shapiro, K. L. 1996 Word meanings can be accessed but not reported during the attentional blink. *Nature* **383**, 616–618. (doi:10.1038/ 383616a0)

Lukatela, G., Frost, S. J. & Turvey, M. T. 1998 Phonological priming by masked nonword primes in the lexical decision task. *J. Mem. Lang.* **39**, 666–683. (doi:10.1006/jmla.1998. 2599)

Mack, A. & Rock, I. 1998 *Inattentional blindness*. Cambridge, MA: MIT press.

Marcel, A. J. 1974 *Perception with and without awareness*. Paper presented at the meeting of the Experimental Psychology Society, Stirling, Scotland.

Marcel, A. J. 1980 Conscious and preconscious recognition of polysemous words: locating the selective effects of prior verbal context. In *Attention and performance, VIII* (ed. R. S. Nickerson). Hillsdale, NJ: Erlbaum.

Marcel, A. J. 1983 Conscious and unconscious perception: experiments on visual masking and word recognition. *Cogn. Psychol.* **15**, 197–237. (doi:10.1016/0010-0285(83) 90009-9)

Martens, S., Wolters, G. & van Raamsdonk, M. 2002 Blinks of the mind: memory effects of attentional processes. *J. Exp. Psychol. Hum. Percept. Perform.* **28**, 1275–1287. (doi:10.1037/0096-1523.28.6.1275)

McCauley, C., Parmelee, C. M., Sperber, R. D. & Carr, T. H. 1980 Early extraction of meaning from pictures and its relation to conscious identification. *J. Exp. Psychol. Hum. Percept. Perform.* **6**, 265–276. (doi:10.1037/0096-1523.6. 2.265)

McGlinchey-Berroth, R., Milberg, W. P., Verfaellie, M., Alexander, M. & Kilduff, P. T. 1993 Semantic processing in the neglected visual field: evidence from a lexical decision task. *Cogn. Neuropsychol.* **10**, 79–108.

McNamara, T. P. 1992 Theories of priming I: associative distance and lag. *J. Exp. Psychol. Learn. Mem. Cogn.* **18**, 1173–1190. (doi:10.1037/0278-7393.18.6.1173)

McNamara, T. P. 1994 Theories of priming II: types of primes. *J. Exp. Psychol. Learn. Mem. Cogn.* **20**, 507–520. (doi:10.1037/0278-7393.20.3.507)

Merikle, P. M. 1982 Unconscious perception revisited. *Percept. Psychophys.* **31**, 298–301.

Merikle, P. M. & Daneman, M. 1998 Psychological investigations of unconscious perception. *J. Conscious. Stud.* **5**, 5–18.

Merikle, P. M. & Joordens, S. 1997 Parallels between perception without attention and perception without awareness. *Conscious. Cogn.* **6**, 219–236. (doi:10.1006/ ccog.1997.0310)

Merikle, P. M., Joordens, S. & Stolz, J. 1995 Measuring the relative magnitude of unconscious influences. *Conscious. Cogn.* **4**, 422–439. (doi:10.1006/ccog.1995.1049)

Merikle, P. M., Smilek, D. & Eastwood, J. D. 2001 Perception without awareness: perspectives from cognitive pychology. *Cognition* **79**, 115–134. (doi:10.1016/S0010-0277(00) 00126-8)

Misra, M. & Holcomb, P. J. 2003 Event-related potential indices of masked repetition priming. *Psychophysiology* **40**, 115–130. (doi:10.1111/1469-8986.00012)

Morris, J. S., Öhman, A. & Dolan, R. J. 1998 Conscious and unconscious emotional learning in the amygdala. *Nature* **393**, 467–470. (doi:10.1038/30976)

Naccache, L. & Dehaene, S. 2001*a* Unconscious semantic priming extends to novel unseen stimuli. *Cognition* **80**, 215–229. (doi:10.1016/S0010-0277(00)00139-6)

Naccache, L. & Dehaene, S. 2001*b* The priming method: imaging unconscious repetition priming reveals an abstract representation of number in the parietal lobes. *Cereb. Cortex* **11**, 966–974. (doi:10.1093/ cercor/11.10. 966)

Naccache, L., Blandin, E. & Dehaene, S. 2002 Unconscious masked priming depends on temporal attention. *Psychol. Sci.* **13**, 416–424. (doi:10.1111/1467-9280.00474)

Naccache, L., Gaillard, R., Adam, C., Hasboun, D., Clemenceau, S., Baulac, M., Dehaene, S. & Cohen, L. 2005 A direct intracranial record of emotions evoked by subliminal words. *Proc. Natl Acad. Sci. USA* **102**, 7713–7720. (doi:10.1073/pnas.0500542102)

Nakamura, K., Dehaene, S., Jorbert, A., Le Bihan, D. & Kouider, S. 2005 Subliminal convergence of Kanji and Kana words: further evidence for functional parcellation of the posterior temporal cortex in visual word perception. *J. Cogn. Neurosci.* **17**, 954–968. (doi:10.1162/0898 929054021166)

Nakamura, K., Hara, N., Kouider, S., Takayama, Y., Hanajima, R., Sakai, K. & Ugawa, Y. 2006 Task-guided selection of the dual neural pathways for reading. *Neuron* **52**, 1–8. (doi:10.1016/j.neuron.2006.09.030)

Neely, J. H. 1991 Semantic priming effects in visual word recognition: a selective review of current findings and theories. In Basic *processes in reading; Visual word recognition* (eds D. Besner & G. Humphreys), pp. 264–337. Hillsdale, NJ: Erlbaum.

Neumann, O. & Klotz, W. 1994 Motor responses to nonreportable, masked stimuli: where is the limit of direct parameter specification? In *Conscious and nonconscious information processing: attention and performance*, vol. 15 (eds C. Umiltá & M. Moscovitch), pp. 123–150. Cambridge, MA: MIT Press.

Nolan, K. A. & Caramazza, A. 1982 Unconscious perception of meaning: a failure to replicate. *Bull. Psychon. Soc.* **20**, 23–26.

Ohman, A. 2002 Automaticity and the amygdala: noncon-scious responses to emotional faces. *Curr. Dir. Psychol. Sci.* **11**, 62–66. (doi:10.1111/1467-8721.00169)

Pierce, C. S. & Jastrow, J. 1884 On small differences in sensation. *Mem. Natl Acad. Sci.* **3**, 75–83.

Perea, M. & Gotor, A. 1997 Associative and semantic priming effects occur at very short stimulus-onset asynchronies in lexical decision and naming. *Cognition* **62**, 223–240. (doi:10.1016/S0010-0277 (96)00782-2)

Perfetti, C. A. & Bell, L. 1991 Phonemic activation during the first 40 ms of word identification: evidence from backward masking and masked priming. *J. Mem. Lang.* **30**, 473–485. (doi:10.1016/0749-596X (91)90017-E)

Perfetti, C. A., Bell, L. & Delaney, S. 1988 Automatic phonetic activation in silent word reading: evidence from backward masking. *J. Mem. Lang.* **27**, 59–70. (doi:10. 1016/0749-596X (88)90048-4)

Perruchet, P. & Vinter, A. 2002 The self-organizing consciousness. *Behav. Brain Sci.* **25**, 297–330.

Perry, C. & Ziegler, J. C. 2002 On the nature of phonological assembly: evidence from backward masking. *Lang. Cogn. Process.* **17**, 31–59. (doi:10.1080/01690960042000157)

Pessoa, L. 2005 To what extent are emotional stimuli processed without attention and awareness? *Curr. Opin. Neurobiol.* **15**, 188–196. (doi:10.1016/j.conb.2005.03. 002)

Pessoa, L., Japee, S. & Ungerleider, L. G. 2005 Visual awareness and the detection of fearful faces. *Emotion* **5**, 243–247. (doi:10.1037/1528-3542.5.2.243)

Pessoa, L., Japee, S., Sturman, D. & Ungerleider, L. G. 2006 Target visibility and visual awareness modulate amygdala responses to fearful faces. *Cereb. Cortex* **16**, 366–375. (doi:10.1093/cercor/bhi115)

Posner, M. I. 1994 Attention: the mechanism of consciousness. *Proc. Natl Acad. Sci. USA* **91**, 7398–7402. (doi:10. 1073/pnas.91.16.7398)

Posner, M. I. & Snyder, C. R. R. 1975 Attention and cognitive control. In *Information processing and cognition: the Loyola symposion* (ed. R. L. Solso), Hillsdale, NJ: Lawrence Erlbaum Associates, Inc.

Posner, M. I., Walker, J. A., Friedrich, F. J. & Rafal, R. 1984 Effects of parietal injury on covert orienting of visual attention. *J. Neurosci.* **4**, 1863–1874.

Pratkanis, A. R. 1992 The cargo-cult science of subliminal persuasion. *Skept. Inq.* **16**, 260–272.

Purcell, D. G., Stewart, A. L. & Stanovich, K. E. 1983 Another look at semantic priming without awareness. *Percept. Psychophys.* **34**, 65–71.

Rastle, K. & Bryasbert, M. 2006 Masked phonological priming effects in English: are they real? Do they matter? *Cogn. Psychol.* **53**, 97–145. (doi:10.1016/j.cogpsych.2006. 01.002)

Rastle, K., Davis, M. H., Marslen-Wilson, W. D. & Tyler, L. K. 2000 Morphological and semantic effects in visual word recognition: a time-course study. *Lang. Cogn. Process.* **15**, 507–537. (doi:10.1080/01690960050119689)

Raymond, J. E., Shapiro, K. L. & Arnell, K. M. 1992 Temporary suppression of visual processing in an RSVP task: an attentional blink? *J. Exp. Psychol. Hum. Percept. Perform.* **18**, 849–860. (doi:10.1037/0096-1523.18.3.849)

Reynvoet, B. & Brysbaert, M. 2004 Cross-notation number priming investigated at different stimulus onset asynchronies in parity and naming tasks. *Exp. Psychol.* **51**, 81–90.

Reynvoet, B., Caessens, B. & Brysbaert, M. 2002 Automatic stimulus-response associations may be semantically mediated. *Psychon. Bull. Rev.* **9**, 107–112.

Reynvoet, B., Gevers, W. & Caessens, B. 2005 Unconscious primes activate motor codes through semantics. *J. Exp. Psychol. Learn. Mem. Cogn.* **31**, 991–1000. (doi:10.1037/ 0278-7393.31.5.991)

Rolke, B., Heil, M., Streb, J. & Henninghausen, E. 2001 Missed prime words within the attentional blink evoke an N400 semantic priming effect. *Psychophysiology* **38**, 165–174. (doi:10.1017/ S0048577201991504)

Rusconi, E., Priftis, K., Rusconi, M. L. & Umilta, C. 2006 Arithmetic priming from neglected numbers. *Cogn. Psychol.* **23**, 227–239.

Schacter, D. L. 1987 Implicit memory: history and current status. *J. Exp. Psychol. Learn. Mem. Cogn.* **13**, 501–518. (doi:10.1037/0278-7393.13.3.501)

Schlaghecken, F. & Eimer, M. 2006 Active masks and active inhibition: a comment on Lleras and Enns 2004 and on Verleger, Jaskowski, Aydemir, van der Lubbe, and Groen 2004. *J. Exp. Psychol. Gen.* **135**, 484–494. (doi:10.1037/ 0096-3445.135.3.484)

Schneider, W. & Shiffrin, R. W. 1977 Controlled and automatic human information processing, vol. I. Detection, search, and attention. *Psychol. Rev.* **84**, 1–66. (doi:10. 1037/0033-295X.84.1.1)

Schnyer, D. M., Allen, J. J. & Forster, K. I. 1997 Event-related brain potential examination of implicit memory processes: masked and unmasked repetition priming. *Neuropsychology* **11**, 243–260. (doi:10.1037/0894-4105. 11.2.243)

Sereno, J. A. 1991 Graphemic, associative, and syntactic priming effects at brief stimulus onset asynchrony in lexical decision and naming. *J. Exp. Psychol. Learn. Mem. Cogn.* **17**, 459–477. (doi:10.1037/0278-7393.17.3.459)

Sergent, C., Baillet, S. & Dehaene, S. 2005 Timing of the brain events underlying access to consciousness during the attentional blink. *Nat. Neurosci.* **8**, 1391–1400. (doi:10. 1038/nn1549)

Shanks, D. R. & St John, M. F. 1994 Characteristics of dissociable human systems. *Behav. Brain Sci.* **17**, 367–447.

Shapiro, K. L., Driver, J., Ward, R. & Sorensen, R. E. 1997 Priming from the attentional blink: a failure to extract visual tokens but not visual types. *Psychol. Sci.* **8**, 95–100. (doi:10.1111/j.1467-9280.1997. tb00689.x)

Shen, D. & Forster, K. I. 1999 Masked phonological priming in reading Chinese words depends on the task. *Lang. Cogn. Process.* **14**, 429–459. (doi:10.1080/016909699386149)

Sidis, B. 1898 *The psychology of suggestion.* New York, NY: Appleton.

Stroh, M. A., Shaw, M. & Washburn, M. F. 1908 A study of guessing. *Am. J. Psychol.* **19**, 243–245. (doi:10.2307/ 1412764)

Sumner, P., Tsai, P. C., Yu, K. & Nachev, P. 2006 Attentional modulation of sensorimotor processes in the absence of perceptual awareness. *Proc. Natl Acad. Sci. USA* **103**, 10 520–10 525. (doi:10.1073/pnas.0601974103)

Swinney, D. 1979 Lexical access during sentence comprehension: (Re)consideration of context effects. *J. Verb. Learn. Verb. Behav.* **18**, 645–660. (doi:10.1016/S0022-5371(79)90355-4)

Taylor, D. A. 1977 Time course of context effects. *J. Exp. Psychol. Gen.* **106**, 404–426. (doi:10.1037/0096-3445. 106.4.404)

Thompson, K. G. & Schall, J. D. 1999 The detection of visual signals by macaque frontal eye field during masking. *Nat. Neurosci.* **2**, 283–288. (doi:10.1038/6398)

Tipper, S. P. 1985 The negative priming effect: inhibitory priming by ignored objects. *Q. J. Exp. Psychol. A* **37**, 571–590.

Tse, P. U., Martinez-Conde, S., Schlegel, A. A. & Macknik, S. L. 2005 Visibility, visual awareness, and visual masking of simple unattended targets are confined to areas in the occipital cortex beyond human V1/ V2. *Proc. Natl Acad. Sci. USA* **102**, 17 178–17 183. (doi:10.1073/pnas.05080 10102)

Tyler, L. K., Bright, P., Dick, E., Tavares, P., Pilgrim, L., Fletcher, P., Greer, M. & Moss, H. 2003 Do semantic categories activate distinct cortical regions? Evidence for a distributed neural semantic system. *Cogn. Neuropsychol.* **20**, 541–559. (doi:10.1080/02643290244000211)

Tzelgov, J., Henik, A. & Porat, Z. 1997 Automaticity and consciousness: is perceiving the word necessary for reading it? *Am. J. Psychol.* **3**, 429–448. (doi:10.2307/ 1423567)

Van Opstal, F., Reynvoet, B. & Verguts, T. 2005*a* How to trigger elaborate processing? A comment on Kunde, Kiesel, & Hoffmann 2003. *Cognition* **97**, 89–97. (doi:10. 1016/j.cognition.2004.12.011)

Van Opstal, F., Reynvoet, B. & Verguts, T. 2005*b* Unconscious semantic categorization and mask interactions: an elaborate response to Kunde *et al.* 2005. *Cognition* **97**, 107–113. (doi:10.1016/ j.cognition.2005.04.005)

Van Voorhis, B. A. & Dark, V. J. 1995 Semantic matching, response mode, and response mapping as contributors to retroactive and proactive priming. *J. Exp. Psychol. Learn. Mem. Cogn.* **21**, 913–932. (doi:10.1037/0278-7393.21.4. 913)

Verleger, R., Jaśkowski, P., Aydemir, A., van der Lubbe, R. & Groen, M. 2004 Qualitative differences between conscious and nonconscious processing? On inverse priming induced by masked arrows. *J. Exp. Psychol. Gen.* **133**, 494–515. (doi:10.1037/0096-3445.133.4.494)

Volpe, B. T., Ledoux, J. E. & Gazzaniga, M. S. 1979 Information processing in an "extinguished" visual field. *Nature* **282**, 722–724. (doi:10.1038/282722a0)

Vuilleumier, P. & Driver, J. 2007 Modulation of visual processing by attention and emotion: windows on causal interactions between human brain regions. *Phil. Trans. R. Soc. B* **362**, 837–855. (doi:10.1098/rstb.2007.2092)

Whalen, P. J., Rauch, S. L., Etcoff, N. L., McInerney, S. C., Lee, M. & Jenike, M. A. 1998 Masked presentations of emotional facial expressions modulate amygdala activity without explicit knowledge. *J. Neurosci.* **18**, 411–418.

Williams, P. & Parkin, A. 1980 On knowing the meaning of words we are unable to report: a confirmation of a guessing explanation. *Q. J. Exp. Psychol.* **32**, 101–107.

10

Neural correlates of the contents of visual awareness in humans

Geraint Rees *

The immediacy and directness of our subjective visual experience belies the complexity of the neural mechanisms involved, which remain incompletely understood. This review focuses on how the subjective contents of human visual awareness are encoded in neural activity. Empirical evidence to date suggests that no single brain area is both necessary and sufficient for consciousness. Instead, necessary and sufficient conditions appear to involve both activation of a distributed representation of the visual scene in primary visual cortex and ventral visual areas, plus parietal and frontal activity. The key empirical focus is now on characterizing qualitative differences in the type of neural activity in these areas underlying conscious and unconscious processing. To this end, recent progress in developing novel approaches to accurately decoding the contents of consciousness from brief samples of neural activity show great promise.

Keywords: consciousness; vision; functional magnetic resonance imaging; awareness

10.1 Introduction

The subjective experience of conscious mental contents is central to our everyday life. Whether the content of such subjective experiences can be reliably decoded and predicted from patterns of brain activity is an empirical question. Techniques for non-invasive measurement of human brain activity such as functional magnetic resonance imaging (fMRI), positron emission tomography, electroencephalography (EEG) and magnetoencephalography (MEG) can reveal the neural substrates of both conscious and unconscious processing underlying these subjective experiences. This review focuses on recent attempts to identify experimentally the neural correlates of the contents of consciousness related to visual perception in humans.

Consciousness and awareness of a stimulus are used interchangeably in this review to indicate the ability of an observer to report either the presence of that stimulus or its identity. In contrast, unconscious or invisible stimuli fail to be reported successfully or are associated with responses that objectively indicate failure to discriminate the presence or identity of the stimulus (e.g. $d' \sim = 0$). The experiments reviewed here relate these differences in the reportability of stimuli (reflecting differences in the subjective contents of consciousness) to brain activity measured using noninvasive imaging techniques. In general, such studies to date have found consistently that both visible and invisible or unreportable stimuli nevertheless undergo processing in both anatomically early and higher levels of the human visual system. This makes a simple division of sensory areas into those supporting conscious or unconscious processing, respectively, increasingly untenable. Instead, the key empirical question is now to

*g.rees@fil.ion.ucl.ac.uk

establish what quantitative and qualitative differences in brain activity distinguish conscious and unconscious processing (Frith *et al*. 1999). Such efforts have benefited from recent developments in analysing fMRI data that focus not only on focal changes in brain activity, but also on decoding the information contained within local spatial patterns of activity (Haynes & Rees 2006; Norman *et al*. 2006). While the application of these techniques is only just beginning, they place new emphasis on determining how much information about mental states can be decoded from functional brain images; and, in turn, they raise the challenge of specifying what information would be sufficient to *decode consciousness*.

10.2 Unconscious processing in human visual cortex

A prerequisite for appreciating how the contents of consciousness might be represented in patterns of brain activity is an understanding of which brain structures and psychological processes are associated with unconscious processing (see also Kouider & Dehaene 2007). Delineating the quantitative and qualitative differences between conscious and unconscious processing is central to identifying the neural basis of consciousness. There is now substantial evidence that processing of sensory stimuli outside awareness can influence behaviour (e.g. Marcel 1983; Naccache *et al*. 2002, though see Holender & Duscherer (2004) for a sceptical critique); but the neural bases of such processing remain under active exploration.

At the anatomically earliest stages of cortical processing, activity in primary visual cortex (V1) can readily be identified even in the absence of visual stimulation. For example, saccadic eye movements or blinks made in complete darkness nevertheless evoke generalized activity in retinotopically defined human primary visual cortex (Bodis-Wollner *et al*. 1999; Bristow *et al*. 2005; Sylvester *et al*. 2005; Sylvester & Rees 2006). Such signals, presumably representing 'efference copy' of the motor command, are usually not associated with any perception of phenomenal content (though see Enoch *et al*. 2003). Activation of V1 *per se* is therefore insufficient for awareness. Activation without awareness in early retinotopic visual areas can be confined to the retinotopic location of an invisible target. When a simple target such as an achromatic disc is briefly flashed, robust activity is elicited in the corresponding retinotopic location of V1 (plus V2 and V3) even when the target is rendered completely invisible by a surrounding mask (Haynes *et al*. 2005*b*). These experiments establish that invisible stimuli can evoke retinotopically specific activity in early visual cortex. However, they do not determine whether the specific neuronal processes elicited within these regions differ for visible and invisible stimuli. Such a determination requires a more direct way of measuring the neuronal representations associated with stimulus presentation.

Neurons in early visual cortex are sensitive to a number of visual features, such as orientation and direction of motion. It is well established that orientation-selective after-effects can result from exposure to grating stimuli that are too fine to be consciously perceived (He & MacLeod 2001), suggesting that orientation-selective but unconscious activation of visual cortex is possible. Direct physiological measurement of such unconscious feature-selective processing in human V1 has proven elusive due to the relatively low spatial resolution (several millimetres) of functional neuroimaging methods when compared with the size of orientation columns in visual cortex (hundreds of microns). However, it has recently become possible to use fMRI even at conventional resolutions (typically, voxels measuring 3×3×3 mm) to obtain a direct measure of orientation-selective processing in V1 (Haynes & Rees 2005*a*; Kamitani & Tong 2005). Many individual fMRI voxels in V1 show subtle but reproducible biases in their activity when differently oriented stimuli are presented to the experimental subject. This is thought to reflect biased sampling by the (relatively) low spatial resolution voxels of the underlying columnar organization of orientation-specific neuronal populations, due to an uneven distribution of different orientation specificities across the cortical surface (for more detailed explanations, see Kamitani & Tong 2005 or Haynes & Rees 2005a). Importantly, this information can be efficiently accumulated across the whole of V1 using multivariate pattern recognition analyses (for reviews, see Haynes & Rees 2006; Norman *et al.* 2006). Such multivoxel pattern analysis can successfully predict which one of the two oriented stimuli a participant is viewing, even when masking renders that stimulus invisible (figure 10.1a,b; Haynes & Rees 2005a). This indicates the presence of feature-selective processing in early visual cortex, even for invisible stimuli. Such analyses thus open up the possibility of probing different levels of neuronal representation associated with conscious or unconscious processing.

Beyond primary visual cortex, the human ventral visual pathway comprises multiple functionally specialized visual areas that respond to different attributes of the visual scene. Activation of such areas (albeit modest in amplitude) is consistently identified for invisible words, faces and objects. For example, masked and invisible words can activate the 'temporal word form area' (Dehaene *et al.* 2001). Dichoptically masked and therefore invisible object and face stimuli can nevertheless activate functionally specialized areas of ventral visual cortex despite their invisibility (Moutoussis & Zeki 2002). Such observations are not restricted to different types of visual masking, as unconscious activation of the ventral visual pathway during the 'attentional blink' can reflect object category (Marois *et al.* 2004) and semantic analysis of visually presented words (Luck *et al.* 1996). Visual motion rendered invisible through 'crowding' can still activate V5/MT (Moutoussis & Zeki 2006). Changes in an object that are not perceived due to introduction of visual flicker between changes nevertheless lead to category-specific activity in the ventral visual pathway that can precede conscious change detection (Niedeggen *et al.* 2001).

Unconscious sensory activation by complex visual stimuli is not confined to the ventral visual pathway, but extends to both dorsal and subcortical structures. Dorsal cortical areas show activation for different types of objects even when observers are completely unaware of their identity through binocular suppression (Fang & He 2005). Moreover, the amygdala can be activated by fearful face stimuli rendered invisible through masking (Morris *et al.* 1999), in response to the emotional content of invisible words (Naccache *et al.* 2005) or during suppression in binocular rivalry (Pasley *et al.* 2004).

Unconscious activation of ventral visual cortex can also be identified following parietal damage causing visual extinction. Patients with visual extinction show deficient awareness for contralesional visual stimuli, particularly when a competing stimulus is also present ipsilesionally. When visual stimuli are presented to patients with visual extinction, areas of both primary and extrastriate visual cortex that are activated by a seen left visual field stimulus are also activated by an unseen and extinguished left visual field stimulus (Rees *et al.* 2000, 2002b; Vuilleumier *et al.* 2001). The unconscious processing of an extinguished face stimulus extends even to face selective cortex in the fusiform face area (FFA; Rees *et al.* 2002b; see also Vuilleumier & Driver 2007).

Taken together, these data present a picture of modest (in terms of the level of activity evoked) but pervasive unconscious processing of visual stimuli throughout the dorsal and ventral visual pathways, plus subcortical structures. In particular, all visually responsive cortical areas appear to show evidence for unconscious visual processing.

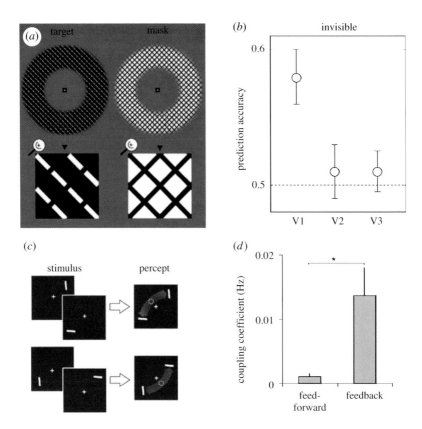

Fig. 10.1 Unconscious and conscious processing in V1. (*a*) An oriented target annulus can be effectively rendered invisible by subsequently presenting a contrast-inverted mask with no specific orientation. (*b*) However, pattern-based decoding applied to V1 activity measured using fMRI can still successfully determine significantly greater than chance which target orientation was presented to a subject. Decoding is not significantly different from chance in V2 and V3. This demonstrates that unconscious information about target orientation must be present in the fMRI signals in V1. Data are from Haynes & Rees (2005*a*). (*c*) Apparent motion on a curved path can be perceived by alternating appearance of tilted line inducers on the horizontal or vertical meridians.(*d*) Perception of apparent motion is associated with significantly enhanced feedback effective connectivity (as assessed with dynamic causal modelling) from V5/MT to the retinotopic location in V1 on the path of apparent motion. Data are from Sterzer *et al.* (2006).

10.3 Conscious processing in human visual cortex

Signals recorded from most, if not all, parts of the human visual pathways can therefore show signals associated with processing visual stimuli that do not reach awareness. However, evidence will now be reviewed indicating that signals recorded from these regions can also show signals strongly correlated with the contents of consciousness.

At the anatomically earliest stages of visual processing, signals in V1 scale linearly with the magnitude of change in retinal illumination, as do subjects' subjective ratings of the perceived brightness of the stimuli (Haynes *et al*. 2004). Such a close correspondence between fMRI signals and phenomenal perception is consistent with a role for these areas in representing conscious contents. More direct evidence has been provided by studies of sensory stimulation at perceptual threshold. For simple grating stimuli, a stimulus that is successfully detected by a subject evokes significantly greater activity in V1 when compared with identical stimuli that do not reach awareness (Ress & Heeger 2003). Such conscious detection of threshold-level stimuli is associated with very early differential electrical signals at posterior electrodes (Pins & Ffytche 2003), suggesting that changes in conscious contents can be associated with activity that is both temporally and anatomically early in processing. However, it is important to note that it is not necessarily the case that conscious and unconscious processing can always be distinguished early in time. In some experimental situations, conscious and unconscious processing can only be dissociated at a much later stage, after several hundred milliseconds (Vogel *et al*. 1998; Sergent *et al*. 2005). Neither need it be the case that such late divergence does not reflect V1 involvement, as such temporally delayed correlates of conscious perception can be identified in monkey V1 (Super *et al*. 2001), supporting theoretical suggestions that conscious perception correlates not with the 'feed-forward' sweep of information processing following stimulation processing but rather with later feedback or recurrent signals, perhaps to V1 (Lamme & Roelfsema 2000).

Retinotopic activity in V1 can reflect conscious perception of illusory features. When a moving grating is divided by a large gap, observers report seeing a moving 'phantom' in the gap and there is enhanced activity in the locations in early retinotopic visual cortex corresponding to the illusory percept (Meng *et al*. 2005). Moreover, when phantom-inducing gratings are paired with competing stimuli that induce binocular rivalry, spontaneous fluctuations in conscious perception of the phantom occur together with changes in early visual activity. Similarly, V1 activation can be found on the path of apparent motion (Muckli *et al*. 2005) and is associated with strengthened feedback connections to that retinotopic location from cortical area V5/MT (Sterzer *et al*. 2006; see figure 10.1*c,d* here). Finally, when two objects subtending identical angles in the visual field are made to appear of different sizes using three-dimensional context, the spatial extent of activation in the V1 retinotopic map reflects the perceived rather than actual angular size of the objects (Murray *et al*. 2006). These data thus show a rather close correspondence between either the level or spatial extent of V1 activation and the perceived phenomenal properties of the visual world.

Such close correspondence between V1 activity and conscious contents also extends to cross-modal influences on visual perception. Irrelevant auditory stimulation can lead to illusory perception of a single flash as two flashes, and primary visual cortex shows enhanced activity when compared with physically identical stimulation that is veridically perceived (Watkins *et al*. 2006). Moreover, these alterations in the contents of visual consciousness are associated with very early modulation of MEG responses over posterior occipital sensors (Shams *et al*. 2005). Responses in human V1 can therefore be altered by sound, and can reflect subjective perception rather than the physically present visual stimulus.

V1 is not the only area in the human visual pathway whose activity can reflect the contents of consciousness. Visually presented objects can be made difficult to identify by degrading them, and in such circumstances, occipitotemporal activity shows a close correlation with recognition performance (Grill-Spector *et al*. 2000). Similarly, conscious detection of changes in a visually presented object is associated with enhanced activity in ventral visual cortex (Beck *et al*. 2001). There are many other examples of similarly close correspondence between the level of activity in the ventral visual pathway and conscious perception. For example, visual imagery activates category-specific areas of visual cortex (O'Craven & Kanwisher 2000), and category-selective neurons in the human medial temporal lobe (Kreiman *et al.* 2000). Contingent after-effects based on colour or motion lead to activation of either V4 (Sakai *et al.* 1995; Barnes *et al.* 1999) or V5/MT (Tootell *et al.* 1995; He *et al.* 1998), respectively, and the time course of such activation reflects phenomenal experience. Perception of illusory or implied motion in a static visual stimulus is associated with activation of V5/MT (Zeki *et al.* 1993; Kourtzi & Kanwisher 2000; Senior *et al.* 2000), whereas perception of illusory contours activates extrastriate cortex (Hirsch *et al.* 1995; Halgren *et al.* 2003). Differential activity in word-processing areas is present when subjects are consciously aware of the presence and identity of visually presented words, but can be absent when they are not (Rees *et al.* 1999). Patients with schizophrenia who experience visual and auditory hallucinations show activity in modality-specific cortex during hallucinatory episodes (Silbersweig *et al.* 1995). Similarly, patients with damage to the visual system who experience hallucinations with specific phenomenal content show activity in functionally specialized areas of visual cortex corresponding to the contents of their hallucinations (Ffytche *et al.* 1998).

Common to all these diverse paradigms are changes in the contents of consciousness without corresponding changes in physical stimulation. Corresponding changes in activity in ventral visual cortex are seen in areas known to represent the attributes represented in the contents of consciousness. Thus, activity in the visual pathway can reflect conscious processing of visual stimuli; but the studies reviewed earlier also indicate that stimuli that are not consciously perceived can also evoke some activation of the same cortical areas, sometimes with comparable amplitude to consciously perceived stimuli (e.g. Rees *et al.* 2000). However, common involvement of a cortical area in both conscious and unconscious processing, as indicated by blood-oxygen-level-dependent (BOLD) signals from large neuronal populations, does not imply that all underlying neuronal processes in that area must be identical for the two conditions. Taken together, these somewhat divergent findings therefore demonstrate the importance of now trying to characterize in more detail whether visible and invisible stimuli elicit qualitatively different *types* of neuronal activity.

Pattern-based decoding approaches have recently been applied to fMRI signals from human ventral visual cortex. These techniques have the potential to reveal qualitative differences in neural processes underlying conscious and unconscious processing in a cortical area. Orientation and direction of motion of simple visual stimuli can be decoded from the local pattern of brain activity (Haynes & Rees 2005a; Kamitani & Tong 2005) and the identity of more complex objects (Haxby *et al.* 2001). Moreover, if subjects are asked to attend one of the two overlapping orientations or motion directions, then patterns of activity in early visual cortex can be used to predict which one is attended (Kamitani & Tong 2005, 2006). These data suggest that reliable decoding of the subjective contents of consciousness, at least under controlled viewing conditions, may be a realistic prospect. Moreover, the ability to provide information about the underlying specificities of the neuronal populations may now provide a future basis for characterizing whether conscious and unconscious stimuli elicit different types of activity in a single cortical region.

The experiments reviewed thus far typically focus on characterizing neural activity evoked by individual visual stimuli that either reach awareness or on other occasions remain invisible. In contrast, when a single ambiguous visual stimulus has more than one possible perceptual interpretation, conscious perception alternates spontaneously and unpredictably between each individual interpretation. Such bistable perceptual phenomena elicit dynamic ongoing fluctuations in the contents of visual awareness, but without any changes in physical stimulation. They have proven extremely popular for studying the neural correlates of consciousness and so relevant empirical data from this particular class of paradigm will now be reviewed separately.

10.4 Neural correlates of bistable perception and binocular rivalry

Binocular rivalry is a particularly well-known bistable phenomenon, and a popular and enduring paradigm for studying the neural correlates of consciousness (Tong *et al.* 2006). When dissimilar images are presented to the two eyes, they compete for perceptual dominance so that each image is consciously visible in turn for a few seconds while the other is perceptually suppressed. Such binocular rivalry is associated with relative suppression of local, eye-based representations that can also be modulated by high-level influences such as perceptual grouping. Since perceptual transitions between each monocular view occur spontaneously without any change in the physical stimulus, neural correlates of consciousness may be distinguished from neural correlates attributable to stimulus characteristics. All stages of visual processing show such activity changes associated with rivalrous fluctuations (Tong *et al.* 2006), which will now be reviewed in more detail.

Even at the earliest subcortical stages of visual processing, signals recorded from the human lateral geniculate nucleus (LGN) exhibit fluctuations in activity during binocular rivalry (Haynes *et al.* 2005a; Wunderlich *et al.* 2005). Regions of the LGN that show strong eye preference independently show strongly reduced activity during binocular rivalry when the stimulus presented in their preferred eye is perceptually suppressed. The human LGN is thus the earliest stage of visual processing that reflects changes in the contents of consciousness, even when physical stimulation is unchanged. Primary visual cortex shows a similar pattern of changes in activity correlated with changes in the contents of consciousness (Polonsky *et al.* 2000; Tong & Engel 2001; Lee & Blake 2002; Lee *et al.* 2005). In general (though see Tong & Engel 2001), such fluctuations in activity are about half as large as those evoked by non-rivalrous stimulus alternation. This indicates that the suppressed image during rivalry undergoes a considerable degree of unconscious processing.

Further along the ventral visual pathway, responses in FFA during rivalry are larger than those in V1 and equal in magnitude to responses evoked by nonrivalrous stimuli (Tong *et al.* 1998). This suggests that neural competition during rivalry has been resolved by these later stages of visual processing, and activity in FFA thus reflects the contents of consciousness rather than the retinal stimulus. However, such an account is inconsistent with the finding that binocularly suppressed faces can nevertheless still activate the FFA (Moutoussis & Zeki 2002). Moreover, Philipp Sterzer, John Haynes and myself have recently re-examined the local spatial patterns of brain activity in FFA when faces are rendered invisible by binocular suppression. Neither invisible faces nor invisible houses 'activated' FFA when fMRI signals were averaged across the whole of FFA, consistent with previous findings. But when local fine-grained spatial patterns of activity were taken into account using multivariate decoding, it was now possible to accurately decode whether the invisible stimulus was a face or house (figure 10.2). These data demonstrate that even during suppression and phenomenal invisibility in rivalry, sufficient information is encoded at high levels of the human visual system to determine the identity of the suppressed stimulus. Future research should now focus on characterizing the nature and extent of such information and whether it differs from conscious perception.

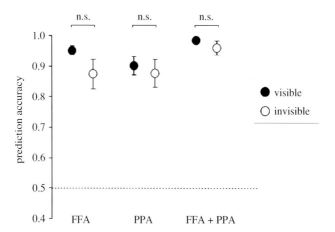

Fig. 10.2 Unconscious representation of face-specific information in FFA. Prediction accuracy of a multivoxel pattern-based decoder for discriminating the presentation of either a face or house from activity recorded in the fusiform face area (FFA) or parahippocampal place area (PPA), respectively. Average prediction accuracies across participants ($n = 5$) for visible faces versus houses are denoted by filled circles (± s.e.m.) and for invisible faces versus houses by empty circles. Performance was uniformly high and significantly above chance level (50%, dotted line) for all pairwise comparisons across participants.

Other forms of bistable perception do not necessarily involve binocular competition. Nevertheless, a repeated finding is that these paradigms lead to activation of visual cortical structures that correspond to the attributes of whichever competing percept the observer is currently aware of (Kleinschmidt *et al.* 1998; Sterzer *et al.* 2002, 2003). This is consistent with the more general observation, reviewed earlier, that visible stimuli often give rise to greater activation in functionally specialized regions of visual cortex corresponding to stimulus type than corresponding invisible stimuli.

Remarkably, the information encoded in early visual cortex during binocular rivalry (as revealed by fMRI) can be sufficient to reconstruct the dynamic stream of consciousness. Information that is contained in the multivariate pattern of responses to stimulus features in V1–V3 as recorded using fMRI can be used to accurately predict, and therefore track, changes in conscious contents during rivalry (Haynes & Rees 2005*b*). Accurate decoding is possible for extended periods of time during rivalry, while awareness undergoes many spontaneous changes (figure 10.3). In that study, successful prediction of rivalry from primary visual cortex activity primarily reflected eye-based signals, whereas prediction in higher areas reflected the colour of the percept. Furthermore, accurate prediction during binocular rivalry could be established in that study on the basis of classifying signals originally recorded during stable monocular viewing, showing that prediction generalizes across different viewing conditions and does not require or rely on motor responses. It is therefore possible to predict the dynamically changing time course of subjective experience using brain activity alone. This raises the possibility that more complex dynamic changes in consciousness might be decoded, though this in turn raises important questions about whether such an approach will be able to generalize to novel mental states (Haynes & Rees 2006).

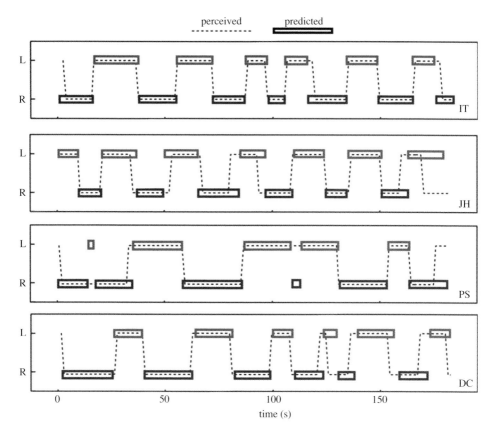

Fig. 10.3 Decoding the stream of consciousness from activity in human V1. A multivoxel pattern-based decoder trained on activity from V1, while participants experience binocular rivalry can successfully decode the stream of consciousness over several minutes. Data are from Haynes & Rees (2005*b*) and show participants' reported percepts (dotted lines) alternating between each monocular view. Blind predictions of conscious contents made from patterns of V1 activity by the decoder are shown (solid lines). A close correspondence between decoded and actual perceptual state is apparent.

10.5 Necessary and sufficient correlates of conscious perception in human visual cortex

fMRI and EEG/MEG studies in normal subjects, such as those discussed above, reveal the correlation between particular contents of consciousness and specific types of neural activity. However, they can neither determine whether this neural activity plays a causal role in determining the contents of consciousness, nor ascertain with certainty the necessary and sufficient correlates of consciousness. In order to do this, neural activity must be manipulated either experimentally (e.g. Vuilleumier & Driver 2007 and this volume) or as a consequence of neurological disease causing brain damage.

In individuals who are blind due to retinal damage, phosphenes can still be elicited by transcranial magnetic stimulation (TMS) of visual cortex (just as in sighted individuals). This suggests that the retina is not necessary for conscious visual experience. Similarly, visual experiences of varying complexity can be elicited by direct electrical stimulation of cortical structures in the ventral visual pathway (Lee *et al.* 2000), suggesting that the LGN may also not be necessary for consciousness. Whether V1 activity is necessary is more controversial. TMS of visual cortex does not elicit phosphenes when blindness results from damage to V1 (Cowey & Walsh 2000), and activation of extrastriate cortex without awareness occurs when the blind visual field is stimulated in patients with damage to V1 (Ptito e*t al.* 1999; Goebel *et al.* 2001). These data suggest that structural integrity of V1 is necessary for at least some types of conscious visual experience, and extrastriate cortical activity alone is not sufficient. But in patients with V1 damage, conscious vision may return over time in previously blind regions of the visual field. Stimulation of such locations in the visual field that gives rise to awareness can be associated with activation of perilesional V1 in some, but not all, patients (Kleiser *et al.* 2001), suggesting that V1 activity is not necessary for conscious awareness in all cases.

One possibility is that some functional aspect of V1 activity, such as its overall level or precise timing, plays a role in determining the contents of visual awareness. Consistent with this, awareness of motion is impaired if feedback signals from V5/MT to V1 are disrupted by TMS (Pascual-Leone & Walsh 2001; Silvanto *et al.* 2005). Similarly, using occipital TMS to disrupt processing of a metacontrast mask presented after a target can lead to unmasking and corresponding visibility of the original target (Ro *et al.* 2003). These data suggest that temporally late signals in V1 representing feedback from other ventral visual (or higher cortical) areas may be required for at least some forms of visual awareness. Findings reviewed earlier that conscious and non-conscious processing can be distinguished by signals occurring several hundred milliseconds after stimulus presentation (Vogel *et al.* 1998; Sergent *et al.* 2005) are consistent with such a role for feedback signals. Similarly, coupling is disrupted between the V1 representation of a target and higher visual areas when the target is rendered invisible by masking (Haynes *et al.* 2005*b*).

10.6 The role of frontal and parietal cortex in visual awareness

Although visual cortex plays a central role in representing the contents of visual consciousness, it has long been recognized that deficits in visual consciousness can result from damage to regions outside visual cortex (see also Vuilleumier & Driver 2007 and this volume). For example, damage to frontal and parietal cortex is commonly associated with visual neglect, where patients often do not perceive or respond to any type of visual stimulus placed in one-half of the visual field, particularly in the presence of competitor stimuli in the other hemifield (Driver & Mattingley 1998). This deficit in the representation of conscious contents is consistent with a general involvement of these structures in representing many different types of conscious contents. Activation of visual cortex or subcortical structures by visual stimuli is insufficient to result in awareness in visual neglect patients (Driver *et al.* 2001). In visual extinction following parietal damage, a proportion of visually presented stimuli reach awareness and in such cases, awareness is associated not only with activation of visual cortical areas (Rees *et al.* 2000, 2002*b*), but also with enhanced covariation of activity between visual cortical areas representing the visual stimulus and undamaged parietal and prefrontal regions (Vuilleumier *et al.* 2001; see also Vuilleumier & Driver 2007 and this volume).

Supporting the notion that regions outside visual cortex play a role in visual awareness, a striking and consistent finding from neuroimaging experiments over the last decade is a strong association of activity in frontal and parietal cortex with changes in the contents of visual consciousness (figure 10.4; see also Kouider & Dehaene 2007). For example, activity during transitions in binocular rivalry, and other forms of bistable perception, is time-locked to frontal and parietal cortex activity (Kleinschmidt *et al*. 1998; Lumer *et al*. 1998; Sterzer *et al*. 2002). Fronto-parietal activity is not simply associated with the requirement that observers report their experience. When binocular rivalry occurs in the absence of behavioural reports, there is a close coupling between activity in early visual cortical areas representing the rivalling stimuli and multiple regions of frontal and parietal cortex previously associated with the report of conscious transitions (Lumer & Rees 1999). Such fronto-parietal involvement in rivalry therefore appears independent of the requirement to make motor reports.

Strikingly, frontal and parietal activity is also associated with spontaneous changes in the contents of consciousness in a variety of perceptual paradigms, such as stereo pop-out (Portas *et al*. 2000), the perception of fragmented figures (Eriksson *et al*. 2004), the detection of change in a visually presented object (Beck *et al*. 2001), conscious perception of flicker (Carmel *et al*. 2006) and successful conscious identification of visually masked words (Dehaene *et al*. 2001). Electrical activity over parietal sensors is associated with the detection of a simple threshold-level stimulus (Pins & Ffytche 2003). Moreover, changes in the contents of consciousness during bistable perception are associated with distributed changes in synchronous electrical oscillations measured on the scalp (Tononi *et al*. 1998; Srinivasan *et al*. 1999; Struber & Herrmann 2002).

These data are consistent with the notion that signals from parietal and prefrontal cortex are necessary for normal conscious perception (Driver & Mattingley 1998; Rees *et al*. 2002*a*). Further direct evidence for such a hypothesis comes from the observation that conscious detection of change is impaired when frontal and parietal cortex is transiently disrupted using TMS (Turatto *et al*. 2004; Beck *et al*. 2006).

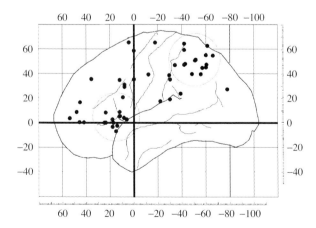

Fig. 10.4 Fronto-parietal activation associated with awareness. Areas of parietal and prefrontal cortex that show activation correlated with changes in visual awareness (Kleinschmidt *et al*. 1998; Lumer *et al*. 1998; Sterzer *et al*. 2002) are plotted on a template brain. Each circle is placed at the centre of a cluster of activation; overlapping loci from the same study are omitted for clarity. There is prominent clustering of activations in superior parietal and dorsolateral prefrontal cortex, highlighted by large, dotted circles.

These data strongly suggest the involvement of prefrontal and parietal cortex in visual awareness, but do not determine the precise functional role of such structures nor clarify the nature of the underlying neural processes. One promising line of future enquiry will be to use the pattern-based decoding approaches that have been used to study representations in ventral visual cortex (reviewed previously here; see also Haynes & Rees 2006) to now probe the nature of the neural representations in frontal and parietal cortex associated with visual awareness.

10.7 Conclusion

The most parsimonious account of currently available data is that the current contents of visual consciousness consist of a representation in primary visual cortex and ventral visual pathway corresponding to the attributes represented in consciousness, together with related activity in specific parietal (and perhaps) prefrontal structures. Information contained within signals in the ventral visual pathway is sufficient to permit accurate decoding both of stable contents of visual awareness and dynamic changes in the stream of consciousness, at least for simple visual paradigms. The challenge for the future is to specify more precisely the interactions between and causal role for each of these areas, and to hence further refine our ability to decode consciousness.

The Wellcome Trust supported this work.

References

Barnes, J., Howard, R. J., Senior, C., Brammer, M., Bullmore, E. T., Simmons, A. & David, A. S. 1999 The functional anatomy of the McCollough contingent colour after-effect. *Neuroreport* **10**, 195–199. (doi:10.1097/00001756-199901180-00037)

Beck, D. M., Rees, G., Frith, C. D. & Lavie, N. 2001 Neural correlates of change detection and change blindness. *Nat. Neurosci.* **4**, 645–650. (doi:10.1038/88477)

Beck, D. M., Muggleton, N., Walsh, V. & Lavie, N. 2006 Right parietal cortex plays a critical role in change blindness. *Cereb. Cortex* **16**, 712–717. (doi:10.1093/cercor/bhj017)

Bodis-Wollner, I., Bucher, S. F. & Seelos, K. C. 1999 Cortical activation patterns during voluntary blinks and voluntary saccades. *Neurology* **53**, 1800–1805.

Bristow, D., Haynes, J. D., Sylvester, R., Frith, C. D. & Rees, G. 2005 Blinking suppresses the neural response to unchanging retinal stimulation. *Curr. Biol.* **15**, 1296–1300. (doi:10. 1016/j. cub.2005.06.025)

Carmel, D., Lavie, N. & Rees, G. 2006 Conscious awareness of flicker in humans involves frontal and parietal cortex. *Curr. Biol.* **16**, 907–911. (doi:10.1016/j.cub.2006.03.055)

Cowey, A. & Walsh, V. 2000 Magnetically induced phosphenes in sighted, blind and blindsighted observers. *Neuroreport* **11**, 3269–3273. (doi:10.1097/00001756-200009280-00044)

Dehaene, S., Naccache, L., Cohen, L., Bihan, D. L., Mangin, J. F., Poline, J. B. & Rivière, D. 2001 Cerebral mechanisms of word masking and unconscious repetition priming. *Nat. Neurosci.* **4**, 752–758. (doi:10.1038/89551)

Driver, J. & Mattingley, J. B. 1998 Parietal neglect and visual awareness. *Nat. Neurosci.* **1**, 17–22. (doi:10.1038/217)

Driver, J., Vuilleumier, P., Eimer, M. & Rees, G. 2001 Functional magnetic resonance imaging and evoked potential correlates of conscious and unconscious vision in parietal extinction patients. *Neuroimage* **14**, S68–S75. (doi:10.1006/nimg.2001.0842)

Enoch, J. M., Choi, S. S., Kono, M., Schwartz, D. & Bearse, M. 2003 Utilization of eye-movement phosphenes to help understand transient strains at the optic disc and nerve in myopia. *Ophthalmic Physiol. Opt.* **23**, 377–381. (doi:10. 1046/j.1475-1313.2003.00120.x)

Eriksson, J., Larsson, A., Riklund, A. K. & Nyberg, L. 2004 Visual consciousness: dissociating the neural correlates of perceptual transitions from sustained perception with fMRI. *Conscious Cogn.* **13**, 61–72. (doi:10.1016/S1053-8100(03)00050-3)

Fang, F. & He, S. 2005 Cortical responses to invisible objects in the human dorsal and ventral pathways. *Nat. Neurosci.* **8**, 1380–1385. (doi:10.1038/nn1537)

Ffytche, D. H., Howard, R. J., Brammer, M. J., David, A., Woodruff, P. & Williams, S. 1998 The anatomy of conscious vision: an fMRI study of visual hallucinations. *Nat. Neurosci.* **1**, 738–742. (doi:10.1038/3738)

Frith, C., Perry, R. & Lumer, E. 1999 The neural correlates of conscious experience: an experimental framework. *Trends Cogn. Sci.* **3**, 105–114. (doi:10.1016/S1364-6613 (99)01281-4)

Goebel, R., Muckli, L., Zanella, F. E., Singer, W. & Stoerig, P. 2001 Sustained extrastriate cortical activation without visual awareness revealed by fMRI studies of hemianopic patients. *Vision Res.* **41**, 1459–1474. (doi:10.1016/S0042-6989(01)00069-4)

Grill-Spector, K., Kushnir, T., Hendler, T. & Malach, R. 2000 The dynamics of object-selective activation correlate with recognition performance in humans. *Nat. Neurosci.* **3**, 837–843. (doi:10.1038/77754)

Halgren, E., Mendola, J., Chong, C. D. & Dale, A. M. 2003 Cortical activation to illusory shapes as measured with magnetoencephalography. *Neuroimage* **18**, 1001–1009. (doi:10.1016/S1053-8119 (03)00045-4)

Haxby, J. V., Gobbini, M. I., Furey, M. L., Ishai, A., Schouten, J. L. & Pietrini, P. 2001 Distributed and overlapping representations of faces and objects in ventral temporal cortex. *Science* **293**, 2425–2430. (doi:10.1126/ science.1063736)

Haynes, J. D. & Rees, G. 2005*a* Predicting the orientation of invisible stimuli from activity in human primary visual cortex. *Nat. Neurosci.* **8**, 686–691. (doi:10.1038/nn1445)

Haynes, J. D. & Rees, G. 2005*b* Predicting the stream of consciousness from activity in human visual cortex. *Curr. Biol.* **15**, 1301–1307. (doi:10.1016/j.cub.2005.06.026)

Haynes, J. D. & Rees, G. 2006 Decoding mental states from brain activity in humans. *Nat. Rev. Neurosci.* **7**, 523–534. (doi:10.1038/nrn1931)

Haynes, J. D., Lotto, R. B. & Rees, G. 2004 Responses of human visual cortex to uniform surfaces. *Proc. Natl Acad. Sci. USA* **101**, 4286–4291. (doi:10.1073/pnas.0307948101)

Haynes, J. D., Deichmann, R. & Rees, G. 2005*a* Eye-specific effects of binocular rivalry in the human lateral geniculate nucleus. *Nature* **438**, 496–499. (doi:10.1038/nature04169)

Haynes, J. D., Driver, J. & Rees, G. 2005*b* Visibility reflects dynamic changes of effective connectivity between V1 and fusiform cortex. *Neuron* **46**, 811–821. (doi:10.1016/ j.neuron.2005.05.012)

He, S. & MacLeod, D. I. 2001 Orientation-selective adaptation and tilt after-effect from invisible patterns. *Nature* **411**, 473–476. (doi:10.1038/35078072)

He, S., Cohen, E. R. & Hu, X. 1998 Close correlation between activity in brain area MT/V5 and the perception of a visual motion aftereffect. *Curr. Biol.* **8**, 1215–1218. (doi:10.1016/S0960-9822 (07)00512-X)

Hirsch, J., DeLaPaz, R. L., Relkin, N. R., Victor, J., Kim, K., Li, T., Borden, P., Rubin, N. & Shapley, R. 1995 Illusory contours activate specific regions in human visual cortex: evidence from functional magnetic resonance imaging. *Proc. Natl Acad. Sci. USA* **92**, 6469–6473. (doi:10.1073/ pnas.92.14.6469)

Holender, D. & Duscherer, K. 2004 Unconscious perception: the need for a paradigm shift. *Percept. Psychophys* **66**, 872 881; discussion 888–895

Kamitani, Y. & Tong, F. 2005 Decoding the visual and subjective contents of the human brain. *Nat. Neurosci.* **8**, 679–685. (doi:10.1038/nn1444)

Kamitani, Y. & Tong, F. 2006 Decoding seen and attended motion directions from activity in the human visual cortex. *Curr. Biol.* **16**, 1096–1102. (doi:10.1016/j.cub.2006.04.003)

Kleinschmidt, A., Buchel, C., Zeki, S. & Frackowiak, R. S. 1998 Human brain activity during spontaneously reversing perception of ambiguous figures. *Proc. Biol. Sci.* **265**, 2427–2433. (doi:10.1098/ rspb.1998.0594)

Kleiser, R., Wittsack, J., Niedeggen, M., Goebel, R. & Stoerig, P. 2001 Is V1 necessary for conscious vision in areas of relative cortical blindness? *Neuroimage* **13**, 654–661. (doi:10.1006/ nimg.2000.0720)

Kouider, S. & Dehaene, S. 2007 Levels of processing during non-conscious perception: a critical review of visual masking. *Phil. Trans. R. Soc. B* **362**, 857–875. (doi:10. 1098/rstb.2007.2093)

Kourtzi, Z. & Kanwisher, N. 2000 Activation in human MT/MST by static images with implied motion. *J. Cogn. Neurosci.* **12**, 48–55. (doi:10.1162/08989290051137594)

Kreiman, G., Koch, C. & Fried, I. 2000 Imagery neurons in the human brain. *Nature* **408**, 357–361. (doi:10.1038/ 35042575)

Lamme, V. A. & Roelfsema, P. R. 2000 The distinct modes of vision offered by feedforward and recurrent processing. *Trends Neurosci.* **23**, 571–579. (doi:10.1016/S0166-2236(00)01657-X)

Lee, S. H. & Blake, R. 2002 V1 activity is reduced during binocular rivalry. *J. Vis.* **2**, 618–626. (doi:10.1167/2.9.4)

Lee, H. W., Hong, S. B., Seo, D. W., Tae, W. S. & Hong, S. C. 2000 Mapping of functional organization in human visual cortex: electrical cortical stimulation. *Neurology* **54**, 849–854.

Lee, S. H., Blake, R. & Heeger, D. J. 2005 Traveling waves of activity in primary visual cortex during binocular rivalry. *Nat. Neurosci.* **8**, 22–23. (doi:10.1038/nn1365)

Luck, S. J., Vogel, E. K. & Shapiro, K. L. 1996 Word meanings can be accessed but not reported during the attentional blink. *Nature* **383**, 616–618. (doi:10.1038/383616a0)

Lumer, E. D. & Rees, G. 1999 Covariation of activity in visual and prefrontal cortex associated with subjective visual perception. *Proc. Natl Acad. Sci. USA* **96**, 1669–1673. (doi:10.1073/ pnas.96.4.1669)

Lumer, E. D., Friston, K. J. & Rees, G. 1998 Neural correlates of perceptual rivalry in the human brain. *Science* **280**, 1930–1934. (doi:10.1126/science.280.5371.1930)

Marcel, A. J. 1983 Conscious and unconscious perception: experiments on visual masking and word recognition. *Cognitive Psychol.* **15**, 197–237. (doi:10.1016/0010-0285 (83)90009-9)

Marois, R., Yi, D. J. & Chun, M. M. 2004 The neural fate of consciously perceived and missed events in the attentional blink. *Neuron* **41**, 465–472. (doi:10.1016/S0896-6273 (04)00012-1)

Meng, M., Remus, D. A. & Tong, F. 2005 Filling-in of visual phantoms in the human brain. *Nat. Neurosci.* **8**, 1248–1254. (doi:10.1038/nn1518)

Morris, J. S., Ohman, A. & Dolan, R. J. 1999 A subcortical pathway to the right amygdala mediating "unseen" fear. *Proc. Natl Acad. Sci. USA* **96**, 1680–1685. (doi:10.1073/ pnas.96.4.1680)

Moutoussis, K. & Zeki, S. 2002 The relationship between cortical activation and perception investigated with invisible stimuli. *Proc. Natl Acad. Sci. USA* **99**, 9527–9532. (doi:10.1073/pnas.142305699)

Moutoussis, K. & Zeki, S. 2006 Seeing invisible motion: a human fMRI study. *Curr. Biol.* **16**, 574–579. (doi:10. 1016/j.cub.2006.01.062)

Muckli, L., Kohler, A., Kriegeskorte, N. & Singer, W. 2005 Primary visual cortex activity along the apparent-motion trace reflects illusory perception. *PLoS Biol.* **3**, e265. (doi:10.1371/journal. pbio.0030265)

Murray, S. O., Boyaci, H. & Kersten, D. 2006 The representation of perceived angular size in human primary visual cortex. *Nat. Neurosci.* **9**, 429–434. (doi:10.1038/ nn1641)

Naccache, L., Blandin, E. & Dehaene, S. 2002 Unconscious masked priming depends on temporal attention. *Psychol. Sci.* **13**, 416–424. (doi:10.1111/1467-9280.00474)

Naccache, L., Gaillard, R., Adam, C., Hasboun, D., Clemenceau, S., Baulac, M., Dehaene, S. & Cohen, L. 2005 A direct intracranial record of emotions evoked by subliminal words. *Proc. Natl Acad. Sci. USA* **102**, 7713–7717. (doi:10.1073/pnas.0500542102)

Niedeggen, M., Wichmann, P. & Stoerig, P. 2001 Change blindness and time to consciousness. *Eur. J. Neurosci.* **14**, 1719–1726. (doi:10.1046/j.0953-816x.2001.01785.x)

Norman, K. A., Polyn, S. M., Detre, G. J. & Haxby, J. V. 2006 Beyond mind-reading: multi-voxel pattern analysis of fMRI data. *Trends Cogn. Sci.* **10**, 424–430. (doi:10.1016/ j.tics.2006.07.005)

O'Craven, K. M. & Kanwisher, N. 2000 Mental imagery of faces and places activates corresponding stimulus-specific brain regions. *J. Cogn. Neurosci.* **12**, 1013–1023. (doi:10. 1162/08989290051137549)

Pascual-Leone, A. & Walsh, V. 2001 Fast back projections from the motion to the primary visual area necessary for visual awareness. *Science* **292**, 510–512.

Pasley, B. N., Mayes, L. C. & Schultz, R. T. 2004 Subcortical discrimination of unperceived objects during binocular rivalry. *Neuron* **42**, 163–172. (doi:10.1016/S0896-6273 (04)00155-2)

Pins, D. & Ffytche, D. 2003 The neural correlates of conscious vision. *Cereb. Cortex* **13**, 461–474. (doi:10. 1093/cercor/13.5.461)

Polonsky, A., Blake, R., Braun, J. & Heeger, D. J. 2000 Neuronal activity in human primary visual cortex correlates with perception during binocular rivalry. *Nat. Neurosci.* **3**, 1153–1159. (doi:10.1038/80676)

Portas, C. M., Strange, B. A., Friston, K. J., Dolan, R. J. & Frith, C. D. 2000 How does the brain sustain a visual percept? *Proc. Biol. Sci.* **267**, 845–850. (doi:10.1098/rspb. 2000.1080)

Ptito, M., Johannsen, P., Faubert, J. & Gjedde, A. 1999 Activation of human extrageniculostriate pathways after damage to area V1. *Neuroimage* **9**, 97–107. (doi:10.1006/ nimg.1998.0390)

Rees, G., Russell, C., Frith, C. D. & Driver, J. 1999 Inattentional blindness versus inattentional amnesia for fixated but ignored words. *Science* **286**, 2504–2507. (doi:10.1126/science.286.5449.2504)

Rees, G., Wojciulik, E., Clarke, K., Husain, M., Frith, C. & Driver, J. 2000 Unconscious activation of visual cortex in the damaged right hemisphere of a parietal patient with extinction. *Brain* **123**, 1624–1633. (doi:10.1093/brain/ 123.8.1624)

Rees, G., Kreiman, G. & Koch, C. 2002a Neural correlates of consciousness in humans. *Nat. Rev. Neurosci.* **3**, 261–270. (doi:10.1038/nrn783)

Rees, G., Wojciulik, E., Clarke, K., Husain, M., Frith, C. & Driver, J. 2002b Neural correlates of conscious and unconscious vision in parietal extinction. *Neurocase* **8**, 387–393. (doi:10.1093/ neucas/8.5.387)

Ress, D. & Heeger, D. J. 2003 Neuronal correlates of perception in early visual cortex. *Nat. Neurosci.* **6**, 414–420. (doi:10.1038/nn1024)

Ro, T., Breitmeyer, B., Burton, P., Singhal, N. S. & Lane, D. 2003 Feedback contributions to visual awareness in human occipital cortex. *Curr. Biol.* **13**, 1038–1041. (doi:10.1016/S0960-9822 (03)00337-3)

Sakai, K., Watanabe, E., Onodera, Y., Uchida, I., Kato, H., Yamamoto, E., Koizumi, H. & Miyashita, Y. 1995 Functional mapping of the human colour centre with echo-planar magnetic resonance imaging. *Proc. Biol. Sci.* **261**, 89–98. (doi:10.1098/rspb.1995.0121)

Senior, C., Barnes, J., Giampietro, V., Simmons, A., Bullmore, E. T., Brammer, M. & David, A. S. 2000 The functional neuroanatomy of implicit-motion perception or representational momentum. *Curr. Biol.* **10**, 16–22. (doi:10.1016/S0960-9822(99)00259-6)

Sergent, C., Baillet, S. & Dehaene, S. 2005 Timing of the brain events underlying access to consciousness during the attentional blink. *Nat. Neurosci.* **8**, 1391–1400. (doi:10. 1038/nn1549)

Shams, L., Iwaki, S., Chawla, A. & Bhattacharya, J. 2005 Early modulation of visual cortex by sound: an MEG study. *Neurosci. Lett.* **378**, 76–81. (doi:10.1016/j.neulet. 2004.12.035)

Silbersweig, D. A. et al. 1995 A functional neuroanatomy of hallucinations in schizophrenia. *Nature* **378**, 176–179. (doi:10.1038/378176a0)

Silvanto, J., Cowey, A., Lavie, N. & Walsh, V. 2005 Striate cortex (V1) activity gates awareness of motion. *Nat. Neurosci.* **8**, 143–144. (doi:10.1038/nn1379)

Srinivasan, R., Russell, D. P., Edelman, G. M. & Tononi, G. 1999 Increased synchronization of neuromagnetic responses during conscious perception. *J. Neurosci.* **19**, 5435–5448.

Sterzer, P., Russ, M. O., Preibisch, C. & Kleinschmidt, A. 2002 Neural correlates of spontaneous direction reversals in ambiguous apparent visual motion. Neuroimage 15, 908–916. (doi:10.1006/ nimg.2001.1030)

Sterzer, P., Eger, E. & Kleinschmidt, A. 2003 Responses of extrastriate cortex to switching perception of ambiguous visual motion stimuli. *Neuroreport* **14**, 2337–2341. (doi:10. 1097/00001756-200312190-00010)

Sterzer, P., Haynes, J. D. & Rees, G. 2006 Primary visual cortex activation on the path of apparent motion is mediated by feedback from hMT+/V5. *Neuroimage* **32**, 1308–1316. (doi:10.1016/j. neuroimage.2006.05.029)

Struber, D. & Herrmann, C. S. 2002 MEG alpha activity decrease reflects destabilization of multistable percepts. *Brain Res. Cogn. Brain Res.* **14**, 370–382. (doi:10.1016/ S0926-6410(02)00139-8)

Super, H., Spekreijse, H. & Lamme, V. A. F. 2001 Two distinct modes of sensory processing observed in monkey primary visual cortex (V1). *Nat. Neurosci.* **4**, 304–310. (doi:10.1038/85170)

Sylvester, R. & Rees, G. 2006 Extraretinal saccadic signals in human LGN and early retinotopic cortex. *Neuroimage* **30**, 214–219. (doi:10.1016/j.neuroimage.2005.09.014)

Sylvester, R., Haynes, J. D. & Rees, G. 2005 Saccades differentially modulate human LGN and V1 responses in the presence and absence of visual stimulation. *Curr. Biol.* **15**, 37–41. (doi:10.1016/j.cub.2004.12.061)

Tong, F. & Engel, S. A. 2001 Interocular rivalry revealed in the human cortical blind-spot representation. *Nature* **411**, 195–199. (doi:10.1038/35075583)

Tong, F., Meng, M. & Blake, R. 2006 Neural bases of binocular rivalry. *Trends Cogn. Sci.* **10**, 502–511. (doi:10. 1016/j.tics.2006.09.003)

Tong, F., Nakayama, K., Vaughan, J. T. & Kanwisher, N. 1998 Binocular rivalry and visual awareness in human extrastriate cortex. *Neuron* **21**, 753–759. (doi:10.1016/ S0896-6273(00)80592-9)

Tononi, G., Srinivasan, R., Russell, D. P. & Edelman, G. M. 1998 Investigating neural correlates of conscious perception by frequency-tagged neuromagnetic responses. *Proc. Natl Acad. Sci. USA* **95**, 3198–3203. (doi:10.1073/pnas. 95.6.3198)

Tootell, R. B., Reppas, J. B., Dale, A. M., Look, R. B., Sereno, M. I., Malach, R., Brady, T. J. & Rosen, B. R. 1995 Visual motion aftereffect in human cortical area MT revealed by functional magnetic resonance imaging. *Nature* **375**, 139–141. (doi:10.1038/375139a0)

Turatto, M., Sandrini, M. & Miniussi, C. 2004 The role of the right dorsolateral prefrontal cortex in visual change awareness. *Neuroreport* **15**, 2549–2552. (doi:10.1097/ 00001756-200411150-00024)

Vogel, E. K., Luck, S. J. & Shapiro, K. L. 1998 Electrophysiological evidence for a postperceptual locus of suppression during the attentional blink. *J. Exp. Psychol. Hum. Percept. Perform.* **24**, 1656–1674. (doi:10.1037/ 0096-1523.24.6.1656)

Vuilleumier, P. & Driver, J. 2007 Modulation of visual processing by attention and emotion: windows on causal interactions between human brain regions. *Phil. Trans. R. Soc. B* **362**, 837–855. (doi:10.1098/rstb.2007.2092)

Vuilleumier, P., Sagiv, N., Hazeltine, E., Poldrack, R. A., Swick, D., Rafal, R. D. & Gabrieli, J. D. E. 2001 Neural fate of seen and unseen faces in visuospatial neglect: a combined event-related functional MRI and event-related potential study. *Proc. Natl Acad. Sci. USA* **98**, 3495–3500. (doi:10.1073/ pnas.051436898)

Watkins, S., Shams, L., Tanaka, S., Haynes, J. D. & Rees, G. 2006 Sound alters activity in human V1 in association with illusory visual perception. *Neuroimage* **31**, 1247–1256. (doi:10.1016/j. neuroimage.2006.01.016)

Wunderlich, K., Schneider, K. A. & Kastner, S. 2005 Neural correlates of binocular rivalry in the human lateral geniculate nucleus. *Nat. Neurosci.* **8**, 1595–1602. (doi:10. 1038/nn1554)

Zeki, S., Watson, J. D. & Frackowiak, R. S. 1993 Going beyond the information given: the relation of illusory visual motion to brain activity. *Proc. Biol. Sci.* **252**, 215–222. (doi:10.1098/rspb.1993.0068)

11

Function and localization within rostral prefrontal cortex (area 10)

Paul W. Burgess*, Sam J. Gilbert, and Iroise Dumontheil

We propose that rostral prefrontal cortex (PFC; approximating area 10) supports a cognitive system that facilitates either stimulus-oriented (SO) or stimulus-independent (SI) attending. SO attending is the behaviour required to concentrate on current sensory input, whereas SI attending is the mental processing that accompanies self-generated or self-maintained thought. Regions of medial area 10 support processes related to the former, whilst areas of lateral area 10 support processes that enable the latter. Three lines of evidence for this 'gateway hypothesis' are presented. First, we demonstrate the predicted patterns of activation in area 10 during the performance of new tests designed to stress the hypothetical system. Second, we demonstrate area 10 activations during the performance of established functions (prospective memory, context memory), which should hypothetically involve the proposed attentional system. Third, we examine predictions about behaviour–activation patterns within rostral PFC that follow from the hypothesis. We show with meta-analysis of neuroimaging investigations that these predictions are supported across a wide variety of tasks, thus establishing a general principle for functional imaging studies of this large brain region. We then show that while the gateway hypothesis accommodates a large range of findings relating to the functional organization of area 10 along a medial–lateral dimension, there are further principles relating to other dimensions and functions. In particular, there is a functional dissociation between the anterior medial area 10, which supports processes required for SO attending, and the caudal medial area 10, which supports processes relating to mentalizing.

Keywords: frontal lobes; executive function; BA 10; anterior prefrontal cortex; neuroimaging; neuropsychology

11.1 Introduction

Area 10 of the brain (also termed 'rostral prefrontal cortex (PFC)', 'anterior PFC' or 'frontopolar cortex') presents one of the most fascinating puzzles in cognitive neuroscience. There are many good reasons to suppose that it plays a critical part in the higher cognitive functions of humans yet, until very recently, virtually nothing was known about the mental processes that it might support.

The first reason for supposing that this region is important for human cognition is simply its size. It is a very large brain region in humans, covering at least 25–30 cubic cm (Christoff *et al.* 2001; Semendeferi *et al.* 2001). Indeed, it is the largest single architectonic region of the PFC (Christoff *et al.* 2001; Ongur *et al.* 2003). The second reason is that it is relatively larger in the human brain than in any other animal, including the great apes (Semendeferi *et al.* 2001;

* Author for correspondence (p.burgess@psychol.ucl.ac.uk).

Holloway 2002). The third reason for supposing that area 10 supports cognition which is both important and peculiar to humans, is its structure. It has a lower cell density in humans than that found in monkeys and apes. This has been interpreted as meaning that the supragranular layers of area 10 in humans have more space available for connections with other higher-order association areas than in other animals (Semendeferi *et al.* 2001). Support from this view comes from findings that the number of dendritic spines per cell and the spine density are higher than in comparable cortical areas (Jacobs *et al.* 2001; Semendeferi *et al.* 2001). Furthermore, area 10 is also unusual in that it is the only PFC region that is almost exclusively connected to other supramodal areas within PFC and elsewhere (for a review, see Ramnani & Owen 2004). The fourth reason for supposing a role for this region in higher cognitive functions is that rostral PFC shows remarkably late developmental maturation. It is probably the last brain region to achieve myelination (Bonin 1950) and is one of the brain regions with the highest rates of brain growth between 5 and 11 years (Sowell *et al.* 2004). Indeed, reductions in grey matter density continue from adolescence to young adulthood (Sowell *et al.* 1999).

On these grounds, it is a reasonable hope that gaining an understanding of the role of this region in human cognition may provide a key to how the brain instantiates some of the behaviours peculiar to humans and, perhaps, thereby the symptoms that accompany its dysfunction (e.g. certain forms of psychological disorder).

However, scientific evidence that might bear on the issue has only begun to emerge over the last 10 years or so. There are many reasons for this situation. For instance, the extreme difference in size and structure of this region in humans when compared with other animals limits the degree to which one might safely generalize from animal data to human experience. Furthermore, it is difficult to record from, and lesion, this region in non-human primates due to practical anatomical considerations. Other cognitive neuroscience methods also face limitations. For instance, until very recently, the available electrophysiological methods have not had the required spatial resolution to collect data from different sub-regions within the frontal lobes. Transcranial magnetic stimulation studies of rostral PFC have also proved difficult for anatomical reasons (although these may not prove insurmountable).

Moreover, human lesion studies into the functions of this area have not, until very recently, been conducted. Partly, this has been due to the length of time it takes to collect sufficient data for this type of investigation (typically several years). But it is also because, traditionally, rostral PFC lesions have been considered neuropsychologically and neurologically 'silent'. In other words, they do not cause impairments easily elicited during the standard neurological or neuropsychological consultation. Thus, until very recently, virtually the only available evidence originated from the relatively new method of functional brain imaging.

Until the late 1990s, these neuroimaging findings were, however, largely restricted to the findings of rostral PFC haemodynamic changes associated with a particular cognitive function (e.g. episodic memory), rather than emanating from investigations that had the specific aim of discovering the functions of the brain region (but see, in particular, the studies by Kalina Christoff, Etienne Koechlin, and Raichle *et al.* 2001).

Unfortunately, these findings did not provide a firm basis for theorizing, since there seemed to be little obvious similarity between the paradigms that provoked area 10 activation. Indeed, area 10 activations could be found during the performance of just about any kind of task, ranging from the simplest (e.g. conditioning paradigms; Blaxton *et al.* 1996) to highly complex tests, involving memory and judgement (e.g. Koechlin *et al.* 1999; Burgess *et al.* 2001, 2003; Frith & Frith 2003) or problem solving (e.g. Christoff *et al.* 2001).

It was in this context that we started our research programme. It differed from most in that it had the specific aim of attempting to discover the cognitive functions of the brain area (BA) 10. This paper describes the stages that we have followed, and our conclusions at this early, but we hope promising, stage. We do not intend to provide an overview of the important work on this topic by our colleagues elsewhere. For this, the interested reader is referred to reviews by Grady (1999), Ramnani & Owen (2004), Burgess *et al.* (2005, 2006*b*) and Gilbert *et al.* (2006*c*).

11.2 Stage 1: Observations of everyday multitasking problems in brain-damaged patients

The starting point for our investigations was a puzzling clinical observation that had been noted since the 1930s (e.g. Penfield & Evans 1935; see also Brickner 1936; Ackerly & Benton 1947). This was that some neurological patients show a marked behavioural disorganization in everyday life, despite little sign of impairment in intellect, memory, perception, motor and language skills—at least according to the evaluative methods available at the time.

It was not until 50 years later, however, that the full extent of this pattern became clear. Eslinger & Damasio (1985) described the case of EVR, who had undergone surgical removal of a large bilateral frontal meningioma. Premorbidly, EVR had been a trusted financial officer, a good father and a respected member of his community. But, following his operation, EVR lost his job, went bankrupt and divorced his wife. Extensive psychological evaluations found no deficit, however, and he was superior or above average on most tests (e.g. Verbal IQ of 125; Performance IQ of 124; no difficulty on Wisconsin Card Sorting Test). Notably, Eslinger & Damasio (1985, p. 1737), however, report prospective memory (PM) problems in everyday life: '. . . it was as if he forgot to remember short- and intermediate-term goals. . .'.

Six years later, Shallice & Burgess (1991*a*) reported three cases with a similar profile in everyday life. None of them showed any significant impairment on formal tests of perception, language or intelligence. Moreover, two performed well on a variety of traditional tests of executive function. Shallice & Burgess (1991*a,b*) measured everyday life problems by inventing a real-life multitasking test carried out in a shopping precinct (the 'Multiple Errands Test'). Participants were required to complete a number of tasks, principally involving shopping in an unfamiliar shopping precinct, while following a set of rules (e.g. no shop should be entered other than to buy something). The tasks varied in terms of complexity (e.g. buy a small brown loaf versus discover the exchange rate of the Euro yesterday), and there were a number of 'hidden' problems in the tasks that had to be appreciated and the possible course of action evaluated (e.g. one item asked that participants write and send a postcard, yet they were given no pen and, although they could not use anything not bought on the street to help them, they were also told that they needed to spend as little money as possible). In this way, the task is quite 'open-ended' or 'ill-structured' (i.e. there are many possible courses of action, and it is up to the individual to determine for themselves which one they will choose). All three of Shallice and Burgess's patients were significantly poorer than a group of age- and IQ-matched healthy controls on this test. The patients made a range of types of error, many of which could be interpreted as PM failures. For instance, they would find themselves having to go into the same shop more than once to buy items that could all have been bought at one visit; they did not complete the tasks that they had previously learnt that they needed to do; and they tended to forget to come over to the experimenter and tell them what they had bought when leaving a shop, which was a pre-learnt task rule. They also made a range of social behaviour errors (e.g. leaving a shop without paying, offering sexual favours in lieu of payment).

11.3 Stage 2: Develop 'models' of the real world with simpler laboratory tasks

Shallice & Burgess (1991a) also developed a laboratory task that aimed to mimic some of the critical demands of the multiple errands test, and thus serve as a 'model of the world' for experimental and assessment purposes. Termed the 'Six Element Test' (SET), this task required subjects to swap efficiently between three simple subtasks, each divided into two sections, while following some arbitrary rules (e.g. 'you cannot do part A of a subtask followed immediately by part B of the same subtask'; figure 11.1). Participants were given 15 minutes to perform the test, which was insufficient for all subtasks to be completed. There were no cues as to when to switch tasks, and although a clock was present it was covered so that checking it had to be a deliberate action. Despite their excellent general cognitive skills, all three cases reported by Shallice and Burgess performed these tasks below the 5% level when compared with the age- and IQ-matched controls.

However, it was not possible from these single case studies to determine the precise location of the lesion that caused this pattern of clinical impairment. Although all these people (and others with similar symptoms) were suffering from lesions affecting rostral PFC, the lesions in each case were large, and invaded a number of prefrontal sub-regions (for brain scan results on these cases, see Shallice 2004; Burgess *et al.* 2005). It was not possible therefore with this small sample to ascertain the critical locus of damage. However, we now had a criterion laboratory measure that we could use for this purpose.

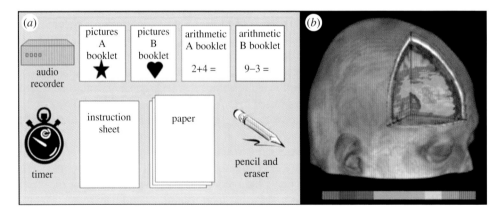

Fig. 11.1 (*a*) Materials for the Modified Six Element Test (Burgess *et al.* 1996). Participants are given 10 minutes to complete at least some of each of the three subtasks, each divided into two parts (i.e. verbal dictation A and B, picture naming A and B, arithmetic A and B), but are not permitted to perform two subtasks of the same type straight after each other (e.g. arithmetic A then arithmetic B). (*b*) Lesion overlap figure from Burgess *et al.* (submitted *b*) for a group of right rostral PFC-damaged participants who made fewer task switches than other patients or healthy controls on a new version of the Six Element Test (right rostrals: mean voluntary task switches 3.0 (s.d. 2.1), other patients mean 6.3 (s.d. 4.0), *p*<0.005).

11.4 Stage 3: Establish the brain regions involved using the human group lesion method

Accordingly, Burgess *et al.* (2000) examined the performance of a series of 60 acute neurological patients (approx. three quarters of whom were suffering from brain tumours) and 60 age- and IQ-matched healthy controls on a multitasking test that shared similar principles with the SET. Called the 'Greenwich Test' this presented participants with three different simple tasks. They were told that they had to attempt at least some of each of the tasks in 10 minutes, while following a set of rules. One of these rules relates to all subtests ('in all three tasks, completing a red item will gain you more points than completing an item of any other colour') and there were four task-specific rules (e.g. 'in the 'Tangled Lines Test' you must not mark the paper other than to write your answers down').

It may be important to note that multitasking tests of this kind differ from most dual-task or task-switching paradigms in that: (i) only one subtask is attempted at any one time (unlike most dual-task paradigms) and (ii) switches of task have to be voluntarily initiated without the appearance of a cue (unlike most task-switching paradigms). In this way, tasks like the SET make strong demands upon PM abilities (i.e. the ability to remember to carry out an intended action after a delay).

The Greenwich Test was administered in a form that allowed consideration of the relative contributions of task-rule learning and remembering, planning, plan-following and remembering one's actions to overall multitasking performance. Specifically, before the participants began the test, their ability to learn the task rules (by both spontaneous and cued recall) was measured. They were then asked how they intended to do the test, and a measure of the complexity and appropriateness of their plans was gained. This enabled us to look at whether their failures could be due to poor planning (e.g. Kliegel *et al.* 2000, 2005). The participants then performed the task itself and by comparing what they did with what they had planned to do, a measure of 'plan-following' was made. Multitasking performance itself was calculated as the number of task switches minus the number of rule-breaks committed. After these stages were finished, subjects were asked to recollect their own actions by describing in detail what they had done and, finally, delayed memory for the task rules was examined.

We found that lesions in different brain regions were associated with impairment at these different stages in the multitasking procedure. Lesions in posterior medial brain regions, including the left posterior cingulate and forceps major, gave deficits on all measures except planning. Remembering task contingencies after a delay was also affected by lesions in the region of the anterior cingulate. Critically, however, Burgess *et al.* (2000) found that patients with left hemisphere rostral PFC lesions, when compared with patients with lesions elsewhere, showed a significant multitasking impairment, despite no significant impairment on remembering task rules. Indeed, the left rostral prefrontal cases showed no significant impairment on any variable except the one reflecting multitasking performance. In other words, despite being able to learn the task rules, form a plan, remember their actions and say what they should have done, they nevertheless did not do what they said that they intended to do.

A subsequent study using a slightly modified form of the SET also showed that it is rostral PFC lesions that can lead to multitasking and PM problems in the context of preserved intellect and retrospective memory (Burgess *et al.* submitted *b*; reported in Burgess *et al.* 2005). In this study, a new version of the Burgess *et al.* (1996) SET was administered to 69 acute neurological patients with circumscribed focal lesions and to 60 healthy controls, using the administration framework of Burgess *et al*. (2000; see also Burgess 2000). Compared with other patients, those whose lesions involved the rostral prefrontal regions of the right hemisphere made significantly fewer voluntary task switches, attempted fewer subtasks and spent far longer on individual subtasks (figure 11.1). They did not, however, make a larger number of rule-breaks (in contrast to the left rostral patients in the Burgess *et al*. 2000 study). As with the study of Burgess *et al*. (2000), these multitasking deficits could not be attributed to deficits in general intellectual functioning, rule knowledge, planning or retrospective memory. Burgess *et al*. (2007*a*) argue that the hemispheric difference between these studies may reflect the differences between these two multitasking tests: the SET differs from the Greenwich Test in that the multitasking score reflects mainly voluntary time-based switching rather than rule-following. (For further discussion of this issue, see Burgess *et al*. in press *a,b*; Okuda *et al*. in press; for other relevant human lesion evidence, e.g. Goldstein *et al*. 1993; Burgess *et al*. 2000; Goel & Grafman 2000; Alexander *et al*. 2003; Bird *et al*. 2004; Picton *et al*. 2006.) Looking back from these group study results to previous case studies of patients with similar symptoms, revealed that all of them had rostral PFC involvement (e.g. Shallice & Burgess 1991 *a,b*; Goldstein *et al*. 1993; Goel & Grafman 2000; see Burgess 2000 for details, and further cases).

11.5 Stage 4: Establish the relation between rostral PFC and a hypothetical function using neuroimaging

Since the patients' problems on the multitasking tests could not be attributed to deficits in memory or planning, we hypothesized that deficits in PM were the core impairment in these people with rostral PFC lesions. If this were the case, then we might expect to see haemodynamic changes in this region when healthy people are performing PM tasks. And indeed, this seems to be the case. Burgess *et al*. (2001) showed, using positron emission tomography (PET), that regional cerebral blood flow (rCBF) increases in lateral BA 10 occur when people are performing a PM task, relative to when they are performing the ongoing task alone (see also Okuda *et al*. 1998). Importantly, these increases were just as large when participants were told that a PM cue might appear, but none actually did. Thus, we could conclude that at least some regions of lateral BA 10 are more involved with the maintenance of an intention rather than cue recognition or intention execution.

A second PET study confirmed this role for lateral BA 10 in PM conditions, and also showed that medial BA 10 is more active in ongoing conditions than PM ones (Burgess *et al*. 2003), i.e. the opposite pattern of results to that observed in lateral BA 10. Furthermore, medial BA 10 was also more active (compared with PM conditions) in a simple attentional baseline condition where the subject (S) just responded as fast as possible to any change in the display. These results raised the possibility that lateral and medial rostral PFC regions support a system that works in concert in PM situations, with a cost to environmental attending (one signature of which is anterior medial area 10 haemodynamic change) that accompanies the need to 'bear the PM intention in mind' (the signature of which is lateral area 10 activation.) (See e.g. Smith & Bayen (2004) for related views from experimental psychology.)

The two PET studies of Burgess *et al*. (2001, 2003) had used a 'multiple task averaging' experimental design. This is where one investigates haemodynamic changes across two or more tasks that putatively stress the process of interest (Shallice 1988), but where the other demands of the tasks are made quite different, for example, using spatial material for one and verbal for the other. Accordingly, Burgess *et al.* (2003) interpreted their results as suggesting that the functions supported by area 10 in PM are 'central' in the respect that they are material non-specific, and unrelated to the precise intention retrieval or cue recognition demands. Instead, Burgess and colleagues favoured an explanation in terms of one of the possibilities raised by Okuda *et al.* (1998), that the rostral PFC rCBF changes were related to the attentional demands made by having to 'bear in mind' an intention while performing an ongoing task.

We subsequently tested this hypothesis. Simons *et al.* (2006*b*) measured brain activity (using functional magnetic resonance imaging (fMRI) and a conjunction of two different PM tasks: 'words' and 'shapes') while manipulating the demands on either recognizing the appropriate context to act ('cue identification') or remembering the action to be performed ('intention retrieval'). A consistent pattern of haemodynamic changes was found in rostral PFC (BA 10) across both types of task and across both PM conditions (compared with the ongoing task alone). There was increased blood oxygen level-dependent (BOLD) signal in lateral BA 10, which was accompanied by decreased BOLD signal in medial BA 10. Direct comparison of the 'high intention retrieval demand' with the 'high cue recognition demand' PM conditions also revealed greater BOLD signal in lateral area 10 regions bilaterally in the intention retrieval condition. These regions were somewhat more medial and caudal to those that showed activation common to both conditions. (For further investigations of the role of BA 10 in PM, see Burgess *et al.* in press)

11.6 Stage 5: Formulate a hypothesis of the critical processing component using constraints from both lesion and neuroimaging data

The studies described earlier suggested that the processes supported by rostral PFC are involved in PM and therefore multitasking. This is useful in understanding how the brain supports these functions. However, area 10 has been implicated as important in supporting many other functions, such as recollection or reflecting on mental states (see Grady 1999; Ramnani & Owen 2004; Gilbert *et al.* 2006*a–c* for review). It therefore seemed plausible that different subsections of area 10 support quite different functions. However, an account of this type raises two problems. The first is the possibility of infinite explanatory regress. Most functions will have sub-functions (or sub-operations) and the localization of each is likely at some level to be different. Moreover, one would be unlikely to discover processing common to many functions with this approach. The second problem is that starting with an assumption of strong modular functional specialization may leave the discovery of the relevant functions essentially to chance. Accordingly, in order to provoke new hypotheses, we proceeded on the basis of the simplifying assumption that BA 10 may support some critical processing component (or 'construct') which is shared by all the implicated functions (for definition of the terms function and construct in this context, see Burgess *et al.* 2006*a, b*).

The challenge was to find a function that fitted the myriad of observations from functional imaging and also those from the human lesion data. This was not straightforward, in particular because the findings from the two methods seemed to present a conundrum. This was that, based on the functional imaging findings of BA 10 activation in a wide range of tasks, an obvious suggestion might be that BA 10 supports some cognitive processing that is important to the performance of all of them. But if this were the case, then one would expect to see performance deficits across a correspondingly wide variety of tasks when this region is damaged in humans. However, this is not the case. As we have seen, neurological patients with rostral PFC lesions need not show impairments on tests of intelligence, clinical (retrospective) memory tests, language, perception and even tests of executive function such as the Wisconsin Card Sorting Test, FAS fluency, etc.

An appropriate account had to accommodate this apparent conundrum and also to be compatible with the other sets of constraints for theorizing presented by these different methods. Burgess *et al.* (2005) list the constraints we took as a starting position. There were seven constraints from human lesion studies and 17 from the functional imaging literature. Examples of the former were: 'rostral PFC lesions disproportionately impair performance in 'ill-structured' situations, in other words where the optimal way of behaving is not precisely signalled by the situation'; and 'rostral PFC lesions need not markedly impair performance on standard tests of intelligence, especially those that measure 'crystallized' intelligence, or those involving the use of over-learned procedures (e.g. arithmetic)'. Examples of the constraints for theorizing presented by the functional imaging literature were, for example, 'rostral PFC activation is not sensitive to the precise nature of stimuli, the nature of the intended action (in PM tasks) nor the precise response method, but is consistently implicated in tasks where one has to 'bear something in mind' while doing something else'.

The account that emerged as a potential solution was termed the 'gateway hypothesis' (Burgess *et al.* 2003, 2005, 2006*b*, 2007*a, b*). This theory of the role of BA 10 in human cognition rests upon a distinction between stimulus-oriented (SO) and stimulus-independent (SI) attending (McGuire *et al.* 1996). SO attending refers to the attending behaviour that is required to concentrate on current sensory input. (Here, we make a distinction between 'attention' as a construct (i.e. a hypothetical processing resource that may operate across a range of operations or functions), and attending behaviour as a function or operation (function, directly observable behaviour; operation, mental experience that may be indirectly inferred from observation, e.g. if presented with the sum 2 + 4 and a person responds '6', one might infer that they have performed a calculation operation; see Burgess *et al.* 2006*a,b* for explanation.)

Examples of SO attending range from performance of vigilance tasks, to reading, watching the television, listening to a conversation and so forth. By contrast, SI attending is the attending behaviour required to effect either self-generated or self-maintained thought. Self-generated thought is cognition that goes beyond the overlearned associations or semantic memories provoked by currently available stimuli. In this respect, the concept shares similarities with that of *N*-order (i.e. second order, third order, etc.) representations used in experimental and developmental psychology and artificial intelligence. By contrast, self-maintained thought is where one deliberately maintains a representation in the absence of the stimuli that provoked it. It is the absence of the stimulus that provoked the representation that defines this operation as belonging to the class of 'SI' cognition. Examples of SI cognition therefore range from task-irrelevant thoughts such as mind-wandering or daydreaming, to goal-directed cognition such as that involved in making up a novel story, or maintaining a representation over a delay period, and so forth.

We assume that many mental experiences which occur over all but the briefest of durations will consist of combinations of SO and SI attending. Accordingly, for empirical purposes, data relating to an SO or SI distinction might be thought of as existing along a continuum of relative proportions of variance. However, at the extremes at least, the distinction may be robust enough for empirical purposes. For instance, we describe four characteristics with which one can imbue a task that would increase the relative demand for SO attending, compared with a task that did not have these characteristics (Burgess *et al.* submitted *a*):

(i)   Requires vigilance (e.g. attending in absence of stimulus or attentional capture).
(ii) Requires stimulus processing, i.e. awareness of stimulus characteristics (e.g. as required for conditional responding of the form 'if characteristic *X*, then respond *Y*').
(iii) The information required to respond appropriately is currently available. For instance, the task that presents subjects with maths problems of the form '4 + 2 =' will be a purer measure of SO attending than one that requires comparing the sum of the currently presented numbers with the sum of two previously (but not currently) seen numbers.
(iv) The operations involved prior to responding are automatic, well learnt or involve retrieval from semantic memory only (i.e. they are not novel).

Similarly, one might describe characteristics with which one might imbue a task which would increase the relative demand for SI attending, thus:

(i) The task encourages mind-wandering, for example, by being easy, monotonous, non-novel and repetitive.
(ii) All the information required to respond appropriately is not currently being presented, and:
   (a) The information that is required in order to respond appropriately is not well learnt or from semantic memory, but comes from a previously witnessed episode (e.g. as in a delay task).
   (b) The task requires the use of self-generated representations (e.g. novel problem solving, imagination).
   (c) The task requires working with representations that were self-generated on a previous occasion and have not been rehearsed in the meantime.

It is important to note that these are not the only characteristics one might outline. An everyday example to demonstrate the contrast between SO and SI modes of attending might be where one is trying to concentrate on a rather dull lecture (SO attending) versus imagining what one might do that evening after the lecture (SI attending). The gateway hypothesis proposes that rostral PFC in part supports a system which operates when one is required to maintain either mode of attending to an unusual degree or switch between them. More specifically, it proposes that medial rostral PFC plays a role in supporting SO attending, and lateral rostral PFC facilitates switching to, maintaining and voluntarily switching away from, SI cognition (figure 11.2). In this way, the cognitive system supported by rostral PFC was characterized as a 'gateway' between mental life and the external world. (For related accounts from neuroimaging, see McGuire *et al.* 1996; Christoff & Gabrieli 2000; Christoff *et al.* 2001, 2003, 2004; Pollmann 2001, 2004; Mason *et al.* 2007.) Within the information processing framework of Shallice & Burgess (1996), it is assumed that this attentional system lies between the contention scheduling (routine schema selection) and the other supervisory system modules (controlled processing), effecting bias between them (see also Shallice & Burgess 1991*b*, 1993)

This potential account, if true, might solve the apparent conflict between the imaging and lesion evidence since (i) the attentional 'gate' would operate in a wide variety of tasks, but not be critical to the performance of tasks that involve routine, informationally encapsulated processing resources or where attending is strongly driven by the environment, (ii) the difficulties that patients with rostral PFC damage experience (e.g. with multitasking and PM) are

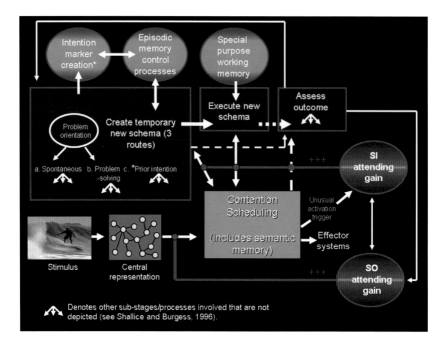

Fig. 11.2 The gateway hypothesis expressed within the framework of Shallice and Burgess (1991a.b, 1993, 1886, Burgess & Shallice, 1996; Burgess et al., 2000). Temporally distinct processing stages effected by the supervisory attentional system (SAS) are shown in dark blue, with a sample of the specialized control resources these stages draw upon shown in green. Selection of an established behavioural routine ("schema") is effected at the "contention scheduling" level. Processing stages between sensory input and the formation of a central representation or schema are not shown (for details of these see e.g. Shallice & Burgess 1996). The influence of the rostral PFC "attentional gateway" is represented by the red ellipses. The gateway hypothesis supposes that some anterior aspects of medial rostral PFC support processing relating to SO attending gain, and some lateral aspects of rostral PFC support processes related to SI attending gain. See Burgess et al., 2005, 2006, 2007b for further details.

those that are particularly likely to require the operation of the attentional gate. This is because multitasking tasks of the type investigated here (i.e. where one task is carried out while bearing in mind that one has to voluntarily switch to another soon) and also typical PM paradigms, both require active intention maintenance (SI cognition) while also engaging with external stimuli (SO attending) in performance of the ongoing task, or current subtask.

11.7 Stage 6: Test the gateway hypothesis

The gateway hypothesis was then tested directly in three ways:

Stage 6(i). Development of direct indicators (i.e. tests) of the proposed function, and investigation of the involvement of area 10 in the performance of the tests using fMRI.

Stage 6(ii). Investigation with neuroimaging and lesion studies of specific functions (e.g. context memory), which should in theory make heavy demands upon this system.

Stage 6(iii). Meta-analyses of functional imaging studies to test the predictions that the theory would make about activation–behaviour associations.

We will consider these in turn.

(a) Stage 6(i)

Gilbert *et al.* (2005) invented three tasks that could be performed either using stimuli that were presented by visual display (i.e. requiring SO attending) or by performing the same tasks 'in one's head' only (i.e. SI attending). In the first task, subjects either tapped a response button in time with a visually presented clock or ignored the visual display (which now presented distracting information) and continued to tap at the same rate. The second task required subjects either to navigate around the edge of a visually presented shape, or, when the shape was replaced by a 'thought bubble', to imagine the same shape and continue navigating as before. In the third task, in the SO condition, participants performed a classification task on sequential letters of the alphabet that were presented on a display. In the SI condition, they mentally continued the sequence and performed the same classification on each self-generated letter. Thus, all three tasks alternated between phases where subjects attended to externally presented information, and phases where they ignored this information and attended to internally represented information instead. We investigated both the sustained neural activity that differed between the two phases, and transient activity at the point of a switch between these two phases. Consistently, across all three tasks, medial rostral PFC exhibited sustained increased activity when participants attended to externally presented information. By contrast, right lateral rostral PFC exhibited transient activity when subjects switched between these phases,

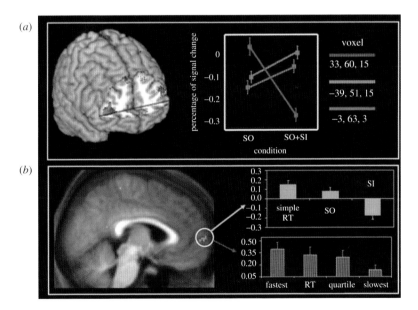

Fig. 11.3 (*a*) Results from Burgess *et al.* (submitted *a*). Tasks requiring SO attending only are contrasted with tasks requiring SO attending plus SI attending (see text for details of the tasks). There is increased BOLD signal bilaterally in lateral area 10 in conditions requiring SI attending. Rostral medial area 10 shows the opposite pattern. The regions rendered on the brain (left) are colour coordinated to the graph (right). Coordinates are MNI. Bars are s.e.m. (*b*) Results from Gilbert *et al.* (2006*a*). Regions of activation revealed in the comparison of SO against SI conditions are shown in yellow. Regions where the BOLD signal correlated with reaction time in a separate simple-reaction time baseline condition are shown in red. This shows that BOLD signal in medial rostral PFC was greater on trials with relatively fast reaction times, ruling out an account of the role of this region in terms of task-unrelated thought during low-demand conditions (since this would be expected to compromise reaction time). (RT, reaction time).

regardless of the direction of the switch. This dissociation between medial and lateral rostral PFC regions was confirmed statistically in all three tasks. Thus, the results of the study strongly supported the hypothesis that rostral PFC is involved in selection between SO and SI attending, and suggested dissociable roles of medial and lateral rostral PFC in this selection process. It also showed that lateral BA 10 is activated at the point when one switches from performing a task in one's head to using displayed stimuli and vice versa.

A further fMRI study (Gilbert *et al.* 2006*a*) demonstrated performance-related activation (i.e. increased activation was associated with faster reaction times) in medial area 10 in simple reaction time conditions that did not require substantial stimulus processing (figure 11.3*b*). Thus, the characterization of medial rostral PFC as most active when an unusual degree of attention to external stimuli is required was supported. Moreover, unpublished data from this second experiment also showed that lateral rostral PFC is activated bilaterally during periods of extended SI cognition, and not only at the SI/SO switch points (SI– SO contrast: left hemisphere, −40, 36, 24, BA 9/46/10, $z = 4.28$, cluster size = 403 voxels; right hemisphere, 38, 44, 32, BA 9/46/10, $z = 4.43$, cluster size = 643 voxels; both $p < 0.001$ uncorrected; S. J. Gilbert 2006, personal communication).

However, there are different forms of both SO and SI attending. Therefore, we next considered whether we could see common BA 10 activations across the different forms, or whether rostral PFC seems to show regional specialization for the different types. Burgess *et al.* (submitted *a*) administered two quite different tasks, each of which consisted of four conditions, in an fMRI conjunction design. The conditions varied in the degree to which they made demands upon five attentional constructs, two of which were stimulus oriented (vigilance and stimulus attending) and three of which were stimulus independent in nature (mind-wandering, use of self-generated representations and maintenance over a delay). Regardless of task, conditions stressing both of the SO attentional forms activated similar regions of rostral medial area 10, and all three that stressed SI cognition activated similar regions of caudal lateral area 10. There was little evidence for further functional specialization within these regions. figure 11.3*a* gives an example of these results, and shows the BOLD signal changes revealed by a contrast between tasks that required stimulus attending (e.g. deciding which of two numbers is the largest) and those that additionally required the use of self-generated representations (e.g. comparing the sum of two currently displayed numbers with the sum of two numbers seen on a previous trial).

(b) Stage 6(ii)

Another way to measure the utility of the gateway hypothesis using neuroimaging is to use it to predict which functions should activate area 10. Clearly, if the investigated function does not involve area 10, then the hypothesis is challenged. We chose a specific form of context memory as a prototype function. Context memory is, *prima facie*, a good candidate for the involvement of a mechanism that plays a role in the control of SI versus SO attending because the recollection of context requires the retrieval of information that goes beyond the associations immediately provoked by the current stimulus. We assume that when a trace is encoded, the strength of the links between elements will be indexed at least in part by what one was attending to at the time, which in turn is influenced by the nature of the task (see Burgess & Shallice 1996 for theoretical background). Thus, being required to recollect details that were part of the event but which were not central to it (or at least to what was attended, i.e. context details) will require the voluntary establishing of a partially new representation, i.e. SI cognition, and integration with the current perceived stimulus (requiring SO attending).

Context memory paradigms should therefore be good examples of memory tasks that require switching between representations directly provoked by current stimuli (i.e. requiring SO attending) and those that are not currently perceived (i.e. SI attending).

Simons *et al.* (2005*b*) asked participants to make two different types of decision about words or famous faces that were presented either on the right or left of a display. They were then shown the words and faces again, while lying in an fMRI scanner, and were asked either which decision they had been required to make about the stimulus ('task memory'), or on which side of the screen the stimulus had appeared ('position memory'). Across both words and faces, activation in lateral rostral PFC regions occurred during both task and position memory conditions compared with a semantic classification baseline task. By contrast, medial BA 10 regions showed significantly increased BOLD signal during the task memory conditions compared with during the position memory ones. In a second study with a similar design (Simons *et al.* 2005*a*), we contrasted task memory with judging which of two previously presented and temporally distinct lists the stimuli belonged to ('list memory'). As with the previous experiment, both experimental conditions activated lateral rostral PFC relative to baseline. However, the aspects of left rostral PFC in both medial and lateral sub-regions additionally showed increased activation during the recollection of task compared with list. Furthermore, the time-courses of the activations in medial and lateral BA 10 were different, with lateral regions more active at the early stages, and medial regions more active at the later stages.

It would probably be premature to take a firm view of the significance of the finer points of these results; this awaits progress in our understanding both of the abilities that area 10 structures support, and of the processing demands made by context memory paradigms. However, it is quite clear from these two studies that: (i) recalling contextual details is associated with very substantial haemodynamic changes in rostral PFC and (ii) there are lateral BA 10 regions that seem to be involved in context memory functions in a surprisingly non-specific way. In this way, the gateway hypothesis intersects with views of BA 10 involvement in memory retrieval (e.g. Lepage *et al.* 2000; Reynolds *et al.* 2006), which is one exemplar of operations whose signature is SI attending.

Remaining within the memory domain, a further prediction we made was that area 10 should be involved in distinguishing between perceived and imagined stimuli (Simons *et al.* 2006*a*). This is because imagining a stimulus is a cardinal form of SI thought, and so therefore must be recalling that memory. However, processing a perceived stimulus in an experimental situation will of course be most effective if one is attending closely to the presented stimuli. Thus, the task will require considerable switching between SI and SO attending states. Accordingly, we showed participants well-known pair phrases (e.g. Romeo and Juliet; Laurel and Hardy) and they were asked to count the number of letters in the second of the pair. This was called the 'perceive condition'. But on some trials the last word was replaced by a question mark (e.g. Romeo and ?), and on these trials, the subjects were required to imagine the word that completed the phrase and count its number of letters 'in their head'. Subsequently, the participants were presented with the first word from these phrases (e.g. 'Romeo') and required either to recall whether (i) the accompanying word had originally been perceived or imagined or (ii) the word-pair had been presented on the left or right side of the screen. We replicated our previous findings of lateral BA 10 activation in recalling which side of the display the stimuli had appeared (versus baseline). However, we also found that on a subject-by-subject basis, people who showed least BOLD signal increase in a particular region of medial rostral PFC (MNI coordinates: $x = 18$, $y = 54$, $z = 6$) tended to be those who made more errors in saying that they had actually witnessed a stimulus that they had in fact imagined (but not vice versa). It is probably too early to attempt a full explanation of these findings in information processing terms, since models of how people decide that they have imagined or perceived items are not sufficiently advanced. Moreover, there is always the possibility that the region of area 10 we identified in this study is not the same as those discussed above (it is, for instance, neither quite as medial nor as lateral as those discussed earlier). However, it does seem probable from these results that area 10 supports processing relevant to determining whether one has perceived or imagined an event. If this is the case, understanding the role this brain region is playing may help us to understand the genesis of disorders where mistaking imaginings for perceived stimuli is a key feature; for example, the hallucinations of schizophrenia. Indeed, when we examined the activation during this experiment in all three brain regions that Whalley *et al.* (2004) have argued show abnormalities in schizophrenia (sections of thalamus, cerebellum as well as the medial rostral PFC region examined here), we found significant BOLD signal increases in all three of these regions when people were engaged in discriminating between perceived and imagined items (relative to position memory).

(c) Stage 6(iii)

The third way in which we have tested the plausibility of the gateway hypothesis is to test a prediction that the theory would make about activation–behaviour associations using meta-analysis of functional imaging studies. If lateral area 10 plays some part in effecting tasks that require the various forms of SI cognition, as the gateway hypothesis proposes, then RTs to tasks that require attending to stimuli plus some form of stimulus-independent thought will be longer, typically, than to tasks that only require the stimulus attending component.

  More specifically, we assume that the anterior medial rostral PFC is involved in simple attending to the outside world, and this can occur under even very low demand conditions (cf. Gilbert *et al.* 2006a). By 'low demand conditions', we mean those conditions that make few demands upon systems other than those involved in attending to the environment. In practice, this means that stimuli will tend to be familiar (and thus easily perceived and understood), conditional responding is either not required (e.g. simple RT paradigms) or taps an established S–R correspondence, and adequate performance of the task is within the capabilities of the individual. We also assume that lateral PFC is involved in SI cognition (e.g. attending to 'the thoughts in our head'; cf. Burgess *et al.* 2007; submitted *a,b*) as described earlier. If this is the case, then medial rostral PFC activations should tend to be associated with paradigms where RTs to the experimental condition are as fast, or faster than, whatever comparison task was used, while lateral rostral activations should be associated with conditions where RTs were slower than in the comparison task. Perhaps the most obvious example comes from the field of PM. Performing an ongoing task while maintaining an intention, and checking for PM cues, is likely to result in slower RTs to stimuli than when one is performing the ongoing task alone. In this case, one would expect where the anterior medial area 10 activations were found, that they would be provoked mainly by the ongoing task alone, and where lateral activations are found they would be principally associated with the PM conditions. This is in fact the case (Burgess *et al.* 2001, 2003).

  Accordingly, Gilbert *et al.* (2006b) analysed the RTs to paradigms from 104 PET/fMRI studies that had reported significant haemodynamic change in area 10. This yielded 133 independent contrasts. The tasks that had provoked these BA 10 activations came from a wide range of functions, e.g. memory, mentalizing, perception as well as tasks that involved multitask coordination (e.g. PM, task-switching, dual-task paradigms, etc.). Similarly, the tasks that had been used for comparison took many forms, and of course differed from study-to-study.

But, if the gateway hypothesis holds, the precise form of neither the task under examination (e.g. memory, perception, etc.) that provoked the area 10 activation nor the comparison task (i.e. the task that had been used as a 'baseline' for the task that provoked the area 10 activation) should matter for these purposes. This is because all cognition consists of varying degrees of SO and SI cognition, so all tasks can be classified according to, for example, the proportion of variance (in BOLD signal change) one might attribute to one attending form or another. We assume that experiments where tasks have been compared that make similar demands upon SO or SI attending will have tended not to have yielded BA 10 activations. Hence, if we examine studies where BA 10 changes have been detected, and where the logic in the paragraph holds, there should be a medial–lateral BA 10 difference by RT.

As predicted by the gateway hypothesis, Gilbert *et al.* (2006*a,b*) did indeed find that RTs to tasks that had provoked lateral area 10 activations tended to be slower than RTs in whatever control task had been used. Furthermore, RTs to tasks that had provoked medial area 10 activations were as fast, or faster, than in the comparison task (figure 11.4*a*). This pattern occurred regardless of the type of task under study, and thus seems to be a general principle of area 10 neuroimaging findings.

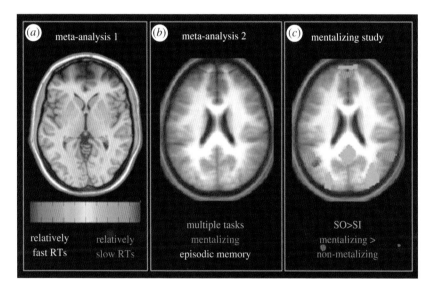

Fig. 11.4 (*a*) Smoothed RT data from a meta-analysis of 104 functional neuroimaging studies reporting activation peaks in rostral PFC (Gilbert *et al.* 2006*b*). On average, contrasts producing activation peaks in regions coloured blue involved faster RTs in the experimental task than the control task against which it was compared. By contrast, those contrasts where the RTs in the experimental condition were slower than in the control condition tended to produce activation peaks in the regions marked in red. This pattern occurred regardless of the type of paradigm under use (e.g. episodic memory, mentalizing, etc.). (*b*) Results of a second meta-analysis of these 104 studies, which investigated the association between different types of task and the location of activation peaks within rostral PFC (Gilbert *et al.* 2006*c*). Note that the studies involving multiple-task coordination tended to yield activation peaks rostral to those involving mentalizing. (*c*) Results of an fMRI study that crossed the factors of attentional focus (SO versus SI) with mentalizing (mentalizing versus non-mentalizing judgments; Gilbert *et al.* 2007*b*). The regions of activation in rostral PFC produced by the SO versus SI contrast were rostral to those produced by the mentalizing versus non-mentalizing contrast. In both (*b*) and (*c*), the results are plotted on an axial slice ($z = 24$) of the participants' mean normalized structural scan.

11.8 Further functional specialization within area 10

Our studies strongly suggest that lateral and medial regions within BA 10 are differentially sensitive to the demands that tasks make upon SO and SI attending, and that this might provide a dimension along which the functional organization of rostral PFC might be understood (see also Koechlin *et al.* 2000, Koechin & Hyafil, 2007). However, it does not provide, nor does it seek to be, a complete account of the relation between structure and function within rostral PFC.

Most importantly, the account presented here does not preclude others. BA 10 is a very large brain region, with many connections to different brain regions. It is certainly possible that while we may have identified a particular function (e.g. attenuating SI versus SO attending), other sub-regions of rostral PFC may perform other unrelated functions. It might even be the case that the same brain regions as we have identified may perform different functions (e.g. by virtue of interactions with other brain regions).

Then, the gateway hypothesis as it currently stands deals only with the functional organization of BA 10 in respect of one spatial dimension: lateral versus medial. Yet, there is strong evidence from our own work and others that principles may emerge for functional organization along other dimensions (i.e. rostral–caudal, dorsal–ventral).

For instance, Gilbert *et al.* (2006*c*) investigated the location of activations within area 10 according to the type of task being used, with the neuroimaging database already described (see §7*c* earlier). The location in *X* and *Y* dimensions of area 10 activations were analysed across 133 contrasts found in the neuroimaging literature according to the type of task which provoked them. A classification algorithm was trained on half of the data and then tested on the other half to see if it could predict the task from the location of each activation peak. This algorithm is represented visually in figure 11.4*b*. Accuracy in the three main categories of task was 71% (chance: 33%; $p < 10^{-39}$). As shown in figure 11.4, episodic memory tasks were associated with lateral area 10 activations. More importantly, however, we found that mentalizing tasks tending to provoke activations within caudal medial aspects of BA 10 (see also Frith & Frith 1999; Gusnard *et al.* 2001), but paradigms that required the coordination of two or more activities (dual task, PM, etc.) were associated with very rostral activations within area 10 (figure 11.4*b*).

In order to investigate this possible rostral–caudal localization distinction further, we conducted an fMRI study that crossed the factors of attentional focus (SO versus SI attending) and mentalizing (mentalizing versus non-mentalizing). Participants performed two of the three tasks investigated by Gilbert *et al.* (2005), which switched between SO and SI phases at unpredictable times. In 'mentalizing blocks', the participants were instructed that the experimenter was in control of the timing of these switches, and that they had to judge whether he had tried to be helpful or unhelpful in that block. In 'non-mentalizing blocks', the participants were instructed that the switches occurred at times randomly selected by a computer, and they were asked to judge whether these switches occurred more or less rapidly than average. In actuality, there was no difference between mentalizing and non-mentalizing blocks, but in post-experiment debriefing participants unanimously described interpreting the timing of switches in the mentalizing blocks in terms of the mental state of the experimenter. For instance, one subject said 'I was thinking about whether you could see if I was stuck . . . and what was coming up on your screen so I did imagine what you were seeing sometimes during the experiment. . . I was more aware of the human element entering into the equation' (Gilbert *et al.* 2007*b*).

The fMRI results were clear. Contrasting SO with SI phases revealed strong activity in the most rostral part of medial PFC. This replicates the earlier finding of Gilbert *et al.* (2005).

Moreover, the contrast of mentalizing with non-mentalizing blocks yielded activity in an adjacent caudal region of medial PFC, as predicted by the meta-analysis (Gilbert *et al.* 2006*c*). Most importantly, however, there was virtually no overlap between the brain regions activated in these two contrasts, and nor were there any regions showing a significant interaction between the mentalizing and attention factors (figure 11.4*c*). Thus, this study confirmed that dissociable, adjacent regions of medial rostral PFC are involved in (i) focusing attention on perceptual versus self-generated information or (ii) mentalizing. Taken with the result of the meta-analysis (figure 11.4*b*), these results suggest that it might be possible to establish a further principle of the functional organization of area 10 based around the rostral–caudal dimension.

11.9 Conclusion

This is an exciting time for scientists involved in trying to discover the functions of rostral PFC (BA 10). For many years, there was essentially little or no evidence that might speak to this issue. Then, the advent of functional neuroimaging placed the functions of this region at the heart of human cognition by demonstrating rostral PFC haemodynamic changes in a very wide range of tasks. However, the sheer volume and variety of these findings provided few constraints for theorizing. But, very recently, some principles have begun to emerge which suggest that achieving an understanding of the functional organization of this large, and uniquely human, brain region may not be an unrealistic aim. For instance, tasks that, in lay terms, require participants to 'bear something in mind while doing something else' very consistently provoke area 10 haemodynamic changes (e.g. Okuda *et al.* 1998, in press; Koechlin *et al.* 1999; Burgess *et al.* 2001, 2003), and these tasks also seem to be performed poorly by patients with damage to this brain region (e.g. Burgess *et al.* 2000). Yet, the functions of this region cannot be reduced to this one alone, since other consistent findings go far beyond this class of task. For instance, tasks that involve episodic recollection, 'mentalizing' and those that provoke mind-wandering are also accompanied by rostral PFC haemodynamic changes in a predictable fashion, as are simple tasks that involve making over-learned responses to environmental stimuli (e.g. Gilbert *et al.* 2005, 2006*a*, *2007a*. For review see Grady 1999; Ramnani & Owen 2004; Gilbert *et al.* 2006*b*,*c*). We have provided a framework that seeks to explain the multiplicity of these findings in a simple way, by invoking a construct that relies on the distinction between SO and SI attending. The experimental predictions that follow have been broadly confirmed in a series of experiments in our own laboratory, and we have also shown with meta-analysis that the hypothesis can explain important aspects of the findings from other laboratories, cutting across gross task characterizations. However, this gateway hypothesis, as it currently stands, seeks only to outline a principle for the functional organization of area 10 along a lateral–medial dimension. The most obvious next candidate discovery at this stage might be a principle that relates to functional organization along a rostral–caudal dimension. Additionally, while we may have discovered one superordinate function of rostral PFC, this precludes neither the discovery of other functions that will provide conceptual challenge nor the possibility of functional specialization within sub-regions of area 10 that do not conform to the principle. In other words, in concentrating on discovering regions of area 10 which provide results that conform to the gateway hypothesis, we have not largely sought to discover those that might not. Nevertheless, we hope that the hypothesis we advance will prove a useful tool for investigation. Currently, it has three advantages over most other accounts of the functions of this brain region. First, it is predicated on the results of both neuroimaging and human lesion data. This is particularly important, since the remarkably specific nature of the deficits shown by people with rostral PFC lesions provides a severe test of many other accounts that have emerged from neuroimaging data alone. Second, it provides a principle by which apparently similar activations (and their behavioural correlates) across tasks of different forms might be investigated. Third, it has received direct empirical examination. Clearly, however, we still have a great deal to learn. But, the special structure of rostral PFC in humans, its size, late development and links to the highest levels of human cognition, give hope that understanding how this fascinating brain region works may reveal key insights into the mental experiences and disorders that are peculiar to humans.

This work was supported by the Wellcome Trust grant number 061171 to P.W.B.

References

Ackerly, S. S. & Benton, A. L. 1947 Report of a case of bilateral frontal lobe defect. Res. *Publ.: Assoc. Res. Nerv. Mental Dis.* **27**, 479–504.

Alexander, M. P., Stuss, D. T. & Fansabedian, N. 2003 California Verbal Learning Test: performance by patients with focal frontal and non-frontal lesions. *Brain* **126**, 1493–1503. (doi:10.1093/brain/awg128)

Bird, C. M., Castelli, F., Malik, O., Frith, U. & Husain, M. 2004 The impact of extensive medial frontal lobe damage on "Theory of Mind" and cognition. *Brain* **127**, 914–928. (doi:10.1093/brain/awh108)

Blaxton, T. A., Zeffiro, T. A., Gabrieli, J. D. E., Bookheimer, S. Y., Carrillo, M. C., Theodore, W. H. & Disterhoft, J. F. 1996 Functional mapping of human learning: a positron emission tomography activation study of eyeblink conditioning. *J. Neurosci.* **16**, 4032–4040.

Bonin, G. von. 1950 *Essay on the cerebral cortex*. Springfield, IL: Charles C. Thomas.

Brickner, R. M. 1936 The *intellectual functions of the frontal lobes: a study based upon observation of a man after partial bilateral frontal lobectomy*. New York, NY: Macmillan.

Burgess, P. W. 2000 Strategy application disorder: the role of the frontal lobes in human multitasking. *Psychol. Res.* **63**, 279–288. (doi:10.1007/s004269900006)

Burgess, P. W. & Shallice, T. 1996 Confabulation and the control of recollection. *Memory* **4**, 359–411. (doi:10.1080/ 096582196388906)

Burgess, P. W., Alderman, N., Emslie, H., Evans, J. J., Wilson, B. A. & Shallice, T. 1996 The simplified six element test. In *Behavioural assessment of the dysexecutive syndrome* (eds B. A. Wilson, N. Alderman, P. W. Burgess, H. Emslie & J. J. Evans). Bury St Edmunds, UK: Thames Valley Test Company.

Burgess, P. W., Veitch, E., Costello, A. & Shallice, T. 2000 The cognitive and neuroanatomical correlates of multitasking. *Neuropsychologia* **38**, 848–863. (doi:10.1016/ S0028-3932(99)00134-7)

Burgess, P. W., Quayle, A. & Frith, C. D. 2001 Brain regions involved in prospective memory as determined by positron emission tomography. *Neuropsychologia* **39**, 545–555. (doi:10.1016/ S0028-3932(00)00149-4)

Burgess, P. W., Scott, S. K. & Frith, C. D. 2003 The role of the rostral frontal cortex (area 10) in prospective memory: a lateral versus medial dissociation. *Neuropsychologia* **41**, 906–918. (doi:10.1016/S0028-3932(02)00327-5)

Burgess, P. W., Simons, J. S., Dumontheil, I. & Gilbert, S. J. 2005 The gateway hypothesis of rostral PFC function. In *Measuring the mind: speed, control and age* (eds J. Duncan, L. Phillips & P. McLeod), pp. 215–246. Oxford, UK: Oxford University Press.

Burgess, P. W. *et al.* 2006a The case for the development and use of "ecologically valid" measures of executive function in experimental and clinical neuropsychology. *J. Int. Neuropsychol. Soc.* **12**, 1–16.

Burgess, P. W., Gilbert, S. J., Okuda, J. & Simons, J. S. 2006*b* Rostral prefrontal brain regions (area 10): a gateway between inner thought and the external world? In *Disorders of volition* (eds W. Prinz & N. Sebanz), pp. 373–396. Cambridge, MA: MIT Press.

Burgess, P. W., Dumontheil & Gilbert, S.J., 2007*b*. The gateway hypothesis of rostal prefrontal cortex (area 10) function. *Trends Cog. Sci.* **11**, 290–298.

Burgess, P. W., Gilbert, S. J. & Dumontheil, I. 2007*a*. A gateway between mental life and the external world: role of the rostral prefrontal cortex (area 10). *Jpn J. Neuropsychol.* **23**, 8–26.

Burgess, P. W., Dumontheil, I., Gilbert, S. J., Okuda, J., Schölvinck, M. L. & Simons, J. S. In press *b*. On the role of rostral prefrontal cortex (area 10) in prospective memory. In *Prospective memory: cognitive, neuroscience, developmental, and applied perspectives* (eds M. Kliegel, M. A. McDaniel & G. O. Einstein). Mahwah, NJ: Erlbaum.

Burgess, P. W., Dumontheil, I., Gilbert, S. J. & Frith, C. D. Submitted *a*. Similar regions of area 10 (rostral PFC) are involved in various forms of stimulus-oriented or stimulus-independent attending.

Burgess, P. W., Veitch, E. J. & Costello, A. Submitted *b*. Multitasking deficits in humans following rostral pre-frontal lesions: the Six Element Test.

Christoff, K. & Gabrieli, J. D. E. 2000 The frontopolar cortex and human cognition: evidence for a rostrocaudal hierarchical organization within the human prefrontal cortex. *Psychobiology* **28**, 168–186.

Christoff, K., Prabhakaran, V., Dorfman, J., Zhao, Z., Kroger, J. K., Holyoak, K. J. & Gabrieli, J. D. E. 2001 Rostrolateral prefrontal cortex involvement in relational integration during reasoning. *Neuroimage* **14**, 1136–1149. (doi:10.1006/nimg.2001.0922)

Christoff, K., Ream, J. M., Geddes, L. P. T. & Gabrieli, J. D. E. 2003 Evaluating self-generated information: anterior prefrontal contributions to human cognition. *Behav. Neurosci.* **117**, 1161–1168. (doi:10.1037/0735-7044.117.6.1161)

Christoff, K., Ream, J. M. & Gabrieli, J. D. E. 2004 Neural basis of spontaneous thought processes. *Cortex* **40**, 1–9.

Eslinger, P. J. & Damasio, A. R. 1985 Severe disturbance of higher cognition after bilateral frontal lobe ablation: patient E. V. R. *Neurology* **35**, 1731–1741.

Frith, U. & Frith, C. D. 1999 Interacting minds—a biological basis. *Science* **286**, 1692–1695. (doi:10.1126/science.286. 5445.1692)

Frith, U. & Frith, C. D. 2003 Development and neurophysiology of mentalizing. *Phil. Trans. R. Soc. B* **358**, 459–473. (doi:10.1098/rstb.2002.1218)

Gilbert, S. J., Frith, C. D. & Burgess, P. W. 2005 Involvement of rostral prefrontal cortex in selection between stimulus-oriented and stimulus-independent thought. *Euro. J. Neurosci.* **21**, 1423–1431. (doi:10.1111/j.1460-9568. 2005.03981.x)

Gilbert, S. J., Simons, J. S., Frith, C. D. & Burgess, P. W. 2006*a* Performance-related activity in medial rostral prefrontal cortex (area 10) during low demand tasks. *J. Exp. Psychol. Hum. Percept. Perform.* **32**, 45–58. (doi:10. 1037/0096-1523.32.1.45)

Gilbert, S. J., Spengler, S., Simons, J. S., Frith, C. D. & Burgess, P. W. 2006*b* Differential functions of lateral and medial rostral prefrontal cortex (area 10) revealed by brain-behavior correlations. *Cereb. Cortex* Jan 18 [Epub ahead of print].

Gilbert, S. J., Spengler, S., Simons, J. S. S., Steele, J. D., Lawrie, S. M., Frith, C. D. & Burgess, P. W. 2006*c* Functional specialisation within rostral prefrontal cortex (area 10): a meta-analysis. *J. Cogn. Neurosci.* **18**, 932–948. (doi:10.1162/jocn.2006.18.6.932)

Gilbert, S. J., Dumontheil, I., Simons, J.C., Firth, C.D., & Burgess, P.W. 2007*a* Comment on 'Wandering minds: the default network and stimulus-independent thought.' *Science* **317**, 43.

Gilbert, S. J., Williamson, I.D.M., Dumontheil, I., Simons, J. S., Frith, C. D. & Burgess, P. W. 2007*b*. Distinct regions of rostral prefrontal cortex supporting social and nonsocial functions. *Soc. Cog. Affect. Neuosci.* **2**, 206–216 (doi: 10.1093/scan/ nsm014)

Goel, V. & Grafman, J. 2000 The role of the right prefrontal cortex in Ill-structured problem solving. *Cogn. Neuropsychol.* **17**, 415–436. (doi:10.1080/026432900410775)

Goldstein, L. H., Bernard, S., Fenwick, P. B. C., Burgess, P. W. & McNeil, J. 1993 Unilateral frontal lobectomy can produce strategy application disorder. *J. Neurol. Neurosurg. Psych.* **56**, 274–276.

Grady, C. L. 1999 Neuroimaging and activation of the frontal lobes. In *The human frontal lobes: function and disorders* (eds B. L. Miller & J. L. Cummings), pp. 196–230. New York, NY: Guilford Press.

Gusnard, D. A., Akbudak, E., Shulman, G. L. & Raichle, M. E. 2001 Medial prefrontal cortex and self-referential mental activity: relation to a default mode of brain function. *Proc. Natl Acad. Sci. USA* **98**, 4259–4264. (doi:10.1073/pnas.071043098)

Holloway, R. L. 2002 Brief communication: how much larger is the relative volume of area 10 of the prefrontal cortex in humans? *Am. J. Phys. Anthropol.* **118**, 399–401. (doi:10. 1002/ajpa.10090)

Jacobs, B. *et al*. 2001 Regional dendritic and spine variation in human cerebral cortex: a quantitative golgi study. *Cereb. Cortex* **11**, 558–571. (doi:10.1093/cercor/11.6.558)

Kliegel, M., McDaniel, M. A. & Einstein, G. O. 2000 Plan formation, retention, and execution in prospective memory: a new approach and age-related effects. *Mem. Cogn.* **28**, 1041–1049.

Kliegel, M., Phillips, L. H., Lemke, U. & Kopp, U. A. 2005 Planning and realisation of complex intentions in patients with Parkinson's disease. *J. Neurol. Neurosurg. Psych.* **76**, 1501–1505. (doi:10.1136/jnnp.2004.051268)

Koechlin, E. & Hyafil, A. 2007 Anterior prefrontal function and the limits of human decision-making. *Science* **318**, 594–598.

Koechlin, E., Basso, G., Pietrini, P., Panzer, S. & Grafman, J. 1999 The role of the anterior prefrontal cortex in human cognition. *Nature* **399**, 148–151. (doi:10.1038/20178)

Koechlin, E., Corrado, G., Pietrini, P. & Grafman, J. 2000 Dissociating the role of the medial and lateral anterior prefrontal cortex in planning. *Proc. Natl Acad. Sci. USA* **97**, 7651–7656. (doi:10.1073/pnas.130177397)

Lepage, M., Ghaffar, O., Nyberg, L. & Tulving, E. 2000 Prefrontal cortex and episodic memory retrieval mode. *Proc. Natl Acad. Sci. USA* **97**, 506–511. (doi:10.1073/ pnas.97.1.506)

Mason, M. F., Norton, M. I., Van Horn, J. D., Wegner, D. M., Grafton, S. T. & Macrae, C. M. 2007 Wandering minds: the default network and stimulus-independent thought. *Science* **315**, 393–395. (doi:10.1126/science. 1131295)

McGuire, P. K., Paulesu, E., Frackowiak, R. S. J. & Frith, C. D. 1996 Brain activity during stimulus independent thought. *Neuroreport* **7**, 2095–2099.

Okuda, J., Fujii, T., Yamadori, A., Kawashima, R., Tsukkiura, T., Fukatsu, R., Suzuki, K., Ito, M. & Fukuda, H. 1998 Participation of the prefrontal cortices in prospective memory: evidence from a PET study in humans. *Neurosci. Lett.* **253**, 127–130. (doi:10.1016/ S0304-3940(98)00628-4)

Okuda, J., Fujii, T., Ohtake, H., Tsukiura, T., Yamadori, A., Frith, C. D. & Burgess, P. W. 2006 Differential involvement of regions of rostral prefrontal cortex (Brodmann area 10) in time- and event-based prospective memory. *Int. J. Psychophysiol*. Nov 23. [Epub ahead of print.]

Ongur, D., Ferry, A. T. & Price, J. L. 2003 Architectonic subdivision of the human orbital and medial prefrontal cortex. *J. Comp. Neurol.* **460**, 425–449.

Penfield, W. & Evans, J. 1935 The frontal lobe in man: a clinical study of maximum removals. *Brain* **58**, 115–133. (doi:10.1093/brain/58.1.115)

Picton, T. W., Stuss, D. T., Shallice, T., Alexander, M. P. & Gillingham, S. 2006 Keeping time: effects of focal frontal lesions. *Neuropsychologia* **44**, 1195–1209. (doi:10.1016/ j.europsychologia.2005.10.002)

Pollmann, S. 2001 Switching between dimensions, locations, and responses: the role of the left frontopolar cortex. *Neuroimage* **14**, S118–S124. (doi:10.1006/nimg.2001. 0837)

Pollmann, S. 2004 Anterior prefrontal cortex contributions to attention control. *Exp. Psychol.* **51**, 270–278.

Raichle, M. E., MacLeod, A.-M., Snyder, A. Z., Powers, W. J., Gusnard, D. A. & Shulman, G. L. 2001 A default mode of brain function. *Proc. Natl Acad. Sci. USA* **98**, 76–682. (doi:10.1073/pnas.98.2.676)

Ramnani, N. & Owen, A. M. 2004 Anterior prefrontal cortex: insights into function from anatomy and neuroimaging. *Nat. Rev. Neurosci.* **5**, 184–194. (doi:10.1038/nrn1343)

Reynolds, J. R., McDermott, K. B. & Braver, T. S. 2006 A direct comparison of anterior prefrontal cortex involvement in episodic retrieval and integration. *Cereb. Cortex* **16**, 519–528. (doi:10.1093/ cercor/bhi131)

Semendeferi, K., Armstrong, E., Schleicher, A., Zilles, K. & Van Hoesen, G. W. 2001 Prefrontal cortex in humans and apes: a comparative study of area 10. *Am. J. Phys. Anthropol.* **114**, 224–241. (doi:10.1002/1096-8644(200103)114:3<224::AID-AJPA1022>3.0.CO;2-I)

Shallice, T. 1988 *From neuropsychology to mental structure*. Cambridge, UK: Cambridge University Press.

Shallice, T. 2004 The fractionation of supervisory control. In *The cognitive neurosciences III* (ed. M. S. Gazzananiga), pp. 943–956. Cambridge, MA: MIT Press.

Shallice, T. & Burgess, P. W. 1991*a* Deficits in strategy application following frontal lobe damage in man. *Brain* **114**, 727–741. (doi:10.1093/brain/114.2.727)

Shallice, T. & Burgess, P. W. 1991*b* Higher-order cognitive impairments and frontal lobe lesions in man. In *Frontal lobe function and dysfunction* (eds H. S. Levin, H. M. Eisenberg & A. L. Benton), pp. 125–138. New York, NY: Oxford University Press.

Shallice, T. & Burgess, P. W. 1993 Supervisory control of action and thought selection. In *Attention: selection, awareness and control: a tribute to Donald Broadbent* (eds A. Baddeley & L. Weiskrantz), pp. 171–187. Oxford, UK: Clarendon Press.

Shallice, T. & Burgess, P. W. 1996 The domain of supervisory processes and temporal organisation of behaviour. *Phil. Trans. R. Soc. B* **351**, 1405–1412. (doi:10.1098/rstb.1996. 0124) Reprinted in *The prefrontal cortex: executive and cognitive functions* (eds A C. Roberts, Robbins, T. W. & Weiskrantz, L.), pp. 22–35. Oxford, UK: Oxford University Press, 1998, 2000.

Simons, J. S., Gilbert, S. J., Owen, A. M., Fletcher, P. C. & Burgess, P. W. 2005*a* Distinct roles for lateral and medial anterior prefrontal cortex in contextual recollection. *J. Neurophysiol.* **94**, 813–820. (doi:10.1152/jn.01200.2004)

Simons, J. S., Owen, A. M., Fletcher, P. C. & Burgess, P. W. 2005*b* Anterior prefrontal cortex and the recollection of contextual information. *Neuropsychologia* **43**, 1774–1783. (doi:10.1016/ j.neuropsychologia.2005.02.004)

Simons, J. S., Davis, S. W., Gilbert, S. J., Frith, C. D. & Burgess, P. W. 2006*a* Discriminating imagined from perceived information engages brain areas implicated in schizophrenia. *Neuroimage* **32**, 696–703. (doi:10.1016/ j.neuroimage.2006.04.209)

Simons, J. S., Schölvinck, M., Gilbert, S. J., Frith, C. D. & Burgess, P. W. 2006*b* Differential components of prospective memory? Evidence from fMRI. *Neuropsychologia* **44**, 1388–1397. (doi:10.1016/j.neuropsychologia.2006.01.005)

Smith, R. E. & Bayen, U. J. 2004 A multinomial model of event-based prospective memory. *J. Exp. Psychol. Learn. Mem. Cogn.* **30**, 756–777. (doi:10.1037/0278-7393.30.4.756)

Sowell, E. R., Thompson, P. M., Holmes, C. J., Jernigan, T. L. & Toga, A. W. 1999 *In vivo* evidence for postadolescent brain maturation in frontal and striatal regions. *Nat. Neurosci.* **2**, 859–861. (doi:10.1038/13154)

Sowell, E. R., Thompson, P. M., Leonard, C. M., Welcome, S. E., Kan, E. & Toga, A. W. 2004 Longitudinal mapping of cortical thickness and brain growth in normal children. *J. Neurosci.* **24**, 8223–8231. (doi:10.1523/JNEUROSCI. 1798-04.2004)

Whalley, H. C., Simonotto, E., Flett, S., Marshall, I., Ebmeier, K. P., Owens, D. G., Goddard, N. H., Johnstone, E. C. & Lawrie, S. M. 2004 fMRI correlates of state and trait effects in subjects at genetically enhanced risk of schizophrenia. *Brain* **127**, 457–459.

12

Is there a dysexecutive syndrome?

Donald T. Stuss, * *and Michael P. Alexander*

The role of the frontal lobes has often been described as a 'paradox' or a 'riddle'. Ascribed to this region has been the loftiest of functions (e.g. executive; seat of wisdom); others contested that the frontal lobes played no special role. There has also been controversy about the unity or diversity of functions related to the frontal lobes. Based on the analysis of the effects of lesions of the frontal lobes, we propose that there are discrete categories of functions within the frontal lobes, of which 'executive' functioning is one. Within the executive category, the data do not support the concept of an undifferentiated central executive/supervisory system. The results are better explained as impairments in a collection of anatomically and functionally independent but interrelated attentional control processes. Evidence for three separate frontal attentional processes is presented. For each process, we present an operational description, the data supporting the distinctiveness of each process and the evidence for impairments of each process after lesions in specific frontal regions. These processes and their coarse frontal localizations are *energization—superior medial, task setting— left lateral* and *monitoring—right lateral*. The strength of the findings lies in replication: across different tasks; across different cognitive modalities (e.g. reaction time paradigms, memory); and across different patient groups. This convergence minimizes the possibility that any of the findings are limited to a specific task or to a specific set of patients. Although distinct, these processes are flexibly assembled in response to context, complexity and intention over real time into different networks within the frontal regions and between frontal and posterior regions.

Keywords: frontal lobes; dysexecutive syndrome; attention; monitoring; energization; task setting

12.1 Introduction

(a) Evolution of the question and initial response

Their relatively large size, late evolutionary development and rich anatomical connectivity all strongly suggest a central role, or roles, for the frontal lobes in human cognition and emotion. That there are so many competing theories about frontal functions despite the many recent advances in lesion and imaging research illuminates the difficulty in understanding this complex region.

The difficulties in studying the frontal lobes are myriad. First, there is no particular predisposition for a neurological disorder to the frontal lobes. Although cerebrovascular disorders may damage only the frontal lobes, the number of individuals with focal frontal pathology is not particularly high. The pressures of publication, the time required to collect an adequate sample of focal frontal lobe lesions and the rapid change in theoretical positions during the period of data accumulation often predispose researchers to use more convenient samples (e.g. undifferentiated traumatic brain injury) as a proxy. Such studies have practical value for

* Author for correspondence (dstuss@rotman-baycrest.on.ca).

understanding the target population, but precise brain–behaviour relationships cannot be determined. Central roles for various frontal regions have been proposed for both cognitive and emotional functions, and both may be recruited for complex tasks—gambling decision, investment planning, etc. Lesions may disrupt either or both, depending on site. It may be the interaction of emotional status and cognition that determines many behaviours, but it is the cognitive aspect of tasks that are defined by executive functions.

Many prominent theoretical positions emphasized the dominant role of the frontal lobes in organizing cognition, thus such terms as *supervisory system* and *central executive*. A controversy within this approach has been related to the unity (Duncan & Miller 2002) versus diversity (Stuss & Benson 1986; Shallice 2002) of executive functions. In the early 1990s, we embarked on a research plan to examine whether such an executive system could be fractionated (Stuss *et al.* 1995). Our approach was different from that often used in neuropsychological research. Instead of selecting one test or one process that was considered executive, we took a 'root and branches' approach. We selected attention (the 'root') as the cognitive focus owing to its prominent role in many influential theories of frontal functions (e.g. Heilman & Watson 1977; Shallice 1982; Mesulam 1985; Norman & Shallice 1986; Posner & Petersen 1990; Knight 1991; Paus *et al.* 1997; Godefroy *et al.* 1999; Sturm & Willmes 2001). We elected to study patients with focal lesions to demonstrate that a region was essential for an attentional process, as opposed to simply being activated during a process (as, say, with functional magnetic resonance imaging, fMRI). All published studies addressing attentional deficits in patients with single focal frontal lesions were reviewed. The tasks used in the various studies could be grouped into a relatively small number of categories. Based on our review of the different papers, we proposed a limited number of distinct frontal lobe processes (the 'branches') which could explain the performance of each task. The reviewed papers also implied potential frontal localization of at least some of these processes. This initial review implied that there was no common central organizing role of the frontal lobes; rather, there were independent control processes related to different brain regions. We concluded that

> If we are correct that there is no central executive, neither can there be a dysexecutive syndrome. The frontal lobes (in anatomical terms) or the supervisory system (in cognitive terms) do not function (in physiological terms) as a simple (inexplicable) homun-culus. Monitoring, energizing, inhibition, etc.—these are processes that exist at many levels of the brain, including those more posterior 'automatic' processes. Owing to their extensive reciprocal connections with virtually all other brain regions, the frontal lobes may be unique in the quality of the processes that have evolved, and perhaps in the level of processing which might be labelled 'executive' or 'supervisory'.
>
> (Stuss *et al.* 1995)

Bolstered by this review and using Norman & Shallice's (1986) supervisory system as our launching point, we undertook a programme of research to examine whether we could differentiate and define frontal processes within a supervisory system. Such processes had to be domain-general, in that they would be necessary for different cognitive modalities (e.g. language, memory) as well as basic attentional tasks such as reaction time (RT). Domain-general implies that different tasks in one modality or similar tasks in different modalities would show similar effects of specific lesions. Finally, the results had to be replicable across different groups of frontal lobe patients to ensure there was no particular subject group bias. Other researchers have embarked on a similar journey (e.g. Shallice & Burgess 1991; Burgess & Shallice 1994; Godefroy *et al.* 1994; Diaz *et al.* 1996; Robbins 1996, 2007; Burgess *et al.* 2007; see also this volume). This paper will necessarily focus on our own programme of research, but results from other laboratories will be presented where appropriate.

(b) Methodological philosophy

We began with three assumptions of what would be necessary for success. First, the history of research on 'executive' functions has conflated psychological theories with anatomical ones, so we focused our investigation on the effects of frontal injuries, not on an investigation of executive functions (which can be examined independently of any brain relationship). This required including only patients with purely focal frontal single lesions. Second, restricting the patients to those with vascular aetiology would profoundly limit the regional representation of frontal lesions, so patients with different aetiologies were accepted if they met specific conditions (see Stuss *et al.* 1995 for a review of these conditions). In addition, we and others have demonstrated several times that, under these conditions, the location is more important than the aetiology (Elsass & Hartelius 1985; Burgess & Shallice 1996; Stuss *et al.* 2005; Picton *et al.* 2006, 2007). Third, in order not to confound acute diffuse problems with more focal impairments, we tested patients in the chronic stage of recovery, ideally after three months. As patients' lesions become more and more chronic, it is possible that brain–behaviour relationships are affected by brain plasticity and reorganization. The evolution of these relationships from acute to post-acute to chronic phases is probably interesting, but would require another programme of research following patients during the course of recovery, supported by imaging. Recent data do suggest that similar patterns of behaviour may be observable in both acute and chronic patients (Stuss *et al.* 1994; Alexander *et al.* 2003; Turner *et al.* in press).

A process must be isolated to demonstrate a specific brain–behaviour relationship. Process dissociation was used for the standard clinical tests where possible. In the experimental tests, the goal was to devise simple tests that probed single processes and then manipulate difficulty and context to probe more complex processes.

The next step was to devise a method to assign frontal lesions to specific frontal regions to determine whether there were any regional effects on each process. There are several different methods to achieve this (Stuss *et al.* 2002*a*). In this paper, we present data from two approaches. In some studies, the frontal patients are compared based on a coarse predominant location of the lesion: left lateral (LL); right lateral (RL); inferior medial (IM); and superior medial (SM). In addition, however, we were able to focus on much more precise architectonic regions with a 'hotspotting' method developed by us (Stuss *et al.* 2002*a*, 2005). The lesion for each patient is mapped onto the Petrides & Pandya (1994) architectonic template. For every patient, each architectonic region is identified as significantly damaged or not. Then, for the measurement in question, the performance of individuals who have damage in a particular region is compared with all those who do not have damage in that region. This hotspotting approach is open to criticism of too many comparisons and the risk of type I error. We have been cognizant of this problem, but given the substantial difficulties of lesion-based research and the potential benefits of identifying specific brain–behaviour relationships, this approach seemed reasonable, at least as a first approximation of focal effects. Furthermore, if the results can be replicated across different tests that demand a similar process, and across different patient groups, the summated evidence for that brain–behaviour relationship is strengthened. At the very least, having these findings in lesion research provides a plausible approach for verification in other studies, or for devising a more specific region of interest hypothesis.

Lesion research demonstrates that some structure within the lesion is critical for impairing a task. Comparing patients with similar, partly overlapping lesions allows increasingly fine identification of which structures are essential. Lesion studies are not equivalent to functional imaging studies that demonstrate activation of a region during defined tasks. The activation may or may not represent a critical role in the performance of the task. Nevertheless, there is considerable convergence of the neuroimaging and lesion studies.

(c) The basic paradigms

If executive functions are truly 'superordinate' and 'domain-general', it should be possible to determine their effects across a variety of tasks. Four different sets of data are used in support of our hypothesis of process fractionation within the frontal lobes. We used classic 'frontal' tasks (Wisconsin Card Sorting Test, WCST, Milner 1963; the Stroop test of interference, Stroop 1935; Comalli *et al.* 1962), other tasks with a control requirement but in different modalities (language— verbal fluency, Borkowski *et al.* 1967; memory—list learning, Delis *et al.* 1987), feature integration test (FIT; Stuss *et al.* 1989, 2002*b*) in which complexity of response distractions could be manipulated, and finally, a novel battery of tests (ROBBIA, ROtman-Baycrest Battery to Investigate Attention; Stuss *et al.* 2005), that systematically

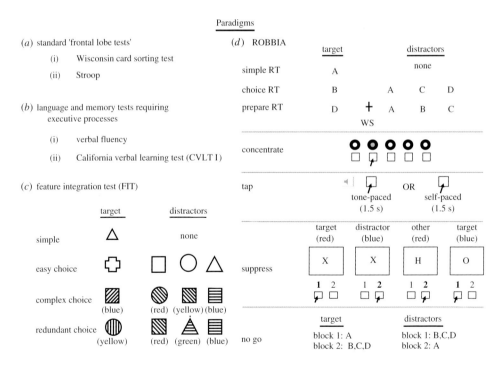

Fig. 12.1 The paradigms used in the various studies. (*a*) Based on commonly used neuropsychological tests of 'frontal lobe' functions: adapted from Wisconsin Card Sorting Test (WCST) and Stroop. (*b*) Language and memory tests that require executive processes: letter fluency and word list learning (CVLT I). (*c*) Three conditions of a FIT are described. (*d*) Finally, several tests from the ROtman-Baycrest Battery to Investigate Attention (ROBBIA) are presented. Test administration and the selected control measures are described in more detail in appendix A.

probe levels of attention and response control (all of the tests are shown and explained in figure 12.1 and appendix A). In each section below, we start with the more precisely defined ROBBIA tests, ending with the more complex clinical tests.

(d) Summary of approach

Our goal was to determine whether all focal frontal lesions produced a similar impairment in cognitive supervisory control or whether lesions in different regions produced specific impairments that might or might not appear on a task depending upon the particular demands of the task.[1] There is currently evidence for at least three separate frontal processes related to attention, each related to a different region within the frontal lobes as illuminated by deficit profiles after injury. We have labelled these processes as *energization*, *task setting* and *monitoring*. For each process, we start with our conclusions, and present a current description of the process and data that support the existence of each distinct process. In some instances, we have reanalysed the original data to be consistent across the tasks. The possibility of a type I error is minimized by the replication of the findings: the replications often occur across the tasks, including tasks of different cognitive modalities (e.g. RT paradigms, memory); the same results can be demonstrated with different patient groups, minimizing the possibility that the results are unique to a specific set of patients[2]; in some cases, there is supporting evidence from other research laboratories.

(e) Definition of 'energization'

Energization is the process of initiation and sustaining of any response. The basis for proposing an energization function comes from neurophysiological observations that there is an internal tendency for any neural activity to become quiescent in the absence of input. A natural extension of the supervisory system model is to assume that, in the absence of external triggers or motivational conditions to optimize responding, lower level perceptual or motor schemata would have to be energized or re-energized when activation becomes low, as would be required, for example, for detecting occasional stimuli or performing occasional motor acts. Without energization, setting and sustaining a specific selected response cannot occur and maintaining performance over prolonged periods of time will waver.

(f) Evidence for energization and putative frontal localization

Deficient energization is most consistently associated with lesions in the SM region bilaterally, with some evidence for a more important role for the right SM area (figure 12.2).

The ROBBIA *simple* and *choice RT* tests differed in that the choice RT tasks required an easy differentiation of the feature of the target stimulus and the presence of distractors (Stuss *et al*. 2005; see figure 12.1 and appendix A for further task details). In both the tests, there was a significant slowing of the SM patients only, with the hotspotting technique highlighting primarily areas 24 and 32 (figure 12.2*a*). The involvement of the SM region appeared to be more pronounced in the somewhat more demanding task. In the simple RT, the SM group was marginally slower than the control group ($p=0.06$); in the choice RT, the significant difference was $p=0.007$. The slowing was not a factor of lesion size, since the SM group was the slowest by far, and there was no relation of lesion size to RT in the SM group (e.g. $p=0.6$–0.9 for the different tasks). Lesion location is a better predictor of response slowing than lesion size.

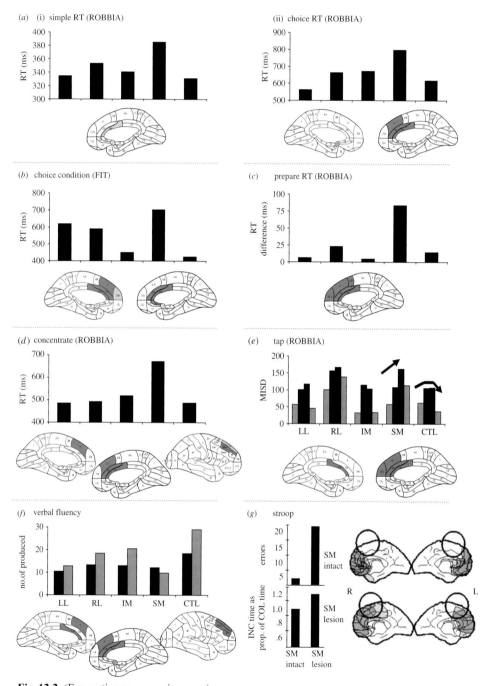

Fig. 12.2 (For caption see opposite page.)

Fig. 12.2 Quantitative data illustrated in graphs for coarse frontal anatomical groupings (most often, left lateral (LL), right lateral (RL), inferior medial (IM) and superior medial (SM)) compared with a matched control (CTL) group (see Stuss *et al.* 1998, for methods), for each illustrated paradigm in figures 12.2–12.4. Note that the baselines may differ from test to test for illustrative purposes. Corresponding to the quantitative data for each test, the architectonic 'hotspots' are depicted in the brain diagrams. Hotspots are those architectonic regions damaged in at least three patients who have significantly impaired performance compared with all other patients who do not have damage in those regions. In the coarse anatomical breakdown used for *x*-axis in graphs, the patient is assigned to a group based on the predominant localization; there may be some overlap with an adjoining region. For example, SM or IM patients may have some overlap into the lateral region. The hotspotting technique emphasizes the specific architectonic localization regardless of coarse grouping. 'Energization' is consistently impaired after damage to the SM region bilaterally, with some emphasis on the right SM area. All measures (except for *g*) are RTs. In the brain diagrams, only the medial regions are illustrated, unless the lateral regions identified by this hotspotting technique are continuous with the medial pathology. In (*a*(i), (ii) and *b*) the simple and choice RTs and (*d*) concentrate, only the RT of the SM group is significantly slower than the CTL group. For prepare RT (*c*), the measure depicts the difference between RTs for the 1 and 3 s warning conditions. The tap measure (*e*) is the mean intra-individual standard deviation (ISD). The light coloured bars indicate externally paced tapping via tones, the dark bars self-paced tapping. The CTL group exhibited greater variability of performance for the self-timed condition compared with the externally timed condition. The SM group increased in ISD in both condition replications and the slowing with replication is indicated by the direction of arrow. The IM and LL were comparable with the control group (see figure 4*b* for interpretation of the RL group). In the verbal fluency task (*f*), the number of words produced in the first 15 s (black bars) was compared with the last 45 s (grey bars). The architectonic hotspot was completed using the difference between these two measures. Analysis of the most important brain region in the Stroop task (*g*) was carried out by comparison of overlapping lesions. If the SM area was damaged, the result was a significantly higher number of errors and slower speed of task completion compared with the colour naming condition. INC, incongruent; COL, colour naming.

The RT results of the *feature integration test* (Stuss *et al.* 2002*b*), similar in design to the simple and choice RT tests of ROBBIA, yielded similar results (figure 12.2*b*).

In the *prepare RT* test (Stuss *et al.* 2005; figure 12.2*c*), we analysed whether a warning stimulus presented either 1 or 3 s prior to a choice RT affected speed of response. In all the three conditions (no warning, 1 s warning and 3 s warning), the overall significant SM slowing remained. All groups benefited from the 1 s warning, and all groups were slower on the 3 s warning condition compared with the 1 s warning. The 3 s warning RT was still faster than without a warning in all but one group, the SM group. Figure 12.2*c* shows the difference in RT between the 3 and 1 s warning conditions. The loss of benefit for the SM group from the longer warning interval is compatible with a deficit in sustaining energized attention and response systems. The fact that there were not significant differences in errors among the conditions suggests that this cannot be secondary to a deficit in noticing and reacting to signals.

The ROBBIA *concentrate* test perhaps illustrates the energization deficit most clearly (Alexander *et al.* 2005; figure 12.2*d*). It is very simple in structure but requires high levels of sustained attention. Only patients with lesions in SM frontal regions had significant RT slowness, and this was consistent across the entire test. This group's mean RT was 33% greater than the other patient groups and the control subjects. The prolonged RT was not simply due to fatigue or errors, as the slowness was evident from the beginning across 500 trials. We had initially hypothesized that the anterior cingulate gyrus (ACG) would be the critical region (Paus *et al*. 1997; Luu *et al*. 2000*a*). However, the critical region was larger and involved supplementary motor area (SMA) and the preSMA region (P & P areas 24, 32, 9 and 46d). The noted slowness with right SM lesions on this test requiring sustained concentration was interpreted as an insufficient energizing of attention to respond.

The ROBBIA *tap* test consisted of two simple timing tasks, one requiring tapping to an externally driven stimulus (every 1.5 s), and another demanding maintenance of the same regular response rhythm without any external stimulus (Picton *et al*. 2006). Normal performance is illustrated in the control group (see CTL in figure 12.2*e*). An increase in the variability of timing performance, *as the task continued* (see rising arrow), was noted in patients with lesions to the SM regions of the frontal lobe (figure 12.2*e*). The SM frontal area is necessary to maintain consistent timing performance over prolonged periods of time.

This energization function was also revealed in two standard clinical frontal lobe tests. An energization function should be applicable to any task. Evidence for this function was observed in a *verbal fluency* language task, requiring the generation of words beginning with a specific letter over 60 s (Stuss *et al*. 1998). All groups produced fewer words over time, but the total of the last 45 s (grey versus black bars in figure 12.2*f*) was greater in all but the SM group. The critical region again was the SM area (figure 12.2*f*).

We administered the classic Comalli *et al*. (1962) *Stroop* version with three conditions: word reading; colour naming of colour patches; and colour naming of colour words printed in a colour different from that of the word (interference; Stuss *et al*. 2001). Patients with frontal and non-frontal pathology were compared with normal control subjects. Patients with posterior lesions were not significantly deficient in any condition. Within the frontal patients, bilateral SM frontal as well as right superior posteromedial lesions were significantly associated with increased errors and slowness in response time for the incongruent condition (figure 12.2*g*), an impairment interpreted as failure of maintenance of consistent activation of the intended response in the incongruent Stroop condition. This inability to maintain an activated response mode appeared consistent with the rapid decline in preparatory activation from 1 to 3 s after a warning stimulus in the prepare RT.

(g) Interim summary for energization

Decreased facilitation (energizing) of the neural systems that are needed to make the decisions (contention scheduling) and initiate the responses (schemata) is impaired after bilateral SM frontal lesions, with suggestion of greater importance for the right SM region. Supportive data came from different RT tasks, from studies in different modalities (RT, language) and across different patients. The SM deficit was demonstrated by prolonged simple RT, proportionately greater prolongation of choice RT, inability to sustain preparation to respond, inability to maintain consistent short time-intervals in a task, diminished output in a verbal fluency test, and increased errors and slower speed in a Stroop test. The localization is similar in each study, although comparison of the different tests suggests that there was some relationship of the severity of the deficit with the demands of the test. The time course across the tasks (e.g. from a few seconds—prepare RT to 1 min— fluency) implies that this region is important for initial energization as well as sustaining of energization; future research might also unveil potential localization or context differences related to the initial energization versus sustaining.

Our data, and we believe our interpretation, appear to support other research and theories of the functions of this region (e.g. Luria 1973; Drewe 1975*b*; Leimkuhler & Mesulam 1985; Passingham 1993; Richer *et al*. 1993; Godefroy *et al*. 1994; Picard & Strick 1996; Paus 2001). It is also compatible with one theoretical explanation of Stroop interference performance, which emphasizes maintenance of the strength of the activated intention, a strength which can wax and wane along a gradient (Cohen *et al*. 1990; West & Baylis 1998; Kornblum *et al*. 1999).

These findings are also concordant with clinical observations. Bilateral damage to ACG and SMA produces akinetic mutism, a dramatic example of deficient energizing (Plum & Posner 1980; Devinsky *et al*. 1995; Alexander 2001). Changes in activity of the cingulate cortex occur as a function of sleep stages (Hofle *et al*. 1997), vigilance (Paus *et al*. 1997) and alertness (Luu *et al*. 2000*a*,*b*). We consider the energizing deficit in SM patients independent of general arousal as, in our studies, there was no correlation or interaction of slowness and reported sleepiness or level of motivation among groups (Stuss *et al*. 2005). We therefore think that energizing schemata is the process that allows subjects to maintain their concentration on a particular task. In the neurological literature, this would correspond to phasic attention (Stuss & Benson 1984, 1986); in the information processing literature, energization would correspond to the effort system of Hockey (1993).

(h) Definition of task setting

Each of the tests in which the task setting attentional process is demonstrated requires the ability to set a stimulus–response relationship. Task setting would be necessary in the initial stages of learning to drive a car or planning a wedding. This may be initiated *a priori* and is most often learned and consolidated through trial and error. In easier tasks, task setting would be more relevant in the early stages. Any deficit would be more evident under conditions that require continuous refreshing and suppression of more salient responses. The establishment of the connection between a stimulus and a response would require formation of a criterion to respond to a defined target with specific attributes, organization of the schemata necessary to complete a particular task and adjustment of contention scheduling, so that the automatic processes of moving through the steps of a task can work more smoothly. Owing to the role of the SM region in energization in some tasks addressing task setting (and monitoring below), there could be evidence of SM involvement. This is not illustrated.

(i) Evidence for the task setting process and putative frontal localization

Task setting is consistently impaired after damage to the LL region of the frontal lobes, most often with a more ventrolateral distribution (figure 12.3).

Errors in the ROBBIA concentrate (see figure 12.1 for task description) task were noted primarily in the first 100 out of 500 trials, and these were made maximally by patients with damage to left frontal P & P Areas 44, 45A and 45B and 47/12 (Alexander *et al*. 2005; figure 12.3*a*). This was not associated with decreased RT (no time–accuracy trade-off) or increased RT (no awareness and monitoring of errors). The difficulty was interpreted as defective setting of specific stimulus– response contingencies (see also Godefroy *et al*. 1994, 1999). Once in 'task responding set' (after the first 100 trials), there were no deficits in any subgroup of patients.

The *suppress* task in ROBBIA was a variant of the Stroop, a test which assesses the ability of patients to control intact cognitive operations under the condition of conflicting possible responses (Alexander *et al*. in press). Lesions of the left ventrolateral region (areas 44 and 45)

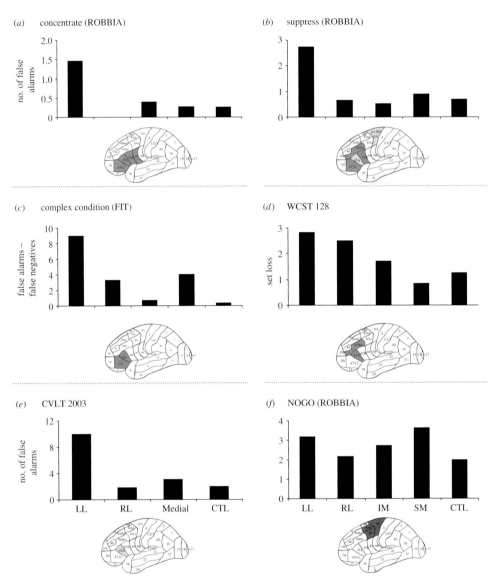

(a) concentrate (ROBBIA)

(b) suppress (ROBBIA)

(c) complex condition (FIT)

(d) WCST 128

(e) CVLT 2003

(f) NOGO (ROBBIA)

Fig. 12.3 'Task setting' process is consistently impaired after damage to the LL frontal region. Figure 12. 3 is organized in a similar manner to figure 12. 2. The tests are illustrated and explained in figure 1 and appendix A. There were no significant impairments after RL pathology. Where the measure is RT, there would also be involvement of the SM region, as described in figure 12. 2. The measure for concentrate is the number of errors in the first 100 out of 500 trials. In suppress, a Stroop-like task, and in NOGO, a motor suppression task, false positives are the dependent measurement. In the complex condition of the feature integration task (FIT), the false positives were subtracted from the number of false negative responses to isolate task setting from monitoring. In the WCST, the coarse anatomical groupings used in the graphs indicate that set loss is evident after pathology in both RL and LL frontal regions. The hotspotting method, however, (brain diagrams) suggests that maximum involvement in this mode of WCST administration is related to the left ventrolateral region. A task setting deficit is evident in memory tasks as well, as noted in the number of false positive responses in the recognition recall of the CVLT. In this study, all patients with medial pathology were originally grouped together.

produced an impairment in setting contingent response rules as indexed by the number of false alarms (figure 12.3*b*).

The importance of isolating the process is illustrated by an analysis of the *feature integration test complex condition* (three features). We had hypothesized that making false positive errors would be an index of task (criterion) setting to respond appropriately to the target as opposed to non-targets (Stuss *et al.* 2002*b*). The first architectonic analysis was surprising—the RL region appeared to be most associated with this type of error (cf. figure 12.4*c*). However, patients with damage to this RL region made errors of all kinds, which we interpreted as a monitoring impairment (see below for analysis of just false negative errors). We subtracted the false negative from the false positive responses to isolate the patients who made primarily the type of errors indicating that they could not set a task criterion to respond 'yes' (response bias—false positives). When the architectonic analysis was redone isolating the false positive responders, the major area of impairment was now focally left frontal (figure 12.3*c*).

Another important example of process isolation, and the need to understand that the experimental manipulation may define what a specific measure may represent, occurred in the analysis of the *WCST* results (Stuss *et al.* 2000). In the 128 card condition, set loss would probably reflect primarily the potential trial and error learning of the correct sorting criterion, in a way similar to the early trial errors in concentrate, as well as some degree of monitoring. In the 64B condition, in which the subject had been informed of the three sorting criteria, what criterion to start with and when the criterion had changed (i.e. the task parameters had been quite specifically established), set loss errors more probably indexed the online monitoring and checking of performance, since the task had been set by the explicit instructions. The hotspot analysis confirmed this hypothesis. In the 128 condition, although set loss problems were apparent after both LL and RL damage, the identified most relevant area was the LL region (areas 9/46v, 45A; figure 12.3*d*); in 64B, set loss was related to damage in the RL region (areas 6B, 44, 45A and 45B; figure 12.4*d*).

Task setting impairment, as indexed by difficulty in establishing an appropriate response criterion, can also be observed in *memory* tasks. We have now administered three different word lists (one of them being the standardized California Verbal Learning Test, CVLT) to three different groups of frontal lobe patients. In the first study, the left frontal group was most impaired in the number of false positives (the hotspotting technique had not yet been developed; Stuss *et al.* 1994). The number of false positives in the CVLT study was associated with damage in the LL area 45A (Alexander *et al.* 2003; figure 12.3*e*).

One task resulted in a more caudal localization than the other task setting effects. In a response inhibition (*NOGO*) task, four equiprobable stimuli (letters A, B, C and D) were presented in two different conditions (Picton *et al.* in press). In the first condition, the subject responded to the letter A only; in the second condition, the subject responded to the letters B, C and D, and not to A. These two conditions were called the 'improbable-go' and the 'improbable-nogo'. An increased number of false alarms (incorrect responses to the nogo stimulus) were found primarily in patients with lesions to left SM (6A) and LL regions' area (8B, area 9/46) of the frontal lobes (figure 12.3*f*). Although our patients were primarily right handed, the involvement of the LL and superior region in nogo motor control is probably independent of response hand (Talati & Hirsch 2005). Our localization results appear comparable to the original nogo study of Drewe (1975*a*,*b*), clinical studies (Verfaille & Heilman 1987) and other human and animal research (Brutkowski 1965; Iversen & Mishkin 1970). Some of the variability of the results in other go–nogo paradigms may derive from the differing cognitive requirements.

(j) Interim summary of task setting

If the task setting process can be isolated, there is consistent evidence that left frontal damage disturbs this process. The task setting–left frontal relationship was observed in different RT tests, the clinical WCST and word list learning. Different patient populations were examined in several of these studies. It is yet uncertain if any variation in task setting localization observed in our tasks is a reflection of inadequate sampling of different brain regions or a reflection of a more general left frontal function interacting with more specific task demands (e.g. response task setting). In general, our findings support Luria's (1966) postulate that damage to the left frontal lobes damages the patient's ability to use task instructions to direct behaviour (verbal regulation of behaviour), even when clearly able to comprehend their meaning.

Other lesion studies using similar patients attempted to identify regional frontal effects using the Stroop task and define underlying impaired neural mechanisms; with some discrepancies in localization details attributable to differences in patient populations and precision of lesion definition, they, in general, support our findings that LL lesions affect setting of stimulus–response contingencies (while SM lesions affect energizing attention to task; Perret 1974; Richer *et al.* 1993).

We believe that fMRI studies using variations of the standard Stroop paradigm also generally support our hypotheses. Derfus *et al.* (2005) completed a meta-analysis of all neuroimaging studies with sufficient data on task switching and the Stroop published from 2000 to 2004. The major localizations for the Stroop studies were in the left inferior frontal gyrus (IFG) (areas 44 and 6; with the next largest clusters in bilateral SM cortex, areas 32/6 and 32/9; see also Brass & von Cramon 2004). Localizations were similar if tasks had similar properties to the Stroop. Their conclusion was that the left VL region was the critical region for updating task representations.

(k) Definition of monitoring

Monitoring is the process of checking the task over time for 'quality control' and the adjustment of behaviour. Monitoring may occur at many levels: the ongoing activity in a task-specific schema; the timing of activity; anticipation of a stimulus actually occurring; detecting the occurrence of errors; and detecting discrepancies between the behavioural response and external reality. If an anomaly or problem is detected by monitoring, then an interrupt or explicit modulation of the ongoing programme would occur.

(l) Evidence for the monitoring process and putative frontal localization

Our results demonstrate that lesions of the RL prefrontal cortex critically impair monitoring as defined previously (figure 12.4).

Interstimulus intervals (ISI) in the ROBBIA simple and choice RT tests provided the opportunity to assess the ability of the different patient groups to monitor the interval between trials. The control group showed a normal foreperiod effect, namely a gradual decrease in RT with ISI (Niemi & Näätänen 1981). Only the RL group exhibited a reverse foreperiod effect, an increase in RT with increasing ISI as opposed to the decrease in the control group and all other patient groups (figure 12.4*a*). This was evident across both tests, although more evident in the more demanding choice RT test. The architectonic hotspotting of the difference in RT between late and short ISI revealed maximum impairment in areas 9, 9/46d and 9/46v. Vallesi *et al.*

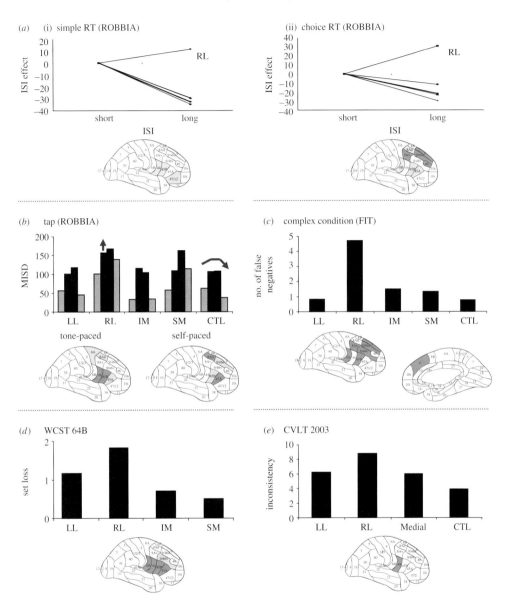

Fig. 12.4 'Monitoring' process is consistently impaired after damage to the RL frontal area. The tests are illustrated and explained in figure 1 and appendix A. The dependent measures vary among tasks. The RTs for the short (3, 4 s) and long (6, 7 s) ISIs are compared among groups by setting the short ISIs for each group to zero, and then illustrating the difference in RT between the long and short ISIs. The measurement for tap is the same as in figure 12. 2—the mean intra-individual variability across repeated taps. The arrow over the RL group indicates that this group has a significantly greater ISD across both conditions and replications. In the FIT complex (three features) condition, the greatest number of errors was associated with damage to the RL region. In this figure, emphasis is placed on the number of false negatives to differentiate from the effect of false positive errors, which reflects task setting also. Set loss for the WCST 128 condition is defined in figure 12. 3. Inconsistency in recall for the CVLT word list learning test indicates the 'in and out' recall of words across the learning trials.

(2007), using TMS over right frontal lateral, left frontal lateral and right angular gyrus in healthy young adults, demonstrated an abnormal foreperiod effect independent of any sequential effect only after RL stimulation. Damage to the RL frontal region impairs the modulation of expectancy. Our study had suggested that this was related to time estimation, but Vallesi used much shorter ISIs (0.5–1.5 s) and revealed the same effect, indicating that the role of RL region in monitoring is not just over longer periods of time. The RL region may be involved in monitoring of temporal information which may be required explicitly as in time reproduction or discrimination tasks (e.g. Basso *et al.* 2003; Lewis & Miall 2003; Picton *et al.* in press) or implicitly as in the foreperiod effect.

In the tap experiment (Picton *et al.* 2007), requiring tapping at a rate of once in every 1.5 s either in response to an external stimulus or self-timed, patients with lesions to the RL frontal lobe, particularly involving P & P area 45 and the subjacent regions of the basal ganglia, had an abnormally high intra-individual variability in both self- and tone-timed conditions (figure 12.4*b*). This impairment was interpreted as deficient monitoring of the passage of the intervals, although a potential role in generating time-intervals could not be excluded.

The monitoring deficit in relation to checking performance of errors was noted in the FIT (Stuss *et al.* 2002*b*). In contrast to the LL group who exhibited false positive errors in the complex three-feature integration condition, the RL group made errors of all kinds: false positives; false negatives; and omissions. Architectonic localization of the false negative errors alone, to minimize any task setting impact, reveals the importance of the RL region in monitoring performance (figure 12.4*c*).

Our modification of the WCST, moving from less (128 card) to more structure (64B condition), revealed that set loss errors were more associated with the LL frontal region, when the task was unstructured and subjects were learning what the criteria were and how to perform the task. But the same measure was associated with the RL region instead when the major task demands have been explained to the patients (informed of the three criteria that colour would be the first and the criterion would change after 10 consecutive correct trials), interpreted as deficient monitoring and checking of performance over time (figure 12.4*d*).

In our original study of *word list learning*, there was an association of RL pathology with two measures that we considered monitoring (Stuss *et al.* 1994). Double recalls were defined as the recall of a word that had already been recalled, but only after at least one intervening word. Inconsistency was a measure of the 'in and out' recall of the same word over different trials. In the replication of this study with the CVLT (Alexander *et al.* 2003), the hotspotting technique did support the predominantly RL (primarily ventrolateral) relationship with the measure of inconsistency. A more direct reflection of this 'checking' role of the RL region was achieved by Turner *et al.* (in press). Functional imaging of memory also indicates an RL role in monitoring of memory (Henson *et al.* 1999; Fletcher & Henson 2001).

(m) Interim summary of monitoring

Lesions of the RL frontal region produce impairments in monitoring and checking of performance over time. This has been shown by a failure to show a decrease in RT with variable foreperiods, contrasted to normally maintained energizing over a fixed warning interval. In essence, the patients fail to note that a stimulus has not yet occurred, hampering their preparedness to respond. The RL group also fail to note that an error has occurred and do not adjust their performance accordingly. These data and interpretation are compatible with imaging and lesion research in 'vigilance' and monitoring (Wilkins *et al.* 1987; Pardo *et al.* 1991; Rueckert &

Grafman 1996; Coull *et al.* 1998; Henson *et al.* 1999; Fletcher & Henson 2001; Shallice 2001, 2002). Functional lesions using transcranial magnetic stimulation over short ISIs suggest that the monitoring is not necessarily limited to 'vigilance' over time in the classic sense (Vallesi et al. 2007).

The difficulty in monitoring the on going passage of the ISI to prepare responsiveness over time is corroborated by the results of the TAP experiment. Although it is possible that prefrontal lesions impair time perception (e.g. Mangels *et al.* 1998), the variability in time perception throughout the entire experiment whether paced or unpaced promotes the idea of a deficit in monitoring a 'clock'.

Comparing the SM and RL groups illuminates the type of regionally specific effects that we originally proposed. The RL group alone revealed an abnormal foreperiod effect (ISI effect) when ISI was manipulated. In the TAP test, the patients with RL pathology showed greater variability of performance throughout the test; the SM patients, on the other hand, showed a significant increase in the variability of the responses as the test continued. Taken together, one might hypothesize that the areas of the RL region may interact with the SM regions to initiate or maintain phasic arousal. The RL frontal lobe is crucially involved in the ongoing control of timed behaviour, either owing to its role in generating time-intervals or in monitoring the passage of these intervals. In contrast, the SM regions of the frontal lobe are necessary to maintain consistent timing performance over prolonged periods of time. Lesions to either of these areas may thus generally slow the responses, but for entirely different reasons that become clear only when the fundamental processes dependent on the different regions are explicitly measured.

12.2 An overview

(a) What of inhibition?

Our model appears to give no special place to a process—inhibition—that classic neuropsychology implies is a major function of the frontal lobes (see also Robbins 2007). The interpretation of our data, including the classic 'inhibitory' tasks such as the Stroop, did not have to rely on inhibition as an explanatory phenomenon. Apparent inhibitory processes can be explained by our triad of frontal processes: energization; task setting; and monitoring. Inhibition clearly does exist neurobiologically and neurochemically. Is it possible that inhibition exists only at the level of biology and not psychology? A different theoretical construct, proposed by Cohen and colleagues (Braver *et al.* 1999), also does not rely on inhibition at an explanatory level. In an earlier study (Stuss *et al.* 1999), in which we did not have the localizing power of later studies, we had suggested that not only are there frontal inhibitory processes, but also there are different frontal inhibitory processes. In retrospect, however, these data could be explained in light of our current triad. Clearly, this is an avenue of future exploration.

(b) Integrated systems and task demands

Demonstrating fractionation of frontal lobe functions does not imply a set of independent processes. These processes are flexibly assembled in response to context, complexity and intention over real time into different networks within the frontal regions (and between frontal and posterior regions; see also Vuilleumier & Driver 2007; and this volume). Depending on task demands, there may be recruitment of processes within the frontal lobes. In some cases, 'top-down' recruitment of posterior processes is demanded. In tasks with simple demands, the more automatic non-frontal processes function independently, but with increase in task requirements, an increased involvement of different frontal (more 'strategic') regions may be required, even to the point where it appears that all frontal regions are involved.

This dynamic interaction can occur among the different domain-general frontal lobe processes, and between the frontal lobe domain-general and more posterior domain-specific functions (see Stuss *et al.* 1999, 2002*a*; Stuss 2006 for illustrations). Examples occur in how we learn (memory), pay attention and communicate. Take the example of language (Alexander 2006). The 'executive' or domain-general frontal lobe processes are not required for answering simple questions, requesting an object or recounting an old familiar story. However, telling a complex narrative, or composing a complicated response to a difficult question requires setting the task goal (what to include, what does the listener already know of the story and what is socially appropriate for this occasion), energization (to plan, and to activate and sustain the intention) and monitoring (keeping track of the objective and content and the listener's response). These frontal lobe operations also demand a series of posterior cognitive operations, and all of these must be recruited and interwoven at different levels and different times.

12.3 Conclusions

Research in patients with focal circumscribed chronic frontal lobe lesions demonstrates that specific, highly differentiated attentional deficits are associated with discrete regional frontal injuries and, at least in patients with single focal circumscribed lesions, there is no undifferentiated 'frontal lobe syndrome' or 'dysexecutive' disorder.

In the area of attention, three separate functions can be demonstrated consistently: energization, related to damage in the SM frontal area, possibly predominantly right; task setting—LL; and monitoring—RL. Further division within the lateral regions, perhaps related to posterior connectivity, has not yet been examined.

These processes are indeed 'supervisory', in that they are important for the control of lower-order processes. Since they interact with many other modular cognitive modalities, these processes are domain-general. The functioning of what has been called the central executive or supervisory system can be explained by the flexible assembly of these processes in response to context, complexity and intention over real time into different networks within the frontal regions, and between frontal and posterior regions. There is no overarching supervisory system—no 'ghost in the machine'—that is higher in the hierarchy.

Funding for the research described in this study was provided primarily by the Canadian Institutes of Health Research Grants no. 108636, and MRC-GR-14974. Thanks to the co-authors on the various papers referenced, all of our staff who have worked on these studies over the years and the patients and subjects who contributed their time. We are especially indebted to Susan Gillingham for figure and manuscript preparation.

Endnotes

1 We believe there is evidence for four categories of frontal lobe functions, which supports the fractionation of frontal lobe functions: executive capacity (which we equate with attentional control), energization, behavioural self-regulation, and metacognition, which are related to different frontal anatomical

regions (Stuss & Levine 2002; Stuss 2007; Stuss & Alexander in press). Only the first two [executive (within this, task setting and monitoring), and energization] are described in this current paper. Other investigators have also considered the frontal lobes to have multiple processes (Burgess *et al.* 2007; Robbins 2007; see also this volume).

2 The following number of frontal patients were assessed in each of the categories of tests: clinical neuropsychological tests, 33–56, depending on the test; FIT, 25; ROBBIA, 43. Overlap of patients was as follows: no overlap between FIT and ROBBIA; 3 patients were common to ROBBIA and clinical neuropsychological tests; 16 of the FIT patients were also assessed in the clinical neuropsychological tests.

Appendix A. Descriptions of tests and measures

(a) Standard 'frontal lobe' tests

Two standard 'frontal lobe' tests were administered and they are described as follows:

(i) Wisconsin Card Sorting Test (WCST; Milner 1963)

In our study (Stuss *et al.* 2000), the test was administered three times in the order described below, each administration increasing in the amount of information and/or external structure provided.

128 cards: all 128 cards were administered, following the administration procedure of Milner (1963).

64 cards (64A): the subject was informed what the three sorting criteria were (colour, form and number), and an additional 64 cards were administered, again starting with colour as the first criterion.

64 cards (64B): the subject was again informed of the three sorting criteria, but now, in addition, was told that colour was the initial sorting criterion, and that the criterion would change after 10 consecutive responses.

The dependent measure used in this paper to illustrate the different attentional processes was 'set loss', defined in our research as the number of times an error is made after at least three consecutively correct responses, one of which has to be unambiguously correct to indicate that there had been experience with the correct sorting criterion. Set loss in conditions 128 and 64B are compared. In condition 128, the subject is hypothetically using trial and error to learn the criteria. Set loss in this condition would be more likely to reflect the discovery and establishment of the correct criterion. In condition 64B, the subject is provided with much more structure and information. Set loss in this case is more probably related to the monitoring of responses rather than setting the response.

(ii) Stroop (Comalli et al. 1962)

In our study (Stuss *et al.* 2001), we used the Comalli *et al.* (1962) version often used clinically. There were three conditions, 100 stimuli in each condition: reading colour words (red, blue and green) printed in black; naming colour patches (R, B and G); naming the colour of ink in which a colour name is printed when the colour is incongruent with the name ('red' printed in the colour green; the Stroop interference effect).

The dependent measurement for this study was the number of errors made in each condition.

(b) Language and memory tests requiring executive processes

(i) Verbal fluency (Borkowski et al. 1967)

We analysed the performance of patients with focal frontal lesions on verbal fluency (Stuss *et al.* 1998). For letter fluency, subjects were required to generate words (no proper names), beginning with letters F, A, and then S, over a duration of 1 min per letter.

For this paper, we compared the number of correct words produced. To isolate the energization process, the time was divided into first 15 and last 45 s. The loss of energization was evaluated by comparing the number of words generated in the first 15 s to that generated in the last 45 s.

(ii) California Verbal Learning Test (CVLT I; Delis et al. 1987)

We (Alexander *et al.* 2003) administered the CVLT to a large group of frontal patients over many years, using the first version of the CVLT, using the standard administration.

Two measures are emphasized in this current paper to illustrate how different attentional processes can be necessary for successful memory performance. A measure of bias in recognition memory, the establishment of a criterion or threshold for saying 'yes' to words presented for recognition, is defined as the number of false positive responses (the number of times a subject says 'yes' to a non-target word). The measure of monitoring we use is 'inconsistency', defined as the number of times a word is recalled on one trial, then forgotten on the next, and so on.

(c) Feature integration test (FIT; Stuss et al. 1989, 2002b)

In each of the following tests of FIT, the subject was asked to respond as quickly as possible but not at the cost of making errors.

 (i) *Simple RT.* One stimulus consisting of a simple shape (e.g. circle) was repeated for 50 trials.
(ii) *Single feature detection (easy choice RT).* Four single geometrical shapes (e.g. circle, square, triangle and cross) were presented randomly. One shape was designated as a target, the other three were non-targets. The subject responded to the target with the dominant hand and to the non-target with the non-dominant hand.
(iii) *Three feature detection (complex RT).* The target was defined as a unique combination of a colour, shape and line orientation within the shape (e.g. a blue circle with horizontal lines inside the circle). The non-targets could share none, one or two features with the target.

Dependent measures were RT speed and the type and number of errors. In this current paper, we present only the results for the three feature detection test (complex RT). Error types analysed were false positives (non-target responded to as a target) and false negatives (target responded to as a non-target).

(d) ROBBIA (ROtman-Baycrest Battery to Investigate Attention; Alexander et al. 2005; Stuss et al. 2005; Picton et al. 2006, 2007)

Several tests were developed as part of the *RO*tman-*B*aycrest *B*attery to *I*nvestigate *A*ttention. Many of them evolved from the FIT.

(i) *Simple RT*. For the simple RT, the capital letter 'A' was presented 50 times repeatedly and subjects responded by pressing button 1 as soon as the letter was presented.

(ii) *Choice RT (single feature choice)*. The target was defined as one of the four letters (A, B, C and D) presented 25% of the time, the remaining letters being non-target feature distractors, each also presented with a probability of 25%. Responses were made to both targets and non-targets as in FIT; button 1 was pressed for the target and button 2 for the non-targets.

Few errors were made in the simple and choice RT tests. The dependent measurements were overall RT, as well as RT divided by interstimulus intervals (ISI). ISIs in the ROBBIA simple and choice RT tests were set at 3,4, 5, 6 or 7 s, with each ISI occurring 10 times in a random order. The ISI was defined as the time from the offset of one stimulus (at the response) to the onset of the next (and is equivalent to response-to-stimulus interval).

(iii) *Prepare RT*. In this condition, choice RT (mentioned previously) with nowarning stimulus was compared with two conditions with warning stimuli, 1 or 3 s prior to the trial.

Again, there were few errors in this test. Dependent measurements were RTs in each condition. The simple, choice and prepare data were presented in detail in Stuss *et al.* (2005).

(iv) *Concentrate*. Concentrate is a rapid serial response task consisting of five LEDs, each of which having a response button directly under the LED (Alexander *et al.* 2005). The LEDs would illuminate randomly. The subject's task was to press the response button directly under the LED when illuminated. Over an approximately 5 min period, 500 trials were presented continuously. Working memory demands are minimized, as the response demands are driven by the light illumination.

Dependent measurements in concentrate were the overall RT, as well as the number of errors, the latter divided by occurrence within each 100 trials.

(v) *Tap* . The primary task in tap was to tap a response button at a rate of once every 1.5 s. There were two conditions, one requiring responding in time with a tone that regularly repeated and another demanding maintenance of the same regular response rhythm without any external stimulus.

The dependent measurement here was the intra-individual standard deviation, a measure of individual variability in performance, assessing the ability to maintain appropriate timing over time.

(vi) *Suppress*. Suppress assesses processes similar to the Stroop. Red or blue letters were presented at a rate of once every 3–4 s. For targets (25%), a red 'X' or a blue 'O', the subject pressed button 1; for all non-targets, button 2. The non-target 'Stroop' distractors (25%) were either a red 'O' or a blue 'X'. Other non-targets (50%) were letters other than 'X' and 'O' in blue or red, excluding the potentially visually confusing letters C,D,G,Q,K and Y (Alexander *et al.* 2007).

Dependent measurement was the number of false positive errors (the identification of any non-target as a target).

(vii) *Nogo*. In this test, we evaluated the ability to withhold responses to stimuli of varying probabilities of presentation (Picton *et al.* 2007). Two conditions were administered; in each, four letters (A, B, C and D) were randomly presented with 25% probability. In the first condition, a response was required to the letter A, but no response for other letters

(B, C and D). In the second half of the experiment, a response was required to the letters B, C and D but not to A.

The dependent measurement in nogo was the number of false alarms (or false positives).

References

Alexander, M. P. 2001 Chronic akinetic mutism after mesencephalic–diencephalic infarction: remediated with dopaminergic medications. *Neurorehabil. Neural Repair* **15**, 151–156.

Alexander, M. P. 2006 Impairments of procedures for implementing complex language are due to disruption of frontal attention processes. *J. Int. Neuropsychol. Soc.* **12**, 236–247.

Alexander, M. P., Stuss, D. T. & Fansabedian, N. 2003 California verbal learning test: performance by patients with focal frontal and non-frontal lesions. *Brain* **126**, 1493–1503. (doi:10.1093/brain/awg128)

Alexander, M. P., Stuss, D. T., Shallice, T., Picton, T. W. & Gillingham, S. 2005 Impaired concentration due to frontal lobe damage from two distinct lesion sites. *Neurology* **65**, 572–579. (doi:10.1212/01.wnl.0000172912.07640.92)

Alexander, M. P., Stuss, D. T., Picton, T., Shallice, T. & Gillingham, S. 2007. Regional frontal injuries cause distinct forms of impaired attention to respond. *Neurology.* **68**, 1515–1523.

Basso, G., Nichelli, P., Wharton, C. M., Peterson, M. & Grafman, J. 2003 Distributed neural systems for temporal production: a functional MRI study. *Brain Res. Bull.* **59**, 405–411. (doi:10.1016/S0361-9230(02)00941-3)

Borkowski, J. G., Benton, A. L. & Spreen, O. 1967 Word fluency and brain damage. *Neuropsychologia* **5**, 135–140. (doi:10.1016/0028-3932(67)90015-2)

Brass, M. & von Cramon, D. Y. 2004 Selection for cognitive control: a functional magnetic resonance imaging study on the selection of task-relevant information. *J. Neurosci.* **24**, 8847–8852. (doi:10.1523/JNEUROSCI.2513-04.2004)

Braver, T. S., Barch, D. M. & Cohen, J. D. 1999 Cognition and control in schizophrenia: a computational model of dopamine and prefrontal function. *Biol. Psychiatry* **46**, 312–328. (doi:10.1016/S0006-3223(99)00116-X)

Brutkowski, S. 1965 Functions of prefrontal cortex in animals. *Physiol. Rev.* **45**, 721–746.

Burgess, P. W. & Shallice, T. 1994 Fractionnement du syndrome frontal. *Revue de Neuropsychologie* **4**, 345–370.

Burgess, P. W. & Shallice, T. 1996 Response suppression, initiation and strategy use following frontal lobe lesions. *Neuropsychologia* **34**, 263–272. (doi:10.1016/0028-3932 (95)00104-2)

Burgess, P. W., Gilbert, S. J. & Dumontheil, I. 2007 Function and localization within rostral prefrontal cortex (area 10). *Phil. Trans. R. Soc. B* **362**, 887–899. (doi:10.1098/rstb. 2007.2095)

Cohen, J. D., McClelland, J. L. & Dunbar, K. 1990 On the control of automatic processes: a parallel distributed processing account of the Stroop effect. *Psychol. Rev.* **97**, 332–361. (doi:10.1037/0033-295X.97.3.332)

Comalli, P. E., Wapner, S. & Werner, H. 1962 Interference effects of Stroop colour-word test in childhood, adulthood, and aging. *J. Gen. Psychol.* **100**, 47–53.

Coull, J. T., Frackowiak, R. S. & Frith, C. D. 1998 Monitoring for target objects: activation of right frontal and parietal cortices with increasing time on task. *Neuropsychologia* **36**, 1325–1334. (doi:10.1016/S0028-3932(98)00035-9)

Delis, D. C., Kramer, J., Kaplan, E. & Ober, B. A. 1987 *California verbal learning test (cvlt) manual.* San Antonio, TX: Psychological Corporation.

Derfus, J., Brass, M., Neumann, J. & von Cramon, D. Y. 2005 Involvement of the inferior frontal junction in cognitive control: meta-analyses of switching and Stroop studies. *Hum. Brain Mapp.* **25**, 22–34. (doi:10.1002/hbm.20127)

Devinsky, O., Morrell, M. & Vogt, B. A. 1995 Contributions of anterior cingulate cortex to behavior. *Brain* **118**, 279–306. (doi:10.1093/brain/118.1.279)

Diaz, R., Robbins, T. W. & Roberts, A. C. 1996 Dissociation in prefrontal cortex of affective attentional shifts. *Nature* **380**, 69–72. (doi:10.1038/380069a0)

Drewe, E. A. 1975*a* An experimental investigation of luria's theory on the effects of frontal lobe lesions in man. *Neuropsychologia* **13**, 421–429. (doi:10.1016/0028-3932 (75)90065-2)

Drewe, E. A. 1975*b* Go–no go learning after frontal lobe lesions in humans. *Cortex* **11**, 8–16.

Duncan, J. & Miller, E. K. 2002 Cognitive focus through adaptive neural coding in the primate prefrontal cortex. In *Principles of frontal lobe function* (eds D. T. Stuss & R. T. Knight), pp. 278–291. New York, NY: Oxford University Press.

Elsass, P. & Hartelius, H. 1985 Reaction time and brain disease: relations to location, etiology and progression of cerebral dysfunction. *Acta Neurol. Scand.* **71**, 11–19.

Fletcher, P. C. & Henson, R. N. 2001 Frontal lobes and human memory: insights from functional neuroimaging. *Brain* **124**, 849–881. (doi:10.1093/brain/124.5.849)

Godefroy, O., Lhullier, C. & Rousseaux, M. 1994 Vigilance and effects of fatigability, practice and motivation on simple reaction time tests in patients with lesion of the frontal lobe. *Neuropsychologia* **32**, 983–990. (doi:10.1016/ 0028-3932(94)90047-7)

Godefroy, O., Cabaret, M., Petit-Chenal, V., Pruvo, J.-P. & Rousseaux, M. 1999 Control functions of the frontal lobes Modularity of the central-supervisory system? *Cortex* **35**, 1–20.

Heilman, K. M. & Watson, R. T. 1977 The neglect syndrome—a unilateral defect of the orienting response. In *Lateralization in the nervous system* (eds S. Harnad, R. W. Doty, J. Jaynes, L. Goldstein & G. Krauthamer), pp. 285–302. New York, NY: Academic Press.

Henson, R. N. A., Shallice, T. & Dolan, R. J. 1999 Right prefrontal cortex and episodic memory retrieval: a functional MRI test of the monitoring hypothesis. *Brain* **122**, 1367–1381. (doi:10.1093/ brain/122.7.1367)

Hockey, G. R. J. 1993 Cognitive energetic control mechanisms in the management of work demands and psychological health. In *Attention: selection, awareness and control. A tribute to Donald Broadbent* (eds A. D. Baddeley & L. Weiskrantz), pp. 328–345. Oxford, UK: Clarendon Press.

Hofle, N., Paus, T., Reutens, D., Fiset, P., Gotman, J., Evans, A. C. & Jones, B. E. 1997 Regional cerebral blood flow changes as a function of delta and spindle activity during slow wave sleep in humans. *J. Neurosci.* **17**, 4800–4808.

Iversen, S. D. & Mishkin, M. 1970 Perseverative interference in monkeys following selective lesions of the inferior prefrontal convexity. *Exp. Brain Res.* **11**, 376–386. (doi:10. 1007/BF00237911)

Knight, R. T. 1991 Evoked potential studies of attention capacity in human frontal lobe lesions. In *Frontal lobe function and dysfunction* (eds H. Levin, H. Eisenberg & F. Benton), pp. 139–153. New York, NY: Oxford University Press.

Kornblum, S., Stevens, G. T., Whipple, A. & Requin, J. 1999 The effects of irrelevant stimuli: 1. The time course of stimulus–stimulus and stimulus–response consistency effects with Stroop-like stimuli, Simon-like tasks, and their factorial combinations. *J. Exp. Psychol. Hum. Percept. Perform.* **25**, 688–714. (doi:10.1037/0096-1523.25.3.688)

Leimkuhler, M. E. & Mesulam, M. M. 1985 Reversible go– no go deficits in a case of frontal lobe tumor. *Ann. Neurol.* **18**, 617–619. (doi:10.1002/ana.410180518)

Lewis, P. A. & Miall, R. C. 2003 Brain activation patterns during measurement of sub- and supra-second intervals. *Neuropsychologia* **41**, 1583–1592. (doi:10.1016/S0028-3932 (03)00118-0)

Luria, A. R. 1966 *Higher cortical functions in man*. New York, NY: Basic Books.

Luria, A. R. 1973 *The working brain: an introduction to neuropsychology*. New York, NY: Basic Books.

Luu, P., Collins, P. & Tucker, D. M. 2000*a* Mood, personality, and self-monitoring: negative affect and emotionality in relation to frontal lobe mechanisms of error monitoring. *J. Exp. Psychol. Gen.* **129**, 43–60. (doi:10.1037/0096-3445.129.1.43)

Luu, P., Flaisch, T. & Tucker, D. M. 2000*b* Medial frontal cortex in action monitoring. *J. Neurosci.* **20**, 464–469.

Mangels, J. A., Ivry, R. B. & Shimizu, N. 1998 Dissociable contributions of the prefrontal and neocerebellar cortex to time perception. *Cogn. Brain Res.* 7, 15–39. (doi:10.1016/ S0926-6410(98)00005-6)

Mesulam, M.-M. 1985 *Principles of behavioral neurology*. Philadelphia, PA: Davis.

Milner, B. 1963 Effects of different brain lesions on card sorting: the role of the frontal lobes. *Arch. Neurol.* **9**, 100–110.

Niemi, P. & Näätänen, R. 1981 Foreperiod and simple reaction time. *Psychol. Bull.* **89**, 133–162. (doi:10.1037/ 0033-2909.89.1.133)

Norman, D. A. & Shallice, T. 1986 Attention to action: willed and automatic control of behaviour. In *Consciousness and self-regulation: advances in research and theory* (eds R. J. Davidson, G. E. Shwartz & D. Shapiro), pp. 1–18. New York, NY: Plenum.

Pardo, J. V., Fox, P. T. & Raichle, M. E. 1991 Localization of a human system for sustained attention by positron emission tomography. *Nature* **349**, 61–64. (doi:10.1038/ 349061a0)

Passingham, R. 1993 *The frontal lobes and voluntary action*. Oxford, UK: Oxford University Press.

Paus, T. 2001 Primate anterior cingulate cortex: where motor control, drive and cognition interface. *Nat. Rev. Neurosci.* **2**, 417–424. (doi:10.1038/35077500)

Paus, T., Zatorre, R. J., Hofle, N., Caramanos, J. G., Petrides, M. & Evans, A. C. 1997 Time-related changes in neural systems underlying attention and arousal during the performance of an auditory vigilance task. *J. Cogn. Neurosci.* **9**, 392–408.

Perret, E. 1974 Left frontal lobe of man and suppression of habitual responses in verbal categorical behavior. *Neuropsychologia* **12**, 323–330. (doi:10.1016/0028-3932 (74)90047-5)

Petrides, M. & Pandya, D. M. 1994 Comparative architectonic analysis of the human and macaque frontal cortex. In *Handbook of neuropsychology* (eds F. Boller & J. Grafman), pp. 17–57. Amsterdam, The Netherlands: Elsevier.

Picard, N. & Strick, P. L. 1996 Motor areas of the medial wall: a review of their location and functional activation. *Cereb. Cortex* **6**, 342–353. (doi:10.1093/cercor/6.3.342)

Picton, T. W., Stuss, D. T., Alexander, M. P., Shallice, T. & Gillingham, S. 2006 Keeping time: Effects of focal frontal lesions. *Neuropsychologia* **44**, 1195–1209. (doi:10.1016/ j.neuropsychologia. 2005.10.002)

Picton, T. W., Stuss, D. T., Alexander, M. P., Shallice, T., Binns, M. A. & Gillingham, S. 2007. Effects of focal frontal lesions on response inhibition. *Cereb. Cortex.* **17**, 826–838

Plum, F. & Posner, J. B. 1980 *The diagnosis of stupor and coma*, 3rd edn. Philadelphia, PA: Davis.

Posner, M. I. & Petersen, S. E. 1990 The attention system of the human brain. *Annu. Rev. Neurosci.* **13**, 25–42. (doi:10. 1146/annurev.ne.13.030190.000325)

Richer, F., Decary, A., Lapierre, M.-P., Rouleau, I., Bouvier, G. & Saint-Hilaire, J.-M. 1993 Target detection deficits in frontal lobectomy. *Brain Cogn.* **21**, 203–211. (doi:10.1006/ brcg.1993.1016)

Robbins, T. W. 1996 Dissociating executive functions of the prefrontal cortex. *Phil. Trans. R. Roc. B* **351**, 1463–1470. (doi:10.1098/rstb.1996.0131)

Robbins, T. W. 2007 Shifting and stopping: fronto-striatal substrates, neurochemical modulation and clinical implications. *Phil. Trans. R. Soc. B* **362**, 917–932. (doi:10.1098/ rstb.2007.2097)

Rueckert, L. & Grafman, J. 1996 Sustained attention deficits in patients with right frontal lesions. *Neuropsychologia* **34**, 953–963. (doi:10.1016/0028-3932(96)00016-4)

Shallice, T. 1982 Specific impairments of planning. *Phil. Trans. R. Soc. B* **298**, 199–209. (doi:10.1098/ rstb.1982. 0082)

Shallice, T. 2001 Fractionating the supervisory system. *Brain Cogn.* **47**, 30.

Shallice, T. 2002 Fractionation of the supervisory system. In *Principles of frontal lobe function* (eds D. T. Stuss & R. T. Knight), pp. 261–277. New York, NY: Oxford University Press.

Shallice, T. & Burgess, P. W. 1991 Deficits in strategy application following frontal lobe damage in man. *Brain* **114**, 727–741. (doi:10.1093/brain/114.2.727)

Stroop, J. R. 1935 Studies of interference in serial verbal reactions. *J. Exp. Psychol.* **18**, 643–662. (doi:10.1037/ h0054651)

Sturm, W. & Willmes, K. 2001 On the functional neuro-anatomy of intrinsic and phasic alertness. *Neuroimage* **14**, S76–S84. (doi:10.1006/nimg.2001.0839)

Stuss, D. T. 2006 Frontal lobes and attention: processes and networks, fractionation and integration. *J. Int. Neuropsychol. Soc.* **12**, 261–271.

Stuss, D. T. 2007 New approaches to prefrontal lobe testing. In *The human frontal lobes: functions and disorders* (eds B. Miller & J. Cummings), pp. 292–305. 2nd edn. New York, NY: Guildford Press.

Stuss, D. T. & Alexander, M. P. In press. Executive functions: is there a frontal lobe syndrome? In *New encyclopedia of neuroscience.*

Stuss, D. T. & Benson, D. F. 1984 Neuropsychological studies of the frontal lobes. *Psychol. Bull.* **95**, 3–28. (doi:10.1037/0033-2909.95.1.3)

Stuss, D. T. & Benson, D. F. 1986 *The frontal lobes.* New York, NY: Raven Press.

Stuss, D. T. & Levine, B. 2002 Adult clinical neuropsychology: lessons from studies of the frontal lobes. *Annu. Rev. Psychol.* **53**, 401–433. (doi:10.1146/annurev.psych.53. 100901.135220)

Stuss, D. T., Stethem, L. L., Hugenholtz, H., Picton, T. W., Pivik, J. & Richard, M. T. 1989 Reaction time after head injury: fatigue, divided and focused attention and consistency of performance. *J. Neurol. Neurosurg. Psychiatry* **52**, 742–748.

Stuss, D. T., Alexander, M. P., Palumbo, C. L., Buckle, L., Sayer, L. & Pogue, J. 1994 Organizational strategies of patients with unilateral or bilateral frontal lobe injury in word list learning tasks. *Neuropsychology* **8**, 355–373. (doi:10.1037/0894-4105.8.3.355)

Stuss, D. T., Shallice, T., Alexander, M. P. & Picton, T. W. 1995 A multidisciplinary approach to anterior attentional functions. *Ann. N. Y. Acad. Sci.* **769**, 191–211. (doi:10. 1111/j.1749-6632.1995. tb38140.x)

Stuss, D. T., Alexander, M. P., Hamer, L., Palumbo, C., Dempster, R., Binns, M., Levine, B. & Izukawa, D. 1998 The effects of focal anterior and posterior brain lesions on verbal fluency. *J. Int. Neuropsychol. Soc.* **4**, 265–278.

Stuss, D. T., Toth, J. P., Franchi, D., Alexander, M. P., Tipper, S. & Craik, F. I. M. 1999 Dissociation of attentional processes in patients with focal frontal and posterior lesions. *Neuropsychologia* **37**, 1005–1027. (doi:10.1016/S0028-3932(98)00158-4)

Stuss, D. T., Levine, B., Alexander, M. P., Hong, J., Palumbo, C., Hamer, L., Murphy, K. J. & Izukawa, D. 2000 Wisconsin card sorting test performance in patients with focal frontal and posterior brain damage: effects of lesion location and test structure on separable cognitive processes. *Neuropsychologia* **38**, 388–402. (doi:10.1016/ S0028-3932(99)00093-7)

Stuss, D. T., Floden, D., Alexander, M. P., Levine, B. & Katz, D. 2001 Stroop performance in focal lesion patients: dissociation of processes and frontal lobe lesion location. *Neuropsychologia* **39**, 771–786. (doi:10.1016/S0028-3932 (01)00013-6)

Stuss, D. T., Alexander, M. P., Floden, D. T., Binns, M. A., Levine, B., McIntosh, A. R., Rajah, M. N. & Hevenor, S. J. 2002a Fractionation and localization of distinct frontal lobe processes: evidence from focal lesions in humans. In *Principles of frontal lobe function* (eds D. T. Stuss & R. T. Knight), pp. 392–407. New York, NY: Oxford University Press.

Stuss, D. T., Binns, M. A., Murphy, K. J. & Alexander, M. P. 2002b Dissociations within the anterior attentional system: effects of task complexity and irrelevant information on reaction time speed and accuracy. *Neuropsychology* **16**, 500–513. (doi:10.1037/0894-4105.16.4.500)

Stuss, D. T., Alexander, M. P., Shallice, T., Picton, T. W., Binns, M. A., MacDonald, R., Borowiec, A. & Katz, D. 2005 Multiple frontal systems controlling response speed. *Neuropsychologia* **43**, 396–417. (doi:10.1016/j.neuropsycho logia.2004.06.010)

Talati, A. & Hirsch, J. 2005 Functional specialization within the medial frontal gyrus for perceptual go/ no-go decisions based on "what," "when," and "where" related information: an fMRI study. *J. Cogn. Neurosci.* **17**, 981–993. (doi:10. 1162/0898929054475226)

Turner, M. S., Cipolotti, L., Yousry, T. & Shallice, T. In press. Qualitatively different memory impairments across frontal lobe subgroups. *Neuropsychologia* **45**, 1540–1552. (doi:10.1016/j. neuropsychologia.2006.11.013).

Vallesi, A., Shallice, T. & Walsh, V. 2007 Role of the prefrontal cortex in the foreperiod effect. TMS evidence for dual mechanisms in temporal preparation. *Cereb. Cortex.* **17**, 466–474. (doi:10.1093/ cercor/bhj163)

Verfaellie, M. & Heilman, K. M. 1987 Response preparation and response inhibition after lesions of the medial frontal lobe. *Arch. Neurol.* **44**, 1265–1271.

Vuilleumier, P. & Driver, J. 2007 Modulation of visual processing by attention and emotion: windows on causal interactions between human brain regions. *Phil. Trans. R. Soc. B* **362**, 837–855. (doi:10.1098/rstb.2007.2092)

West, R. & Baylis, G. C. 1998 Effects of increased response dominance and contextual disintegration on the Stroop interference effect in older adults. *Psychol. Aging* **13**, 206–217. (doi:10.1037/0882-7974.13.2.206)

Wilkins, A. J., Shallice, T. & McCarthy, R. 1987 Frontal lesions and sustained attention. *Neuropsychologia* **25**, 359–365. (doi:10.1016/0028-3932(87)90024-8)

13

Shifting and stopping: fronto-striatal substrates, neurochemical modulation and clinical implications

*T. W. Robbins**

The neuropsychological basis of attentional set-shifting, task-set switching and stop-signal inhibition is reviewed through comparative studies of humans and experimental animals. Using human functional neuroimaging, plus neuropsychological investigation of patients with frontal damage quantified by structural magnetic resonance imaging, and through parallels with effects of specific lesions of the prefrontal cortex (PFC) and striatum in rats and marmosets, it is possible to define both distinct and overlapping loci for tasks such as extra-dimensional shifting and reversal learning, stop-signal reaction time and task-set switching. Notably, most of the paradigms implicate a locus in the right PFC, specifically the right inferior frontal gyrus, possibly associated with processes of response inhibition. The neurochemical modulation of fronto-striatal circuitry in parallel with effects on task performance has been investigated using specific neuropharmacological agents in animals and by human psychopharmacological investigations, sometimes in conjunction with functional imaging. Evidence is provided for double dissociations of effects of manipulations of prefrontal cortical catecholamine and indoleamine (5-HT) systems that have considerable implications in the treatment of disorders such as Parkinson's disease, attention deficit/hyperactivity disorder and depression, as well as in theoretical notions of how 'fronto-executive' functions are subject to state-dependent influences, probably related to stress, arousal and motivation.

Keywords: prefrontal cortex; striatum; neurotransmitters; switching; inhibition

13.1 Introduction

About a decade ago, a Discussion Meeting of the Royal Society that was dedicated to the functions of the prefrontal cortex (PFC; Roberts *et al.* 1998) helped to crystallize a number of issues that have since been the subject of intense theoretical and empirical effort. At that time, considerable attention was being paid to the concept that the PFC helped to mediate aspects of 'working memory' and its role in generating representations of the world, although the evidence from non-human primates (Goldman-Rakic 1998) did not always map convincingly onto the so-called executive aspects of human working memory (Baddeley & Della Salla 1998). Part of the reason for this mismatch arose from differences in the use of the term 'working memory'. Goldman-Rakic emphasized the maintenance operation of working memory, i.e. the capacity to hold stimuli 'on-line' and protect them from disruption, whereas the human theories of working memory (e.g.Baddeley1986) placed more weight on understanding how information stored in modality-specific short-term memory buffers was used and the coordination of these buffers by a hypothetical (and vaguely specified) 'central executive' (see also D'Esposito 2007). There was nevertheless a superficial coherence in terms of studies

*twr2@cam.ac.uk

attempting to localize working memory functions in humans (Owen *et al.* 1990; Smith & Jonides 1995) and monkeys (Goldman-Rakic 1998).

One productive approach was to break down working memory functions into components such as those specified by the Baddeley model. This led to the suggestion that anatomically separate loci might mediate functions such as 'holding stimuli online' (ventrolateral PFC) and the manipulation of its contents using strategic encoding (dorsolateral PFC) (Owen *et al.* 1996; Petrides 1998; Robbins 1998; Bor *et al.* 2003). Further work has shown that the role of the PFC in response-selection processes in standard working memory paradigms may have been underestimated (e.g. Rowe *et al.* 2000): the role of the PFC in response selection had been a major theme of the early Shallice and Norman's model of PFC as a 'supervisory attentional system' (Shallice 1982).

Another consistent theme emerging about PFC function was the role of the ventromedial orbitofrontal cortex in emotional decision making, as determined especially by the study of single cases with damage including that region (Damasio 1998). This led to speculations about how these regions of the PFC, with their classical limbic connectivity, interacted with dorsolateral PFC regions in the control of cognition and behaviour. One promising basic neuroscience approach has been to track the impact of rewarding feedback in discrimination tasks in rhesus monkeys on single-cell activity throughout the PFC during the course of learning and performance (Hollerman *et al.* 2000; Miller & Cohen 2001). Another has been to postulate different forms of 'marker' that are monitored by the PFC to guide optimal performance (Damasio 1998; Shallice & Burgess 1998). A third, mainly employing functional brain imaging, has focused directly on the hypothesis that parts of the human medial and orbitofrontal cortex (OFC) mediate 'reward' or 'goal' representations (O'Doherty *et al.* 2001). In general, the OFC has been implicated in choice mechanisms that are recruited to deal with complex contingencies, as often occur, for example, in an economic context (Rogers *et al.* 1999*a*; McClure *et al.* 2004; Huettel *et al.* 2006; see also Dolan 2007; and this volume).

This implication of the OFC in reward processes also had to be integrated with growing evidence of the importance of specified subcortical circuitry in the mediation of reward processes, notably dopamine-dependent functions of the nucleus accumbens (Robbins & Everitt 1992). This has led to a growing realization of the nodal position of the PFC in 'loop' circuitries involving connections between the OFC, other limbic structures, the nucleus accumbens, mediodorsal thalamus and ventral pallidum. Such neuroanatomical loops link other sectors of the PFC and functionally related regions of the striatum in a cascading series of serial as well as parallel circuitries (Alexander *et al.* 1986; Haber *et al.* 2000). The functioning of the cortico-striatal loops is also influenced by a number of ascending 'neuromodulatory' chemical neurotransmitter systems, notably the catecholamines (dopamine and noradrenaline), the indoleamine serotonin or 5-hydroxytryptamine (5-HT) and acetylcholine (Robbins 2000). These neurochemical systems, which are implicated in stress, arousal and mood as well as reward processes (see Robbins & Everitt 1992; Arnsten & Robbins 2002), may themselves, to some extent, be regulated by the descending influences of the PFC (e.g. Amat *et al.* 2005). In general, these cortico-striatal systems can be understood as incorporating mechanisms for the optimal selection of goals and responses, and for the optimal preparation of appropriate response outputs. Phasic activity in some of the neuromodulatory systems, especially the mesolimbic dopamine pathway, has been implicated in the mechanisms of learning, for example reflecting 'error prediction signals' (Schultz & Dickinson 2000). In addition, tonic levels of activity in the neuromodulatory systems can be understood as representing different states, in which various types of 'executive operation' are recruited and performed. Implementation of some tasks requiring executive control may be optimally performed in different states (e.g. of 'arousal', 'fatigue' or 'mood'; Robbins 2000). Executive control refers to the collection of mechanisms that serve to optimize behavioural and cognitive output, and includes the regulation of input (e.g. over posterior cortical processing), output (e.g. via the basal ganglia and the associated cortico-striatal loops) and also the activity of the ascending neuromodulatory systems.

A particular function of the PFC in response selection becomes evident in fluctuating or ambiguous circumstances, for example in dual-task control, attentional conflict (e.g. Stroop interference) and changes in background distracting stimuli or instructions (e.g. contextual control; Cohen *et al.* 1998), as well as following changes in rewarding and error feedback (e.g. Wisconsin Card Sort Test, WCST). Most of these situations underline the principle that the supervisory attentional system of Shallice and Norman (Shallice 1982) becomes especially important in the selection of rapid responses to novel, often stressful situations, for example by adding more 'weight' or bias to particular representations. In neurobiological terms, this cognitive flexibility may correspond to the recruitment of the same sort of plastic mechanisms implicated in rapid learning itself, involving for example the phenomenon of long-term potentiation and the involvement of glutamate receptors, especially of the NMDA receptor subtype (Moghaddam 2004; Robbins & Murphy 2006). However, although the PFC has long been implicated in the mechanisms of cognitive flexibility, a conceptual basis for understanding this typically 'executive' function has been elusive or described only globally in terms of 'behavioural inhibition'. The most potent way of effecting behavioural change is either to withdraw rewarding feedback for a particular response or shift it to another option. This feedback may be associated with particular stimuli or responses, or more usually with classes or categories of input and output, including perceptual dimensions and 'task sets' (i.e. specifications of particular stimulus–response (S–R) links). Moreover, the shifts in reinforcement contingencies may occur occasionally and encompass new learning (Slamecka 1968; Roberts *et al.* 1988), or may instead occur frequently for well-established responses or task sets (Monsell 2003). Thus, the subject may have to shift rapidly between responding to one of two established task sets such as naming digits and naming letters, when both are present in the array. Alternatively, the 'task set' may be to respond according to a choice reaction time procedure as rapidly as possible, but occasionally to cancel or countermand responding altogether, in the presence of a so-called 'stop-signal' (Logan & Cowan 1984).

In this paper, the neural substrates and their chemical neuromodulation of basic operations such as shifting and stopping are surveyed, drawing upon evidence from experimental animals and humans. It has become evident that, despite the considerable heuristic usefulness of the Norman and Shallice model, it is not feasible to make any more than a coarse mapping of their influential concepts of 'attention to action' onto the matrix of specific neural and neurochemical dissociations among different types of cognitive flexibility to be described below. The paper begins with the example of attentional set-shifting, which has been used, in both experimental animals and humans, to decompose the types of processes engaged by tests such as the WCST. This test is sensitive not only to deficits of cognitive rigidity in frontal patients, but also to a number of other disorders ranging from Parkinson's disease to schizophrenia. Two further paradigms used to model certain components of executive control processes in humans, task-set switching and stop-signal inhibition, will also be analysed. The structure of the paper will depend first on defining the types of operation that are measured in these paradigms and their neural correlates. These having been established, it is logical to examine in each case their neurochemical modulation by the chemically defined ascending systems. The relevance of these analyses to several neurological and neuropsychiatric disorders that exhibit substantial deficits in certain ones of these cognitive tests will then be made clear, an important link being that many of the medications employed in these disorders have selective actions on the chemical modulatory systems.

13.2 Attentional set-shifting

A major new finding presented at the Royal Society Discussion Meeting of 1996 was relevant to the issue of the role of the PFC in 'cognitive flexibility': two apparently similar forms of cognitive flexibility were mediated by very different regions of the PFC in the marmoset (Dias *et al.* 1996; Robbins 1998). Thus, when responding to complex (compound) stimuli was governed by a particular perceptual dimension (such as shapes, as distinct from an alternative dimension of superimposed lines; see figure 13.1), new learning was impaired in monkeys with lesions of the lateral PFC when the reinforcement contingencies were switched so as to render the previously irrelevant dimension relevant (figure 13.2). This shifting requirement is conceptually equivalent to the 'category shift' required in the WCST, as it involves a shift of responding that entails a switching of attention between two perceptual dimensions; hence the description 'extra-dimensional shift' (ed-shift). (An intra-dimensional shift (id-shift) occurs, by contrast, when new stimuli or exemplars are presented, but the subject has to continue to choose the same perceptual dimension (or 'follow the same rule') when responding to them. In this sense, each normal trial of the WCST (i.e. when there is no requirement to shift the rule) is akin to an id-shift.) A category shift in the WCST may also engage other processes

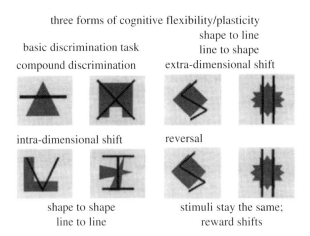

Fig. 13.1 Compound stimuli used in discrimination learning paradigm. The perceptual dimensions were shapes and lines. Exemplars of these dimensions could occur in combination with one another on successive trials, one exemplar of one dimension being correct. Three types of shift are shown: an intra-dimensional shift (ids) occurs when novel stimuli are used but the relevant stimulus dimension (i.e. shapes or lines) stays the same; an extra-dimensional shift (eds) occurs when an exemplar from the previously irrelevant dimension becomes correct. Reversal learning can occur at several stages, e.g. at the compound discrimination stage or after the id- or ed-shift. Here, the stimuli remain the same, but the exemplar that was previously correct is now incorrect and vice versa. See Dias *et al.* (1996, 1997) for further details.

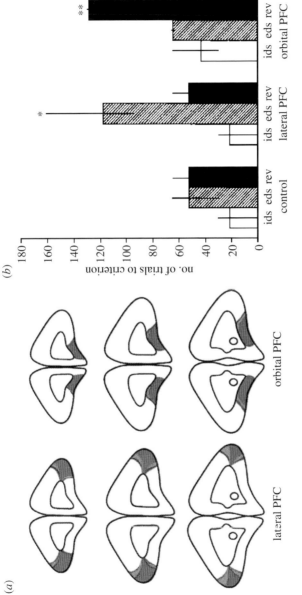

Fig. 13.2 (a) Representative coronal sections through the marmoset PFC showing the extent of lesions made to the lateral or orbitofrontal PFC, together with (b) doubly dissociable behavioural deficits on id-shifting, ed-shifting and reversal shifts (rev; *p<0.05, **p<0.01) (reproduced with permission from Dias *et al.* 1996, modified with permission from the publishers).

besides switching; for example, the subject also has to identify the correct new category and resist the fact that previously it has been irrelevant ('learned irrelevance'). They also have to realize that a shift is now necessary owing to the altered feedback. The precise nature of any failure to make the category shift can be analysed by further variations of the id-/ed-shift procedure, as implemented by Owen *et al.* (1993), in a study of frontal patients.

The lateral PFC-lesioned monkeys were not impaired when they were required merely to shift responding to the previously rewarded alternative ('reversal learning'), suggesting that their deficit at the ed-shift stage was not simply a failure to detect the altered feedback. By contrast, lesions of the OFC produced exactly the opposite pattern: no deficit on the ed-shift, but impaired reversal learning. While these empirical data were clear and replicable (e.g. Dias *et al.* 1997), they provided several new challenges in terms of interpretation. For example, what was the theoretical significance of the findings, in particular the double dissociation, and were they of any significance for understanding the functions of the human PFC? Some advance has been made in addressing these issues. The most obvious point is the implication that both the lateral and OFC regions of the PFC are active during discrimination learning but have different functions in behavioural plasticity. The lateral PFC was implicated in the shifting of responding between abstract perceptual dimensions, whereas the OFC was necessary for the shifting of responding between different stimuli or objects with specific associations with reinforcement. This implies a hierarchical organization of function between lateral and OFC regions of the PFC, analogous to other proposed hierarchical relations between ventrolateral and dorsolateral PFC (Petrides 1998) and between the rostral PFC and other regions of PFC (Koechlin *et al.* 2003). The reason that this putative organization is suggested to be hierarchical, rather than just another example of functional specialization, is that discrimination learning is based on simple concrete features (e.g. triangle, curly) in the case of reversal learning, but entire, abstract dimensions (e.g. 'shape', 'line') in the case of ed-shifting. Moreover, an influential theory of discrimination learning (Sutherland & Mackintosh 1971) held that discrimination learning proceeds in a hierarchical fashion: first attention is attracted by feedback to a specific perceptual dimension; then, it must be identified which exemplar of the dimension is rewarded and which is punished prior to response selection. Presumably, these different stages of discrimination learning correspond to different functions mediated by the lateral PFC and the OFC.

The findings of Dias *et al.* (1996, 1997) also appear to show that, although both deficits can be classified as reflecting deficits in behavioural inhibition (owing to perseverative responding, either to previous exemplars or to dimensions in the face of non-reward), a process of response inhibition *per se* is not represented simply within a single PFC region. This had been previously mooted, for example, by Fuster's (1989) review, which suggested that the OFC had a function of behavioural inhibition. Rather, it appeared that the lateral PFC also performed inhibitory functions in response selection. Thus, response inhibitory functions are distributed widely within the PFC, analogous to Goldman-Rakic's view that working memory was organized on a modular basis within the PFC, subsuming processes of inhibition and selection, as well as holding stimuli online.

The second major question was whether the double dissociation of ed-shifting and reversal learning in the marmoset, a non-human primate, had any relevance for defining the functions of the human PFC. Although it might have been thought rather straightforward to test this relevance in humans, it has proved in fact to be more problematic than translating the basic findings to other species such as the rat. Birrell & Brown (2001) used an ingenious digging task for food rewards that required rats to discriminate between rough and smooth sand, or different smells associated with it. Rats with different lesions of PFC subregions were exposed to the same sequence of discrimination learning stages as the marmoset, including reversal learning, id-shifting and ed-shifting. A similar anatomical dissociation of effects of medial PFC and lateral portions of the OFC lesions was found on shifting and reversal, respectively (Brown & Bowman 2002). These data provide interesting pointers on homologies between the rodent and primate brain. In fact, there is now considerable evidence that lateral OFC lesions in the rat produce impairments in reversal learning in a number of sensory modalities (Schoenbaum *et al.* 2002; Chudasama & Robbins 2003). The evidence for neuroanatomical homologies between the primate and rodent brain suggests that the rat OFC is indeed related to the primate OFC (Preuss 1995; Brown & Bowman 2002); hence, their common involvement in reversal learning could be expected. The common involvement of the rat medial PFC and the primate lateral PFC in ed-shifting might also be expected on the grounds of the putative homology of these regions, although this is more controversial (Brown & Bowman 2002).

Is the same true of the human brain? One difficulty in investigating this possibility is that reversal learning for humans is generally a much easier task than the ed-shift. Using similar visual stimuli to those employed in the work with marmosets, it was nonetheless possible to show relatively selective deficits in reversal learning in patients with frontal-variant fronto-temporal dementia, for whom hypoperfusion initially occurs in the OFC (Rahman *et al.* 1999). Several other groups have also confirmed that the OFC mediates aspects of reversal learning (Fellows & Farrah 2003; O'Doherty *et al.* 2003; Hornak *et al.* 2004) on the basis of neuropsychological testing of patients or functional neuroimaging. However, none of these studies included a test of ed-shifting. We have been unable to pinpoint precisely those regions of the PFC that are especially implicated in the ed-shift from neuropsycho logical studies of cases with PFC damage. However, it is apparent that in two series of patients with damage to different regions of the PFC, arising from diverse aetiology and with largely lateral lesions that spared the OFC, the greatest deficit was in ed-shifting. Performance of the reversal stages of the tasks was not significantly affected (Owen *et al.* 1991).

The other main technique that can be employed is that of functional neuroimaging. Our early attempt (Rogers *et al.* 2000) to study reversal learning and ed-shifting in a functional imaging context using H_2O^{15} positron emission tomography (PET) was unsuccessful in showing activations in the OFC, presumably owing to limitations of the block design employed. Thus, reversal and shifts occur quite quickly and so any effects on cerebral activity may be diluted if it is averaged over many trials that include just one shift; an event-related designis thus to be preferred. However, there was activity shown in the ventromedial caudate nucleus for the contrast between an id-shift and reversal, suggesting that reversal is mediated in part by a cortico-striatal loop. This loop includes the OFC, given the anatomical connectivity existing between these regions, even if activation of the OFC itself was not evident. Moreover, a similar contrast between ed-shifting and id-shifting showed activity in the rostral and dorsolateral PFC. However, a recent elegant event-related functional magnetic resonance imaging (fMRI) study using methods that allowed resolution of activity within the OFC region has considerably clarified the situation: Hampshire & Owen (2006) had volunteers shift between attending to photographs of houses or faces when both were present within the same stimuli. They found that reversal was indeed associated with blood oxygen level-dependent (BOLD) signals in the OFC (as well as reductions in the activation of the medial PFC), whereas ed-shifting was associated most obviously with ventrolateral PFC activity (figure 13.3). Thus, it could be argued that there is considerable concordance between the findings for the marmoset and human functional neuroimaging. The lateral PFC lesion in the marmoset may

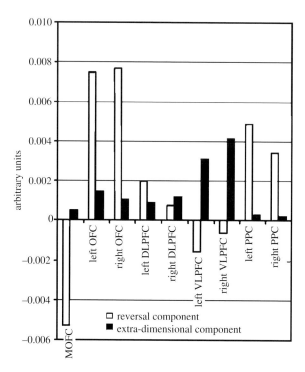

Fig. 13.3 Results of an fMRI study on reversal learning, id-shifting and ed-shifting in human subjects. The regional cortical BOLD activations for contrasts involving reversal and ed-shifting are shown. Note the double dissociation between activations for reversal learning and ed-shifting. DLPFC, dorsolateral prefrontal cortex; VLPFC, ventrolateral pre frontal cortex; PPC, posterior parietal cortex. Adapted with permission from Hampshire & Owen (2006) and publishers of *Cerebral Cortex*, Oxford University Press.

correspond to the ventrolateral PFC highlighted in the Hampshire & Owen (2006) study. Nevertheless, it is significant that although the dorsolateral PFC was not specifically associated with responding at any one stage, it was active during most of the task, possibly reflecting an overall role in strategic processes contributing to problem solution.

13.3 Effects of manipulating chemical neuromodulatory systems on attentional set-shifting and reversal learning

Hypoactivity of the mesocortical dopamine projection has been implicated not only in working memory dysfunction (Goldman-Rakic 1998), but also in clinical disorders such as schizophrenia and attention deficit/ hyperactivity disorder (ADHD). Consequently, initial studies focused on the effects of profound (greater than 85%) dopamine depletion from the entire PFC in the marmoset and found surprisingly that, if anything, ed-shifting was not impaired but actually enhanced (Roberts *et al.* 1994). However, this was later found probably to result from a failure of the monkey to form stable attentional sets in the first place. This was shown by the fact that serial id-shifting, which normally leads to the establishment of an attentional 'set',

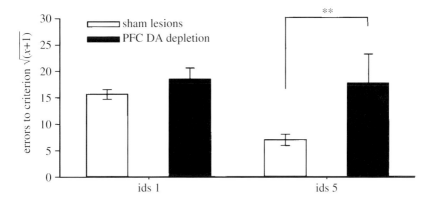

Fig. 13.4 Effects of prefrontal dopamine depletion on the first and fifth stages of a serial id-shifting task, showing deficits in the lesioned group. *$p<0.05$, **$p<0.01$.

was profoundly impaired (figure 13.4) and there were additional signs of attentional lability (Crofts *et al.* 2001). It is important to note that there were no other effects on discrimination or reversal learning (Roberts *et al.* 1994), even in the serial condition (Clarke *et al.* 2005). By contrast, selective 5-HT depletion had no effect on ed-shifting or serial id-shifting, but produced a large deficit in reversal learning (Clarke *et al.* 2004, 2005, 2007; see figure 13.5), largely due to perseverative responding to the previously rewarded object. Thus, these manipulations of two different monoamine pathways that innervate the PFC clearly have distinct effects on PFC-dependent mechanisms of cognitive flexibility. Although both systems

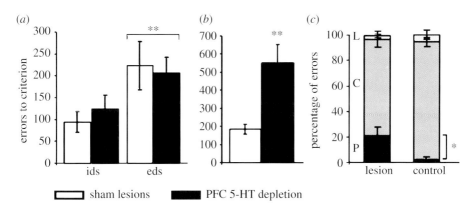

Fig. 13.5 Effects of selective prefrontal 5-HT (serotonin) depletion on id-shifting, ed-shifting and reversal learning; note the selective effect on the latter: (*a*) ed-shift, (*b*) reversal and (*c*) reversal error type. *$p<0.05$, **$p<0.01$. Adapted with permission from the Society for Neuroscience (© 2005) from Clarke *et al.* (2005).

innervate the entire PFC, they appear to have differential impact in distinct regions. Thus, for example, it is 5-HT depletion in the OFC that is implicated in reversal learning and we have not been able to discern so far any impact of 5-HT depletion on the performance of tasks (such as ed-shifting) dependent on lateral PFC regions in the marmoset.

There is some resonance of this work on reversal learning with what has been shown in human volunteers following transient depletion of central 5-HT by the tryptophan depletion technique. Park *et al.* (1994) first reported the effects on discrimination learning that were especially evident for reversal learning and Rogers *et al.* (1999*b*) also found that such depletion led to relatively selective effects on reversal learning in human subjects (but see also Talbot *et al.* 2006), with no effect on ed-shifting (Rogers *et al.* 1999*b*) or spatial working memory (Park *et al.* 1994). However, for mesocortical dopamine, the position is less clear owing to the difficulty in manipulating this system selectively in human subjects. However, studies on polymorphism for a gene controlling catechol-o-methyltransferase (COMT), which has been postulated to have a selective effect on PFC dopamine, have been shown to affect WCST performance, although the nature of the deficits are more in keeping with a difficulty in ed- than id-shifting (Mattay *et al.* 2003). Additional work in the rat with a pharmacological inhibitor of COMT, tolcapone, also showed improvements at the ed-stage in the rat version of the id-/ed-shift task, possibly as a consequence of enhanced PFC dopamine activity (Tunbridge *et al.* 2004). Thus, while the mesocortical dopamine projection has been implicated in both id- and ed-shifting, there is agreement of a lack of effect on reversal learning at the cortical level.

Recent work in the rat task has also shown an important role for PFC noradrenaline at the ed-shifting stage (Lapiz & Morilak 2005; Tait *et al.* 2007). This is consistent with data in humans in some respects, showing that both the noradrenergic agents, clonidine and idaxozan, produce detrimental effects at the ed stage, especially in combination (Middleton *et al.* 1999). It is intriguing that the three forms of shift described are each associated with a different mono-amine operating probably in different sectors of the PFC; thus, reversal (5-HT), id-shifting (dopamine) and ed-shifting (noradrenaline) may be differentiated to some extent. The findings thus confirm the view that these ascending monoaminergic systems have distinct functions, and future work must be aimed at understanding the conditions or states under which they are active. One such state is stress, which is known to activate the monoaminergic systems (Arnsten & Robbins 2002). The finding by Liston *et al.* (2006) that chronic stress in rats that causes a retraction of dendritic arbours in the medial PFC, but not lateral OFC, selectively impairs attentional set-shifting but not reversal learning, is clearly a step in the direction of further analysis along these lines.

13.4 Attentional set-shifting: possible fronto-striatal substrates and clinical implications

Patients with basal ganglia diseases, such as early-in-the-course Huntington's and Parkinson's diseases, show impairments in ed-shifting, suggesting some mediation by striatal structures. In late Huntington's disease, the impairments are in simple reversal learning and patients rarely progress sufficiently to even attempt the ed-shift stage. This pattern of initial deficits in ed-shifting to reversal learning suggests a dorsal-to-ventral spread in pathology (Lange *et al.* 1995). Performance in the early stages of the id-/ed-shift task was remediated by L-Dopa medication in patients late-in-the-course with Parkinson's disease, although there was no conclusive evidence on whether ed-shifting was affected (Lange *et al.* 1992). In fact, subsequent work has largely cast doubt on the hypothesis that the ed-shift is dopamine (DA) dependent. Two studies of Parkinson's disease both on- and off-L-Dopa (Cools *et al.* 2001; Lewis *et al.* 2005) did not show a significant difference in the Parkinson's disease deficit at this stage, and studies of the effects of a D2 receptor antagonist (sulpiride) in normal volunteers showed only weak and inconsistent effects in normal subjects on a single (latency) measure (Mehta *et al.* 1999, 2004). Consequently, from human studies alone it is far from clear that dopamine, whether in the PFC or striatum, is implicated in the ed-shift.

This conclusion is supported by further studies in the marmoset in which dopamine was selectively and profoundly depleted in the caudate nucleus. Such depletion caused deficits in a spatial delayed response task indexing working memory and also produced reduced distract-ibility in the id–ed-shift task (Collins *et al.* 1998; Crofts *et al.* 2001). However, the striatal depletion had no effect on discrimination learning or reversal, id- or ed-shifting. The one defi-cit that was observed occurred at the end of the id-/ed-shift series, in which a novel shift was interpolated; namely, an ed-shift back to the previously reinforced dimension. Under these conditions a deficit was revealed, which had not been apparent in the parallel studies of PFC lesions (Dias *et al.* 1997). The finding has some theoretical significance as it suggests that the striatum and its dopaminergic innervation are important in the mediation of shifts between already established sets: the striatal dopamine-depleted animals were impaired when faced with an ambiguous choice of selecting one of the two options that had both previously been successful. In the case of the initial ed-shift of course, the animal is learning a new set of associations for a dimension that has never been reinforced.

These considerations suggest that the ed-shift, probably as distinct from reversal learning, does not depend so much upon striatal mechanisms and implicates, for example, PFC interac-tions with other cortical regions, especially in the parietal and temporal cortices (Rogers *et al.* 2000; Hampshire & Owen 2006). The deficits observed in ed-shifting in Parkinson's and Huntington's diseases may thus reflect the extra-striatal pathology, possibly in the PFC. On the other hand, reversal learning does implicate subcortical structures, including the striatum, based on several lines of evidence including effects of lesions in monkeys (Divac *et al.* 1967) and rats (Dunnett & Iversen 1981), as well as functional neuroimaging in humans. Indeed, there are indications that a probabilistic reversal task (where options are reinforced on a 80–20 or 70–30 basis, rather than 100–0) activates not only regions of the OFC, medial PFC and inferior frontal cortex, but also the ventral striatum (Cools *et al.* 2002). Furthermore, patients with Parkinson's disease are impaired on such a task following L-Dopa medication, which appears to alter signals related to the final response shift during reversal within the nucleus accumbens (Cools *et al.* 2007).

Other work from a slightly different perspective is consistent with the view of a separation of function between the PFC and striatum. Thus, Cools *et al.* (2004) found that switching responding between objects produced activations in fMRI for both the PFC and striatum in normal human volunteers, whereas activations following rule alternation were only seen in the PFC. A similar dissociation has been reported for patients with PFC and striatal lesions: the latter (though mainly comprising lesions of the putamen and not the caudate nucleus) were unimpaired in responding to higher-order 'rules' but exhibited problems alternating between objects (Cools *et al.* 2006). Overall, these latter studies are consistent with the view that the striatum exhibits control in the lower-order function of switching or shifting between objects, akin to reversal learning, rather than between more abstract rules, analogous to ed-shifting.

The modulatory role for dopamine in the nucleus accumbens of probabilistic reversal learning in humans contrasts with the role of OFC 5-HT in reversal learning in monkeys. However, the 5-HT system also evidently has a modulatory role. Evers *et al.* (2005) recently showed that a dorsomedial PFC locus was affected by tryptophan depletion during the performance of the probabilistic reversal task. Tryptophan depletion affected the BOLD signal specifically associated with negative feedback, a finding of relevance to our understanding of the cognitive deficits in depression, which is associated with disorders of 5-HT regulation. Depressed patients are especially sensitive to spurious feedback in the probabilistic reversal task, switching responding inappropriately (Murphy *et al.* 2002). The effects of low tryptophan depletion in the functional imaging task of normal volunteers contrasted with those of methylphenidate (a catechol-aminergic agent) and sulpiride (a dopamine D2 receptor antagonist), both of which modulated the activity produced by a reversal shift in the inferior frontal gyrus (Clark *et al.* 2004). These data again suggest that these monoamine systems have distinct modulatory effects on task performance.

13.5 Task-set switching

One of the difficulties in interpreting changes in id- and ed-shifting, as well as reversal, is that they all depend on learning; the main measures are thus generally errors or trials to criterion. Although the paradigm includes internal controls for basic deficits in discrimination learning, it is possible that the task demands, for example, of attentional set-shifting, are conflated by the learning requirement. Set-shifting has recently been studied in other ways that allow a more analytic approach in a paradigm termed 'task-set switching' (Allport & Wyllie 1999; Monsell 2003). Formally, the human participant responds to a stimulus on each trial according to a well-established S–R rule specific to that task, but on different trials may have to respond according to a different rule defined by a different task. A task set is thus a set of processes linking sensory analysis, including identification and categorization, to particular responses and motor outputs; task sets frequently require reconfiguration if rules change. However, in the basic paradigm, the subject shifts and has to reconfigure between two well-established task sets. The critical issue is the processing cost of shifting from one task to another. This is frequently measured in an AABB design, which can isolate the latencies to repeat a task and to shift from one to the other; the difference between the two being called the 'switch cost'. The fundamental finding is that shifting between the two tasks incurs a switch cost (in terms of errors as well as latencies). The major difference between the task-set and id-/ed-shifting paradigms is that task-set switching occurs between two well-established habits, such as naming digits or naming letters, and so no new contingency learning is required. Moreover, after minimal practice, reaction times remain stable over repeated testing. The switch cost may be reduced to some extent by preparation. Thus, if the interval between the response and stimulus (response–stimulus interval; RSI) is lengthened, then the switch cost is reduced as the subject presumably is able to reconfigure the tasks in advance. However, it is notable that there remains a 'residual switch cost' even under these conditions. Explanations of the residual switch cost are controversial and include the effects of persistent interference from previous task sets and a need to complete the reconfiguration of the task via an exogenous control process cued by the new task-set cue (i.e. a control process that is triggered by the external cues associated with each task set, see Monsell 2003). There are also a number of other variables that can affect performance on the task-set switching paradigm, including for example the congruence or S–R compatibility of the task sets and the amount of interference between the two task sets, e.g. if the cues for both tasks remain present in the array, thus causing inevitable interference through 'crosstalk' between the two.

13.6 Neural substrates of task-set switching

The neural substrates of task-set switching continue to provoke debate, with most of the evidence deriving from human functional neuroimaging or neuropsychological studies of groups with frontal brain damage or neurodegenerative diseases of the basal ganglia. A number of studies have suggested that left prefrontal cortical damage is especially important for task-set switching. Our own study (Rogers *et al*. 1998) showed that patients with left PFC damage had switch deficits but only in conditions in which there was interference between the two task sets. This was in agreement with the findings of Mecklinger *et al*. (1999) who found that patients with speech and language difficulties had the greatest switch deficits, implicating the left hemisphere, and also a single case described by Keele & Rafal (1999). Neuroimaging studies suggest that the maintenance and establishment of task set are functions mediated by the middle gyrus (MFG) of the left dorsolateral PFC (MacDonald *et al*. 2000; Garavan *et al*. 2002).

In a follow-up study to that of Rogers *et al*. (1998), we tested 36 patients with unilateral damage to either the right or left PFC, and used a novel structural imaging method to quantify the volume of damage to the defined regions of interest (ROI) on both sides: the superior frontal gyrus, middle frontal gyrus (MFG), inferior frontal gyrus (IFG), orbitofrontal and medial— see Aron *et al*. (2004*a*,*b*) for methods. A task-set shifting paradigm was used that included predictable shifts and a variation of the RSI ('short' and 'long') to allow different degrees of preparation for task-set reconfiguration. The tasks were (i) a word task in which stimuli were composed of a word ('left' or 'right ') inside a shape (left arrow, right arrow or rectangle) and (ii) an arrow task in which stimuli comprised either a left or right arrow shape surrounding a letter string ('LEFT', 'RIGHT ' or 'XXX'; figure 13.6*a*). These three conditions of congruency, incongruency and neutrality also enabled the effects of congruency on task-set switching to be studied.

The behavioural results were complex but informative (figure 13.7). The left PFC group showed a general impairment in imposing the appropriate task set—as indicated by larger switch costs at both short and long RSIs. By contrast, the right PFC group had deficits in reaction time switch cost at the longer RSI. In addition, the right PFC group had difficulty in suppressing inappropriate responses or task sets, especially at short RSIs, as shown by a greater switch cost in errors for incongruent compared with congruent trials. Parametric correlational analysis of the structural imaging data with various parameters of task-set switching performance established that the only significant relationship to survive correction for multiple testing and also partial correlation was between right IFG damage and the residual switch cost ($r = 0.82$, $p < 0.005$; figure 13.7). The particular region implicated was the right pars opercularis (brain area (BA) 44). The left PFC group exhibited no reliable correlations for any of the switch cost measures, at any ROI. However, there were significant correlations for some of the congruency and interference measures; damage to the left MFG correlated with the difference between congruent and incongruent response latencies at the long RSI and with the difference between congruent and neutral conditions at short RSIs. Thus, the greater the MFG damage within the left PFC, the greater the tendency to activate the competing task and the incongruent response, even on no-switch trials (figure 13.7). This result suggests a basic deficit in

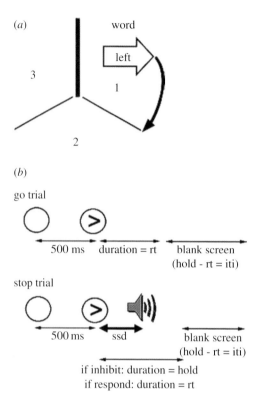

Fig. 13.6 Versions of tasks used in (a) task switching and (b) stop-signal inhibition paradigms. For task-set switching, the subject moves around the spatial array in positions 1, 2 and 3 on successive trials, cued to respond to the arrow or word. For stop-signal inhibition, on a proportion of trials, an auditory stimulus signals not to respond on that trial of a choice reaction time paradigm. rt, reaction time; ssd, stop-signal delay; iti, inter-trial interval. Modified with permission from the publishers of *Brain*. The Clarendon Press, Oxford University Press (Aron *et al.* 2004*b*) and the Society for Neuroscience © 2006 (Aron & Poldrack 2006).

endogenous task-set control (i.e. those aspects of task set that are controlled by 'stimuli' arising from internal processes such as response preparation).

To summarize the main components of task set, performance appears to be a product of an interaction between task-set inertia (the persistence of activation or inhibition from previous trials; Allport & Wyllie 1999), exogenous task-set activation and endogenous control. Exogenous task-set activation is cued by the stimulus and this is likely to happen inappropriately on switch trials. To overcome these biases, endogenous control is required, which biases attention to a particular S–R rule, along the lines originally suggested by Gilbert & Shallice (2002). On the other hand, endogenous control seems unable fully to overcome some forms of inappropriate responding, for example, caused by interference arising from incongruency.

The pattern of results described indicates that left PFC-lesioned patients did not have difficulty in suppressing the inappropriate response on switch trials at short RSIs. They showed a more general difficulty in imposing the appropriate task set at both short and long RSIs,

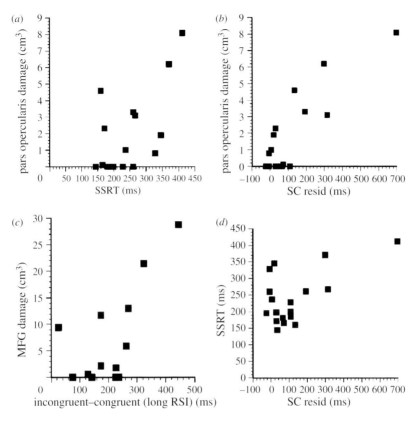

Fig. 13.7 Main results from Aron *et al.* (2004*a,b*).(*a*) Relationship between stop-signal reaction time (SSRT) and volume of damage to the right pars opercularis. (*b*) Relationship between residual switch cost (SC resid) and volume of damage to the right pars opercularis. (*c*) Relationship between volume of damage to the medial gyrus of the left PFC and a measure of task congruency at long response–stimulus intervals. (*d*) Significant correlation between stop-signal reaction time performance and residual switch cost. Modified from Aron *et al.* (2004*b*), with permission from the publishers, The Clarendon Press (Oxford University Press).

consistent with a reduction of endogenous control and thus leading to an exaggerated influence of the exogenous cueing of task set. By contrast, the clear-cut deficits shown in the right PFC group strongly suggest that the right PFC has an important role in reactive inhibition, which becomes especially important under conditions of weak endogenous control. We know from functional neuroimaging studies that many cortical structures are active during complex situations such as task-set switching. Thus, the anterior cingulate cortex is likely to detect a conflict in task setting and the right IFG is likely to be recruited to inhibit the irrelevant response activation (Gehring & Knight 2000). In general, it is clear that several different regions of the PFC are implicated in task-set switching (Derrfuss *et al.* 2005), although we would argue for a specific role for the right IFG in response inhibition in certain circumstances. The earlier demonstrations (e.g. Dias *et al.* 1996) that behavioural inhibition is apparently a function of many prefrontal areas mean that we have to define in more detail what precisely these circumstances might be. A further attempt to do this is provided in §7, where inhibition has to be applied following response initiation. The conclusion that the right IFG is implicated in response inhibition is supported by several experiments using functional neuroimaging. Two particularly salient studies are by Konishi *et al.* (1999) and Swainson *et al.* (2000), both of which directly compared response inhibition with switching and found a locus in right IFG common to both. Swainson and colleagues' study is particularly convincing as the right IFG was implicated specifically in a Go–NoGo version of the task-set switching paradigm for the shift to stopping ('suppression mode').

Although the right IFG is activated by a large number of conditions (Duncan & Owen (2000) for a meta-analysis), there is a preponderance of studies that have specifically focused upon response inhibition (Garavan *et al.* 1999; De Zubicaray *et al.* 2000; Menon *et al.* 2001; Bunge *et al.* 2002; Garavan *et al.* 2002; Rubia *et al.* 2003) and also reversal or shifting (Dove *et al.* 2000; Nagahama *et al.* 2000; Monchi *et al.* 2001; Cools *et al.* 2002; Nakahara *et al.* 2002; Hampshire & Owen 2006). The latter two of these studies are of special interest, as they investigate the WCST and the ed-shift, respectively. While it is sometimes difficult to compare exact loci of activation sites across studies and tasks, it would appear that there is at least a rough association between the neuroanatomical areas subserving task-set switching and edshifting. A parsimonious account of this observation is that there are some shared processing resources between tasks requiring task-set switching and the ed-shift, presumably related to the shift or switch itself, and thereby contributory response selection, including inhibitory processes. Alternatively, given the prominence ascribed to an area somewhat posterior to the right IFG, the so-called 'inferior frontal junction' from meta-analyses of functional imaging data in related aspects of response control (Derrfuss *et al.* 2005), it may be that there is more differentiation of function within this region than this parsimonious view. In fact, careful scrutiny of the Hampshire and Owen activation suggests that the peaks were in BA 47 in the left hemisphere and the border of BA 47 and 45 on the right, which suggests caution in attributing too many functions to the pars opercularis in the right IFG. Nevertheless, the strength of the lesion data is that the precise regions within the right IFG are necessary for adequate task-set switching performance, thus demonstrating the causal importance of the right IFG, particularly the pars opercularis, in this situation.

Unlike ed-shifting, task-set switching appears to depend to a greater extent on basal ganglia mechanisms. Patients with Huntington's disease have profound problems in elementary aspects of task-set switching (Aron *et al.* 2003*a–c*), although the neuropathology of this disease may well encompass more than simply the basal ganglia. In Parkinson's disease, there are significant impairments in task-set switching under certain conditions (Cools *et al.* 2001). In particular, Parkinson patients were most impaired at short RSIs (Cools *et al.* 2003), but such deficits were remediated by L-Dopa, suggesting a dopaminergic modulation of striatal function. Mehta *et al.* (2004) also found recently that the dopamine D2 receptor antagonist sulpiride significantly increased switch cost in a standard task-set switching paradigm in human volunteers. This was striking, owing to the relative lack of effect of the drug on performance on an id-/ ed-shifting task in the same subjects. Evidently, as well as the similarities described above in their requirements for response inhibition, there may be important differences between ed-shifting and task-set switching. The continuous nature of the latter task, and the need to shift rapidly between well-established motor sets, may make the latter task more dependent on basal ganglia functioning, whereas the ed-shift task has fewer motor components and may recruit additional associative and attentional mechanisms that are more dependent on posterior cortical structures (Rogers *et al.* 2000; Corbetta & Shulman 2002).

13.7 Stop-signal inhibition

The stop-signal inhibition paradigm (Logan & Cowan 1984) at first sight is unrelated to task-set switching and ed-shifting, although it also incorporates a major inhibition component. It is a sophisticated Go–NoGo task in which subjects are required to make speeded responses on 'Go' trials in choice reaction time procedure, but to inhibit responding on 'NoGo' trials; for example, to an auditory 'beep' that sounds on approximately 25% of the trials (figure 13.6b). This stop-signal is programmed to occur at different delays following the imperative signal, thus occurring at different times after the initiation of the response, and progressively taxing the ability of subjects to impose its suppression. A key parameter of the paradigm is the time it takes to inhibit a response, i.e. the stop-signal reaction time (SSRT), which can be computed from the response time distributions and is usually measured when the probability of a successful response inhibition is set at 0.5, taking into account also the variable delays after the imperative signal. The 'race' model explicitly assumes that there is a competition between hypothetically independent 'go' and 'stop' processes that determine performance (see Logan & Cowan (1984) and Aron et al. (2003a–c) for a more detailed account of the race model), although there may well be other ways of conceptualizing the component processes of this task. While the human version of SSRT invariably requires suppression of limb responses, it has also been employed in a saccadic variant in rhesus monkeys (Schall et al. 2002). These authors were able to show that temporally coincident with the suppression of responding by a stop-signal was an inhibition of neuronal firing in the vicinity of the animal's frontal eye fields, demonstrating in this preparation at least that psychological inhibition imparted by the SSRT task is translated into physiological inhibition.

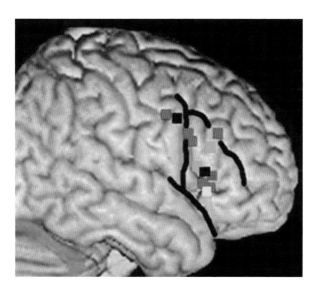

Fig. 13.8 Talairach coordinates plotted from six neuroima ging studies of switching, sorting and reversing and boundaries of inferior frontal gyrus (for further details see Aron et al. 2004a,b). Adapted from Aron et al. (2004b), with permission from the publishers, The Clarendon Press (Oxford University Press).

13.8 Neural substrates of SSRT

Early primate studies showed that lesions of the inferior convexity, a likely homologue in macaques of the right IFG in humans, produced impairments in Go–NoGo performance (Iversen & Mishkin 1970). The likely role of the right IFG in response inhibition has already been mentioned, and several neuroimaging studies of Go–NoGo or SSRT performance in human subjects have confirmed this (Konishi *et al.* 1998; Garavan *et al.* 1999; Menon *et al.* 2001; Rubia *et al.* 2003; figure 13.8). We were also able to use the same group of unilateral frontal patients to compare their deficits in task-set switching (above) and SSRT. As before, we were able to relate the volume of damage in pre-defined ROI, including the right IFG, specifically to aspects of SSRT performance, notably the Go reaction time and the SSRT itself. We found that there was a significant slowing of SSRT in patients with right PFC but not left PFC damage. Furthermore, there was a highly significant correlation ($r=0.83$, $p<0.005$) between SSRT and volume of damage in the right IFG (figure 13.7). While there were weaker correlations between SSRT and damage to other sectors, they disappeared if account was taken of the fact that damage to some of these sectors was inevitably related to damage to the right IFG itself, because lesions typically extended across ROI. There was also a significant correlation ($r=0.59$, $p<0.005$) between the SSRT and the residual task switch cost in these same patients (figure 13.7), strongly supporting the hypothesis that the two tasks share some common processes, some of which are mediated by the right IFG region. There was no significant correlation between right IFG damage and Go reaction time ($r=0.14$), suggesting that the right IFG was specifically implicated in response inhibition processes.

A recent functional neuroimaging study (Aron & Poldrack 2006) has substantiated this conclusion, while going on to suggest distinct anatomical networks for the go and stop processes. Specifically, 'Going' significantly activated motor areas contralateral to the response hand including primary motor cortex, supplementary motor area (SMA), the putamen and the pallidum, whereas 'Stopping' significantly activated the right IFG, the pre SMA, the globus pallidus and the right subthalamic nucleus (STN), a putative component of the 'indirect' pathway of the basal ganglia. Activation was significantly greater in the right IFG for subjects with faster SSRTs. These neuroimaging data have also been supported by a recent study showing that transcranial magnetic stimulation also impaired SSRT when applied over the right IFG region(Chambers *et al.* 2006).The activations of the right IFG and STN were correlated, consistent with the possibility of direct anatomical connections between the two areas (Aron *et al.* in press). This new study certainly suggests that the balance between 'Going' and 'Stopping' may be mediated by different portions of the fronto-striatal–pallidal systems.

However, it may be premature to assume that the STN itself is the key subcortical structure. Eagle *et al.* (2007) have found, using a version of the SSRT task for rats, that lesions to the STN globally disrupt performance, thus greatly complicating interpretation. By contrast, lesions of the medial striatum, but not the core region of the nucleus accumbens, do impact more selectively on SSRT performance (Eagle & Robbins 2003*a,b*). Of course, caution has to be exercised when extrapolating across species from rats to humans, but the structure of the basal ganglia has largely been conserved in evolutionary terms, making it likely that these areas are homologues of what is found in humans. The medial striatum is generally considered, for example, to be equivalent to the caudate nucleus. The situation is more complicated in the PFC; here, lesions of the OFC sector but not the infralimbic (ventromedial PFC) in rats selectively impair SSRT (Eagle & Robbins 2003*b*; Eagle *et al.* 2007). It is not yet clear how these results relate to the focus in human studies on the right IFG.

13.9 Neurochemical modulation and clinical implications

The SSRT task has proven useful for measuring deficits in impulsivity in juvenile and adult ADHD (Solanto *et al.* 2001; Aron *et al.* 2003*a–c*). It is significant that the SSRT deficit in these conditions responds well to methylphenidate medication (Aron *et al.* 2003*a–c*), suggesting modulation by catecholamine systems, and is consistent with one model of subtypes of ADHD, suggesting a right frontal hypoplasia associated with problems in motor inhibition (Castellanos & Tannock 2002). These clinical observations raise several issues, including whether it is noradrenaline or DA (or both) that are responsible for the therapeutic effects of methylpheni-date in ADHD and how they modulate the activity of the right IFG. A recent psychopharma-cologi cal study in human volunteers has shown that the relatively selective noradrenaline re-uptake blocker atomoxetine improves SSRT without affecting measures of attention and learning, whereas the selective serotonin re-uptake inhibitor, citalopram, affected learning but not attention or SSRT (Chamberlain *et al.* 2006). Other data are consistent with this selectivity; thus, both L-Dopa and tryptophan depletion (Clark *et al.* 2005) has relatively little effect on SSRT performance, suggesting that dopaminergic and serotoninergic influences on SSRT performance are only minor.The question of modulation of the right IFG can be addressed by pharmacological functional magnetic imaging studies. The results described above for the modulation of right IFG in probabilistic reversal learning may be salient. It is shown that methylphenidate (and also sulpiride) did modulate BOLD signals within the right inferior PFC (Clark *et al.* 2004), but that tryptophan depletion had no effect (Evers *et al.* 2005).

13.10 Conclusions

Studies of ed-shift, task-set switching and stop-signal inhibition have been reviewed. While these paradigms each have their distinctive features, they probably share some processes in common, related for example to response shifting and response inhibition in the context of behavioural change and cognitive plasticity. On the one hand, they appear to engage different networks within the cortico-striatal circuitry and probably have distinct interactions between the PFC and posterior cortical regions. On the other hand, they also appear to share some crucial neural substrates such as the inferior PFC, and this gives us potentially a powerful way of isolating executive functions thought to be mediated by the PFC. The evidence for this is based on the effects of precise lesions in monkeys and, in some cases, in rats on the perform-ance of tasks that bear some clear relationship to some of those also used in humans (e.g. the id-/ed-shifting test). Lesions in humans are less readily quantified, but we (and others, e.g. Stuss *et al.* 1999; see also Stuss & Alexander 2007) have developed a method for this based on quantitative structural imaging. The crucial importance of such evidence from lesion and also transcranial magnetic stimulation studies is that it enables a determination to be made of the causal significance of an activation of a particular region in a functional imaging study. The advantage of the latter, of course, is that it is possible through neuroimaging to determine the entire neural network engaged by a particular task.

Although structures such as the right IFG within the inferior PFC have been implicated in the component process of many tasks (Duncan & Owen 2000), its role in tests requiring inhibition across a wide variety of tasks, including switching into a suppression mode (Swainson *et al.* 2000), is significant. This role may possibly extend to other situations such as dual-task interference (Herath *et al.* 2001), 'memory inhibition' (Anderson *et al.* 2004) and the modulation of anxious reactions (Bishop *et al.* 2004), through influences mediated to the hippocampus and amygdala, respectively. Indeed, the IFG is one of the most densely connected regions of the PFC (Miller & Cohen 2001) and is one of the last to develop in both ontogenetic and phylogenetic terms (Pandya & Barnes 1987).

Functions such as stopping, shifting and switching are influenced by internal state and are thus susceptible to modulation by ascending neurotransmitter systems mediating functions such as stress, arousal and motivation. We have explored the potentially distinct functions of the monoamine systems by means of selective neuropsychopharmacological manipulations of the dopamine, noradrenaline and serotonin systems in experimental animals and, where feasible, in humans. By using intra-cerebral treatments in animals or combining functional imaging and psychopharma cological investigations, we have shown how it is possible to gain some idea about how processing in different regions may be influenced by distinct neurochemical mechanisms. Such evidence of course is crucial for understanding how medications for conditions such as ADHD and depression actually work in neuropsychological terms.

Using these methods, we have gained some evidence for a separation of PFC regions in the mediation of id-and ed-shifting and reversal learning that holds across species. Even more surprising is that there is evidence for precise modulation of these functions by different monoamine systems projecting to the PFC in the marmoset, and also in humans (see Robbins & Roberts (2007) for a more detailed review of this evidence in infrahuman animals). It is also striking how performance on certain tasks, such as reversal learning, is so susceptible to manipulations of 5-HT, whereas other functions such as stop-signal inhibition are insensitive in our hands. By contrast, extrapolating across species, it appears that noradrenaline is implicated in both stop-signal inhibition and ed-shifting, with obvious implications for conditions such as ADHD. Furthermore, it is important to point out that neurotransmitter influences are determined by the neural context in which they occur; for example, there is evidence that striatal, but not PFC, DA modulates reversal learning.

The theoretical and adaptive significance of this complexity is still being addressed. The fact that the different neurotransmitter systems innervating the PFC and striatum not only interact with one another, but also exert specific functions, suggests that the functioning of the fronto-circuitry is state dependent, and that different aspects of executive control may need to be recruited to optimize behavioural and cognitive performance in those states. Understanding the nature of these states, by determining the precise circumstances in which these systems operate, should be a major goal of research in the next decade. Central to this effort will be the need to solve a modern version of an old conundrum: how basic functions mediated by the subcortical systems interact with higher cognitive processing? One distinct possibility is that it is achieved partly in a 'top-down' manner, i.e. those regions of the PFC that are engaged by particular task operations recruit activity in the neurochemically differentiated systems by means of descending projections to their sources in subcortical sites (e.g. Amat *et al.* 2005; Robbins 2005). Unravelling this form of 'executive control', with its implications for optimizing cognitive functioning and understanding of psychopathology and its treatment, is undoubtedly a challenge for the future.

I wish to thank A. Aron and A. Roberts for discussion and all of my other collaborators over the last decade who have contributed to the research reviewed here. This work was supported by programme grants from the Wellcome Trust. The Behavioural and Clinical Neuroscience Institute is supported by a joint award from the MRC and the Wellcome Trust.

References

Alexander, G., DeLong, M. & Strick, P. L. 1986 Parallel organisation of functionally segregated circuits linking basal ganglia and cortex. *Annu. Rev. Neurosci.* **9**, 357–381. (doi:10.1146/annurev.ne. 09.030186.002041)

Allport, A. & Wyllie, G. 1999 Task-switching: positive and negative priming of task-set. In *Attention, space and action: studies in cognitive neuroscience* (eds G. W. Humphreys, J. Duncan & A. Treisman), pp. 273–296. Oxford, UK: Oxford University Press.

Amat, J., Baratta, A., Paul, E., Bland, S. T., Watkins, L. R. & Maier, S. F. 2005 The ventral medial prefrontal cortex determines how behavioral control over stress impacts behavior and dorsal raphé nucleus activity. *Nat. Neurosci.* **8**, 365–371. (doi:10.1038/nn1399)

Anderson, M. C., Ochsner, K. N., Kuhl, B., Cooper, J., Robertson, E., Gabrieli, S. W., Glover, G. H. & Gabrieli, J. D. E. 2004 Neural systems underlying the suppression of unwanted memories. *Science* **303**, 232–235. (doi:10.1126/science.1089504)

Arnsten, A. F. T. & Robbins, T. W. 2002 Neurochemical modulation of prefrontal cortical functions in humans and animals. In *The prefrontal cortex* (eds D. Stuss & R. Knight), pp. 51–84. New York, NY: Oxford University Press.

Aron, A. R., Behrens, T. E., Frank, M. J., Smith, S. & Poldrack, R. A. In press. Triangulating a cognitive control network using diffusion-weighted MRI and functional MRI. J. *Neurosci.*

Aron, A. R. & Poldrack, R. A. 2006 Cortical and subcortical contributions to stop signal response inhibition: role of the subthalamic nucleus. J. *Neurosci.* **26**, 2424–2433. (doi:10.1523/JNEUROSCI. 4682-05.2006)

Aron, A. R., Fletcher, P. C., Bullmore, E. T., Sahakian, B. J. & Robbins, T. W. 2003a Stop-signal inhibition disrupted by damage to right inferior frontal gyrus in humans. *Nat. Neurosci.* **6**, 115–116. (doi:10.1038/nn1003)

Aron, A., Watkins, L., Sahakian, B. J., Monsell, S., Barker, R. A. & Robbins, T. W. 2003b Task-set switching deficits in early-stage Huntington's disease: implications for basal ganglia function. J. *Cogn. Neurosci.* **15**, 629–642. (doi:10. 1162/jocn.2003.15.5.629)

Aron, A., Dowson, J., Sahakian, B. J. & Robbins, T. W. 2003c Methylphenidate response inhibition in adults with attention-deficit/hyperactivity disorder. Biol. Psych. **54**, 1465–1468. (doi:10.1016/ S0006–3223(03)00609–7)

Aron, A. R., Robbins, T. W. & Poldrack, R. A. 2004a Inhibition and the right inferior frontal cortex. Trends *Cogn. Sci.* **8**, 170–177. (doi:10.1016/j.tics.2004.02.010)

Aron, A. R., Monsell, S., Sahakian, B. J. & Robbins, T. W. 2004b A componential analysis of task-switching deficits associated with lesions of left and right frontal cortex. Brain **127**, 1561–1573. (doi:10.1093/brain/awh169)

Baddeley, A. D. 1986 *Working memory*. Oxford, UK: Clarendon Press.

Baddeley, A. & Della Salla, S. 1998 Working memory and executive control. In *The prefrontal cortex: executive and cognitive functions* (eds A. C. Roberts, T. W. Robbins & L. Weiskrantz), pp. 9–21. Oxford, UK: Oxford University Press.

Birrell, J. M. & Brown, V. J. 2001 Medial frontal cortex mediates perceptual attentional set shifting in the rat. J. *Neurosci.* **20**, 4320–4324.

Bishop, S., Duncan, J. & Lawrence, A. D. 2004 Prefrontal cortical function and anxiety: controlling attention to threat-related stimuli. *Nat. Neurosci.* **7**, 184–188. (doi:10.1038/nn1173)

Bor, D., Duncan, J. & Owen, A. M. 2003 Encoding strategies dissociate prefrontal activity from working memory demand. *Neuron* **37**, 361–367. (doi:10.1016/S0896-6273 (02)01171-6)

Brown, V. J. & Bowman, E. 2002 Rodent models of prefrontal cortical function. *Trends Neurosci.* **25**, 340–343.

Bunge, S. A., Dudukovic, N. M., Thomason, M. E., Vaidya, M. & Gabrieli, J. D. E. 2002 Immature frontal lobe contributions to cognitive control in children: evidence from fMRI. *Neuron* **33**, 301–311. (doi:10.1016/S0896-6273(01)00583-9)

Castellanos, F. X. & Tannock, R. 2002 Neuroscience of attention-deficit/hyperactivity disorder: the search for endophenotypes. *Nat. Rev. Neurosci.* **3**, 617–628.

Chamberlain, S. R., Muller, U., Blackwell, A. D., Clark, L., Robbins, T. W. & Sahakian, B. J. 2006 Neurochemical modulation of response inhibition and probabilistic learning in humans. *Science* **311**, 861–863.

Chambers, C. D., Bellgrove, M. A., Stokes, M. G., Henderson, T. R., Garavan, H., Robertson, I. H., Morris, A. P. & Mattingley, J. B. 2006 Executive 'brake failure' following deactivation of human frontal lobe. *J. Cogn. Neurosci.* **18**, 444–455.

Chudasama, Y. & Robbins, T. W. 2003 Dissociable contributions of the orbitofrontal and infralimbic cortex in pavlovian autoshaping and discrimination reversal learning: further evidence for the functional heterogeneity of the rodent frontal cortex. *J. Neurosci.* **23**, 8771–8780.

Clark, L., Cools, R., Evers, L. E., van den Veen, F., Jolles, J., Sahakian, B. J. & Robbins, T. W. 2004 Neurochemical modulation of prefrontal cortex function. *FENS Abstr.* **2**, A205.1.

Clark, L., Roiser, J. P., Cools, R., Rubinsztein, D. C., Sahakian, B. J. & Robbins, T. W. 2005 Stop signal response inhibition is not modulated by tryptophan depletion or the serotonin transporter polymorphism in healthy volunteers: implications for the 5-HT theory of impulsivity. *Psychopharmacology* **182**, 570–578. (doi:10. 1007/s00213-005-0104-6)

Clarke, H. F., Dalley, J. W., Crofts, H. S., Robbins, T. W. & Roberts, A. C. 2004 Cognitive inflexibility following prefrontal serotonin depletion. *Science* **304**, 878–880. (doi:10.1126/science.1094987)

Clarke, H. F., Walker, S. C., Crofts, H. S., Dalley, J. W., Robbins, T. W. & Roberts, A. C. 2005 Prefrontal serotonin depletion affects reversal learning but not attentional set shifting. *J. Neurosci.* **12**, 532–538. (doi:10.1523/JNEUR-OSCI.3690-04.2005)

Clarke, H. F., Walker, S. C., Dalley, J. W., Robbins, T. W. & Roberts, A. C. 2007 Cognitive inflexibility after prefrontal serotonin depletion is behaviorally and neurochemically specific. *Cereb. Cortex* **17**, 18–27. (doi:10.1093/cercor/ bhj120)

Cohen, J. D., Braver, T. S. & O'Reilly, R. C. 1998 A computational approach to prefrontal cortex, and schizophrenia: recent developments and current challenges. In *The prefrontal cortex: executive and cognitive functions* (eds A. C. Roberts, T. W. Robbins & L. Weiskrantz), pp. 195–220. Oxford, UK: Oxford University Press.

Collins, P., Roberts, A. C., Dias, R., Everitt, B. J. & Robbins, T. W. 1998 Perseveration and strategy in a novel spatial self-ordered sequencing task for non-human primates: effects of excitotoxic lesions and dopamine depletions of the prefrontal cortex. *J. Cogn. Neurosci.* **10**, 332–354. (doi:10.1162/089892998562771)

Cools, R., Barker, R., Sahakian, B. J. & Robbins, T. W. 2001 Enhanced or impaired cognitive function in Parkinson's disease as a function of dopaminergic medication and task demands. *Cereb. Cortex* **11**, 1136–1143. (doi:10.1093/ cercor/11.12.1136)

Cools, R., Clark, L., Owen, A. M. & Robbins, T. W. 2002 Defining the neural mechanisms of probabilistic reversal learning using event-related functional magnetic resonance imaging. *J. Neurosci.* **22**, 4563–4567.

Cools, R., Barker, R., Sahakian, B. J. & Robbins, T. W. 2003 L-Dopa medication remediates cognitive inflexibility, but increases impulsivity in patients with Parkinson's disease. *Neuropsychologia* **41**, 1431–1441. (doi:10.1016/S0028-3932(03)00117-9)

Cools, R., Clark, L. & Robbins, T. W. 2004 Differential responses in human striatum and prefrontal cortex to changes in object and rule relevance. *J. Neurosci.* **24**, 1129–1135. (doi:10.1523/JNEUROSCI. 4312-03.2004)

Cools, R., Lewis, S. J., Clark, L., Barker, R. A. & Robbins, T. W. 2007 L-Dopa disrupts activity in the nucleus accumbens during reversal learning in Parkinson's disease. *Neuropsychopharmacology.* **32**, 180–189. (doi:10.1038/sj. npp.1301153)

Cools, R., Ivry, R. B. & D'Esposito, M. D. 2006 The human striatum is necessary for responding to changes in stimulus relevance. *J. Cog. Neurosci.* **18**, 1973–1983. (doi:10.1162/jocn.2006. 18.12.1973)

Corbetta, M. & Shulman, G. L. 2002 Control of goal-directed and stimulus-driven attention in the brain. *Nat. Rev. Neurosci.* **3**, 215–229. (doi:10.1038/nrn755)

Crofts, H. S., Dalley, J. W., Collins, P., Van Denderen, J. C. M., Everitt, B. J., Robbins, T. W. & Roberts, A. C. 2001 Differential effects of 6-OHDA lesions of the prefrontal cortex and caudate nucleus on the ability to acquire an attentional set. *Cereb. Cortex* **11**, 1015–1026. (doi:10.1093/cercor/11.11.1015)

Damasio, A. R. 1998 The somatic marker hypothesis and the possible functions of the prefrontal cortex. In *The prefrontal cortex: executive and cognitive functions* (eds A. C. Roberts, T. W. Robbins & L. Weiskrantz), pp. 36–50. Oxford, UK: Oxford University Press.

D'Esposito, M. 2007 From cognitive to neural models of working memory. *Phil. Trans. R. Soc. B* **362**, 761–772. (doi:10.1098/rstb.2007.2086)

De Zubicaray, G. I., Andrew, C., Zelaya, F. O., Williams, S. C. & Dumanoir, C. 2000 Motor response suppression and the prepotent tendency to respond; a parametric fMRI study. *Neuropsychologia* **38**, 1280–1291. (doi:10.1016/ S0028-3932(00)00033-6)

Derrfuss, J., Brass, M., Neumann, J. & von Cramon, D. Y. 2005 Involvement of the inferior frontal junction in cognitive control: meta-analyses of switching and Stroop studies. *Hum. Brain Mapp.* **25**, 22–34. (doi:10.1002/hbm. 20127)

Dias, R., Robbins, T. W. & Roberts, A. C. 1996 Dissociation in prefrontal cortex of affective and attentional shifts. *Nature* **380**, 69–72. (doi:10.1038/380069a0)

Dias, R., Robbins, T. W. & Roberts, A. C. 1997 Dissociable forms of inhibitory control within prefrontal cortex with an analogue of the Wisconsin card sort test: restriction to novel situations and independence from 'on-line' processing. *J. Neurosci.* **17**, 9285–9297.

Divac, I., Rosvold, H. E. & Szwarcbart, M. K. 1967 Behavioral effects of selective ablations of the caudate nucleus. *J. Comp. Physiol. Psychol.* **63**, 184–190. (doi:10.1037/h0024348)

Dolan, R. J. 2007 The human amygdala and orbital prefrontal cortex in behavioural regulation. *Phil. Trans. R. Soc. B* **362**, 787–799. (doi:10.1098/rstb.2007.2088)

Dove, A., Pollman, S., Schubert, T., Wiggins, C. J. & von Cramon, D. Y. 2000 Prefrontal cortex activation in task switching: an event-related fMRI study. *Brain Res. Cogn. Brain Res.* **9**, 103–109. (doi:10.1016/ S0926-6410(99) 00029-4)

Duncan, J. & Owen, A. M. 2000 Common regions of the human frontal lobe recruited by diverse cognitive demands. *Trends Neurosci.* **23**, 475–483. (doi:10.1016/S0166-2236(00)01633-7)

Dunnett, S. B. & Iversen, S. D. 1981 Learning impairments following selective kainic acid-induced lesions within the neostriatum in rats. *Behav. Brain Res.* **2**, 189–209. (doi:10.1016/0166-4328 (81)90055-3)

Eagle, D. M. & Robbins, T. W. 2003a Inhibitory control in rats performing on the stop-signal reaction time task: effects of lesions of the medial striatum and D-amphet-amine. *Behav. Neurosci.* **117**, 1302–1317. (doi:10.1037/ 0735-7044.117.6.1302)

Eagle, D. M. & Robbins, T. W. 2003b Lesions of the medial prefrontal cortex or nucleus accumbens core do not impair inhibitory control in rats performing a stop-signal reaction time task. *Behav. Brain Res.* **146**, 131–144. (doi:10.1016/ j.bbr.2003.09.022)

Eagle, D. M., Baunez, C., Hutcheson, D. M., Lehmann, O., Shah, A. P. & Robbins, T. W. 2007. Stop-signal reaction time performance: role of prefrontal cortex and subthalamic nucleus. *Cereb. Cortex.* (doi: 10.1093/cerca/bhm/044)

Evers, E. A., Cools, R., Clark, L., van der Veen, F. M., Jolles, J., Sahakian, B. J. & Robbins, T. W. 2005 Serotonergic modulation of prefrontal cortex during negative feedback in probabilistic reversal learning. *Neuropsychopharmacology* **30**, 1138–1147. (doi:10.1038/sj.npp.1300663)

Fellows, L. K. & Farrah, M. J. 2003 Ventromedial frontal cortex mediates affective shifting in humans: evidence from a reversal learning paradigm. *Brain* **126**, 1830–1837. (doi:10.1093/ brain/awg180)

Fuster, J. M. 1989 *The prefrontal cortex: anatomy, physiology and neuropsychology of the frontal lobe.* New York, NY: Raven.

Garavan, H., Ross, T. J. & Stein, E. A. 1999 Right hemispheric dominance of inhibitory control: an event-related functional MRI study. *Proc. Natl Acad. Sci. USA* **96**, 8301–8306. (doi:10.1073/pnas. 96.14.8301)

Garavan, H., Ross, T. J., Murphy, K., Roche, R. A. & Stein, E. A. 2002 Dissociable executive functions in the dynamic control of behavior: inhibition, error detection and correction. *Neuroimage* **17**, 1820–1829. (doi:10.1006/nimg.2002. 1326)

Gehring, W. J. & Knight, R. T. 2000 Prefrontal–cingulate interactions in action monitoring. *Nat. Neurosci.* **3**, 516–520. (doi:10.1038/74899)

Gilbert, S. J. & Shallice, T. 2002 Task switching: a PDP model. *Cogn. Psychol.* **44**, 297–337. (doi:10.1006/cogp. 2001.0770)

Goldman-Rakic, P. S. 1998 The prefrontal landscape: implications of functional architecture for understanding human mentation and the central executive. In *The prefrontal cortex: executive and cognitive functions* (eds A. C. Roberts, T. W. Robbins & L.Weiskrantz), pp. 87–102. Oxford, UK: Oxford University Press.

Haber, S. N., Fudge, J. L. & McFarland, N. R. 2000 Striatonigrostriatal pathways in primates form an ascending spiral from the shell to the dorsolateral striatum. *J. Neurosci.* **20**, 2369–2382.

Hampshire, A. & Owen, A. M. 2006 Fractionating atten-tional control using event-related fMRI. *Cereb. Cortex* **16**, 1279–1289.

Herath, P., Klingberg, T., Young, J., Amutis, K. & Roland, P. 2001 Neural correlates of dual task perform-ance can be dissociated from those of divided attention: an fMRI study. *Cereb. Cortex* **11**, 796–805. (doi:10.1093/cercor/11.9.796)

Hollerman, J. R., Tremblay, L. & Schultz, W. 2000 Involvement of basal ganglia and orbitofrontal cortex in goal-directed behavior. *Prog. Brain Res.* **126**, 193–215.

Hornak, J., Bramham, J., Rolls, E. T., Morris, R. G., O'Doherty, J., Bullock, P. R. & Polkey, C. E. 2004 Reward-related reversal learning after surgical excisions in orbitofrontal or dorsolateral prefrontal cortex in humans. J. *Cogn. Neurosci.* **16**, 463–478. (doi:10.1162/08989290 4322926791)

Huettel, S. A., Stowe, C. J., Gordon, E. M., Warner, B. T. & Platt, M. L. 2006 Neural signatures of eco-nomic preferences for risk and ambiguity. *Neuron* **49**, 765–775. (doi:10.1016/j.neuron.2006.01.024)

Iversen, S. D. & Mishkin, M. 1970 Perseverative interference in monkeys following selective lesions of the inferior frontal convexity. *Exp. Brain Res.* **11**, 376–386. (doi:10. 1007/BF00237911)

Keele, S. W. & Rafal, R. 1999 Deficits in task set in patients with left prefrontal cortex lesions. In *Control of cognitive processes: attention and performance XVIII* (eds S. Monsell & J. Driver), pp. 627–651. Cambridge, MA: MIT Press.

Koechlin, E., Ody, C. & Kouneiher, F. 2003 The architecture of cognitive control in the human prefrontal cortex. Science **302**, 1181–1185. (doi:10.1126/science.1088545)

Konishi, S., Nakahama, K., Uchida, I., Kameyama, M. & Miyashita, Y. 1999 Common inhibitory mechanism in human inferior prefrontal cortex revealed by event-related fMRI. *Brain* **122**, 981–991. (doi:10.1093/brain/122.5.981)

Konishi, S., Nakajima, K., Uchida, I., Sekihara, K. & Miyashita, Y. 1998 No-go dominant brain activity in human inferior prefrontal cortex revealed by functional magnetic resonance imaging. *Eur. J. Neurosci.* **10**, 1209–1213. (doi:10.1046/j.1460-9568.1998.00167.x)

Lange, K., Robbins, T. W., Marsden, C. D., James, M., Owen, A. & Paul, G. M. 1992 L-Dopa withdrawal selectively impairs performance in tests of frontal lobe function in Parkinson's disease. *Psychopharmacology* **107**, 394–404. (doi:10.1007/BF02245167)

Lange, K. W., Sahakian, B. J., Quinn, N. P., Marsden, C. D. & Robbins, T. W. 1995 Comparison of executive and visuospatial function in Huntington's disease and dementia of the Alzheimer-type matched for degree of dementia. J. *Neurol. Neurosurg. Psych.* **58**, 598–606.

Lapiz, M. D. S. & Morilak, D. A. 2005 Noradrenergic modulation of cognitive function in rat medial prefrontal cortex as measured by attentional set shifting capability. *Neuroscience* **137**, 1039–1049. (doi:10.1016/j.neuro-science.2005.09.031)

Lewis, S. J. G., Slabosz, A., Robbins, T. W., Barker, R. A. & Owen, A. M. 2005 Dopaminergic basis for deficits in working memory but not attentional set-shifting in Parkinson's disease. *Neuropsychologia* **43**, 823–832. (doi:10.1016/j.neuropsychologia.2004.10.001)

Liston, C., Miller, M. M., Goldwater, D. S., Radley, J. J., Rocher, A. B., Hof, P. R., Morrison, J. H. & McEwen, B. S. 2006 Stress-induced alterations in prefrontal cortical dendritic morphology predict selective impairments in perceptual attentional set-shifting. *J. Neurosci.* **26**, 7870–7874. (doi:10.1523/JNEUROSCI.1184-06.2006)

Logan, G. D. & Cowan, W. B. 1984 On the ability to inhibit thought and action: a theory of an act of control. *Psychol. Rev.* **91**, 295–327. (doi:10.1037/0033-295X.91.3.295)

MacDonald, A. W., Cohen, J. D., Stenger, V. A. & Carter, C. S. 2000 Dissociating the role of the dorsolateral prefrontal cortex and anterior cingulate cortex in cognitive control. *Science* **288**, 1235–1238. (doi:10.1126/science. 288.5472.1835)

Mattay, V. S., Goldberg, T. E., Fera, F., Hariri, A. R., Tessitore, R., Egan, M. F., Kolachana, B., Callicot, J. H. & Weinberger, D. R. 2003 Catechol O-methyltransferase val158-met genotype and individual variation in the brain response to amphetamine. *Proc. Natl Acad. Sci. USA* **100**, 6186–6191. (doi:10.1073/pnas.0931309100)

McClure, S., Laibson, D. I., Loewenstein, G. & Cohen, J. D. 2004 Separate neural systems value immediate and delayed monetary rewards. *Science* **306**, 503–507. (doi:10.1126/science.1100907)

Mecklinger, A. D., von Cramon, D. Y., Springer, A. & Matthes-von Cramon, G. 1999 Executive control functions in task-switching: evidence from brain-injured patients. J. *Clin. Exp. Neuropsychol.* **21**, 606–619.

Mehta, M. A., Sahakian, B. J., McKenna, P. J. & Robbins, T. W. 1999 Systemic sulpiride in young adult volunteers simulates the profile of cognitive deficits in Parkinson's disease. *Psychopharmacology* **146**, 162–174. (doi:10.1007/ s002130051102)

Mehta, M. A., Manes, F. F., Magnolfi, G., Sahakian, B. J. & Robbins, T. W. 2004 Impaired set-shifting and dissociable effects on tests of spatial working memory following the dopamine D2 receptor antagonist sulpiride in healthy volunteers. *Psychopharmacology* **176**, 331–342. (doi:10.1007/ s00213-004-1899-2)

Menon, V., Adleman, N. E., White, C. D., Glover, G. H. & Reiss, A. L. 2001 Error-related brain activation during a Go/No Go response inhibition task. *Hum. Brain Mapp.* **12**, 131–143. (doi:10.1002/ 1097-0193(200103)12:3!131:: AID-HBM1010O3.0.CO;2-C)

Middleton, H. C., Sharma, A., Agouzoul, D., Sahakian, B. J. & Robbins, T. W. 1999 Idazoxan potentiates rather than antagonizes some of the cognitive effects of clonidine. *Psychopharmacology* **145**, 401–411. (doi:10.1007/s00213 0051074)

Miller, E. K. & Cohen, J. D. 2001 An integrative theory of prefrontal cortex function. *Annu. Rev. Neurosci.* **24**, 167–202.

Moghaddam, B. 2004 Targeting metabotropic glutamate receptors for treatment of the cognitive symptoms of schizophrenia. *Psychopharmacology* **174**, 39–44. (doi:10.1007/s00213-004-1792-z)

Monchi, O., Petrides, M. P., Petre, V., Worsley, K. & Dagher, A. 2001 Wisconsin Card Sorting revisited: distinct neural circuits participating in different stages of the test identified by event-related functional magnetic resonance imaging. J. *Neurosci.* **21**, 7733–7741.

Monsell, S. 2003 Task switching. *Trends Cogn. Sci.* **7**, 134–140.

Murphy, F. C., Michael, A., Robbins, T. W. & Sahakian, B. J. 2002 Neuropsychological impairment in patients with major depressive disorder: the effects of feedback on task performance. *Psychol. Med.* **33**, 455–467. (doi:10.1017/ S0033291702007018)

Nagahama, Y., Okada, T., Katsumi, Y., Hayashi, T., Yamauchi, H., Oyanagi, C., Konishi, S., Fukuyama, H. & Shibasaki, H. 2000 Dissociable mechanisms of atten-tional control within the human prefrontal cortex. *Cereb. Cortex* **11**, 85–92. (doi:10.1093/cercor/11.1.85)

Nakahara, K., Hayashi, T., Konishi, S. & Miyashita, Y. 2002 Functional MRI of monkeys performing a cognitive set-shifting task. *Science* **295**, 1532–1536. (doi:10.1126/ science.1067653)

O'Doherty, J., Kringelbach, M. L., Rolls, E. T., Hornak, J. & Andrews, C. 2001 Abstract reward and punishment representations in the human orbitofrontal cortex. *Nat. Neurosci.* **4**, 95–102. (doi:10.1038/82959)

O'Doherty, J., Critchley, H., Deichmann, R. & Dolan, R. J. 2003 Dissociating valence of outcome from behavioral control in human orbital and ventral prefrontal cortex. J. *Neurosci* **23**, 7391–7939.

Owen, A., Downes, J. J., Sahakian, B. J., Polkey, C. E. & Robbins, T. W. 1990 Planning and spatial working memory following frontal lobe lesions in man. *Neuro-psychologia* **28**, 1021–1034. (doi:10.1016/0028-3932(90) 90137-D)

Owen, A. M., Roberts, A. C., Polkey, C. E., Sahakian, B. J. & Robbins, T. W. 1991 Extra-dimensional versus intra-dimensional set shifting performance following frontal lobe excision, temporal lobe excision or amygdalo-hippo-campectomy in man. *Neuropsychologia* **29**, 993–1006. (doi:10.1016/ 0028-3932(91)90063-E)

Owen, A. M., Roberts, A. C., Hodges, J. R., Summers, B. A., Polkey, C. E. & Robbins, T. W. 1993 Contrasting mechanisms of impaired attentional set-shifting in patients with frontal lobe damage or Parkinson's disease. *Brain* **116**, 1159–1179. (doi:10.1093/brain/116.5.1159)

Owen, A. M., Morris, R. G., Sahakian, B. J., Polkey, C. E. & Robbins, T. W. 1996 Double dissociations of memory and executive functions in working memory tasks following frontal lobe excision, temporal lobe excisions or amygdala-hippocampectomy in man. *Brain* **119**, 1597–1615. (doi:10.1093/brain/119.5.1597)

Pandya, D. N. & Barnes, C. L. 1987 Architecture and connections of the frontal lobe. In *The frontal lobes revisited* (ed. E. Perecman), pp. 41–68. Hillsdale, NJ: Lawrence Erlbaum.

Park, S. B., Coull, J. T., McShane, R. H., Young, A. H., Sahakian, B. J., Robbins, T. W. & Cowen, P. J. 1994 Tryptophan depletion in normal volunteers produces selective impairments in learning and memory. *Neuro-pharmacology* **33**, 575–588. (doi:10.1016/0028-3908(94) 90089-2)

Petrides, M. 1998 Specialized systems for the processing of mnemonic information within the primate frontal cortex. In *The prefrontal cortex: executive and cognitive functions* (eds A. C. Roberts, T. W. Robbins & L. Weiskrantz), pp. 103–114. Oxford, UK: Oxford University Press.

Preuss, T. M. 1995 Do rats have a prefrontal cortex? The Rose–Woolsey–Akert Program reconsidered. *J. Cogn. Neurosci.* 7, 1–24.

Rahman, S., Sahakian, B. J., Hodges, J. R., Rogers, R. D. & Robbins, T. W. 1999 Specific cognitive deficits in mild frontal variant frontotemporal dementia. Brain **122**, 1469–1493. (doi:10.1093/brain/122.8.1469)

Robbins, T. W. 1998 Dissociating executive functions of the prefrontal cortex. In *The prefrontal cortex: executive and cognitive functions* (eds A. C. Roberts, T. W. Robbins & L. Weiskrantz), pp. 117–130. Oxford, UK: Oxford University Press.

Robbins, T. W. 2000 Chemical neuromodulation of frontal-executive function in humans and other animals. *Exp. Brain Res.* **133**, 130–138. (doi:10.1007/s002210000407)

Robbins, T. W. 2005 Controlling stress: how the brain protects itself from depression. *Nat. Neurosci.* **3**, 261–262. (doi:10.1038/nn0305-261)

Robbins, T. W. & Everitt, B. J. 1992 Functions of dopamine in the dorsal and ventral striatum. In *Seminars in the neurosciences* (ed. T. W. Robbins), pp. 119–127. London, UK: Saunders.

Robbins, T. W. & Murphy, E. R. 2006 Behavioural pharmacology: 40C years of progress, with a focus on glutamate receptors and cognition. *Trends Pharmacol. Sci.* **27**, 141–148. (doi:10.1016/j.tips.2006.01.009)

Robbins, T. W. & Roberts, A. C. 2007. Differential regulation of fronto-executive function by the monoamines and acetylcholine. *Cereb. Cortex.* **17**, i151–i160.

Roberts, A., Robbins, T. W. & Everitt, B. J. 1988 Extra- and Intra-dimensional shifts in man and marmoset. Q. J. *Exp. Psychol.* B **40**, 321–342.

Roberts, A. C., De Salvia, M. A., Wilkinson, L. S., Collins, P., Muir, J. L., Everitt, B. J. & Robbins, T. W. 1994 6-hydroxydopamine lesions of the prefrontal cortex in monkeys enhance performance on an analogue of the Wisconsin card sorting test: possible interactions with subcortical dopamine. J. *Neurosci.* **14**, 2531–2544.

Roberts, A. C., Robbins, T. W. & Weiskrantz, L. 1998 *The prefrontal cortex: executive and cognitive functions.* Oxford, UK: Oxford University Press.

Rogers, R. D., Sahakian, B. J., Hodges, J. R., Polkey, C. E., Kennard, C. & Robbins, T. W. 1998b Dissociating executive mechanisms of task control following frontal lobe damage and Parkinson's disease. *Brain* **121**, 815–842. (doi:10.1093/brain/121.5.815)

Rogers, R. D., Owen, A. M., Middleton, H. C., Williams, E. J., Pickard, J. D., Sahakian, B. J. & Robbins, T. W. 1999a Choosing between small, likely rewards and large unlikely rewards activates inferior and orbital prefrontal cortex. J. *Neurosci.* **20**, 9029–9038.

Rogers, R. D. *et al.* 1999b Tryptophan depletion impairs stimulus-reward learning while methylphenidate disrupts attentional control in healthy young adults: implications for the monoaminergic basis of impulsive behaviour. *Psychopharmacology* **146**, 482–491. (doi:10.1007/PL00 005494)

Rogers, R. D., Andrews, T. C., Grasby, P. M., Brooks, D. & Robbins, T. W. 2000 Contrasting cortical and sub-cortical PET activations produced by reversal learning and attentional-set shifting in humans. J. *Cogn. Neurosci.* **12**, 142–162. (doi:10.1162/089892900561931)

Rowe, J. B., Toni, I., Josephs, O., Frackowiak, R. S. J. & Passingham, R. E. 2000 The prefrontal cortex: response selection or maintenance within working memory? *Science* **288**, 1656–1660. (doi:10.1126/science.288.5471.1656)

Rubia, K., Smith, A. B., Brammer, M. J. & Taylor, E. 2003 Right inferior cortex mediates response inhibition while mesial prefrontal cortex is responsible for error detection. *Neuroimage* **20**, 351–358. (doi:10.1016/S1053-8119(03) 00275-1)

Schall, J. D., Stuphorn, V. & Brown, J. W. 2002 Monitoring and control of action by the frontal lobes. *Neuron* **36**, 309–322. (doi:10.1016/S0896-6273(02)00964-9)

Schoenbaum, G., Setlow, B. & Ramus, S. 2002 Orbitofrontal lesions in rats impair reversal but not acquisition of go, no-go odour discriminations. *Neuroreport* **13**, 885–890. (doi:10.1097/00001756-200205070-00030)

Schultz, W. & Dickinson, A. 2000 Neuronal coding of prediction errors. *Annu. Rev. Neurosci.* **23**, 473–500. (doi:10.1146/annurev.neuro.23.1.473)

Shallice, T. 1982 Specific impairments of planning. *Phil. Trans. R. Soc. B* **298**, 199–209. (doi:10.1098/rstb.1982.0082)

Shallice, T. & Burgess, P. 1998 The domain of supervisory processes and the temporal organisation of behaviour. In *The prefrontal cortex: executive and cognitive functions* (eds A. C. Roberts, T. W. Robbins & L. Weiskrantz), pp. 22–35. Oxford, UK: Oxford University Press.

Slamecka, N. J. 1968 A methodological analysis of shift paradigms in human discrimination learning. *Psychol. Bull.* **69**, 423–438. (doi:10.1037/h0025762)

Smith, E. E. & Jonides, J. 1995 Working memory in humans: neuropsychological evidence. In *The cognitive neurosciences* (ed. M. Gazzaniga), pp. 109–120. Cambridge, MA: MIT Press.

Solanto, M., Abikoff, H., Sonuga-Barke, E., Schachar, R., Logan, G. D., Wigal, T., Hectman, L., Hinshaw, S. & Turkel, E. 2001 The ecological validity of delay aversion and response inhibition as measures of impulsivity in AD/HD: a supplement to the NIMH multi-modal treatment study of AD/HD. *J. Abnorm. Child Psychol.* **29**, 215–228. (doi:10.1023/A:1010329714819)

Stuss, D. T. & Alexander, M. P. 2007 Is there a dysexecutive syndrome? *Phil. Trans. R. Soc. B* **362**, 901–915. (doi:10. 1098/rstb.2007.2096)

Stuss, D. T., Toth, J. P., Fianchi, D., Alexander, M. P., Tipper, S. & Craik, F. 1999 Dissociation of attentional processes in patients with focal frontal and posterior lesions. *Neuropsychologia* **37**, 1005–1027. (doi:10.1016/ S0028-3932(98)00158-4)

Sutherland, N. S. & Mackintosh, N. J. 1971 *Mechanisms of animal discrimination learning.* New York, NY: Academic Press.

Swainson, R., Cunnington, R., Jackson, G. M., Rorden, C., Peters, A., Morris, P. G. & Jackson, S. R. 2000 Cognitive control mechanisms revealed by ERP and fMRI: evidence from repeated task-set shifting. *J. Cogn. Neurosci.* **15**, 785–799. (doi:10.1162/089892903322370717)

Talbot, P. S., Watson, D. R., Barrett, S. L. & Cooper, S. J. 2006 Rapid tryptophan depletion improves decision-making cognition without affecting reversal learning or set-shifting. *Neuropsychopharmacology* **31**, 1519–1525. (doi:10.1038/sj.npp.1300980)

Tait, D.S., Brown, V.J., Farovik, A., Theobold, D.E., Dalley, J.W. & Robbins, T.W. 2006 Lesions of the dorsal noradrenergic bundle impair attentional set-shifting in the rat. *Euro. J. Neuurosci.* **25**, 3719–3724.

Tunbridge, E. M., Bannerman, D. M., Sharp, T. & Harrison, P. J. 2004 Catechol-*o*-methyltransferase inhibition improves set-shifting performance and elevates stimulated dopamine release in the rat. *J. Neurosci.* **24**, 5331–5335. (doi:10.1523/JNEUROSCI.1124-04.2004)

14

Should I stay or should I go? How the human brain manages the trade-off between exploitation and exploration

Jonathan D. Cohen,* Samuel M. McClure, and Angela J. Yu

Many large and small decisions we make in our daily lives—which ice cream to choose, what research projects to pursue, which partner to marry—require an exploration of alternatives before committing to and exploiting the benefits of a particular choice. Furthermore, many decisions require re-evaluation, and further exploration of alternatives, in the face of changing needs or circumstances. That is, often our decisions depend on a higher level choice: whether to exploit well known but possibly suboptimal alternatives or to explore risky but potentially more profitable ones. How adaptive agents choose between exploitation and exploration remains an important and open question that has received relatively limited attention in the behavioural and brain sciences. The choice could depend on a number of factors, including the familiarity of the environment, how quickly the environment is likely to change, and the relative value of exploiting known sources of reward versus the cost of reducing uncertainty through exploration. There is no known generally optimal solution to the exploration versus exploitation problem, and a solution to the general case may indeed not be possible. However, there have been formal analyses of the optimal policy under constrained circumstances. There have also been specific suggestions of how humans and animals may respond to this problem under particular experimental conditions as well as proposals about the brain mechanisms involved. Here, we provide a brief review of this work, discuss how exploration and exploitation may be mediated in the brain and highlight some promising future directions for research.

Keywords: uncertainty; learning; neurotransmitters; prefrontal cortex; decision making; norepinephrine; dopamine

14.1 Introduction

Should I stay or should I go now?
If I go there will be trouble
And if I stay it may be double
So come on and let me know
Should I stay or should I go?

(The Clash)

Every researcher has personal experience with the exploration–exploitation dilemma. At some point in the conduct of a study, when the data are still inconclusive, it may become necessary to decide how to proceed. On the one hand, there is the option to continue with the experiment, in the hope that with more effort and data, the results will look more promising. Alternatively, the experiment can be scrapped in favour of a modified experimental design,

*Author for correspondence (jdc@princeton.edu).

a new approach to the problem, or an entirely new research topic. That is, the experimenter faces a trade-off between the value of exploitation versus exploration. This example highlights the importance of this problem in decision making, one that has typically been ignored in psychological research on cognitive control and executive function.

The need to balance exploitation with exploration is confronted at all levels of behaviour and time-scales of decision making from deciding what to do next in the day to planning a career path. It is confronted by individuals in love (as captured by the lyrics above) and by entire armies at war (should a campaign focus intensively on one battle or seek to identify new opportunities to surmount the enemy). Nor is it limited to human behaviour. It is confronted by fungi deciding whether to concentrate growth at a local site or send out hyphae to sample more distant resources (Watkinson *et al.* 2005); by ant colonies exploring options for a new nest before settling on and exploiting a particular site (Pratt & Sumpter 2006); by engineers generating algorithms to deploy a fleet of automata to map the expanses of a new environment (Leonard *et al.* in press) and by machine learning theorists—who coined the phrase 'exploration versus exploitation'— in their efforts to improve the ability of reinforcement learning (RL) algorithms to function adaptively in changing environments (e.g. Kaelbling *et al.* 1996).

In general, how agents should and do respond to the trade-off between exploration and exploitation is poorly understood. In part, this reflects the difficulty of the problem: there is no known optimal policy for trading off exploration and exploitation in general, even when the objectives are well specified. Gittins & Jones (1974) and Gittins (1979) presented a strategy and proved its optimality for a limited class of problems in which the decisions are made from a finite number of stationary bandit processes (e.g. options for which the reward is delivered with *unknown* but *fixed* probabilities), and when the agent discounts their value exponentially over time. Gittins proved that if being optimal consists of maximizing the cumulative reward over an infinite horizon when the value of each reward is discounted exponentially as a function of when it is acquired, then the optimal policy is to calculate the expected total future rewards associated with each option at a particular time—a value known as the Gittins index— and to select that bandit with the greatest Gittins index (Gittins & Jones 1974; Gittins 1979). The significance of Gittins' contribution is that it reduced the decision problem to computing and comparing these scalar indices. In practice, computing the Gittins index is not tractable for many problems for which it is known to be optimal. However, for some limited problems, explicit solutions have been found. For instance, the Gittins index has been computed for certain two-armed bandit problems (in which the agent chooses between two options with independent probabilities of generating a reward), and compared to the foraging behaviour of birds under comparable circumstances; the birds were found to behave approximately optimally (Krebs *et al.* 1978).

While the Gittins index lends formal rigour to the problem of exploration versus exploitation, proof of its optimality requires strong assumptions about the environment and the agent. The properties of the individual bandits must be frozen unless acted upon (i.e. the pay-off structure of the environment must be stationary), all options must be available at all decision points (i.e. there cannot be any 'side paths') and agents must discount the value of rewards exponentially into the future (Gittins 1979; Berry & Fristedt 1985; Banks & Sundaram 1994). Real-world problems typically violate one or more of these assumptions.

Perhaps, the most important exception to Gittins' assumptions is that real-world environments are typically non-stationary; i.e. they change with time. To understand how organisms manage the balance between exploration and exploitation in non-stationary environments, investigators have begun to study how organisms adapt their behaviour in response to the experimentally induced changes in reward contingencies. Several studies have now shown that both humans and other animals dynamically update their estimates of rewards associated with specific courses of action, and abandon actions that are deemed to be diminishing in value in search of others that may be more rewarding (e.g. Sugrue *et al.* 2004; Daw *et al.* 2006; Nieuwenhuis Gilzenrat & Cohen in preparation). At the same time, there is also longstanding evidence that humans sometimes exhibit an opposing tendency. When reward diminishes (e.g. following an error in performance), subjects often try harder at what they have been doing rather than less (e.g. Rabbitt 1966; Laming 1979; Gratton *et al.* 1992). The balance between exploration and exploitation also seems to be sensitive to time horizons. Humans show a greater tendency to explore when there is more time left in a task, presumably because this allows them sufficient time later to enjoy the fruits of those explorations (Carstensen *et al.* 1999). A full account of how people regulate the balance between exploration and exploitation must account for these diverse, and in some cases seemingly discrepant, patterns of behaviour.

Recent findings are also beginning to shed light on the neural mechanisms that underlie exploratory and exploitative behaviours. These findings consistently implicate the involvement of neuromodulatory systems thought to be involved in assessing reward and uncertainty. The midbrain dopamine system has been implicated in the signalling of reward prediction errors critical for learning the value of specific actions (Montague *et al.* 1996; Schultz *et al.* 1997) and for decision-making based on those values (McClure *et al.* 2003). The locus coeruleus (LC) noradrenergic system has been proposed to govern the balance between exploration and exploitation in response to reward history (Aston-Jones & Cohen 2005). And the basal forebrain cholinergic system together with the adrenergic system have been proposed to monitor uncertainty, signalling both expected and unexpected forms, respectively, which in turn might be used to promote exploitation or exploration (Yu & Dayan 2005).

Regulating the balance between exploitation and exploration is a fundamental need for adaptive behaviour in a complex and changing world. In the rest of this article, we consider the progress outlined above that has been made in understanding this problem in formal terms and in identifying the mechanisms that have evolved in natural organisms for meeting this challenge. While there has been recent progress in identifying relevant empirical phenomena and candidate neural mechanisms, such work is still in the earliest stages. Accordingly, the connection between theory and data remains largely speculative. Our primary purpose here is to call attention to the problem and point to relevant lines of research that show promise in addressing it.

14.2 Optimal performance in stationary environments: the Gittins index

In a landmark paper, Gittins & Jones (1974) developed a straightforward means for calculating the optimal strategy for decision making in multi-armed bandit problems. Bandit problems are well suited for studying the tension between exploitation and exploitation since they offer a direct trade-off between exploiting a known source of reward (continuing to play one arm of the bandit) and exploring the environment (trying other arms) to acquire information about other sources of reward (Kaelbling 1996).

For an *n*-armed bandit problem, an agent is required to choose between *n* options, each of which delivers reward with a probability p_i. The probability of obtaining reward from a bandit, p_i, may change through time but, in this case only when a choice is made for that bandit. The goal for the agent is to maximize expected rewards, V_i, where rewards earned in the future are discounted by an exponential discount factor $\delta \in (0, 1)$.

Gittins & Jones proved that optimal performance can be obtained by tracking a single index υ_i of the form

$$v_i = \sup_{T>0} \frac{\left\langle \sum_{t=0}^{T} \delta^t R_i(t) \right\rangle}{\left\langle \sum_{t=0}^{T} \delta^t \right\rangle}, \tag{14.2.1}$$

for each of the bandits, which is a normalized sum of future rewards discounted by the delay until they are accrued. The sum is taken until a time T, which is defined as the stopping time, or the point at which selecting from bandit i will be terminated. Gittins & Jones proved that optimal behaviour is assured as long as that action is always taken which has the greatest index value. Critically, the Gittins index for any given bandit is independent of the expected outcomes of all other bandits. This implies that once the bandit with greatest index is known, behaviour should continue on this bandit until its index value falls below its original value. This is true because the index values for all other bandits do not change as long as these bandits are not selected. Computationally, calculating the Gittins index (equation (14.2.1)) is demanding and may not reasonably be expected to be calculated in the brain.

The Gittins index provides a normative account of how agents should act when faced with a particular form of the exploration–exploitation dilemma. Krebs *et al.* (1978) tested whether the foraging behaviour of birds is optimal when confronting a two-armed bandit problem similar to that solved by the Gittins index. In the experiment, the birds were presented with two feeding posts that gave food reward with fixed probability. The problem was a simplification of the general problem solved by the Gittins index, since the probability of obtaining reward from a feeding post was not allowed to change when selected and since the experiment was of finite length. The investigators found that the time at which birds stopped exploring (operationalized as the point at which they stayed at one feeding post) closely approximated that predicted by the optimal solution. Despite their findings, Krebs *et al.* (1978) recognized that it was highly unlikely that their birds were carrying out the complex calculations required by the Gittins index. Rather, they suggested that the birds were using simple behavioural heuristics that produces exploration times that qualitatively approximate the optimal solution. However, there are more fundamental problems with the Gittins index, beyond complexity of calculation.

As noted earlier, Gittins' proof requires that rewards should be discounted exponentially for delay (Berry & Fristedt 1985) whereas it is generally accepted that most animals (including humans) show hyperbolic discounting (e.g. Ainslie 1975). Additionally, if there is a cost associated with switching from one behaviour to another, then not only is the Gittins index no longer optimal, but also there is *no* optimal index that may be calculated independently for each bandit (Banks & Sundaram 1994). It is well recognized that, under many conditions, humans exhibit costs when switching from one task to another (e.g. Allport *et al.* 1994; Rogers & Monsell 1995). Most importantly, the Gittins index assumes that, although the pay-offs for each bandit are probabilistic and each must be sampled sufficiently to determine its expected value, the *actual* expected value of each remains fixed except when acted upon. That is, if nothing is done to a bandit, then its true value remains stable across time. However, both the needs of most organisms and the environments in which they live are not stable in this way. Things change over time, even when they are not acted upon, and often in unpredictable ways. To date, no universally optimal algorithm has been described that prescribes how to trade-off between exploration and exploitation in non-stationary environments, and it is not clear that doing so is possible. Thus, understanding how animals respond to this problem must also be guided by empirical investigation, both of behaviour and underlying neural mechanisms.

14.3 Modelling exploitation versus exploration in non-stationary environments

Daw *et al.* (2006) recently addressed this problem in a study that used a variant of the *n*-armed bandit problem in which the pay-offs of each bandit changed slowly over time (figure 14.1). In this setting, therefore, the cost of persisting with one behaviour (i.e. playing only one bandit) was not only the opportunity cost of failing to learn more about the value of the others, but also the possibility that what has already been learned about them will fall out of date. Daw *et al.* (2006) proposed three possible models for how subjects might guide their choices in this situation.

The first model used a simple decision rule, in which the subject maintains a record of the expected value for each option, based on past experience, and usually chooses the option with the greatest value (exploitation) though sometimes, with a fixed probability, picks randomly among the other alternatives (exploration). This is sometimes referred to as the 'epsilon-greedy' algorithm (Sutton & Barto 1998). According to a second model, options are chosen by probability matching, i.e. with a probability weighted by their estimated values. This is often referred to as the 'soft max' decision rule (e.g. Thrun 1992), as it favours choosing the option with the maximum value (this option will have the highest probability), though this tendency is 'softened' by both the value of the competing options as well as randomness (noise) added to the decision rule. Thus, in this model, the balance between exploitation and exploration is governed by both the relative value of the alternatives as well as a parameter (referred to as gain or, inversely, temperature) that determines how tightly decisions are constrained by the contrast of value among the alternatives: with higher gain, decisions are determined more by relative value (exploitation); with lower gain, decisions are more evenly distributed at random (exploration).

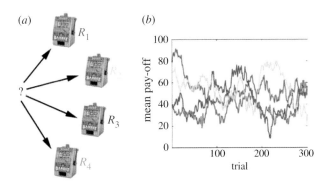

Fig. 14.1 Daw *et al.* (2006) examined how subjects handle the exploration–exploitation problem in a four-armed bandit problem. (*a*) In each trial of their task, subjects selected one of the four bandits and received a reward based on its current mean pay-off perturbed by noise. (*b*) The expected value of each bandit changed continuously over time.

Finally, they entertained a third model, according to which choices are made using the soft max decision rule, but with a critical added factor: options that have not been selected receive an 'uncertainty bonus' that augments their probability of being chosen (i.e. promotes exploration). This captures the opportunity cost that is formalized by the Gittins index for stationary environments, and that is particularly important in non-stationary environments: the more time allocated to one option the less one knows about the others, which may be (or have become) more valuable.

Daw *et al.* (2006) compared the behaviour of subjects playing their *n*-arm bandit task to predictions from each of the three models. The model that provided the best fit was the soft max decision rule. Importantly, although subjects did periodically explore options other than the one currently deemed to be most valuable, they did not find evidence that this was driven by an uncertainty bonus (i.e. growing uncertainty about the competing alternatives). However, there are several caveats that must be kept in mind. First, it is possible that the specifics of the environment did not adequately favour the use of an uncertainty bonus. For example, the pay-offs of each bandit changed continuously and relatively slowly over time in their experiment. In the real world—to which real-world organisms are presumably adapted—the dynamics of environmental change may be very different, and therefore call for a different policy of exploration (and computation of uncertainty bonus) than was assumed by Daw *et al.* (2006). Another important factor may be social context—people may be enticed to explore the environment when they have information about the behaviour of others, and they may also place a greater premium on exploration when they face competition from others for resources.

These are questions that beg more detailed formal analysis. Nevertheless, to our knowledge, the Daw *et al.* (2006) study was the first to address formally the question of how subjects weigh exploration against exploitation in a non-stationary, but experimentally controlled environment. It also produced some interesting neurobiological findings. Their subjects performed the *n*-armed bandit task while being scanned using functional magnetic resonance imaging (fMRI). Among the observations reported was task-related activity in two sets of regions of prefrontal cortex (PFC). One set of regions was in ventromedial PFC and was associated with both the magnitude of reward associated with a choice, and that predicted by their computational model of the task (using the soft max decision rule). This area has been consistently associated with the encoding of reward value across a variety of task domains (O'Doherty *et al.* 2001; Knutson *et al.* 2003; McClure *et al.* 2004; Padoa-Schioppa & Assad 2006). A second set of areas observed bilaterally in frontopolar PFC was significantly more active when subjects chose to explore (i.e. chose an option other than the one estimated by their model to be the most rewarding) rather than exploit. This finding is consistent with the hypothesis that more anterior and dorsal regions of PFC are responsible for top-down control, biasing processes responsible for behaviour in favour of higher level goals, especially when these must compete with otherwise prepotent behaviours (e.g. Miller & Cohen 2001). Such top-down control may be important for exploration, insofar as this involves selecting an action that has been less recently associated with reward. That is, when a decision is made to pursue an exploratory behaviour, this may rely on support from higher level control processes. However, this begs the question of how the system decides when it is appropriate to explore. That is, what mechanisms are responsible for assessing the reliability and value of current rewards, and using this information to determine when to continue to pursue current sources of reward (exploit) or take a chance in pursuing new behaviours (explore). Several lines of investigation have begun to address this question.

14.4 Uncertainty and exploitation versus exploration

One line of work that has direct relevance addresses the question of how the brain encodes different forms of uncertainty. Yu & Dayan (2005) proposed that a critical function of two important neuromodulators— acetylcholine (ACh) and norepinephrine (NE)—may be to signal expected and unexpected sources of uncertainty. While the model they developed for this was not intended to address the trade-off between exploitation and exploration, the distinction between expected and unexpected uncertainty is likely to be an important factor in regulating this trade-off. For example, the detection of unexpected uncertainty can be an important signal of the need to promote exploration. To see this, consider the following scenario.

You are asked to observe a series of coin tosses, told that the coin is biased, and your job is to determine whether it is biased towards heads or tails. The first several tosses produce the following sequence: heads, heads, tails, heads, heads, heads, heads. If you are forced to choose at this point, like most observers, you would probably say that the coin is biased towards heads. If the next flip comes up tails, that is OK. You know that the outcome of any particular toss is uncertain. This represents an *expected* form of uncertainty. However, consider what happens if the subsequent set of tosses is: heads, tails, tails, tails, tails, tails, tails. ... NAt some point, you will revise your determination and say that the coin is biased towards tails. Perhaps, the coin was surreptitiously switched (i.e. the world has changed) or your determination was wrong in the first place. In either case, having come to assume that the coin is biased towards heads, you have now been confronted with an *unexpected* form of uncertainty and must revise your model of the world accordingly, along with the choice of any actions that depend on it.

This problem is closely related to the example we gave at the beginning of this article (concerning the collection of experimental data), and as we have noted elsewhere (Aston-Jones & Cohen 2005), the distinction between expected and unexpected forms of uncertainty may be an important element in choosing between exploitation versus exploration. As long as prediction errors can be accounted for in terms of expected uncertainty—that is the amount that we expect a given outcome to vary—then all other things being equal (e.g. ignoring potential non-stationarities in the environment), we should persist in our current behaviour (exploit). However, if errors in prediction begin to exceed the degree expected— i.e. unexpected uncertainty mounts—then we should revise our strategy and consider alternatives (explore).

Yu & Dayan (2005) proposed that ACh levels are used to signal expected uncertainty, and NE to signal unexpected uncertainty. They describe a computationally tractable algorithm by which these may be estimated that approximates the Bayesian optimal computation of those estimates. Furthermore, they proposed how these estimates, reflected by NE and ACh levels, could be used to determine when to revise expectations

$$NE > \frac{ACh}{(0.5 + ACH)}. \tag{14.4.1}$$

They showed that this closely approximates the Bayesian optimal solution to, and people's behaviour in, a variant of a commonly used selective attention task (the 'Posner paradigm'; Posner *et al.* 1980).

This work provides another instructive example of the value in conducting a mathematical analysis of optimal performance in a task, and using this to guide the generation of hypotheses about the specific mechanisms—in this case neural—that govern behaviour in that task.

Furthermore, it lends precision to hypotheses about the function of neuromodulatory systems. Despite their ubiquity in the brain, theories about these systems have typically been vague, proposing non-specific functions such as the mediation of motivation and arousal. Yu and Dayan's model assigns precise functions to ACh and NE, specified in mathematical form, that can be used to generate specific testable predictions.

As suggested above, it is not hard to imagine how the functions ascribed to ACh and NE in representing estimates of expected and unexpected forms of uncertainty might play an important role in regulating the balance between exploitation and exploration. As estimates of unexpected uncertainty rise, and NE approaches the threshold defined by equation (14.4.1), the system promotes a revision of current expectations. This could be an important signal to search for a new model of the environment and a corresponding behavioural strategy— i.e. exploration. Sometimes, however, unexpected events are followed by the opposite tendency: an increase in commitment to the current behavioural strategy. For example, following errors in simple reaction time tasks people often become more cautious and improve their performance (i.e. become more accurate; Rabbitt 1966; Laming 1979). Similarly, following interference in selective attention tasks, subjects typically increase the focus of their attention and improve performance (Gratton et al. 1992), especially when such interference is relatively rare (Carter et al. 2000; Kerns et al. 2004).

The Yu & Dayan model also sensibly predicts that performance should be best when expectations are most accurate. However, when outcomes in a task become too predictable, people often become bored and look for other things to do (explore). Video game programmers learned this lesson long ago, and routinely include multiple levels in a game, so that when it becomes too predictable, it is made more difficult in order to retain players' interest (i.e. keep them exploiting).

These observations suggest that additional mechanisms may be involved in evaluating expectations and in regulating the trade-off between exploration and exploitation. Another closely related line of investigation has sought to address some of these observations. It too has suggested an important role for NE, building on detailed physiological observations about the dynamics of NE release, and proposing how this may relate to assessments of reward as well as uncertainty.

14.5 Utility and exploitation versus exploration

Virtually all of the NE released in the neocortex originates from a small brainstem nucleus called the locus coeruleus (LC). Aston-Jones et al. (1994, 1997) have observed that in the awake behaving monkey the LC shifts between two operating modes that correspond closely with behavioural performance in a simple target detection task. In the 'phasic mode,' when the animal is performing well (no misses and very few false alarms), the LC shows only moderate levels of tonic discharge, but responds phasically with a burst of activity to target stimuli (but not to distractors). In the 'tonic mode', the baseline level of discharge is higher, but there are diminished or absent phasic responses to target stimuli. In this mode, reaction time to targets is slower and the animal commits a greater number of false alarms to distractors. These two modes most probably represent a continuum of LC function, consistent with the formal theories described below. However, we will continue to refer to two modes for expository purposes, because the distinction between them (or the extremes of function they represent) has been proposed to be an important factor in influencing the balance between exploration and exploitation.

Usher *et al.* (1999) developed a biophysically detailed model of the LC that accounted for the physiological observations outlined above and suggested that these may play a role in regulating the balance between exploitation and exploration. They proposed that the phasic mode favours exploitation by releasing NE specifically when a task-relevant event occurs, thereby facilitating processing of that event. In contrast, in the tonic mode, sustained release of NE indiscriminately facilitates processing of all events irrespective of their relevance to the current task and thereby favours exploration. Note that the latter aligns well with the role of NE proposed by Yu & Dayan (2005), favouring exploration, if it is assumed that NE in their model corresponds to tonic release.

The Usher *et al.* (1999) model describes physiological mechanisms by which the LC may contribute to regulating the balance between exploitation and exploration. However, it does not specify what drives the LC towards the phasic (exploitation) or tonic (exploration) modes. Recently, Aston-Jones & Cohen (2005) have proposed that this may be governed by ongoing assessments of utility carried out in ventral and medial frontal structures. As noted earlier, there is extensive evidence that ventral regions within PFC form part of a circuit responsible for encoding reward value (e.g. Knutson *et al.* 2003; O'Doherty *et al.* 2001; McClure *et al.* 2004; Padoa-Schioppa & Assad 2006). There is also now a substantial body of evidence that medial frontal structures, and in particular the anterior cingulate cortex (ACC), encode costs. Regions within the ACC have consistently been observed to respond to pain, negative feedback, errors in performance, conflicts in processing and even mental effort, all of which represent or are indicative of various forms of cost (e.g. Miltner *et al.* 1997; Carter *et al.* 1998; Peyron *et al.* 2000; Botvinick *et al.* 2001; Holroyd & Coles 2002; Yeung *et al.* 2004). Furthermore, recent anatomic evidence indicates that these ventral and medial frontal structures provide dense projections to the LC (Rajkowski *et al.* 2000; Aston-Jones *et al.* 2002).

Based on these findings, Aston-Jones & Cohen (2005) have proposed that ongoing assessments of utility carried in frontal structures are used to govern the mode of LC and thereby regulate the balance between exploitation and exploration. Specifically, they propose that assessments of utility are carried out over both short (e.g. seconds) and long (e.g. minutes) time-scales and that this can reconcile the opposing tendencies (to 'try harder' versus 'give up') following periods of poor performance noted above. For example, consider the following two circumstances. In one, performance in a task has been good and there are still rewards to be accrued from the task, but there are occasional lapses in performance producing transient decreases in utility (e.g. on single trials). In this case, following such a lapse the agent should act to restore performance. That is, exploitation should be promoted when long-term utility has been high, but there has been a momentary decrease. In contrast, consider a second situation in which performance has been poor and utility has progressively declined. At some point, this should encourage disengagement from the current task and exploration of alternative behaviours. That is, how the system responds to a current decrease in utility should depend upon the context of longer term trends in utility, favouring exploitation if long-term utility has been high, but favouring exploration if it has been low. A relatively simple equation can capture these relationships,

Engagement in current task

$$
\begin{aligned}
= &\left[1 - logistic\left(\text{short-term utility}\right) \right] \\
&\times \left[logistic\left(\text{long-term utility}\right) \right],
\end{aligned}
\tag{14.5.1}
$$

where *logistic* refers to the sigmoid function $1/(1+e^{-utility})$. Aston-Jones & Cohen (2005) proposed that high values of this equation favour the LC phasic mode (exploitation), whereas low values favour the tonic mode (exploration; figure 14.2). Usher *et al.* (1999) and Brown *et al.* (2005) both suggest the ways in which this can be accomplished through the regulation of simple physiological parameters (such as electronic coupling and/or baseline afferent drive) within the LC.

This model can also be related to the soft max mechanism that Daw *et al.* (2006) found best fits decision-making behaviour in their *n*-armed bandit task. The effect of the LC can be thought of as tuning the softmax function, sharpening it (phasic mode) and biasing decisions towards the most recently rewarded choices (i.e. exploitation) when long-term utility is high, and flattening the function (tonic mode) promoting a more uniform distribution of choices (exploration) when long-term utility is low. Whether such effects are observed in a suitably designed *n*-armed bandit decision-making task remains to be tested. However, recent findings from a simpler, two-armed decision-making task, that used pupilometry to index LC activity (Aston-Jones & Cohen 2005), have corroborated predictions of the model regarding the relationship of LC activity to decision-making performance (Nieuwenhuis, Gilzenrat & Cohen in preparation). This work has also recently been extended to explore the interaction between these mechanisms and those underlying RL.

14.6 Reinforcement learning and exploitation versus exploration

The trade-off between exploration and exploitation has long been recognized as a central issue in RL (Kaelbling 1996, 2003). RL mechanisms act by strengthening associations (e.g. between a stimulus and an action) when these have been associated with a reward (e.g. Sutton & Barto 1998). There is now strong reason to believe that the dopaminergic (DA)

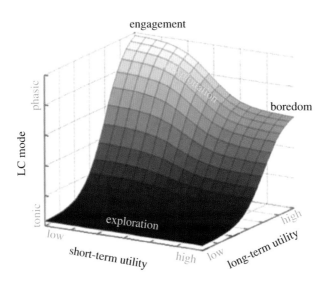

Fig. 14.2 Aston-Jones & Cohen (2005) propose that exploration and exploitation may be mediated by separate short- and long-term measures of utility (cost and reward). Exploration and exploitation, in this model, are mediated by the firing mode of norepinephrine neurons in the locus coeruleus (LC).

system implements such a mechanism (Montague *et al.* 1996; see Montague *et al.* 2004 for a recent review). RL mechanisms function well in stationary environments, in which progressive strengthening of associations makes them robust and efficient, allowing the agent to exploit the current environment. However, this also makes them resistant to change, which is problematic in non-stationary environments when the system must be able to explore and learn new contingencies.

The simplest example of this is a reversal conditioning paradigm, in which the agent learns a set of associations (e.g. that a purple light calls for a response and a pink light does not) and once they are learned the contingencies are reversed. If the RL mechanism ensures rapid and strong learning of the initial association, then it will be difficult to adjust to the change (the purple light will continue to elicit a response). However, if RL operates more weakly, then it will take longer to learn the initial association. A common solution to this problem is to introduce an annealing mechanism. When new learning is required (i.e. there is uncertainty about the environment, and/or utility declines), noise is added to the system, allowing it to randomly explore new associations; noise is then progressively reduced as newly rewarded associations are discovered and these are strengthened. This is similar to the tuning of the softmax decision function described above. Indeed, McClure *et al.* (2006) have described a model showing how the frontal and LC mechanisms described above can function as such an annealing mechanism when integrated with a DA-based RL mechanism (figure 14.3).

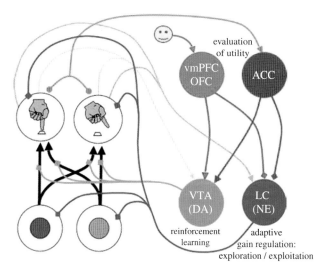

Fig. 14.3 A neural network model of how reward and cost are integrated in the locus coeruleus to adaptively change between exploration and exploitation, as proposed by McClure *et al.* (2006). The left side shows a simple network for decision making in the task. The right side shows evaluative and neuromodulatory mechanisms that regulate the decision-making mechanisms. The model proposes that information about cost (calculated by the anterior cingulate cortex (ACC)) and reward (calculated by the ventromedial prefrontal cortex (vmPFC) and orbitofrontal cortex (OFC)) converge on both the ventral tegmental area (VTA) and the locus coeruleus (LC). This information is used by the VTA to implement a reinforcement learning algorithm that adjusts the weights in the decision network. In the LC, evaluative information sets the mode of responding (phasic or tonic), which, through norepinephrine (NE) release and gain modulation of units in the decision network, regulates the balance between exploration and exploitation (see text for more detailed description).

Furthermore, they have shown that the behaviour of the LC in this model closely parallels observations that have been made from LC recordings in a reversal conditioning paradigm using a target detection task (Aston-Jones *et al.* 1997). Performance of the task following acquisition of the initial target was associated with the LC phasic mode. When the contingencies were reversed, LC tonic activity increased and phasic responses diminished. Then, as the new target was acquired, the LC returned to the phasic mode of responding. These findings provide growing support for the view that the LC noradrenergic system plays an important role in mediating the balance between exploitation and exploration. As the work of Aston-Jones & Cohen (2005) and Yu & Dayan (2005) suggests, ongoing assessments of both uncertainty and utility are likely to be important in regulating this balance.

14.7 Open questions and challenges

In this article, we hope to have drawn attention to the fact that managing the trade-off between exploitation and exploration is a fundamental challenge for the adaptive control of behaviour. While traditionally this has not occupied centre stage in research on executive function and cognitive control, we have reviewed several lines of work that have productively begun to address this issue. Nevertheless, many important questions remain.

First, it is should be noted that some of the work we have reviewed addresses the estimation of uncertainty (e.g. Yu & Dayan 2005), while other work focuses more on the computation of utility and action selection (e.g. Usher *et al.* 1999; Aston-Jones & Cohen 2005; Daw *et al.* 2006). All of these are likely to be critical elements in determining the trade-off between exploitation and exploration. However, the specific relationship between these remains to be examined directly. For example, it would be valuable to understand how the mechanisms proposed by Yu & Dayan (2005) to compute assessments of uncertainty (i.e. prediction errors) can be coupled to action selection, and how this relates to the algorithm described by equation (14.5.1)— proposed by Aston-Jones & Cohen (2005) to relate assessments of utility to LC function and decision-making performance.

It seems inescapable that, in addition to uncertainty and utility, social signals are a critical factor adjudicating the trade-off between exploitation and exploration. Observing others can provide critical counterfactual information about the reward value of behavioural strategies that one has not yet pursued oneself (Montague *et al.* in press). Competition within a social context may also help explain aspects of boredom—i.e. the perplexing tendency to explore alternatives to current behaviour when certainty of outcome (including reward) is at its highest. If it is assumed that more difficult tasks are both more remunerative and less competitive (because fewer agents possess the skills necessary to perform them), then performing a task below one's skill level carries an opportunity cost. That is, it should be possible to find another task for which one is still adequately competent, but that is more difficult and less competitive, and therefore more remunerative. Thus, boredom may in part reflect an adaptive bias towards exploration when performance at ceiling suggests that a more remunerative task can be found (M. Todd 2006, personal communication).

An important super-ordinate question is whether the trade-off between exploitation and exploration should be considered a single problem addressed by a unitary set of mechanisms in the brain, or whether it represents a family of problems spanning different scales, that are addressed by different mechanisms. The time-scale of neuromodulatory function suggests that these mechanisms influence decisions that take place over seconds or minutes. However, faster processes (e.g. saccadic search mechanisms) and longer ones (planning a career) may involve very different mechanisms.

Finally, an equally pressing question is whether it is best to distinguish qualitatively between exploitation and exploration, or whether these represent the extremes of a continuum. For example, the models we have discussed have, for the most part, treated exploration as random search (e.g. increasing noise in an annealing procedure). However, search can often be structured by relatively sophisticated, domain-specific heuristics (for example, in problem solving tasks; Newell & Simon 1972). Such search processes may involve temporally extended, goal-directed behaviours that rely on mechanisms of cognitive control similar to those required for exploitation within the context of simpler tasks. Indeed, the findings of an association between PFC activity and exploration in the Daw *et al.* (2006) study may provide an example of this. These considerations help underscore the need for a precise formulation of the exploitation–exploration trade-off within specific task environments.

More generally, this issue brings into focus an important dimension for considering the trade-off between exploration and exploitation: the extent to which the environment to be explored is well-structured (whether static or changing in predictable ways) versus unknown and unpredictable. To the extent that it is structured, then it should be possible to explore it in a systematic fashion (we might refer to this as 'controlled exploration'). That is, at least from the theorist's perspective, it should be possible to identify an optimal strategy for exploration that takes account of knowledge about the various behavioural alternatives (the Gittins index represents a special case of this). Under such conditions, the decision of whether to exploit or explore should weigh both the value of current pursuits as well as informed expectations about the alternatives, and exploration should be deterministic. Indeed, to the extent that an optimal strategy can be found, this might be thought of simply as higher level exploitation. Of course, for realistically complex environments, theoretically optimal strategies are likely to be computationally intractable, at least for biological mechanisms (this is so for the Gittins index, even given its simplifying assumptions). Thus approximations, including stochastic ones (such as some of the mechanisms reviewed in this article) may be more biologically realistic.

At the other end of this dimension are unknown and unpredictable environments. Under such conditions, the decision of whether to exploit or explore may focus more profitably on assessments of performance in the current task rather than on expectations about alternatives. Similarly, strategies for exploration will necessarily rely on cruder assumptions about behavioural alternatives and search among them will be less structured and presumably more stochastic. Consideration of these factors may be useful in guiding the next generation of hypotheses about the mechanisms governing exploitation and exploration in biological organisms.

14.8 Summary and conclusions

This article began by reviewing efforts to formalize the optimal solution to the trade-off between exploitation and exploration. The Gittins index provides such a solution, but applies to restricted circumstances (e.g. only stationary environments). As yet, no general solution has been found for non-stationary environments and, depending upon the breadth and characteristics of the environment to be considered, this may not be possible. Nonetheless, empirical studies of both behaviour and neural mechanisms have begun to reveal mechanisms that animals may use to adapt to changes in the environment, by regulating the balance between exploitation and exploration. These studies appear to be converging on the view that neuromodulatory systems—in particular, ACh and NE, interacting with DA-mediated RL mechanisms—may play a critical role in regulating this balance within certain domains of behaviour. These systems appear to be responsive to both estimates of uncertainty and utility. However, social signals are also likely to be an important source of information. More generally, the trade-off between exploitation and exploration represents a challenge to behaviour at all levels and over multiple time-scales. It is not yet clear whether neuromodulatory mechanisms serve the same function at all of these levels and time-scales, or whether this relies on other mechanisms that remain to be discovered. Given these considerations, it seems probable that further research will require a mixed (though not yet fully informed) strategy of continuing to exploit promising lines of recent work, while considering new ones to explore.

This work was supported by NIHM grants P50 MH062196 (J.D.C.), F32 MH072141 (S.M.M.) and the NIMH Quantitative Neuroscience Training Grant (MH65214). We thank Gary Aston-Jones, Eric Brown, Mark Gilzenrat, Phil Holmes and Leigh Nystrom for their close collaboration in the development of many of the ideas presented in this article. We would also like to thank Nathaniel Daw, Yael Niv and Greg Stephens for their valuable discussions related to this work, as well as Peter Dayan and an anonymous reviewer for their useful suggestions regarding this article. Finally, we would like to offer a profound and heartfelt thanks to Tim Shallice, not only for his comments on this article, but more importantly for the decades of inspiring work and visionary leadership that he has provided to our field.

References

Ainslie, G. 1975 Specious reward: a behavioral theory of impulsiveness and impulse control. *Psychol. Bull.* 82, 463–496. (doi:10.1037/h0076860)

Allport, A., Styles, E. & Hsieh, S. 1994 Shifting intentional set: exploring the dynamic control of task. *In Attention and performance XV* (eds C. Umilta & M. Moscovitch), pp. 421–452. Cambridge, MA: MIT Press.

Aston-Jones, G. & Cohen, J. D. 2005 An integrative theory of locus coeruleus-norepinephrine function: adaptive gain and optimal performance. *Annu. Rev. Neurosci.* 28, 403–450. (doi:10.1146/annurev. neuro.28.061604.135709)

Aston-Jones, G., Rajkowski, J., Kubiak, P. & Alexinsky, T. 1994 Locus coeruleus neurons in monkey are selectively activated by attended cues in a vigilance task. *J. Neurosci.* **14**, 4467–4480.

Aston-Jones, G., Rajkowski, J. & Kubiak, P. 1997 Conditioned responses in monkey locus coeruleus neurons anticipate acquisition of discriminative behavior in a vigilance task. *Neuroscience* **80**, 697–715. (doi:10.1016/ S0306-4522(97)00060-2)

Aston-Jones, G., Rajkowski, J., Lu, W., Zhu, Y., Cohen, J. D. & Morecraft, R. J. 2002 Prominent projections from the orbital prefrontal cortex to the locus coeruleus in monkeys. *Soc. Neurosci. Abstr.* **28**, 86–89.

Banks, J. S. & Sundaram, R. K. 1994 Switching costs and the Gittins index. *Econometrica: J. Econ. Soc.* **62**, 687–694.

Berry, D. A. & Fristedt, B. 1985 *Bandit problems: sequential allocation of experiments*. London, UK: Chapman and Hall.

Botvinick, M. M., Braver, T. S., Barch, D. M., Carter, C. S. & Cohen, J. D. 2001 Conflict monitoring and cognitive control. *Psychol. Rev.* **108**, 624–652. (doi:10.1037/0033-295X.108.3.624)

Brown, E., Gao, J., Bogacz, R., Gilzenrat, M. & Cohen, J. D. 2005 Simple neural networks that optimize decisions. *Int. J. Bifurc. Chaos* **15**, 803–826. (doi:10.1142/S021812 7405012478)

Carstensen, L. L., Isaacowitz, D. & Charles, S. T. 1999 Taking time seriously: a theory of socioemotional selectivity. *Am. Psychol.* **54**, 165–181. (doi:10.1037/0003-066X.54.3.165)

Carter, C. S., Braver, T. S., Barch, D. M., Botvinick, M. M., Noll, D. C. & Cohen, J. D. 1998 Anterior cingulate cortex, error detection and the on-line monitoring of performance. *Science* **280**, 747–749. (doi:10.1126/science. 280.5364.747)

Carter, C. S., Macdonald, A. M., Botvinick, M., Ross, L. L., Stenger, V. A., Noll, D. & Cohen, J. D. 2000 Parsing executive processes: strategic vs. evaluative functions of the anterior cingulate cortex. *Proc. Natl Acad. Sci. USA* **97**, 1944–1948. (doi:10.1073/pnas.97.4.1944)

Daw, N. D., O'Doherty, J. P., Seymour, B., Dayan, P. & Dolan, R. J. 2006 Cortical substrates for exploratory decisions in humans. *Nature* **441**, 876–879. (doi:10.1038/ nature04766)

Gilzenrat M. S. & Cohen J. D. In preparation. The role of locus coeruleus in mediating between exploration and exploitation in nonstationary environments: an empirical test in a changing utility task.

Gittins, J. C. 1979 Bandit processes and dynamic allocation indices. *J. R. Stat. Soc. B* **41**, 148–177.

Gittins, J. C. & Jones, D. M. 1974 A dynamic allocation index for the sequential design of experiments. In *Progress in statistics* (ed. J. Gans), pp. 241–266. Amsterdam, The Netherlands: North-Holland.

Gratton, G., Coles, M. G. H. & Donchin, E. 1992 Optimization in the use of information: strategic control of activation and responses. *J. Exp. Psychol. Gen.* **4**, 480–506. (doi:10.1037/0096-3445.121.4.480)

Holroyd, C. B. & Coles, M. G. H. 2002 The neural basis of human error processing: reinforcement learning, dopamine, and the error-related negativity. *Psychol. Rev.* **109**, 679–709. (doi:10.1037/ 0033-295X.109.4.679)

Kaelbling, L. P. 1996 Gittins Allocation Indices. See http://www.cs.cmu.edu/afs/cs/project/jair/pub/ volume4/ kaelbling96a-html/node9.html.

Kaelbling, L. P. 2003 *Learning in embedded systems*. Cambridge, MA: MIT Press.

Kaelbling, L. P., Littman, M. L. & Moore, A. W. 1996 Reinforcement learning: a survey. *J. Artif. Intell. Res.* **4**, 237–285.

Kerns, J. G., Cohen, J. D., MacDonald, A. W., Cho, R. Y., Stenger, V. A. & Carter, C. S. 2004 Anterior cingulated conflict monitoring and adjustments in control. *Science* **303**, 1023–1026. (doi:10.1126/ science.1089910)

Knutson, B., Fong, G. W., Bennett, S. M., Adams, C. M. & Hommer, D. 2003 A region of the mesial prefrontal cortex tracks monetary rewarding outcomes: characterization with rapid event-related fMRI. *Neuroimage* **18**, 263–272. (doi:10.1016/S1053-8119(02)00057-5)

Krebs, J. R., Kacelnik, A. & Taylor, P. 1978 Tests of optimal sampling by foraging great tits. *Nature* **275**, 27–31. (doi:10.1038/275027a0)

Laming, D. R. J. 1979 Choice reaction performance following an error. *Acta Psychologica* **43**, 199–224. (doi:10.1016/ 0001-6918(79)90026-X)

Leonard,N.E.,Paley,D.,Lekien,F., Sepulchre, R.,Fratantoni, D. M. & Davis, R. E. In press. Collective motion, sensor networks and ocean sampling. *Proc. IEEE*, **95**.

McClure, S. M., Daw, N. D. & Montague, P. R. 2003 A computational substrate for incentive salience. *Trends Neurosci.* **26**, 423–428. (doi:10.1016/S0166-2236(03) 00177-2)

McClure, S. M., Laibson, D. I., Loewenstein, G. & Cohen, J. D. 2004 Separate neural systems value immediate and delayed monetary reward. *Science* **306**, 503–507. (doi:10.1126/ science.1100907)

McClure, S. M., Gilzenrat, M. S. & Cohen, J. D. 2006 An exploration–exploitation model based on norepinephrine and dopamine activity. In *Advances in neural information processing systems*, vol. 18 (eds Y. Weiss, B. Sholkopf & J. Platt), pp. 867–874. Cambridge, MA: MIT Press.

Miller, E. K. & Cohen, J. D. 2001 An integrative theory of prefrontal cortex function. *Annu. Rev. Neurosci.* **24**, 167–202. (doi:10.1146/annurev.neuro.24.1.167)

Miltner, W. H. R., Braun, C. H. & Coles, M. G. H. 1997 Event-related potentials following incorrect feedback in a time-estimation task: evidence for a 'generic' neural system for error detection. *J. Cogn. Neurosci.* **9**, 788–798.

Montague, P. R., Dayan, P. & Sejnowski, T. J. 1996 A framework for mesencephalic dopamine systems based on predictive Hebbian learning. *J. Neurosci.* **16**, 1936–1947.

Montague, P. R., Hyman, S. E. & Cohen, J. D. 2004 Computational roles for dopamine in behavioral control. *Nature* **431**, 760–767. (doi:10.1038/nature03015)

Montague, P. R., King-Casas, B. & Cohen, J. D. In press. Imaging valuation models in human choice. *Annu. Rev. Neurosci.* **29**, 417–448. (doi:10.1146/annurev.neuro.29. 051605.112903)

Newell, A. & Simon, H. A. 1972 *Human problem solving.* Englewood Cliffs, NJ: Prentice-Hall.

O'Doherty, J., Kringelback, M. L., Rolls, E. T., Hornak, J. & Andrews, C. 2001 Abstract reward and punishment representation in the human orbitofrontal cortex. Nat. *Neurosci.* **4**, 95–102. (doi:10.1038/82959)

Padoa-Schioppa, C. & Assad, J. A. 2006 Neurons in the orbitofrontal cortex encode economic value. *Nature* **441**, 223–226. (doi:10.1038/nature04676)

Peyron, R., Laurent, B. & Garcia-Larrea, L. 2000 Functional imaging of brain responses to pain: a review and meta-analysis. *Neurophysiol. Clin.* **30**, 263–288. (doi:10.1016/ S0987-7053(00)00227-6)

Posner, M. I., Snyder, C. R. R. & Davidson, B. J. 1980 Attention and the detection of signals. *J. Exp. Psychol. Gen.* **109**, 160–174. (doi:10.1037/0096-3445.109.2.160)

Pratt, S. C. & Sumpter, D. J. T. 2006 A tunable algorithm for collective decision-making. *Proc. Natl Acad. Sci. USA* **103**, 15 906–15 910. (doi:10.1073/pnas.0604801103)

Rabbitt, P. M. A. 1966 Errors and error-correction in choice-response tasks. *J. Exp. Psychol.* **71**, 264–272. (doi:10.1037/ h0022853)

Rajkowski, J., Lu, W., Zhu, Y., Cohen, J. D. & Aston-Jones, G. 2000 Prominent projections from the anterior cingulate cortex to the locus coeruleus in Rhesus monkey. *Soc. Neurosci. Abstr.* **26**, 838.15.

Rogers, R. & Monsell, S. 1995 The costs of a predictable switch between simple cognitive tasks. *J. Exp. Psychol. Gen.* **124**, 207–231. (doi:10.1037/0096-3445.124.2. 207)

Schultz, W., Dayan, P. & Montague, P. R. 1997 A neural substrate of prediction and reward. Science **275**, 1593–1599. (doi:10.1126/science.275.5306.1593)

Sugrue, L. P., Corrado, G. S. & Newsome, W. T. 2004 Matching behavior and the representation of value in the parietal cortex. *Science* **304**, 1782–1787. (doi:10.1126/ science.1094765)

Sutton, R. S. & Barto, A. G. 1998 *Reinforcement learning: an introduction.* Cambridge, MA: MIT Press.

Thrun, S. B. 1992 The role of exploration in learning control. In *Handbook of intelligent control: neural, fuzzy, and adaptive approaches* (eds D. A. White & D. A. Sofge), pp. 527–559. Florence, KY: Van Nostrand Reinhold.

Usher, M., Cohen, J. D., Rajkowski, J. & Aston-Jones, G. 1999 The role of the locus coeruleus in the regulation of cognitive performance. *Science* **283**, 549–554. (doi:10. 1126/science.283.5401.549)

Watkinson, S. C., Boddy, L., Burton, K., Darrah, P. R., Eastwood, D., Fricker, M. D. & Tlalka, M. 2005 New approaches to investigating the function of mycelial networks. *Mycologist* **19**, 11–17. (doi:10.1017/S0269915 X05001023)

Yeung, N., Botvinick, M. M. & Cohen, J. D. 2004 The neural basis of error detection: conflict monitoring and the error-related negativity. *Psychol. Rev.* **111**, 931–959. (doi:10. 1037/0033-295X.111.4.939)

Yu, A. & Dayan, P. 2005 Uncertainty, neuromodulation and attention. *Neuron* **46**, 681–692. (doi:10.1016/ j.neuron. 2005.04.026)

Index